People Resourcing

Fourth edition

Stephen Taylor

Published by the Chartered Institute of Personnel and Development,
151, The Broadway, London, SW19 1JQ

This edition published 2008
First published 1998
Reprinted 1998, 1999, 2000, 2001
Second edition published 2002
Reprinted 2002, 2003, 2004 (twice)
Third edition published 2005
Reprinted 2006, 2007

Typeset by Curran Publishing Services
Printed in Spain by Graphycems

British Library Cataloguing in Publication Data
A catalogue of this publication is available from the British Library

ISBN 978 184398 198 5

The views expressed in this publication are the author's own and may not necessarily
reflect those of the CIPD.

The CIPD has made every effort to trace and acknowledge copyright holders. If any
source has been overlooked, CIPD Enterprises would be pleased to redress this in
future editions.

Chartered Institute of Personnel and Development, CIPD House, 151, The Broadway,
London, SW19 1JQ

Tel: 020 8612 6200
E-mail: cipd@cipd.co.uk Website: www.cipd.co.uk
Incorporated by Royal Charter. Registered Charity No. 1079797.

People Resourcing

Fourth edition

Stephen Taylor

The CIPD would like to thank the following members of the CIPD Publishing editorial board for their help and advice:

- Pauline Dibben, Sheffield University
- Edwina Hollings, Staffordshire University Business School
- Caroline Hook, Huddersfield University Business School
- Vincenza Priola, Keele University
- John Sinclair, Napier University Business School

The Chartered Institute of Personnel and Development is the leading publisher of books and reports for personnel and training professionals, students, and all those concerned with the effective management and development of people at work. For details of all our titles, please contact the publishing department:

tel: 020-8612 6204

e-mail publish@cipd.co.uk

The catalogue of all CIPD titles can be viewed on the CIPD website:

www.cipd.co.uk/bookstore

In memory of Dr C. S. Govendar 1932–2002

Contents

Figures

Tables

Abbreviations

ACAS	Advisory, Conciliation and Arbitration Service
BPS	British Psychological Society
CIPD	Chartered Institute of Personnel and Development
CPIS	computerised personnel information system
CSSB	Civil Service Selection Board
CV	curriculum vitae
DDA	Disability Discrimination Act
DfEE	Department for Education and Employment
DTI	Department of Trade and Industry
EAP	employee assistance programme
ELUS	Employer's Labour Use Survey
EQ	emotional intelligence
ESRC	Economic and Social Research Council
GAAP	generally accepted accounting practices
GHQ	General Health Questionnaire
HR	human resources
IDS	Incomes Data Services
IiP	Investors in People
IPD	Institute of Personnel and Development
IPM	Institute of Personnel Management
IRS	Industrial Relations Services
MbO	management by objectives
OFI	operating financial review
OSI	Occupational Stress Indicator
P&D	personnel and development
PBDI	patterned behaviour description interview
PEO	professional employment organisation
PRP	performance-related pay
SAF	standard application form
SSP	statutory sick pay
TQM	Total Quality Management
TUPE	Transfer of Undertakings (Protection of Employment) Regulations
WERS	Workplace Employee Relations Surveys

CHAPTER 1

Introduction

Effective hiring and firing, attracting the best candidates, reducing staff turnover and improving employee performance are fundamental management functions. They are as relevant for a small family business as for a major international PLC. They are, however, carried out in a variety of different ways, and people have differing views about which approach is best in different circumstances. These functions have come to form the backbone of generalist personnel and development (P&D) work. The ability to make sure that they are done well has thus become a basic requirement for any successful P&D career. Together they form the body of managerial skill and knowledge now described by the Chartered Institute of Personnel and Development (CIPD) as 'the people resourcing function'.

The principal aim of this book is to act as a general, comprehensive introduction to the learning material contained in the current CIPD professional standards for people resourcing. However, it is not designed only for students studying for CIPD qualifications. It has also been written to meet the needs of personnel and development practitioners, general managers and consultants who are interested in refreshing and updating their knowledge or in thinking about different approaches to familiar resourcing problems. It will also be of interest to those studying for other qualifications that cover staffing issues.

The primary purpose of this introductory chapter is to define the term 'people resourcing' and to explain both how it relates to other areas of P&D activity and how it supports the achievement of wider organisational objectives. In addition a number of perspectives are introduced which underpin the rest of the material included in the book – including those that are given particular prominence in the CIPD's people resourcing standards. In this context we consider the different ways in which resourcing activity can 'add value' for an organisation, and look at some of the constraints that threaten to stop this being achieved. Finally we outline three distinct paradigms or ways of thinking about the resourcing function that can be used to inform decision-making in this field. In so doing it is hoped that a key message is put over, particularly for those sitting CIPD exams. That is that there is always more than one way to skin a cat. Different circumstances require different tools and techniques to be used. There is no one right way of carrying out the resourcing function and no one simple definition of 'professionalism' in this field.

LEARNING OUTCOMES

By the end of this chapter readers should be able to:

- define the term 'people resourcing'

- distinguish between different kinds of organisational objectives that are met, in part, through resourcing activities

- evaluate resourcing practices against key criteria

- point out the different ways in which a resourcing specialist can 'add value' on behalf of an organisation

- identify different types of constraint that need to be managed in order to achieve resourcing objectives.

In addition, readers should be able to understand and explain:

- how 'people resourcing' differs from and complements the other generalist elective subjects that make up the CIPD's standards

- the purpose of the resourcing function and the contribution it makes to the achievement of organisational goals

- the importance of administrative excellence as the basis for P&D credibility and influence within an organisation

- the contribution effective P&D management can make to long-term organisation success

- the significance of environmental constraints in the activities of a resourcing professional

- the types of paradigm that govern the assumptions behind different approaches to people resourcing.

EXERCISE BOXES

EXERCISE

Throughout each chapter of the book a number of exercises have been included in boxes such as this. For the most part these are based on articles published in the CIPD's fortnightly journal *People Management*. If you are a student member of the CIPD you will be able to access these articles directly through the Institute's website www.cipd.co.uk. You just need to follow the links provided to the People Management archive and use the search facility to locate the relevant article. If you are not a member of the CIPD you can subscribe to *People Management* and gain access to the archive in the process, but you may also find that your college library subscribes and has both web-access and hard copies of recent editions.

KEY ARTICLES

A new feature for this fourth edition of *People Resourcing* is the further text boxes which draw your attention to a recent, seminal or particularly thought-provoking article published in an academic journal, many of which take a critical view of P&D practices. Wherever possible these articles have been selected from those that can be accessed via the online journals service operated by CIPD through its website at ‹www.cipd.co.uk/onlineinfodocuments/journals› or which are readily available electronically through most university libraries. In each case the article is briefly described and questions or an exercise provided for you to complete while you are reading it.

RESOURCING ACTIVITIES

People resourcing is the broadest of the four generalist modules that those studying for the CIPD graduate qualification can choose to study. Because, as a whole, it is less specialised than employee reward, employee relations or employee development, it is also harder to define meaningfully. Indeed, in some ways it is probably best defined simply as the range of activities undertaken by P&D professionals that do not readily fit into the other three main generalist areas. Essentially, however, it covers the range of methods and approaches used by employers in resourcing their organisations in such a way that they can meet their key goals. The resourcing function can thus be usefully said to comprise a set of management activities that facilitate the achievement of four fundamental groups of P&D objectives: staffing, performance, administration and change management.

STAFFING

Staffing objectives are concerned with ensuring that an organisation is able to call on the services of sufficient numbers of staff to meet its objectives. These people may be employed in a variety of different roles, but one way or another they must be able to carry out the tasks and duties needed for the organisation to function effectively. This is often summed up in the phrase 'Securing the services of the right people, in the right place, at the right time'. To achieve this, there is a need to recruit new employees, to retain existing employees and, on occasions, to dismiss others. In recent years the term 'talent management' has become widely used to describe the way that organisations increasingly manage these activities, along with the development of their people, in a coherent fashion. As a result, it is not unusual nowadays to read about the organisations pursuing defined 'talent management strategies'.

PERFORMANCE

Performance objectives pick up from the point at which the staffing objectives have been achieved. The aim here is to ensure that, once assembled, the staff are absent as little as possible, and are well motivated and willing to perform to the best of their abilities. To achieve this, there is a need first to monitor individual and group performance and then to develop means by which these can be improved. There are always two distinct areas of performance management activity. The first concerns the identification of sub-standard performance and measures taken to improve it. This can be focused either on groups of employees or on individuals. The second concerns policies and practices which have as their aim the maximisation of performance in a more general sense. In recent years the emphasis here has tended to be on managing people in such a way as to encourage them to demonstrate 'discretionary effort'. The most successful organisations are those whose people are sufficiently committed that they are prepared to work beyond the strict requirements of their contracts in order to help achieve the organisation's aims.

ADMINISTRATION

Administration objectives are concerned with ensuring that the employment relationships formed are managed efficiently, as well as in accordance with the law, professional ethics and natural justice. In order to achieve these aims consistently, it is necessary to write P&D policies, to develop accepted procedures and to draw up other documents relating to the employment of individuals (eg job descriptions, offer letters, contracts and disciplinary warnings). Effective job and organisation design can also be cited as significant administrative activities. It is often argued that these kinds of activities represent a cost to organisations, amount to bureaucratic requirements and do not add value. While this is true of over-elaborate and unnecessarily unwieldy practices, it is not the case in more general terms. The truth is that the management of every organisation includes an administrative element. Carrying out those tasks more effectively and efficiently than others is therefore one way in which the P&D function contributes to the achievement of competitive advantage.

CHANGE MANAGEMENT

A fourth type of objective draws on elements of the first three but is usefully treated as being distinct in nature. This ensures that proper recognition is given to the significance of change in organisations and its effective management. Increasingly it is argued that we operate in a business environment that is subject to continual change. For many businesses, it is no longer a question of managing a discrete episode during which change occurs, but managing processes through which organisations progressively evolve in terms of both their structure and their culture. The resourcing function can act as an important 'change agent' through the mechanisms whereby it attracts, retains and motivates staff. Charles Darwin famously argued that the biological species that survive most effectively and thrive are not those that are strongest or most intelligent, but those that are best at adapting to change. The more volatile, competitive and unpredictable our business environment becomes, the more relevant this idea is to the world of employment. The organisations that develop the best capacity for flexibility are those that are best placed to seize opportunities as they arise.

Each of the major components that make up the employee resourcing function is thus concerned with meeting one or more of these objectives. The major activities are as follows:

- forecasting the demand for employees

- forecasting the supply of employees

- drawing up job descriptions and person specifications

- recruiting new employees

- selecting new employees

- issuing offer letters and contracts of employment

- the induction and socialisation of new employees

- monitoring employee performance

- improving employee performance

- reducing absence

- reducing employee turnover

- managing redundancies

- managing retirements

- carrying out dismissals.

If employee resourcing activity is to make a real, long-term contribution to the success of an organisation, it is not sufficient simply to set out to achieve the above tasks and objectives. Because the environment is continually changing and developing, and because there are always other organisations with which one must compete, there is always a need to look for ways of improving the methods used to achieve fundamental resourcing objectives. In other words, there is a need regularly to review the policies and practices used in order to maximise the contribution of the resourcing function to organisational success. It is thus necessary to adjust or rethink the approaches used from time to time, with a view to meeting the requirements of new business circumstances. The objectives do not change, but over time the tools used to achieve them may do so, and to a considerable degree.

People resourcing specialists must therefore evaluate their activities, periodically if not continually, in order to establish whether or not improvements could or should be made to their policies and practices. Key skills thus include the development of a capacity for constructive criticism, as well as a knowledge and understanding of the various possible courses of action that could be taken in any given situation. In Chapter 20 we examine evaluation methods in further detail, but it is important at this stage to set out some basic principles.

It is helpful, when formally evaluating specific resourcing policies and practices, to think about them with three basic questions in mind:

- Are we achieving our objectives as effectively as we could?

- Are we achieving them as efficiently as we could?

- Are we achieving them as fairly as we could?

These three broad criteria (effectiveness, efficiency and fairness) underpin much of the evaluative material included in this book. Where the literature indicates that a variety of different approaches is or can be used to tackle a particular set of resourcing objectives or problems, each of the major options is assessed and its merits considered against the backdrop of different environmental circumstances and with these three basic considerations in mind. Courses of action are thus evaluated not in isolation but in comparison with other possible approaches. This reflects what has to happen in practice. Perfection is rarely possible: what is important is that the best approach is taken when compared with other options. It is also often necessary to compare taking action in a particular field with the results of not taking action, or with the approaches used by competitor organisations.

REFLECTIVE QUESTION

Which resourcing activities does your organisation formally evaluate on a regular basis? What are the main criteria used?

ADDING VALUE

It is always important to remember that many organisations, including some that are large and successful, find it possible to manage quite happily without employing P&D specialists. In many others the function is responsible purely for the accomplishment of basic administrative tasks, or is outsourced altogether and devoid of any meaningful influence on the direction of organisational policy. Although we may consider that we and our function carry out indispensable work, other managers often see things rather differently. Unless we are perceived clearly to add value to the organisations we serve, no future existence can be assured and we rapidly find ourselves disrespected and lacking in credibility. Much of this book is thus concerned with pointing out the ways in which professionally qualified P&D specialists, working through resourcing policies and practices, can add value for their organisations. The alternative is a function that represents little more than a 'cost' on an organisation's balance sheet.

'Adding value' is a term that is used more often than it is clearly understood. What does it actually mean in practice? The answer lies in three separate types of contribution: delivering business objectives, providing an excellent administrative service and acting as a champion for effective people management.

DELIVERING BUSINESS OBJECTIVES

The most important way in which resourcing activities add value is by playing a significant role in the achievement of strategic objectives. Not all organisations have a clearly articulated business strategy, and sometimes where they do it is expressed in language that is too vague to be usefully translated into practical goals to be achieved in a defined time frame. Nonetheless, it can be said that all organisations exist for some purpose and that all should, at the very least, be striving to meet a set of aims or aspirations as effectively as possible. However clearly defined these objectives are, the P&D function via resourcing activities needs to be contributing, and must be able to demonstrate that it is doing so.

Key business objectives change over time, often for reasons wholly outside the control of managers. An organisation that is expanding one year may find itself needing to contract substantially in the next. Indeed many organisations nowadays find that they are both contracting and expanding at the same time, as one area of activity prospers while another flounders. Either way, resourcing activity is central to maximising the extent to which objectives are met effectively, efficiently and fairly. Expansion requires proficient recruitment and selection of new employees. It also requires the development of staff retention practices that minimise avoidable turnover of valuable people. It usually requires attention to be given to job analysis and the organisation of work so as to maximise the efficiency with which staff are deployed once recruited. Resourcing practice is also central when an organisation, or part of an organisation, contracts. The aim here is to shed staff in as professional and inexpensive way as possible, while minimising the damage done to long-term business prospects. Badly handled downsizing programmes not only cost a great deal more than is necessary (often at a time when the financial situation is tight), but also have a knock-on effect on the morale, commitment and performance of surviving staff, and can have a profoundly damaging effect on an organisation's image in the wider world.

Organisational performance is another key component of many business strategies. The aim is continually to improve the quality of products and services, or to maintain standards that have already been achieved. Frequently this has to be striven for in the face of stiff competition from other organisations and despite tightening cost constraints. Here too the resourcing function can play an important role. One way of adding value is through cost-effective recruitment and selection of people who are able to meet performance expectations. Once they have been hired, the need is to ensure that the individuals concerned are managed appropriately so that they are willing, as well as able, to perform to the expected levels. In tight labour markets particularly, where individuals can leave with relative ease, a sophisticated approach to the management of performance is required. Here P&D specialists work together with line managers to develop approaches that maximise the chances of success.

Effective change management is frequently required in order to ensure that business aims are met. However, it is often carried out incompetently by managers who are inclined to give people management considerations a low priority. Whether the change sought is essentially structural or cultural in nature (or both), the chances are that objectives will be met less effectively, or not met at all, without the contribution of P&D professionals focused on employment implications. Managing people's expectations is important here, as is proper employee involvement. Above all there is a need to manage the process sensitively with an eye to the long-term future. The alternative is a demoralised staff with little trust in those appointed to lead them, and inclined to look for jobs with competitor organisations should the opportunity arise. The result for the organisation is a failure to realise the advantages planned for the change, or more commonly, avoidable expenditure.

ADMINISTRATIVE EXCELLENCE

The idea of P&D functions supporting the achievement of business strategies has received such prominence in recent years that readers might be forgiven for considering it to be the only way in which the profession can add value. This is not the case. Helping to achieve business objectives is an essential part of the role, but it is insufficient on its own. Resourcing specialists also have tasks to achieve that may be less glamorous and more mundane, but that are equally important.

Whether we like it or not, it is important to recognise that all organisations need to be managed. They do not and cannot run themselves. The larger and more complex the organisation, the more administrative activities of one kind or another are necessary. Moreover, because organisations compete with others (or in the case of the public sector are answerable to taxpayers), there is an imperative to perform these necessary administrative activities as effectively as possible and at the lowest possible cost. Achieving this with maximum effectiveness and efficiency becomes a potential source of competitive advantage for the organisation. Since much administrative activity is the responsibility of P&D personnel, the P&D function adds value by ensuring that these tasks are achieved to a higher standard and more cost effectively than by competitors.

A great deal of resourcing activity falls into this category, the major examples being the following:

- human resource planning
- job analysis
- developing competency frameworks
- drawing up job descriptions, person specifications and accountability profiles
- administering recruitment and selection procedures
- training managers to recruit and select effectively
- drawing up contracts of employment
- managing induction processes
- issuing statements of terms and conditions of employment
- administering and recording absence
- developing effective training in performance management
- advising line managers and senior managers on matters relating to employment law
- drawing up appraisal documentation
- managing dismissal processes effectively, fairly and lawfully
- carrying out exit interviews with leavers
- processing documentation when someone leaves
- managing redundancy programmes

- handling retirements properly

- drawing up and reviewing P&D policy across all these areas of activity

- evaluating the effectiveness of P&D activity in the organisation.

There is another reason for striving towards administrative excellence. This derives from the fact that many P&D functions are established and maintained principally in order to carry out the kinds of activities listed above. It is thus essential that they are carried out professionally and competently if the function, and its managers, are to gain and maintain credibility within the organisation. If this is not achieved they will not be listened to by other managers and stand no chance whatever of gaining sufficient influence to participate in the direction of wider organisational decision-making. Administrative excellence is a prerequisite for more ambitious aims such as those described above in the context of the achievement of strategic objectives, and those discussed in the next paragraphs.

ACTING AS A CHAMPION FOR PEOPLE MANAGEMENT

In recent years a great deal of robust research evidence has been published showing the existence of clear links between effective people management practices and business success. Writers disagree about the precise nature of these links and their magnitude in terms of statistical significance, but most now agree with the claim that organisations that are good at managing their staff increase their chances of achieving long-term competitive advantage in their industries (see Boselie *et al* 2005, for a review of this literature). However, despite the published evidence and the inherent logic underlying the proposition, it remains the case that many managers are unconvinced of its validity. Their scepticism is often hidden behind a general adherence to statements about the importance of people to organisations, but is nonetheless demonstrated in their actions. Again and again P&D specialists find that their priorities are not shared by their bosses, who are more inclined to focus on short-term financial objectives and on devising means of enhancing effective management control over their organisations. This does not occur because chief executives and other senior directors are incompetent or unscrupulous, but because they are required to answer first and foremost to shareholders whose interest is often short-term financial gain. These are matters with which P&D specialists must also be concerned, but they also have a particular responsibility to argue for the very real contribution effective people management can make to the achievement of financial success over the longer term.

This is not to say that all organisations, whatever their financial or labour market position, must put in place 'gold-plated' resourcing policies and practices. It does not make good business sense for all organisations to seek to be 'employers of choice' or to invest more than all their competitors in the most expensive human resource systems that the market has to offer. However, there remains a need for P&D people continually to explain and demonstrate the worth of effective people management practices to a somewhat sceptical audience. If they don't no one else will, and the result is likely to be lost opportunities and, over time, loss of competitive advantage. It is really a question of playing the role of advocate for people management and seeking to ensure that staffing considerations are taken into account when business decisions are being taken. Value is only added if P&D professionals are able to remind other managers of the potential impact their actions can have on employee satisfaction, staff turnover rates, performance levels, the incidence of absence and the organisation's reputation in its key labour markets.

REFLECTIVE QUESTION

To what extent do you think the P&D function in your organisation 'adds value'? How would you go about demonstrating that this was the case?

EXERCISE 1.1

MAKING A DIFFERENCE

People management

Read the article Survival strategy (*People Management*, 28 October 2004, pp46–47). This can be downloaded from the *People Management* archive on the CIPD's website (www.cipd.co.uk).

This article consists of an exchange of letters or e-mails between two senior HR professionals: Neil Hayward of Serco, a large private sector company, and Hilary Douglas who is responsible for HR at the Treasury. They are discussing the future of the HR function in their different sectors, with a particular focus on the ways in which the function can 'make a difference' in organisations.

Questions

1   Which of the four main areas of resourcing activity identified above are cited in the article as being of particular importance now and in the future? Why do you think this is the case?

2   In what ways do you think people resourcing activities need to be organised and managed in order to achieve Hilary Douglas's vision of 'falling costs and rising value – a winning combination'?

3   Write a short list of the key points on which the two authors agree and those where there is some disagreement or difference of emphasis. To what extent can their differences be explained by the fact that they work in different sectors?

ORGANISING FOR ADDED VALUE

Traditionally, where a specialist P&D function had been established all of the above types of activity were carried out by the same team of people, and this remains the case in many organisations. This traditional approach thus involves teams of P&D generalists taking responsibility for delivering business objectives, achieving administrative excellence and also acting as champions for effective people management. Indeed, in many cases the traditional P&D role involves acting as an advocate in management circles not only for the effective management of people, but for the interests of employees too.

In recent years, however, mainly because of increased pressure on P&D departments to demonstrate that they are adding value, there has been a pronounced tendency, particularly in larger UK organisations, for the traditional P&D role to be split up. The work of the American academic and consultant Dave Ulrich has been particularly influential in this regard, his 'three-legged model' of the HR function having been put into practice in many organisations. Under such arrangements there are three distinct groups of P&D professional employed, each with a different function, and who may have relatively little to do with one another, at least on a day to day basis:

- A central shared service centre responsible for the provision of HR administration across the whole organisation. These roles are often based in call-centre operations, much communication also occurring via a corporate intranet site.

- Business partners are P&D specialists who operate at a local level, often reporting to business unit (ie divisional or departmental) managers undertaking case work and operating as part of a wider management team to help deliver the organisation's objectives through P&D activities.

- Centres of expertise, like service centres, operate from a central base but their role is to provide specialist advice to managers on, for example, legal matters, diversity, resourcing issues or reward practices. They also take the lead in developing organisational policy in these areas.

The advantage of the three-legged model over the traditional model is the achievement of greater efficiency. A large organisation can provide administrative excellence more cheaply and more effectively by centralising this service and making maximum use of technology in delivering it. This frees up the business partners and experts to focus all their efforts on activities which can be shown to add value because they help the organisation to achieve set objectives. Critics of the newer approaches, such as Francis and Keegan (2006), point out that there is a major flaw in that there is less room, and sometimes no room at all, for the P&D specialist to play the employee champion role. They go on to argue that this may well have negative long-term consequences if it results in less attention being given to employee well-being (see Key Article 1).

People management

EXERCISE 1.2

HM PRISON SERVICE

Read the article Cell block HR by Claire Warren (*People Management*, 12 October 2006, pp26–31). This can be downloaded from the *People Management* archive on the CIPD's website (www.cipd.co.uk).

This article describes the recent move by the HR function in the prison service away from a traditional model of P&D provision, with separate HR divisions within each prison, to a system that resembles Ulrich's three legged model. The key people resourcing issues facing the service are also discussed along with an assessment of the extent to which the P&D has and has not succeeded in adding value.

Questions

1   What are the key people resourcing problems currently facing HM Prison Service?

2   What steps have been taken to help solve them? To what extent have these been successful?

3   How is it anticipated that reorganising the P&D function will help to add greater value?

KEY ARTICLE 1

Helen Francis and Anne Keegan, The changing face of HRM: in search of balance. *Human Resource Management Journal*, Vol. 16, No. 3, pp231–249 (2006)

In this article the authors report their interviews with several dozen HR practitioners and people associated with the CIPD's professional development scheme about their perceptions of the term 'the thinking performer' – the idea which underpins all the Institute's professional standards, including those in the field of people resourcing. In the process they observe how influential David Ulrich's model has become, and in particular how focused people are on the 'business partner' role. They go on to analyse this trend from a critical perspective, noting that it involves the P&D function leaving behind to a great extent the traditional role it often played as an employee champion. Some long-term consequences which are undesirable both from an employer and employee perspective are then identified.

Questions

1   To what extent do you think the sample of people interviewed by the authors for this study is appropriate as a means of discovering opinion across the P&D profession? Who else might they have interviewed?

2   To what extent do you agree with the view that moves towards a 'business partner' view of the P&D manager's role will lead to a reduction in the extent to which employee interests are championed?

3   What consequences do the authors argue are likely to occur which will have a negative impact on organisations as well as their employees?

4   What practical lessons can be learned from the authors' analysis for P&D managers with responsibility for resourcing issues in particular?

MANAGING WITHIN CONSTRAINTS

Above we have set out what P&D professionals should strive to achieve. In an ideal world such would be the case. We would meet our staffing, performance, administration and change management objectives with relative ease. We would also manage to support the achievement of business objectives, function administratively to an excellent standard, and successfully convince our fellow managers of the merits of our priorities. Unfortunately, of course, our world is far from ideal. We may (and indeed must) strive to achieve these objectives, but we also need to recognise that doing so is often a hard, uphill struggle during which many setbacks can occur. No manager, least of all P&D professionals, can exercise total control over the environment in which an organisation operates. Managers are thus faced with significant constraints on their power to achieve exactly what they want. We may be able to set out plans to help our organisations meet their core objectives, but we will only be able to put these into practice after first negotiating a variety of obstacles. A good case can thus be made for arguing that the effective P&D manager is someone who is able through professional knowledge and experience to help steer an organisation past, through or over these obstacles. It follows that resourcing policy and practices must be informed by both the need to underpin the achievement of organisational goals and the need to manage activities within the constraints of the business environment. It would be great if the former could be achieved without giving much attention to the latter, as sometimes appears to be assumed by management theorists, but this is not a practical possibility.

Figure 1.1 Factors influencing resourcing activities

There are all manner of constraints which can act as barriers which get in the way of the smooth and speedy achievement of P&D objectives. However, from a resourcing point of view it is possible to identify five which are particularly significant: labour market conditions, regulation, employee attitudes, poor line managers and trade unions.

LABOUR MARKETS

Labour market conditions often act as a major constraint on the activities of resourcing specialists by ensuring that it is not always possible to attract and retain the staff that are needed at a particular time or at a given level of reward. Commentators often seem to forget that employers are obliged to compete in labour markets for employees and that this sometimes makes it difficult (or even impossible) to fulfil business objectives. When labour markets are relatively loose, for example at times of high unemployment, the constraint is less problematic. The problem arises when labour markets are tight and staff with the required skills or attitudes are hard to come by. The professional P&D manager will always be aware of this constraint and of the need to operate effectively as a labour market competitor. This will ensure that the organisation is best placed to secure the services of the people it needs. Effective labour market competition involves the following:

- Understanding the dynamics of the labour markets that are most important to your organisation (What makes them tick? Why do people switch jobs? Why do people join a particular profession? What alternative job opportunities are available for your own staff?).

- Considering the long-term implications of management actions for the organisation's labour market position (What is the impact on the ability to attract new recruits? Will a change in policy or practice serve to improve or worsen employee turnover rates?).

- Acting to bolster the organisation's labour market reputation (What can we do to improve the way we are perceived as an employer by potential employees, current employees and ex-employees?).

In Chapter 3 you will read about these issues in more depth, focusing in particular on the problems and opportunities that tight labour markets pose for P&D practitioners.

REGULATION

A second major constraint on actions in the resourcing field is imposed by employment legislation, which can seriously limit the room we have for manoeuvre in certain areas of activity. The ever-growing volume of regulation serves to make this particular constraint harder and harder to negotiate with each passing year. While it is true that much employment law is inadequately policed and unknown to employees, professional P&D managers will not be prepared to allow their organisations to act unlawfully in the hope that no consequences will follow. When Employment Tribunal cases are brought, the task of defending them is always most likely to fall on the P&D manager's desk.

The major areas of relevance for day-to-day resourcing practice are discrimination law, unfair dismissal law, maternity and parental leave regulations and the various EU directives that now give protection to groups of atypical workers such as those employed on fixed-term or part-time contracts. Developments in this field are reviewed in greater detail in Chapter 4.

EMPLOYEE ATTITUDES

A further constraint on the power of managers to meet their objectives in a manner of their own choosing derives from the unwillingness, in certain situations, of employees to comply. Poor people management breeds low-trust relationships and greatly increases the likelihood that individual employees will fail to perform to the best of their ability. It is to some extent possible to select people in the first place on grounds of their attitude, giving prominence to attributes such as conscientiousness or evidence of a strong work ethic. It is also possible to make inferences from past actions about likely future attitudes. However, such approaches cannot alter the fact that people, no matter what their individual attitudes towards work, tend to respond negatively when they believe that they or their colleagues are being treated inequitably, inconsistently or arbitrarily by their managers. The result is a situation in which poor employers find themselves having to cope with high turnover and absence rates, adversarial employee relations and generally with a workforce that is demotivated and unwilling to 'go the extra mile' in order to satisfy customers. All these are signs of a P&D function that is failing to deliver on its key objectives.

The professional resourcing specialist recognises these realities and seeks to ensure that employees, within reason, are not given cause to become dissatisfied. Much, of course, is outside our control. Pay levels, for example, are often a major source of low motivation, but are inevitably determined by business conditions. Nonetheless, there is a great deal that a well-respected, influential P&D manager can do to provide a good platform for positive employee attitudes. First, it is important to ensure that people are treated equitably and that an approach akin to 'the rule of law' is followed. This means that everyone is subject to the same set of rules and is judged according to the same principles. There should be no perception of favouritism and no examples of people being victimised simply because a particular manager has taken a dislike to them. Such an approach ensures that everyone knows where they stand and that managers do not act arbitrarily in disciplining their staff, distributing work or managing performance. Second, there is a need to ensure that everyone who is employed, in whatever capacity, is treated with respect. There is nothing more unhealthy than a workplace in which managers give the appearance of abusing their positions by treating subordinates rudely or harshly simply because they can get away with doing so. Proper selection and training of managers is important here, as is effective ongoing assessment of their performance as supervisors. Finally, there is a great deal to be said for encouraging a culture of employee involvement. Institutions through which employees' voices are heard can help in this respect, but it just as important to find ways of eliciting opinions from individuals about their own areas of work. This ensures that they are treated with basic courtesy and respect – essential prerequisites for genuine employee commitment.

POOR LINE MANAGERS

Line managers, particularly front-line supervisors who have day-to-day responsibility for managing the employment relationship that an organisation has with individual employees, can either hinder the effective realisation of HR objectives or contribute greatly to their achievement. Their key role as mediators between HR policy and its implementation in practice is increasingly being recognised as more and more studies are carried out which focus on employee attitudes and the sources of satisfaction and dissatisfaction at work. In the United Kingdom, recent studies carried out by John Purcell and his colleagues have shown that achieving superior employee performance, a high instance of discretionary effort, low employee turnover and a positive reputation as an employer require both appropriate human resource policies and their full and effective implementation in practice (see Purcell and Kinnie 2007, Purcell and Hutchinson 2007 and Purcell *et al* 2003a). The latter is the job of first line managers, who by implication can therefore constrain the achievement of the objectives if they fail to give effect to the policies through incompetence, lack of effort or active opposition.

In most organisations many key people resourcing activities are carried out by front line managers, often alone or only with quite limited guidance from P&D specialists. They are frequently the key decision-makers when selection decisions are being made, central to performance appraisal procedures, the major people responsible for deciding whether and how to discipline staff or to reward them, and the people P&D specialists rely on to carry out any new policies they develop. From the employees' point of view the front line manager is the face of management that they have to deal with on a day-to-day basis, and hence the person who is able far more than anyone else to motivate them positively or to demotivate them. If these management tasks are carried out ineffectively, the objectives of the P&D function will not be achieved.

There are two major implications for P&D specialists. First, it is necessary to pay particular attention to the selection, development and ongoing appraisal of line managers. Time, effort and resources are well spent on trying to ensure that line managers have the right attitudes and skills to carry out their job effectively. Too often we promote people into supervisory positions on the basis of seniority or technical skill, without giving proper consideration to people-management skills. Often we simply make the assumption that people will be able to mange others without training them or supporting them in what can be a very demanding and difficult role. Second, it is necessary for P&D specialists to maintain an effective working relationship with line managers in their organisations. The relationship should be characterised by high levels of trust, respect and shared aims. Too often this is not the case, often because P&D specialists allow themselves to be seen as unhelpful, somewhat distant and prone to preventing line managers from running their departments as they see fit. The relationship works best when both parties see it as a partnership of equals in which neither pulls rank over the other, when each actively seeks to understand the other's perspective, respects the other's spheres of expertise and takes steps to assist the other in achieving their objectives.

John Purcell and Sue Hutchinson, Front-line managers as agents in the HRM–performance causal chain: theory, analysis and evidence. *Human Resource Management Journal,* **Vol. 17, No. 1, pp 3–20 (2007)**

KEY ARTICLE 2

This article looks in detail at the role played by front-line managers with direct supervisory responsibility for employees in applying HR policies and practices. The results of two separate but linked pieces of research are presented which together make a strong case for focusing on the effective selection and development of line managers. The first is quantitative in nature. The authors present an analysis of 40 interviews carried out with randomly selected samples of 40 employees in 12 UK organisations. This demonstrates a correlation between, on the one hand, various measures of organisation commitment and job satisfaction, and on the other, perceptions of HR practices and the 'leadership behaviours' demonstrated by front-line managers. The second piece of research that is presented is a longitudinal study based at one of the 12 organisations – the Selfridges department store in the Trafford Centre, Manchester. This shows that active steps taken by senior managers to improve the quality of front-line management in the store had a markedly positive impact on employee turnover and performance in a relatively short time.

Questions

1   Explain the concept of the 'causal chain' identified by Purcell and Hutchinson in this article. Why is it helpful in understanding the role played by front-line managers in implementing P&D policies and practices?

2   What are the key findings of the first research study described in the article? How convincing do you find the authors' conclusions and why?

3   What are the key findings of the second research study described in the article? To what extent do they add further weight to the findings of the first study?

4   What are the main practical lessons to be learned from this article for a P&D manager with particular responsibility for people resourcing activities in an organisation?

TRADE UNIONS

Trade unions should not necessarily be characterised as acting as a constraint on management action in the resourcing field. Where trust is established, perhaps through some form of partnership agreement, a healthy, co-operative relationship can flourish, bringing benefits to employer and employee alike. However, it remains the case in many organisations that the presence of well-trained, effective union officials acting with the backing of the workforce does in practice limit the freedom of P&D people to carry out the resourcing aspects of their role. This is especially true of situations in which dismissal is a possible, if distant outcome, as in the case when managing cases of poor performance, unsatisfactory attendance, ill health, misconduct or redundancy. The truth is that when a union official is involved, P&D managers often have to tread more carefully than when they are dealing with employees who are not effectively represented. This occurs in part because union officials are more detached from the individual employee's predicament, and can thus display greater confidence in advocating their interests, but also in part because union officials tend to know their employment law and are familiar with the way the organisation's policies have been applied previously.

Many organisations are not unionised, while as many as 49 per cent employ no one at all who is a union member (Kersley *et al* 2006, p110), but it must be remembered that there is now a right for all employees to be represented by a union official at a serious disciplinary or grievance hearing. It is therefore necessary for all professional P&D managers to develop the capacity to manage this kind of relationship effectively. The key requirements are the following:

- Act in a straight and professional manner, taking account of the union official's legitimate interests.

- Ensure that you are fully prepared and briefed before any meeting at which a union official will be present – both about the facts of the matter in hand and the legal implications of any proposed actions.

- Do not allow yourself to be put on the back foot or required to react defensively. When in doubt of your position, adjourn the meeting and take time to form a considered response.

- Ensure that you treat people consistently in similar sets of circumstances to avoid any just accusations of unfairness.

REFLECTIVE QUESTION

What other constraints can you think of which need to be negotiated in order to achieve organisational goals? How relevant are these to the activities of people resourcing specialists?

EXERCISE 1.3

WILLIAM HILL

Read the article by Steve Smethurst, Onto a winner (*People Management*, 29 January 2004, pp35–36). This can be downloaded from the *People Management* archive on the CIPD's website (www.cipd.co.uk).

The article describes the major environmental pressures that drive and constrain the P&D function at the William Hill chain of betting shops.

Questions

1   What are the major environmental developments that are determining the change in direction of William Hill's business strategy?

2   What are the major implications for people resourcing activities?

3   In what ways is the company's freedom of manoeuvre constrained by other developments in its business environment?

INTEGRATION WITH OTHER P&D ACTIVITIES

It is important to remember that the term 'people resourcing' is an invention of the CIPD. Its purpose is to serve as a means of distinguishing the management activities described above from those covered by the other CIPD elective subjects: employee relations, training and development, and reward management. In practice there is no real barrier between these different areas of activity and none should be created, even where each is the responsibility of a different manager. Activity in the resourcing field often has an impact on what happens in the other areas and vice versa. Moreover, solutions to problems are frequently to be found through the agency of 'joint actions' that draw on thinking and practice from more than one specialist area. Some examples are as follows:

- A skills shortage can be eased through resourcing activities (eg better recruitment, more effective retention, better deployment of skilled staff), but also hugely benefits from intervention on the training and development front.

- Activities in the development, reward and relations fields are significant in their ability to underpin job satisfaction. They thus play a major role in reducing staff turnover and making an employer a more attractive proposition for potential employees.

- Maximising individual levels of performance and addressing poor performance is a central resourcing role. These are also, however, key objectives of reward systems, achieved through the use of incentive schemes and the achievement of perceived equity in terms of pay distribution.

- The effective introduction and utilisation of performance management initiatives are also matters that affect collective employment relationships and are thus a concern of employee relations specialists.

- Poorly introduced initiatives in the resourcing field (eg a new absence management policy, changed contractual terms or redundancy programmes) often have very profound employee relations implications.

- The effectiveness of the training and development function has important implications for human resource planning activity and is central to the effective induction of new employees.

Many other examples could also be cited to illustrate the futility, and indeed danger, of seeing resourcing activity as discrete or being undertaken in a theatre which is in some way distinct from the other major P&D functions. In practice the lines between each is blurred. It is important to remember this when analysing the likely effectiveness of a future resourcing intervention and when evaluating existing organisational practice. It is particularly important to think about the links between the different areas of HR practice (horizontal integration) and with the business strategy of the organisation (vertical integration) if you are preparing to sit CIPD exams. The ability to demonstrate a full understanding of these links and their practical significance is something that many exam questions across all the papers often seek to test.

APPROACHES TO PEOPLE RESOURCING

The CIPD's standards for people resourcing specifically set out three distinct paradigms, or frames of reference, that managers can adopt when dealing with resourcing matters. The implication is that none of the three in itself constitutes the 'right' approach and that there is a good case for all to be adopted in different types of situation. The three are assessed below.

THE TRADITIONAL PARADIGM

The traditional paradigm represents established 'good practice' thinking about the management of the resourcing function. It might be characterised as comprising traditional 'textbook' approaches, and is often thought of as the basis for a definition of professionalism in this field. Several features of this paradigm can be identified:

- It tends to assume that organisations are of medium or large size and that they are traditionally structured with a management hierarchy, clear lines of accountability and well-defined roles assigned to the people who are employed.

- It tends see the resourcing function in terms of a chronological process mirroring an individual's employment. This starts with human resource planning, before moving on through job analysis, recruitment, selection and performance management, and ending with resignation or dismissal.

- Another background assumption is that organisations are able to exercise a fair degree of control over their business environments and that they are reasonably stable from one year to the next. The drawing up of policy documents and job descriptions thus makes sense.

- There is a tendency to assume that people all work under contracts of employment and that they perceive themselves as belonging to an organisation. Working relationships that are voluntary in nature, casual or based on self-employment are perceived as 'atypical' or contrary to the norm.

- There is an assumption that organisations operate in competitive environments, be they in the private or public sectors.

There is nothing at all wrong with these assumptions or with the traditional paradigm. Despite the evolving change in the business context, it remains entirely appropriate for most organisations. However, it is important that we do not consider it to be the only valid approach, or condemn as being in some way 'unprofessional' alternative approaches that may make good business sense.

THE CONTINGENCY-BASED PARADIGM

As defined in the CIPD standards, this paradigm can be characterised as accepting that rather different approaches to people resourcing can and *should be* used in different types of situation. The assumptions set out above, which form the background to the traditional paradigm, do not apply here. Instead the only assumption is that organisations vary considerably in terms of their environments, their aims and their structures. What is appropriate for one is often inappropriate for others.

The assumptions behind the traditional paradigm are, for example, irrelevant in the case of many small firms with few resources. There is often only one manager in such concerns, with other staff assuming responsibilities here and there on an ad hoc basis. Management may be carried out in a very informal, personal manner, with no written policies, as little employment documentation as possible, and certainly no P&D specialists. The same is true of organisations that rely on large numbers of voluntary workers, or of those experimenting with a 'virtual' approach where pretty well everyone is employed on a subcontracted basis. In all these types of situation there is a need to approach resourcing activities from a different angle, while seeking ultimately to achieve the same basic objectives. Above all such organisations are likely to find the formality of procedures that are central to the traditional paradigm unnecessarily stifling and restrictive.

Formality is also inappropriate for some larger organisations in certain types of situation. It is important to understand that organisations hit serious crises from time to time that necessitate very quick and profound change. In such circumstances it is simply absurd to expect or argue for a 'by the book' approach to people management. There is no time to respect the professional niceties if the organisation is to survive. In such circumstances the traditional paradigm has to be abandoned and a less predictable, disordered approach adopted that may itself need to change on a daily basis.

Another example of an organisational type that does not fit the traditional paradigm is one that is transient: set up for a limited period of time to carry out a particular function and then closed. Events management is the most common example, where a 'company of players' is assembled and required to perform in close-knit teams, often quite intensely, but for just a few weeks or months. There is no expectation of long-term employment on the part of participants; indeed there is no possibility of such employment. Hence, traditional approaches to performance management and employee retention, for example, are irrelevant. The nature of the contracts too, both legal and psychological, is necessarily very different from the norm.

Then there are not-for-profit organisations, which are not required to adopt a competitive stance. Their role is to co-operate with others, to undertake joint projects or simply to undertake charitable activities. While they still have to compete with other employers for staff, they are not faced with the same commercial pressures as private sector companies and increasing numbers of public sector organisations. The rationale behind their resourcing activities is thus different, as are the benchmarks against which their performance is judged. This has consequences for most of their resourcing practices. They will look to recruit people with a different orientation and different ambitions from those sought by commercial organisations, and will subsequently manage their performance differently. Importantly, because of the lack of competitive pressure, different criteria will determine the methods used to encourage good performance.

These are all clear examples of contingencies that are unfavourable for the adoption of the traditional paradigm. There are many other examples of situations where a less total adaptation is required, maybe involving just one part of a larger organisation or lasting only for a limited period of time. What is important is that resourcing specialists should not resist moves away from the traditional paradigm where alternatives make good business sense. Adopting different sets of assumptions, provided they are lawful and ethical, need not compromise professionalism.

NEW PARADIGMS

Even where the organisation you work for takes a traditional form, it is important not to assume that the traditional paradigm has to be the one that you work within. Innovation is not usually incompatible with professionalism, and is certainly not incompatible with the achievement of competitive advantage. While it is true that research has found strong correlations between traditional 'good practice' approaches and business success, this does not mean that organisations that manage people differently cannot achieve even greater success. Indeed, it is often because of the willingness of maverick figures to 'think outside the box' that major advances in professional practice are brought about. Several examples of this occurring in practice, including areas of resourcing policy, are provided by Marcus Buckingham and Curt Coffman (1999) in their influential book *First break all the rules: what the world's greatest managers do differently.*

The approach they advocate is uncomplicated, but tends to be one that many of us recoil from, largely because we lack the confidence to take on 'received wisdom' or to question established ways of doing things. You simply start with a blank sheet of paper and focus on your end goal. You then start thinking of the most straightforward, commonsensical means of achieving the objective. This is done without making assumptions about what is currently considered to be the right way. Most of the examples given in Buckingham and Coffman's book tell of managers replacing organisationally prescribed practices – often bureaucratic ones – with simpler approaches that are more effective. For example, in their chapter on performance management they cite examples of managers being impatient with 'the complexity of most company-sponsored performance appraisal schemes'. These are thus abandoned in favour of 'a format that allows them to concentrate on the truly difficult work: what to say to each employee and how to say it'. Other features of the innovative approach they describe include very frequent meetings to discuss performance (as opposed to once a year, as prescribed in most appraisal schemes), future focus and giving employees responsibility for keeping track of their 'own performance and learnings'. In each respect (ie simplicity, frequency, focus and responsibility), this approach turns the one commonly associated with the traditional paradigm on its head.

It is necessary to accept that the kind of solutions to issues that are reached via innovative thinking about resourcing processes may not always work in practice. It may also be inappropriate to use this approach across a whole organisation, but there is nonetheless a good case for experimenting from time to time. Managers who want to think differently and develop new approaches should not therefore be seen by P&D professionals, as they often are, as nuisances or awkward customers. Instead they should be encouraged to experiment and supported wherever it is practicable to do so. The result may just be a better way of doing things, and one that competitors will find it hard to replicate.

EXERCISE 1.4

NORWICH COMMUNITY HOSPITAL

Read the article by Rima Manocha, Game plan (*People Management*, 6 November 2003, p39). This can be downloaded from the *People Management* archive on the CIPD's website (www.cipd.co.uk).

The article describes the way in which an NHS Trust managed to improve its efficiency considerably, reducing the average length that patients stayed in its beds, by identifying weaknesses in its systems.

Questions

1 To what extent do you think this hospital applied the principles described here under the heading 'new paradigms'?

2 Why do you think the hospital was so successful in gaining the support of its staff for the changes it introduced?

3 Aside from efficiency savings, what other benefits resulted from the changes from a P&D perspective?

CHAPTER SUMMARY

- The 'people resourcing function' is concerned with meeting our different types of organisational objective. These are staffing objectives, performance objectives, administration objectives and change management objectives.

- It is important to review the contribution made by resourcing practices regularly. Key criteria are effectiveness, efficiency and fairness.

- Resourcing specialists principally 'add value' for their organisations by supporting the achievement of organisational objectives and providing 'administrative excellence'. A third way is through acting as a champion of effective people management.

- Good P&D professionals accept that they can only achieve their objectives by managing within the constraints of the business environment. The major constraints that resourcing specialists must negotiate are provided by the labour market, employment legislation, employee attitudes and trade unions.

- It is possible to identify three types of paradigm that determine the assumptions that underpin resourcing activity. These are the traditional paradigm, the contingency-based paradigm and the new paradigm.

CHAPTER 2

The competitive environment

P&D professionals can only make a full contribution to the management of their organisations if they gain a full understanding of the factors in the business environment that are having the biggest impact. They need to understand the commercial pressures that drive decision-making and the formation of strategy if they are to develop policies and practices that genuinely support the achievement of organisational goals. However, this in itself is insufficient, because P&D people are hired, at least in part, to advise their organisations about developments in the employment environment. It is thus important to be able to grasp and articulate the key developments in the world outside the organisation itself that most affect the resourcing function. In addition to current developments, it is necessary to anticipate future environmental trends as far as is possible. This allows plans to be drawn up in plenty of time, with the result that your organisation is better placed to respond than your competitors.

It is not possible in one chapter to review all factors in the business environment that have an impact on resourcing activity. Other CIPD books provide a far more comprehensive coverage of these matters (eg Farnham 2005, Stredwick and Kew 2005, Daniels 2004, Lewis and Sargeant 2007). It is, however, useful to point to the most important developments and to reflect directly on what they mean, and will mean in the future, for the resourcing function. All the themes covered here are returned to later in the book in the context of the chief operational tasks carried out by resourcing specialists, but it is only here that they and their general significance are explained at any length. This chapter is the first of three that look at different aspects of the business environment, focusing on the key developments and their consequences for people resourcing functions. Here we assess key trends in today's commercial environment. In Chapter 3 we look at labour market issues and in Chapter 4 at developments in the field of employment regulation.

LEARNING OUTCOMES

By the end of this chapter readers should be able to:

- advise on the resourcing implications of increased volatility in product markets

- advise on P&D activities during merger and acquisition situations

- identify key technological developments and appreciate their likely future impact on organisations

- evaluate the significance of increased international economic activity for their industry and for the P&D function

- contribute towards the management of resourcing policy when an organisation internationalises its operations

- appreciate the consequences for resourcing practice of increasing customer expectations.

In addition, readers should be able to understand and explain:

- the reasons for increased commercial volatility

- the types of P&D activity required during mergers and acquisitions

- major trends in the technological environment

- the forces underpinning internationalisation of business

- the implications from a P&D perspective of trends towards globalisation.

THE COMMERCIAL ENVIRONMENT

There are clearly a huge number of diverse trends that are responsible for shaping the contemporary business environment. It is impossible in a few short paragraphs to analyse all the relevant factors and their potential impact on resourcing practice. However, it is possible to argue that the net effect, at least for most organisations, is the emergence of a commercial world that is a good deal more volatile and unpredictable than was the case a decade or two ago. The extent of competitive intensity in an industry is very difficult to measure objectively or to track over time because so many factors need to be taken into account. All the anecdotal evidence, however, strongly suggests that organisations in all sectors of the economy are subject to a good deal more competition than was the case a decade ago, and very much more than they were 20 years ago. The term 'hyper-competitive' is sometimes used to describe the evolving commercial environment, indicating that the speed of change is far greater than has been the case previously in human history (Sparrow 2002). This change has been brought about principally through the interaction of three developments. The first derives from information technology, the second from the process of internationalisation and the third from government policies designed actively to promote competition. The result is a world in which competition between organisations is fiercer and the stakes higher.

Volatility has been further strengthened by the creation of much more choice for consumers as to how they spend their money. The sheer range of products and services on offer is far greater than previously, making customers more fickle, keen to try alternatives, less loyal to producers and generally rather harder to please. The more choice there is on offer, the more likelihood there is that customers will exercise their choices and transfer their business to other organisations. We thus have to work much harder at satisfying existing customers and at selling our products and services to new ones. Below we look in more detail at the specific consequences of these forces for resourcing activities. First it is necessary to focus more generally on the notion of volatility and on its impact. The key trends were effectively articulated and accurately anticipated by Stalk *et al* (1992) in an often-quoted article in the *Harvard Business Review*. They compare the 'old' commercial world with the 'new' as follows:

Key features of the old world

- a relatively static economy

- relatively static business strategies

- durable products

- stable customer needs

- well-defined markets

- clearly identified competitors.

Key features of the new world

- a fast-changing economy

- continually evolving business strategies

- short product life-cycles

- changing customer needs

- a global market place

- thousands of potential competitors.

The result, according to the Stalk *et al* analysis (1992, p62), is a shift from an environment in which 'companies occupied competitive space like squares on a chess board' to one in which 'competition is a war of movement in which success depends on anticipation of market trends and quick response to changing customer needs'. They go on to argue that the consequence is a need for successful competitors to 'move quickly in and out of products, markets, and sometimes even entire businesses' in 'a process more akin to an interactive video than to chess'.

REFLECTIVE QUESTION

To what extent do you recognise your own organisation's environment in the analysis of Stalk *et al* (1992)? Is strategic management more like chess or an the interactive video game?

As with many articles of this kind, the case is somewhat overstated. There remain many organisations that can still, to an extent at least, work according to the 'old rules'. But for a growing proportion the 'new' world described by Stalk and his colleagues has become or is becoming a reality. For these organisations, success – or even survival – does very much depend on their ability to anticipate consumer tastes, to respond quickly to opportunities and threats, and to provide the best possible service to their customers at the lowest possible price. There are major and profound consequences for the resourcing function. The most important are as follows:

- the need to find people to work in organisations that are regularly contracting and expanding in different directions

- the need to manage people during frequent periods of structural change and reorganisation, including mergers and acquisitions

- the need to cope with situations of rapid growth in numbers and rapid decline

- the need to recruit and motivate people to work effectively in organisations or parts of organisations which are transient (ie set up to meet a temporary need or opportunity, or to carry out a short project).

These types of situation affect almost every aspect of the resourcing function. First, they call into question the usefulness of traditional, long-term human resource planning activity. Why plan for the long term when there is such uncertainty ahead or where there is no long term for the organisation? Human resource planning is still needed, but it has to be more focused on specific episodes in an organisation's existence, and broader in terms of what factors are incorporated into the plan. The same is true of job analysis and more generally of policy-making across the resourcing field. All these types of activity must be more adaptable to change than was hitherto the case. Second, there is a need to manage expectations very differently in order to recruit and retain the best available employees. It is no longer possible to promise stable, long-term employment. Instead organisations have to offer enhanced employability to their recruits, so that they leave with useful experience, greater knowledge or a better-developed capacity to carry out a range of activities. Third, there is a need to select the people who are most likely to be able to adapt, and subsequently to encourage and reward such behaviour. Innovation needs to bolstered and ways found to persuade people to acquire new skills on a regular basis. This has implications for traditional top-down approaches to supervision, which have tended to stifle creativity, to discourage the open exchange of new ideas and to eschew employee involvement in decision-making. Finally there is of course a need to embrace flexibility in terms of the types of contractual arrangement offered by organisations, and for the P&D function itself to become adaptable and open to new approaches.

HOW NOT TO MANAGE CHANGE

People management

EXERCISE 2.1

Read the article by Lynne Baxter and Alasdair Macleod, Unhappy endings (*People Management*, 5 April 2007, pp38–40). This can be downloaded from the *People Management* archive on the CIPD's website (www.cipd.co.uk).

This article summarises the main findings of an extensive longitudinal research project in which the authors studied change management episodes in a variety of organisations, all of which were aimed at increasing quality or efficiency. In many cases the results were very disappointing because they were handled poorly by the managers concerned. Interestingly though, few admitted their failures, many taking steps to make it look as if they had actually been successful.

Questions

1   What, according to the authors, were the major reasons for the failure of the initiatives in the companies studied?

2   What were their major observations about organisations where the initiatives succeeded?

3   What do you think are the main negative consequences of organisations 'creating an impression of improvement' when they have failed to bring about material change?

KEY ARTICLE 3

Louise Amoore, Risk, reward and discipline at work. *Economy and Society*, Vol. 33, No. 2, pp174–196 (2004)

In this lively and thought-provoking article written from a very critical perspective, Louise Amoore argues that organisations, consultants and government ministers have accepted too readily the idea that organisations must increase flexibility in order to survive in a much more uncertain and volatile business environment. The extent to which developments outside the organisation have contributed to the growth of volatility has been overstated, while the substantial contribution made by the organisational response (outsourcing functions, employing people on a more flexible basis and managing performance by requiring employees to 'embrace risk') has been understated. In other words, it is argued that organisational policy is as much to blame for creating economic uncertainty as developments in the wider business environment. The result is a situation in which organisations have managed to displace the risk from themselves and on to their employees.

Questions

1   To what extent have you observed initiatives that seek to persuade employees of the need to 'embrace uncertainty' in your own working life?

2   How far have these been genuine responses to increased uncertainty in the business environment?

3   To what extent do you agree that initiatives aimed at increasing flexibility on the part of employees themselves serve to increase the volatility of the environment?

4   Is it fair to see these initiatives as being a method of protecting the interests of powerful groups at the expense of employees' interests?

5   What alternative approaches might be adopted in order to ensure the prosperity of organisations in a more competitive global economy?

MERGERS AND ACQUISITIONS

An increasingly common feature of corporate life that results from increased volatility in product markets is the selling off of businesses (or parts of businesses) to new owners and the merging of organisations to create a much larger, more efficient, and if all goes well more commercially robust entity. There are over 1,000 mergers and acquisitions involving public companies each year in the United Kingdom, to which can be added thousands more in the small firms sector and equivalent reorganisations involving public sector organisations. The amount of such activity has grown markedly in recent years, making it likely that all P&D professionals will be involved in the management of a merger or acquisition at some stage in their careers. The term 'merger and acquisition' can be used to describe a variety of different situations, some of which have a far greater impact on P&D activities than others. The most important distinction is between processes in which partners of broadly equal size join forces (a merger of equals) and a combination that involves the merging of a small organisation into a rather larger one. In the latter case, although it may technically be a merger rather than an acquisition, the practical reality as experienced by employees is something akin to a takeover of one organisation by another. Indeed, mergers of equal partners often feel more like takeovers for the staff involved when the 'new' senior management team is largely composed of people only from one or other of the partners.

Some mergers and acquisitions have very little impact on the day-to-day management of an organisation, at least in the short term. This occurs when a business changes ownership, but still continues to operate as a separate entity (as in the case of Asda and Wal-Mart). Over time structural changes are made, new people brought in and some assimilation of cultures encouraged, but little occurs overnight. By contrast there are many examples of organisations that work to some kind of 'D-day' timetable. After a predetermined date their identities are wholly merged, teams brought together under a unitary management structure, terms and conditions harmonised, uniform policies adopted and logos changed (eg Price Waterhouse with Coopers and Lybrand). In between are operations that involve bringing together central management functions while allowing the individual business units or branches to continue operating as before (eg Lloyds and TSB). Another difference is between processes that result in significant job losses and those that do not. The final major distinction is between mergers and acquisitions that are organised very quickly, often because they are kept confidential until carried out, and those that are planned quite openly over years or months before being formalised.

Each of the above situations has rather different implications from a P&D perspective. Some amount to profound and complex change management scenarios requiring careful planning and implementation. Others can be handled more steadily and opportunistically over time as two or more organisations gradually assimilate their practices. It is therefore difficult to set out general advice or 'good practice' for use during mergers and acquisitions. Too much depends on the particular circumstances facing individual organisations. However, what is clear is that a heavy amount of P&D

involvement of one kind or another is necessary if the benefits of these processes are to be fully realised.

The major reasons for mergers and acquisitions relate to the achievement of greater competitive advantage. By and large, when they are well managed, larger organisations are better placed than smaller ones to compete effectively in global markets. They can withstand commercial shocks more effectively and can harness economies of scale to cut their costs. The result is a better-quality product or service, offered at lower price and with a higher profit margin. Larger organisations are also better placed than their smaller rivals to promote themselves effectively, to expand overseas and to raise money for the development of new product lines. The result should therefore be a substantially improved business position, measured in terms of profitability, productivity or market share. However, research into the results of mergers and acquisitions strongly suggests that around half can be described as failures when judged against their original objectives (Cartwright and Schoenberg 2006, ppS1). Moreover, a number of studies have shown that in many of these cases the failure results from a mishandling of the 'people issues' (CIPD 2003a). Often this occurs simply because senior managers are so focused on strategic, financial and legal issues that they do not make the time to consider the implications for or concerns of staff. The results include the following:

- loss of commitment to an organisation that has ceased to exist

- uncertainty about roles and job security leading to voluntary resignations

- loss of productivity as merger activities take up people's time and effort

- conflict between different cultures after mergers

- low morale and undue stress as inadequate resources are set aside for merger activities

- organisational inertia during mergers as people focus on themselves and their own futures rather than on achieving business objectives.

Some consequences of this kind are inevitable during any change management process. There will always be winners and losers, and there will always be anxiety created. However, the extent to which such matters are able to harm organisational effectiveness can be greatly reduced by paying proper attention and assigning sufficient resources to the management of the human dimension.

An important task for organisations embarking on a merger or acquisition is the need to manage employee expectations effectively. According to Hubbard and Purcell (2001, p31), this can be achieved successfully and, once achieved, will bring forward the time at which people stop focusing on internal changes and turn their minds to business issues:

> The vast majority of employees we interviewed at all levels wanted to know the vision, the way forward for the newly-acquired company and where they 'fitted in'. It appeared that, once the plan for the company was known, beyond the initial hype, and their own position was made clear, employees were reasonably

secure and willing to continue in their work capacity. It was almost as if they needed to rationalise the changes in their own minds – any additional information provided accelerated that process.

This quotation raises some interesting questions. First it seems to suggest that the more information given to employees, the better. Yet at the same time there is clearly a need to avoid confusing them or, worse still, misleading them by providing too much information. Central to Hubbard and Purcell's findings is the need for managers to maintain high levels of credibility and trust. Once people perceive that they are being misled by managers or manipulated into accepting arrangements with which they are uncomfortable, that trust is lost. The result thereafter is an uphill struggle for managers to make a success of the merger. At the other end of the scale, providing too little information will send rumour mills into overdrive, which can be equally damaging if they result in unfounded fear of future outcomes. There is also a need to balance the need to provide accurate, comprehensive and up-to-date information about proposals with the need to consult employees as much as is possible.

Reassurance is important to successful outcomes in all change management scenarios, but so is a sense that staff have participated in decision-making. The problem is that consultation takes time and can easily cause an 'information interval' during which damaging rumours get spread around. The business of managing expectations is thus difficult and requires skilful handling. There is a need to provide very regular updates via e-mail, newsletters and face-to-face meetings through which the process is explained to employees. There is also a need to invite views and take on board suggestions, making it clear where matters have and have not been finalised. This process has to be planned, but not set in stone. Managers have to keep their ears to the ground so that they can establish very quickly where misinformation is being spread and respond very quickly to put the record straight. Throughout the process, however, they need to ensure that they only put out information that is wholly accurate and cannot be interpreted in different ways. False statements of reassurance are just as damaging in the long term when it comes to managing employee expectations as false rumours of gloom and doom.

Aside from communication and the effective management of expectations, the other 'soft' issue that needs to be managed during a merger or acquisition process is cultural assimilation. Another major root cause of failure is a difficult post-merger phase in which groups with very different established norms and ways of working are expected to work together fruitfully. Where cultures are very different, some kind of clash is likely as former teams jostle for position in the new organisation. However, such disruption can be minimised with planning and preparation. Cartwright and Cooper (2000, pp81–93) advocate a pre- and post-merger process by which the parties seek to understand the prevailing 'culture-in-use' in the organisation (or part of it) with which they will be merging. The suggestion is that focus groups and questionnaire surveys are used to identify the major cultural attributes of future partners. Once these are understood, it is possible to set out via some form of mission statement the values that the merged organisation will seek to espouse. The result is a situation in which all mergees know ahead of time something of what to expect, where the tension points are likely to lie, and how the organisation expects these to be resolved.

It would be a mistake to think that the P&D role in mergers and acquisitions is primarily the management of soft issues such as those described above. There is also an important job to do on the 'hard' side too, and this is no less problematic thanks to the vagaries of Transfer of Undertakings legislation (the TUPE regulations). The principal activities are as follows:

- the design of new post-merger organisation structures and reporting lines

- harmonisation of terms and conditions of employment

- the management of redundancies arising from post-merger downsizing programmes

- merging together of existing HR functions

- standardisation of P&D policies and practices across the new organisation.

The TUPE regulations, despite recent reform, are still widely considered to be over-complex. While the principles are clear, it is not always at all easy to establish what are the precise expectations of the law about specific issues. Employers thus frequently do not know what they can and cannot do or where the major risk points are as far as possible litigation is concerned. Where P&D managers are unsure of their position, it is thus necessary to take specialist legal advice. The key requirements are threefold:

- Individual terms and conditions of employment, along with collective agreements and continuity of employment, continue after a merger or acquisition has taken place. New owners cannot change these unilaterally when a business (or part of any organisation) changes hands.

- It is considered unfair in law to dismiss someone for a reason directly related to the transfer of an organisation (or part of an organisation) unless there is an acceptable alternative 'economic, technical or organisational' explanation.

- There is a requirement for both the transferor and the transferee organisations to consult with staff representatives about planned changes at the earliest practicable opportunity.

Legal requirements thus ensure that each employee's contract of employment remains unchanged even though after a merger or acquisition they are employed by a different legal entity. Altering terms and conditions, particularly pay scales and benefit entitlements, so as to harmonise them across the new organisation is thus problematic. Essentially there is a need to persuade people to switch to new terms and conditions by making them sufficiently attractive. Forcing changes runs the risk of legal actions based on the TUPE regulations or from constructive dismissal claims brought by former employees who would rather leave than accept new contracts.

Although it is less often a legal question, damaging results can also result from an ill-considered harmonisation of P&D policies. The danger arises from the appearance of adopting more from one former organisation than from the other (or others). Even in clear-cut acquisition situations, where one firm very obviously takes over another, negative consequences (eg low morale, reduced commitment and high staff turnover) result from the perception that one organisation's identity is being wholly subsumed by that of another. Such an impression is very easily created, especially where the new policies are less attractive from the employee perspective than those they have replaced. Care thus has to be taken to avoid these appearances. The best way of doing so is to avoid adopting the language or idiosyncrasies associated with the practices of either pre-merger organisation. The emphasis needs to be forward looking, using the opportunity created by the merger to review past practice and to fashion something for the future that is evidently new.

A BADLY HANDLED ACQUISITION

In their article entitled 'Managing employee expectations during acquisitions', Nancy Hubbard and John Purcell (2001) describe at some length the case of a large-scale acquisition that appears to have been very poorly managed from a P&D perspective at virtually every stage. It serves as an excellent lesson in what not to do. The case concerned the sale of a security firm given the pseudonym 'Quality Guarding' from one large PLC to another labelled 'Service Conglomerate'. The former employed 12,000 staff in seven regional offices; the latter had a chief executive with 'a ruthless reputation in the industry'. The different elements that made up the mishandling included the following:

- Announcements about future arrangements were given to the press before managers and staff in the affected organisation had been informed.

- The sale of Quality Guarding came as a complete shock to its own managers, who had been told that a sale was 'out of the question' a few months earlier.

- Service Conglomerate wrote letters to all Quality Guarding employees stating that business was to continue as previously and that major changes were not envisaged.

- Within a few months a cost-cutting plan was announced and implemented that involved many redundancies in Quality Guarding at senior and middle-management level.

- Redundancies were announced very quickly in face-to-face meetings with personnel staff who were often using out-of-date information. A number of people were mistakenly told that their job was going when it was not.

- Managers who remained employed were put under pressure to lie about the reduced quality of support services following further cost reductions.

- Survivors sometimes ended up working 70 hours a week to carry out their jobs to the standard they were accustomed to achieving.

It is clear that substantial cost savings were made as a result of this takeover, but the manner in which the process was carried out substantially reduced the quality of future service provision and wholly destroyed trust between the new owners and those staff who remained employed after the redundancies had been announced. The ones who kept their jobs were horrified at the way their former colleagues had been treated. The result was a huge loss in levels of commitment. After four months, 15 per cent of the remaining managers had left voluntarily, while half of all employees surveyed said that they were actively looking for another job. It is hard to avoid concluding that much of this damage was caused by incompetent management.

EXERCISE 2.2

SUCCESSFUL AND UNSUCCESSFUL MERGERS

Read the following four articles featured in *People Management*. They can be downloaded from the *People Management* archive on the CIPD's website (www.cipd.co.uk):

- Anat Arkin, Perfect fit (25 September 2003)

- Jon Watkins, Direct line (15 May 2003)

- Rosie Blau, Creative fusion (18 April 2002)

- Rebecca Johnson, The nicer splice (22 February 2007).

The first article gives examples of some unsuccessful mergers and takeovers, and identifies better approaches. The second describes the takeover of Park HR by Work Communications, and the third the merger that created the AstraZeneca chemical company. The fourth describes the approach taken by P&D managers at LogicaCMG during a series of recent mergers and acquisitions.

Questions

1. Seen from a P&D perspective, what would you say are the main dangers associated with mergers and acquisitions?

2. How can these be minimised?

3. What specific examples of good practice in the management of mergers and acquisitions are described in these articles?

TECHNOLOGY

There can be few organisations that have not changed their operations considerably over the past generation in response to technological developments. The impact has been, and continues to be, particularly pronounced in manufacturing, where the manner in which components are designed and made, and products assembled, has often been revolutionised and then revolutionised again in the space of a few years. Furthermore, of course, the nature of the products themselves has frequently had to change too in response to technological innovation and development. The effect in other sectors has been profound too, and can be expected to continue to be so. Developments in the fields of computers, lasers, telecommunications, transport and biotechnology have all played a major role in reshaping industrial activity. New technologies make it possible for businesses to do more things and to them at a cheaper rate. Nearly all sectors are being affected. Extraction technologies, for example reduced the costs of oil and gas production by 30 per cent during the 1990s (Grayson and Hodges 2001, p21), while service providers now routinely sell their products through web-based agencies and retailers. Media industries have grown very rapidly on the back of technological developments that allow everyone access to millions of television channels, radio stations and websites at a time of their own choosing. It goes without saying that almost no organisation that wants to stay at all competitive can fail but to embrace the challenges of technology and the world of e-commerce decisively. Moreover, there is no sign that developments are going to slow down. Anticipating future advances and understanding their business implications has thus become central to the business of establishing competitive advantage.

The specific effects on resourcing practice, like the changes themselves, vary greatly from organisation to organisation. However, there are a number of common threads running across the industrial sectors. First and foremost, there are the fundamental changes that technological developments impose on the way work is organised. New machinery requires new skills, and the inability of an existing workforce to adapt can mean bringing in new people and dispensing with the services of others. This may be the case even where relatively minor changes are brought in, such as new software for use in an administration or distribution operation, as well as where new production processes are being introduced. Second, the make-up of specific jobs or the terms and conditions on which people are employed may change. One person may be able to carry out the tasks formerly done by three. Alternatively it may be possible or necessary to subcontract work previously undertaken in house, or to bring people in on temporary contracts during a period in which major changes are occurring.

Technology brings with it the need to resource the organisation with new skills, and can create whole new occupations and career paths. A major example is the rise of call centre work which makes efficient use of telecommunications and information technologies. Over 950,000 people are now employed in UK call centres (ContactBabel 2007). This represents 3 per cent of the workforce, yet this industry was hardly even thought of 20 years ago. Such developments mean that established labour market dynamics alter over time, with some groups who were once hard to recruit now in plentiful supply, and vice versa. This will affect recruitment and selection practices while also altering the extent to which the retention of particular staff groups is significant.

Last but not least it is important to point to the impact of information technologies on the operation of the P&D function itself. An excellent summary of up to date research in this area is provided by Parry and Tyson (2007). The key points of relevance to the resourcing function are as follows:

- The capacity of human resource information systems to store and manipulate data has grown substantially in recent years. Provided accurate and complete data is entered, it becomes possible to generate user-friendly reports that improve knowledge of what is happening in the organisation. Better control of absence and staff turnover, for example, can be exerted as a result.

- Bespoke software is increasingly available at an affordable price to assist P&D managers in meeting their objectives. Examples are programmes for use in human resource planning, psychometric testing and payment administration. Computers also make more sophisticated evaluation of HR activity possible.

- Internet and cd-rom technologies allow P&D managers access to huge amounts (whole libraries) of information at the touch of a keyboard. This enables us, for example, to keep right up to date with the latest developments in employment law without the need to employ specialist lawyers or to subscribe to paper-based briefings that quickly become out of date.

- A great deal of time used to be taken up in HR departments informing callers (managers and staff) about P&D policy, terms and conditions, the content of collective agreements, pay scales and available training courses. Much of this time can now be saved by loading all the relevant data onto an organisation's intranet system.

- Outsourcing of the HR function itself (or part of it) becomes more plausible with the advent of the above technologies. There is no longer a need for the routine aspects of the role necessarily to be carried out in house because so much is automated.

REFLECTIVE QUESTION

Make a list of the five or six technological developments that have had most impact on your organisation in recent years. Which have had the biggest effect on the P&D function? What do you anticipate will be the most important developments in the next five years?

INTERNATIONALISATION

A major theme of management writers in recent years has been the contention that national economies are fast being subsumed into a single global economy in which huge companies operate across national boundaries, serving worldwide markets and locating production wherever it is most cost effective to do so. As with so much that is written about the major economic trends, there is some truth in the picture drawn, but also a great deal of exaggeration. It is true that international trade is growing faster than world output, and it is also true that the amount of direct foreign investment undertaken by companies is growing faster still. It is also interesting to observe that the sales of some multinational corporations are larger than the gross domestic products (GDPs) of some developed countries. However, these are not new phenomena, nor should we fall into the trap of assuming that further internationalisation is inevitable.

The volume of economic activity carried out internationally has been growing steadily since the 1950s by a few percentage points each year (Dicken 2007, pp35–36), but there have in this period been times when it has slowed or even reversed – during the 1970s in particular. We must also recognise that history has seen very pronounced reversals in the extent of international economic activity. The volume of the United Kingdom's GDP accounted for by foreign trade (around 25 per cent) is still less than was the case before the First World War (Wes 1996, p5), while several writers have argued that the world economic system we are building contains the seeds of its own destruction. It would not be the first time that such structures have come tumbling down. It happened before, in living memory, during the 1930s (see James 2001). There is also little evidence, as yet, to show that companies are becoming 'stateless' operators. Instead, the current picture is overwhelmingly one in which nationally based organisations undertake international trade. What we are increasingly seeing is regional economic activity (pan-European, pan-American etc), which has different consequences from true globalisation (Rugman 2000, Dicken 2007).

Nevertheless, while it is important not to be taken in by the wilder predictions, it remains the case that current trends point to a continued, if steady, growth in international trade and that its net effect over the next decades will be an increase in the number of businesses that operate internationally or compete with others that do so. There are good reasons to predict such an outcome. The most convincing concern the prospects of countries in the former Eastern bloc, China, India and in the developing world, all of which now embrace market principles as the best means of creating wealth. In short, the size of the international market is growing, providing more business opportunities for organisations than have been seen for a generation. This has several implications for employee resourcing activities, and there is thus a need for specialists in the field to develop an awareness of how exactly it will affect their industries and organisations.

There is also a need to develop an understanding of the reasons for increases in international economic activity in different industries. In many cases these are primarily technological, with the development of faster and cheaper international transport and communication links. Not only is it now economically viable to travel across the world in search of markets, it is also far easier to communicate with representatives, subsidiaries or licensees based in foreign locations. The recent extensions of e-mail and Internet services to new areas of the world, along with developments in mobile telecommunications technology, serve to speed up the communication process further. Developments in freight transport also underlie the continued increase in the volume of international trade. Container ships now transport vast quantities of goods between continents more cheaply, securely and conveniently than ever before, and at greater speed. The biggest ships now travel at the equivalent of 20 to 30 miles an hour round the clock, meaning that goods can be shipped from China to the United Kingdom and vice versa in less than three weeks. Air freight services also continue to develop. The result is a world that is far smaller, with the capability of transporting people and goods from one hemisphere to the other in little more than a single day at an affordable cost. To these technological developments are added the many measures taken in recent years to liberalise trade between countries through the removal or reduction of tariff barriers. There is thus both an increasing ability as well as an enhanced willingness to extend global economic exchanges.

It is difficult to make meaningful generalisations about the internationalisation of P&D activity, because it has a variety of different outcomes depending on individual business circumstances. Furthermore, because it does not accelerate at a uniform pace, we currently have a situation in which some industries (notably manufacturing and finance) are having to adapt far more dramatically and swiftly than others. Indeed, there are some sectors that have yet to be internationalised at all to any great degree, remaining nationally based in terms of both their product and labour markets (eg the public services, newspapers, many small businesses and much of the retailing sector). In short, the effects come in a number of different shapes and forms, and thus have rather different implications in terms of evolving employee resourcing policy. It is helpful to view the internationalisation process in terms of a continuum. At one end is a situation in which organisations take on what commentators describe as a 'global' or 'transnational' character, while at the other organisations remain entirely nationally based and may (or may not) be faced with the need to compete with commercial rivals based overseas. In between is a range of other states encompassing the development of sizeable export markets, the purchasing or setting up of overseas subsidiaries and the building of strategic alliances with foreign organisations. The picture is often made more complex by the fact that different divisions within the same organisation can operate at different points along the continuum.

By far the most generally applicable result of these trends is the increased competition they bring. Few commercial organisations are not now touched by the presence of more overseas competitors for their products in home markets, even if they themselves do not export goods to any great degree. In some respects the rest of this book is concerned with the various choices open to P&D specialists who are faced with the need to assist their organisations to compete more effectively. For most, this means helping to create a workforce capable of enhancing the quality of the goods and services produced, and possessing the capacity both to adapt to change and to generate innovative approaches. In employee resourcing terms, this means finding and then retaining the best-qualified and most able individuals available. Once that part of the equation has been 'solved', there is then a need to address individuals' performance so as to ensure that the organisation gets the best return possible on its investment over the long term.

At the global end of the spectrum are organisations that have developed a transnational structure. Not only are their products sold all over the world, but they are also conceived, designed, manufactured, marketed, distributed and serviced in different locations. In some cases a number of stages in the manufacturing process are carried out in separate countries. Such organisations are still relatively uncommon, because most international corporations still perform the preponderance of their activities in a single country, but the number is growing. The implications for the P&D specialist are profound. Not only is there a need to compete internationally, as described above, but there is also a need to create, manage and develop workforces in a variety of different places. It may be, for example, that a company designs products at a head office in the United Kingdom, manufactures them in Eastern Europe, and then markets and distributes them from a further dozen locations around the world. The need to exercise control over such an organisation while ensuring that it retains a common identity and sense of purpose requires the acquisition and development of a sizeable expatriate workforce to live and work for periods overseas. Other staff will need to travel a great deal from location to location, commuting from country to country while being based elsewhere. In addition, there is a compelling need to communicate effectively with all of the international arms and to put in place, as far as is practical or possible, common standards of P&D practice.

Many organisations have moved beyond national boundaries in some respects but do not or cannot aspire to develop into full-blown global operators such as those described above. For some, this will involve developing durable export markets in different countries. Others go further by taking over foreign-based companies, setting up overseas subsidiaries or merging with organisations that are based abroad but operate in similar product markets. A third group enters into strategic alliances with overseas competitors with a view to enhancing shared competitive advantage. A fourth group operates internationally but not globally, for example restricting their activities to the European market or to one or two EU countries. In each case there is a need in P&D terms to move some of the way down the globalisation road. While there will be less of a requirement for expatriate employees, there will be much more need for key players to travel and to spend substantial periods of time in foreign locations. There is also an important communication job to do, preparing employees for change, involving them in the process, informing them of new individual opportunities and reassuring them about their own futures.

The major day-to-day practical implications from a resourcing perspective arise when nationally based organisations, either through acquisition or expansion, start to operate overseas. This brings with it all manner of developments related to the employment of expatriates and the need to take account of unfamiliar systems of employment legislation.

REFLECTIVE QUESTION

Are your major competitors UK-based or international? What difference does it make in terms of their ability to compete with you and you with them?

EMPLOYING STAFF TO WORK OVERSEAS

Torrington (1994, p6), in his study of international HRM, divides overseas employees into a number of distinct categories. The most important are:

- expatriates (staff who live and work in an overseas location for a year or more)

- occasional parachutists (staff who spend shorter periods overseas, often working on specific projects such as setting up new production processes)

- cosmopolitans (mostly management staff who travel from location to location throughout their working year, spending little more than a week or two in each country before moving on).

Each has different requirements from the employee resourcing function, in particular in terms of recruitment, selection and performance management.

To survive and succeed professionally in any one of these three roles is difficult. It is not something that will automatically occur when someone is posted overseas. It is thus important to select people carefully and to make sure that they have the support they need during the period that they are abroad. Ideally, the nature and extent of overseas working in a job will be identified at the HR planning stage. It will then form an integral part of written job descriptions and person specifications, feature in recruitment advertisements, form a major criterion at the selection stage, and then be explicitly incorporated into individual contracts of employment. This will ensure that only people with relevant language skills and whose personal circumstances are conducive to overseas working are considered for employment in such roles. Remuneration packages designed to attract and retain such staff can then be developed along with appropriate performance management systems.

In today's volatile business environment, however, situations often arise that do not permit such a well-planned resourcing exercise to take place. Companies often need to act speedily and opportunistically to secure business and existing, nationally based staff may have to be involved. As a result, the time available for preparation is brief, and any training given has to be intensive. Where such opportunities involve staff who have not specifically been selected for overseas work, there will thus often be a need to provide more structured and extensive support once the individual concerned has taken up his or her post.

That said, it is clearly not usually in the interests of an organisation to encourage people to spend time travelling or to take up positions abroad against their wishes. Wherever possible, therefore, those who are likely to be asked to do so need to be recruited, at the very least, with that possibility in mind. The following factors thus need to be considered in the recruitment and selection process:

- existing language skills

- capacity to learn new languages

- awareness of relevant overseas cultures

- ability to adapt to specific overseas values and norms

- preparedness for living conditions in particular foreign counties (ie rented accommodation or hotels)

- domestic circumstances.

This last point has to be handled very carefully to avoid breaching sex discrimination legislation. However, in most cases of overseas working it will inevitably arise and have to be dealt with at the selection stage. Of course, employers can do a great deal to help individuals to juggle international employment and family life by providing regular flights home or by making funds available for spouses and families to join employees while they are abroad. Help can also be given by granting additional holidays or the opportunity to take sabbatical leave.

In recent years UK-based organisations have increasingly employed people from overseas to work here. The major issues that P&D managers need to tackle are thus more likely to emanate from situations in which the expatriate comes from overseas to work among UK-based staff, serving UK-based customers. We shall look in more detail at these issues in Chapter 3. For now though, it is useful to consider what can be learned about the effective recruitment and management of migrants from overseas from the experience of and literature about sending UK staff abroad on expatriate assignments.

CULTURAL VARIATIONS

A second topic of general importance for the development of employee resourcing policy in international organisations is the need to manage within the grain of different national cultures. While it is sometimes claimed that culturally the world is becoming more homogeneous, for the foreseeable future very substantial differences between different national cultures will clearly continue. Getting to grips with these and developing an effective understanding of different norms, values and assumptions are therefore prerequisites for successfully doing business in different places. For transnational organisations, where people based in one country are managed by people based elsewhere, there is an even greater need to appreciate cultural differences and to understand how they affect employee resourcing practice.

In recent years a number of studies have been carried out among employees and managers in different countries in an effort to 'map' or categorise in some way the cultural variations between them. The best known and most influential are the studies by Hofstede (1980 and 2005) and Lewis (1996). These are all fascinating, but inevitably tend to oversimplify the picture by categorising whole nations into particular cultural groups. Hence, according to Hofstede, the United Kingdom is characterised as a 'village market', in which organisations tend to have less formal hierarchical structures than elsewhere, with much decentralisation of authority, a relatively relaxed view of change and a preference for keeping emotions hidden. Clearly there is some truth in this, especially when these characteristics are compared with those that appear prevalent elsewhere. However, there are also plenty of organisations, communities and individuals that do not share these cultural norms, so we should be wary about simply 'reading off' a set of national characteristics from such typologies.

Lewis's studies classified national cultures into three broad categories, each of which consists of a long list of characteristics covering human relationships, work styles, perceptions of time and preferred approaches to the collection and communication of data. The three were labelled respectively as 'linear-active', 'multi-active' and 'reactive'. Linear-active cultures, according to Lewis, include the English-speaking nations and much of Northern Europe. People originating from these areas are respectful of authority, unemotional, relatively patient and keen to keep their private lives to themselves. They also tend to be analytical, making decisions based on firm data rather than hunches or personal recommendations. In terms of work organisation, the preference is for order and planning, with each task carried out separately and in accordance with agreed schedules. As a result, time is seen as scarce, and great emphasis is placed on punctuality.

By contrast, multi-active cultures are shared by people originating from Southern Europe, Africa, the Middle East and Latin America. Here the social norms include a greater willingness to display emotion and to appeal to a sense of emotion rather than logic when seeking to persuade. Family relationships are closer and less likely to be kept separate from work than in linear-active cultures. Body language is far more expressive, and punctuality regarded as less important. At work there is relatively little delegation of authority, the most senior figure taking decisions according to personal perceptions. Agreed plans or procedures are thus readily altered without the need to consult others.

The third culture is labelled 'reactive', and incorporates the Eastern countries, along with Russia, Finland and Turkey. Here there is great emphasis on listening and the avoidance of confrontation in relationships with others. People are often inscrutable and will go to more extreme lengths than elsewhere to avoid losing face. Decision-making tends to take a long time but, by the same token, will be done so as to last for the long term. Great emphasis is placed on integrity and reliability, but it takes time to build up the trust required. Discussion and negotiation thus tend to take time, each party avoiding direct answers or even eye contact but preferring instead to listen and react after careful consideration.

Hofstede (1980) focused more directly on work organisation, and has identified four dimensions that allow different national characteristics to be classified or mapped. These are:

- power distance (the extent to which members of a society accept that power in institutions is distributed unequally)

- uncertainty avoidance (the extent to which people feel threatened by ambiguous situations and have created beliefs and institutions that try to avoid these)

- individualism (the extent to which people believe that they have responsibility for looking after themselves and their own families, as opposed to institutions)

- masculinity (the extent to which the dominant values in society are success, money and material acquisitions).

More recently, Hofstede (2005) has refined his uncertainty avoidance dimension somewhat to take account of the long-term orientation of Eastern cultures compared with those prevalent in the West. In this, like Lewis, he is recognising the important differences that exist in the field of time perception, with its implications for reactive decision-making, perseverance and face-saving. Hofstede has also produced a typology of cultures based on his first two dimensions (uncertainty avoidance and power distance), which has led him to identify four basic organisational categories associated with particular countries. These are the 'pyramid of people', the 'well-oiled machine', the 'village market' and the 'family', and are best illustrated graphically (see Figure 2.1).

Inevitably, it has been possible here only to outline some of the main contours of research findings in the field of cultural variations. Readers are referred to more specialist texts, such as those referenced above, for more detailed material on specific countries. However, it is clear even from the briefest of surveys that assumptions about work relationships and organisations vary considerably

UNCERTAINTY AVOIDANCE

HIGH

Pyramid of people

Japan
France
Pakistan
South America
Arabic-speaking
Southern Europe

Well-oiled machine

Germany
Finland
Austria
Israel
Switzerland
Costa Rica

POWER DISTANCE
HIGH   LOW

Family

India
Malaysia
Singapore
Indonesia
East and West Africa
Hong Kong

Village market

United Kingdom
United States
Canada
Sweden
The Netherlands
Australia

LOW

Figure 2.1 Typology of cultures
Source: Hofstede (1980).

CULTURAL DIFFERENCE AND HRM

People management

EXERCISE 2.3

Read the following two articles featured in *People Management*. They can be downloaded from the *People Management* archive on the CIPD's website (www.cipd.co.uk):

- Philip Stiles, A world of difference (15 November 2007)

- Wes Harry, East is east (29 November 2007).

These two articles both concern the extent to which HR practices in multinational companies reflect differences in national culture. Stiles explains how his research suggests that cultural differences are becoming less important as multi-national organisations increasingly adopt standardised international approaches and downplay local differences. Wes Harry, by contrast argues that cultural differences remain pronounced and that the experience of working in a western-owned organisation is very different from working in one which has eastern roots.

Questions

1   In what ways does Stiles criticise Hofstede's research in the first article? How do his conclusions differ?

2   What are the major points made by Harry?

3   Can you reconcile these two points of view? If so, how?

around the globe. In employee resourcing terms, this means that the approaches prevalent in the United Kingdom, or even defined here as constituting 'best practice', will often be seen as foreign and ill-judged if imposed elsewhere. In managing international organisations there is thus a need to study, and gain an understanding of, the key differences in work cultures, and then to develop policies that take the variations into account.

TRANSNATIONAL ORGANISATIONAL STRUCTURES

A third issue of underlying significance for employee resourcing practices in international organisations concerns the internal structures and reporting lines. These are complex issues at the best of times for large organisations, and they are made a great deal more involved when geographically diverse workforces are included. The problem is best illustrated with a fictional example: a catering conglomerate that operates only within the United Kingdom and runs a chain of restaurants and a chain of hotels. How should it structure itself? One option is for the two product groups to be managed separately, with two managerial hierarchies, each with its own maintenance, marketing, finance and personnel functions, and both reporting at the very senior level to corporate directors. Alternatively, the whole group could be managed functionally, all the chefs (from both hotels and restaurants) reporting to regional food and beverage managers, and the housekeepers, accountants, maintenance, finance, marketing and personnel people doing likewise. The third option is to organise the whole company into separate regional divisions so that there are managers with responsibility for both restaurants and hotels operating in the South-East, Midlands, Scotland and so on. All three are plausible approaches. Because one language is spoken and one broad organisation culture shared, and because operations are confined to a reasonably small geographic area, any inherent tensions can be resolved relatively easily. Hence, if the organisation is structured regionally, it is still very easy for maintenance staff based in different locations to communicate, share their expertise and equipment, and come together to take part in project work. The same goes for general managers of hotels in different regions and wine-buyers within the restaurant chain. In other words, it is possible for each member of staff to have a single line manager who appoints and appraises him or her, but it is also possible to work to or with others on a regional or functional basis.

The larger and more complex an organisation becomes, the harder it is to resolve the tensions described in the example given above. Once international divisions are established, a further tension emerges in the form of the need for the organisation to have a common strategic focus while simultaneously taking account of local cultural norms and organisational traditions. Hence, to take the catering example further, there is a need in an international hotel chain for all units to adhere to the same basic standards so that they can be marketed as a group, while at the same time they will be managed very differently depending on the country in which they are based. So to whom should the sales manager at the Hong Kong unit report? Should it be the hotel's general manager, a worldwide director of sales or a manager with responsibility for sales and marketing activity within South-East Asia? In practice, the answer will vary, depending on the established traditions in the company, the political strength of particular managers, and the costs and benefits associated with each option.

A further option is for organisations to develop matrix structures, whereby there is no single reporting line, so that employees may be accountable to a number of different individuals at the same time. In the above example, that might mean that an aspiring sales manager for the Hong Kong hotel would be interviewed by all three potential bosses but would report to each about different areas of work. Day-to-day supervision might come from the local general manager, but this would not prevent the regional sales and marketing managers overseeing much of the individual's work. In addition, he or she might be involved in some international project work, which would require work to be undertaken for the international director. Ideally this would maximise the individual's contribution while ensuring that responsibilities at organisational, regional and unit level were all met. Such matrix structures are becoming increasingly common in international companies, because they permit cost-effective achievement of organisational objectives, but in different ways depending on local conditions. Further information on different approaches to such arrangements, together with a number of examples in the international field, are provided by Sparrow and Hiltrop (1994, pp288–298) and Jackson (2002).

Linked to the question of the overall structure is the issue of who should manage plants or other units located in countries other than that of the corporate headquarters. In a truly global organisation, where the original location of the headquarters is irrelevant to staffing policy, and perhaps where ownership is no longer concentrated in one country, the nationality of each unit manager is less of an issue. The corporate culture supersedes separate national cultures, and it becomes possible simply to promote people to new positions across different countries on the basis of individual merit. Hence someone who is Dutch can be appointed to manage a Polish factory owned by a US-based corporation. It is also more common for people based in subsidiaries to spend time working at the corporate headquarters as much as the other way round. However, as has already been pointed out, this kind of global organisation remains relatively rare at present, with most multinationals dominated by a strong nationally based headquarters that keeps a tight rein on its overseas subsidiary units. In such situations, the choice in the above example would more typically be between a local Polish manager and an expatriate American one. The advantage of the former is local knowledge and language skills; the latter has the advantage of knowledge of organisational culture and strategy, together with expertise in the international aspects of the operation. Again, as in the case of matrix organisation structures, the usual solution is to try to achieve the best of both worlds by employing local and home country nationals to work together, perhaps one acting as deputy to the other. Hall (2005) has made a particular study of how the HR function is best organised in multi-national organisations. He suggests that where functions are global in nature (typically, pay strategy, succession planning, management development) the reporting structures should operate at a global level. By contrast where the functions carried out are more local (recruitment and selection for example), reporting lines should be to local managers. In other cases there will be a need for a matrix structure.

THE COMPASS GROUP

Read the article by Rima Manocha, Bonding agents (*People Management*, 11 November 2004, pp38–39). This can be downloaded from the *People Management* archive on the CIPD's website (www.cipd.co.uk).

The article describes how the Compass Group (the ninth largest employer in the world) set about developing an international corporate identity for itself. This giant catering conglomerate has grown over the years by buying up smaller organisations based in 90 countries. As a result its staff tend to identify with their local division or brand-group rather than seeing themselves as working for a major and highly successful international company.

Questions

1   Why did senior managers at Compass identify a need to develop an international identity among their 415,000 staff?

2   What cultural variations did they encounter during this process and how did they overcome them?

3   From a P&D perspective, what advantages do you think the company will gain over the long term as a result of the initiative described in this article?

INSTITUTIONAL VARIATIONS

Just as workplace cultures vary considerably from country to country, so of course do the institutional structures that govern the way organisations operate. While larger international organisations can impose their own cultural norms to some extent, they are pretty well always obliged to manage within the requirements of a country's legal system. It is also unwise and usually unnecessary to seek to work outside accepted national training systems or established employee representative institutions. An understanding of these latter two areas is are particularly important when employing people in Germany, for example, where there is a strongly entrenched national training system of very different hue to that of the United Kingdom and where industry level collective bargaining thrives. The established works council system also greatly affects the way that P&D policy is developed. However, these are not issues that are of strict relevance to resourcing policy. Legal regimes, and particularly different approaches to employment regulation, are of more direct relevance.

Historically three different models of employment regulation have developed in different countries. Although we are now witnessing some convergence, for example through the development of EU employment law, the three different approaches are clearly discernible:

- Systems with common law origins include those of the United Kingdom, Eire, the United States, and the other Anglo-Saxon countries. Here the individual contract of employment forms the centrepiece of employment law, although in some countries (not in the United Kingdom) collective agreements made with trade unions also have contractual status. In these jurisdictions the tradition is for the state (ie the law) to avoid too great an involvement in the determination of the terms and conditions that prevail in the workplace. These are left for the parties to contracts to determine for themselves. The role of the law is to provide a means whereby these contracts, once agreed, can be effectively enforced.

- Codified systems are associated with much of the European Union, the Eastern European countries and Far Eastern countries such as Japan and China. Partly as a result of EU membership, and partly because of more regulation introduced by successive governments, the UK employment system is beginning to take on more of a codified character than was the case historically. However, the level of regulation remains a great deal less detailed than is the case in most other European countries. There a range of minimum standards are set by the state and usually supported by some form of policing system. Employees who believe they have been badly treated can take cases to court on their own account, but they are backed up by inspectorates of one kind or another that have substantial powers. For employers, breaching employment law is thus often a criminal matter and not simply something to be resolved by the affected parties in the civil courts.

- Theocratic systems are the third variety. Here employment regulation and contractual relationships are based on religious principles and sacred texts. Nowadays such systems survive principally in the Islamic states of the Middle East and southeast Asia. The major distinction from codified systems is the fact that they derive their principles from ancient documents. This means, first, that the principles cannot easily be changed by governments (although there can be flexibility in interpretation), and second, that they do not reflect modern employment scenarios. They are, for example, often associated with the subordination of female employees.

For resourcing purposes, the main areas of legal regulation that matter in practical terms are discrimination law and dismissal law. In both areas there are very wide differences in the approaches used in different jurisdictions. An example is the scope of anti-discrimination measures. Most developed countries have in place regulations that seek to deter unfair discrimination on grounds of sex and race. However, in some countries little more is done than to provide a mechanism for 'minority groups' to complain when they are treated less favourably than the 'majority group'. Elsewhere, as in the United Kingdom, various additional legal measures are present to protect the interests of particular groups, such as maternity laws, and statutes giving rights to part-time workers. In a number of countries, such as the United States and New Zealand, there are well-established laws outlawing discrimination on grounds of age and disability. In most of the European Union such regulations were only introduced for the first time in 2006. In the United States, except for certain states, there is no law on equal pay (or comparative worth) as between men and women, yet over the border in the Canadian province of Ontario, the Pay Equity Act has set up one of the most far reaching and widely admired systems for enforcing equal pay principles anywhere in the world. In much of the developing world and in several Eastern European counties, there is very little by way of anti-discrimination law at all.

There are also substantial variations in the approaches used to protect people from being dismissed for reasons other than those linked to unfair discrimination. Here the United Kingdom can be characterised as having a system that lies somewhere in between two extremes. We have a system that protects most workers (but by no means all) by providing a means for them to gain compensation when dismissed for an unfair reason or in an unreasonable manner. This acts as something of a deterrent to employers, but there is no absolute right to reinstatement when a case is won by an applicant, while compensation levels remain low in most situations. In the United States the doctrine of 'employment at will' is established, meaning that there is very little general statutory protection for those who are dismissed unfairly. However where 'unlawful discharge' is found to have occurred, for example where someone refuses to obey an instruction to act unlawfully, levels of damages are a great deal higher than is the case in the United Kingdom. Another interesting feature of the US system is the way that remedies have been developed using the common law. In the absence of statutory protection, dismissed employees have brought cases alleging defamation when, for example, they believe themselves to have been wrongly accused of a disciplinary offence. They can also sometimes bring breach of contract claims when established disciplinary procedures are not adhered to. At the other extreme are systems such as that used in the Netherlands. Here, with some important exceptions, the rule is that a person cannot be dismissed until the employer has first gained the written approval of a District Labour Office. In the most straightforward situations a license to dismiss takes several weeks to obtain, during which time pay continues even if the employee concerned is suspended. In practice only 5 per cent or so of dismissal requests are turned down, and the criteria are similar to those set out in the UK unfair dismissal law, but institutionally the arrangement is wholly different. There are also major differences between the regimes that exist for redundancies and ill health dismissals.

Institutional variations of the kind described above clearly need to be understood and taken on board by organisations employing people in overseas countries. Importantly, however, the existence of diverse forms of employment law also helps inform decisions about where to locate different organisational functions. Indeed, the fact that the United Kingdom is relatively unregulated is often held up as the reason for its comparative success in attracting foreign investment. Knowledge of different systems and how they operate in practice is thus a key competence for employee resourcing specialists in international undertakings to gain.

CUSTOMER RELATIONSHIPS

Seen from an organisational perspective, the net effect of internationalisation, deregulation and new technologies is to create intensified commercial competition. New technologies help lift the 'barriers to entry' into an industry by making it cheaper to carry out complex activities. They also allow smaller organisations to compete effectively with their better-established, larger rivals. At

KEY ARTICLE 4

Boyd Black, National culture and labour market flexibility. *International Journal of Human Resource Management*, Vol. 10, No. 4, pp592–605 (1999)

In this often-cited article Boyd Black focuses both on the institutional differences between countries that affect the way that the employment relationship is managed and on cultural differences of the kind identified by Hofstede in his research (see above). He concludes that the two should not be seen as separate dimensions of international diversity, but as two sides of the same coin. Embedded cultural differences explain not only diversity of practices in the workplace, but many of the institutional differences too. In particular he finds that the labour market rigidities associated with many European countries (centralised bargaining, restrictive employment legislation, the level of unemployment benefit etc) are associated with the national cultures of those countries. By contrast individualistic cultures, such as the United Kingdom's, have tended to create a preference for more flexible labour markets.

Questions

1   Make a list of the key findings that underpin Boyd Black's conclusions.

2   What criticisms could you make of his methods and conclusions?

3   What are the practical implications of the conclusions for the future development of pan-EU employment policies and institutions?

the same time, the development of international markets for products and services makes it harder for one or two larger producers to dominate an industry as they could when markets were predominantly national. It is now possible, at least in theory, for any business to sell its products to any consumer anywhere in the world through the use of the Internet. Internationalisation thus massively increases the number of potential competitors an organisation faces. In practical terms this means much more consumer choice. Whereas previously our options as to where to buy any particular product were restricted, a far greater range of spending opportunities are becoming available to us. Any brief comparison of the consumer lives led by our grandparents with ours today shows this to be the case. There are two evident consequences: first, consumers now experience a broader range of experiences (good and bad), and second, power has shifted from providers to their customers.

The result is a customer population that has ever-higher expectations, is more intolerant of poor service, more willing to complain and a lot more likely to seek out alternative providers (Armistead *et al* 2001). People are less likely to put up with poor service than they were ten years ago. If they experience faults in systems, poor service from staff or a failure to deliver on 'promises' made, they are more inclined to take their business elsewhere. They do so, because there is more choice available to them. These trends are already well established and there is every reason to predict that they will strengthen in the future.

The public sector is cushioned to an extent from some of these forces because of the monopoly position it occupies in the provision of certain services. Where consumer choice is limited, customers have to tolerate less than satisfactory service if they want to have access to the product. The extent to which the sector is cushioned from these forces is, however, becoming increasingly limited. First, of course, we have seen and continue to see greater commercialisation of the public services. Most state-run corporations in the United Kingdom have now been privatised, while state-provided services such as the NHS and education systems have been required to manage their activities along more commercial lines. They also compete with thriving and growing private sector providers. Second, we are now clearly witnessing a situation in which public concern about public service delivery (or lack of it) is moving to the top of the political agenda. In the absence of major ideological differences between the political parties, we have instead competition based on who can best deliver public services that are high in quality and good value for taxpayers. Intolerance of poor service is thus just as important an issue for public sector managers as it is for those working in the private sector.

For all organisations, it is thus fair to conclude that achieving and sustaining service excellence is a major management objective. A great deal can be achieved through effective selling and the development of trusted brands, but these need to go hand in hand with effective service if long-term competitive advantage is to be achieved. This means meeting customer expectations and surprising customers with the quality of the service that they receive. It means getting the logistics right, delivering on time, treating people with courtesy and providing good value for money.

It is also an objective that the P&D function has a central role in achieving. Resourcing activities contribute in several different ways:

- Recruitment campaigns need to attract staff with a customer orientation by reflecting the type of commercial reputation that the organisation wishes to establish.

- Employee selection processes need to focus on attributes such as conscientiousness, a concern for detail and a willingness to seek continuous improvement.

- Interviews and induction programmes need to convey the significance of customer service objectives for the organisation.

- Performance management and promotion systems need to reward commitment to customer service and be seen to do so.

However, there is rather more to it than this. Research by Johnson (2001c) and his colleagues at Warwick University suggests that good people management practices tend to be associated with workforces that are highly rated as service providers. If you want to create a body of employees who consistently achieve high standards, who show genuine commitment to the organisation, stay for a good length of time and act conscientiously, you have to treat them well. According to Johnson a feature of the most successful organisations, when judged on customer ratings, is the adult nature of the relationship that exists between staff and management. There is mutual respect, trust and openness, employee involvement and plenty of career development opportunities. Discipline and management control are exercised, but sanctions are applied fairly and consistently so that all concerned know exactly where they stand. We can thus conclude with the observation that the general orientation of P&D management is as important in achieving service excellence as are the more obvious practical steps that need to be taken in the resourcing field.

REFLECTIVE QUESTION

Think of an example of a time recently when you experienced poor service and an occasion when you observed service excellence. To what extent do you think the difference could be held to be the responsibility of the resourcing function in the organisations concerned?

EXERCISE 2.5

NANDO'S RESTAURANTS

People management

Read the article by Steve Smethurst, Chicken coup (*People Management*, 13 January 2005, pp34–36). This can be downloaded from the *People Management* archive on the CIPD's website (www.cipd.co.uk).

The article describes some of the approaches to people management used by managers at the Nando's restaurant chain. These are highly unusual in the catering industry and are believed to make a major contribution to the organisation's success. The approach is based on their motto: 'If you look after your people, the customers will have a good time and you'll make money'.

Questions

1   Identify the major features of the management approach adopted at Nando's that make it different from most other businesses, particularly in the hospitality sector.

2   Why do you think that line managers at Nando's are likely to be more effective people managers than their equivalents in competitor companies?

3   To what extent do you agree with the view advanced in the article that many organisations agree with the Nando's approach, but fail to introduce it in practice? Why do you think this might be the case?

KEY ARTICLE 5

James Harter, Frank L Schmidt and Theodore L Hayes, Business-unit-level relationship between employee satisfaction, employee engagement and business outcomes: a meta-analysis. *Journal of Applied Psychology*, Vol. 87, No. 2, pp268–279 (2002)

This article represents the most comprehensive analysis in an academic journal of the Gallup Organisation's studies into employee engagement. For over 30 years now Gallup has been

carrying out quite a simple employee attitude survey consisting of 12 questions, often returning to the same organisations to re-test and carrying out comparisons between levels of employee engagement in different business units in the same organisation. The amount of data they have collected is huge, comprising questionnaire returns from almost 200,000 employees and nearly 8,000 separate business units. The organisations studied come from across the business sectors and are based in a number of different countries. What makes the study so important, however, is the simultaneous collection of further data on customer satisfaction levels, employee turnover rates, productivity and profitability in many of the business units studied. This has enabled the authors of this article to carry out a statistical analysis to establish how great the links are between levels of employee engagement in a business unit and measures of its business performance. This article shows that the links are significant: put crudely, that the happier

a workforce is, the better the service it tends to provide to its customers and the more profitable the business unit tends to be.

Questions

1 How effective do you consider the 12-question survey to be as a means of establishing how engaged employees are in their jobs?

2 What is the main message from the study concerning the link between customer satisfaction and the way employees are managed?

3 What practical measures would you recommend were taken in an organisation in which customer satisfaction rates were lower than those being achieved by major competitors?

CHAPTER SUMMARY

- Increased volatility in product markets is the major feature of our evolving commercial environment. Its major causes are new technologies, the internationalisation of commerce, and the willingness of customers to exercise the choice that they increasingly enjoy.

- The major implications for resourcing activity are a reduced ability to put in place long-term policies or to offer long-term employment, the need to develop the capacity to manage overseas operations and expatriate workers effectively, and the need to focus on service excellence when recruiting and motivating staff.

- Once an organisation becomes international and starts employing people in different countries, its resourcing specialists need to

acquire new competencies. The major areas for consideration are the employment of expatriate workers, the need to manage within the grain of overseas cultures, the development of structures that facilitate effective international operations, and the need to understand the implications of diverse institutional arrangements.

- Mergers and acquisitions often fail when judged against their original objectives because of poor handling of P&D issues. There is a need to spend time and resources attending to soft issues (eg cultural assimilation and managing expectations) as well as the 'hard' issues such as organisation design, harmonising policies and conditions, and managing redundancies.

EXPLORE FURTHER

- The topics covered in this chapter are covered extensively in texts on the business environment. Wetherly and Otter (2008) and Farnham (2005) provide a good introduction, as do Brooks and Weatherston (2004) and Morris *et al* (2002). A rather more sceptical eye is cast by Grayson and Hodges (2001) in a book which boasts an introduction by Prince Charles.

- Many books deal with globalisation issues and their significance for people management. Perkins (1997) is a useful introduction. Other recommended texts include those by Joynt and Morton (1999) and Dicken (2007). Editions of IDS Focus in 2000c and 2001a dealt very effectively with the impact of new technology and globalisation on P&D practice. A good summary of academic research in this field is provided by Parry and Tyson (2007).

- More detailed treatment of P&D issues is found in Derek Torrington's *International human resource management* (1994) and in more recent books by Jackson (2002) and Sparrow *et al* (2004).

Many aspects of the current and future impact of new technologies on P&D practice are discussed in Holman *et al*'s recent book on 'the new workplace' (2005) and in Garsten and Wulff (2004). Both of these consist of articles written by experts on particular areas of technology and their impact. The potential long-term impact of evolving technologies is discussed in two *People Management* articles by Claus (2007) and Philpott (2007).

- Useful general guides to P&D involvement in mergers and acquisitions are provided by Holbeche (1999), Cartwright and Cooper (2000), IRS (2000g), Burke (2002) and Stevens (2005, Chapter 6). Interesting case studies are described in the articles by Devine and Lammiman (2000), IRS (2000b), Hubbard and Purcell (2001), Dempsey and McKevitt (2001) and Morris (2001). Nikandrou *et al* (2000) are particularly good on communications issues. A special edition of *British Journal of Management* published in 2006 contains several articles that have relevance to the P&D aspects of managing mergers and acquisitions.

CHAPTER 3

The employment market

As explained in Chapter 1, the view that P&D activities can neatly be derived from an analysis of an organisation's business plan or strategic objectives is overly simplistic, although it is commonly advanced from conference platforms and in business magazine articles. This is because the P&D manager is also required to take account of developments in other areas that may restrict the degree to which an organisation is able to move in a particular direction. One of these is employment regulation, which we will look at in Chapter 4. The other major area comprises the employment (or labour) markets in which organisations are obliged to compete with one another in order to acquire the services of employees. The need to take account of developments in employment markets is not new but it has become a good deal more important in the UK context over recent years. This is for two reasons. First, because the economy has performed well and because of long-term demographic trends, labour has become more scarce in general terms. Second, the nature of the work that we carry out is steadily becoming more specialised in nature. More jobs are advertised that require applicants to hold some kind of professional qualification or to have achieved a defined level of educational performance. At the same time less unskilled work is available. Not only does this create acute skills shortages in some areas, but it also makes the recruitment and training of new people more expensive.

We thus have a situation in which the loss of effective performers through voluntary resignation creates many more problems for organisations and is much more costly than it was when most jobs required few skills and could readily be filled by a pool of unemployed people. Yet many managers still give the impression that they are operating in a former era, taking little care about how they manage their people. Maintaining their own career progression and strengthening their own authority over their subordinates remain their priorities, even if this means treating people with disrespect and seeking to force them to work longer and more intensively than is good for them. The result, inevitably, is a recruitment and retention problem. While this is by no means true of all industries and regions, it is increasingly the case that organisations are having to adjust to the realities of an unfamiliar business environment in which managers are required to take greater care in the way they manage people, and to put a good deal more effort into finding and keeping their employees. In this chapter we start by looking in detail at the major underlying labour market trends and at their general consequences for organisations. We go on to introduce four specific topics, each of which has risen up the management agenda in recent years, in large part because of changed labour market conditions. These are work–life balance initiatives, employer branding, employing people from overseas and the more general question of ethical approaches to people management.

LEARNING OUTCOMES

By the end of this chapter readers should be able to:

- distinguish between 'tight' and 'loose' labour market conditions
- identify the demographic trends and developments in employee attitudes of importance to the future of their organisation
- evaluate the arguments in favour of the introduction of work–life balance initiatives in organisations
- develop plans for the application of ideas about 'employer branding'
- advise about the employment of overseas nationals in the United Kingdom
- deploy effective arguments as a means of achieving ethical outcomes in P&D decision-making.

In addition, readers should be able to understand and explain:

- the importance of labour markets for the resourcing function
- the concepts of work–life balance initiatives and employer branding
- the nature of the ethical dilemmas which face resourcing specialists and responses to these.

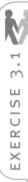

IMPROVING BASIC SKILLS

EXERCISE 3.1

Read the article by Lucie Carrington, The skills equation (*People Management*, 23 August 2007, pp24–28). This can be downloaded from the *People Management* archive on the CIPD's website (www.cipd.co.uk).

In 2006 the Leitch Report looking at the skills base of the UK population was published. It concluded that far too great a proportion of the population lacked the basic literacy and numeracy skills required to sustain a career in the contemporary business world. The government responded with a white paper in July 2007, World class skills: implementing the Leitch Review of Skills in England, and separate responses were issued by devolved governments elsewhere in the United Kingdom. Several of the initiatives suggested involve employers working with government agencies and funding bodies to provide basic skills training to employees who have left school without a defined level of qualification. Some of the costs are shouldered by employers because time must be made available to employees for training purposes. This article looks at organisations that are committed to providing basic skills training of this kind.

Questions

1   What methods are available to help employers move towards formal provision of basic skills training for employees?

2   Apart from improved skills, what other benefits accrue to employees who participate on these schemes?

3   What are the major advantages for employers?

LABOUR MARKET CONDITIONS

People resourcing, like other P&D activities, must focus on supporting the organisation in achieving its core product market objectives. However, this can only be accomplished through successful competition in the labour market. The use of employees as a means of achieving particular organisational goals is no more than an aspiration if it is not possible, in practice, to find people of the required skills and attitudes who are prepared to work at the rates and in the conditions that the organisation is able to provide. Resourcing specialists thus have to be as interested in what is happening in their labour market environment as they are in the wider commercial environment. For most jobs, the focus will be on the local labour market and what is happening in the 'travel to work areas' from which staff are recruited. However, for the better-paid positions that people will happily relocate to secure, the focus must be regional, national or even international.

Labour market conditions vary considerably over time and across different types of employment. A 'tight' labour market is one in which employers are obliged to compete fiercely to secure the services of the people they need. This state of affairs arises when there are fewer people looking for jobs than there are jobs available. Some labour markets are always tight, whatever the prevailing economic conditions, because the skills required are relatively scarce. In recent years the major examples have been the IT and sales professions, where really effective people have tended to be in short supply. By contrast, when people are in plentiful supply, labour markets can be characterised as being 'loose'. Such situations are a great deal easier to manage from a resourcing perspective. Vacancies are easy and cheap to fill quickly, while managers have to tread less carefully in the way they treat staff because there are fewer alternative job opportunities for dissatisfied employees to take up. This is not to say that staff can be treated badly, as doing so will tend to demotivate them and lead to poorer performance, but there is less of an imperative to ensure that individuals are satisfied with their employment.

The years following the end of the 1989–92 recession saw a steady, year-on-year tightening of labour markets in the United Kingdom as unemployment fell to the lowest levels for a generation. Economic confidence has grown and there has been an increase in the variety of career opportunities open to individuals. Labour market conditions still vary considerably with different lines of work. There also remain areas of the country in which unemployment is high and job opportunities few, but by and large the late 1990s and first years of the twenty-first century have been good for employees with skills that are in demand, and consequently tougher for employers wanting to recruit the best available people. This has led a number of commentators to talk in terms of 'a war for talent' (see Hiltrop 1999, Williams 2000, Cappelli 2000, Larkan 2007), by which they mean the development of hyper-tight labour markets and 'no holds barred' skirmishes between employers to compete for their services.

There is some debate over how long this situation will last. On the one hand there is a convincing case for seeing the tightening and loosening of labour market conditions as cyclical in nature. As the economy expands and contracts, moving from recession to recovery and back to recession again, so labour markets become more or less competitive. If this is the case, we can expect to see some loosening of the current situation in future years as the effects of economic slowdowns filter through to the UK labour force. Indeed, some economists see tight labour markets and the skills shortages they cause as a primary cause of economic recession (Lind Frogner 2002). An alternative point of view suggests that tight labour markets are more likely to become the norm in the foreseeable future, because other underlying trends are operating to mitigate the countervailing influence of recessionary pressures. It is pointed out, for example, that the size of the potential working population is ceasing to expand and will begin to decline in years to come. This is because more older people are retiring each year than there are younger people entering the workforce. Moreover, the nature of the work that we are now required to do (requiring more sophisticated technical or social skills) can be said to be creating a situation in which good performers are necessarily in relatively short supply. Commentators also point to a general decline in the extent to which employees are inclined to remain loyal to one employer for any length of time. There is a greater willingness to switch jobs as well as more opportunity to do so. The result is a labour market environment that is more competitive than it once was, all other things being equal.

REFLECTIVE QUESTION

How far has your personal experience of the labour market changed in recent years? Are you harder to recruit and retain than you were a year or two ago? Do you have a wider range of alternative employment possibilities?

COMPETING IN A TIGHT LABOUR MARKET

What are the practical consequences for organisations of tightening labour markets? The answer is, a reduction in the number of people with the required attributes looking to work in the jobs that are available. This means that it becomes progressively harder to find new recruits and that good people, who have the skills that are most in demand, are more likely to leave their current employment in order to work for another organisation or to set up their own businesses. It also tends to alter, however subtly, the power balance within organisations. People who are hard to replace are less easily controlled by management. They are in a position to demand greater autonomy over their own areas of work, more flexibility, better working conditions and more developmental opportunities, in addition to competitive rates of pay. This has an impact on the means used to achieve performance and change management objectives, as well as those related to staffing. Resourcing policies and practices have to reflect employee interests as well as those of the employer, while more care has to be taken over the manner in which people are treated by their managers. People who can, if they wish, resign and find another job elsewhere, are less likely to put up with arbitrary and iniquitous treatment than is the case when alternative career opportunities are few and far between. There is therefore a general effect on the whole portfolio of resourcing activity – consequences that need to be taken on board if organisations are going to compete effectively for key staff. However, the major immediate impact of tightening labour market conditions is in the staffing arena. Here several alternative approaches need to be developed and pursued:

- **Recruitment initiatives.** Employers can allocate a greater budget for recruiting staff by designing more sophisticated advertising and seeking to ensure that it has greater reach. They can also look to recruit people from outside their customary sources. Some of the best-known recent examples have been in the NHS, where recruiters have looked overseas in a bid to meet their specialist staffing needs. Efforts have also been made to lure back into work people who have previously left for family reasons or to take early retirement.

- **Retention initiatives.** When labour markets tighten, employers can work harder at retaining the staff that they already employ. The key here is understanding why people leave and then acting accordingly. The main approaches used are described in Chapter 17. They include attitude surveys, exit interviews and surveys of former employees. People resign jobs for a wide variety of reasons, so employers are foolish to make any rash assumptions.

- **Reorganisations.** A third response to skills shortages is to reorganise tasks among existing staff in such a way as to reduce the extent of dependence on hard-to-recruit groups. The term 'skill mix review' is used frequently to describe this process. The aim here is to ensure that people who are in greatest demand (normally those with the rarest skills or qualifications) spend 100 per cent of their time doing what only they are qualified to do. Other activities (eg managerial or administrative tasks) should be carried out by support staff who are easier to recruit.

- **Development initiatives.** The fourth response involves developing home-grown talent rather than seeking to buy it in 'ready-made'. This takes rather longer to achieve and can be the most expensive approach, but should form part of a longer-term strategy for tackling skills shortages. The approach simply involves employing people who do not have the requisite skills and experience, and then giving them the opportunity to lean and develop.

DEMOGRAPHIC TRENDS

Over the longer term it is likely that labour markets will tighten further as the proportion of the population that is of working age begins to stagnate and then fall. Reductions are expected to begin after 2010 as the bulk of the 'baby boomer' generation (the large number of people born between 1945 and 1965) retire. Fewer births in the years since 1965 mean that there will not be enough younger people to replace them. However, the shortages are expected to become noticeable before then as the size of the working population ceases to expand. This is a reversal of the trend in recent years, which has seen a steady growth in the number of people entering the labour market, mainly due to increased participation on the part of women over the past 25 years. The government has stated that it wishes to see a higher proportion of young people taking up university places in these coming years, so that a situation is reached in which 50 per cent of all school leavers go on to degree courses. This is likely to fuel greater demand for postgraduate courses too, as the brighter students seek to differentiate themselves by going on to secure specialist qualifications after graduating.

There has been considerable mitigation of tight labour market conditions in the United Kingdom in the form of more overseas immigration (especially from Eastern Europe following the expansion of the European Union), a tendency to retire later, and the evolution of labour-saving technologies, but employers must nonetheless now accept that a new type of labour market environment is evolving. The main implications are as follows:

- The average age of the working population will increase over time. This means fewer opportunities to employ young people with a view to training them and securing many years' return on that investment. Employers will be obliged either to compete a great deal harder to secure the services of young workers, or accept that they need to resource their organisations from other sources.

- P&D policies will have to be adjusted in order to attract people of an older generation into jobs that have traditionally been filled by school leavers or graduate recruits. Flexible working practices are critical here as a means of recruiting for those with family responsibilities and older workers looking for part-time work.

- Greater attention will need to be given to human resource planning (HRP) processes. Systematic human resource planning has tended to be carried out less frequently in recent years as other P&D priorities have come to the fore. There is a strong case, in a world in which the working population is static or falling, to revive interest in HRP techniques. This will help ensure that organisations are in a position to manage the consequences of demographic change before it starts to damage their ability to compete effectively.

- The presence of an ageing population means that it will be progressively harder for the state to provide adequate pensions for older people. Individuals will thus be required to take greater responsibility for funding their own pensions, making the subject one in which everyone will have to take a greater interest. Employers who provide particularly good occupational pensions and who are able to communicate this fact to their workforces should gain an advantage in the labour market over less generous rivals.

EXERCISE 3.2

SHORT IN SCOTLAND

People management

Read the article by Katie Hope, Scots mist (*People Management,* 13 October 2005, pp16, 17). This can be downloaded from the *People Management* archive on the CIPD's website (www.cipd.co.uk).

Across the United Kingdom as a whole the population is now rising rapidly, principally as a result of increased migration from overseas. However, the increases are heavily concentrated in south-east England. Other parts of the country continue to see alarming falls in population levels, not least because so many people are drawn towards London

early on in their careers. This article focuses on the response to this issue of the devolved government in Scotland.

Questions

1   How are Scottish employers tending to address the issue of skills shortages at present?

2   Why is this approach unlikely to provide a viable long-term solution?

3   What longer-term approaches is it argued should be considered?

ATTITUDES TO WORK AND THE WORKPLACE

Another factor for resourcing specialists to take into account is the possibility that the attitudes of future generations towards work, careers and employment will evolve and be different from those of past and current generations. It is impossible to predict what will happen here with any degree of accuracy, because generational attitudes are to a large extent shaped by the life experiences that members of each generation face. As yet we cannot know what the major factors shaping the views of today's children will turn out to be. We cannot be certain if they will in fact be markedly different in any way from those of their parents and grandparents. Nonetheless it is possible to put forward an informed opinion and to speculate with some degree of confidence about likely developments. For example, we can draw on the limited evidence that is available of prevailing attitudes among those coming up through schools and universities, and who have graduated relatively recently (see Zemke *et al* 2000, Pollock and Cooper 2000, Sparrow and Cooper 2003, Brown *et al* 2007). It is important to be wary of generalisations and to accept that no one set of beliefs or perspectives is shared by an entire generation. Nonetheless it would seem that the members of 'Generation Y' or the 'nexters' as they are variously called (people born after 1980) tend to share some views in common that are relevant to the workplace and differ to an extent from those of other generations. Some of the most frequently made points are as follows:

- ease with and acceptance of ongoing technological change

- strong intolerance of intolerance in respect of minority groups

- a wish to achieve a greater work–life balance than their parents managed

- a commitment to ethical practices (eg environmental concerns) and an attraction to ethical organisations

- a global perspective (ie not European)

- a resistance to tight systems of control and bureaucratically imposed rules

- greater ease with insecurity than previous generations.

If these findings are correct, and the attitudes do not change as this generation ages and takes on domestic responsibilities, there are important messages for organisations seeking to recruit and retain its members. First we can predict that employees in the future will be less accepting of management prerogative than has been the case in recent decades. There is a possibility that this will herald renewed interest in trade unionism, but the strong individualistic streak picked up by researchers working in this field suggests that a more common form of protest will be to resign and look for work elsewhere. Employers will thus have to get used to a world in which employees are less predisposed to be loyal and less easily bought with pay and perks. Bad management will lead to recruitment and retention problems, and it will be progressively harder to shed an unethical reputation once gained. Hand in hand with less loyalty, goes less respect for management and a greater tendency to question. This suggests that the organisations that are most successful in resourcing terms in the future will be those with flat hierarchies, decentralised power structures and democratic cultures. Tolerance of alternative lifestyles and needs arising outside the workplace are also likely to be essential features of successful future organisations.

While employers will probably have to take greater care than they have to date in promoting an acceptable workplace culture, they are likely to have fewer problems in the future securing acceptance of structural and technological change. Generation Y appear to be a great deal more relaxed about this than their parents were and still are. It will be easier for organisations to reinvent themselves, to merge with others and to restructure as and when required by their business environments. Ongoing change is seen as part of life by the younger generation and is thus less likely to be greeted with suspicion. On the other hand of course, there are disadvantages for employers as the same 'relaxed attitude' to change will mean that employees in the future are more likely to switch jobs or even careers than their predecessors. The price to pay for greater acceptance of organisational change is thus higher staff turnover and an inability to rely on traditional mechanisms of staff control. In short, people in years to come are likely to be less attached to their jobs and workplaces, as well as less concerned about their likely future prospects in any one organisation.

REFLECTIVE QUESTION

What do you think of these findings on new attitudes to work and the workplace among younger people? To what extent are they demonstrating an idealism that can be expected to fall away as they encounter career pressures later in life?

EXERCISE 3.3

TARGETING THE OLDER GENERATION

People management

Read the article by Roger Trapp, *Older and wiser* (*People Management*, 23 December 2004, pp40–41). This can be downloaded from the *People Management* archive on the CIPD's website (www.cipd.co.uk).

This article focuses on the experiences of two companies operating in different sectors (B&Q and Barclays Bank) that have helped to resolve staff shortages by employing older people.

Questions

1   Aside from skills shortages, what other factors might lead employers to target older workers in their recruitment campaigns?

2   What evidence is presented of the business advantages associated with employing older people?

3   The article debunks some common myths about the employment of older workers, suggesting that they are often better employees than younger colleagues. How far do you agree with this view? What genuine disadvantages could you cite?

WORK–LIFE BALANCE

Work–life balance initiatives have become prominent in recent years for several reasons. In some situations they are introduced primarily to meet the operational requirements of organisations rather than the preferences of employees. Much of the growth in part-time working, for example, has come about because employers in the service sector require additional staff over and above their full-time cohort to help them meet peaks in demand that occur at certain times of the week or day. The fact that such initiatives can also serve to meet the needs of employees with caring and childcare responsibilities is essentially coincidental. You will read more about flexible forms of working of this kind in Chapter 7.

A second important factor is the move we have increasingly witnessed in recent years towards far longer hours of operation for many organisations. Only a few years ago most shops opened only during office hours, closing on Wednesday afternoons. Conversely, the pubs, bars, restaurants and other leisure services opened only once the shops and offices had closed. Working hours thus equated to hours of operation. An organisation did business for 40–45 hours a week, employing managers and staff to work those hours. The norm now is for such organisations, and all the others that provide services of one kind or another, to operate at full pace throughout the daytime and evenings, not to mention

Sundays and bank holidays. This trend has provided opportunities for the employment of staff on unconventional shift patterns, some of which can help people achieve a better balance between the needs of their work and those of their home-based activities. For example, they allow older people to reduce their hours of work steadily over a number of years rather than transferring from full-time working to total retirement in one jump.

Regulation has played a major part in pushing work–life balance issues up the P&D agenda (see Chapter 4), while major social changes have also had an important impact. Organisations a generation ago could broadly assume that most of their employees lived in households in which men were the breadwinners and the women primarily looked after the home and children, but this is no longer the case. Dual income earning is now the norm, with many women earning more than their male partners, while single-parent households are commonplace.

Despite all these factors, it remains the case that most work–life balance initiatives are introduced for labour market reasons. In other words, employers are moving in this direction because their employees and potential employees are seeking a greater work–life balance, and helping them to achieve it is thus a good way of acquiring a loyal and effective workforce. CIPD (2005) shows clearly that the major motivations for introducing work–life balance options for employees are to improve recruitment and especially to retain staff. However, it is not just a question of providing existing employees with a more desirable package in order to dissuade them from looking elsewhere for employment. Importantly, initiatives in the field of work–life balance also help to provide organisations with an entree into parts of the labour market to which they have hitherto been unable to gain access. Organisations suffering from skills shortages are obliged to look beyond their customary recruitment sources (typically people looking for full-time employment during conventional working hours). Once a more flexible approach is adopted, interest can be engendered among groups of people who are interested in working some hours each week or year, but who are either unwilling or unable to take up a traditional full-time role.

IDS (2000d) provides an excellent survey of the various types of elements that make up a work–life balance policy. It identifies four major categories of initiative.

Flexible working

This comprises patterns of working hours that differ from the traditional 9–5 working day. Part-time working is the most common, but it is also possible to offer compressed hours, whereby people work a full complement of hours each week, but concentrate them into three or four days. Term-time working is attractive to parents with children of school age, as are shifts that allow parents to divide childcare responsibilities between them. Job-sharing, flexitime (see Chapter 7) and homeworking are other types of arrangement that can be adopted. Finally, of course, it is possible simply to meet the needs of particular individuals, either for a temporary period or permanently, by altering established patterns of working.

Leave and time off

Allowing staff to take extended periods of leave on an unpaid basis and to return to their jobs at a later date is another significant type of work–life balance initiative that employees value. In practice the vast majority will never take up the opportunities offered to them, but many find it comforting to know that the possibility is there and are likely to opt to work for organisations that have schemes of this kind. The law now requires organisations to allow people a few days off at short notice to make arrangements for the care of dependents when they become ill, but it does not provide for any longer periods away. If it can be afforded and does not reduce productivity it can make good business sense in labour market terms to go beyond the minimum requirements of the law and offer a more generous entitlement. Permitting people to take career breaks or sabbaticals for longer periods (eg six months or a year) once they have become established employees is also a valued benefit.

Childcare facilities

The third type of initiative that forms part of a work–life balance policy involves providing direct assistance with childcare. It is common for larger organisations to provide nurseries for children who are below school age, but other types of approach are also in operation. After-school clubs and school holiday clubs are the major examples. Some organisations also provide equivalent facilities to help meet the needs of older people for whom employees have a caring responsibility. The Peugeot 'granny crèche' in Coventry is a well-publicised example.

Health and well-being

The final category includes the provision of any other service that aims to assist employees to reach a better work–life balance for themselves. Occupational health services have long been run by larger employers as a means of helping to ensure that employees remain fit and well. But it is possible to extend these so that they also provide confidential counselling and advisory services that provide practical assistance to employees who are finding it difficult to juggle their domestic and working lives.

While the extent of work–life balance initiatives has grown considerably in recent years (Fleetwood 2007), many commentators agree that a great deal more benefit could be gained for employers than is currently the case. This is because there remains a strong tendency for managers and employees alike to perceive them as being relevant only for women with young children and not for the generality of people (CIPD 2002a). This leads to the presence of strong cultural barriers that prevent men and women who do not have young children from taking up opportunities offered by the initiatives that might help them to achieve a better work–life balance. While many state that they would be interested in working fewer hours or taking a sabbatical, they chose in practice not to because they perceive that their careers would suffer over the long term. Kodz *et al* (2002) found substantial evidence of such effects in their research, as well as a lack of enthusiasm on the part of line managers. Organisations, it would seem, are happy to embrace the principles of work–life balance and develop initiatives centrally, but are less able to develop a supportive culture that enables the idea to become a reality.

People management

EXERCISE 3.4

BT

Read the article by Claire Seneviratna, Dependant's day (*People Management*, 6 December 2001, pp38–40). This can be downloaded from the *People Management* archive on the CIPD's website (www.cipd.co.uk).

The article describes the development of a wide suite of family-friendly policies at BT designed to help its employees achieve a better work–life balance. The positive results of the policies are also set out.

Questions

1   Write down a list of the various different work–life balance initiatives that are mentioned or alluded to in the article.

2   What were the main reasons for their introduction?

3   What benefits does BT point to in its evaluation of its policies?

KEY ARTICLE 6

Jane Sturges and David Guest, Working to live or living to work? Work life balance early in the career. *Human Resource Management Journal,* Vol. 14, No. 4, pp5–20 (2004)

This article looks in detail at the perspective of young graduate recruits on the issue of work–life balance. The results of two surveys are presented, one questionnaire-based and one interview-based. The article is interesting because of the way that the authors try to reconcile two apparently contradictory findings. Why is it, they ask, that graduate recruits profess to be very interested in achieving a good work–life balance, but at the same time stay in jobs which require them to work long hours and hence prevent them from achieving one?

Questions

1   What do the findings presented show about the employees' attitudes towards work–life balance?

2   Why are they prepared to work such long hours?

3   What are the major lessons to be learned from these findings from a practical P&D management perspective?

EMPLOYER BRANDING

Employer branding is an idea that was developed in the last years of the twentieth century as labour markets tightened and it became harder to recruit and retain staff. At base what is involved is the application of branding techniques long used when competing in product markets to an organisation's labour markets. It is primarily concerned with improving an organisation's ability to compete for new staff, but it is also believed to improve retention rates and to contribute more generally to employee commitment and motivation.

Nearly 70 per cent of employers responding to a recent CIPD survey claimed that their organisations had an employer brand (CIPD 2007a, p22), but the extent to which this amounts to more than a spin put on recruitment advertising campaigns is less clear. Responsibility for the development of the employer brand is much more often carried by public relations or marketing departments than by the HR function (Willock 2005), and there remains considerable disagreement among P&D professionals about what the term 'employer brand' really means. Edwards (2005) helpfully makes a clear distinction between 'employer branding', which is clearly aimed at attracting and retaining staff, and 'employee branding' which is more concerned with helping to ensure that employees are willing and able to assist the organisation in communicating the brand image associated with its products in the marketplace. The former relates to competition for staff in the labour market, the latter may be an important part of someone's job duties, but it is a completely different process.

Effective branding is universally recognised to be of central importance in consumer marketing strategies. A strong brand is one which consumers recognise and trust. They are thus more likely to buy a strongly branded product than one which is just as good in terms of quality and price, but less effectively branded. Quite ordinary products (such as soft drinks, soap powder or indigestion pills) can only be differentiated from one another by their branding. At a recent CIPD conference, Mark Ritson illustrated the value and power of a strong brand with the example of Haagen Dazs ice cream, a product that in terms of its taste and quality is not very different from that produced by hundreds of other manufacturers. What makes it highly successful is its brand image, which is sexy and sophisticated. This enables a premium price to be charged and helps maintain a huge international market. The brand image has also been designed to appeal to a particular segment of the market (people who are young, urban and reasonably well-off) because this is where the product's marketers believe there to be most scope for sales. The same is true of most of the products and services we buy. Brands are thus very valuable indeed to producers, their major merits being the following:

- A strong brand signifies a product or service of recognisable quality, reliability or value for money.

- Brands help to differentiate a product or service from others being offered by competitors.

- Brands convey familiarity on a product or service, attracting customers away from offerings of competitors.

- Customers have a tendency to become loyal to brands, reducing the likelihood that they will switch to products or services offered by competitors.

- Customers will pay a premium price for brands with which they identify.

- Less money has to be spent on advertising when there is already strong brand recognition.

Employer branding seeks to apply these same principles to the field of employment and to labour markets. The aim is for organisations to develop and maintain a strong brand image as employers that will reinforce their efforts to attract and subsequently retain the most effective performers. The term 'employer of choice' is often used in this context to describe the situation in which potential employees actively seek to work for a particular employer. An employer of choice is one with strong brand recognition. The name immediately conjures up in people's minds certain desirable qualities, giving people a favourable impression of the experience of working there.

Employer branding should in fact be seen as only one part of a wider process through which organisations seek to build and maintain a strong reputation in the world generally. We are talking here about an overall corporate image rather than perceptions of particular goods and services, but the principles are the same: 'Corporate brand equity occurs when relevant constituents hold strong, favourable and unique associations about the corporate brand in memory' (Keller 2000, p115).

Target audiences are customers, employees and potential employees, but also a range of other constituents such as investors, business analysts, financial journalists, regulatory bodies, potential business partners and government policy-makers. Employer branding thus constitutes the P&D contribution to the wider reputation-building process.

It is important not to get too carried away with the idea of applying consumer marketing principles to the employment field. Labour markets and product markets are dissimilar beasts, operating in different ways. While an employer may seek to 'sell' a job to a potential employee, it is the employer who will be paying the money. In return the employee gives time and effort. This is a different type of economic exchange from purchasing a product. The decision is also a great deal more important from the employee's perspective. Most of us only have 10 or 12 jobs in a lifetime, so the decision to join an organisation is a major one, affecting our lives profoundly for an extended period, and thus requires a great deal of consideration. Like buying a house, we need to think carefully about all the advantages and disadvantages before committing ourselves. As a result we are perhaps less likely to be swayed by surface level perceptions or a 'brand image' alone.

Despite these differences, anecdotal evidence strongly suggests that employers can gain an edge in the labour market through the development of a good brand, as the experience of Charles Schwab, a US investment bank shows:

> *Having a strong brand for employees is a competitive advantage and a strategic advantage. ... It really does help us to attract the best candidates. Someone glances at an ad in the newspaper and says 'Oh yeah, Schwab. I hear they are a great place to work'. Or we're recruiting executives and a headhunter calls us with a client who's willing to listen because we're Schwab.*

The Conference Board (2001, p5)

Employer branding is particularly useful for organisations that do not have a strong corporate brand. Household names, especially those that are instantly recognised by their strong consumer brand image (eg Mars, Virgin or easyJet) can benefit from employer branding exercises, but can live without them perfectly satisfactorily because they are already well known and successful. They already have a brand image established by virtue of their products that will attract the interest of potential job applicants. This is not the case for smaller organisations, start-ups or larger employers who are regionally based or little known by consumers but who wish to tap into wider labour markets. For them, there is a real benefit to be gained by thinking strategically about their position in the labour market and using branding as a means of improving it.

A common myth about strong brands is that they can be built simply through the use of effective advertising. This is not the case. Advertising has a role to play in shaping perceptions and reinforcing existing beliefs about a good or service, but it is not sufficient on its own to achieve a positive and strong brand image. The product itself must live up to expectations and deliver consistent value for the customer. Marketing textbooks are full of examples of companies that have tried to rebuild tarnished reputations through slick advertising campaigns, but have failed because their advertisements simply did not reflect the reality. The starting point must therefore be the product itself, and in the case of employer branding, this means the actual, lived experience of working for a particular organisation. This point is in fact more important for employer branding than consumer branding. Unjustified hype in advertising campaigns for products will simply lead to lost business as people's experience fails to live up to expectations. In the employment field, however, the costs are potentially rather greater. This is because a disgruntled employee who performs poorly or is looking for another job all the time is a direct cost to the business, not just a lost opportunity. So it is very important not to use recruitment advertising as a means of exaggerating the attractiveness of a workplace or to make any kind of misleading claim about the experience of working there.

There are therefore two stages that need to be considered when branding an organisation for employment market purposes. First, it is necessary to work out what features of the employee experience are appreciated and differentiate you as an employer from your competitors. This process is variously labelled as 'defining the brand identity' (Whitenack 2001, p2) and 'formulating the employee value proposition' (Michaels *et al* 2001, p67). Essentially this stage involves determining, in practice, what you have to offer as an employer. This then forms the basis of the branding exercise. The second stage involves communicating your brand message effectively to your target audience. Fields (2001, pp101–102) cites ideas developed by the McKinsey consulting organisation suggesting that there are four core types of employer brand, meaning four types of proposition that employers can use in developing their brand image:

- Prestige. For example, we have a great reputation in our business; working for us will enhance your long-term career opportunities.

- Cause. For example, we undertake work that is meaningful and socially important; working for us will provide you with the opportunity to help humankind.

- **High risk/big potential.** For example, we are a small but growing organisation; working for us will enable you to grow alongside us to reap big long-term rewards.
- **Work–life balance.** For example, we will provide you with a good job, but also allow you plenty of time to spend doing other things.

It is possible to think of other types of brand identity as well. One example would be an organisation that is able to offer job security, another would be opportunities to work overseas, another the opportunity to work in a close-knit friendly team. In each case the aim is to identify the key messages on which to base the branding exercise. Where it is not obvious what the unique selling points of an organisation are, it is necessary to carry out research. This involves running focus groups with employees (particularly recent hires), undertaking questionnaire surveys and, if possible, talking to ex-employees and rejected job applicants too.

Once the key elements of the employment experience that are valued and that differentiate the organisation from its labour market competitors have been identified, communication exercises can begin. This stage involves 'leveraging the brand' by finding creative ways to communicate the core messages. A brand image is developed by repeating the same basic points consistently across different types of media over a prolonged period. Logos and slogans are useful at this stage to convey the main points, but beneath them must lie a more detailed account of what is on offer. This will provide the basis, for example, of what is said to potential applicants when they call to express an interest, of the message given to undergraduates at an employer presentation, and subsequently what is said at the interview stage. That way, over time, the positive brand image becomes established in the minds of potential employees.

Style of presentation is also important, particularly when an organisation wishes to focus its labour marketing efforts on a particular sector of the community. If young people are the target audience, then the message has to be conveyed in language and in a manner that they find appealing. A rather different approach would be used for 30-somethings and a different one again used for older people. Market research is necessary at this stage too, so that the most effective approaches can be adopted.

While the focus of much employer branding effort is on new employees, if it is carried out effectively there should also be a positive impact on existing employees. The branding exercise will make them more appreciative of their employment experience and give them a slightly less favourable impression of competitors. This occurs because of the deliberate use of branding to differentiate the current employer from others. The result should be lower turnover rates and a higher level of motivation. As yet there is no extensive body of empirical research available to prove or disprove these claims, but they are intuitively attractive.

EMPLOYER BRANDING AT ERICSSON

The telecommunications company, Ericsson, claims to have gained substantial benefits from carrying out an extensive employer branding exercise. Its major target market was new MBA graduates from the world's top business schools. Its aims were to improve the quality of the people it recruited from this source and to retain more of its new recruits for longer.

The company started by using polling and focus group activities to establish what were the key features of the Ericsson brand from an employee perspective. Four phrases were then selected that summed up these up:

● world citizenship

● forefront of technology

● connected to the best minds

● inspiring possibilities.

The 'world citizenship' idea was given particular prominence for MBA graduates, because it was found to stress the aspects of employment that they found especially appealing. The international career opportunities offered by Ericsson were thus placed at the forefront of its recruitment campaign, along with other messages about exposure to the newest technology and the practice of board level directors acting as mentors.

The result was a greatly improved retention rate among new graduate recruits (perhaps because more appropriate people were self-selecting into the applicant pool), a substantial reduction in recruitment costs (because advertising and other approaches were more effective) and lower employment costs (because people wanted to work for Ericsson sufficiently that they accepted a lower initial salary).

Source: Presentation by Sven-Ake Damgaard at the 2001 CIPD Conference, Harrogate.

EXERCISE 3.5

EMPLOYER BRANDING CASE STUDIES

People management

Read the following three articles featured in *People Management*. Each represents a good case study of an organisation seeking to establish a clear, well-differentiated, positive brand image in its labour markets. The organisations are Axa, the Environment Agency and McDonald's. The articles can be downloaded from the *People Management* archive on the CIPD's website (www.cipd.co.uk).

● Karen Higginbottom, Image conscious (6 February 2003, pp44–45)

● Jane Simms, Blue skies thinking (8 December 2005, pp24–26)

● Stephen Overrell, Fast forward (9 February 2006, pp26–31).

Questions

1   How would you define in a few sentences the different types of employer brand that each of these organisations is seeking to develop?

2   How far do you find their values to be attractive brand propositions from an employment perspective?

3   What evidence is provided of actual or potential problems being encountered in the process of establishing a positive employer brand image?

KEY ARTICLE 7

Kristin Backhaus and Surinder Tikoo, Conceptualizing and researching employer branding. *Career Development International*, Vol. 9, Nos. 4/5, pp501–516 (2004)

This is one of relatively few academic journal articles focusing specifically and exclusively on the subject of employer branding. It is interesting and useful because it discusses the idea of employer brands in the context of established theories in the fields of marketing and HRM. Towards the end a future research agenda is set out.

Questions

1 Explain how our understanding of 'employer branding' can be enhanced with reference to theories about:

i   the resource-based view of the firm

ii   the psychological contract

iii brand equity

iv   social identity theory

v   brand loyalty.

2 How, in theory, does employer branding serve to enhance an organisation's performance?

3 What type of research study would be required to test whether or not there is a link between employer branding and organisational performance?

EMPLOYING PEOPLE FROM OVERSEAS

For most of the past 50 years the UK population grew at a slow, steady rate. A growth of 4.9 per cent occurred between 1971 and 1999, which was considerably lower than was experienced in almost every other industrialised country in the world. However, since the turn of the millennium net migration into the country has grown at a much faster pace, causing the total population to increase by some 2 million between 2000 and 2006 (Blanchflower *et al* 2007, p2). A major factor in this acceleration was the accession of 10 new countries into EU membership in May 2004, the United Kingdom being one of just three existing member states to permit their citizens to enter freely in order to seek work. People migrating to the United Kingdom from countries such as Poland, Latvia, Hungary and the Czech Republic are legally required to register with the government in order to work in the United Kingdom, but this does not apply to self-employed people, and it is thought that many others simply do not bother to register as there is no penalty to pay for failing to do so.

As a result there is substantial disagreement about the precise number of recent arrivals from Eastern European countries. Around 500,000 registered to work in the United Kingdom between May 2004 and October 2006, but no record is kept of the numbers leaving to return to their countries of origin, and by definition, there are no official figures available for those who fail to register. Notwithstanding this debate, it is apparent that in recent years substantially more people have come to the United Kingdom from overseas than have emigrated to other countries. In the year to April 2007, for example, 713,000 new national insurance numbers were issued by the UK government to employees from overseas who had secured jobs in the United Kingdom (Taylor 2007). When it is considered that the total working population in the United Kingdom numbers 29 million, by any standards this represents a highly significant trend. Over the course of the past decade we have seen an increase of 70 per cent in the number of people working in the United Kingdom who originate from elsewhere (Caldwell 2007). Across the country as a whole, one in every eight employees was born overseas, but the proportion is much higher in London and other major cities where immigrant communities are concentrated.

The rise in overseas migration into the United Kingdom has helped to ameliorate skills shortages and has kept wage inflation low during a period of strong economic growth. However, from a practical operational P&D management point of view the key outcome is the presence of a much more culturally and racially diverse workforce than was the case just a few years ago. It is not uncommon now for major employers in urban areas to employ people with origins in dozens of different countries and for a substantial proportion of job applicants to be from overseas.

In Chapter 2 we explored the work of researchers such as Gert Hofstede, who have sought to identify and 'map' major differences that exist across the world as far as working and workplace cultures are concerned. Their findings have long informed the way that organisations in the United Kingdom prepare employees for overseas assignments, but they are less frequently used as a means of helping workers coming from overseas to adjust to the prevailing culture in UK organisations. Yet, as a result of increasing diversity in the labour market, there is now a strong case for taking this issue seriously and investing considerable time and effort in developing P&D policies and practices which are culturally sensitive. The result should be more effective recruitment, retention and motivation of overseas workers. In particular, there is every reason for managers to gain an understanding of the major differences between UK workplaces and those in other countries so that the expectations of people coming from overseas can be met and managed more effectively. This should result in fewer early resignations and a faster period of adjustment, leading to the achievement of higher levels of performance at an earlier stage. Addressing the issue is not difficult, all that is required is effective training of managers in cultural differences and effective cross-cultural communication. The outcome should be greater sensitivity to differences in expectations and hence more effective interpersonal management.

This is an evolving area of HR expertise which at the time of writing (late 2007) has yet to generate many substantial academic research studies. However, a great deal of work in the field is carried out by specialist consultants, and they have begun to publish books and articles which are useful and thought-provoking. Tokarek (2006) and Laroche and Rutherford (2007) both draw on their experience to pinpoint practices and approaches which appear wholly natural in workplaces in the United Kingdom, United States and Canada, but which are carried out very differently in other countries. The following are examples of particular relevance to people resourcing activities:

- In Anglo-Saxon workplaces it is expected that employees will be open about personal ambitions and will promote themselves and their interests in the workplace. In many other cultures modesty is the norm, people being asked to contribute rather than being expected to push themselves forward. Elsewhere, in many Asian countries, the maintenance of group harmony is more significant, leading individuals to promote the interests of others rather than themselves. Hence in selection interviews they will prefer to talk about 'our accomplishments', referring to their team, rather than to draw attention to their own individual contribution.

- By comparison with workplaces in most countries, those in Anglo-Saxon cultures are egalitarian in nature. People are expected to challenge the ideas of those higher up the organisational hierarchy. This does not happen where 'power distance' as defined by Hofstede is high and a more autocratic approach is followed. Deference to more senior figures is expected, while delegation of tasks is limited. The Anglo-Saxon approach of delegating a task, including decision-making, is not the norm.

- Another major difference relates to the way that business meetings are organised. In Western countries the norm is to get straight down to business and to follow a pre-agreed agenda, especially in negotiation situations. In many Eastern countries this is seen as impolite, there being a need to develop a personal relationship with other participants, while agendas are only loosely adhered to.

- In Anglo-Saxon countries there is less reverence for educational qualifications in the selection of employees than is the case in many other cultures. Having a doctorate in a relevant field is not enough to secure a job in competition with less well-qualified candidates if they have greater practical skills or experience. In many Eastern countries educational qualifications carry a great deal more weight and hence tend to be at the top of a CV in front of personal achievements in job roles.

- Anglo-Saxon cultures sit in the middle as far as direct and indirect styles of communication are concerned. People from Northern European backgrounds tend to be a great deal more direct, saying exactly what they think and seeing no need to dress the message up at all to make it more polite. Elsewhere, for example in Japan, the level of directness that a UK manager communicates with is seen as impolite.

EXERCISE 3.6

MIGRATION FROM EASTERN EUROPE

Read the article by John Philpott and Gerwyn Davies, No turning back? (*People Management*, 14 September 2006, pp26–30). This can be downloaded from the *People Management* archive on the CIPD's website (www.cipd.co.uk).

In this article the authors ask a number of questions about the recent increases in immigration to the United Kingdom from Eastern Europe, particularly Poland. Why have so many more people come than the government predicted? What are the implications for employers and employees in the United Kingdom? Have the numbers of migrants now peaked, or are we likely to see continued immigration at similar levels for some time to come?

Questions

1   Why have around a million people

moved from Eastern Europe to the United Kingdom since 2004?

2   What have been the major advantages and disadvantages for the United Kingdom as a whole?

3   Who are the major winners and who are the major losers from this trend? Why?

KEY ARTICLE 8

Mary Trefry, A double-edged sword: organizational culture in multicultural organizations. *International Journal of Management*, Vol. 23, No. 3, pp563–576 (2006)

This article explores the potential advantages and disadvantages of multicultural organisations, by which the author means workforces made up of people from several diverse national backgrounds. She concludes that there are huge potential benefits to be gained if cultural diversity is nurtured, managed effectively and harnessed to bring maximum advantage. However, where this does not happen, multicultural workforces can be less effective than those dominated by a single culture. The key to ensuring that an organisation falls into the first rather than the second category is the development of an appropriate organisational culture. This article draws on evidence presented elsewhere to develop its arguments. No original empirical research is presented.

Questions

1   What positive outcomes can be found to result from the employment of staff from a variety of different cultural backgrounds?

2   What problems can arise?

3   What steps would you advise an organisation with a multicultural workforce to take in order to minimise the problems and maximise the benefits?

ETHICAL QUESTIONS

The field of business ethics, and its connection to HRM, is fascinating and is developing significantly at present. It is also quite complex, dealing in ideas which are beyond the scope of this book to explore in any depth. Readers are referred to recent publications such as those by Legge (1997), Fisher and Rice (1999), Woodhall and Winstanley (2001), Ackers (2005) and Torrington *et al* (2008) for good general introductions to the topic. Our purpose here is to raise the issue of ethics in general terms and to focus on its practical application in day-to-day P&D management.

These matters are difficult to resolve because it is often far from clear what the 'ethical path' is in certain situations. In fact it is often possible to construct two quite contrary arguments for different courses of action, both of which are apparently built on solid ethical principles. This state of affairs derives from the presence of two quite different perspectives on the whole question of business ethics. On the one hand are the views of authorities such as Milton Friedman (1963) and developed by others such as Henderson (2001) which see the market economy (ie, the capitalist system of economic organisation) as virtuous in its own right. As the engine of wealth creation its long-term health is seen as being in the interests of everyone across the globe, rich and poor alike. Actions which restrict free competition between organisations only serve to reduce our prosperity. It thus follows that companies are acting ethically when they act uniquely in their own self-interest, working for the benefit of shareholders and paying less attention to the interests of other stakeholders such as employees. Individuals may suffer when this approach is taken, but the long-term effect is a better life for all (less unemployment, better education, longer life expectancy etc). Provided basic standards of honesty and lawfulness are abided by, the ends thus justify the means.

The contrary view takes issue with the idea that all benefit from the advance of 'unbridled capitalism'. Some benefit far more than others, while a third group hardly benefit at all. A different conception of business ethics is advanced, based on notions of human rights and the presence of responsibilities which are owed by the relatively strong to the relatively weak. According to this perspective, employees have legitimate interests which employers are under a moral duty to protect. Poor treatment of staff is thus unethical in itself and can not be justified by reference to a need to create wealth.

In an era of tight labour markets the need to manage staff within an ethical framework that they and their potential successors share is particularly important. Nothing is more likely to promote dissatisfaction at work and hence voluntary resignations than the perception that people are being treated unfairly. If employees feel that they are being exploited to too great a degree, treated inequitably compared with other employees or friends working for other organisations, or simply that insufficient attention is given by managers to their legitimate needs and interests, they are less likely than they once were to take it on the chin or to grin and bear it. They may protest informally in some shape or form by reducing their commitment, and or formally through participation in more adversarial forms of industrial relations, but in today's business environment it is far more likely that they will simply start looking for another job. They are also very likely to tell others about their experiences. Existing employees are likely to become less satisfied with their employment as a result, while potential staff will be a good deal less likely to apply in the first place. Isolated incidents of this kind need not trouble managers too much. All organisations make mistakes in the way that they treat their people from time to time and no major corporate damage results. But an organisation that gets a reputation for treating people badly is likely to suffer economically. In a tight labour market situation, unethical management practices leave organisations at a competitive disadvantage because they find it harder than others to secure the services of effective performers.

The application of ethical principles to P&D activities is also necessary for another reason, namely the part that having good employment relations plays in securing the organisation's broader corporate reputation. Increasingly consumers take into consideration their perception of an organisation's ethicality when deciding how to spend their money (Harrison *et al* 2005), and this in turn affects the assessment of opinion-formers and investors about its likely future financial health. The share price of public limited companies and the ability of other types of organisation to raise finance is thus tied in part to their ethical reputation. There is nothing more likely to put a potential backer off investing than the fear that a corporate brand may soon become contaminated by association with unethical practices. The activities of a P&D function can quite easily become the source of such contamination, as has happened in some high-profile cases of apparent exploitation of workers at home and the employment of child labour overseas.

A good starting point for an exploration of the application of ethics to P&D work is the CIPD's own codes and guides. The CIPD graduateship is a professional qualification, and therefore carries with it not only proof of an ability to carry out the P&D function effectively but also an obligation to uphold a high standard of professional ethics. Like most professional bodies, the CIPD has a disciplinary procedure to which complaints of unprofessional conduct can be made. Under its terms, a disciplinary panel can be set up to consider complaints against members who are accused of actions that 'appear likely to bring discredit to the Institute or the profession'. Where a complaint is substantiated by the panel, a number of possible disciplinary actions can be taken, ranging from formal warnings through suspension to expulsion.

Nevertheless, the standards of professional conduct to which CIPD members are expected to adhere, and which form the basis of decisions under the disciplinary procedure, are general rather than specific. They are concerned with ensuring that members practise P&D work with a high standard of honesty, intelligence and diligence, that they act within the law at all times, that they respect confidentiality, that they recognise their own limitations and that they continually update their skills and knowledge. In addition, members are expected to promote the removal of employment practices that unfairly discriminate against people on any grounds (ie not simply on those that are currently outlawed). The CIPD code of professional conduct provides a sound basis for the development of ethical practices, but is not intended to give detailed guidance on how to handle day-to-day P&D decision-making. It sets a general standard, but does not specify what courses of action are considered ethical and unethical. In particular, it gives no guidance on what approach should be taken when conflicts arise between the legitimate needs of the organisation and the duty to maintain high standards of people management.

First and foremost it is necessary to recognise that P&D professionals are regularly faced with ethical dilemmas, and have to make decisions and take actions that do not always sit easily with individual consciences. At base, these arise because the employment relationship, while technically an agreement freely entered into by two parties, is in fact very unequal. Except in the case of individuals, such as some of the knowledge workers referred to above who can be said to be members of a 'headhunted class', the employer always has some degree of power over the employee – and often a great deal. In many situations, where the law does not effectively intervene, it is very easy for employers to abuse this power. Indeed, because much employment law is inadequately policed, abuse often extends into these areas too, so that unfairness and discrimination of one sort or another continue to occur in spite of legislation.

Dealing with abuses of power is no easy matter for most P&D professionals for a number of reasons, not least because decisions in these areas are very often made by others. P&D specialists rarely become chief executives. Thus they nearly always report ultimately to managers whose career path has been based on the capacity to deliver wider organisational objectives. While it would clearly be very unfair generally to characterise such people as being capable of unethical actions, in practice many situations that occur which are potentially questionable in ethical terms arise as a result of pressure from the 'I'm going to show him who's boss – I want her out now' brigade. Organisational politics play an important part in this, people who wish to advance themselves putting their own careers and financial interests before notions of ethicality (see Badaracco and Webb 1995).

The second reason that it is difficult to define the ethical path in P&D arises because there is often a genuine conflict between the interests of employees and the interests of the organisation. It may be ethically justifiable to make substantial alterations to a set of premises to accommodate disabled workers, and it may also be ethically wrong to put pressure on someone with family responsibilities to remain at work until 8.00 at night, but in both cases the business needs of the organisation may demand that 'unethical' courses are taken. Third, as has already been indicated, there is no clear statement of what *is* ethical, aside from what has been stated by Parliament and the courts. So even where a P&D specialist wishes to pursue an ethical path, it is not always easy to gain acceptance for the view that it is an ethical question at all.

In an ideal world, these issues would be resolved by each organisation's adopting a firm and agreed statement of business ethics covering the treatment of employees and potential employees, as well as customers and local communities. The statement would not only be endorsed from the top of the organisation, but would also be well enforced, with career progression and performance appraisal ratings determined in part by the presence of a good 'ethical record'. Furthermore, the statement would be well publicised and employees given the opportunity to make reference to its terms in grievance procedures that they were not fearful of invoking. Some organisations are moving in this direction, but it is difficult to avoid suspecting that, in some cases at least, their reasons have more to do with public relations (internal and external) than with practical decision-making.

For most P&D professionals, therefore, a less ambitious view has to be taken. Where ideals cannot be attained, the best that can realistically be achieved is to push decision-making and policy-making in an ethical direction. To achieve this, however, two issues have to be considered. First, it is necessary to establish a general ethical standard so that it is possible to determine what can and what cannot be regarded as an ethical issue. Second, there is a need to develop methods for influencing decision-making, given the restricting factors described above. As has already been indicated, the first of these is a matter for debate. What follows, therefore, is a suggested set of general principles that could be used in formulating a notion of P&D ethics. Readers might like to consider how far it accords with their own views on this subject.

- A balance has to be found between ethical considerations and the long-term survival and financial success of an organisation. This reflects a pragmatic view of organisational decision-making, based on the notion that there is no point in taking a strong ethical stand over an issue if the result is poor corporate performance and the consequent need to lay people off. It also accepts that ethical decision-making is often about choosing 'least of all evils' options in situations where all paths are unpalatable to some degree. However, it also recognises that a distinction must be made between actions that harm the interests of the organisation and those that damage the political interests of specific individuals, and that where an ethical stance does not damage the organisation, it should be pursued.

- Ethical P&D practice requires that all employees are treated consistently. Double standards should not be applied. All employees, whatever their status, length of service, sex, race, age or experience, should thus be accorded equal respect and be subject to the same rules and expectations.

- Basic principles of natural justice should apply. Aside from consistency, employees should be treated by managers in the way that managers themselves would wish to be treated – that is, with honesty and fairness. All sides of a case should thus be aired prior to decisions being taken about an employee's future, and issues should be looked at from a variety of perspectives. By and large this involves extending the principles (if not the procedures) set out in the Advice, Conciliation and Arbitration Service (ACAS) codes of conduct on the handling of dismissal across the whole raft of P&D decisions with an ethical dimension.

- Wherever possible, argument and not power should be used to determine actions. While it is inevitable that power will be distributed unequally in organisations, it should also be recognised that there is no need for the employment relationship to take on a feudal character. Power should be used sparingly, with implied or explicit threats made only when it is absolutely necessary, and after careful consideration. It follows that it is unprofessional and unethical to treat employees other than as adults with whom the organisation has an economic relationship. There should thus be no justification for playing games with employees or for unfairly manipulating expectations through hints, half-truths or misleading statements.

Once the principles have been established, it is possible to address possible ways of influencing the actions and approaches of senior managers and line managers with whom decision-making responsibility is shared. Where general agreement to enforceable organisation-wide standards cannot be secured, it is necessary to deploy other arguments on a case-by-case, situation-by-situation basis. Broadly, these fall into three categories: a moral, a business or a legal case.

A MORAL CASE

It is possible to appeal purely on moral or ethical grounds, putting across principles such as those outlined above, with eloquence and a degree of passion. In other words, an ethical dilemma can be treated purely on its own terms and resolved by appealing to a decision-maker's sense of reasonableness, of right and wrong, or of duty.

A BUSINESS CASE

Second, an argument based on the long-term needs of the organisation can be formulated. Decision-makers can be urged to consider the possibility of adverse publicity or potentially damaging effects of particular actions on the ability of the organisation to attract and retain the best employees. Such arguments are most commonly associated with issues of consistency, and particularly with the case for positive action in the equal opportunities field. In some situations it should be possible to present plausible evidence from published research or from the experience of other organisations to back up these kinds of argument.

A LEGAL CASE

The third kind of argument is often the most effective, because it raises the prospect not only of financial loss but also of the need to appear in court and be subjected to cross-questioning about one's actions. Clearly it can be deployed only where the decision in question has potential legal consequences and where the deployer has a good knowledge of legal principles.

Where pure argument fails, it is necessary either to accept the situation or to deploy other tactics. These involve first of all seeking to negotiate an ethical outcome by conceding other points, or ultimately, if the situation became intolerable, a threat of resignation. Professional P&D managers should clearly not take the decision to resign lightly, but where professional and ethical standards are clearly being breached and cannot be changed, this course of action is necessary. It particularly occurs in situations where the P&D professional is being required to break the law in a fundamental way (for example, by pursuing recruitment policies that unfairly discriminate or by dismissing people without first following the accepted procedural steps). In such cases, of course, the resigner may well have a very good case for pursuing a claim of constructive dismissal – another potential weapon to deploy where the most basic ethical standards are being compromised.

REFLECTIVE QUESTION
What types of argument have you used in seeking to persuade someone that an ethical course of action should be taken? Which approach have you found to be most successful?

EXERCISE 3.7

ETHICS TRAINING

People management

Read the article by John Drummond, A matter of principle (*People Management*, 17 June 2004, p42) This can be downloaded from the *People Management* archive on the CIPD's website (www.cipd.co.uk).

In this opinion piece the author draws on his experience of implementing programmes designed to improve awareness of ethical issues in organisations to argue that the HR function has an important role to play.

Questions

1 Assume that you have been asked to run a training programme for P&D

personnel using the approach outlined by John Drummond in this article. What everyday ethical dilemmas might you draw on as a means of engaging the interest of your trainees?

2 What arguments would you use to persuade a board of directors that the following would be good investments:

i ethics awareness training for all staff employed by the organisation?

ii ethics awareness training focusing specifically on the management of people?

KEY ARTICLE 9

Michelle R. Greenwood, Ethics and HRM: a review and conceptual analysis. *Journal of Business Ethics*, Vol. 36, No. 3, pp261–279 (2002)

This article asks the question 'What is an ethical approach to HRM?', looking for possible routes towards an answer in different theories of ethics such as the Kantian and utilitarian perspectives. The use of a stakeholder perspective is advocated as a useful way forward for future analysis. The article is particularly helpful from a student's point of view because it starts with a lengthy review of the literature, before going on to develop an interesting line of argument. The author is an Australian academic, but many of the references in the article are to the work of UK scholars and to UK-based journals.

Questions

1 What are the major gaps in the current literature on ethics and HRM identified by Michelle Greenwood in this article?

2 On what grounds does she argue that neither the established Kantian or utilitarian perspectives can provide an adequate ethical basis for HRM as practised in most contemporary organisations?

3 To what extent do you agree that treating employees with respect and refraining from undermining their autonomy are useful criteria for evaluating the extent to which HR practices can be described as being 'ethical'?

- In recent years labour markets have tended to tighten. This has had important implications for the resourcing function, which has no longer been able to assume the presence of a steady supply of people. New initiatives in recruitment, retention, work organisation and employee development have resulted.

- Resourcing specialists need to anticipate likely future labour market developments. The numbers of potential employees is important, but attention also needs to be given to the attitudes future staff are likely to display.

- A major way in which employers have responded to skills shortages has been through the provision of opportunities for employees to achieve a greater work–life balance. This widens the labour market and helps to retain existing staff. In many organisations, however, there is low take-up of these opportunities on the part of staff because of cultural barriers and a lack of interest on the part of line managers.

- 'Employer branding' involves applying established consumer marketing ideas and techniques to an organisation's relationship with its labour markets. The first stage requires the organisation to gain an understanding of its 'employee value proposition' (what it uniquely offers employees which is valued). The second stage involves projecting this message consistently and appropriately across all recruitment activities.

- A third development of significance has been an increase in the number of people working in the United Kingdom who were born overseas. Managing these groups effectively requires cultural sensitivity on the part of managers and an adjustment of expectations.

- P&D practitioners making resourcing decisions find it impossible to avoid difficult ethical dilemmas. Sometimes opposite courses of action can be chosen, each of which can be justified in ethical terms. More often there are unethical dimensions present in each alternative course, making it necessary to choose the least worst option.

EXPLORE FURTHER

- There are few general introductions to labour market trends which take a management perspective. Capelli (1999) makes most of the important points, and there are introductions in the textbooks by Torrington *et al* (2008) and Beardwell and Claydon (2007). Government publications such as *Economic and Labour Market Trends* (monthly) and *Labour Market and Skill Trends* (yearly) contain statistics and in-depth analysis.

- Work–life balance issues are well-covered in the literature. CIPD published a wide-ranging *Guide to work–life balance* in 2002 (CIPD 2002b) in which several authors write about different aspects of introducing initiatives in the field. The Institute of Employment Studies research report by Kodz and her colleagues (2002) provides much food for thought about the practical and cultural barriers which often prevent organisations from reaping the full benefit from such policies. A special supplement on work–life balance issues was published with *People Management* in September 2002. It contains several useful case studies and opinion-based articles. In more recent years a lively critical perspective has been developed. The articles by Fleetwood (2007) and Eikhof *et al* (2007) and the book by Gambles *et al* (2006) are useful introductions.

- There is an increasing literature on employer branding, but the field remains under-researched. The best source of general information is the Internet, where thousands of sites can be accessed which make use of the term. Fombrun (1996) and Schultz *et al* (2000) are substantial texts which look in general terms at the development of a positive corporate reputation. Fields (2001) and Reed (2001) contain short, but very useful passages on the practicalities of employer branding exercises. The most useful discussions are those by Edwards (2005) and by the various authors who contributed to the CIPD publication, Employer branding: the latest fad or the future of HR? (CIPD 2007b).

- Ackers (2005) and Bevan (2007) probably represent the most accessible and clear introductions to ethical issues in P&D work. Aside from the other authors cited in the text above, books on business ethics which include particularly useful sections on the employment relationship are Sorell and Hendry (1994) and Beauchamp and Bowie (1997). A major book of articles contributed by various authors and edited by Pinnington *et al* (2007) represents the most detailed academic treatment of the subject to date. From time to time *People Management* publishes interesting articles about companies seeking to improve their ethical reputations. Two interesting cases are the pieces about British American Tobacco by Anat Arkin (2005a) and Citigroup by Sarah Butcher (2005).

CHAPTER 4

The regulatory environment

There can be no question that one of the most significant current developments in the P&D business environment is the growing volume of regulation that governs the employment relationship in the United Kingdom. Every year more areas of organisational life are subject to new regulation, while the trend is very much to tighten and to extend existing regulation in other areas. Much of the most significant new law (eg on working time, data protection and age discrimination) originates in European Union institutions and thus applies across all 25 member states, but a good deal more has a UK origin (eg the national minimum wage, trade union recognition laws and family-friendly measures).

Employment law has moved in 15 years from being perceived by lawyers as something of a 'poor relation' to a major area of practice attracting top legal brains. Whole chambers of barristers now specialise in the field, while solicitors and consultancy firms devoted to employment law have also grown and prospered. More than 80 different types of case can now be heard by employment tribunals (Shackleton 2005), to which must be added the various claims that are brought to the county courts in the fields of health and safety and breach of contract. As more opportunities are given to people to pursue legal actions against their employers, more choose to take them up. While the figures vary somewhat from year to year, it is clear that the total number of claims processed annually by the Employment Tribunal Service is now three, or even four times what it was ten years ago, and that these are tending to be more complex and to cover more issues than used to be the case (ETS 2007). As a result, many more organisations report that they are facing increasing numbers of legal claims than state that their litigation rates are decreasing (White *et al* 2004, p155).

The impact of increased regulation on P&D specialists is significant. On the one hand it provides an important new source of authority for members of the profession, giving them the opportunity to use their expertise to make a greater contribution to the effective management of their organisations. But dealing with regulatory matters also eats up a great deal of time that could better be spent proactively enhancing the organisation's competitive position. Astonishingly, according to a recent CIPD report (CIPD 2002c), two-thirds of P&D specialists now spend in excess of 20 per cent of their time 'dealing with employment law issues'. Moreover, a quarter report that over 40 per cent of their working days are spent in this way. It is, in short, now quite impossible for anyone who is serious about developing a career in the P&D field to do so without gaining a good working knowledge of the law and how it affects decision-making. This is particularly true of the people resourcing function, where the law in some shape or form has something to say about almost all the core activities carried out.

In this chapter our focus is on six areas where regulation is playing and will increasingly play an important role as far as people resourcing activities are concerned: discrimination law, dismissal law, the law of contract, family-friendly legislation, working time regulations and confidentiality laws. Most are addressed again later in the book in the context of specific management activities, but it is important first to summarise their major points and to introduce some of the wider debates about the purpose, effectiveness, rights and wrongs of employment regulation. The law relating to Transfer of Undertakings (TUPE) was briefly summarised in Chapter 2 in the context of mergers and acquisitions.

LEARNING OUTCOMES

By the end of this chapter readers should be able to:

- advise on the legal principles governing activities in the people resourcing field

- appreciate the relatively rapid evolution of employment legislation and its consequences for employing organisations

- participate in debates and consultation exercises concerning the future direction of employment regulation.

In addition, readers should be able to understand and explain:

- the reasons for the development of employment regulation in the United Kingdom

- the major areas of law that impact on resourcing activities and their consequences

- the major strands of the arguments for and against further employment regulation.

SCOPE AND DEVELOPMENT

Employment law is a relatively recent development as far as the United Kingdom is concerned. Until the 1960s, with the exception of regulations outlawing the exploitation of children, some basic health and safety rules and the limited protection provided by the common law, employers were able to manage their organisations without the limitations that are now imposed through statute. Managers could dismiss staff as and when they pleased, could require them to work whatever hours were deemed necessary, and were in no way restrained by the law if they wished to discriminate against women or members of the ethnic minorities. Indeed it was common to have separate pay scales for male and female employees.

For many employees this unregulated world of work meant a life of insecurity and, in some cases, grievous exploitation. But for the majority this was not the case because trade union membership was high – covering 40 per cent to 50 per cent of the total workforce in the post-war period. Moreover, a good majority of staff worked in unionised environments and were covered by national-level collective agreements that operated across whole industrial sectors, and to which all organisations in those industries signed up. The same approach remains in place to a great extent in the public sector today, most staff still being employed on nationally agreed terms and conditions that cover everyone in particular professional groups.

Protection from abuse of power on the part of employers was thus effectively provided through non-legal mechanisms. This voluntarist system of industrial relations had evolved over decades and appears to have suited both employers and trade unions reasonably well, but it was very different from the traditions of active state involvement that were being developed in other European countries at the time. Whereas in the United Kingdom the way that workplaces operated vis-à-vis employees was almost exclusively determined with reference to contracts of employment, negotiated collective agreements and informal arrangements developed through custom and practice, elsewhere on the continent labour codes created and enforced by government agencies had become the norm.

Over the past 40 years the United Kingdom's situation has changed to a very considerable extent. The first major reform came in 1965 with the introduction of statutory redundancy payments and a fledgling industrial tribunal service to enforce the new law. Henceforth staff could not be laid off without a minimum level of compensation being paid by their employers at a level determined by Parliament. The 1970s then saw the introduction of unfair dismissal law, equal pay legislation and protection from discrimination at work on grounds of sex and race. Health and safety regulation was also greatly extended at this time and protection introduced for employees whose organisations were taken over by or merged with others. During the 1980s the pace of law-making in the employment field slowed down as the Thatcher government sought to fight off the demands of those who argued for greater levels of protective regulation. Recessionary conditions and high unemployment would remain, it argued, if additional costs and regulatory burdens were placed on businesses. What was required were incentives for organisations to employ people and to attract investment into the United Kingdom from foreign firms. Attention was given to reforming the trade unions through the development of a regulatory regime that they had to comply with and by taking steps that reduced their ability to organise lawful industrial action.

The past 15 years have seen a reversal of this position in an era of far lower unemployment. The trade union laws have largely stayed in place, but we have also seen a substantial increase in the extent to which the individual employment relationship is subject to state-imposed regulation. 1995 saw the introduction of disability discrimination law, and 1998 the establishment of a national minimum wage, working time regulations and a comprehensive data protection law. In subsequent years we have seen protection introduced for part-time workers and people employed on fixed-term contracts, and measures outlawing discrimination on grounds of sexual orientation, religion and age. Maternity rights have been vastly extended and rights for fathers, parents of young children and carers of disabled adults introduced for the first time. There are now circumstances set out in law in which an employer must recognise a trade union, and others in which employers are required to consult with workforce representatives about a broad range of management issues. In short, we have moved a very great distance from a voluntarist regime towards one that has a great deal more in common with the 'codified' approaches of our continental neighbours.

There are no straightforward answers to the question of why the United Kingdom has seen such a transformation in the nature and extent of employment regulation in a single generation. The process has not been a planned one and progress continues to be made in a piecemeal, step-by-step fashion. No grand overarching strategy on the part of any government can clearly be identified. However, it is interesting to note how rarely a piece of regulation has been repealed by an incoming government with different priorities from its predecessor. Once in place, employment law appears to be very difficult to displace, suggesting that there is a broad level of agreement among the electorate in favour of the regulatory structure that has been steadily erected. Despite the lack of any single dominant explanation, it is possible to identify a number of factors that have contributed significantly to this transformation:

- UK membership of the European Economic Community (EEC) and now the European Union (EU) has clearly played a major role. A great deal of the employment legislation originates in Europe and would probably not be on our statute books were it not for our membership of the EU. This is particularly true of the many measures that have been introduced in recent years following the decision of the Blair government to sign the Social Chapter of the Maastricht Treaty in 1997. Through this route have come the regulations protecting part-time and fixed-term workers, anti-discrimination measures that extend protection to people who suffer adverse treatment on grounds of their religion, age or sexuality, and the requirement for employers to consult with their workforces about major employment issues.

- The decline in trade union membership and activism the country has witnessed over 25 years has also played an important part. As collective bargaining structures have been dismantled and the numbers joining unions have fallen, new institutional arrangements have had to be put in place to ensure that people are protected against unfair treatment and undue health risks while they are at work. In many important respects employment law now fills this gap. Indeed, one of the major reasons for the introduction of unfair dismissal law was the aim of reducing the number of strikes that were precipitated when employers were perceived to have fired someone unjustly (Davies and Freedland 1993, pp199–200). Whereas 30 years ago employers would be deterred from making unjust decisions by the presence of strong unions, it is anxiety about possible employment tribunal claims that now makes them think twice. Many would argue that the law is less effective at carrying out this job, but at least it covers everyone, including those working in small enterprises where union organisation was never common.

- Government economic policy has also played an important role in helping to shape employment regulation through the decades and continues to do so. In the 1980s the focus was on using legislation to tame trade union power so as to boost UK productivity and the capacity of the economy to change in response to emerging global industrial trends. By contrast, in the past decade a major driving force behind employment regulation has been the government's desire to encourage people to 'come off welfare and into work'. To that end various regulatory changes have been made to remove barriers that act to deter people from entering (or in the case of mothers with small children from returning to) the workforce. Both the national minimum wage and the wide range of recent family-friendly employment rights were justified by the government using these arguments. Other measures are aimed at promoting the growth of a partnership approach to the management of employee relations, as this is believed by the government to promote growth and hence job opportunities.

- The growth of employment regulation can also be viewed in a far wider perspective as just one of the many areas of national life that have become regulated or that have seen an expansion of their regulatory regimes in recent years. It is not only the employment relationship that has seen its traditional 'voluntarist' nature dismantled in recent decades. The same kind of processes have occurred in the professions, in the City of London (see Moran 2003), in the world of pensions, and more generally across most industry sectors. Everywhere informal, locally established ways of running institutions have been replaced since the 1970s with new formalised structures that impose standard rules on everyone, and help ensure that institutions are accountable for their actions and open to far greater public scrutiny.

- Finally, it is very reasonable to assert that plain political expediency has also played a part. Much of the regulation that has been introduced has been politically popular either in a general sense or among particular constituencies that governments have needed to court in order to gain electoral advantage. This was true of the anti-union measures introduced by the Thatcher governments, of the Disability Discrimination Act introduced by the Major government, and of much of the employment protection legislation brought onto the statute books by the Blair government. In the latter case, care was taken to advance the regulatory agenda in a step-by-step fashion so as not to alienate the business community. But from time to time, in an equally carefully paced way, ministers introduce a measure that pleases their trade union constituency and helps to ensure its continued support.

People management

HISTORICAL ROYAL PALACES

EXERCISE 4.1

Read the article by Elizabeth Davidson, A break with tradition (*People Management*, 10 July 2003, pp38–40). This can be downloaded from the *People Management* archive on the CIPD's website (www.cipd.co.uk).

The article begins by describing the action taken by managers of some of London's major historical tourist attractions to ensure that their organisation complied with new and existing employment law. It goes on to report more generally about the rapid growth of consultancies and training arms of law firms whose role is to brief managers about the evolving law.

Questions

1 What combination of circumstances caused Historical Royal Palaces to alter their established approach to ensuring legal compliance?

2 Why do you think that this organisation has a particular incentive to ensure that it does not breach employment legislation?

3 To what extent do you agree with the final comment in the article: 'There is a whole new generation of employees who know their rights. They know what they can do and what they are entitled to. That can only be a good thing'?

DISCRIMINATION LAW

Discrimination law has two basic aims. First, it seeks to ensure that employers treat people equally whatever their gender, race, nationality or other distinction. Second, it seeks to protect groups who are vulnerable to discrimination from less favourable treatment on the part of employers. This is the rationale behind the Disability Discrimination Act and measures designed to protect the rights of trade unionists and ex-offenders. The presence of discrimination law should be taken into account whenever decisions are being taken that may adversely affect a par group more than another (eg women or members of ethnic minorities) and whenever an individual might have a just claim that he or she is being unfairly discriminated against on unlawful grounds. The following are the major examples in resourcing:

- drawing up person specifications

- recruitment advertising

- short-listing

- selecting employees

- promoting employees

- setting performance appraisal criteria

- absence management

- redundancy selection

- dismissing people.

Anti-discrimination laws in the United Kingdom cover detrimental treatment on the following grounds:

- sex

- marital status

- race

- national origin

- ethnicity

- disability

- sexual orientation

- religion or belief

- age

- being an ex-offender whose conviction is spent

- union membership/non-membership/union activities

- working on a part-time contract

- working on a fixed-term contract.

Each of these measures works in rather different ways. In some cases (eg sex, race and disability) all 'workers' are covered, meaning everyone who works under any type of contract. In other cases (eg trade union grounds, fixed-term work) most of the protective measures only effectively apply to 'employees'. Some give a very wide degree of protection, offering employers very little scope to defend themselves (direct sex and race discrimination), while others permit discrimination in certain circumstances provided it can be objectively justified (eg disability, age and part-time workers). Under the Rehabilitation of Offenders Act, there are several occupations that are exempted altogether and in which there is no protection from much discrimination. Importantly, the regulations on fixed-term work go further than offering protection from discrimination. They also mean, that in certain circumstances, fixed-term contracts are to be considered as indefinite contracts once someone has been employed for four years.

EXERCISE 4.2

DISCRIMINATION LAW AND DIVERSITY

Read the article by Rima Evans, Variety performance (*People Management,* 23 November, 2006, pp26–31). This can be downloaded from the *People Management* archive on the CIPD's website (www.cipd.co.uk).

This article looks at past, present and future developments in discrimination law.

Various experts are quoted giving their assessments, many of which are critical about what has been achieved to date.

Questions

1   In what ways have UK workplaces made progress towards greater equality over the past 30 years?

2   In what ways has progress been disappointing?

3   To what extent can the legal framework be seen as having failed to meet its objectives?

4   What reforms of discrimination law would you like to see and why?

DISMISSAL LAW

This is described in some detail in Chapters 18 and 19, so it only needs to be flagged up at this stage. Most cases are brought under the law of unfair dismissal, but there are two other types of claim that can be made:

• **Unfair dismissal** is defined as a dismissal in breach of statute. It means that the reason for the dismissal and/or the manner in which it was carried out falls short of the expectations of legislation.

• **Wrongful dismissal** is a dismissal in breach of contract. This means that the way the dismissal was carried out breached the employee's own contract of employment. Wrongful dismissal cases are quite rare these days, but were more common prior to the introduction of unfair dismissal law in 1971.

• **Constructive dismissals** occur when an employee resigns as a direct result of unreasonable conduct on the part of the employer. Cases hinge on whether or not the employer can be said to have repudiated the contract of employment through its actions. Most cases result from unilaterally imposed pay cuts or other contractual changes, but some relate to breaches of implied terms such as 'the duty of care' or 'the duty to maintain a relationship of mutual trust and confidence'. It is through this latter route that the law has evolved to provide some legal redress for employees who suffer from sustained campaigns of bullying at the hands of their managers.

Around 40,000 claims of unfair dismissal are made each year to employment tribunals, making it a very common occurrence. It is highly unlikely that any P&D professional will proceed through their career these days without having to defend such a case at some stage.

Measures introduced in 2004 (under the Statutory Dispute Resolution Regulations) aimed to reduce the number of cases coming to tribunal. These provided strong incentives for dismissed employees to make use of appeal mechanisms that all employers must provide as part of their disciplinary procedures. A failure to appeal a decision to dismiss led to reduced compensation should the claimant subsequently show themselves to have been unfairly dismissed at the employment tribunal. Importantly, from the employer's perspective, failure to provide a basic procedure or to follow one led to additional compensation having to be paid if the ex-employee wins the case. However, in March 2006 the Gibbons Report reached the conclusion that these procedures had not met their objectives. In response the government announced that they would be repealed. At the time of writing (late 2007) it is unclear exactly from when this will happen, but April 2009 is the most likely date.

THE LAW OF CONTRACT

The law of contract forms part of the common law. It is thus largely judge-made and has not been created through Acts of Parliament. It is, however, no less important for that and must be taken account of in decision-making on resourcing matters. The key points are as follows:

- Employers need to be aware that a contract of employment is only established when a clear, unambiguous and unconditional offer has been made and a clear, unambiguous and unconditional acceptance has been received. In addition there must be an intention to create legal relations and some form of consideration (eg wages) made to bring it into existence.

- In principle contracts cannot be changed unilaterally by one party. An employer wishing to make significant changes must first secure the agreement of the employees concerned. Where this is not forthcoming the employer needs to consider making the change financially attractive or, where there is no alternative, dismissing and re-hiring on new terms. The latter course leaves open the possibility of an unfair dismissal claim. It is thus best to include in all contracts of employment one or more flexibility clauses that give the employer the right to make reasonable changes from time to time.

- Once a contract of employment is established it confers duties on both parties. Both henceforward owe a duty of mutual trust and confidence to one another. In addition the employer owes a duty of care along with several other duties, while the employee owes a duty of fidelity and the duty to exercise reasonable skill and care. If either side breaches one of these implied terms of contract, it can lead to breach of contract proceedings or can form the basis of a constructive dismissal claim.

There are a number of practical consequences for employers. First, care must be taken to ensure that the employees' understanding of what constitutes the key terms of their contracts matches what the employer believes the contracts to contain. This is best achieved through the existence of written statements of terms and conditions that are given to new employees before they commence their jobs. It is not necessary to issue everyone with a formal, written contract of employment extending to many pages. A simple offer letter accompanied by a basic summary of the key terms is all that is required. This helps to create certainty and should ensure that accusations of breaches of contract do not occur.

Second, it is essential that employers explicitly build a degree of flexibility into the contracts they offer employees. In other words, one of the terms of the contract needs to give the employer the right to make reasonable changes to terms and conditions from time to time in order to meet business requirements.

Third, it is important that everyone who undertakes a supervisory role is provided with basic training on the law of contract, and in particular on the issue of implied terms. The majority of managers in the United Kingdom remain blissfully unaware of the existence of such law and its potential significance, and it is this ignorance that leads to situations in which employees (and more commonly ex-employees) find themselves with a strong legal claim to pursue.

FAMILY-FRIENDLY STATUTES

Recent years have seen the introduction of a range of new rights designed to make it easier for people with family responsibilities to combine these with a career. In addition, we have seen the extension of existing rights, notably the provisions for statutory maternity leave and pay. It is beyond the scope of this book to describe or evaluate these in any detail, but it is important that readers appreciate the extent of the rights that now exist and will be granted in the near future. They are significant from a resourcing point of view because they provide rights for employees to be away from the workplace for much longer than has been the case historically. Aside from the need to administer such matters professionally, resourcing specialists also need to build assumptions about the take-up of these rights into their human resource planning activities. The upshot is a need to hire more people to work on a temporary or casual basis (to cover absences), to increase staffing generally and to think more openly than has been the tendency to date about job-sharing arrangements and the possibility of allowing much more flexible working. The key areas of law that fall into this category are the following:

- the right to maternity leave/right to return

- the right to maternity pay

- the right to unpaid parental leave

- the right to time off to care for dependents

- the right to paid paternity leave

- the right to request flexible working.

This is an area of law in which employees' rights have improved very considerably over time in incremental steps. New rights and extensions of existing rights are introduced every two or three years. At the time of writing (late 2007) the government is proposing to extend the period of paid maternity leave to which all employed mothers are entitled from nine to 12 months, and to permit part of this to be taken by fathers instead should that be the preference of the couple concerned.

REFLECTIVE QUESTION
How far do you agree with these proposals for the extension of family-friendly law? From an employer's perspective what would be the major advantages and disadvantages?

WORKING TIME

The Working Time Regulations were introduced in 1998 and have been amended twice since then. The regulations are complex and have been heavily criticised for lacking clarity. The major rights they include are as follows:

- a working week limited to a maximum of 48 hours (averaged over 17 weeks)

- four weeks paid annual leave per year (in addition to bank holidays)

- a limitation on night working to eight hours in any one 24-hour period

- 11 hours rest in any one 24-hour period

- an uninterrupted break of 24 hours in any one seven-day period

- a 20-minute rest break in any shift of six hours or more

- regular free health assessments to establish fitness for night working.

When first introduced the regulations contained more stringent requirements in the case of young workers as well as exceptions for certain industries and professions (eg junior doctors). Many of these either have been or soon will be phased out. There is currently a right for employees to opt out of the 48-hour week, and it remains lawful for employers to require that such a step is taken as a condition of a job offer. However, less known is the existence of a right to opt back in again without suffering any kind of detriment. There is a considerable question mark over whether the right of employees to 'opt out' of their rights under these regulations will survive into the long- term future.

Working time is clearly central to human resource planning and to the organisation of work generally. Hitherto, because of the opt-outs, the lack of clarity about some terminology and the lack of an effective policing regime, many employers have found themselves to be affected by these regulations only to a limited degree. This could well change in the future if the United Kingdom is required by the European Union to accept forms of regulation that have long been standard in many other European countries.

CONFIDENTIALITY ISSUES

A range of new regulations have been introduced in recent years that affect the use of information in the workplace. The Public Interest Disclosure Act 1998 and The Telecommunications (Lawful Business Practice) (Interception of Communications) Regulations 2000 deal respectively with the rights of 'whistle-blowers' and of employers to snoop on their employees' phone calls and e-mails. A third piece of legislation, The Data Protection Act 1998, is of greater direct relevance to resourcing activities. This is because it sets out to prescribe what kinds of information can be held on employee files and for how long. It also gives employees rights of access to information held on them. The Act covers paper records and information that is held electronically, so it should determine how an organisation uses data held in a computerised personnel information system. It requires organisations to appoint a 'data controller' to take responsibility for this area of activity. Typically this person will be a P&D specialist. It is best understood in terms of eight 'data protection principles' that data controllers are obliged to observe:

- Personal data should be processed fairly and lawfully.

- It should be collected for specified purposes and used accordingly.

- It should be adequate, relevant and not excessive for the purpose proposed.

- It should be accurate and up to date.

- It should not be kept longer than is necessary.

- It must be processed in accordance with the rights of employees.

- It must be safeguarded against unlawful processing, accidental loss, damage or destruction.

- It must not be transferred to a country outside the European Economic area unless that country recognises equivalent rights.

The Act gives workers the right to see any files kept on them, to receive copies of the data held and to correct inaccurate information. Employers are required only to process personal data that is 'necessary' and 'justifiable' and must only keep it for as long as is strictly necessary. Adequate security measures must also be taken. Stricter rules apply to 'sensitive data', such as information that relates to people's ethnic origins, religious beliefs, health records or past criminal convictions. This cannot be kept or processed without the employees' express consent. Fines of up to £5,000 can be levied for breaches of the Act.

In 2003 in the case of Durrant *v* Financial Services Authority the Court of Appeal appeared to cut down the scope of the data protection legislation by a large measure. In considering what classes of information could be described as being 'personal data' and thus disclosable under the Act the Lords of Appeal concluded that data is not 'personal' unless it focuses on the person concerned. Data that merely mentions the individual's name or concerns him/her in some way and that does 'not affect his privacy' should not to be considered as 'personal data'. They ruled that 'the mere fact that a document is retrievable by reference to a name does not entitle someone to a copy of it under the Act. This clearly narrows the number of documents that can be defined as comprising 'personal data' very considerably. Time will tell exactly what types of personnel data are and are not covered by this ruling, but it would appear to restrict it to documents or records that have an individual as their focus.

DEBATES ABOUT EMPLOYMENT REGULATION

As the regulatory revolution in employment matters continues to run its course it is not surprising that it has generated much debate among managers, employers associations, commentators, trade unions, political bodies, think-tanks and academic researchers. There are basically two types of debate that can be identified. First there is much discussion and disagreement about the effectiveness of particular pieces of legislation. Second, there is a more general debate concerning the rights and wrongs of regulating the labour market through employment protection legislation. We shall now briefly look at each of these in turn.

MICRO-DEBATES

It is not at all difficult to find fault with many individual pieces of employment legislation. Those representing employee interests or those who come to the debate from a social democratic or Marxist perspective tend to argue that measures 'do not go far enough', while employer associations and those who take a liberal or conservative perspective are typically to be found arguing that business is now over-regulated and that individual statutes 'go too far'. Hence, for example, unfair dismissal law is criticised both for favouring employers and for making it too difficult to dismiss under-performing employees. Data-protection legislation can be criticised for being backed by inadequate sanction and thus being too easy for employers to ignore, but also for being a wholly unnecessary set of regulations that create red tape and give employees rights they have no real interest in having. The law of indirect discrimination can penalise employers who have absolutely no intention whatever of discriminating unfairly against an individual, but can also be criticised for providing a defence that allows employers to justify practices that have the effect of perpetuating sexual and racial inequality. However, there are some areas of employment regulation that are generally agreed to function badly and several types of criticisms that are made by protagonists from all sides of the debate:

- It is argued that some employment law fails to meet its own objectives in practice. It is thus both burdensome from an employer point of view and ineffective when seen from the perspective of the employee. Equal pay law is a good example. Although this has been on the statute books for over 30 years now, women's hourly rates of pay remain only 82 per cent of those enjoyed by men. Female part-time workers earn only 63 per cent of the male full-time rate – a figure that has hardly narrowed at all since 1970 and is also widening.

- Some employment law is very badly drafted leaving much uncertainty about whether or to what extent it applies in particular situations. Too often, it is argued, governments have passed legislation or issued statutory regulations that lack clarity. It then takes several years for the courts to establish what employers actually have to do in practice through the establishment of precedents in individual cases. The best examples are the Working Time Regulations and the Transfer of Undertakings Regulations. The latter apply in some (but not all) cases in which a business or part of an organisation is taken over or merged with another. The volume of case law in this field is immense, yet after 25 years and major reform in 2006, there are still many grey areas.

- Unnecessary complexity is another general criticism of much UK employment law. Again, this creates uncertainty and makes it hard for employers to act within the law when carrying out their activities, even when they wish to. The best example is the law on employment status. Many statutes give rights only to 'employees' (eg unfair dismissal and parental leave) whereas others apply to all 'workers' (eg discrimination law and the national minimum wage). Yet these terms are not fully defined. So over the years the courts have had to devise tests to establish who is an 'employee', who is a 'worker' and who is neither. The law in this area has become far too complex and subject to change, leaving major groups such as agency workers unclear about what rights they have, if any.

EXERCISE 4.3

EUROPEAN LABOUR LAW

Read the following two articles featured in *People Management*. They can be downloaded from the *People Management* archive on the CIPD's website (www.cipd.co.uk):

• Anna Czerny, Double trouble (24 February 2005)

• James Brockett, Flexicurity knocks (19 April 2007).

Both articles concern proposals put forward by the European Union to form part of a possible new regulatory agenda for the coming 10 years.

Questions

1   To what extent is it possible to articulate a clear sense of direction for the future of EU employment regulation from these proposals?

2   Why do you think proposals from the EU appear to point in different directions at the same time?

3   How would you like to see the EU's agenda develop in this field and why?

MACRO-DEBATES

At a broader level, a further set of debates focuses on the full range of employment regulation. The question about which the protagonists disagree can basically be summed up as follows: 'Is increased employment regulation beneficial or harmful to the United Kingdom's economy and people?'

Those who tend as a rule to argue that it has harmful effects include the Confederation of British Industry (2000), the Institute of Directors (see Lea 2001) and pro-business research organisations such as the Institute of Economic Affairs (2001). At the heart of their argument is the claim that much employment regulation serves to place substantial additional costs on employers and that this has the effect of making UK businesses less competitive in international markets than they would otherwise be. While it is accepted that most Western European countries impose even greater costs on their employers, this is not true of the rest of the world. Hence, in an increasingly global economy, regulation reduces the capacity of organisations to match the prices of goods and services originating in other countries. Small firms in particular are hit hard because they do not have the flexibility, profit margins or expertise to work within the requirements of the ever-growing volume of employment regulation. According to the CBI the cost to businesses of implementing just the National Minimum Wage and the Working Time Regulations amounted to over £10 billion (CBI 2000, p9). The costs can be categorised under several headings.

- First, there are the direct costs that employers assume as a result of employment regulation. Examples are the costs associated with the payment of statutory sick pay, maternity pay, increased numbers of paid holidays and complying with the expectations of disability discrimination law.

- Second, there are knock-on costs that arise as a result of employees exercising their rights. A good example is the recruitment of temporary workers to cover when someone exercises the right to time off to care for a dependent relative or takes a period of paternity leave.

- Third, there are costs that derive from lost opportunities. Instead of spending their time running competitive businesses or providing efficient public services, managers are occupied in finding out how to comply with regulations, making changes to ensure that they act within the expectations of the law and showing regulatory bodies that they are complying in practice.

- Finally there are the costs associated with litigation itself. Employers and their representatives often complain that even those who act entirely lawfully are often called upon to defend their actions in employment tribunals. Ex-employees can bring cases at no risk to themselves and, even if they lose, cause considerable expense to the responding employer in legal fees and management time.

The total impact of these costs is to reduce competitiveness and hence slow down the growth of jobs. Moreover, where budgets and profit margins are tight, the net effect is to cause employers to shed labour and thus create unemployment. Over the longer term, employment regulation serves to give organisations a preference for expansion based on capital expenditure (buildings, machinery etc) rather than expanding the number of employees. It also tends to encourage investment overseas in Eastern European and developing countries where employing people is a great deal less restrictive and costly. The net impact is fewer job opportunities for the UK workers whose interests the law is intended to serve.

This argument about employment law being counterproductive is often extended to focus on particular groups of workers. The most significant example is the position of women with young children or those whom an employer suspects are likely to start a family in the near future:

> *It is clear that many business people are very supportive of maternity benefits and rights (nearly a fifth of members provided more than the statutory maternity benefits in terms of leave or pay). But there is a clear warning from our survey. Already 45% of our members feel that such rights are a disincentive to hiring women of prime child-rearing age. If the regulations are made even more burdensome then employers will be even more reluctant to employ these women.*
> (Lea 2001, p57)

According to critics, another way that employees suffer as result of increased regulation arises from its tendency to impose on organisations single, standard ways of doing things. As a result local flexibility is reduced. Whereas once individual workplaces or even departments within larger organisations could devise their own informal workplace rules that met the needs of employer and employee alike, everyone now has to comply with a single, centralised and often bureaucratic approach, often imposed by a strengthened corporate HR function. Local management discretion over pay, benefits, and terms and conditions, for example, has had to be curtailed in order to ensure that equal pay claims can be defended. All manner of informal practices have had to be ditched thanks to data protection law. Not because any employee complained or ever would complain in practice, but because the law expects all organisations to standardise arrangements in ways approved of by the Information Commissioner. Too often, the changes introduced in response to such regulations serve to reduce the quality of working life enjoyed by employees rather than raise it. In particular it militates against local, team-based decision-making and enhances the power and reach of administrators (often of the P&D variety).

REFLECTIVE QUESTION

It is sometimes argued that smaller firms should be exempted from much employment law. What are the arguments for and against this proposition? To what extent do you agree with the idea that employment law should only fully apply to larger organisations?

According to Davies (2004) there are two types of argument that are commonly deployed against the critics of increased employment regulation. The first type revolves around notions of human rights and social justice, the second around its economic impact. The social justice arguments are the most straightforward to grasp. There may well be costs that have to be borne by employing organisations as a result of greater regulation, it is claimed, but these are justified because without it employees would suffer unreasonably as a result of the actions of employers. Employment law is necessary to protect vulnerable people who might otherwise be unjustly exploited by far more powerful employers. In the absence of effective trade unions, the state must step in to provide such protection. Much employment law is intended to give employees a degree of power to resist unjust treatment and hence to help reduce social injustice generally. There are several obvious examples:

- Discrimination law is necessary because without it the position at work and in the labour market of women and certain minority groups would be a great deal worse. This is true of ethnic minorities who suffer from racial and religious discrimination, of gay and lesbian people, of trade union activists, older workers and ex-offenders, all of whom had fewer opportunities and suffered greater prejudice at work in the days before they were protected by law.

- Health and safety law is necessary to help prevent accidents and psychological injury occurring in the workplace. Without it, managers looking for opportunities to cut costs and increase margins would cut corners and take undue risks with their workers' health. This occurs in many developing countries and certainly occurred in the United Kingdom before the modern regulatory regime was established along with its inspectorates.

- Dismissal law serves to protect employees from being fired by their employers for no good reason or without first being given a reasonable opportunity to put right whatever fault the employer finds with their work. The alternative is a world of insecure employment where no employee, however effective and long-serving, can be sure that his or her job is safe from the whims or prejudices of maverick managers.

REFLECTIVE QUESTION

Which of these areas of law do you consider to be the most effective at achieving its aims in practice? Which is the least effective? Why do you think this is?

The economic arguments in favour of employment regulation are harder to summarise briefly and include several distinct strands. Further information is provided by Davies (2004) and in many publications of the Institute of Employment Rights (eg Deakin and Wilkinson 1996, IER 2000). However, the broad conclusion reached by their proponents is that over the long term the UK economy, as well as employing organisations, stands to benefit rather than to suffer from the regulation of labour markets. There are costs to be borne over the short term, but the overall effect is positive.

An important part of this case concerns one of the topics we discussed in Chapter 3: tight labour markets. According to many influential economists, the major threat to the future growth of the UK economy is a lack of qualified people to carry out jobs, coupled with chronic skills shortages in particular industries. A recession may be precipitated simply because the United Kingdom finds itself without the human resources needed to keep its economic engine running at full speed. This is a far greater threat to our international competitiveness than the costs associated with employment regulation. It is therefore in our economic interests for our government to force employers provide workplaces in which people want to work and terms and conditions that attract them into employment.

Too many people do not work for one reason or another. Some take early retirement, others take time out to care for young children or elderly relatives, some are constantly leaving one job and taking time out while they search for something more satisfactory, while a third group find that they are better off overall by claiming state benefits of one kind or another. Some of these people have skills that are not currently being placed at the disposal of the economy, while others have the potential to gain these skills. Without employment regulation, it is argued, the numbers of such people would be higher because working in UK organisations would often be less attractive than it is now.

Moreover, further regulation that serves to improve the experience of work, by making workplaces equitable and forcing organisations to employ people on decent terms and conditions, will encourage more people back into work and discourage others from leaving. Importantly, by the same token, employment protection legislation can help the United Kingdom to attract skilled workers from overseas to fill vacancies. The better the deal offered by UK employers, the more likely it is that talented people will want to come to live and work here.

A rather different economic argument is also commonly deployed by advocates of employment regulation. Here the focus is on the appropriate long-term strategy for the UK economy as a whole. It starts with an acceptance of the proposition that the United Kingdom is not, and will not be for the foreseeable future, able to compete internationally on the basis of low labour costs. However little employment regulation we have, developing countries will always be able to undercut us when it comes to the costs associated with employing people. It follows that some other basis has to be found on which to base our competitive future in a global economy. The only realistic choice is to focus on the development of high-tech and knowledge-intensive industries that compete through their capacity to innovate and to produce high quality products and services.

Where we can compete on a cost-reduction basis, it will only be through the development of machinery that reduces the need to employ people. It follows that employment law must play its part in pushing sometimes reluctant employers in this direction. If low-quality jobs, low pay and sweatshop-type conditions are effectively outlawed, the only alternative is for employers to pay well and to create higher-skilled jobs that enable them to compete on grounds other than price. In turn this requires them to invest in training and hence gives them a strong incentive to retain people they have trained. Hence, employment regulation along with complementary measures taken in fields such as education and research funding is helping UK industry over time to transform itself so as to enable it to compete effectively in the modern global economy.

The third principal economic argument concerns productivity. To a great extent the government accepts the arguments long advanced by researchers in the employment field that good P&D practice is linked to improved business performance. If you treat people well in the workplace they will respond with greater loyalty and with a willingness to work with greater effort. Moreover, they will choose to remain employed and will not continually be looking out for a job move. Beyond this general point is a strong belief on the part of ministers that partnership approaches to the relationship between management and staff are far more likely to bring about business success than autocratic styles or adversarial relationships.

Employment regulation can promote the establishment and maintenance of fruitful partnerships between staff (and their representatives) and management. This is partly achieved through requirements to recognise trade unions where that is the will of most staff, and partly through various requirements in the legislation to inform and consult with the workforce. More generally employment legislation serves to make it harder for employers to treat their staff in an inequitable or repressive manner. In so doing it plays a role in helping to create workplaces that are well managed and hence stand the best chance of achieving competitive advantage.

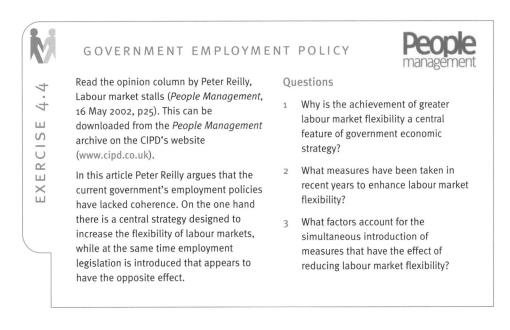

EXERCISE 4.4

GOVERNMENT EMPLOYMENT POLICY

People management

Read the opinion column by Peter Reilly, Labour market stalls (*People Management*, 16 May 2002, p25). This can be downloaded from the *People Management* archive on the CIPD's website (www.cipd.co.uk).

In this article Peter Reilly argues that the current government's employment policies have lacked coherence. On the one hand there is a central strategy designed to increase the flexibility of labour markets, while at the same time employment legislation is introduced that appears to have the opposite effect.

Questions

1   Why is the achievement of greater labour market flexibility a central feature of government economic strategy?

2   What measures have been taken in recent years to enhance labour market flexibility?

3   What factors account for the simultaneous introduction of measures that have the effect of reducing labour market flexibility?

KEY ARTICLE 10

Susan Marlow, Regulating labour management in small firms. *Human Resource Management Journal*, Vol. 12, No. 3, pp25–44 (2002)

This article reports the results of a qualitative survey involving interviews with the owners and employees of small businesses. They were asked about the likely future impact of what was at that time a good deal of new legislation. The findings are interesting because of what they have to say about the attitudes of small business owners to labour market regulation. The views of the employees are also interesting and somewhat surprising in some respects.

Questions

1   Why were the managers interviewed as part of this research unconcerned about new employment regulation?

2   In what ways did the managers say that the new regulation might have the effect of working against the interests of employees?

3   Why did the employees who were interviewed say that the new regulation would have little impact on them?

CHAPTER SUMMARY

- One of the most important trends in the context of people resourcing activities is the ever-growing volume of employment regulation that employing organisations are required to take account of and act upon. Employment law in the United Kingdom has developed over a 40-year period, its complexity and importance growing significantly over the past decade.

- This regulatory revolution has occurred as a result of EU membership and the decline in the influence of trade unions in the workplace, and in order to meet governments' economic and political objectives. It can also be seen as part of a wider trend in recent years to bring all institutions with a public function under a regulatory umbrella.

- The major areas of law that play a role in the management of resourcing activities are discrimination law, dismissal law, the law of contract, family-friendly statutes, the working time regulations and the law covering confidentiality issues.

- Critics of employment regulation believe that the costs associated with compliance are substantial and that this adversely affects the capacity of organisations to compete internationally. Moreover, regulation makes organisations (particularly small businesses) less inclined to create jobs.

- Supporters of employment legislation point to its role in promoting social justice, attracting people into work, creating a high-skill/knowledge-based economy and improving productivity.

EXPLORE FURTHER

- Keeping up with major legal developments is quite a task these days as the volume of new law, and particularly case law, is continually growing. *People Management* contains legal briefings in every issue and regular features about coming legislation. *IRS Employment Review* also contains a fortnightly summary that covers current developments in greater depth. A similar function is provided by the excellent *IDS Brief*. There are also numerous websites of variable quality that keep subscribers informed of unfolding developments.

- There are several good introductions to employment law available. But because they tend to become out of date quickly, it is important to ensure that you read the latest edition. Lewis and Sargeant (2007) and Daniels (2004) are published by CIPD. Pitt (2007), Lockton (2006), Willey (2003) and Taylor and Emir (2006) have also written good student-friendly introductions.

- Debates about employment law are rarely summarised succinctly in one place. *Perspectives on labour law* by Anne Davies (2004) provides the best general summary available. The major arguments against employment regulation are effectively advocated by the CBI (2000) and those in favour by the Institute of Employment Rights (2000).

CHAPTER 5

Human resource planning: methods and applications

The techniques of human resource (HR) planning are some of the most involved and complex activities carried out by employee resourcing professionals. By contrast, the basic principles on which they are founded are straightforward, with a potential significance that is readily understood. HR planning is also an area of P&D work that has often been denigrated in recent years, with the result that it has received relatively little attention in the literature and has become less widely used in organisations. Criticism of the HR planning function has tended to come from two directions. On the one hand, it has been seen as overly mathematical and so scientifically sophisticated as to render it remote and irrelevant from day-to-day management concerns; on the other, it has been branded oversimplistic, with critics challenging the very notion that it is possible to plan the staffing of an organisation with such confidence in a fundamentally unpredictable business environment.

In this and the following chapter the practice of HR planning is examined and its relevance to organisations today discussed. Here, our focus is on the practicalities. The term 'human resource planning' is defined, followed by a description of the various activities that have traditionally been undertaken by HR planners. In the next chapter, the wider debate about the usefulness of HR planning in the current environment is examined, and the purposes to which HR plans can be put are discussed.

LEARNING OUTCOMES

By the end of this chapter readers should be able to:

- design and implement a system for human resource planning

- estimate the future demand for labour

- measure current levels of employee utilisation, productivity and performance

- forecast the extent to which human resource needs can be met internally

- assess how far and by what means the demand for human resources can be met by external labour markets

- provide advice concerning the use of information technology in undertaking the above activities

- give advice on strategies to reconcile labour supply and demand.

In addition, readers should be able to understand and explain:

- the terminology used in the practice of human resource planning

- the principles underlying effective human resource planning.

A NOTE ON TERMINOLOGY

As in so many areas of P&D, there is some confusion about the precise meanings of the terms used to describe the human resource planning function. Here, as elsewhere, developments in terminology have moved on at different speeds and in different directions from developments in the activities themselves, leading to something of a mismatch between the concepts and the labels used to describe them. As with the term 'human resource management', there are in the field of human resource planning different uses of key terms by different authors. The main distinction is between those who see the term 'human resource planning' as having broadly the same meaning as the longer-established terms 'workforce planning' and 'manpower planning', and those who believe 'human resource planning' to represent something rather different.

Notable among the second group are John Bramham (1987, 1988, 1994), Sonia Liff (2000), Hazel Williams (2002) and Dipak Bhattacharyya (2002), who make a significant distinction between 'manpower planning', which they see as being primarily quantitative in nature and concerned with forecasting the demand and supply of labour, and 'human resource planning'. They give the latter a wider meaning, encompassing plans made across the whole range of P&D activity (including soft issues such as motivation, employee attitudes and organisational culture). Bramham's book *Human resource planning*, published in 1994, is thus very different in terms of its content from his earlier *Practical manpower planning* (1988). According to this definition 'human resource planning' is essentially a planned approach to the management of human resources, linking practice to an organisation's strategic objectives and planning responses to prevailing labour market conditions.

For others (eg Reilly 1996, McBeath 1992, Burack and Mathys 1996, Heneman *et al* 2000), the term 'human resource planning' is simply a more modern and gender-neutral term with essentially the same meaning as 'manpower planning'. Both are concerned with looking ahead and using systematic techniques to assess the extent to which an organisation will be able to meet its requirements for labour in the future. They are thus undertaken in order to assess whether an organisation is likely to have 'the right people, with the right skills, in the right places at the right time'. According to this definition, human resource planning is a relatively specialised sub-discipline within the general activity undertaken by human resource managers. More recently the term 'workforce planning' appears to be being used more frequently again, while other terms which have essentially the same meaning, such as 'workforce analytics' (Schuyler 2006) and 'workforce alignment' (Dyer and Ericksen 2007), are finding their way in to the American P&D literature.

For the purposes of this chapter we shall accept this latter definition. While the term 'human resource planning' will be used throughout, it can thus be taken by readers to refer to the same disciplines and activities traditionally encompassed by the terms 'manpower' and 'workforce' planning. The focus is on forecasting the supply and demand of labour and developing plans to reconcile any future gap that is identified between the human resources an organisation needs and those to which it is likely to have access.

This approach should not be taken to mean that the broader definition of 'human resource planning' is mistaken in any way. Indeed, its concerns, aims and objectives are reflected throughout the rest of the book. It does, however, recognise that longer-established 'manpower planning' approaches continue to be useful in many situations, that they merit specific attention and are competencies that resourcing specialists can benefit from developing.

EXERCISE 5.1

THE LONDON OLYMPICS

Read the article by Lucy Phillips, Games of skill (*People Management*, 31 May 2007, pp24–29). This can be downloaded from the *People Management* archive on the CIPD's website (www.cipd.co.uk).

This article discusses the major HR challenges associated with mounting a successful Olympic Games in London in

2012. The sheer size of the need for people is set out along with an explanation of where they will be found and why.

Questions

1   What factors make the workforce planning activities associated with the

Olympic Games more complex than would be the case with a more typical commercial project involving the recruitment of thousands of people?

2   In what ways are workforce planning activities focused on a wider agenda than the Olympic Games themselves, and why?

3   What skills required for the running of the Games do managers believe are in short supply? What steps are being taken ahead of time to ameliorate this situation?

STAGES IN HUMAN RESOURCE PLANNING

Human resource planning is principally concerned with assessing an organisation's position in relation to its labour markets and forecasting its likely situation in years to come. It is thus mostly used to formulate the data on which plans of action can be based, rather than in the actual drawing up those plans. If, for example, a supermarket chain is planning to open a large new store for which it believes there is a demand, the human resource planning function would be responsible for identifying how easily – given previous experience of opening superstores of a similar size – the organisation will be able to recruit the staff it needs from internal and external sources to launch its new venture. It is thus concerned with identifying potential or likely problems with staffing the store and not with the development of specific plans to recruit and develop the employees needed. John Bramham, in defining manpower planning, used the metaphor of a ship at sea to illustrate the distinction between planning in general terms and the devising of specific plans of action (Bramham 1988, pp5–6). Seen in this way, human resource planning has more in common with navigation than piloting. It is about assessing the environment and bringing together the data required to plan the direction the organisation needs to take if it is to achieve its goals.

STAGES IN AN HR PLANNING CYCLE

1   Forecasting future demand for human resources.

2   Forecasting future internal supply of human resources.

3   Forecasting future external supply of human resources.

4   Formulating responses to the forecasts.

The forecasting function has three general stages, which will be dealt with one by one in this chapter. The fourth stage involves the formulation of a response to the forecasts. This will involve activities covered elsewhere in the book. First, there is the need to assess what demand the organisation will have for people and for what skills as its business plans unfold. This stage is therefore about distilling the human resource implications from overall organisational strategies. If the business aim is expansion to new product markets or regions, then calculations need to be made about how many people, with what training, will be required at different stages. If the business strategy emphasises consolidation and innovation rather than growth, there is still a need to assess what new skills or competencies will be required if the plan is to be met. Once the likely demand for labour is determined, the next two stages involve assessing the potential supply of human resources. First, there is a need to look at internal supply: at the likelihood that those already employed by the organisation will be able, or indeed willing, to remain in it and develop sufficient skills and gain enough experience to be capable of meeting the demand identified in the first stage. The final stage considers any gap between likely demand and likely supply identified in stages one and two. Here the planner is concerned with forecasting how far skills and experience not available internally will be obtainable externally through the recruitment of new employees.

HRP AT A HIGH-STREET CHEMIST

A good illustration of the application of human resource planning principles and techniques described in this chapter was the plan drawn up by a chain of high-street chemists to cope with an expected recent shortfall in the number of pharmacists.

Here, the starting point was a change in the external environment: the expansion of the UK pharmacy degree course from three to four years after 1997. The company has always hired substantial numbers of qualified pharmacists to work in their stores straight from university, so they were faced with a significant problem in 2001, when no new pharmacists graduated.

In order to address the problem, in 1997 the company undertook a human resource planning exercise to forecast the likely demand for and internal supply of staff in the years following 2001. The demand analysis included consideration of the following factors:

- the number of new stores that the chain planned to open

- the staffing implications of Sunday trading and extended weekday opening hours

- the changing roles undertaken by pharmacists.

Having worked out how many pharmacists would be required, the planners then undertook an analysis of how many they would be likely to have in post, were they to continue operating established recruitment practices. This exercise involved consideration of likely staff turnover figures for pharmacists between 1997 and 2001, but also took account of expected maternity leave and secondments out of high-street stores.

The final stage involved determining how great the shortfall was likely to be and formulating plans to fill the gap with additional recruitment in the years prior to 2001. In addition, P&D policies were developed to reduce turnover among pharmacists so as to keep to a minimum the magnitude of the skill shortage.

A similar exercise has had to be carried out in the social services departments of local authorities in more recent years. Here too the main degree programme that graduate recruits complete has moved from being of three to four years duration, creating a fallow year.

FORECASTING FUTURE DEMAND FOR HUMAN RESOURCES

The process of assessing demand is defined by Smith (1976, p20) as 'Analysing, reviewing and attempting to predict the numbers, by kind, of the manpower needed by the organisation to achieve its objectives'.

The ability of human resource managers to predict accurately how many people will be required and with what skills depends on a number of factors. First, there is the timescale that the forecast is intended to cover. Except in the most turbulent of environments, it is possible to look forward one or two years and make reasonable assumptions about what staffing requirements will be. It gets far harder when timescales of three, five or ten years are contemplated. This is because relevant technological or economic developments that will have a profound effect on the level and kind of activity carried out by the organisation may not yet even have been contemplated.

The other major variable is the nature of the activities carried out by the organisation. Those in relatively stable environments are able to forecast their needs with far greater confidence than those operating in inherently unstable conditions. An example of the former might be a government department such as the Foreign Office or a local authority social services department. Here, relatively little is likely to change, except at the margins, over the foreseeable future. Such change as there is will probably be gradual and brought in steadily over a manageable period. It is therefore quite possible to make reasonable estimates of how many diplomats, administrators or social workers will be needed in five or ten years' time. While there may be increases in productivity brought about through re-organisation and new working methods, such matters are predictable to a considerable degree. By contrast, a company with a relatively small market share of an international market can make such forecasts with far less confidence. Even looking forward one year, it is difficult to say for certain how many will be employed, or what roles they will be undertaking.

The timescale and the nature of the business will influence which of the various available techniques are used to forecast the demand for human resources. We divide these into four basic categories: systematic techniques, managerial judgement, combining systematic and subjective approaches, and working back from costs.

SYSTEMATIC TECHNIQUES

At root, most mathematical and statistical techniques used in demand forecasting are concerned with estimating future requirements from an analysis of past and current experience. A number of distinct approaches are identified in the literature, including time series analysis, work study and productivity trend analysis. Time series or ratio–trend analyses look at past business patterns and the numbers of people employed in different roles to make judgements about how many will be required to meet business targets in the future. Such an approach is straightforward, but appropriate only in relatively stable business environments. Common examples are found in the public services, where the number of school children or elderly patients that require education or treatment is predicted some years in advance on the basis of population trends. In such circumstances it is possible to project how many teachers, nurses, doctors and support staff will be needed, given the staff–student or staff–patient ratios of the past.

The method is also helpful in businesses subject to cyclical fluctuations over time. Where it is known, on the basis of past experience, that the number of customers is likely to increase and decrease seasonally or in tandem with economic cycles, it is possible to plan future staffing requirements accordingly. The principle is best illustrated graphically. Figure 5.1 (overleaf) shows past occupancy and staffing rates in a large seaside hotel employing 250 full-time staff. The thin line represents occupancy rates and the thick line the number of whole-time equivalent staff employed. Future projections are shown as broken lines. Here there is a clear pattern of full or near-full occupancy in the summer and very low occupancy in the spring, with an intermediate position at Christmas. The projections of future occupancy are based on the average figures for past years. The number of seasonal, temporary staff needed in the future at particular times of the year can be estimated using the scale marked on the y-axis. Thus, for December 2009 the hotel will need to hire and train around 40 temporary staff to assist its 250 full-timers.

This is, of course, a very simple example used to illustrate a planning technique that is potentially far more complex. In practice, most organisations would have to analyse separate time series for different departments or grades of staff to obtain useful information. It is also likely that, for many, the fluctuations will be less predictable, requiring predicted levels of business to be adjusted as the date in question approaches. The more complex the organisation and the variations in staffing levels, the more useful are computer programs designed to assist in this kind of analysis.

The work study approach has a different basis. Here, instead of assuming that the ratio of business to staff will remain broadly constant, special studies are undertaken of individual tasks or processes carried out by the organisation in order to establish the numbers required to complete them most effectively and efficiently. The method is thus suitable in situations where there are no clear past trends to examine, or where wholly new production or service methods are being planned. Work study is most commonly associated with manufacturing industries where the work is readily divisible into discrete production-line tasks (for example, when a new plant is being brought into service using hitherto untried production methods). The work study specialist then observes employees undertaking each task involved in the manufacturing process during the development stage. Once the most productive systems have been observed, it is possible to compute the number of staff required and the type of skills they will require.

According to Silver (1983, pp49–60), a further approach involves incorporating productivity trends into the time series calculation. This method removes from the time-series analysis described above the assumption that the ratio of staff to work (labour to capital) will remain constant over time. Instead, improvements

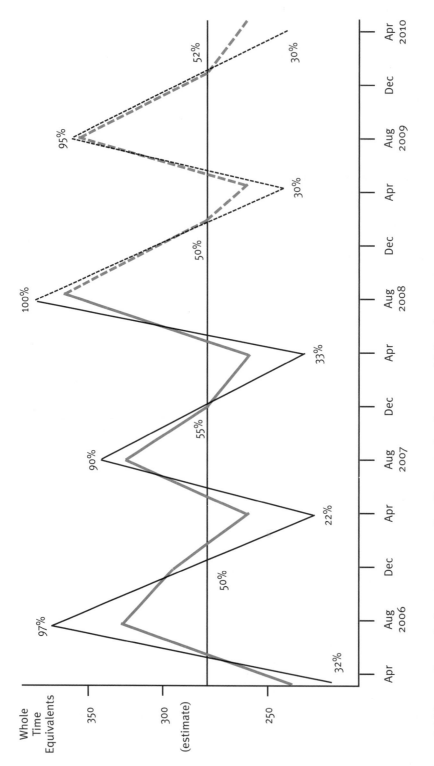

Figure 5.1 Time series analysis: occupancy and staffing rates in a large seaside hotel

in productivity over past years are calculated and extrapolated forward when calculating future human resource requirements. The approach is best suited to long-term forecasting, perhaps when major capital investment is being contemplated that has a long lead time. An industry for which such an approach might be feasible today would be banking, where large organisations employing skilled employees have seen very considerable productivity improvements in recent years. Given this experience, it would be appropriate to take account of that productivity trend, as well as the likely volume of work in the future, when forecasting the numbers to be hired and trained over future years.

MANAGERIAL JUDGEMENT

A different approach to forecasting demand dispenses to some degree with systematic approaches. Instead, it bases forecasts on the subjective views of managers about likely future human resource needs. Clearly, in situations where the business environment is highly volatile and where future staffing patterns may well bear little resemblance to past experience, there is no alternative, if planning is to occur, to using informed opinion as a basis for estimates. According to Stainer (1971, p98) there are three principal advantages to this approach:

- It is quick and requires little or no data collection.

- Basically intangible factors, such as changes in fashion, social opinion and taste, can be brought into account.

- The opinion of managers from different organisations as well as that of other experts can be used, as far as they are available.

This last point is probably less relevant in the current environment, where competition between employing organisations has replaced central planning, even in much of the public sector. Nevertheless, it is possible to envisage situations in which managers from other organisations who have experienced a particular set of changes might be able to offer valuable assistance in planning for similar developments elsewhere. An example is the NHS Unit Labour Costs scheme, which puts managers from hospitals in one part of the country in touch with others elsewhere to exchange such information. Another approach commonly used is the recruitment of new managers from organisations that have a similar pattern of development. Thus a British car manufacturer wishing to adopt certain Japanese production techniques might well hire senior figures with direct experience of managing such plants. Their judgement as to the number and type of staff required in the future will clearly be invaluable. Management consultants with similar experience can also be brought in to assist in demand forecasting.

A method that has received considerable attention in the literature on human resource planning is known as the 'delphi technique'. It is a systematic approach to decision-making that aims to introduce a measure of objectivity into the process by which forecasts are made on the basis of managerial judgement. According to Jackson and Schuler (1990, p163), its principal aim is to 'maximise the benefits and minimise the dysfunctional aspects of group decision-making', which is achieved by removing group dynamics and political considerations from the process. In human resource planning the delphi technique requires several managers and experts to submit their own forecast in writing (often anonymously) to a central contact, who then circulates the estimates among the other members of the group. Each then revises his or her own forecasts, taking account of the factors suggested in colleagues' submissions. Sometimes several rounds of adjustments are undertaken before a consensus forecast emerges.

In Stainer's view, there are great disadvantages to relying on managerial judgement alone in demand forecasting exercises (Stainer 1971, pp98–99). He believes that the complexity of the process and the number of factors at work are often too great for a single brain or group of brains to cope with. Furthermore, he expresses the view that organisational politics and 'emotional attachments' almost inevitably get in the way of objective decision-making when forecasts of this kind are made. There is therefore a good case for incorporating both statistical analysis and managerial judgement into the demand forecasting process. Computer modelling enhances the possibility of merging the two approaches successfully, because it permits many more variables to be included in the statistical formulae used than is practicable when calculations are done manually. Such approaches involve statistical analysis, but the assumptions made in the calculations are based on managerial or expert judgement.

Leap and Crino (1993, pp179–181) give an example of a formula that fits this description:

$$E = \frac{(L+G)\ 1/X}{Y}$$

Here E represents the number of staff required at a particular date in the future, L the current level of business expressed in terms of turnover, G the expected growth in business level, X the productivity improvement expected during the planning period, and Y the amount of business activity divided by the number of staff (ie the staff–business ratio). In the following example it is assumed that a health authority currently employing 1,200 GPs is considering how many will be needed in the year 2012.

L (current budget for GPs):	£180 million
G (expected growth in budget due to increased patient numbers and inflation):	£10 million
X (expected productivity growth):	1.02 (indicating an expected productivity improvement of 2 per cent)
Y (current budget per doctor):	£150,000

$$E = \frac{(180 + 10) \times 1/1.02}{150,000}$$

$$E = \frac{186.3}{150,000} = 1,242$$

The conclusion is that a total of 1,242 GPs will be needed in the year 2012.

WORKING BACK FROM COSTS

Bramham (1987, 1988) outlines an alternative approach to demand forecasting that removes past experience from the equation altogether. Here the process begins with the future budget: the amount of money the finance department expect to be available for staff costs in coming years. The human resource planner then works out, given that constraint, how many people at what salary level will be affordable. Current methods, ratios and productivity levels are thus ignored, the focus being on designing organisational structures and methods of working that will permit the budget to be met.

In recent years such approaches have been adopted far more frequently in the public services than in the past. With governments continually pressing for greater productivity, the emphasis in planning terms has been less on how many people are required to deliver a particular service given past experience, and more on what the taxpayer is prepared to spend or the government happy to allocate, given its public-spending targets. In the jargon of politicians, resource-based provision has replaced that based on need. The future budget has thus been the starting point in HR planning rather than the cost of providing the service in question in the past.

REFLECTIVE QUESTION

How far does your organisation go in forecasting future demand? To what extent is it possible to do so, given your business environment?

EXERCISE 5.2

NOTTINGHAM CITY COUNCIL

People management

Read the news item by Julie Griffeths, Council taps new talent pools to ease shortages (*People Management*, 16 September 2004, p13). This can be downloaded from the *People Management* archive on the CIPD's website (www.cipd.co.uk).

The article describes how a chronic shortage of support staff in social services was alleviated by targeting unemployed people and providing them with training.

Questions

1 What evidence is there in this article to suggest that the council does not carry out effective human resource planning?

2 To what extent would HRP have allowed the council to avoid the chronic staff shortages it faced?

3 What other initiatives would you advise the council to consider in order to fill its vacancies?

FORECASTING INTERNAL SUPPLY

There are a number of techniques used to assess the extent to which the demand for human resources can be met by the existing staff employed by an organisation. However, all share the same basic characteristic: they involve analysing the current workforce department by department or grade by grade before estimating the numbers likely to remain employed and the skills they are likely to possess. As in the case of demand forecasting described above, most of the tools used rely on a mixture of statistical analysis and managerial judgement in assisting planners to make informed forecasts. The key here is detailed analysis. In forecasting internal supply, overall figures about staff turnover rates are of little help. What is important is the likely turnover rate among specific groups of staff, such as those of a particular age, those with a defined length of service or those employed at different levels to do different jobs.

Predicting likely staff turnover (better described from the perspective of P&D managers as 'wastage') with any degree of accuracy is a complex activity, because people leave their current jobs for a variety of reasons. The following list covers many of these, but is by no means exhaustive:

- internal promotion
- internal transfer
- internal demotion
- to take up a different job offer elsewhere
- to retire
- to enter full-time education
- through illness
- redundancy or end of temporary contract
- dismissal for misconduct or incapability
- to take a career break
- to set up a new business
- as a result of a spouse or partner's relocating.

While the incidence of some of these can be increased or reduced by actions taken in the employing organisation, many are linked to factors in the wider environment – social, political, economic and technological. Others are linked to the age of the employee concerned. All these factors need therefore to be considered when developing meaningful forecasts of turnover rates in the future. Edwards (1983, p62) makes the following general observations, which continue to hold true.

- Wastage rates decrease with increasing age.
- They decrease with increasing length of service.

- They decrease with increasing skill and responsibility.

- They are higher for female than for male staff.

- They decrease when the general level of unemployment rises.

However, the experience of particular organisations or individual departments may well not correlate with these general observations, or may do so only to a limited extent. Meaningful forecasts of turnover must thus incorporate consideration of the organisation's experience, while building in assumptions about the probable future effects of environmental and demographic factors. Past figures are primarily analysed using the wastage and stability indices, together with analysis of specific employee cohorts and internal promotion patterns.

WASTAGE ANALYSIS

The wastage index is one of the basic formulae used by human resource planners in calculating likely future turnover rates. It is calculated thus:

$$\frac{\text{Number of leavers in a specified period}}{\text{Average number employed in the same period}} \times 100$$

The raw calculation is multiplied by 100 to allow the result to be expressed as a percentage. As has previously been stated, general organisation-wide turnover statistics are of limited use. While they may be helpful in making broad year-on-year comparisons or for general target setting, they are misleading if used as the basis for forecasting future internal supply. This is because the overall figure may mask very great differences between separate departments in the organisation and different groups of employees. In particular, raw figures do not take into account the tendency, identified above, for wastage to decrease with tenure and age. It is quite possible to envisage circumstances in which an organisation with a very low wastage rate might see it increase several times over when it embarks on a programme of expansion – particularly if it brings in large numbers of younger people in the process. Moreover, the overall wastage figure may mask big differences in turnover rates between different posts in the organisation. Hence an organisation with 60 per cent turnover may actually have quite low wastage in most posts, but a very high rate in others.

FORECASTING STAFF TURNOVER

Forecasting turnover rates among any particular staff group is inexact because so many different factors can have an effect. The number of leavers may rise or fall simply as a result of the appointment of new managers or the implementation of new policies. However, it is possible to make useful predictions by looking at economic trends and at how past economic conditions have affected wastage rates.

Regular government surveys are undertaken to establish staff turnover trends in the economy, while the CIPD and the CBI publish annual benchmarking studies. These show that job tenure among men has steadily increased over the past 20 years, while turnover among women has decreased. However, the figures also show that wastage rates decline substantially during recessions (when alternative jobs are hard to come by) and increase when an economy performs well. There are also substantial regional variations reflecting economic conditions in different parts of the United Kingdom.

In 1992, turnover levels in the United Kingdom as a whole were as low as 10 per cent. In 2004, when jobs were plentiful, the figure was 20 per cent, representing a doubling of the figure recorded in the pit of the previous recession. In 2007 the figure recorded by CIPD was 18 per cent. Reasonable estimates of future turnover can be made using information such as this in combination with authoritative economic forecasts for the economy as a whole and for specific industries.

STABILITY ANALYSIS

The method used to give more meaning to wastage rates is the stability index, also expressed in percentage terms:

$$\frac{\text{Number of employees with } n \text{ years' service at a given date}}{\text{Number employed } n \text{ years ago}} \times 100$$

Thus, if an organisation employs 1,000 people at the start of 2008, and calculates at the end of the year that 800 remain in their jobs, it would have a stability rate of 80 per cent. It thus looks at staff turnover from the opposite angle, focusing on the proportion of human capital that is retained, and not on the numbers lost.

COHORT ANALYSIS

Cohort analysis is used for forecasting in an effort to further improve the accuracy of wastage predictions. Here, instead of focusing on the stability and turnover of the staff generally, separate figures are calculated for each cohort of staff – usually the group hired in a particular year. The stability index is therefore adjusted somewhat to calculate a 'survival rate' for each cohort. In effect this involves simply calculating, on an annual basis, a different stability index for each year's intake of new employees. An example is shown in Table 5.1, focusing on stability rates among a cohort of a company's 150 graduate trainees starting in January 2001.

Table 5.1 Cohort analysis for graduate trainees starting in 2001

Year	Number employed at year end	Survival rate (%)
2001	120	80
2002	90	60
2003	67	45
2004	48	32
2005	41	27
2006	36	24
2007	30	20
2008	24	16

Again, as with the other approaches, the purpose of cohort analysis for human resource planners is to enable them to focus on past trends and use them as the basis for forecasting the extent to which an organisation is likely to be able to meet its future demand for labour internally. With cohort analyses it is common to calculate 'half-lives' for each group under examination. This is the length of time, expressed in years or months, that it takes for each cohort to halve in size. In the example in Table 5.1, 50 per cent is reached between two and three years, after 32 months or so. The half-life figure can then be readily used to compare one group of jobs in an organisation with another, allowing meaningful predictions to be made about likely future internal supply.

INTERNAL PROMOTION ANALYSIS

In larger organisations with well-defined hierarchies there is a need, when forecasting internal supply, to take account of movement up the ranks or grades, in addition to general wastage rates. It is important to know not only how many trainees remain employed, but also how many are likely to achieve promotion to different levels in the organisation. In a department store, for example, knowledge of the stability and wastage indices for shop supervisors is meaningless if account is not also taken of the fact that 90 per cent of supervisor vacancies are filled through internal promotion.

A variety of statistical models has been developed to assist in predicting human resource flows into, out of and up graded hierarchies. The best known is the Markov model, in which past data is used to work out the statistical probability that vacancies at each level will be filled internally. A straightforward example might be a traditional restaurant, where waiting staff are graded as follows:

a) junior waiter

b) *chef de rang*

c) restaurant supervisor

d) restaurant manager.

Past patterns of promotion can then be used to work out how often, in practice, vacancies at each level are filled through internal promotion from the grade below. In many restaurants, the majority of those in grades (b) and (c) will have been promoted through the ranks. An understanding of such processes and their frequency is essential if employee resourcing specialists are to forecast accurately how far future demand for *chefs de rang* and supervisors will be met internally, and thus how many vacancies will have to be filled externally. A simple example of a Markov analysis, using the restaurant example is as follows:

STEP 1: Analysing historical promotion patterns

In 2004 a restaurant chain employed a total of 750 people as junior waiters. Three years later in 2007 some of this cohort had been promoted once, some twice and a few three times, while others had left the organisation. The figures were as follows:

Still employed as junior waiters:	147	20%
Employed as *chefs de rang*:	110	15%
Employed as restaurant supervisors:	78	10%
Employed as restaurant managers:	9	1%
Left the organisation:	406	54%

STEP 2: Forecasting using these figures

In 2008 the restaurant chain has expanded considerably. It now employs 1,300 junior waiters. It uses the figures from the past analysis to predict likely internal promotion patterns in the coming three years. By 2011, it calculates, the 1,300 will be distributed as follows:

Still employed as junior waiters (1,300 × 20 per cent):	260
Employed as *chefs de rang* (1,300 × 15 per cent):	195
Employed as restaurant supervisors (1,300 × 10 per cent):	130
Employed as restaurant managers (1,300 × 1 per cent):	13
Will have left the organisation: (1,300 × 54 per cent):	702

STEP 3: Calculating external recruitment needs

It is planned that the chain should continue expand between 2008 and 2011, but at a slower pace. By 2011, it is anticipated that 2,460 staff will be employed as waiting staff. The Markov analysis can be used to establish how many vacancies will need to be filled using external recruitment. Estimates for this stage of the analysis (ie junior waiter promotions) are as follows:

Junior waiters in 2007:	1,440	(−260)	=	1,180
Chefs de rang in 2007:	720	(−195)	=	525
Restaurant supervisors in 2007:	240	(−130)	=	110
Restaurant managers in 2007:	60	(−13)	=	47

This is only one stage of the analysis. The company would also have to undertake similar analyses of promotions from the ranks above junior waiter level as well in order to establish the total number of external recruits required. The method used, however, would be the same. Recruitment and training budgets could then be set accordingly.

As was indicated in the section on demand forecasting, in most situations there is a need to combine these statistical forecasts based on past activity with the judgement of managers and other informed observers as to what factors are likely to change the patterns in the future. The result will be a final forecast based on analysis of past wastage that also takes into account some of the factors listed above, such as unemployment rates, anticipated retirements, likely promotions and any other actions taken by managers or planned for the future that might alter the prevailing trends.

REFLECTIVE QUESTION

Which of the above techniques have you observed being used? Which do you think is most appropriate for your organisation?

FORECASTING EXTERNAL SUPPLY

Having established the future demand for different kinds of employee, and how far these needs will or will not be met internally, it is necessary to give attention to filling the gap and reconciling supply and demand using the external labour market. While internal data can help planners make judgements about trends in different labour markets (eg response rates to advertisements, the proportion of turnover explained by individuals leaving to join competitors, the performance of new starters), relevant information is most often found outside the organisation.

Most labour markets are local. That is to say, applications for vacancies will come from people already living within commuting distance of the principal place of work. The trends that are important in such circumstances, from an employer's point of view, are thus those occurring within the relevant 'travel to work area'. For other jobs, usually those requiring greater levels of skill or commanding higher salary rates, the relevant labour markets will be national or even international. In either case there is a need for human resource planners to gain an understanding of the dynamics of these labour markets and to update their plans as trends change and develop. As far as the immediate travel to work area is concerned, the following statistics are the most helpful:

- general population density
- population movements into and out of the area
- age distribution
- social class
- unemployment rates
- school leavers
- the proportion with higher education
- skill levels.

Statistics of this nature for each local authority area are collected by the government and published in the monthly journal *Economic Labour Market Trends*. Other useful publications include *Labour Market Quarterly*, the annual *Social Trends* survey and the reports that are published following each national census (undertaken every ten years). In addition there are commercial organisations, often specialising in particular groups of employees or industries, that collate information from other sources and undertake research themselves. An example is a consultancy set up to provide information to NHS units in England, which produces a quarterly journal as well as providing specific advice to individual trusts. In addition to the basic statistics, there is a need to apply judgement and experience to assess the potential impact of other local factors. Those that might be relevant include any developments in the local transport network that might effectively expand or contract the travel to work area, the opening or closure of other units and the construction of new housing developments.

Where employers operate in national labour markets there is far less meaningful information available, because only the more significant trends are likely to have a substantial impact on future recruitment and retention exercises. The fact that unemployment increases or decreases nationally may well have little or no impact on specific labour markets; this was shown in the recessions of the 1980s and 1990s, when skill shortages remained in some areas despite the large number of people seeking work. That said, there are national statistics that may be of relevance in specific circumstances, particularly for larger employers. These would include statistics on the number of individuals leaving higher education with specific qualifications, and the number of employers competing for their services.

As is the case with local labour markets, there is also a need to keep an eye on any other major developments that might have an impact on the organisation's ability to recruit sufficient numbers in the future. Examples would include new government initiatives in the field of education and training, and the manner in which particular jobs or professions are portrayed by the media.

For some employers developments in international labour markets are important too. Where there are significant skills shortages in a particular country, employers will look abroad to find the people they need. In the United Kingdom in recent years, shortages of front-line medical staff has led to very substantial overseas recruitment, with particular attention being given to Spain where there is a surplus of trained medical professionals. Conversely, we have seen a net outflow of executives and IT staff from the United Kingdom to the United States during the same period.

LONG-TERM FORECASTS OF LABOUR DEMAND

An important variable in estimating external labour supply is the extent to which other employers will be competing for the available talent. It is useful here to look at long-term forecasts of which professional groups are going to be most sought after and which will be easier to recruit than is currently the case.

Estimates carried out by advisors to the Leitch Review have produced estimates for the years to 2004–2020. They calculate that UK employers will have to fill 18.4 million vacancies in total during this period, taking account of retirements, likely voluntary turnover and increases or decreases in overall demand.

The biggest growth in demand is expected in management jobs, where 2 million more posts will exist in 2020 than did in 2004, professional roles (1 million new jobs) and lower-skilled service-sector jobs (several hundred thousand new posts). By contrast there will be rather fewer jobs overall in the administrative and secretarial fields, and a fall of over 850,000 in the total number of unskilled jobs.

Source: Beavan *et al* (2005).

HRP CASE STUDIES

EXERCISE 5.3

Read the following two articles featured in *People Management*. They can be downloaded from the *People Management* archive on the CIPD's website (www.cipd.co.uk).

- Bruce Tulgan, Drill inspection (22 February 2007, pp44–45)

- Lucie Carrington, A bridge too far? (11 August 2005, pp24–28).

These articles concern leadership development in two very different organisational scenarios, the US military and professional services firms. However, the situations described are also useful to consider from an HR planning perspective.

Questions

1   What techniques would be best to use for forecasting the future demand for leaders in these organisations?

2   What factors described in the article might mean that internal supply forecasts might have to be adjusted from their current levels?

3   What approaches should be considered as a means of reconciling gaps between supply and demand?

COMPUTER APPLICATIONS

There are many different ways in which information technology can be used to support and undertake human resource planning. They can be divided into three broad categories: information provision, modelling and presentation. An important role played by computer databases is storing the information required to undertake meaningful forecasts of staffing demand and internal supply. Not only do computerised personnel information systems (CPISs) allow more data to be stored about jobs, employees and past applicants, they also permit far swifter generation of reports summarising the data than is ever possible using manual information storage systems. The larger and more complex the organisation, the more added value is gained by the presence of a CPIS with such capabilities.

Much information held in CPISs can be used in human resource planning, and forms the basis for the calculations and judgements referred to above. The following list is indicative but by no means comprehensive:

- sex

- age

- start date

- pay levels

- test scores at selection

- internal career history

- career history prior to joining

- educational qualifications
- skills/training completed
- performance/productivity ratings
- sickness/absence records
- promotion record
- turnover record.

Data such as this, analysed for hundreds or thousands of present and past employees, provides raw data for the calculation of formulae such as the wastage and stability indices, and for the analysis of cohorts and promotion patterns. It also permits HR planners to calculate correlations between wastage and variables such as age, sex, type of job and pay rate. In addition it facilitates analysis of the organisation's bank of skills when calculations are being made about its ability to meet future demand internally. Furthermore, the reporting facilities built into personnel databases readily permit comparative analysis between one department and another so as to make forecasts more accurate.

The second major application of information technology in human resource planning is in the field of modelling. The ability of a computer to handle vast quantities of data permits highly complex formulae containing numerous variables to be built up and results to be calculated in seconds. While specialist modelling programmes are available on the market, most human resource forecasting can be undertaken using basic spreadsheet programmes – best illustrated with an example. Table 5.2 shows a fictional spreadsheet application for a computer software company. The columns each represent a different variable.

Table 5.2 Spreadsheet application

	A	B	C	D	E	F	G
Manager	20	15%	20%	60%	3.6	1.44	7,200
Administrator	28	15%	20%	3%	5.04	4.9	7,350
Accountant	12	10%	20%	10%	1.44	1.3	3,250
Sales executive	40	60%	30%	5%	31.2	29.64	59,280
Software developer	35	12%	30%	20%	5.46	4.37	6,555
Software support	30	23%	30%	7%	8.97	8.34	12,510
Total					55.71	49.99	£96,145

Key
A   Total number of whole time equivalents in post at 1 January
B   Turnover rate based on past trends
C   Increased demand expected during the coming year
D   Number of vacancies typically filled by internal promotion
E   Number of vacancies expected in the coming year
F   Number of posts to be filled externally in the coming year
G   Recruitment costs per job group for the coming year (£s)

Columns A, B, C and D are calculated using analysis of past data, adjusted as is seen fit, given environmental changes. Columns E and F are calculated using statistical formulae that include the variables A, B, C and D. In this case E is calculated using the formula $[(A \times C) + A] \times B$. The number of vacancies is therefore calculated with reference to current numbers, likely growth and expected turnover rates. By contrast, F is calculated using the formula $E - (E \times D)$. It thus takes into account both the number of vacancies and the number of internal promotions.

Even with a small-scale exercise of this kind, looking at forecasts for one year in a relatively small company, the assistance of a computer makes the planning process far quicker than would be the case if the calculations were undertaken using a calculator. The advantage becomes far greater when more rows and columns are added, incorporating additional variables, forecasts for a number of years ahead and the building-in of further cost assumptions. In the above example it would be very straightforward to add columns representing forecasts for 2003, 2004 and beyond, and others calculating the costs of training new staff members in the various categories. Spreadsheets also permit the development of far more complicated formulae involving averages, fractions, logarithms, standard deviations, variances and many other statistical tools. It is also possible to build IF ... THEN ... ELSE commands into the formulae used (eg IF $(A \times C) >$ B THEN E ELSE $A \times B$).

Perhaps the greatest advantage of the computer in human resource planning, examined in more detail in the next chapter, is the ability it gives the planner to undertake 'What if?' or scenario analyses, altering figures or formulae to calculate what the implications would be, were key trends to change. In the example given here, the effect of increased or reduced turnover on the future supply of and demand for labour could be calculated with great ease; it would simply be necessary to alter the figures in column B and to watch while the computer recalculated the figures in columns E and F.

The third major contribution of computer technology in the human resource planning field is the capacity of proprietary systems to generate attractive and user-friendly reports and summaries. The advantage of innovations in this area is the relative ease with which data is interpreted. It is possible to present senior managers with well laid out graphics that summarise forecasts without the need to spend time drawing up such documents separately. The credibility and efficiency of the P&D function in general, as well as the HRP function in particular, is thus increased.

REFLECTIVE QUESTION

In what ways could human resource planning in your organisation be improved with greater use of computer applications? Could such activities be justified in cost terms?

HR PLANNING IN THE CONTEMPORARY BUSINESS ENVIRONMENT

EXERCISE 5.4

Read the article by Duncan Brown, Success in all shapes and sizes (*People Management*, 24 October 2002, p25). This can be downloaded from the *People Management* archive on the CIPD's website (www.cipd.co.uk).

In this opinion piece Duncan Brown describes the breadth of skills shortages that employers face. He also reflects on the paradox that organisations now often need to hire new people to work in some parts of their operation while making redundancies in others.

Questions

1   What evidence is provided in this article of HR planning activity in organisations?

2   Why are employers apparently moving away from planning (or talent management) systems which focus uniquely on elite performers?

KEY ARTICLE 11

Stella M. Nkomo, Human resource planning and organization performance: an exploratory analysis. *Strategic Management Journal,* Vol. 8, pp387–392 (1987)

In recent years there have been very few articles published in academic journals about human resource planning. It is not a fashionable area of research, despite the claims that are frequently made for the benefits that it can bring. This article does explore the subject and, in the process, provides one possible explanation why human resource planning has apparently fallen off the agenda of academic researchers. The principal finding is that there is no clear link between the presence of HR planning in organisations and measures of their relative business performance.

Questions

1   How robust do you consider the research design described in the article? How might it be improved?

2   Which of the possible explanations for the findings put forward in the concluding paragraphs do you find the most persuasive?

3   Having read the article, to what extent would you agree with the view that organisations are better off not bothering to undertake human resource planning at all? Why?

CHAPTER SUMMARY

- Different writers use the term 'human resource planning' in different ways. For some it is equivalent to 'manpower planning'; for others it is a broader concept describing a 'planned' or 'strategic' approach to P&D practice.

- There are four distinct stages in the HRP process: forecasting future demand for people, forecasting internal supply, forecasting external supply, and developing plans to respond to the forecasts.

- Three approaches to demand forecasting can be identified: projecting past trends forward, managerial judgement and working back from costs.

- Future internal supply can be estimated using wastage analysis, stability analysis, cohort analysis and internal promotion analysis.

- External supply is forecast by looking at developments in key labour markets, including the activities of competitors, numbers of school leavers and graduates, and likely unemployment rates.

- There are several ways in which computer technology facilitates effective HRP. The use of spreadsheet programmes provides a means of calculating different variables speedily, estimating recruitment and training costs and undertaking scenario forecasting.

EXPLORE FURTHER

- Little has been written in very recent years about the practice of human resource planning, so students are forced to rely on older texts. Some of these are now out of print, but were until recently widely available and widely read. You may well find multiple copies in your college library.

- The best general introduction to the practice of human resource planning is John Bramham's well-established text *Practical manpower planning* (1988). Other books that cover the topics include *The handbook of human resource planning* by Gordon McBeath (1992), *Human resource planning: a pragmatic approach to manpower staffing and development* by Elmer Burack and Nick Mathys (1996), *Human resource planning: an introduction* by Peter Reilly (1996), and *Staffing organizations* by Herbert Heneman *et al* (2000).

- There are also a number of edited texts containing short articles about different aspects of human resource planning and the various statistical techniques used. An good example is *Manpower planning: strategy and techniques in an organizational context* (1983) by John Edwards *et al*.

- The specific topic of the use of computers in human resource planning is covered by Bramham (1988) and in *Human resource management systems: strategies, tactics and techniques* by Vincent Ceriello (1991).

- Debates about terminology and the distinction between 'human resource planning' and 'manpower planning' are covered by Liff (2000), Williams (2002), Beardwell and Claydon (2007) and Torrington *et al* (2008).

CHAPTER 6

Human resource planning: relevance and debates

In the previous chapter, the various forecasting techniques developed by human resource (HR) planners were described and their objectives discussed. In this chapter we turn our attention to broader issues in the field of HR planning, and in particular to the question of its relevance to organisations operating in the contemporary business environment, which is often turbulent and unpredictable. Our focus therefore switches from the tools used to undertake HR planning to the utility of formulated plans and the fundamental problems associated with this area of P&D work. In addition, three other specific issues are explored: the extent to which HR planning is undertaken in practice, methods used in its evaluation, and approaches to planning human resources in international organisations.

LEARNING OUTCOMES

By the end of this chapter readers should be able to:

*   evaluate HR planning activity

*   assess the extent to which forms of HR planning can benefit organisational effectiveness

*   give advice concerning the application of HR planning in international organisations.

In addition, readers should be able to understand and explain:

*   the main arguments against comprehensive HR planning

*   the potential benefits of HR planning

*   the relationship between HR plans and key environmental trends.

THE USE OF HR PLANNING IN PRACTICE

The research evidence about how many employers currently carry out systematic HR planning is unclear but tends to indicate that the majority of employers do not give the function a high profile. In recent years few surveys have looked directly at the use or lack of use of specific HR planning techniques, preferring instead to look at wider issues. It is thus necessary to make inferences about the extent to which they are in fact used from surveys on computer usage, the introduction of 'strategic HRM' and the activities of human resource managers.

A study for the (then) Institute of Personnel Management (IPM – now the Chartered Institute of Personnel and Development) by Cowling and Walters (1990) asked a range of questions to establish whether or not particular activities associated with systematic HR planning were carried out. In each case respondents were asked to state whether the operation was undertaken 'on a formal and regular basis', 'as an ad hoc activity' or 'not at all'. The results indicated that only three activities were undertaken formally and regularly by a majority of respondents: the identification of future training needs, analysis of labour costs and productivity, and an assessment of the need for structural change resulting from business plans. Fewer than half, therefore, carried out formal forecasts of supply and demand of labour, and less than 20 per cent formally monitored HR planning practices. However, the figures rose considerably when the number of respondents claiming to carry out these activities on an ad hoc basis was added.

When it is considered that the response rate for this survey was only 2.45 per cent, it is difficult not to conclude that a large majority of UK employers see HR planning activities of the kind described in the previous chapter as a low priority for their organisations. Only in a minority of cases could a fully fledged HR planning function be said to have been established. Further evidence of informal and unsystematic approaches comes from surveys of computer use in P&D departments. According to a survey undertaken in 1993, 75 per cent of UK P&D departments used computers, but only a third of these (25 per cent of the total) used them for purposes related to HR planning (Kinnie and Arthurs 1993). *Personnel Today* (1995, p33) barely registered any use of planning at all in their survey, although respondents did suggest that they believed such applications would become important in the future. More recently, the CIPD (2003a) and IRS (2004a) have reported the results of surveys into the purposes for which employers used their computerised HR systems. Only a minority stated that they used such systems for workforce planning purposes.

The Workplace Employee Relations Surveys (WERS) ask P&D managers to indicate for which of a list of management activities they are responsible. In 2004, the most recent survey, 90 per cent stated that they carried responsibility for 'staffing or manpower planning' (Kersley *et al* 2006, p48). However, this term is too broad and subject to different interpretations to allow us to reach firm conclusions about the type of HR planning activity that is carried out. There is some evidence of renewed interest in traditional approaches to HR planning in the public sector, notably in the NHS where it forms an explicit part of the 'agenda for change' programme, and in local government (IRS 2003a). But no equivalent revival appears to be taking place in the private sector.

The overall picture painted by these and other research projects (see Rothwell 1995, pp175–178, Florkowski 1998, pp113-114, Liff 2000, pp96-98 and Johnson and Brown 2004) strongly suggests that systematic HR planning carried out in the manner advocated by writers in the 1960s and 1970s is now rarely found in UK industry or elsewhere in the world. Its use is mainly restricted to large public-sector organisations and firms operating in reasonably stable, capital-intensive industries. Others, if they use it at all, do so in a more casual and irregular way – perhaps relying more on managerial judgement and intuition than on established statistical approaches.

A variety of reasons have been put forward to explain the apparent abandonment of HR planning techniques – as far as they were ever well established – by employers in the UK (see Rothwell 1995, pp178–180, Marchington and Wilkinson 2002, pp278–279, Johnson and Brown 2004, pp386-387). These include the following:

- There is hostility to the use of statistical techniques in place of managerial judgement.

- It is believed that HR planning, while desirable, is not essential to organisational effectiveness; funding therefore tends to be funnelled elsewhere.

- The prevalence of a short-termist outlook in UK industry leads to a belief that individual managerial careers are unlikely to be enhanced by long-term activities such as HR planning.

- There are practical problems associated with inadequate historical data on which to base forecasts.

- There is ignorance of the existence of HR planning techniques and their potential advantages for organisations.

- Similarly, there is a more general ignorance or fear of mathematical methods.

It can be further argued that HR planning, as traditionally practised, simply no longer 'fits' the approach to P&D and to management generally that many employers now prefer. An example can be found in the way contemporary organisations, in both the public and private sectors, have moved towards decentralised forms of structure. Responsibility for employment resourcing issues is thus no longer held centrally, but by managers operating in independent business units whose small size makes detailed HR planning impractical. Organisation structures themselves are also increasingly impermanent and are staffed by people who expect to move on after a relatively short period. Time horizons, both individual and collective, are thus limited, ensuring that long-term planning is a low priority. Moreover, flexibility among staff is increasingly expected. The traditional model in which an organisation was made up of clearly defined jobs occupied by people employed on standard contracts has begun to break down. Instead, organisational life is becoming more and more fluid. We are expected and expect to be members of teams rather than occupants of defined jobs, and we are employed under a greater variety of contractual arrangements. None of these trends are compatible with the systematic application of the techniques outlined in the last chapter.

A further probable reason for decline in the extent to which HR planning is carried out relates to complexity and turbulence in the business environment. The result is a preference on the part of managers to wait until their view of the future environment clears sufficiently for them to see the whole picture before committing resources to preparing for its arrival. This forms the background to the major academic criticisms that have been made about HR planning, a subject to which we now need to turn.

THE CASE AGAINST HR PLANNING

The essence of the argument against the HR planning function is based on the simple proposition that it is unfeasible to forecast the demand for and supply of labour with any accuracy – a classic case of a brilliant theory being undermined by insurmountable problems when put into practice. In recent years, the most celebrated critic of business planning processes in general (ie not just those in the HR field) has been Henry Mintzberg. In a series of books and articles he has advanced the view that, in practice, most forecasts turn out to be wrong and that, as a result, the planning process tends to impede the achievement of competitive advantage (eg Mintzberg 1976, 1994). His points were further developed and applied specifically to the P&D field by Flood *et al* (1996).

The main problem with forecasting, so the argument goes, is its reliance on past experience to predict future developments. The main techniques involve the extrapolation of past trends and predictions based on assumptions about the way organisations interact with their environments. In practice, according to Mintzberg, this means that one-off events that fundamentally alter the environment cannot be included in the forecasts:

> *When it comes to one-time events – changes that never occurred before, so-called discontinuities, such as technological innovations, price increases, shifts in consumer attitudes, government legislation – Makridakis argued that forecasting becomes 'practically impossible'. In his opinion, 'very little, or nothing can be done, other than to be prepared in a general way to react quickly once a discontinuity has occurred'.*
>
> (Mintzberg 1994, p231)

The point about discontinuities is that not only is the event or trend difficult to predict in itself, but there is also a whole set of problems associated with assessing its likely impact on the organisation over time. As a result, except in situations where the organisation itself is able to exert control over future developments, all forecasts are inevitably based on questionable assumptions. It therefore follows that preparations undertaken to meet inaccurate predictions may well cause the long-term interests of the organisation greater harm than would have been the case had a less definite view been taken of unfolding developments.

The general case against HR planning was acknowledged to have some relevance in the 1960s and 1970s in the context of a relatively stable business environment, when organisations were being urged to 'take the plunge' despite understandable reservations about 'taking a long-term view on assumptions that are decidedly shaky' (Department of Employment 1971, p8). It is therefore unsurprising that it should be more widely accepted in the increasingly unpredictable world of the twenty-first century. What was appropriate for large organisations with a dominant or complete share of national markets in 1970 is no longer of any use to organisations with a relatively small share of an international market. The problems are summed up in the following quotation from the Institute of Employment Studies:

> Firms at the moment are very uncertain about what to expect in the future in terms of their size, structure and the design of jobs. Some companies may know what business they will be in a few years time, but they don't know how they will be doing it.

> (Speechly 1994, p45)

Competitive advantage today, according to critics of strategic planning, comes from generating responses to fast-changing circumstances that are swifter, more creative, more innovative and more flexible than those of key competitors – qualities that are stifled by the bureaucratic characteristics of planning processes (Smith 1996, p31). In other words, it is claimed that because the world is increasingly complex and unpredictable it is not worth trying to predict what will happen more than a year ahead. Any plans that are made will, in all likelihood, have to be revised several times in the light of changing environmental developments. Using Mintzberg's terminology, the number of obstacles to effective planning, in the form of discontinuities, are now so legion as to render the long-term planning process effectively redundant.

Many examples of discontinuities can be cited, some of which have had negative consequences for organisations and whole industries. A prominent example is the fate of the tourist industry over the past few years. In 1998 and later, the analysts confidently predicted steady and strong growth in the number of tourists, in air ticket sales and receipts from tourism (see *Economist* 1997, 1998, 1999, 2000). The Millennium Dome was widely expected to be capable of attracting 12 million visitors, and the UK tourist industry looked set to increase its size and wealth considerably. A number of factors then came along, one after another, which have led to a substantial contraction on a scale that no analyst, however well informed, could have predicted. First there was the rise in the value of the pound sterling against other currencies in the late 1990s and early 2000s, making the United Kingdom a more expensive destination than had been the case for many years. Then in 2001 the industry was hit first by the outbreak of foot-and-mouth disease and then by the fall in air passenger numbers following terrorist attacks in the United States and elsewhere. Thousands of jobs were lost, while the industry contracted in size by 20 per cent.

REFLECTIVE QUESTION

Consider what discontinuities have occurred in your organisation's business environment over the past two or three years. How far were these predicted? Would it have been possible to predict them?

THE TIME-BOMB THAT FAILED TO EXPLODE

A classic example of mis-forecasting is described by Sisson and Timperley (1994, pp169–171) in their discussion of the response of UK firms in the late 1980s to predictions concerning the impending explosion of a 'demographic time-bomb'. Declining birth rates after 1960, combined with a steep growth in the number of young people remaining in full-time education after the age of 16, led many commentators and government agencies to warn employers that there would be a severe drop in the number of 16–20-year-olds entering the labour market in the 1990s. Organisations were therefore advised to develop plans to enable them to cope with the labour shortage when it occurred. Among the measures suggested were the reorganisation of working methods, the recruitment of older workers, retraining programmes for unemployed people and the development of long-term plans to compete more effectively for the services of the limited number of younger workers looking for employment.

In the event, of course, the time-bomb failed to explode at the expected time. Instead, the early 1990s saw the onset of a deep economic recession and very high levels of unemployment. Instead of difficulties in

recruiting young people, employers were faced with a glut of applicants, many with qualifications for which there was no market. In effect, therefore, the exact opposite of what was predicted occurred, owing to circumstances that few in government or industry had foreseen. Those employers who failed to draw up plans to cope with demographic downturns were thus left no worse off and, in many cases, better off than their counterparts who had developed elaborate strategies.

Planners in the NHS, praised by Sisson and Timperley for their 'considerable imagination' in anticipating change, were actually left to cope with the aftermath of the implementation of inaccurate plans. In fact, two planning mistakes were made. In the late 1980s, too much new nurse training was commissioned, at considerable cost to the tax-payer. When it became clear, some years later, that an error had been made and that there would be too many trained nurses looking for work, the NHS overcompensated by reducing the number of training places being offered. The result in the early twenty-first century is a chronic shortage of trained nurses coming onto the labour market and a need to recruit large numbers from overseas.

WEMBLEY STADIUM

EXERCISE 6.1

Read the article Underneath the arches by Tim Smedley (*People Management,* 26 July 2007, pp28-31) This can be downloaded from the *People Management* archive on the CIPD's website (www.cipd.co.uk).

This article describes some of the problems that faced the HR team at Wembley Stadium during the period when it was supposed to open, but didn't, and some of the key threats to smooth operations that have appeared since the opening occurred.

Questions

1   To what extent does this episode support Henry Mintzberg's view that discontinuities will always occur rendering HR planning useless?

2   How far could the problems have been alleviated with more effective human resource planning?

3   What future developments in the stadium's HR business environment need to be taken into account when undertaking workforce planning for the coming few years?

THE CASE FOR HR PLANNING

A number of writers working in the P&D field have taken issue with the arguments put forward by critics of business planning. In addition to generally restating the potential advantages of HR plans, they also reject the assertion that because accurate forecasting is complex, difficult and subject to error, it follows that organisations should abandon long-term planning altogether. Two main arguments are put forward: the need to view plans as adaptable, and the greater attention to planning required by a more turbulent environment. A third set of arguments focuses on the practical outcomes of human resource planning, suggesting that they are both useful for organisations and can make a positive contribution to the achievement of business objectives.

THE NEED TO VIEW PLANS AS ADAPTABLE

The point is made that HR planning has never been intended to produce blueprints that determine the direction recruitment and development policy should take years in advance. Instead, it is viewed as a less deterministic activity, in which plans are continually updated in the light of environmental developments:

Pin-point accuracy in forecasting is rarely essential; the real purpose of looking ahead is to do as much as possible to reduce the area of uncertainty, to minimise the unknown factor.... Few major changes in a company's operations take place overnight and cannot be anticipated in some measure. If there is some agreed procedure for examining closely the manpower implications at an early stage, both the company and its employees will reap substantial benefits from the longer period they will have to prepare for change.

(Department of Employment 1971, p8)

Mintzberg's central point about discontinuities rendering plans redundant is thus disputed. In practice, it is said, changes in the environment rarely occur as suddenly as he suggests. As a result, when unforeseen developments do occur, there is time for plans to be adapted and updated to enable the implications to be met.

In fairness to Mintzberg, it must be stressed that his arguments concern business planning in general and are not related only to the management of people. When making long-term plans for major capital investment projects (building new plants, research and development of new technologies and the like), discontinuities potentially interfere far more dramatically. The time horizons for P&D practitioners are not so long, except in the case of the development of highly skilled employees. A great deal more can be adapted and changed in six months in the P&D field than is the case for capital investment in new plant and machinery. It thus follows that Mintzberg's arguments, while valid from a general management perspective, may have less relevance to P&D.

TURBULENCE REQUIRES MORE ATTENTION TO PLANNING

Linked to the first argument is the idea that, because the business environment is becoming increasingly turbulent and unpredictable on account of the threat from potential discontinuities, there is an even greater need for organisations to develop the capacity to plan accurately. Bramham (1988, p7) puts the case as follows:

> It is of course a paradox that as it becomes more difficult to predict and select, so it becomes more necessary to do so. The nineteenth-century businessman would have found his twentieth-century counterpart's obsession with planning strange. But, of course, the environment is now changing more rapidly and the conflicting pressures are greater. The modern manager must develop the systems and controls that increase the likelihood of the environment being controlled to a reasonable extent. Without an accurate awareness of his position, a manager will quickly lose his way in this rapidly changing environment.

In effect, what is being argued is that it is both possible and desirable to plan for uncertainty. When faced with an unpredictable environment, employers have two basic choices: they can abandon formal planning activity and rely on intuition – reacting swiftly and decisively at the point at which a clear picture of the future comes into view – or they can plan their HR policies so as to enable them to meet the future with a variety of different responses. If the second course is taken, the emphasis in HR planning will be on maximum future flexibility. In theory, the organisation will then have the capability to respond even more quickly than rivals who pursue the first approach.

The point is perhaps best illustrated with an example. Among the industries currently facing considerable uncertainty, even turbulence, are providers of Internet services. For some years a consensus has developed around the proposition that the evolution of the World Wide Web is set to change the business environment fundamentally. The view was expressed that it would kick forward the pace of globalisation several-fold, that retailing would be transformed as we swapped browsing in shops for browsing on net sites, that there would no longer be a need for books and that we would all seek to educate ourselves on a distance-learning basis via downloads from virtual universities. These revolutionary predictions were based on the belief that Internet usage would continue to grow at the same pace until everyone was connected. The Web has, of course, led to many changes and to important business opportunities, but the predictions about continued growth in usage have turned out to be wildly over-optimistic. The rate of growth in the United Kingdom slowed after 2000, then started to grow slowly again with the introduction of broadband technologies. By 2007 60 per cent of households had access. But far from revolutionising our lives for ever, the Internet has begun to seen like any other major new consumer product. Books, high-street shopping and traditional classroom-based university courses are all very much still with us and thriving. From the point of view of Internet service providers this creates major dilemmas. On the one hand, they may see their markets grow very rapidly in the future. On the other, they may now have reached their peak and be about to fall. In between the two extremes lie a range of other possibilities.

The P&D practitioners responsible for staffing these operations therefore have a difficult judgement to make. Is it worth their while to undertake detailed HR forecasting or not? Does the uncertainty they face mean that HR planning is so hazardous as to be a waste of resources, or should they take the view that in order to maximise their future profits they need to plan for all possible contingencies? In the case of these industries there are particularly difficult judgements to make, because the labour market for IT people with up-to-date skills is always very tight.

Supporters of HR planning would advise planning for all contingencies. The aim of doing so would not be to follow any plan to the letter, but to create a flexible scheme covering different possibilities that can later be updated as knowledge of the future environment becomes clearer. To achieve maximum potential competitive advantage, HR planners need to ensure that they have committed people with the right skills to exploit whatever opportunities arise. It is therefore the uncertainty that provides the rationale for increased attention to thinking ahead.

Dyer and Ericksen (2007) propose that organisations operating in turbulent environments should aim for 'workforce scalability', a concept that combines a form of HR planning labelled 'workforce alignment' with a very different idea labelled 'workforce fluidity'. Like the traditional approach to HRP explored in this and the previous chapter, workforce alignment is concerned with ensuring that an organisation 'has the right number of the right types of people in the right places at the right times doing the right things right' (Dyer and Erickson 2007, p268), but both managers and employees accept that no one configuration will last for long if competitive advantage is to be maintained. Regular realignments are necessary, but these should be planned strategically and are best achieved if the impetus for them comes 'from the bottom up' rather than being solely determined by senior managers and then imposed 'from the top down'. HR planning is thus effectively carried out by the employees themselves 'initiating salient moves on their own'. This will happen, it is argued, if the leaders in organisations ensure 'workforce fluidity' which essentially means a flexible mindset on the part of employees, and combine this with clear and inspirational direction from the top about the organisation's vision and its business model. The authors illustrate how the approach can work by describing its successful use by Yahoo! in establishing itself as a leading internet search portal. Yahoo!'s success is contrasted with the failure of a rival organisation called 'Excite' which no longer exists.

REFLECTIVE QUESTION

What are the main uncertainties faced by your organisation at present? To what extent could plans be put in place to enable these to be met more effectively by you than by your competitors?

OUTCOMES OF HRP

The clearest summary of the reasoning behind HR planning in a less obviously volatile business environment was given in a discussion paper published by the government as long ago as 1968 when encouraging HRP was government policy (Department of Employment 1971, pp5–7). Bramham (1987, pp56–57) also discusses the key objectives. Between them, six basic objectives of HR planning are identified, all of which can play a useful role in the management of organisations.

Recruitment

HR planning provides the information on which recruiters base their activities. It reveals what gaps there are between the demand for and supply of people with particular skills and can thus underpin decisions about whom to recruit and what methods to use in doing so. HR planning aims to ensure that there are neither too many nor too few recruits to meet the organisation's future needs.

Training and development

In forecasting the type of jobs that will need to be filled in the future, as well as the number, HR planning aims to reveal what skills training and development activities need to be undertaken to ensure that existing staff and new recruits possess the required skills at the right time. The longer and more specialised the training, the more important accurate HR planning is to the organisation's effective operation.

Staff costing

The accurate forecasting of future staff costs is an important activity in its own right. HR planning assists in cost reduction by aiming to work out in advance how organisational operations can be staffed most efficiently. It is also significant when new ventures or projects are being considered, because it provides information on which to base vital decisions. Too high a labour cost, and the project will not go ahead; too low an estimate, and profit levels will be lower than expected.

Redundancy

HR planning is an important tool in the anticipation of future redundancies. It therefore allows remedial action to be taken (recruitment freezes, retraining, early retirements and similar measures) so as to reduce the numbers involved. As a result, considerable savings in the form of avoided redundancy payments can be made. While redundancies may not be avoided altogether, adequate warning will be given, thus reducing the adverse impact on employee relations associated with sudden announcements of dismissals and restructuring.

Collective bargaining

In organisations with a strong trade union presence, HR planning provides important information for use in the bargaining process. It is particularly significant when long-term deals are being negotiated to improve productivity and efficiency. In such situations, the information provided by HR forecasts enables calculations to be made concerning how great an increase in pay or how great a reduction in hours might be conceded in exchange for more productive working methods and processes.

Accommodation

A final practical advantage associated with HR planning is the information it provides about the future need for office space, car parking and other workplace facilities. Such considerations are of most importance when organisations expect fast expansion or contraction of key operations. As with the other objectives described above, the basic rationale is that planning enhances cost control over the long term because it helps avoid the need to respond suddenly to unforeseen circumstances.

KEY ARTICLE 12

Gilbert L. Johnson and Judith Brown, Workforce planning not a common practice, IPMA-HR study finds. *Public Personnel Management,* Vol. 33, No. 4, pp379–388 (2004)

IPMA-HR is an association based in the United States called the International Public Management Association for Human Resources. It represents people working in P&D roles in local, state and federal government. This article discusses the results of a survey carried out among members of the association. It finds that the majority of the organisations where respondents work do not have workforce plans, and sets out the reasons for this. However it also goes on to cite the benefits those who have workforce plans find they bring to their work.

Questions

1   On what grounds do the authors argue that the incidence of workforce planning is actually rather lower than that revealed by their formal survey?

2   Why is so little HR planning, including succession planning, carried out in US government organisations?

3   What arguments are advanced in favour of HRP in public sector organisations?

ADAPTING TRADITIONAL HR PLANNING

It can be argued that in this debate, as in so many featured in the management literature, there is no clear right or wrong answer. It is not a question of whether or not HR planning per se is a good or a bad thing, but of the extent to which it is appropriate in different circumstances. This is not a field in which general theories or sweeping judgements can be applied at all usefully. As was shown in the examples given in Chapter 5, there remain employers for whom traditional approaches to HR planning (the use of systematic techniques to forecast supply and demand three to five years ahead) are very appropriate – at least for certain staff groups. These share the following characteristics:

- being large enough to be able to dedicate resources to the establishment and maintenance of an HR planning function

- operating in reasonably stable product and labour markets

- having key staff groups who require lengthy or expensive training

- competing in industries in which decisions concerning future investment in plant and equipment are made a number of years ahead and are essential to effective product market competition (ie capital-intensive industries).

In the United Kingdom, many organisations share most or all of these distinguishing features. In addition to the major public services (health, education, social services, defence, local and central government), many larger companies would also be included (utilities, oil producers, major banks and building societies, large retailers and so on). In all of these cases, while change may be occurring quickly, it is relatively predictable over the short term. The closure of departments or plants, expansion into new markets and changes in organisation do not take place overnight. Typically there will be at least six months' warning of likely changes, allowing time for established HR forecasts to be adapted and revised plans established. For such organisations, the criticisms of the HR planning process described above are applicable in relatively few situations and for relatively few staff groups. It can thus be plausibly argued that the absence of an HR planning function in such organisations will mean that they are not maximising their long-term efficiency and effectiveness.

The traditional approach to HR planning has a great deal less relevance for other employers (those that are small players in their industries, operating in a fast-changing technological field, or unable to know from one quarter to the next what turnover is likely to achieved). For such organisations the case against HR planning presented above will have greater resonance. The establishment of a formal, systematic planning function to make forecasts on the basis of past trends and managerial judgement is not a cost-effective proposition. The market and the organisational structures are simply too unpredictable to enable meaningful forecasts to be made and plans to be established concerning staffing needs a year or more ahead. However, that is not to say that such employers should not plan – merely that the traditional approach to planning described in Chapter 5 has little to offer. A case for these organisations to undertake some form of HR planning can still be made, but it involves methods that have somewhat different features.

What is needed is an adaptation of the principles underlying HR planning, together with the development of newer techniques and approaches. Many of these – now well covered in the literature – are also relevant for the larger, more stable organisations, where they can be used in addition to the longer-established HR planning techniques. Here five of these adaptations are described. In three cases the HR planning process becomes less all-encompassing and instead aims to focus on specific organisational developments or groups of employees. In a further two, the nature of the forecasting operation moves away from focusing simply on 'the right people in the right jobs, at the right time'. None are mutually exclusive, so all could be usefully adopted in tandem in a single organisation.

MICRO-PLANNING

The first alternative is to move away from a planning function that focuses on the organisation as a whole, and instead concentrate on forecasting the demand and supply of defined staff groups or on specific organisational developments. Planning activity is thus discrete and centres on potential problem areas. The techniques described in Chapter 5 are used, but their scope is limited. The major examples are as follows:

- Tight labour markets in which the organisation is obliged to commit substantial resources to compete effectively (see the example of pharmacists in Chapter 5).

- Major new business developments such as an expansion/contraction, a merger or acquisition, the development of a new line of business activity or a reorganisation.

- The need to respond to a significant environmental development (eg regulation, activity of a competitor, negative publicity or a new business opportunity).

- Where it is practicable and cost effective (eg where the required information is readily available and the outcome of an HRP exercise is clearly of use to the organisation).

Micro-planning is also often time limited. It can be carried out as a one-off project, rather than on an ongoing basis. This is usually because the organisational issues themselves are transient and cease to be problem areas once the planning process has been carried out and effective responses formulated.

Examples of contemporary situations that require focused micro-planning from an employment resourcing point of view include the following:

- the extension of the Working Time Directive to junior doctors after 2009, bringing their hours down to a maximum of 48 a week

- the secondment and employment of people to run major sporting events such as the Commonwealth Games which took place in Manchester in 2002 and the London Olympic Games being mounted in 2012

- the planned increase in the number of student places to be provided in universities by 2010 to accommodate half of all school leavers

- the opening of a new superstore or academy school where staffing numbers and structures can be planned ahead of time.

CONTINGENCY PLANNING

Contingency planning is rarely given more than passing reference by authors assessing the worth of HR planning, yet it can be seen as an approach that is almost universally applicable. Instead of seeing the HR planning process as one in which a single plan is developed and then adapted as the environment changes, contingency planning involves preparing possible responses to a variety of potential environmental developments. The result is that HR planning effectively switches from being a reactive process undertaken in order to assist the organisation achieve its aims, and becomes a proactive process undertaken prior to the formulation of wider organisational objectives and strategies. The purpose of contingency planning in the HR field is thus the provision of information on which to base decisions about the future direction the organisation takes.

As was argued in Chapter 5, the development of computer applications that permit 'what if' analyses greatly assists the contingency planning process. They are particularly useful in their capability to calculate very rapidly the cost implications of certain courses of action or shifts in environmental conditions, a basic spreadsheet program being all that is necessary to undertake these activities. Once developed, it is a very straightforward process to alter one or more sets of figures or assumptions to forecast what would happen in HR terms were certain scenarios to unfold or be pursued.

A straightforward example is a retailer who has to decide whether to open a new store and what size it should be. A spreadsheet could be constructed in which assumptions were made about the number and type of staff that would be required, the likely turnover rate in the first year and the cost of recruiting and training the new employees required to fill the posts. Different figures could then be plugged into the program representing different scenarios in terms of costs, training times, difficulty in recruiting staff, turnover, wage rates, business levels and so on. Particularly useful is the capacity such approaches have for calculating, in cost terms, potential best and worst scenarios. In the case of the retail company, such analysis would produce estimates of the highest and lowest possible costs associated with opening the new store. A range of other estimates could also be generated, given a variety of different potential outcomes. Senior managers, charged with making the decision about whether or not to invest in a new store, would then base this partly on information provided by the HR planner.

CONTINGENCY PLANNING IN A MANUFACTURING COMPANY

An example known to the author of the effective use of contingency planning occurred recently in a major manufacturing organisation. The company produces two distinct household products under a well-known brand name, and until 1995 did so in three separate plants in Italy, Germany and the United Kingdom. At that time it was decided to rationalise the company's operations and concentrate the manufacturing of each item on one site, a decision that necessitated the closure of one of the three plants. The question was, which should close?

While many considerations were taken into account in making the decision, HR issues played their part. Plans were thus drawn up looking at the outcomes in cost terms of different contingencies: closing the UK plant and focusing production of one product in Italy and one in Germany, closing the Italian plant and producing the products in Germany and the United Kingdom, and so on. In the event the decision was taken to close the German factory and to produce one of the two principal products in the United Kingdom

and the other in Italy. The cost in HR terms of each scenario was a significant factor in the final decision and was informed by the HR planning programme.

In the following year, managers at the UK plant had to retrain large numbers of employees in new production processes, made some redundant and hired others with particular skills. However, as a result of the contingency planning process, it had a very good idea of when each stage in the restructuring programme had to take place (ie what staff it needed in what jobs at what time) and a good estimate of the programme's cost in terms of recruitment, redundancy and retraining.

EXERCISE 6.2

LONG-TERM SCENARIO PLANNING

People management

Read the article The generation game by Anat Arkin (*People Management*, 29 November, 2007, pp24–27). This can be downloaded from the *People Management* archive on the CIPD's website (www.cipd.co.uk).

This article describes some examples of organisations thinking about different future scenarios. The organisations include PricewaterhouseCoopers, BUPA and Shell.

Questions

1   How plausible do you consider some of the long-term business scenarios described here? Why?

2   What unexpected advantages accrued to the organisations carrying out these exercises?

3   What does the article say about the decline of traditional HR planning since 1990?

SUCCESSION PLANNING

Another adaptation of the principles of traditional HR planning is the development, mostly in larger organisations, of a succession planning function, nowadays sometimes seen as forming part of a 'talent management' programme. The objective here is to focus HR planning activity on the recruitment and development of individuals to fill the top few posts in an organisation. Succession planners are mainly interested in ensuring that their employer has enough individuals with the right abilities, skills and experience to promote into key senior jobs as they become vacant. While some organisations have succession plans covering several hundred top jobs, for many the focus of attention is on 'once-in-a-generation' appointments such as the chief executive, board-level directors, hospital consultants, professors, newspaper editors, ambassadors and top civil servants. These jobs typically represent the pinnacle of an individual's career, and tend to be occupied by a single employee for between five and twenty-five years. Needless to say, ensuring that the right people are available to fill these posts at the right time is particularly important to the ongoing achievement of organisational success. According to Jackson and Schuler (1990, p171), succession planning differs from traditional HR planning in that:

> *the prediction task changes from one of estimating the percentage of a pool of employees who are likely to be with the company x years into the future, to one of estimating the probability that a few particular individuals will be with the company x years into the future.*

In other words, the planning process covers a narrower group of employees but does so with a higher degree of intensity; because plans concern relatively few, they can be considerably more sophisticated. The time horizons involved are also longer than is the case with traditional HR planning. Succession plans, by their very nature, often involve forecasting and planning the progress of individuals 20 years or more ahead.

The technique is most often associated with hierarchical organisations in which individuals develop careers by moving upwards and sideways over a number of years as they acquire the required skills and experience. The aim is to ensure that enough individuals with the potential to succeed to senior positions are available when an appointment needs to be made. Rothwell (1995, p189) reports that three candidates are typically identified for each senior post:

- one who is ready now and could succeed immediately if necessary

- one who will be ready, if needed, in two to three years' time

- one who will be ready in five years' time.

In addition, succession planners have an input into decisions about the numbers and kinds of graduates that are employed on graduate training programmes each year. While it is rare for individuals to be earmarked for senior posts at this stage, a major purpose of the graduate recruitment process for many employers is the development of a pool of people with the potential to reach the highest levels.

In technical terms, succession planning involves collecting and manipulating data about individuals, and tracking their performance and progress as they move from job to job over a period of time. Files therefore have to be kept containing information about training programmes, results of performance appraisals, and career histories and qualifications, as well as details of any potential constraints that might hold their development back (such as a disinclination to move to a new region or country). Customised and proprietary computer systems are now available to help match people to jobs (IRS 1990, p16), although some of these appear to be too sophisticated and prescriptive to be of any great practical use (O'Reilly 1997, p4). Examples of recent approaches are provided by IRS (2000a), while the wider aspects of contemporary HR planning, including succession planning, are covered in depth by Berger and Berger (2004) in their book about talent management.

The alternative is to recruit people from other organisations into leadership roles when vacancies come available. This approach, as demonstrated by Riddell (2001, p37), has been increasingly used of late to fill major posts that have traditionally been resourced through internal promotion. Advantages include original ideas, a new-broom approach and the perception of a fresh start. The disadvantages are the time it often takes to fill the post and greater uncertainty about how the 'outside appointments' will fit into their new environment.

EXERCISE 6.3

NURTURING SENIOR MANAGERS

People management

Read the article by Jane Simms, also entitled The generation game (*People Management*, 6 February 2003, pp26–31). This can be downloaded from the *People Management* archive on the CIPD's website (www.cipd.co.uk).

In the article it is argued that traditional approaches to succession planning that fell out of fashion in the 1980s and 1990s are making a comeback under the new title of 'talent management'. It also considers whether it is better to recruit senior managers externally or to promote people from within.

Questions

1 Why did succession planning become unfashionable over the past 20 years?

2 Why is it now undergoing a renaissance in many organisations?

3 Summarise the arguments for and against promoting senior managers from inside the organisation rather than recruiting them from outside.

KEY ARTICLE 13

Sally Sambrook, Exploring succession planning in small, growing firms. *Journal of Small Business and Enterprise Development*, Vol. 12, No. 4, pp579–594 (2005)

In this article the author discusses her interviews with four senior managers (two of whom are owner-managers) of small but fast-growing firms based in Wales. The particular issues associated with identifying and developing successors to top roles in small organisations are explored in detail. Particular problems are identified along with steps that need to be taken to ensure an effective transition over time from one leader to another.

Questions

1 Why is succession planning a particularly necessary activity in small, growing firms like those featured in this article?

2 Why is it a more problematic process than in larger organisations?

3 What key steps are identified as being necessary if succession planning is to be effective in small firms?

4 What might larger organisations learn from the discussion about effective succession planning in this article?

SKILLS PLANNING

A further adaptation of traditional HR planning principles to meet new circumstances is a shift away from a focus on planning for people towards one that looks first and foremost at skills. Instead of forecasting the future supply of and demand for employees (expressed as the numbers of whole-time equivalents required or available), skills planning involves predicting what competencies will be needed one to five years hence, leaving open the question of the form in which these will be obtained.

The approach is novel in so far as it acknowledges that as product markets have become increasingly turbulent, new forms of employment (such as those described in Chapter 7) have developed to meet the employers' need for labour flexibility. It therefore abandons the assumption inherent in the traditional model of HR planning that organisations in the future will employ staff in the same manner as they have in the past. Skills-based plans thus incorporate the possibility that skill needs will be met either wholly or partially through the employment of short-term employees, outside contractors and consultants, as well as by permanent members of staff. Examples of the adoption of this approach are reported by Speechly (1994, pp45–47).

Skills planning is particularly appropriate in situations where there are various different methods by which employee resourcing needs can be met. An example might be a computer company launching a new software package for use in industry. Its managers may have a rough idea of how many licenses they will sell, but cannot predict how much training customers will require or what type of servicing operation will be necessary. They need to put in place plans that focus on their ability to provide different levels of training and service, but because these services will be provided by temporary employees and subcontractors as much as by permanent members of staff, there is no point in making plans that focus on the number of new staff posts needed. Instead, the plans focus on the possible skill requirements and form the basis of strategies designed to make sure that those skills are obtainable in one form or another.

SOFT HUMAN RESOURCE PLANNING

There is a degree of disagreement in the literature about the use of the term 'soft human resource planning' and its precise meaning. Marchington and Wilkinson (2005, p89) define it broadly as being 'synonymous with the whole subject of human resource management' while others, such as Torrington *et al* (2008, p53), accept a narrower definition involving planning to meet 'soft' HR goals – particularly cultural and behavioural objectives. Torrington *et al* use the label to give meaning to a distinct range of HR activities that are similar to hard HR planning in approach, but that focus on forecasting the likely supply of and demand for particular attitudes and behaviours rather than people and skills. Soft HR planning can thus be seen as a broadening of the objectives associated with the traditional approaches described above.

Like skills planning, soft HR planning accepts that for organisations to succeed in the current environment they need more than the right people in the right place at the right time: they also need to ensure that those people have an appropriate outlook and set of attitudes to contribute to the creation of a successful organisational culture. More importantly, undertaking systematic soft HR planning can alert organisations to long-term shifts in attitudes to work among the labour force in general, allowing them to build these considerations into their general planning processes. An example might be a need on the part of an employer for sales staff who are not just appropriately trained, but who also exhibit the behaviours required to interact successfully with customers. There is thus a requirement for staff with a particular set of attitudes, so that an effective customer-focused culture develops. Traditional, hard HR planning takes no account of such issues, a deficiency corrected with the addition of a soft dimension.

Techniques for assessing the internal supply or availability of people with the desired attitudes and behaviours are described by Torrington *et al* (2008, pp61–62). They include the use of staff surveys, questionnaires and focus groups to establish the nature of employee motivation, the general level of job satisfaction and commitment and the extent to which certain behaviours are exhibited. Methods for analysing external supply are discussed by Jackson and Schuler (1990, p157). The emphasis here is on making an assessment of the likely impact of general societal attitudinal change on the future needs of the organisation. Published surveys are the main source of external data. Among the changes in attitudes they report in the United States are the following:

- Employees are becoming increasingly resistant to relocation.

- There is a general reduction in loyalty towards individual employers.

- Younger workers have considerably less trust in and respect for authority than their older counterparts.

- Younger workers tend to look for work that is fun and enjoyable, whereas older workers see it as 'a duty and a vehicle for financial support'.

- Younger workers have a different conception of 'fairness' in the work context than older colleagues. They see it as involving being tolerant towards minorities and allowing people to be different, while older workers define it as 'treating people equally'.

Advocates of soft HR planning argue that such matters can and should be considered when forecasting future needs, in addition to data concerning the numbers of staff and skills that are likely to be available.

An interesting example of a 'soft' trend in the United Kingdom and the response of employers is described by Wills (1997, pp31–34). She observes that, in response to the decline in the number of 'jobs for life', employees are increasingly viewing their employment first and foremost as a means by which they can gain work experience and boost their own employability. As a result, less attention is given to securing promotion by impressing managers and to focusing on achieving organisational goals. The response of companies who wish to retain staff in whom they have invested a great deal of time and resources is to give greater attention to career management, developing a network of mentors and advisors who try to ensure that internal moves are available so as to retain the interest and loyalty of employees.

HR PLANNING IN AN INTERNATIONAL CONTEXT

The globalisation of organisations has a number of distinct implications for the HR planning function, raising fundamental questions about the extent to which it is useful to carry it out and about the level at which such activity should be undertaken. In practical terms, there are two major implications for international organisations: the requirement for language skills and the need to move skilled employees and managers from country to country. Both complicate the planning process and make forecasting supply and demand for key groups of employees a considerably harder task. Added to this is the inherent instability associated with much international business activity. Companies are bought, reorganised and resold regularly, production is shifted from country to country as economic conditions change, and strategic alliances are formed that can easily alter a company's HR planning needs overnight.

In forecasting the demand for and supply of language skills, the HR planning function has a potentially crucial role to play, so fundamental is the need for effective communication between employees in different countries. Forecasting demand a year or so ahead is not a major problem, nor is forecasting the probable internal supply. The problem arises in estimating the external supply by accessing data on the number of people in different countries proficient in different languages at different levels. As a result, accurate forecasting of the amount of language training that needs to be provided is necessarily problematic. However, the importance of the issue and the length of time needed for most people to acquire reasonable proficiency in a new language mean that factoring such considerations into the HR planning process is an important potential source of increased organisational effectiveness.

The practice of succession and career planning also becomes more complex and more important when organisations become international. This is because to develop people so that they are ready to take on senior roles at a later date, it is necessary for them to undertake international careers, including spells working as expatriates in one or more foreign countries. Succession planners therefore have to add to the considerable amount of data they already hold further information about language, the willingness of individuals to work abroad (together with spouses and families) and the costs associated with organising overseas postings.

However, these complexities are small fry when general HR planning in international organisations is considered. It is hard enough, as was illustrated above, to generate accurate forecasts for the supply of and demand for employees in one country; doing so across several countries renders the process a great deal more complicated. Not only do basic labour market conditions vary considerably between countries over time, there are also, as Hofstede (1980) and others have shown, substantial differences between the attitudes and expectations of different national workforces towards their jobs, their careers and their employers. When the problems associated with obtaining access to robust external labour market data in different countries are added to the equation, it becomes clear that the operation of a single headquarters-based HR planning function is unlikely to be a practical option for international companies. Instead, what is required, if HR planning is to be carried out in any meaningful way, is separate regional or national HR planning functions, each focusing on developments in its own labour market and reporting to a central co-ordinating department. This will ensure that HR planning is carried out for each key labour market and that information is provided from each in a similar format. Planning data can then be used to inform decision-making about future investment and downsizing programmes.

EVALUATING HR PLANNING PROCESSES

In 1992, the (then) IPM issued a Statement on Human Resource Planning that suggested three criteria for evaluating the process:

- the extent to which the outputs of HR planning programmes continue to meet changing circumstances

- the extent to which the programmes achieve their cost and productivity objectives

- the extent to which strategies and programmes are replanned to meet changing circumstances.

The last two apply to the HR planning function the same kind of evaluation criteria as might be applied to any department of an organisation. They simply ask how far the day-to-day objectives are met effectively and efficiently. By contrast, the first advocates the evaluation of the plans themselves.

Were HR planning exercises one-off affairs, making single sets of long-term forecasts, evaluation would be a very straightforward matter. An organisation would simply ask how far the forecasts of demand for and supply of labour in fact proved to be accurate. However, as has been made clear, HR planning is an ongoing activity in which forecasts are continually reviewed, updated and adjusted as circumstances change. What is important is how effective the whole HR planning process is in supporting the achievement of wider organisational objectives. Ultimately therefore, as argued by Rothwell (1995, p197) and Jackson and Schuler (1990, pp173–174), it is the effectiveness of strategies developed on the back of the HR planning process that provides the most meaningful evaluation criteria. The planning process itself is thus less significant than the extent to which it supports the evolution of training and development programmes, recruitment policy and P&D interventions aimed at reducing turnover. In the case of planning for a reduction in the number of employees, the appropriate criteria would be the number of compulsory redundancies avoided as a result of planning activity.

In addition, as with all evaluation activity in the P&D field, there is a need to estimate the value of a particular intervention against the likely outcome of not intervening, and a need to compare outcomes with those of key competitors. In the HR planning field this will involve asking the following kinds of questions:

- Does the presence of a long-term HR planning function contribute to the achievement of organisational objectives?

- What would have been the result in recent years had no such function been present?

- Does the function justify its presence in cost terms?

- How does our organisation's performance compare with that of competitors who have either a (more or less) sophisticated HR planning function, or no such function at all?

CHAPTER SUMMARY

- Evidence on the extent to which organisations carry out systematic human resource planning is unclear. However, most authorities agree that the major approaches used in practice are qualitative and informal in nature.

- Reasons put forward to explain the reluctance to carry out HRP include practical problems, lack of appreciation of its potential contribution, trends in organisation structure and trends in the business environment.

- A case against HRP has been articulated in recent years by authors who consider the practice to be, at best irrelevant, and at worst damaging to organisations.

- The case for HRP rests on practical outcomes of the process, the need to plan more carefully in turbulent times and the need to view HR plans as adaptable.

- Adaptations of traditional approaches include micro-planning, contingency planning, succession planning, skills planning and soft HR planning.

- HR planning is particularly problematic in international organisations. Here there is a need to balance the need for pan-national planning to ensure that the organisation can draw on the required reservoir of skills, and country-specific approaches that focus on specific labour market developments.

- A variety of approaches are available as a means of evaluating an HRP exercise. Many focus more on the success or failure of outcomes from HRP than on HRP itself.

EXPLORE FURTHER

- The specific issue of the case for and against HR planning in the current environment has rarely been addressed in a balanced way in the literature. It is thus necessary to look in different places for the arguments on either side. The case against is best articulated by Henry Mintzberg (1994) in *The rise and fall of strategic planning*, but is also covered more briefly by Flood *et al* (1996) in *Managing without traditional methods* and by Micklethwait and Wooldridge (1996) in *The witch doctors*. The counter-arguments in favour of HR planning are best articulated in Bramham (1988), Torrington *et al* (2008) and Marchington and Wilkinson (2005). The chapter by Dyer and Erickson (2007) in John Storey's *HRM: a critical text* is an excellent contribution to the debate.

- Up-to-date case-studies focusing on the aims and outcomes of HR planning are also relatively rare. However, Terry Hercus (1992) describes the approaches taken in eight organisations based in the United Kingdom, and Jackson and Schuler (1990) include good examples from the United States in their article Human resource planning: challenges for industrial/organisational psychologists. Current public sector developments are summarised by the IRS (2003a).

- Several articles about succession planning being carried out in contemporary organisations have been published recently in *People Management*. Examples are those about Hilton Hotels and the Broadway charity for homeless people in the 19 April 2007 edition.

- Evaluation issues are covered in some detail by Jackson and Schuler (1990) and by Sheila Rothwell (1995). A good summary of the international issues is found in Damian O'Doherty's (2000) chapter on HR planning in the textbook edited by Beardwell, Holden and Claydon (2004).

CHAPTER 7

Flexibility

In recent years flexibility issues have become a major preoccupation of managers and commentators interested in resourcing practice. These issues have come to the fore for many different reasons, but underlying all is the belief that organisations that gain a capacity for greater flexibility can develop sustained competitive advantage. This occurs for three distinct, but equally important reasons:

- An organisation that is flexible is able to deploy its people and make use of their talents more effectively and efficiently than one that is not.

- The more flexible an organisation becomes, the better able it is to respond to and embrace change.

- Flexibility, particularly in terms of hours of work, is valued by employees and can thus help to recruit and retain strong performers.

The term 'flexibility' covers a broad range of different areas of activity. It is useful to categorise these under two general headings; namely structural flexibility and cultural flexibility. The first refers to the types of contract under which people work and the architecture of the organisation. An organisation that is structurally inflexible could be characterised as one that employs everyone on the same basic set of terms and conditions, is made up of fairly narrowly defined 'jobs' into which people are required to fit themselves, and is managed via a traditional hierarchical structure. A flexible organisation, by contrast, deploys people as and when they are needed using a variety of contractual arrangements, and expects its people to work in a variety of different roles as and when required. These characteristics mean that it is better placed to respond quickly to changed circumstances and evolving customer expectations. Cultural flexibility is the other side of the same coin, being concerned with beliefs, attitudes and values. It is little use having an organisation that is structurally flexible if its people do not share a flexible mindset. Willingness to respond to change is as important a capacity to develop as the ability to do so, but it is harder to develop. Ultimately it can only be achieved by gaining the commitment of staff through promoting a working environment characterised by high levels of trust, partnership and mutual respect.

The notion that flexibility is invariably a positive aspiration to be welcomed has, however, been extensively challenged. For many the term 'flexibility' is synonymous with 'insecurity' and thus has many negative connotations. Critics rightly point to the ease with which short-sighted managers can damage an organisation's long-term prospects by introducing flexibility carelessly or too quickly. They remind us that developing a capacity for flexibility is difficult, and that it is easy to make serious mistakes when embarking on such exercises.

In this chapter readers are introduced to all these issues. We start by defining the term 'flexibility', before evaluating the major reasons for increased interest in the concept. We go on to examine how far, in practice, organisations are becoming more flexible, and assess the major advantages and disadvantages of different types of contractual relationship. The chapter ends with a short section outlining the major criticisms of moves towards greater flexibility and the lessons that can be learned from these perspectives.

LEARNING OUTCOMES

By the end of this chapter readers should be able to:

- distinguish between the concepts of functional, numerical and temporal flexibility

- lead/contribute to a programme of increased functional flexibility or multi-skilling

- advise on the main advantages and disadvantages of employing people on part-time or fixed-term contracts

- advise on the merits of using subcontractors or homeworkers to carry out organisational activities

- determine the extent to which different forms of temporal flexibility are appropriate in particular circumstances

- assess the advantages and disadvantages of outsourcing functions, including those traditionally within the remit of P&D managers.

In addition, readers should be able to understand and explain:

- the content and underpinning rationale of flexible resourcing practices

- contextual factors underlying increased interest in flexible working practices

- key UK trends in the field of flexibility

- the major arguments against increased flexible working practices

- the concept and role of 'employability'.

DEFINING FLEXIBILITY

Any survey of flexibility does well to start with a description of the work of John Atkinson and, in particular, his proposed model of the 'flexible firm'. For the purposes of this chapter, this model will be used as the basic definition of the term 'flexibility'. Published in 1984, Atkinson's model has been very influential and has led to the development of a vigorous academic debate about its merits as a tool of description, prescription and prediction. Its main feature is the suggestion that a flexible firm (by which Atkinson means one that is competitive in the modern business environment) is composed of three basic groups of employees: core workers, peripheral workers, and a third group who are employed only on some kind of subcontracted basis. The basic model is illustrated in Figure 7.1.

Central to the model are two distinct types of flexibility: functional and numerical. The former is applied specifically to the core workers: that is, people who are employed on standard, permanent, full-time contracts and who undertake the tasks that are central to the success of the organisation. They are

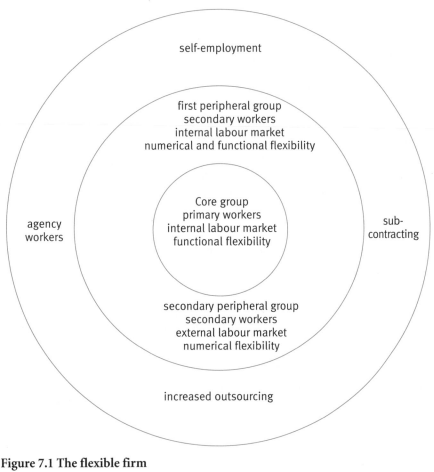

Figure 7.1 The flexible firm
Source: Atkinson (1984).

functionally flexible, in that they do not work to rigid job descriptions but carry out a broad range of duties. Moreover, they do not restrict their activities to work at a particular level. Instead, they carry out complex tasks associated with managerial or professional jobs as well as more mundane activities, depending on the day-to-day needs of the organisation.

The peripheral group can also be functionally flexible, but in the model is more strongly associated with the term 'numerical flexibility'. Atkinson divided peripheral workers into primary and secondary categories, the first forming part of the firm's internal labour market. These people are mainly full-time and have a certain degree of permanence, but tend to have lower skills than colleagues who enjoy the status of core employees. As individuals they are less central to the organisation's success because their skills are more widely available in the labour market. They therefore enjoy lower job security than the core workers and will be among the first to have their hours cut or to be laid off when business downturns are experienced. The secondary peripheral group are in an even more precarious position, because they are brought in mainly to help cover peaks in business or short-term needs resulting from the absence of other staff. They are employed on either a part-time or temporary basis.

The final group, located beyond the periphery, consists of people who are not employees of the firm but who are hired on a subcontracted basis to undertake a particular task or set of tasks. In the vast majority of cases, their contracts will be temporary, and hence insecure, although it is possible for a series of fixed-term contracts to follow one after another. Some may be professionally qualified people working on a self-employed basis; others may work for an agency or some other service provider. In both cases they are perceived by the other groups as being external to the organisation and thus readily replaceable by a competitor should their work prove to be unsatisfactory or more cheaply provided elsewhere.

Over the years others have proposed similar models (eg Loveridge and Mok 1979, Handy 1989), but none has entered managerial language or generated as much debate as that proposed by Atkinson. The most useful addition to his core concepts have been two other forms of flexibility (ie other than functional and numerical):

- temporal flexibility (meaning flexibility in terms of when people work)

- financial flexibility (referring to variable payment systems that increase the extent to which wage costs are flexible and mirror an organisation's income).

The latter is primarily a concern for remuneration specialists, and is covered extensively in books on reward management, including a number published by CIPD.

The other major development of Atkinson's ideas has come from analysts who believe that his model does not go far enough in its portrait of a truly flexible organisation. They suggest that technological and competitive pressures will grow to such an extent over the coming years that the number of people employed in what Atkinson describes as core jobs will decline very rapidly, leaving most skilled people with no choice but to operate as peripheral employees. This will involve working part time for a number of employers on a series of fixed-term contracts or on a self-employed basis. For those seen by Atkinson as currently belonging to the peripheral groups, the future is bleaker still, with writers predicting substantial reductions in demand for their services over the next few decades.

In *The empty raincoat,* Charles Handy (1994) suggests that employers will increasingly wish to buy a specific service from a worker rather than that person's time. The result will be a situation in which, for most people, there will be little opportunity to enjoy the security of a long-term, full-time job. Instead, Handy believes, people will have to develop portfolio careers in which they earn money by 'looking for customers, not bosses'. Employers will be far less willing or able to employ people (especially professionals or 'knowledge workers') to come to their premises for a fixed number of hours each week. Rather, they will say: 'Do this by this date; how you do it is up to you, but get it done on time and up to standard'. The term 'job' will thus revert to its original meaning of a specific task or project rather than an occupation or profession, while individual ambitions will focus more on the achievement of employability than on the status of being an employee. Organisations will thus become increasingly 'virtual' and society increasingly 'jobless'. The same kind of analysis also underlies other influential publications concerned with the future of work, with some writers going further than Handy in their assessments of the speed with which and the extent to which these developments will occur (eg Bridges 1995, Rifkin 1995, Davison and Rees Mogg 1997, Greenfield 2003, 2006). These and other ideas about the future of work are discussed at length in Chapter 22.

The final point to make by way of introduction is to stress that the model of flexibility advanced by Atkinson and others, despite the use of the word 'firm', is not intended to be restricted to the private sector. The principles of efficiency and responsiveness to change are just as applicable in the public sector. Indeed, some studies have shown that in many respects the principles of the 'flexible firm model' have been adopted to a greater degree in public organisations than in private companies (Bryson 1999, p69).

KEY ARTICLE 14

Laura Hall and Carol Atkinson, Improving working lives: flexible working and the role of employee control. *Employee Relations,* **Vol. 28, No. 4, pp374–386 (2006)**

In this article the authors draw on extensive semi-structured interviews and sessions with a focus group made up of staff employed in an NHS trust. Their aim is to explore employees' perceptions of flexible working practices, having been asked by the trust's HR department to investigate why so few staff were taking advantage of the extensive range of flexible working options available to them. They found that most staff were unaware of formal flexible working policies and did not see them as being relevant to them. However, by contrast the interviewees expressed considerable interest in and satisfaction with informally arranged flexible working practices.

Questions

1. Why were the staff in this trust unaware of the range of flexible working opportunities available as part of formal P&D policies?

2. Why did they see these policies as being irrelevant to them?

3. Why were the informal practices of so much greater interest?

4. What practical lessons can be learned from this research about ways of introducing more flexible working opportunities in organisations?

REASONS FOR INCREASED INTEREST IN FLEXIBILITY

Organisations have always sought to achieve a degree of flexibility. For centuries workers have been laid off (either permanently or temporarily) when business levels dipped, and offered premium overtime rates to work additional hours during periods of peak demand. Moreover, as Pollert (1987, 1998) has shown, employers have always shed subcontractors and peripheral workers first. What is new is the propagation of flexibility in the form of a model intended to guide management actions. In other words, it is the idea that organisations should deliberately develop core and peripheral structures as part of a considered strategy that represents a departure from past practice.

People have different ideas about why interest in this subject should have grown so greatly over the past two decades. In truth, the reasons are many and varied, encompassing several of the major contextual developments outlined in Chapters 2, 3 and 4. The following list of factors draws on the analyses of Blyton (1998), Bryson (1999), Heery and Salmon (2000) and Reilly (2001):

*   Companies must be able to respond to increased volatility in product markets. Globalisation and e-commerce mean that businesses are required to expand and contract more frequently in order to compete in markets that become more unpredictable every year.

*   New technologies have provided more scope for businesses to act opportunistically in response to customer demands. Smaller production runs are possible, as is the production of bespoke goods and services, meaning that flexibility is becoming more central to the achievement of competitive advantage.

*   Ongoing interest in established Japanese management techniques has also fuelled interest in flexibility. The Japanese have long used approaches that are similar to that advocated in Atkinson's model. Functional flexibility for core workers employed on a long-term basis is a particular feature of the traditional Japanese approach.

*   The decline in the size and influence of trade unions over the past 20 years has made it easier for managers to introduce a greater degree of flexibility. There are less resistance to change and fewer demarcation disputes.

- Increased female participation in the labour market, together with greater interest in work–life balance issues, has meant that a greater proportion of potential employees are looking for atypical working arrangements.

- Encouragement from successive governments seeking to create 'flexible labour markets' is a further factor. Both the New Labour and previous Conservative administrations sought to minimise unemployment by encouraging economic dynamism. Responsiveness to change and a high degree of efficiency are central components of this, along with encouragement of 'lifelong learning' and measures to remove barriers preventing people from participating in the workforce.

- A tendency towards short-term thinking in financial markets has been demonstrated through an increased emphasis on maximising shareholder value. This, it is argued, leads managers to think in terms of short-term horizons. Long-term commitment to individuals is thus less necessary than it used to be in order to develop a financially successful organisation.

- The growth of private service sector employment as a proportion of the total, together with the evolution of a '24-hour society' are also cited as factors. This kind of employment, by its nature cannot be of the traditional 9–5 variety. Customers need to be satisfied when they want to be satisfied. This requires far greater flexibility on the part of suppliers of services.

PRODUCTIVITY AND FLEXIBILITY

EXERCISE 7.1

Read the article by Lynda Gratton, Feel the burnout (*People Management*, 15 July 2004, page 22). This can be downloaded from the *People Management* archive on the CIPD's website (www.cipd.co.uk).

In this excellent opinion piece, Lynda Gratton concludes that there is a very strong case for much more flexible working in the United Kingdom and in other Western economies, but that this is rather more difficult to achieve in practice than many people think. Unless we become a great deal more productive as an economy, she argues, flexible working of the kind that employees like will not be available for most.

Questions

1   What are the major arguments in favour of flexible working?

2   Why are so many managers reluctant to move in this direction?

3   What are the implications of globalisation for the United Kingdom's prospects of expanding flexible working?

4   To what extent do you agree with Lynda Gratton's conclusion about the way forward for UK industry?

FUNCTIONAL FLEXIBILITY

Most writers on functional flexibility focus on developments in manufacturing, where change in this field has been most pronounced, but the principles are equally applicable in all industrial sectors. A programme aimed at increasing an organisation's functional flexibility is essentially one that promotes multi-skilling. The aim is that people should increase the range of tasks that they are willing and able to perform. This may involve learning to carry out colleagues' jobs, it may involve picking up duties currently carried out by either their bosses or their subordinates, or it may involve developing new skills that are anticipated to become more significant in the future.

Greater functional flexibility is associated with the following processes:

- The number of different job descriptions in an organisation is reduced (ie less demarcation between jobs).

- More teamworking, so that instead of employees A, B and C undertaking tasks 1, 2 and 3 respectively, all work together on all three types of task.

- Hierarchies are flatter, with fewer levels of grades defined by the type of work that is performed, and more people employed on the same grades carrying out the full range of activities.

- Job rotation helps ensure that as many people as possible are familiar with as many roles as is practicable.

It is probably best understood by illustrating how an organisation suffers when it is not functionally flexible. The following example from the past is provided by Reilly (2001, p50):

> A maintenance electrician would not adjust a bolt on a pipe; a mechanical craftsman would not isolate a piece of equipment. Neither of them was trained to assist production, and the operators, for their part, would not take on any craft duties.

The advantages of creating a functionally flexible workforce are evident. First, it means that people can be deployed where they are most needed at any particular time. If one area of activity is busy and another slack, multi-skilled employees based in the slack area can be moved to the busy area. This is an efficient use of staff and should mean that overall headcount can be minimised. It also makes it easier to cover for absence and lateness. Not only are costs saved, it also means that customers are served more quickly and to a higher standard. Second, it allows faster response to change. If one area of the business grows, there is a ready supply of people familiar with its operations able to transfer over without needing extensive training.

There are, however, potential drawbacks as well. First of all, improving functional flexibility is costly. Training programmes have to be organised for larger numbers of people than in an organisation with clear lines of demarcation between jobs. In addition, there are administrative costs associated with recording skills learned and organising job rotation systems. Second, there may be resistance to overcome, particularly where staff have been employed with the expectation that they will be specialising in one line of work. Forcing them to multi-skill against their will can then easily lead to dissatisfaction and the loss of good performers to competitors. Third, it is possible that some skills are too complex or specialised to be shared by several people. Forcing the pace then leads to dilution, a group of people each of whom is unable to carry out the job as effectively as one highly-trained individual with long experience.

Introducing functional flexibility is thus something that has to be carried out with care. Employees need to be involved as much as possible, and their legitimate concerns about its effect on them addressed sensitively. It is also important to accept that there are limits to functional flexibility and that it must be introduced within reasonably defined parameters. In many organisations it is neither practicable or desirable for everyone to be able to carry out everyone else's job.

BEING FUNCTIONALLY FLEXIBLE

The author's first job after leaving university was a graduate traineeship with a hotel chain. The scheme started with each management trainee being posted to a large city-centre hotel for six months and spending a few weeks working in each department. The idea was that by the end all would be basically proficient in the tasks undertaken by all staff in the kitchen, restaurants, housekeeping department, banqueting suite, bar, reception desk and so forth.

Unfortunately for the trainees the scheme worked rather too well for their own sanity. By the end of the six months they were able to undertake just about any job in the hotels to a reasonable standard. The temptation to deploy them where they were most needed at any one time became too great for managers. As a result instead of moving on properly to the next stage of their training (ie

gaining experience of management activities), they were forever being called down to help out wherever it was busy at any particular time. Much time that was supposed to be devoted to gaining experience of sales management or finance or P&D was thus actually spent serving breakfast, checking people in or making up rooms. Sometimes they would even be called away for weeks on end to work at other locations where high-profile conferences were being held and additional staff were needed.

The problem arose because the graduate trainees were the only genuinely multiskilled people employed in the hotels. How much more efficient they could have been if many more staff had been given the opportunity to move from job to job in the same fashion.

NUMERICAL FLEXIBILITY

While functional flexibility is principally intended to be promoted among the 'core' workforce, the peripheral workforce in the Atkinson model is defined in terms of numerical flexibility. The central contention is that employers seeking flexibility should employ people on different forms of 'atypical contract' so that they can deploy people where they are most needed at the times when they are needed. The extent to which different types of contractual arrangement are appropriate in different industries varies greatly. For example, part-time working is necessarily restricted in manufacturing industry because of the need to maintain a common shift system. Subcontracting, however is very common. In contrast, the use of fixed-term contracts has grown most in the public services, where funding to undertake specific projects is limited in terms of time. Such contracts are also used extensively by employers whose workload increases and decreases on a seasonal basis (eg in tourism and agriculture), and have necessarily become highly significant in sectors where most employees are female, as a result of the greater take-up of the right to maternity leave in recent years.

For the P&D manager, therefore, the most important questions to ask are the following:

- In respect of the particular industry and labour markets in which my organisation operates, what opportunities exist to increase the proportion of employees on non-standard contracts?

- What are the potential short and long-term advantages and disadvantages of doing so?

Clearly the answer to these questions will vary from situation to situation. What follows, therefore, is a brief survey of some of the factors that might need to be taken into account for each of the major categories of atypical work.

PART-TIME CONTRACTS

Part-time working is by far the most common form of atypical working. In the United Kingdom just over a quarter of the workforce are part-timers, 80 per cent of these being women (National Statistics 2006). Within certain sectors the figures are far higher. Over 40 per cent of all hotel and catering employees are women who work part-time; the figures for the health and education sectors are 51 per cent and 47 per cent respectively. By contrast, the numbers employed outside the service sector are considerably smaller, with a heavy concentration in clerical and secretarial roles. The biggest period of growth in part-time work was during the 1960s, when the proportion of the total workforce that worked part-time increased from 9 per cent to 16 per cent. After that it continued to rise steadily, along with the overall female participation rate, but has begun to fall slightly since 2004.

In past decades there were clear incentives for organisations to employ two part-timers instead of one full-timer. This resulted from an inequality of treatment in legal terms, whereby part-timers could be denied pension scheme membership and other fringe benefits and had to wait five years before they were entitled to bring cases of unfair dismissal. In the 1990s the courts ruled such practices to be indirectly discriminatory towards women, leading to several legislative amendments. Then in 2001 the UK government implemented the EU's Part-Time Workers Directive, which makes any discrimination on the grounds that someone works part-time potentially unlawful. Treating part-timers less favourably than full-timers is thus now a risky approach to take. However, it remains the case that at the lowest pay levels part-timers often earn less than the lower National Insurance threshold, meaning that employers do not have to pay contributions when these workers are appointed.

There are two main reasons for the creation of a part-time post. The first, and most common, is to enable an organisation to respond more efficiently to peaks and troughs in demands for its services. Hence shopworkers are hired to work part-time on busy days or to cover the busiest hours of the day. The second reason is to respond to a demand from employees or potential employees for part-time jobs to be created. The most common situation in which this occurs is when a woman who has previously worked on a full-time basis wishes to return as a part-timer following her maternity leave. In many cases, organisations find ways of accommodating such requests, either by re-organising job duties or by advertising for another part-timer to share the job. However, generally speaking, the inflexibility of such arrangements makes them less easy to organise for managerial employees who need to be present throughout the week in order to supervise their departments effectively. Often a difficult choice has to be made between accommodating employee wishes in this regard or losing a valued member of staff. The presence of reputable childcare services can reduce the likelihood of this issue arising. Indeed there is evidence from the continent that suggests part-time working on the part of women with children is less common in countries where there is good and widely available childcare provision (Brewster *et al* 1993, p17).

Creating part-time jobs can thus bring considerable advantages to an organisation. It can reduce costs dramatically by making sure that people are present only when required, and can also attract well-qualified people who, because of childcare or other commitments, are looking for less than 40 hours' work each week. Other parts of the labour market to which employers can look include retired people and students in full-time education. Another possible advantage in some situations is the apparent lack of interest among part-timers in trade union activity.

There are of course potential disadvantages too. First, there is the possibility that part-timers, because of other obligations and the fact that theirs is often not the main family income, will show less commitment to their work than their full-time colleagues. The problem is potentially compounded by the lack of promotion opportunities open to them. Part-timers can also be inflexible in terms of the hours they work because of the need to honour their other commitments. They are often attracted to the job in the first place because they need to be guaranteed fixed weekly hours (eg 12.00–2.00, or Wednesdays and Thursdays) and will thus be either unwilling or unable to change these too much. There is also the more general issue of training investment. Where two or three part-timers are employed in place of one full-timer to undertake the same role, the training time and cost will be two or three times higher. A well-rooted myth about part-time workers is the notion that they are harder to retain than full-timers, a belief that presumably arises from more general perceptions of a lack of commitment. In fact, there is little evidence to support this perception, with 40 per cent staying with their employers for five years or more (IDS 1995c, p4).

LEGAL PROTECTION FOR PART-TIME WORKERS

The Part-Time Workers (Prevention of Less Favourable Treatment) Regulations came into force on 1 July 2000. They implement into UK law the 1997 EU Part-Time Worker's Directive. The rights apply to all workers irrespective of their length of service.

- Part-time workers who believe that they are being treated less favourably than a full-time colleague in a similar role can write to their employers asking for an explanation. This must be given in writing within 14 days.

- Where the explanation given by the employer is considered unsatisfactory, the part-time worker may ask an employment tribunal to require the employer to affirm the right to equal treatment.

- Employers are required under the regulations to review their terms and conditions and to give part-timers pro rata rights with those of comparable full-timers.

- There is a right not to be victimised for seeking to enforce rights under the part-time workers regulations.

The regulations define a 'part-time worker' as someone who works fewer hours a week than recognised full-timers do in the organisation in question.

Any term or condition of employment is covered, as is any detriment at work (like access to training, promotion or redundancy selection). The major exception built into the regulations is overtime payments. Part-timers only have the right to enhanced hourly rates when they work more hours than is usual for full-timers in the organisation concerned.

Tribunals are free to award whatever compensation they consider to be 'just and equitable in the circumstances'.

TEMPORARY CONTRACTS

The term 'temporary worker' covers a variety of situations. On the one hand there are staff who are employed for a fixed term or on a seasonal basis to carry out a specific job or task. This category includes well-paid or senior people such as football players or public officials, as well as individuals brought in to undertake more ordinary work on a fixed-term basis. A second group are people who are employed temporarily but for an indefinite period. Their contracts thus state that they will be employed until such time as a particular project or body of work is completed. Again, this category can encompass well-paid individuals such as TV presenters and actors, in addition to those occupying less glamorous positions. A third category includes temporary agency staff who are employed via a third party to cover short-term needs.

Currently in the United Kingdom 5.6 per cent of all employees are contracted to work on a temporary or fixed-term basis, but the figure rises somewhat during the summer months as a result of seasonal work in the tourism and agricultural sectors (National Statistics 2006). The number of such workers tends to fluctuate with economic conditions, so we saw a rise in the early 1980s, followed by a slight reduction, before the figure rose steeply again in the early 1990s. It has now been falling back again from the peak of 1.8 million who were employed on temporary contracts in 1998. Since then the only group to have grown in number is those working for agencies on a temporary basis (ie agency temps). As with part-time working, there is very great variation between the different industrial sectors, the service and agricultural sectors accounting for a high proportion of the total. As many as 10 per cent of public sector staff are now employed on a fixed-term basis, with some positions, such as those of researchers in higher education, now usually paid for through one-off grants or single allocations of funds.

While somewhat dated, the Department of Employment's Employer's Labour Use Survey (ELUS), carried out in 1987, provides a good summary of the great variety of reasons employers have for employing temporary staff:

- to give short-term cover for absent staff (55 per cent of employers)

- to match staffing levels to peaks in demand (35 per cent)

- to deal with one-off tasks (29 per cent)

- to help adjust staffing levels (26 per cent)

- to provide specialist skills (22 per cent)

- to provide cover while staffing levels are changed (19 per cent)

- because applicants request temporary work (8 per cent)

- to screen for permanent jobs (4 per cent)

- because temporary workers are easier to recruit (4 per cent)

- to reduce wage costs (1 per cent)

- to reduce non-wage costs (1 per cent).

    (Source: McGregor and Sproull 1992, p27)

From the employer's perspective there is thus a number of compelling reasons to consider offering fixed-term contracts to certain groups of staff. They are particularly useful when the future is uncertain, because they avoid raising employee expectations. It is far easier, when departments close or businesses begin to fold, not to renew a fixed-term contract than it is to make permanent employees redundant. During the run-up to redundancies it is also useful to be able to draw on the services of temporary staff to cover basic tasks, freeing permanent employees who are under threat of redundancy to spend time seeking new jobs.

A note of caution is needed for those with responsibilities for the employment of staff in other EU countries, because a number have considerably greater restrictions on the employment of temps than is the case in the United Kingdom and the Irish Republic. In Italy, for example, the number of temporary workers is relatively small, despite the presence of a substantial tourism sector, because the law restricts the ability of employers to offer temporary work. Unless it can be shown that the employment has been offered to cover absence or to deal with a temporary increase in workload, it can be declared unlawful. Moreover, fixed-term contracts can stand only for three months (or six months if the work is seasonal), and temporary employment agencies are illegal. Other countries have less rigorous laws, but most have legislated in some way to discourage temporary employment (Brewster *et al* 1993, pp20–22). In the United Kingdom, the level of regulation is restricted to the requirements of the EU's Fixed-Term Worker's Directive, which was introduced into our law via the Employment Act 2002. This aims to protect people from being treated adversely at work simply because they work on a temporary contract. It also requires employers to notify their temps of any permanent vacancies, and limits the number of times that a fixed-term contract can be renewed without good reason. Since July 2006 if someone has been employed on a fixed-term basis for four years or more, their contracts can become permanent unless the employer is able to provide objective justification for a continuation of the existing contractual arrangements.

KEY ARTICLE 15

Kevin Ward, Damien Grimshaw, Jill Rubery and Huw Benyon, **Dilemmas in the management of temporary work agency staff.** *Human Resource Management Journal*, Vol. 11, No. 4, pp3–21 (2001)

In this article the authors explore a range of HR and employee relations issues arising from increased use of agency temps. Drawing on extensive numbers of interviews with managers and employees in two large private sector organisations, they set out a variety of reasons for the increased use of temporary staff, discuss some of the consequences, and at the end, question the business case for and long-term sustainability of a P&D strategy which relies on the heavy usage of agency temps.

Questions

1   What were the major reasons for increasing the number of temporary staff supplied by agencies in the two companies studied?

2   What problems arose?

3   To what extent is it possible to sustain a P&D strategy which has as a central component the employment of large numbers of temporary staff? Why?

SUBCONTRACTORS

Apart from the use of temporary agency workers, subcontracting comes in two basic forms. First, there is the use of consultants and other self-employed people to undertake specific, specialised work. Such arrangements can be long-term in nature, but more frequently involve hiring someone on a one-off basis to work on a single project. The second form occurs when a substantial body of work, such as the provision of catering, cleaning or security services, is subcontracted to a separate company. The latter form is examined in the later section on outsourcing (see pages 172–179). Both varieties have become more common in recent years, leading to a rise in the number of agency employees and self-employed people.

One per cent of the total workforce (270,000) now work as agency staff, and a further 13 per cent are self-employed (Forde and Slater 2005, p249; National Statistics 2006, p23). Self-employment is focused in the fields of technical and professional services, the majority of self-employed workers being relatively well-paid men. Most of the traditional professions provide opportunities for self-employment, but the highest concentrations are in the fields of draughting, design engineering, computing and business services. According to the ELUS survey described above, the main reasons given for using self-employed subcontractors were as follows:

- to provide specialist skills (60 per cent)

- to match staffing levels to peaks in demand (29 per cent)

- because workers prefer to be self-employed (28 per cent)

- to reduce wage costs (9 per cent)

- because the self-employed are more productive (8 per cent)

- to reduce non-wage costs (6 per cent)

- to reduce overheads (4 per cent)

- other reasons (11 per cent).

(Source: McGregor and Sproull 1992, p27)

Again, the figures in parentheses represent the percentages of employers stating that the reason was one of significance in their use of subcontractors who are self-employed. As with temporary workers, it is interesting how cost-cutting opportunities appear to be so much less significant than the need to bring in specialists. This may be because, hour for hour, the employment of a self-employed contractor is often a good deal more expensive than hiring a temporary employee. Even when the absence of National Insurance and pension contributions is taken into account, along with other on-costs associated with standard employment contracts, it is usually more costly to bring someone in on a consultancy basis.

Aside from cost considerations, there are also other potential disadvantages from the employer's perspective. First, it is often suggested that self-employed people, like agency workers, inevitably have less reason to show a high level of commitment. They have no long-term interest in the organisation and are thus less likely than conventional employees to go beyond the letter of their contracts. In turn this leads to suspicions about the quality and reliability of the services they provide. Only where there is a clear possibility of an ongoing relationship in the form of further work does the contractor have a serious economic incentive to overservice the client. Such a perception is of course a generalisation and is probably unfair to the majority of self-employed people, but organisations have to take such thoughts into consideration when considering whether to subcontract work and to whom. In some situations there is no choice, because all the specialists in a field have chosen to work for themselves. One such example is in parts of the computer industry, where people with expertise in particular programs or operations know that they are in a sellers' market and that they can earn more, while keeping control of their own working lives, if they take up self-employed status.

Another possibility to consider, which is relatively common now, is the rehiring of retired employees on a self-employed basis. Both parties stand to gain from such arrangements where the retired person has a reasonable income from his or her pension. The company draws on organisation-specific expertise, but pays for it only when there is a particular demand. The retired person draws a pension and supplements it by undertaking a modest amount of work when he or she wishes to.

HOMEWORKING

The employment of people to work either wholly or partly from home is another trend which has aroused the interest of researchers. We are not looking here at self-employed people or casual workers, but at people whose contracts of employment are standard in other respects. The extent to which this kind of arrangement currently occurs is not easy to state with certainty because many people work from home only for a proportion of their time, but according to government statistics there are around 3 million people who work from home all or most of the time. This represents 8 per cent of the total UK workforce (National Statistics 2006, p24), but includes within it self-employed people – a very considerable number of whom work from home. Interestingly the number of employees who are based at home is very small indeed – around 200,000, a further 350,000 being mobile and working some of the time from home (IDS 2005a, p2). This is surprising given the potential for growth with the expansion of computerised communication technology and improvements in telecommunications.

For the employer, the main advantage is a reduction in the size of premises required. Savings are thus made in terms of office rents, business rates, heating and lighting. The main disadvantages relate to the low morale that homeworkers often suffer as a result of their isolation from co-workers. A different kind of supervision is thus required, along with control systems that assess performance on the basis of the quantity and quality of each batch of work undertaken. Because it is clearly not possible to oversee each individual's work, there is no opportunity either to encourage or correct when mistakes are made or when the pace of work slackens. As yet there is little specific employment law concerned with protecting the rights of homeworkers. However, campaigns are launched from time to time by trade unions and other bodies concerned about low pay and lack of employment protection, so it is reasonable to expect that legislation may soon be introduced along continental lines. This will ensure that homeworkers enjoy the same terms and conditions as other employees and the same access to training, and that they are offered the full range of fringe benefits. There is also a strong case for bringing homework stations within the ambit of organisations' health and safety responsibilities.

The biggest problem in managing a home-based workforce is the maintenance of effective communication – a particularly important issue where members of the 'core' workforce are employed on a teleworking basis. If such arrangements are to work, more is needed than simple electronic communication. There is also a need to hold regular team meetings, as well as face-to-face sessions between supervisors and staff. In practice, as has been pointed out, most homeworking of this kind is carried out part-time, the employee performing some work at the office and some at home. When managed well, this can provide the best of both worlds, in that effective communication is retained while savings in terms of office space and energy use are also achieved. Of course, this can occur only if employees forgo the privilege of having their own office or desk at work and accept 'hot-desking' arrangements, whereby they occupy whichever workstation or computer terminal is free when they are not working at home.

EXERCISE 7.2

AA

Read the following two articles from *People Management*, which can be downloaded from the *People Management* archive on the CIPD's website (www.cipd.co.uk):

- Andrew Bibby, Home start (10 January 2002, pp36–37)

- Catherine Edwards, Remote control (16 June 2005, pp30–32).

The first article describes the ups and downs of the Automobile Association's (AA's) experiences of employing call-centre workers on a homeworking basis. Aside from initial technical problems, the company found that the main issue was the need to adapt its approaches to people management.

The second article reflects more generally on the advantages and disadvantages of introducing homeworking, suggesting ways of helping to ensure it works effectively.

Questions

1   Why did the AA decide to employ call-centre workers on a homeworking basis?

2   What were the major problems it encountered?

3   How has it had to adjust management practices in order to make the new approach work effectively?

4   What other steps could be taken to improve the situation?

TEMPORAL FLEXIBILITY

A form of working arrangement that, evidence suggests, is becoming more common involves a move away from setting specific hours of work. While such contracts come in several different forms, all help in some way to match the presence of employees with peaks and troughs in demand. They thus help ensure that people are not being paid for being at work when there is little to do, while at the same time avoiding paying premium overtime rates to help cover the busiest periods. Three types of arrangement are common: flexitime, annual hours and zero-hours schemes.

FLEXITIME

The most common, and least radical, departure from standard employment practices is the flexitime scheme. Precise rules vary from organisation to organisation, but generally involve employees' clocking in and out of work or recording the hours they work each day. Typically such schemes work on a monthly basis, requiring employees to be present for 160 hours over the month, but permitting them and their managers to vary the precise times in which they are at work in order to meet business needs and, where possible, their own wishes. Often such schemes identify core hours when everyone must be at work (eg 10–12.00 and 2–4.00 each day), but allow flexibility outside these times. It is then possible for individuals who build up a bank of hours to take a 'flexiday' or half-day off at a quiet time.

The number of situations in which flexitime can operate and in which it is appropriate to do so are quite limited. Clearly, it is not a good idea where the presence of a whole team throughout the working day is important. It would thus not be used for roles where there is direct contact with customers or where a manufacturing process required a large number of employees to be present at the same time. It is also inappropriate where organisational objectives and culture focus heavily on the maximisation of effort and the completion of specific tasks. In such workplaces, the hours worked are often long, and there is a need to encourage employees to concentrate more on the achievement of goals and less on the actual time they are spending at work. Hence flexitime would be inappropriate for newspaper journalists, because the hours worked are inevitably determined by the requirement to chase and write stories. In any case, the whole idea of clocking in or recording hours worked on a time sheet is seen by many organisations as undesirable in itself and representative of an approach to management from which they wish to move. According to IRS (1997a, p7), this was the major reason for the abandoning of flexitime by Cable and Wireless after privatisation in 1981. Its objection was the way in which the system 'symbolised a relationship between management and employees far removed from the one to which it aspired – namely one based on trust and shared responsibility'.

However, flexitime remains in many organisations – particularly where large numbers of clerical and secretarial workers are employed to look after a range of different bodies of work. Where deadlines are relatively unimportant, where individuals have responsibility for carrying out a prescribed range of tasks, and where there is no requirement to be available to members of the public all day long, there is a good case for using flexitime to maximise organisational efficiency. This is because it cuts out the need to pay overtime and keeps the overall headcount to a minimum. It is thus unsurprising that it is mostly used in government departments, local authorities and other public sector organisations. In the private sector it is used mainly in larger financial services companies for clerical staff working in back-office roles.

ANNUAL HOURS

A more radical form of flexitime is the annual hours contract. The principle is the same, only here the amount of time worked can vary from month to month or season to season as much as from day to day. A significant difference from typical flexitime systems is that variations in hours are decided by the employer, without much choice being given to the employee. Each year all employees are required to work a set number of hours (usually 1,880), but to come in for much longer periods at some times than others. Pay levels, however, remain constant throughout the year. Again, from the employer's point of view, the aim is to match the demand for labour to its supply and thus avoid employing people at slack times and paying overtime in busier periods. Variations can occur seasonally or monthly, or can follow no predictable pattern at all. In tourism or agriculture, where the summer is busy and the winter quiet, this can then be reflected in the time put in by employees. In an accountancy firm, where month and year-end reports need to be produced to tight deadlines, employees can then work long weeks followed by compensation in the form of shorter ones.

In the early 1990s, according to Brewster *et al* (1993), the incidence of annual hours schemes increased to a level at which they covered some 6 per cent of the UK working population. However, more recent figures (see Bell and Hart 2003) show a rather lower level of coverage at 4.5 per cent, strongly suggesting that the incidence of such schemes has not taken off as many predicted would be the case.

Their relative scarcity is interesting when their potential advantages from the perspective of both employers and employees is considered. In part, this is explained by the presence of similar objections as those described above in the case of flexitime, but there are also practical difficulties. A major problem concerns what to do when an employee leaves, having worked only during a slack period, but having also drawn the full monthly salary. It can also be difficult to predict the supply of work, so that an organisation ends up either paying overtime anyway or employing more people than it actually needs to cover the work. However, where such issues can be overcome, annual hours can be attractive to employees, leading to lower levels of staff turnover and absence.

EXERCISE 7.3

THE CASE FOR ANNUAL HOURS

People management

Read the article by Kevin White, Year we go, year we go (*People Management*, 17 June 2004, p23). This can be downloaded from the *People Management* archive on the CIPD's website (www.cipd.co.uk).

In this article Kevin White puts a strong case for the adoption of annual hours systems, but he also considers the main reasons that they are not adopted in practice despite the potential advantages. He concludes by suggesting some possible solutions.

Questions

1   What are the main strands of the case for the adoption of annual hours systems?

2   Why are managers and staff often resistant to changing established rostering systems?

3   What approaches are suggested in order to gain support for annual hours systems among staff?

ZERO HOURS

At the other end of the scale is the zero-hours contract, which organisations use in the case of casual employees who work on a regular basis. They are most suitable for situations in which there are frequent and substantial surges in demand for employees on particular days or weeks of the year, but where their instance is unpredictable. An example is the employment of couriers in the travel industry. A company needs to have a body of trained courier staff it can call on to look after clients, but is unable to predict exactly how many it will need and on what dates. It therefore hires people on a casual basis, gives them training and then calls on their services as required during the holiday season. Another common example is the employment of waiting staff for banquets and Christmas parties in hotels and restaurants. Because the staff involved have no great expectation of substantial amounts of work, they usually combine casual employment with other activities. Many have other jobs too, or are in full-time education. Employers can thus not always rely on their availability at short notice and have to ensure that enough trained people are kept on their books to cover their needs at any time.

A variation on the zero-hours approach is a system that guarantees casual employees a minimum number of hours a week or days a year. IRS (1997a, p8) reports that Tesco uses such an approach in some of its stores. The company guarantees employees between 10 and 16 hours' work a week, but then adds to this if the workload increases or in order to cover absences among non-casual employees. The core guaranteed hours are fixed week by week, but additional hours are flexible and can be arranged as little as a day in advance.

OUTSOURCING

A form of flexibility that appears on the outermost peripheral circle of Atkinson's flexible firm model is 'outsourcing', a topic that has attracted a considerable amount of interest over the past ten years. In the literature the term is usually defined in one of two subtly different ways. Some see at as involving the purchase from external providers of services that could be carried out internally, while others are more specific in referring to the provision of activities that were previously carried out internally. In fact outsourcing covers both types of situation and more besides. At one end of the spectrum it is more or less synonymous with subcontracting: an organisation purchasing a service from another which is better placed to provide it. At the other, as is shown by Kakabadse and Kakabadse (2002, p31), it takes the form of a franchising arrangement or joint venture, with a supplier taking over the running of core business functions. They give the example of the Virgin Group, which has regularly entered into agreements 'whereby they provide the brand name and marketing flair and the other parties, the production facilities and capital'. For our purposes we will take the term to describe the situation in which an organisational function that is customarily carried out on an in-house basis by the organisation's own employees is instead purchased from a specialist provider.

In itself, like most features of the flexible firm model, outsourcing is not remotely new. Indeed, historically it was a good deal more common than is now the case. Smaller firms, in particular, have long found it necessary, and indeed desirable, to buy in certain services rather than hire employees to carry them out on their behalf. This is because they are not large enough to be able to justify the employment of specialists such as lawyers, accountants, maintenance engineers or IT staff. Some important new features are, however, clearly discernible:

- the widespread use of outsourcing by larger private sector companies

- substantial increases in the extent to which public sector organisations buy in externally provided services

- the development of a view that sees the decision to outsource a function as a central plank in an organisation's business strategy

- the extent to which organisations are prepared to replace established in-house functions with externally provided alternatives, often involving large-scale redundancies.

As far as the United Kingdom is concerned, there is extensive and compelling evidence to show that outsourcing is a form of flexibility which has become much more common in the past two decades. Colling (2005, pp93–95), drawing on statistics from the Workplace Employment Relations Surveys, government figures and other studies shows that there were very substantial extensions of outsourcing during the 1990s. Kersley *et al* (2006, pp105–106) show that the trend has continued in the first years of the twenty-first century, but they also balance this by recording many instances of previously outsourced functions being brought back in-house. Their figures show that 16 per cent of workplaces contracted out a service in the previous five years, but that 11 per cent had also insourced a service that had previously been subcontracted.

The main areas in which outsourcing occurs are as follows:

- cleaning premises

- security services

- building maintenance

- transport of documents/goods

- catering

- computing advice and maintenance

- legal services

- market research.

Almost half of the recent growth in outsourcing in the 1990s originated in the public sector and was the direct result of government requirements to introduce forms of competitive tendering (Reilly 2001, p33), but much was also accounted for by decisions taken in private corporations. Several different reasons have been put forward to explain the trend. First, we have seen an increased desire on the part of organisations to focus efforts on 'core activities', by which is meant those activities that are the source of competitive advantage. It follows that where a 'marginal activity' such as security, maintenance or cleaning can be effectively provided externally, it makes good business sense to employ a specialist company to provide such services. This frees the organisation to throw all its energy into seeking and maintaining competitive advantage over its rivals. Stredwick and Ellis (2005, pp147–148) give the following example to illustrate this point:

> British Airways has taken this policy to the extreme in the 1990s, looking at every activity to see if it can be outsourced. The airline's core activity is regarded as flying passengers, not as providing their meals, moving their baggage or seeing to their security. All these are ancillary activities and can be put out to tender if suitable contracts can be negotiated. In 1997 BA transferred 85 per cent of its ground fleet services staff (415 employees) to outsource provider Ryder under a five year deal. The airline believes it can now concentrate on building its flight network, increasing its reliability and serving its customers.

Another way in which competitive advantage can be promoted through outsourcing is in the achievement of substantial cost savings. This arises because of the economies of scale that are achieved by the providers of the outsourced services and is, according to Kakabadse and Kakabadse (2002, p18), the most common reason that organisations give for considering outsourcing existing activities. A large, well-established, specialist provider of catering or security services is often able to provide as good a service (or a better one) than can be achieved by a far smaller, internally run department. They have access to the newest and best equipment, are able to offer superior professional training, and can readily replace staff who leave or go absent. Moreover, because they are obliged to compete for the contract to provide the service, they have an incentive to keep costs as low as possible by maximising the efficiency of their operations.

Expertise in the provision of ancillary services also leads to reduced costs. Colling (2000, p71) makes the point that organisations often have 'little idea of the market rate for such activities', typically relating the pay of the staff employed to carry them out to established payment systems for core employees. In doing this, they commonly end up paying higher rates than is necessary given labour market conditions. This is particularly true of the public sector, where ancillary staff are frequently paid a great deal more than people carrying out equivalent roles on behalf of specialist private sector service providers. Where outsourcing has occurred, according to the Audit Commission, savings of 20 per cent or more have readily been achieved (see Stredwick and Ellis 2005).

It is not surprising, therefore, that successive governments have used outsourcing as means of reducing public expenditure. Under the Conservatives the terms used were 'compulsory competitive tendering' and 'market testing'; under Labour we have moved to 'best value' and 'private finance initiatives'. All in their different ways involve the state (or local government institutions) seeking ways of reducing costs by hiring private sector companies to undertake certain activities. Of course, the contracts are sometimes won by the existing public sector providing units – but only after a process in which they are obliged to compete with outsiders for the right to continue their activities. Under the current government, outsourcing of public sector activities has been extended well beyond the provision of ancillary services. Moreover, it has been suggested that private sector companies should be contracted to build and run NHS hospitals on behalf of the Department of Health, while firms specialising in education management should be invited to bid for the right to run state schools. Similar policies are also being extended into fields that have always been considered to be central obligations of the state. Privately managed prisons and a privately run air traffic control service already exist, while the armed forces are engaged in negotiations with private sector companies to provide equipment and training for their personnel. In the future it will not be unusual for airforce personnel to be trained by defence contractors and to fly planes that are leased from the contractors by the government. The airfields and ground maintenance crews will also all be managed by private sector suppliers.

A third major reason for outsourcing is the opportunity it gives organisations to make use of services that are provided at the desired level of quality without having to achieve this themselves. When an outsourced service is considered to be operating unsatisfactorily, providers can be warned that they will lose the contract if they do not make immediate improvements. It is great deal easier to issue such a threat than it is to manage an in-house performance improvement programme. All responsibility for achieving quality standards (along with the hassle) is passed to the supplier. The extent to which this theory operates in practice is a moot point. There have been many criticisms made of the quality standards achieved by private sector contractors operating in some public sector organisations, while private sector employees often suspect that efficiency (ie cost savings) are in fact more important than quality criteria in determining which firms win contracts to supply ancillary services.

A fourth reason for increased outsourcing activity in recent years simply derives from the fact that there is more opportunity for organisations to contract out their non-core activities. The growth during the past two decades of companies

Table 7.1 Reasons for contracting out and contracting in

Reasons for contracting out	
To achieve cost savings:	47%
To improve services:	43%
To focus on core business activities:	30%
To achieve greater flexibility:	10%
Due to government regulation or policy:	2%
Reasons for contracting in	
To achieve cost savings:	57%
To improve services:	51%
Sufficient in-house capacity:	8%
Staff/union pressure:	1%

Source: Kersley *et al* (2006, pp105–107).

specialising in the provision of such services is itself a factor in the trend. It was not so easy 20 years ago as it is now to find a good external supplier of security or catering services, and there was less competition between the providers who were in business. Now we have large (even international) operations that are very efficiently managed, and that have access to equipment, expertise and personnel that make them a great deal more attractive as potential service suppliers. In a sense, therefore, the process has developed its own momentum. The bigger the outsourcing industries get, the more able they are to supply services at the price and of the quality that organisations require.

PROBLEMS WITH OUTSOURCING

The theoretical case for outsourcing is readily understood and compelling from a management point of view. However, survey evidence suggests that the reality often disappoints in practice. Outsourcing a function, particularly where it is well established internally, is a problematic experience for many. According to Reilly (2001, p135), the following difficulties are common:

- legal disputes over the meaning of contractual terms

- inability of organisations to manage the relationship with contractors properly

- poor levels of service

- communication difficulties between client and contractor

- problems in evaluating/monitoring performance levels achieved.

At base there is the fundamental issue of a difference of interest between the two parties. The client (the outsourcer) wants a decent level of service provided on an ongoing basis at a reasonable cost. By contrast, the contractor has a desire to maximise profits and reduce its costs wherever possible. In Reilly's view this often 'imperils the whole venture'. Where contracts are agreed on a fixed-price basis, contractors tend to 'skimp on the service as much as possible' by interpreting service level agreements quite narrowly. Conversely, where the price is variable, the client being billed according to the amount of work done in a particular week or the type of services provided (a cost-plus contract), contractors try to 'gild the lily' by overstaffing and providing too good a standard of service. Promises are often made (or half-made) during the negotiation process that do not subsequently materialise in practice, and it is frequently difficult in practice to develop a really fruitful, high-trust relationship between the two parties.

Were there perfect competition in the outsourcing industry such problems would be rare, but when contracts are signed for periods of five years or more following tendering exercises the two parties are obliged to work together. It is not easy, in practice, to ditch one contractor and immediately employ another. Aside from practical problems, legal action can easily ensue, with the courts having to decide on the correct interpretation of particular contractual terms. In addition, of course, there is a range of employee relations and regulatory issues that prevent the swift despatch either of an internally provided service or one staffed and managed by an external contractor. Such processes often result in redundancies and are, of course, governed by the requirements of the Transfer of Undertakings Regulations.

There is also some question over the extent to which outsourcing exercises save money in practice. The 1998 Workplace Employment Relations Survey (cited by Reilly 2001, p136) found that costs had fallen as a result of outsourcing in only a third of the cases reported by respondents. This is because there are costs associated with outsourcing that are not immediately apparent. An example is the complexity of the contracts that need to be drawn up between the client and the contractor. Stredwick and Ellis (2005) state that 'contracts can, almost literally, weigh a ton', running to hundreds of pages even for the provision of quite straightforward services. These are often major deals worth millions over several years. Hence there is a need to involve firms of commercial lawyers in drafting, and subsequently interpreting, agreements. Further problems occur when contractors are not as viable commercially as they appear during the tendering process. The highly competitive nature of the businesses in which they operate means that margins are necessarily tight. Even if there are no problems at all with the performance of the contract in your organisation, your provider may have to pull out or re-negotiate terms because of difficulties in other organisations that they supply. It is not uncommon for service providers to fold altogether, leaving the client with no service at all.

Finally there are problems that result from the organisation forfeiting control over the outsourced functions. From a P&D perspective, this means losing control over who is hired to undertake roles, the approach used to performance

---

KEY ARTICLE 16

Mari Sako, Outsourcing and offshoring: implications for productivity of business services. *Oxford Review of Economic Policy*, Vol. 22, No. 4, pp499–512 (2006)

This article focuses in detail on the ways in which productivity is enhanced as a result of outsourcing services to specialist providers that were previously provided in-house. It goes on, in rather less detail, to look at the offshoring of services to providers based in other countries where lower wages can be paid. By focusing on the figures for employment growth and productivity growth in different types of outsourcing business, the author poses an interesting question about the future of outsourcing. The article is particularly interesting from a P&D perspective because HR outsourcing is used as an example to illustrate many of the points made.

Questions

1   Why has employment in the business services sector grown so much in recent years?

2   Why has this sector become so much more productive?

3   In the context of future business strategy for business service providers, explain why there is a tension between focusing on the provision of 'customised services' and 'standardised services'.

management and the management of discipline and dismissal for unsatisfactory staff. Where problems arise (absence, lateness, poor service provision and so on), solving them is outside the control of the purchasing organisation. It can complain and put pressure on the contractor to address the issue, but cannot deal with the problems itself. Where outsourced services have a direct impact on the effective performance of core functions, this loss of control can be a major drawback that has severe negative implications for the business.

Colling (2005) stresses the significance of employee relations and the way that they are often damaged as a result of outsourcing. Low trust follows and, often, a reduced willingness to be flexible and work beyond contract.

OUTSOURCING P&D FUNCTIONS

Despite the presence of a great deal of hype in the P&D press about the outsourcing of P&D departments, survey evidence shows that the vast majority of employers in the United Kingdom have not chosen to take this path. IDS (1999, p14) is right to complain about a dangerous tendency for commentators to mistake a few high-profile examples for an 'inexorable trend'. In fact, as is demonstrated by a recent major CIPD survey into developments in HR provision (CIPD 2007e), the big majority of UK organisations continue to provide all the core HR activities in-house. Moreover, in recent years there have been several examples of large corporations contracting HR services back in house (Pickard 2007). There has been some growth in the extent to which the payroll function has been contracted out in recent years, while organisations seem more willing to draw on external expertise when recruiting and training people, but there is nothing new about this at all. The truth is that organisations have long drawn on external providers in a range of P&D support roles and they continue to do so. A number of these are directly relevant to the material covered in this book. The most commonly outsourced areas in the United Kingdom are the following:

- training
- recruitment
- payroll management
- safety and security monitoring/advice
- occupational health services
- legal advisory services
- childcare facilities
- employee welfare and counselling services.
- pre-employment testing
- HR information services
- salary surveys
- benefits

- relocation

- organisational development.

Despite the patchy rate of expansion, it is true that there has been greater interest recently in the idea of outsourcing HR. It is also the case that organisations have given greater consideration to the possibility. We are seeing, for example, moves in some larger organisations towards the establishment of a 'shared services model' for P&D. This means that the function is set up as a separate business within the organisation and is required to sell its services to other business units. P&D departments in this position are not being outsourced, but the arrangement is a step in that direction and does require them to compete with external agencies for business. The other development that is clearly recognised in the literature is the trend for businesses that are too small to retain the services of P&D employees to buy in specialist advice from outside providers. Whereas previously such organisations would have used an external pension provider and payroll administration service, they are now increasingly likely to purchase a wider range of advisory services externally. The growth in the volume of employment legislation partly explains this trend, but it also derives from the greater presence of consultancies specialising in HR issues.

Other factors may also explain the growth in interest in HR outsourcing. Reed (2001, p120) sees globalisation as a significant factor. The need to expand operations internationally leads to the employment of overseas workers by employers who are not familiar with prevailing employment rights and customs in foreign countries. They are therefore obliged to hire external advisors. Another factor, according to IDS (2000b, p2), is the development of new technologies:

> The increasing sophistication of HR software is enabling more routine elements of HR work to be automated. The parallel advance in corporate intranet technology is also transforming the ways in which line managers and employees can access HR information. But the investment that these developments entail in building and maintaining IT systems has led some employers to seek specialist suppliers capable of delivering this new model of HR administration on their behalf, while freeing up core HR staff to concentrate on more strategic issues.

There are therefore good reasons for believing that larger organisations might outsource more P&D activity in the future than they have in the past. However, it is likely that in most cases this will be restricted to basic administrative matters that have no role in adding value. Going much further, for example by using an outside agency to run all HR affairs, may well be dangerous and is opposed by the CIPD (see Pickard 2000, p50). Far from allowing flexibility, such arrangements are often rather inflexible as the purchasing company is obliged to accept whatever standard package of services the contractor is set up to provide.

EXERCISE 7.4

ACCENTURE AND BT

Read the article by Jane Pickard, Should I stay or should I go? (*People Management*, 25 March 2004, pp31–36). This can be downloaded from the *People Management* archive on the CIPD's website (www.cipd.co.uk).

This article describes the experiences of BT following its decision in 2000 to outsource much of its HR administration to Accenture. The deal was initially set up as a joint venture, but BT sold its stake in 2001, so Accenture now provide the service to BT entirely on a subcontracted basis. This was a five-year deal, so BT's managers had to decide in 2005 whether to continue the existing arrangement, outsource to another company or take back some of the functions to provide on

an in-house basis. In the event, they decided to sign a further agreement with Accenture. The article describes many of the problems that were encountered during the first years of the outsourcing arrangement.

Questions

1   What features of this particular outsourcing deal gave it a good chance of succeeding?

2   What were the major problems encountered? What was their cause?

3   What changes were made some years into the arrangement to make it work better?

CRITICISMS OF FLEXIBILITY

The above discussion shows that there are many disadvantages as well as advantages associated with flexible working practices, and these probably account for the rather modest moves towards the flexible firm model undertaken by employers in practice. Those who have made a good living out of predicting revolutionary change in this area appear to have been proved wrong, at least for the time being. However, there remains a school of thought that supports the ideas associated with flexibility and argues that we should be moving in that direction a great deal faster than we are. Advocates of greater flexibility believe that there will be no other way to compete in a post-industrial world, and that organisations that do not maximise their flexible capabilities are likely to founder when facing competition from others that do. This is by no means a view that is universally shared. Many take issue with the central thesis of those arguing in favour of flexibility, and put forward compelling arguments in support of their position. The major strands of the critical case are set out below. All are characterised by a tendency to equate the concept of 'flexibility' with that of 'employment insecurity'. Readers seeking more detailed treatments of these debates are referred to two excellent books of articles edited by Heery and Salmon (2000) and Burchell *et al* (2002).

The major management objection to the principles of the flexible firm model relate to its supposed incompatibility with high-commitment P&D practices. It is argued that organisations cannot have it both ways in this regard. They cannot, on the one hand, create a situation in which human resources are deployed as and when required so as to maximise short-term efficiency, while on the other requiring staff to exhibit a high degree of commitment. It is argued that flexibility, because it creates insecurity, is associated with low commitment on the part of employees. In consequence, staff turnover rates will be higher in flexible firms, while employees are less likely to perform above and beyond the basic requirements of their contracts. There is more likely to be cynicism on the part of staff and less identification with the aims of the organisation. The result, over the long term, is a low level of performance, resulting from the presence of unenthusiastic staff and recruitment and retention difficulties. In short, the suggestion is that people who perceive themselves to be peripheral to the operation (a large proportion in the flexible firm model) will act accordingly.

A development of these points forms the second major strand of the argument against flexibility. This relates to the health of the national economy as a whole, with important implications for individual organisations. It is argued that a situation in which all organisations evolve into flexible firms will have negative long-term consequences for the country. First and foremost, there is concern that in flexible organisations employers tend to seek staff who are already trained, and refrain from developing people themselves. Why invest in training people who are classed as peripheral and with whom the organisation expects to have a relatively short-term relationship? Ultimately the result will be (and some would argue already is) a situation in which there are chronic skills shortages. The result is reduced output as employers find themselves unable to take up business opportunities and, over time, economic decline. Instead, the critics argue, employers should be actively encouraged (or even forced) to invest in people with whom they expect to have a long-term relationship. It follows that the best interests of economy over the longer term are met by expanding rather than contracting the size of the 'core' in the Atkinson model.

A third strand of argument brings in ethical considerations. The concern here is that managers will inevitably be tempted to use the development of a peripheral workforce to exercise too great a degree of power. People who perceive their position at work to be precarious are understandably keen to seek greater security. Peripheral workers will thus try, wherever they can, to gain admittance to the core. This, it is argued, gives employers considerable leverage over them – power that can easily be abused. The result is a situation in which managers intensify work to an unacceptable degree, require people to work longer hours than is good for them and generally exploit their vulnerability. From a management perspective, such a situation is only viable in the short term. Over time the organisation's reputation in the labour market slips, making it harder to recruit and retain people. It can potentially also lead to legal action where levels of employer-induced stress lead to ill health.

A fourth set of arguments is more political in nature, but also carries important implications for organisations. The suggestion here is that widespread adoption of the flexible firm model will lead to a more unequal society (even more unequal than it currently is). We will see a clearer evolution of two distinct classes of employed persons, one of which consists of people in secure, well-paid employment, while the other is composed of insecure, peripheral people. The result will be (and many would argue already is) a substantial rise in crime, in the incidence of family breakdown and in political alienation – all outcomes that arise when society becomes less socially cohesive. This in turn requires government intervention, which necessitates higher taxation and less demand for privately produced goods and services.

EMPLOYABILITY AND MUTUAL FLEXIBILITY

On the surface it appears that two irreconcilable positions have been summarised in this chapter. On the one hand, there is a strong commercial case for moving towards greater flexibility on the grounds that it brings with it greater efficiency and the ability to cope well with change. On the other, there are serious arguments against such a trend, based on the long-term harm that results from the creation of insecurity. How, if at all, can these points of view be reconciled and a sound conclusion be reached?

First of all, it is necessary to accept that the term 'flexibility' as developed in Atkinson's model of the flexible firm covers several very distinct types of employment practice. Not all of these are necessarily equated with insecurity. Indeed, functional flexibility is fully associated with the employment of 'core' workers with whom a long-term association is desirable, while many other practices are potentially as attractive to employees as to employers. The main examples are flexitime, part-time working and homeworking, but it is clear from the experience of people working in the IT industry that subcontracting is also a form of relationship that some find both comfortable and profitable. It is important, therefore, not to tar all forms of flexible working with the brush of 'insecurity'.

Second, there is merit in the argument that, in a changing world, staff have more to gain in the long term from improving their 'employability' than they do from remaining in employment with one organisation. The argument is based on the presumption that no job can be particularly secure in the contemporary business environment because technological developments are evolving at such a great a speed. It follows that none of us should expect to remain employed in the same occupation through to retirement and that our best hope of remaining in work is to build up a portfolio of varied experience on which to draw as and when required. New opportunities should thus be welcomed and not feared, because they are the source of our future employability.

Looking at the issues from this perspective it is possible, at least in theory, to argue that it is possible for organisations to become more flexible while at the same time avoiding the generation of additional insecurity. Such a conclusion is reached by Reilly (2001) in his work on the concept of 'mutual flexibility', by which he means forms that bring benefits to both employees and employers. Central to Reilly's argument is the role of partnership and negotiated changes. Involving staff in decision-making about greater flexibility, and taking their concerns on board, is a good way of ensuring that the interests of both employer and employee are properly addressed.

In addition it is argued that employers should focus their attention on the types of flexible working practice that employees appreciate. Those that breed perceptions of insecurity, such as zero-hours contracts and the widespread use of fixed-term contracts, should thus be avoided except where they are strictly necessary. Moreover, functional flexibility should be promoted as an alternative to the numerical and temporal forms where it is in the interests of employees that it should be. Finally, there should be a genuine commitment on the part of employers seeking more flexibility to enhance their people's future prospects (their employability) by actively developing them through the provision of relevant training and experience. In these ways insecurity can be minimised and sustainable flexibility maximised.

EXERCISE 7.5

WORKING AT FLEXIBILITY

People management

Read the article by Rebecca Clake, How to make flexible working work (*People Management*, 11 January 2007, pp48–49). This can be downloaded from the *People Management* archive on the CIPD's website (www.cipd.co.uk).

In this short article the author makes a series of practical and very sensible suggestions for how an organisation should go about introducing greater flexibility if it wants to maximise the chances of its objectives being met.

Questions

1   What are the major benefits that can be gained as a result of introducing flexible working?

2   What situations can arise which hinder the success of flexible working initiatives?

3   How can these be avoided?

CHAPTER SUMMARY

- Increased volatility in the competitive environment together with other factors have led to increased interest in flexible working practices during the last 20 years.

- There have been marked, but not dramatic, increases in the employment of people on atypical forms of contract in recent years. These are international trends that have not disproportionately affected the United Kingdom.

- The major forms of non-standard contracts are part-time, fixed-term, temporary, subcontracting and homeworking. The major practical forms of temporal flexibility are flexitime, annual hours and zero-hours arrangements.

- The past two decades have seen a substantially increased trend towards outsourcing of non-core activities. The public sector has been particularly affected.

- Increased interest in outsourcing P&D activities has not, as yet, been borne out in practice. There remain, however, compelling reasons for organisations to consider taking such an approach in the case of routine administrative matters.

- The concept of flexibility and the model of the flexible firm have been subjected to substantial critical scrutiny. Arguments against the usefulness of the approach reveal many weaknesses as well as strengths.

EXPLORE FURTHER

- The topic areas looked at in this chapter are covered in several recent books. Among the most useful are *Flexible working* by John Stredwick and Steve Ellis (2005) and *Flexibility at work* by Peter Reilly (2001).

- Several textbooks contain articles looking at forms of flexible working, their advantages and disadvantages. These include work by Bryson (1999), Campos E Chuna (2002) and Colling (2005).

- Critical perspectives are well covered in the books edited by Heery and Salmon (2000) and Burchell *et al* (2002), and in articles by Allen (2000) and Ward *et al* (2001).

- Outsourcing is debated effectively by Baron and Kreps (1999), Kakabadse and Kakabadse (2002) and IDS (2000b). In recent years each February *People Management* has published a special supplement focusing in detail on HR outsourcing issues.

- Case studies of flexible working in practice are provided by Edwards and Robinson (2001) and IRS (2001a). In addition, IDS has published a series of studies focusing in detail on the experience of organisations introducing different types of flexible working. Recent studies have covered flexitime, annual hours, teleworking and the outsourcing of the HR function (see IDS 2002a, 2002b, 2002c, 2003a, 2005a, 2006a, 2006b and 2006c).

CHAPTER 8

Job analysis and job design

Once the need for additional employees has been identified, a series of distinct steps has to be taken before the new people are both established in their jobs and performing satisfactorily. Two of these, namely soliciting applications and employee selection, account for a substantial portion of the resourcing specialist's work, and are covered extensively in the following four chapters. Here the focus is on the other tasks and processes that need to be completed, in some shape or form, if human resource plans are to be effectively realised.

Effective job analysis has long been considered to be the essential foundation of any 'good practice' approach to the recruitment and selection of staff. Systematic analysis of the duties that make up any vacant or newly created job, it is argued, allows recruitment and selection to proceed, drawing on objectively gathered information about the attributes required of the job-holder. It thus minimises the extent to which recruiters allow subjective judgements to creep into their decision-making and helps ensure that people are selected fairly. Not only does this mean that unlawful discrimination does not occur (and is seen not to occur); it also makes sure that the best candidate is chosen for the job. In good practice, model job descriptions and person specifications are derived from job analysis and form the principal tools used by recruiters in devising their advertisements or briefing agencies, and by selectors in developing interview questions or interpreting the results of selection tests. In recent years, however, a rival good practice approach has achieved some prominence. Focusing on the attributes of the most effective performers in an organisation, competency frameworks also result in the formulation of recruitment and selection documentation using objective criteria. Both approaches are assessed in this chapter.

In the second half of the chapter our attention focuses to the different principles that can underlie job design and redesign exercises, processes that have to be carried out a great deal more often in a volatile business environment. Finally we look briefly at a relatively new idea, labelled 'job sculpting', which involves designing jobs around people rather than searching for people to fit pre-defined job requirements. This turns on their heads the established approaches described earlier in the chapter, but will it ever become at all widespread?

LEARNING OUTCOMES

By the end of this chapter readers should be able to:

- undertake job analysis

- write job descriptions and accountability profiles

- draw up person specifications

- advise on the establishment of competency frameworks

- debate the merits of competing approaches to job design

- argue the cases for and against job sculpting.

In addition, readers should be able to understand and explain:

- the principles underpinning job analysis

- critiques of traditional job-based approaches to pre-recruitment activities

- the Taylorist and humanist approaches to job design

MANAGING VACANCY SCENARIOS

For many years P&D professionals have accepted an established view of what constitutes 'good practice' when an organisation decides to recruit new employees. This traditional approach is best understood as a process comprising a series of defined stages linking job analysis (the starting point) with employee induction (the final stage). It is illustrated on the left-hand side of Figure 8.1.

The later stages of the traditional approach are generally accepted to be necessary, although there is a good deal of debate about how exactly they should be carried out. Most critical attention in recent years has been focused on the earlier stages, namely job analysis and the subsequent development of job descriptions and personnel specifications, which many academics and consultants now see as being outdated. Yet this traditional approach remains by far the most common. IRS (2003b) surveyed 250 organisations, large and small, from across the public and private sectors and found that 82 per cent of employers continue to use job descriptions and 72 per cent person specifications.

The best articulated critiques have come from those who advocate the use of different approaches based on competency frameworks that are person-focused rather than job-focused. These, it is argued afford greater flexibility, require less administration and facilitate quicker and more effective recruitment decisions. Moreover, advocates contend that they are just as fair to potential candidates as

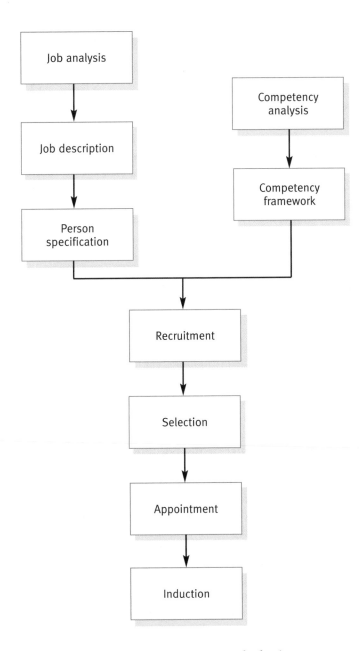

Figure 8.1 Stages in good practice recruitment and selection

the more established job-based approaches (see the right-hand side of Figure 8.1). However, competency frameworks themselves are not without their critics, some of whom have argued persuasively that they tend to produce workforces that lack diversity.

JOB ANALYSIS

Formal analysis of the jobs that make up an organisation can form the basis of much P&D activity. Apart from its role in recruitment and selection, which is our concern here, job analysis also has a central part to play in the determination of pay differentials, the identification of training needs, the setting of performance targets and the drawing-up of new organisational structures. Furthermore, without effective and objective job analysis as their foundation, it can be difficult to justify decisions in the fields of promotion, redundancy, disciplinary action for poor performance and changes in rates of pay. As such, while essentially being a technical administrative task, job analysis (also known as occupational analysis) can be convincingly characterised as a process that adds value to an organisation's activities.

> *Occupational analysis is a business investment – it requires considerable expenditure of funds, human effort, and time. These costs, however, can be amortized over a period of time, during which the data base can be used to avoid costs, tailor programs, increase efficiency and flexibility, improve quality control, and effect operational change. The data developed during occupational analysis can serve initially to validate existing programs, to document or articulate specific program needs, and to influence almost every aspect of the personnel management program within that occupation.*
>
> (Legere 1985, p1327)

In the fields of recruitment and selection, job analysis is important because it provides the information on which to base two documents: the job description and the person specification. The first summarises the tasks that make up a job, together with statements of reporting lines, areas of responsibility and performance criteria. The second identifies those human attributes or personality traits that are considered necessary for someone holding the job in question. Of course, it is quite possible to draw up written job descriptions and person specifications without first undertaking rigorous job analysis. Indeed, it is often the case that job advertisements are compiled and interviewing processes undertaken entirely without the assistance of these documents. However, in such cases, when no alternative is used, the likelihood that selection decisions will be properly objective and capable of identifying the most appropriate candidates for appointment is reduced.

Pearn and Kandola (1993, p1) see job analysis as a form of considered research, and define it simply as 'a systematic procedure for obtaining detailed and objective information about a job, task or role that will be performed or is currently being performed'. It is therefore a process, or a means to an end, rather than an end in itself. This definition is a general statement of what job analysis involves. In practice, a wide range of distinct approaches has been developed that analyse jobs in different ways and at different levels.

The first question to ask when approaching a job analysis exercise is, 'What type of information is sought?' Only then can appropriate decisions be taken on the method that will be used. If the analysis is to form the basis of personnel selection decisions, there is a need to focus not just on the tasks carried out but also on the skills deployed in the job, the equipment used and the environment within which the various activities are carried out. The Position Analysis Questionnaire, one of a range commercially produced for use as job analysis tools, gathers six distinct classes of information:

- the source of information used to perform the job

- the kind of mental processes used to perform the job

- the output expected and methods used

- the types and levels of relationships with others

- the physical and social context in which the job is performed

- other job characteristics and activities not covered by the above (eg hours, payment arrangements, level of responsibility).

Job analysis is thus not merely concerned with data on the content of a job or the tasks that it entails. It also looks at how each job fits into the organisation, what its purpose is, and at the skills and personality traits required to carry it out.

A number of distinct methods of gathering job analysis data are employed, some more straightforward than others. The most basic of all simply involves observing a job-holder at work over a period of time and then recording what has been observed. In most cases the observation is supplemented with an interview carried out at the same time or later to clarify points and gather information about mental activities that are less readily observable. The main drawback concerns the length of time it takes to get a full picture of the tasks carried out by any one job-holder. Where the job varies from one day or week to the next, with certain aspects only taking place occasionally, observation cannot be the main tool of analysis used. It is most appropriate in the case of straightforward jobs that are primarily physical and involve carrying out the same tasks in the same setting each day. One would thus expect to see observation used in the case of low-skilled manual work or in situations where the work, though more complex, is carried out cyclically, with each day's routine broadly resembling that of the next (eg shop assistants, nursery school assistants, clerical workers).

The great weakness of the observation method is the strong possibility that the individuals being observed are unlikely to behave as they usually do, given the presence of a job analyst. Some will feel threatened, others will be out to impress; few will find themselves able to ignore the observer and continue as if no job analyst were there. Some have suggested that this kind of distorting effect can be reduced if observers are carefully trained and then introduced to the workplace tactfully. The need is to build trust with those being observed and to tell them the purpose of the exercise. Another method used to reduce the distorting effects of observation is the use of video cameras placed at a discreet distance from the place in which the observee is working. Again, this may have an effect if the individuals concerned are well prepared, but is unlikely to render an altogether accurate picture of day-to-day work, because people inevitably alter their behaviour when they know they are being watched.

The second approach is the job analysis interview. Here trained analysts ask job-holders (as well as their supervisors and colleagues) to describe the job concerned, how it fits into the organisation and what it involves. Wherever possible, interviewees are invited to open up and discuss particular events or occurrences to illustrate the points they are making. Interviews also provide the opportunity to probe points made by job-holders and to clarify any areas of uncertainty. Information given can then be checked against answers given by colleagues and managers.

Here too there is always a danger that interviewees will 'talk up' their work in a bid to impress. They will downplay the more routine aspects of their work and seek to focus on the more interesting and significant parts. There is also a tendency for people to believe that they have greater authority and influence than they do actually enjoy – especially in situations where a degree of decision-making authority has been delegated but is still exercised under reasonably close supervision. Interviewees with a number of years' experience in the job being analysed are thus often less suitable than colleagues who have only spent one or two years in that role. As with work observation, it is possible to train job analysts to recognise such problems and to focus the attention of interviewees on the nuts and bolts aspects of what they do. Above all, it is important to make it clear that it is the job that is being analysed and not the individual's performance in the job. Where these approaches fail, another method used to ensure that individuals do not puff themselves up too much is to conduct a group interview with several job-holders at the same time.

Aside from the group approach, a number of specific job analysis interviewing techniques have been developed in a bid to overcome the problems described above and to ensure that only the most important information is gathered. One of these is known as the 'critical incident technique' and involves focusing the attention of interviewees on only those aspects of their jobs that make the difference between success and failure. The starting point here is a study of the key job objectives, so a critical incident interview always begins by establishing with the interviewee the central performance indicators or outcomes that are expected of any job-holder. The interview then proceeds with the interviewee's being asked to describe actual events or incidents that resulted in key objectives' being either met or not met. In addition to describing the critical incident, interviewees are also asked to describe the background and to state specifically what their own contribution to the outcome was. The advantage of this approach is that it forces the people being interviewed to think about specific occurrences and not to dwell on general points. As a result, far more detailed and specific information is gathered to help the analyst build up a picture of what the most significant job tasks are, the environment in which they are performed and what type of behaviours determine the extent to which success is achieved.

Another method that focuses on key aspects of jobs, but that requires a greater level of training, is the repertory grid approach. It involves first compiling a list of the tasks that form part of a job and then comparing and contrasting each task with the others in terms of the skills or abilities needed to carry it out effectively. Random pairs or trios of tasks are usually selected and analysed by job-holders, their supervisors and other colleagues until no new information on the skills required to perform the job is forthcoming. The lists of tasks and skills are then placed at right-angles to each other on a repertory grid so that each skill can be rated in terms of its significance to the achievement of each task (a very simple illustrative example is shown in Table 8.1). A seven or five-point rating scale is usually used, a score of 1 indicating that the skill is not relevant to the accomplishment of a task and 5 or 7 signifying that the skill is crucial or essential to its successful completion.

Computer programs can then be used to analyse the scores and to establish which skills or personality attributes are most important overall. This part of the process goes beyond job analysis to the development of person specifications, but that does not negate the potential usefulness of the earlier stages as analytic tools. As with the critical incident approach, through breaking the job down into its constituent parts and reflecting on the detail of each, the process is made more structured, thorough and objective than is the case with a straightforward interview.

The third commonly used approach is the administration of a prepared job analysis questionnaire. While it is possible for employers to develop their own, many either adapt or directly administer a proprietary scheme that they obtain a license to use. The more reputable providers also give training in the use of the questionnaire and in its analysis. Where the jobs involved are not too unusual, this approach is probably the most efficient and straightforward to use. Because all interviewees are asked identical questions there is less opportunity for interviewer bias to creep in, and so there is a higher level of objectivity than is the case with observation or conventional job analysis interviews.

There are a number of questionnaires on the market, two of which are very well-established: the Work Profiling System and the Position Analysis Questionnaire. All the better products contain hundreds of questions and have been developed using data gathered from a very broad cross section of job types from a number of industries. Most are now computerised, which greatly speeds up the analysis of data collected, and permits the generation of reports summarising key tasks and the competencies that are most important to perform the job successfully. They also have the advantage in that where 'yes/no' answers are inappropriate, a series of descriptive statements is provided from which the most appropriate response can be chosen. The following examples come from the Medequate Job Analysis Questionnaire developed by KPMG for use in the NHS.

Why do people seek advice from the job-holder?

i)   First point of contact (the job-holder is readily available).

ii) Recognised authority (the job-holder is the first source of advice within

Table 8.1 An example of a repertory grid for an office receptionist

Duties	Skills/competencies							
	Sensitivity to customer needs	Ability to plan own work	Good spoken communication skills	Reliability	Ability to analyse straightforward data	Typing skills	High level of personal presentation	Initiative
Open and close premises	1	1	1	5	1	1	1	4
Maintain filing system	1	4	1	5	4	2	1	4
Order office supplies	1	5	2	5	3	1	1	4
Deal with telephone enquiries	5	1	5	3	4	1	1	4
Welcome visitors	5	1	5	3	4	1	5	4
Type documents	1	3	1	4	5	5	1	2
Postal distribution	1	4	1	5	5	1	1	4
Arrange appointments	4	4	5	4	3	1	2	2

a particular function and can handle standard/routine requests for advice within their particular field. The job-holder would pass on detailed/difficult/out of the ordinary requests to a senior authority).

iii) Senior authority (the job-holder would handle more involved/out of the ordinary requests for advice leaving the more routine requests to subordinates).

iv) Acknowledged expert/specialist (the job-holder is a respected source within an area of expertise/specialism; only in exceptional circumstances would the job-holder need to refer to a higher source or a second opinion).

v) Ultimate authority/expert (as a result of experience and authority, the job-holder is seen as the organisation's ultimate source of information in a certain field and would be expected to provide expert advice within their own specialty; the job-holder would be consulted in all the most difficult/complex cases).

Describe the nature of the majority of the decisions taken by the job-holder.

i) Straightforward choices (little scope for decision-making, eg yes and no answers).

ii) Few and well-established (the decisions made will be few in number and will follow well-established procedures or precedents).

iii) Many and well-established (decision-making will be frequent and over a wide range of topics, but each decision will follow well-established procedures or precedents).

iv) Unprecedented (decision-making will be over a wide range of topics but will often be outside existing procedures and no precedents may exist).

Organisations also employ other methods of job analysis that do not fit into any of the three broad categories identified above. These include asking individuals to complete work diaries detailing the tasks they complete each day, the use of documentary evidence such as performance appraisal results and training manuals, and consultation with experts in particular fields. In most cases these methods will be insufficient in themselves, but may well assist in so far as they back up or contradict the results of job analysis exercises using the more conventional approaches. The use of panels of experts is particularly useful when a job that does not yet exist is to be analysed. In these circumstances, where there is no job-holder to question or observe, there is no real alternative but to ask well-informed people what the key job tasks and competencies are most likely to be.

REFLECTIVE QUESTION

Which of the above approaches would you consider to be most appropriate to employ when analysing complex, senior job roles?

EXERCISE 8.1

HOLLYWOOD FILM-MAKERS

People management

Read the article by Angus Strachan, Lights, camera, interaction (*People Management*, 16 September 2004, pp44–46). This can be downloaded from the *People Management* archive on the CIPD's website (www.cipd.co.uk).

This article relates one person's experienced but subjective view about the attributes required in film directors, production co-ordinators and assistant directors working in film production in Hollywood.

Questions

1　If a formal job analysis was to be carried out for the roles of production co-ordinator and assistant director, for what purposes could the results be used?

2　Which method (or combination of methods) of job analysis would you recommend in order to gain sufficient data to develop a useable job analysis profile?

3　What practical problems would you anticipate and how might these be overcome?

JOB DESCRIPTIONS

A written job description or job summary is the main output from the job analysis process. As has been stated, it can form the basis of a variety of decisions and processes across the range of P&D activity, including the drawing-up of training plans and the determination of pay rates. However, it is no less important in the staffing field where, once compiled and filed, it is used in five specific ways:

- **As a tool in recruitment.** Job descriptions are used to assist in the writing of job advertisements and will be given to agents hired to undertake all or part of the recruitment process. Copies are also typically sent to people who enquire about specific jobs, along with application forms and person specifications. IRS (2003b, p43) found that over 75 per cent of employers include copies of job descriptions in application packs and that 82 per cent use them when drawing up job advertisements.

- **As a tool in selection.** Decisions about whom to employ from among a range of possible candidates can be taken with reference to job descriptions. This helps ensure that there is a clear match between the abilities and experience of the new employee and the requirements of the job.

- **As the basis of employment contracts.** Frequently organisations make specific reference to job descriptions in their contracts of employment. They can thus have an important legal significance if someone is dismissed for failing to reach expected performance standards or resigns and claims constructive dismissal after being unreasonably told to undertake duties that lie outside the terms and conditions of employment. IRS (2003b, p44) found that nearly 40 per cent of employers (53 per cent in the public sector) make direct reference to job descriptions in their contracts.

- As part of an employer's defence in cases of unfair discrimination. Where an individual has been refused employment or promotion and believes that this is on account of direct or indirect discrimination, he or she may threaten the employer with legal action. The presentation in court of a job description can then be used as part of a case to establish that the selection decision in question was carried out objectively and that other candidates were judged to be more suitable than the complainant. As is so often the case with employment law, the existence of evidence of this kind is most important in so far as it deters people from bringing actions in the first place.

- As a means by which the employer's expectations, priorities and values are communicated to new members of staff. Statements can be included in job descriptions that make clear what the employee is expected to achieve and how he or she will be rewarded for so doing.

Job descriptions are among the best-established institutions in the P&D field. As a result, a consensus has grown up about what they should include and the level of detail that should be used. They thus vary surprisingly little from one organisation to another in terms of style and coverage. Typically the following headings are included:

- job title

- grade/rate of pay

- main location

- supervisor's name/post

- details of any subordinates

- summary of the main purpose of the job

- list of principal job duties together with very brief descriptions

- reference to other documents (such as collective agreements) that may clarify or expand on other items.

Most will also include a date at the end indicating the point at which the document was last updated. In most cases they will also include some kind of general statement indicating that other duties may be carried out by the job-holder from time to time. Where the job description is explicitly incorporated into the contract of employment, it is also wise to state that the content and reporting lines may be reviewed, and that they cannot be assumed to remain the same indefinitely.

ACCOUNTABILITY PROFILES

A problem with the format of job descriptions is the stress that is placed on the tasks that are performed by the job-holder. This, it can be argued, encourages people to think of their jobs as being made up of defined activities or duties, rather than to think in terms of what they are responsible for achieving for their employers. In response many organisations have moved towards the adoption of 'accountability profiles' or 'role profiles' that focus on achievement rather than a straightforward description of the job.

Armstrong (2003, pp198–199) advocates the use of such approaches, offering useful advice about the language that should be used in compiling the documentation and the methods that can be used to edit it down to a manageable length. He suggests that each item in the job description/accountability profile should relate to the 'outputs' or 'key result areas' that the job-holder will be expected to achieve or produce, and that each should therefore state what the job-holder can be held responsible for. Where a job task is performed under supervision, that should be clearly stated. Likewise, where there are deadlines to work to, those too should be included, or at least their existence recognised. Fine and Getkate (1995, pp2–3) go further in proposing that the language used should always refer to 'what gets done' rather than 'what workers do', on the grounds that this allows far more effective description and less room for ambiguity. So, rather than state that the job involves 'consulting' (ie what is done), the job description should use terms such as 'communicates with', 'explains', 'clarifies', 'discusses' or 'informs', which give a more precise meaning to the activity being described.

REFLECTIVE QUESTION

Do you have a job description or accountability profile? If so, which of the above items are included? How could it be improved?

EXTRACT FROM A JOB DESCRIPTION AND AN ACCOUNTABILITY PROFILE FOR A DOCTOR'S RECEPTIONIST

Job description
Main duties:

Opening and closing the premises

Checking heating

Reconnecting the regular telephone service

Opening and distributing mail

Answering general enquiries

Registering patients

Making appointments

Filing and extracting patient records

Receiving and logging samples

Accountability profile
Key result areas:

Ensures that the premises are opened on time and secured at the end of surgery hours

Checks that heating equipment is in working order and that correct temperatures are maintained

Reconnects the regular telephone service at the start of surgery hours

Opens all mail on receipt and takes responsibility for its prompt distribution to each doctor

Ensures that all enquiries are dealt with promptly and courteously

Completes all procedures associated with the registration of new patients

Accurately maintains appointment records

Ensures the accurate extraction and filing of patient records

Receives and logs all samples received promptly and accurately

PERSON SPECIFICATIONS

The second piece of documentation that is derived from the job analysis process is the person or personnel specification. Here the emphasis is not on what the job involves but on the attributes that are required of someone aspiring to fill the role. Effectively it lists the criteria the organisation proposes to use in short-listing and selecting an individual to fill the job concerned. Typically, person specifications include information under a number of headings such as skills, knowledge, personality attributes, education, qualifications and experience. Where the hours of work deviate from standard patterns or where the work is carried out on a number of sites, the ability and willingness to meet these requirements will also be included. It is also common for items in the person specification to be divided into 'desirable' and 'essential' characteristics.

The repertory grid method described above (see Table 8.1) is a useful tool to use in developing a person specification. An advantage is the way in which each attribute that is required by a job-holder is scored in terms of its significance to the achievement of each job task. These scores can then be added up to produce a list of attributes in rank order, providing a straightforward and objective means of establishing which are 'essential' and which are 'desirable'. However, in order to ensure an accurate outcome it is necessary to weight the tasks or duties according to their relative significance in the job. Otherwise attributes of relatively minor importance can easily be given undue prominence.

A further well-known, if somewhat dated, tool for drawing up person specifications is Rodger's seven-point plan, first published in 1952. This suggests that each of the following are considered:

- physical make-up
- attainments
- general intelligence
- special aptitudes
- interests
- disposition (personality)
- circumstances.

Munro-Fraser's five-fold grading system has a slightly different emphasis, but sets out to achieve the same broad objectives:

- impact on others (appearance, manner etc)
- acquired qualifications
- innate abilities
- motivation
- adjustment (stability, resilience etc).

It is unlikely that all of these points will be relevant for any one job, and some of the headings will be of significance only in the case of appointments to specialised roles. Nevertheless, the two systems taken together are useful as check-lists covering possible points to include, and can also be used in preparing questions to ask at interview.

That said, care must of course be taken to include in a written person specification only items that really are 'essential' or 'desirable' in someone appointed to a particular job. The presence of a professionally compiled document will be of no help in front of an employment tribunal when a case of unfair discrimination is brought by an aggrieved candidate who failed to be appointed or promoted to a new job. It is the responsibility of the P&D specialist to make sure that problems of this kind do not arise and that the items included can clearly be objectively justified.

IRS (2003b, p47) found that the following areas were covered in the person specifications used by the majority of their respondents:

- skills

- experience

- qualifications

- education

- personal attributes.

Interests and motivation are not included by the majority, but according to this survey are included by 40 per cent of employers.

DISCRIMINATION LAW AND PERSON SPECIFICATIONS

Care needs to be taken when developing person specifications that items included do not indirectly discriminate on grounds of sex or race. If they do, aggrieved job applicants who fail to be selected on these grounds can bring their case to an employment tribunal. Over the coming years, new grounds for discrimination claims are due to be added to the list with the adoption of the EU's Equal Treatment Directive: namely, sexual orientation, religious belief, political views and age. We are also likely to see a broadening of existing disability discrimination law to encompass the notion of indirect discrimination.

The P&D professional thus needs to ensure that any criteria included in a person specification, whether 'essential' or 'desirable' in job-holders, do not leave the organisation open to legal actions. In practice this means insisting that any criteria that is potentially discriminatory against a protected group is objectively justifiable. It must therefore be genuinely necessary for the performance of the job in question and not a device to benefit members of one group in the population.

Two reported cases are worth looking at in this regard. In Hussein v Saints Complete House Furnishers (1979) a firm limited recruitment to people living within certain postal districts of Liverpool. A tribunal ruled that this indirectly discriminated against certain ethnic minorities because applications from the postal districts in which they were concentrated were rejected. More recently, in Northern Joint Police Board v Power (1997), a senior police officer won his case having argued that he had been indirectly discriminated against on grounds of his national origin. Mr Power was an Englishman who had failed in his bid to be appointed as a chief constable because the appointment board thought it desirable that the post be occupied by a Scottish person.

PROBLEMS WITH THE JOB ANALYSIS APPROACH

Now we have put the case for detailed job analysis and the production of written job descriptions and person specifications, it is necessary to point out some of the drawbacks. One, which has already been alluded to, concerns the problems inherent in carrying out the analysis. Some argue that any exercise of this kind, even when its sole purpose is to support fair decision-making in recruitment and selection, is so difficult to achieve objectively that it is not an appropriate way to use organisational resources. According to this point of view, all the main methods used are deficient in some shape or form: observation, because of people's suspicion and their tendency to behave differently when being watched; interviewing, because of people's tendency to puff up their own importance; and questionnaires, because they are unable to include all aspects of a job role. The result, therefore, is inaccurate job descriptions and misleading person specifications, a bureaucratic procedure that takes up time and effort that could be more usefully employed elsewhere (see Searle 2003, pp44–48 for a detailed discussion of accuracy in job analysis).

The problem of inaccuracy is compounded in situations where jobs change in terms of their content, character or complexity. Where this occurs, the written job descriptions can very easily become outdated, with the result that they are of little or no use as the basis of a recruitment and selection programme (let alone the other P&D functions that draw on job descriptions). For organisations operating in fast-changing environments where job-roles evolve and re-evolve rapidly, the problem of obsolescence of job descriptions and person specifications means that their use is of questionable value. Aside from dispensing with detailed job analysis altogether, there are two methods that can be used to minimise this effect: regular updating and looser approaches.

REGULAR UPDATING

Once job descriptions for all positions have been established, each line manager can be asked formally to review their content on an annual basis. The best time to do this is when the individual job-holder is receiving his or her formal yearly appraisal. The process can then be tied in with a general review of the role, and the job description can anticipate future changes, rather than simply reflect those that have already occurred. However, this only seems to be done by a minority of organisations (IRS 2003b, p46). It is more common for updates only to occur at the time that a job becomes vacant.

FUZZY DESCRIPTIONS

Where jobs are genuinely subject to substantial, ongoing change, job analysis can be undertaken on a looser basis, with the result that job descriptions are couched in less precise language than is usually the case. Parker and Wall (1998, p102) describe this as making job descriptions 'fuzzy to allow for greater flexibility'. Instead of specifying the exact job duties and responsibilities, the focus is on the general level of the work and the degree of skill employed. So, instead of stating explicitly that the job involves supervising three administrators performing specific tasks, a more general statement is included simply making clear that the job-holder is expected to undertake supervisory duties across a more broadly defined field.

A third commonly cited drawback associated with job analysis and the development of written job descriptions relates to the fact that they may be used by employees as part of a case for refusing to follow reasonable management instructions. In other words, it is argued that people cannot say 'I'm not doing that – it's not in my job description' if they have no documentation to refer to. Linked to this is the suggestion that, where job duties are written down, managers are liable to be required to negotiate changes with employees or their representatives and that this tends to decrease organisational effectiveness. Again, this problem can be minimised to a great extent if care is taken in drawing up job descriptions and person specifications. Not only should clear and explicit reference always be made to the possibility that other duties may be undertaken from time to time, but the job description can also contain some reference to the possibility that duties will change over time and that the job-holder will be expected to co-operate where such changes are reasonable.

The fourth criticism is similar to one that is made about traditional approaches to human resource planning: namely that the perspective is job-based. There is an underlying assumption that organisations can usefully be seen as comprising a collection of identifiable 'jobs' into which people are slotted and remain until promoted or shifted sideways into another predesigned and discrete 'job'. A further associated assumption is that the 'jobs' are all to be offered on a standard contractual basis, identical in terms of hours, payment arrangements, holidays and other conditions of employment. Such thinking can be convincingly characterised as being inflexible as well as inefficient on the grounds that it encourages people to see themselves as employed 'in a job' and not 'for an organisation' or 'in a team'. At best this results in a narrow focus on particular job duties, at worst in an 'I know my place' attitude that prevents people from contributing all the skills and ideas that they could if encouraged to do so.

The job-based focus and inflexibility associated with job descriptions and person specifications derived from them may also serve to deter bright, flexible and ambitious people from taking up opportunities in the organisation. This is particularly so in tight labour markets where organisations have to offer jobs that match the requirements of individuals (rather than the other way around) if they wish to attract and subsequently retain them. Why work for an organisation that expects you to fit into its predetermined job structure when competitors offer more flexible roles that you have the opportunity to shape yourself?

COMPETENCY FRAMEWORKS

The major alternative approach to the job analysis/job description/person specification process involves the development of a competency framework that avoids many of the drawbacks set out above. 'Competencies' were famously defined by Boyzatis (1982, p21) as ' an underlying characteristic of a person which results in effective and superior performance in a job'. Competency frameworks are therefore not very different from person specifications in terms of their broad appearance and function. What makes them different is the way that they are developed and the fact that they can be generic to an organisation (or a part of an organisation) rather than specific to defined jobs.

A competency approach is person-based rather than job-based. The starting point is thus not an analysis of jobs (in the manner described above) but an analysis of people and what attributes account for their 'effective and superior performance'. This involves first identifying people in the organisation whose performance is consistently impressive vis-à-vis that of average performers. Personality questionnaires, interviews or a combination of both are then used to establish what attributes the high achievers share that differentiate them from other employees. The resulting profile is then used to inform recruitment and selection processes in the same way as a person specification derived from an analysis of job tasks. Repertory grid approaches can be used here too, along with interviews that focus on individual responses to 'critical incidents' that have occurred in the past.

The precise range of competencies that explain superior performance will clearly vary from job-role to job-role (particularly those that are skills-based), but it is often possible to identify competencies that are more broadly present among top performers, which can then be sought in all applicants for roles in the organisation. Some examples are given by Karen Moloney (2000, p44).

For companies launching on the Internet and experiencing rapid market growth and change, for example, competencies such as breadth of vision, opportunism and drive will be important. For firms rethinking their strategy in the face of stiff competition – Marks & Spencer, for instance – competencies such as mental toughness, attention to detail and prudence will be crucial.

Some organisations, notably those with Japanese parent companies, go a step further and base all their recruitment and selection on generic competencies of this kind, all but dispensing with skills-based criteria altogether. Personality attributes, and particularly attitudes towards work, are the major yardsticks used to judge the suitability of candidates. Recruiters want to be sure that the workforce shares the key characteristics associated with high levels of performance in current and previous employees. Having recruited people with these desired 'competencies', the employer then takes responsibility for equipping them with the skills they need to do the job. This turns established practice on its head because most organisations select primarily on the basis of skills, then subsequently use a variety of methods (performance management systems, reward systems and the like) to influence attitudes.

THE MOST COMMONLY SOUGHT COMPETENCIES

According to an analysis carried out by Wood and Payne (1998, p27), the most commonly adopted competencies in UK organisations were the following:

- communication

- achievement/results orientation

- customer focus

- teamwork

- leadership

- planning and organising

- commercial/business awareness

- flexibility/adaptability

- developing others

- problem solving

- analytical thinking

- building relationships.

EXERCISE 8.3

LOCAL GOVERNMENT MANAGERS

Read the article by Beverly Alimo-Metcalfe and John Alban-Metcalfe, Under the influence (*People Management*, 6 March 2003, pp32–35). This can be downloaded from the *People Management* archive on the CIPD's website (www.cipd.co.uk).

This article describes a major research project that sought to identify the competencies associated with effective managers in the local government sector. It provides an excellent case study of the competency-based approach in action.

Questions

1   Why do you think so many senior

managers in local government appear to lack the competencies their role requires?

2   To what extent would this change if recruitment and promotion processes were based around a competency framework rather than a job description/person specification approach?

3   How would you go about introducing a competency-based approach for this group of managers? What practical problems might you expect to meet when doing so?

CRITICISMS OF THE COMPETENCY APPROACH

Despite the many advantages associated with the use of competency frameworks as the basis for recruitment and selection, several significant criticisms have been made of this approach. Debates about these can be found in Wood and Payne (1998, pp29–33), Moloney (2000) and Whiddett and Kandola (2000).

The most persuasive critiques are those that suggest that competency-based recruitment and selection lead to a form of cloning, all new recruits tending to be similar types of people to those already in post. Over time there is a risk that everyone behaves and approaches problems in the same way. The advantages springing from the employment of a diverse group of people are thus lost. The result is less creative tension, fewer voices arguing for different ways of looking at things, and less innovative thinking. Whiddett and Kandola (2000, p33) show how in many organisations competency frameworks are reflected very strongly in job advertisements, leading to a situation in which people who could play an effective role, but do not share the defined competencies, are put off from applying. They are thus not even the given the chance to impress at the selection stage.

Another criticism is the tendency for competency frameworks to reflect what attributes were needed to be effective in the past and not those that the organisation needs to move forward in the future. This occurs because the methods used to identify the competencies (especially interviews with effective performers) inevitably focus on their past activities. Not only, therefore, is there a danger of recruiting 'clones', but clones whose attributes have been superseded by developments in the business context! Other criticisms reflect bad practice in the development of competencies rather than the method itself. They serve as a reminder that establishing a meaningful competency framework is a specialised and difficult task, but do not undermine the fundamental principles of the approach.

EXERCISE 8.4

GENDER BIAS IN COMPETENCY FRAMEWORKS

People management

Read the article by Julie Griffeths, Masculine wiles (*People Management*, 27 October 2005, pp20–21). This can be downloaded from the *People Management* archive on the CIPD's website (www.cipd.co.uk).

This article criticises the competency frameworks that are most frequently used by leading UK corporations in the selection of leaders and the identification of future leadership potential. They are one of the main reasons, according to the researchers quoted, that there are so few women on the boards of top companies.

Questions

1   In what ways do competency frameworks tend to echo 'masculine' leadership attributes?

2   What alternative attributes could be included?

3   What business case can be advanced for taking action in this field?

4   What, according to commentators quoted in the article, is the case for retaining existing competency frameworks?

REFLECTIVE QUESTION

Which competencies do you consider are shared by the better performers in your organisation? To what extent do these form the basis of recruitment and selection at present?

KEY ARTICLE 17

C. M. Siddique, Job analysis: a strategic human resource management practice. *International Journal of Human Resource Management,* Vol. 15, No. 1, pp219–244 (2004)

This is a rare example of an article reporting research which seeks to test the business case for carrying out job analysis. The author is based in Dubai and the research is based on a survey of companies in the United Arab Emirates. The underlying hypothesis is straight forward. Job analysis produces information that is subsequently used to underpin a variety of other P&D practices and decisions, and hopefully improves their quality in the process. If this is so we would expect to see a correlation between the use of job analysis and the performance of organisations.

The author goes further than this, however, in distinguishing between companies that use the conventional approach to job analysis and those that have adopted the competency approach. A variety of other factors are included too as moderating, control and dependent variables. The key finding was a strong positive association between 'proactive job analysis' and firm performance. However, the extent to which a competency-based approach is associated with superior performance was less clear from the results.

Questions

1 What measures of firm performance were found to be positively correlated with the presence in an organisation of job analysis?

2 How convincing do you find the research findings described here? How might the methodology be criticised?

3 What practical lessons can be learned from this research from the perspective of a UK-based P&D function?

JOB DESIGN

Job design, or job redesign as it is usually more accurately described, is concerned less with what is in a job or what its purpose is, and more with what duties should make it up. When a vacancy occurs an opportunity is often created to re-organise duties among a team, thus redesigning the vacant job. When an organisation expands it may be necessary to decide on the design of several new jobs, but the same process occurs whenever any major re-organisation occurs, following redundancies or a merger between two organisations for example. The more volatile and unpredictable the business environment, the more frequently jobs need to be redesigned.

Cordery and Parker (2007, pp190–192) identify six core features of work content which have to be determined for each job and which can be altered from time to time:

- scope (the breadth and level of the tasks carried out)

- discretion (the amount of control the employee exercises over the operational aspects of their work)

- variability (the extent to which a job remains the same day by day or is subject to flexibility)

- demands (workload as well as the physical and emotional demands placed on the job holder)

- feedback (the speed and effectiveness with which a job holder gains information on their level of performance)

- interdependence (how reliant on other team members the job holder is to perform tasks).

This is an interesting area of HRM to study, because the central debate about the best principles for managers to use when designing (or redesigning) jobs is one of the oldest in the field, dating back to the foundations of P&D as a management discipline and field of academic enquiry in the early twentieth century. Two distinct traditions, based on totally opposing principles can be identified. The first is known as the scientific management or Taylorist approach, after Frederick W. Taylor who pioneered these principles when designing jobs in the first factories to make use of large-scale production lines. The second is often referred to as the humanist approach, pioneered by managers who saw that a fundamental flaw in Taylorist principles was their tendency to dehumanise work.

TAYLORIST PRINCIPLES

The Taylorist approach to job design is systematic and very logical. It involves examining in great detail all the individual tasks that need to be carried out by a team of workers in order to achieve an objective. The time it takes to accomplish each task is calculated, and jobs are then designed so as to maximise the efficiency of the operation. In short an analyst works out on paper how many people need to be employed, carrying out which tasks and using which machinery. Waiting time and duplication of effort is minimised to reduce costs. Moreover, work is so designed as to minimise the number of more skilled people the organisation requires. This is done by packaging all the specialised tasks to form one kind of job, which is then graded more highly than others that are made up of less specialised, lower skilled tasks. The workforce is thus deployed with machine-like efficiency. Each plays a very defined role in a bigger process that is overseen, supervised, controlled and maintained by managers.

While originally developed in for use in engineering and car assembly plants, the principles of Taylorism live on and are still widely deployed. For example, call centres are very much organised along Taylorist principles, each employee having a tightly defined role and being responsible for hitting targets of the number of calls made or answered in each hour of work. The aim is to keep costs as low as possible given the expected throughput of work. The public sector too makes heavy use of Taylorist principles in designing and redesigning jobs so as to maximise efficiency. In recent years many skill-mix reviews have been carried out in hospitals, for example, the aim being to re-allocate duties between staff and achieve cost savings in the process. This is done by seeking to ensure that highly qualified (and highly paid) staff spend 100 per cent of their time carrying out duties that only they can perform. Lower skilled activities are then packaged together into jobs carried out by support workers. Similar approaches have been used in the police and in schools with the creation of more support roles, 'freeing' qualified teachers and police officers to focus on the more demanding tasks.

> **REFLECTIVE QUESTION**
>
> Skill-mix reviews in the public sector have often proved to be highly controversial and have been firmly resisted by trade unions and professional bodies. Why do you think this is?

HUMANIST PRINCIPLES

In the post-war era, a number of management thinkers began to challenge what had by then become a Taylorist orthodoxy. The major criticism made of scientific management was that it was dehumanising and therefore, ultimately bad for business. The argument was that the adoption of Taylorist principles led to the creation of jobs that were tedious, repetitive and unpleasant to perform. The result was a disengaged workforce and hence absenteeism, high staff turnover and the development of adversarial industrial relations. It also generally created resentment among people forced into workplace 'straitjackets', leading to low motivation and commitment, and hence poor performance. Some also wrote about sabotage of operations by disgruntled employees denied a 'humanistic' work environment (Fried *et al* 1998, p533). Moreover, more supervisors were needed than would be the case if people were positively motivated by the content of their jobs. Ultimately, therefore, Taylorism was not the most efficient approach over the long term, and an alternative set of principles were developed.

Instead of scientific management an approach evolved that draws on notions of intrinsic motivation and involves designing jobs that engage and even excite people. The alternative principles start with the idea that employees achieve higher levels of motivation, satisfaction and performance if the jobs they do are made more interesting and challenging. The key is to maximise the enjoyment that job-holders derive from their work. While it must be accepted that many jobs are never going to be highly enjoyable, it can be argued that managers should nonetheless try to design them in such a way as to maximise the satisfaction that the job-holders derive from them.

Traditionally, the main vehicles for achieving this have been job rotation, job enlargement and job enrichment. In each case, jobs are redesigned so as to make them less monotonous. Job rotation, for example, involves training employees to undertake a variety of jobs in an organisation so that different groups of tasks are performed on different days, weeks or months. In a manufacturing plant the rotation is likely to be daily or weekly, so that each employee works on different pieces of machinery and takes responsibility for different parts of the production process at different times. In other environments, perhaps where jobs take somewhat longer to learn, the rotation may be organised on a six-monthly or yearly basis. In each case the aim is to reduce the likelihood that people undertaking routine tasks become bored and uninterested in their work.

The use of job enlargement and job enrichment to improve workforce motivation are chiefly associated with the work of Frederick Herzberg (1966, 1968). Both approaches were defined as ones by which employees were given a wider variety of tasks to undertake, but in the case of job enrichment these required the acquisition of a higher level of skill. Hence, in addition to making jobs more interesting, enrichment also opens up wider developmental and career opportunities. Further, work carried out by Eric Trist and others (eg Trist *et al* 1963) led to the evolution of the socio-technical systems perspective on job enrichment, which sought to identify the key features needed in a job if it is to be motivating. In addition to a requirement for interesting work with opportunities for development and advancement, they stressed the importance of decision-making autonomy and discretion over the way the work is organised. The implication is that the less overt control is exercised over employees at work, the more motivated they will be and the higher their standard of performance will be.

According to Buchanan (1982), job enrichment had something of an 'unhappy history' in the 1960s and 1970s, with far more interest shown in its possibilities by academic researchers than by managers in organisations. However, in recent years interest has grown substantially, so that it is now very common to hear managers talking about empowering employees, developing new work roles, multi-skilling their workforces and refashioning reporting structures. Total Quality Management (TQM), a fashionable management philosophy of the 1980s and 1990s, also draws on many of these assumptions with its emphasis on self-supervision and the 'flattening' of management hierarchies. It is probably still the case that the rhetoric is more common than the reality, but the ideas that underpin job enrichment theories are now accepted with a great deal less scepticism than was the case 15 or 20 years ago.

One method of altering work arrangements to improve efficiency and quality that has received a great deal of attention is teamworking. The approach is derived from Japanese management practices and involves giving autonomous or semi-autonomous groups of employees responsibility for carrying out a particular task or group of tasks. How different elements of work are divided among them is a matter for the groups themselves to determine, so it is for them to decide how best to maintain high levels of motivation and performance. Job enrichment thus goes beyond the development of challenging roles and the reduction of direct management control to include systems of social support and interdependence among members of each team. Not only is the job itself made intrinsically more pleasurable, it also provides a basis for the development of valued social relationships. However, it is not always necessary to alter working arrangements quite so radically to generate performance improvements. It is quite possible to move down this kind of route a short step at a time by adjusting the content of jobs, the level of autonomy or the amount of teamworking as opportunities to do so arrive.

REFLECTIVE QUESTION

In what ways could your job be enlarged or enriched? How far would this increase your level of motivation, and why?

These ideas were taken forward in the influential work of Hackman and Oldham (1980) with the development of their 'job characteristics model' and applied to a wider variety of job types. They propose that job satisfaction, motivation and high work effectiveness occur when five 'core job characteristics' are present. These are as follows:

- skill variety (the degree to which a job draws on a job-holder's different skills and talents)

- task identity (the degree to which a job involves completing an identifiable piece of work from start to finish with a visible outcome)

- task significance (the degree to which a job has an impact on the lives of others)

- autonomy (the degree to which the job-holder has freedom, independence and discretion in carrying out the work)

- job feedback (the degree to which the job provides the job-holder with direct information about his or her effectiveness).

However, they also found that these job characteristics are not guaranteed to produce high work performance. Other factors also need to be present. First, the job-holders must possess the knowledge and skills necessary to carry the job out effectively. If they do not, however much autonomy is given and however meaningful the job may be, they are likely to struggle. Second, the job-holders must be psychologically in a position to appreciate the opportunities provided by the job and willing to grow through their work. In other words, they must want to develop in a role and not simply be interested in working because they have to in order to earn a living. Finally, the work context must be satisfactory. Poor pay, difficult co-workers or poor managers can easily undermine the potential of the five job characteristics to deliver improved performance.

EXERCISE 8.5

BMW

Read the article by Jon Watkins, A Mini adventure (*People Management*, 6 November 2003, pp29–32). This can be downloaded from the *People Management* archive on the CIPD's website (www.cipd.co.uk).

This article focuses on major changes made to working practices at the BMW (formerly Rover) plant at Cowley in Oxford. A major job redesign exercise placed workers into self-steering teams of 8–15 people, carrying out a far wider range of tasks than had previously been the case.

Questions

1 What evidence is presented in the article of job rotation, job enlargement and job enrichment?

2 What cost savings do you think are likely to have been gained as a result of the job redesign process and the other changes described?

3 From an HR perspective, what other advantages have accrued as a result of the changes?

KEY ARTICLE 18

Jed DeVaro, Robert Li and Dana Brookshire, Analysing the job characteristics model: new support from a cross-section of establishments. *International Journal of Human Resource Management,* Vol. 18, No. 6, pp986–1003 (2007)

This is an article written by a group of American researchers, but which draws on UK data in the form of the very substantial, government-funded Workplace Employment Relations Survey which is carried out every few years. The aim here is to use this large data base to test some of the claims made for Hackman and Oldham's 'job characteristics model' described in this chapter. The research is quantitative in nature, looking for correlations between, on the one hand, productivity, product quality and worker satisfaction, and on the other, task variety and worker autonomy. They conclude that there are not only positive associations, but that these are rather stronger in the case of the link between job design and productivity than that between job design and worker satisfaction.

Questions

1 On what basis do the authors claim that their research is of greater value than previous studies looking at the validity of the job characteristics model?

2 What limitations do the authors acknowledge could lead to valid criticisms being made of their findings? Can you suggest any others?

3 What practical lessons can be learned from this research and applied in the workplace?

JOB SCULPTING

Finally in this chapter we need to introduce an idea that has yet to gain much following, but may be applied more commonly in the future. Job sculpting turns almost all of the management approaches and processes discussed so far in this chapter on their heads, creating a wholly different way of managing this area of P&D work. Essentially it involves designing jobs around the needs, ambitions and capabilities of people rather than expecting people to fit themselves into a job designed for them by the organisation. Instead of recruiting new staff to fill defined roles, effective performers are recruited and asked to develop their own roles or, effectively, to write their own job descriptions.

Such an approach has always been used in the case of very talented individuals whose services an organisation wishes to secure and whose skills can be deployed in varied ways without the need to fit into any established role. It has also long been the case that long-serving staff are able, incrementally, to grow their own roles in directions that best suit them and make best use of their abilities. But job sculpting goes much further than this, beginning with the principle that contemporary organisations need to gain a capacity for flexibility and creativity above all things in order to attain competitive advantage. To achieve this they need to attract and retain effective people and develop strong, cohesive teams of individuals who can deliver changing organisational objectives. In a tight labour market, where skills are in short supply, it is argued that there is no alternative but to move at least some way down the road towards job sculpting. Hirsch and Glanz (2006) see the adoption of such an approach as entirely logical. Like employer branding (see Chapter 2), job sculpting draws on the experience of consumer marketing techniques whereby customers are increasingly engaged in the design of customised products and services.

Butler and Waldroop (1999) have created a framework around which job sculpting exercises can take place. Their research, involving in-depth interviews with 650 employees, has led them to conclude that there are eight major 'life interests' that motivate people as far as the content of their jobs is concerned. Most people, they claim, are primarily motivated by one or two of these. The eight can be summarised as follows:

- The application of technology. People who are interested in how things work and want to find ways of making them work more effectively.

- Quantitative analysis. People who are interested in numbers and mathematics and who like using quantitative approaches to analyse issues.

- Theory development and conceptual thinking. People who tackle problems using theory and abstract thinking.

- Creative production. Imaginative people who think original thoughts and enjoy innovating. They are particularly drawn to setting up new systems or projects.

- Counselling and mentoring. People who like to teach, coach and guide others.

- Managing people and relationships. People who derive satisfaction from getting objectives achieved through others.

- Enterprise control. People who like leading, making decisions and taking responsibility for the completion of projects.

- Influence through language and ideas. People who gain satisfaction through writing and speaking. Excellent communicators.

A method of job sculpting involves establishing which of these eight 'life interests', or indeed others, motivate individual staff or job applicants and then seeking, as far as is practically possible, to develop jobs that meet their particular preferences or aspirations.

REFLECTIVE QUESTION

Which of Butler and Waldroop's eight life interests carries most resonance for you? To what extent would it be possible for your current job to be resculpted to meet these preferences? Would this increase or decrease your effectiveness?

CHAPTER SUMMARY

- Two distinct approaches are used to determine which attributes an organisation will seek in applicants for vacant job roles. The longer established one makes use of job analysis, the other focuses on competency frameworks.

- Job analysis is carried out by observation, interviewing or the use of questionnaires. Job descriptions, accountability profiles and person specifications are derived from this data.

- Criticisms of the job analysis approach include inaccuracy and inflexibility. It is also cumbersome and time-consuming.

- Competency-based approaches focus on the characteristics of superior performers rather than on the attributes of job-holders generally. Competency frameworks can be generic across organisations, but are criticised for failure to deliver a diverse workforce.

- Job design and redesign exercises can be carried out according to Taylorist or humanist principles. While the two are wholly different, it is possible to use a blend of both when designing individual groups of jobs.

- Job sculpting provides a wholly different way of thinking about job design issues. It involves designing jobs and allocating duties to fit the preferences and strengths of effective individuals rather than seeking people who can fit themselves into a predesigned role.

EXPLORE FURTHER

- Michael Pearn and Rajvinder Kandola's *Job analysis: a manager's guide* (1993) provides a thorough overview of different approaches to the topic and contains a number of short case-studies outlining the methods used by four organisations. The wider issues are well covered in the following American textbooks: *Staffing organisations* by Heneman, Judge and Heneman (2000), *Human resource management* by Carrell, Elbert and Hatfield (1995), and *Personnel/human resource management* by Leap and Crino (1993).

- The debate about competencies is covered effectively by Robert Wood and Tim Payne in *Competency based recruitment and selection* (1998) and by Gareth Roberts (2000) in *Recruitment and selection: a competency approach*.

- The case for a competency approach, together with a guide to the major models used, is provided by Dalziel (2004).

- Searle (2003) contains a chapter that offers a critical perspective on job analysis, the views of its detractors its contemporary uses.

- Job design is covered in detail by Parker and Wall (1998). The rival claims of the Taylorist and humanist approaches are summarised very effectively by Fried *et al* (1998).

- A thoughtful assessment of the practice of writing job descriptions that are appropriate to the contemporary business environment is provided by Marie Gan and Brian Kleiner (2005).

CHAPTER 9

Recruitment advertising

The recruitment of new employees is an area of work in which all human resource professionals are involved in some way. According to the CIPD (2007a), the cost of replacing someone when they leave an organisation averages over £7,750, the large majority of which is spent on recruitment processes. The costs, of course vary greatly from job to job. Filling a vacancy can be inexpensive if internal candidates are promoted, job centre candidates chosen or informal word-of-mouth recruitment used. But these methods, by their nature, heavily restrict the applicant pool and often mean that the 'best' available candidates are not even considered for vacant roles. To secure applications from a reasonable field of candidates, more usually needs to be spent on either advertising, agency fees or attending careers events of one kind or another. It is thus not unusual for a sum equal to 2–3 per cent of an employer's total wage bill to be spent on recruitment advertising and agency fees. For a company employing 100 people at national average earnings this would mean that around £50,000 a year was committed to recruitment, before taking account of administration costs. For larger organisations employing in excess of 3,000 people, the annual cost will amount to millions of pounds.

Recruitment can also take up a great deal of time. One survey suggested that on average this area of work accounts for 16 per cent of a typical personnel department workload (*Personnel Today*, April 1996, p3). It is thus important to appreciate how recruitment arrangements can be managed as efficiently as possible while making sure, at the same time, that the approaches chosen remain effective and do not breach the law.

In this chapter and the next we assess the key decisions that need to be taken in managing recruitment processes and consider the skills needed to undertake them with maximum effectiveness, efficiency and fairness. The different kinds of recruitment methods that can be used are described and the advantages and disadvantages of each assessed. In this chapter the focus is on recruitment advertising and the fast-developing area of Internet or e-recruitment. In Chapter 10 we look at other approaches such as informal recruitment, the use of agents and education liaison. In addition, issues of more general significance are also discussed. Recruitment advertising agencies are covered in Chapter 10.

LEARNING OUTCOMES

By the end of this chapter readers should be able to:

- distinguish between recruitment strategies based on internal and external sources

- draft advertisements for filling vacancies and select appropriate media for specific cases

- evaluate advertising media and other methods of recruitment

- advise organisations on the options for e-recruitment.

In addition, readers should be able to understand and explain:

- the cases for and against internal and external recruitment

- different recruitment advertising strategies

- the advantages and disadvantages of Internet recruitment.

DEFINING RECRUITMENT

The terms 'recruitment' and 'selection' are often considered together, but they are in fact distinct human resource management activities. While recruitment involves actively soliciting applications from potential employees, selection techniques are used to decide which of the applicants is best suited to fill the vacancy in question. We can thus characterise recruitment as a positive activity that requires employers to sell themselves in the relevant labour markets so as to maximise the pool of well-qualified candidates from which future employees can be chosen. By contrast, selection can be seen as a negative activity, in so far as it involves picking out the best of the bunch and turning down the rest.

An important question to ask whenever recruitment is being considered is whether or not there really is a need to recruit outside the organisation at all. Giving thought to alternative approaches might lead to the development of effective solutions at considerably lower cost. An interesting example is the experience of the UK Air Directorate.

RECRUITING AIR TRAFFIC CONTROLLERS

During the 1980s, the UK Air Directorate was faced with a shortage of applicants for enrolment as air traffic control cadets. The problem arose for a number of reasons. It was partly caused by increased traffic in UK airspace, but also arose because of competition for air traffic controllers from overseas operators and a substantial number of early retirements.

External recruitment was deemed necessary,

but its scale was greatly reduced in two important ways. First, the training programme was shortened very considerably, allowing cadets to graduate after 18 months rather than two years. This involved forcing cadets to specialise at a far earlier stage but had the advantage of bringing them into control centres much sooner. Second, air traffic control assistants were actively encouraged to apply for promotion to the rank of controller, a career move that had occurred only rarely previously.

Source: G. Brown (1993).

Once we have made the distinction between selection and recruitment, it is important to understand that there are times when selection techniques have a recruitment role and vice versa. An employment interview, for instance, while primarily a tool of selection, is also an experience that enables applicants to evaluate the organisation and to decide whether or not they wish to take up any offer of employment that may be made. Similarly, there is a strong element of selection in many recruitment processes. For example, one aim of a good job advertisement is to enable potential applicants to self-select, so that only those who truly have the required qualifications and attributes make formal applications.

The relative significance of each stage in terms of costs, management time and organisational success varies with the state of the labour market. When labour markets are tight, as they have been in the United Kingdom in recent years, recruitment activities assume a greater importance. This occurs because it becomes harder to find staff of the calibre and skills required, so more time and expense is necessary on the part of organisations. Conversely when labour markets are loose and jobs are in short supply, there is no shortage of qualified applicants for vacant positions. Less attention is thus given to recruitment and more to the selection stage as organisations look for ways of effectively differentiating between candidates. The more considered and sophisticated approaches to recruitment assume significance when unemployment among target groups is low; sophisticated selection rises up the corporate agenda when it is high. These realities are reflected in the activities of those whose job is to research and write about human resource management, the 1980s and early 1990s being a period in which much was written about selection, more recent years seeing something of a switch of interest towards recruitment.

INTERNAL RECRUITMENT

Most private sector employers, as a matter of course, attempt to fill vacancies internally before they consider looking for people outside the organisation (Newell 2005, p122; CIPD 2007a, p8). In the public sector, by contrast it is more common to advertise internally and externally at the same time. Fuller and Huber (1998, p621) identify four distinct internal recruitment activities:

- promotions from within

Table 9.1 Recruitment methods

Internal methods	internal promotion lateral transfers job rotation schemes re-hiring former staff		college tutors careers advisors student societies
		Other media	direct mail local radio teletext billboards Internet TV and cinema
Printed media	national newspapers local newspapers trade and professional journals magazines		
External agencies	job centres outplacement consultants headhunters employment agencies Forces Resettlement Agency recruitment consultants	Professional contacts	conferences trade union referrals suppliers industry contacts
		Other methods	'factory gate' posters past applicant records open days word of mouth poaching
Education liaison	careers service careers fairs		

- lateral transfers

- job rotation

- rehiring former employees.

In each case current or former staff are made aware of opportunities to develop a new role in the organisation before external candidates are considered. There are a number of advantages for organisations. First, of course, internal recruitment is very cost effective. Vacancies can be advertised at no cost at all using staff noticeboards, newsletters or intranet systems. It also helps in the establishment of a strong internal labour market, giving people a reason to stay in the organisation rather than moving on to develop their careers elsewhere. This means that the organisation is maximising its return on investment in staff training, while also enhancing motivation and commitment among existing staff. Other advantages include better knowledge on the part of new appointees about the way the organisation operates and what to expect in the job. Learning times for new job-holders are thus shorter, while early leaving as a result of dashed expectations is less likely. The time taken to fill a vacancy is usually quicker in the case of internal recruits, leading to further cost savings and greater organisational effectiveness. Finally, selection is based on greater knowledge of the individuals' merits and prospects, being less of a 'shot in the dark' than it is with external recruits.

There are also strong arguments to put against internal recruitment. Foremost is the way that it tends to perpetuate existing ways of thinking and carrying out tasks. Fresh blood is often needed to challenge the status quo, particularly at more senior levels, and this can only come through external recruitment. If all recruitment to such positions is internal the result is sterility, lack of originality and a decline in the breadth of an organisation's collective knowledge base. Second, it is very likely that the 'best' person for the job is not currently working for the organisation. An employer that is genuinely seeking to excel by attracting and retaining the most talented people is obliged not only to recruit externally, but to take some time and effort doing so. Finally there are arguments based on equality, the suggestion being that a reliance on internal recruitment tends to perpetuate existing imbalances in the make-up of the workforce. Hence if ethnic minorities are not currently well represented, promoting from within will do nothing to create greater diversity, particularly among the management team.

Heneman *et al* (2000, pp327–331) make a useful distinction between 'traditional mobility paths' and 'innovative mobility paths' in their discussion of internal recruitment. Traditional approaches start with the assumption that individuals can expect to be promoted upwards through some form of organisational hierarchy. Internal recruitment is thus focused on people on the rung beneath that on which a new vacancy becomes available. Jobs are thus advertised narrowly, this group expecting to compete with one another for the promotion opportunity. Innovative paths are more appropriate in organisations operating in less predictable waters and in those that have sought to flatten their hierarchies by stripping out many middle management posts. Here the focus is on lateral and cross-functional moves, with individuals being given the opportunity to build a broader portfolio of experience as a means of enhancing their long-term employability. In practical terms, this means advertising posts much more widely within an organisation and avoiding making assumptions about who could and who could not undertake the role.

IRS (2002c) correctly points to an important and problematic feature of internal recruitment, namely the need to manage situations in which candidates are unsuccessful. Turning external candidates down is a great deal more straightforward, because there are no long-term consequences for the day-to-day management of the organisation. By contrast, turning down internal candidates sometimes creates a difficult situation that needs immediate and careful management. Otherwise there are likely to be deeply dissatisfied staff who feel let down and unappreciated, and relationships in which the level of trust has been reduced. IRS (2002c) quotes the findings of an IES study into these issues (Hirsh *et al* 2000) that recommends managers be trained in how to 'rehabilitate' failed internal candidates so as to avoid impaired performance, unwanted resignations and a breakdown in workplace relationships. But they also stress that these outcomes are easiest to avoid by running an open contest based on selection criteria that are both fair and seen to be fair.

Exclusive use of internal recruitment is good deal less common in public sector organisations, where it is generally considered good practice to advertise all vacancies externally. They do so because they need to give full opportunity to all those who fund them (ie tax payers) to apply and because it is considered important that their staff, at all levels, reflect the make-up of the whole community. Hence NHS, educational and local government organisations prefer to advertise all jobs in newspapers, even where there are strong internal candidates around whose attributes specific jobs have been designed. There are exceptions (eg senior civil service posts and judicial appointments), but most public sector roles, even at the highest levels, are open to applications from everyone. In theory this both allows public sector organisations to select the best candidate and ensures that they are seen to be doing so. In practice, because they know the interviewers and have greater knowledge of the job, internal candidates tend to enjoy a considerable advantage over those from outside. This allows them to triumph with relative ease at the selection stage. The process can thus be criticised for wasting the time and energies of external candidates, as well as a good deal of public money.

> ### REFLECTIVE QUESTION
>
> Think about people you know who have been recruited to senior posts internally and externally. What different qualities do you think each brings to their role?

EXTERNAL RECRUITMENT

There are numerous different approaches used to attract applications from prospective external employees, some more conventional than others. In practice, for most jobs the formal methods can be listed under the following five headings: printed media, external agencies, education liaison, other media and professional contacts (see Table 9.1). In addition, there are informal methods that can be used, whereby employees' families, suppliers or personal acquaintances get to hear about a vacancy via word of mouth or the 'grapevine'. All these methods are used to a greater or lesser degree. Some, like job centres or word of mouth, cost next to nothing. Others, including national newspaper advertising and the employment of headhunters, require considerable expenditure. A few methods, such as the use of cinema and television, are only realistic propositions for the largest employing organisations seeking to recruit substantial numbers. An example would be the use of such media by army and navy recruiters.

When deciding which method to use, a variety of other considerations must also be taken into account. For example, it is necessary to consider how precisely the approach adopted will hit its target audience. We can safely conclude that it would be as inappropriate to advertise for a new chief executive in a job centre as it would be to place an advertisement for an engineer in a medical journal. Recruiters also need to be mindful of the image of their organisation they are portraying in the labour market. While a small local newspaper advertisement might attract large numbers of applicants, there is a case for spending rather more on a substantial advertisement set by professionals as a means of suggesting to job seekers that the organisation compares favourably with others as a place to work.

Some methods are ruled out because of time constraints. Most P&D specialists will at some time have experienced pressure from line managers to fill vacancies within days rather than weeks, with the result that the range of possible recruitment methods is severely restricted. In such cases the only realistic options are employment agencies, job centres, personal contacts and those local papers that advertise positions on a daily basis.

Another important consideration is the volume of applications that each method is likely to yield and the ability of the personnel department to administer them effectively. While it would be grossly inefficient to choose a method that brought in hundreds of applications for a single unskilled job vacancy, there are situations in which it is necessary to attract very large numbers. One example would be advertisements seeking applications for very senior jobs where the widest possible pool of appropriately qualified individuals is needed to enable the organisation to screen out all but the very best candidates. Another common instance is the opening of a new plant or store leading to the creation of hundreds of new jobs.

THE NATIONAL LOTTERY

A high-profile example of mass recruitment occurred when Camelot was successful in its bid to run the national lottery in May 1994. The lottery itself was launched only six months later – in the event, very smoothly – but prior to this the company needed to recruit over 500 people and then train them. For most this was, quite literally, a whole new ball game: few can have had experience of running a similar operation because none had existed in the United Kingdom. Recruiting staff was made particularly difficult by the tight timescales involved. A proportion had to be employed in planning functions prior to the announcement of which consortium had won the contract to operate the lottery. Their posts were necessarily temporary in the first instance.

In the event a variety of different recruitment sources were tapped and several recruitment methods employed. About 10 per cent of the staff were recruited from within the companies backing the Camelot bid. Others were recruited through two specialist employment agencies that focused on management and technical functions respectively. A further source of candidates was the Watford Job Centre, situated close to the company's headquarters. The Employment Service then passed details of the jobs on to other centres around the country. The final source of candidates was the thousands of speculative applications Camelot received as a result of the publicity surrounding its successful bid. In total, using all four methods, over 16,000 applications were received. Turning these into 500 employees occupied 20 personnel officers for several months.

Source: G. Huddart (1995).

People
management

EXERCISE 9.1

LONDON BOROUGHS

Read the article by Rebecca Johnson, Sharing the load (*People Management*, 9 August 2007, pp40–42). This can be downloaded from the *People Management* archive on the CIPD's website (www.cipd.co.uk).

This article describes a complex project whereby 16 separate London boroughs have partially merged together their recruitment services and outsourced different parts to three separate private sector providers. The aim is to save money while also substantially improving the quality of recruitment activities.

Questions

1 Why do you think that so many people working in the private sector have such a negative image of public sector work?

2 In what ways might the project described in this article help improve the reputation of London local authorities as employers?

3 What other advantages is it anticipated will accrue?

4 Why are some London boroughs unwilling to take part?

RECRUITMENT ADVERTISEMENTS

According to Ri5 (2007), well over £1 billion is now spent each year on recruitment advertising in the United Kingdom, including £215 million on online ads. Advertising space in newspapers is generally sold in units of 3cm by 1cm. An advert measuring 10cm by 6cm will thus involve purchasing 20 of these blocks of space. The cost of each unit is known as the 'single-column centimetre rate', which varies very considerably between different publications and over time. The marketplace is highly competitive, particular newspapers offering a range of preferable rates to employers and agents who place large volumes of business with them. Over the last 20 years the *Guardian* newspaper has managed to gain a substantial share of the national market (35–40 per cent in most years) with very competitive pricing. As a result it now tends to dominate public sector and middle-range management job advertising. The market for senior management positions, by contrast, is divided between other quality papers like the *Sunday Times* and the *Daily Telegraph* – which charge rather more per single-column centimetre than the *Guardian*. These papers, along with the *Financial Times*, carry the vast bulk of national newspaper advertising.

The choice of publication will depend very much on the target audience. Opinion poll research has indicated that around 70 per cent of people buy a different newspaper when they are looking for a new job (*Recruitment Today*, June 1995), so information about readership levels and profiles is only of limited use in deciding where to place a job advertisement. The first question to ask is whether or not there is a need to advertise nationally. For most jobs, local newspapers are preferable, because they reach potential applicants only within the relevant travel-to-work area. It is only necessary to advertise on a national basis for relatively specialised vacancies for which there is a national labour market. An example of this distinction would be the labour markets for kitchen employees in expensive hotels and restaurants. In order to recruit a kitchen porter or junior chef it will probably only be necessary to advertise locally. A national advertisement might well not yield many responses, because these are not generally jobs that people would happily move house to take up. On the other hand, the market for top head chefs is national or even international – so a local paper would clearly be inappropriate in these cases. The higher the salary and the more specialised the job, the more geographically widespread the labour market will be.

Another consideration is the possibility of placing recruitment advertisements in trade and professional journals. These tend to cost rather less than either local or national papers but have a far lower readership than either. Again the decision will depend on the nature of the labour market concerned. Some industries, by nature or tradition, offer clearer career prospects to individual entrants than others. Some also tend to favour internal candidates over outsiders because of the need to recruit individuals with industry-specific skills or competencies. Where this is the case and a national or international labour market exists, there is a strong case for advertising in the relevant trade journal. An example might be the *Nursing Times*, which serves the largest single professional group of staff in the United Kingdom.

REFLECTIVE QUESTION

Where does your organisation advertise? What considerations are taken into account in deciding which papers or journals are most appropriate?

STYLE AND WORDING

Any cursory flick through the appointments pages of newspapers and journals reveals how different one recruitment advertisement is from another. There is clearly no one best approach, because in this field 'best' can often mean 'distinctive'. Some of the key decisions that recruiters face in drawing up effective advertising copy are examined in the following paragraphs.

WIDE TRAWLS VERSUS WIDE NETS

A fundamental decision is the number of applications it is intended should be received. Wide trawls bring in lots of different fish, while wide nets only catch the biggest. According to the Newspaper Society (2005, p7), 11 per cent of the of the population of working age are always actively looking for a new job, while a further 11 per cent are looking for a new job at any one time. In addition, 32 per cent of the working population say that they would consider a new job 'if they came across it'.

So in principle it is not difficult to attract very large numbers of applicants. The question is how useful or desirable such an approach might be.

Where a wide trawl is required the advert has to be striking in appearance. It will probably be large and make use of pictures or unusual graphics. It will then be placed prominently, on several occasions, in the places where possibly interested people are most likely to see it. By contrast the wide net approach requires less razzmatazz. The key aim here is to reach a relatively narrow audience and then to encourage self-selection on the part of job seekers. This often means including a substantial quantity of detailed information about the job and the kind of candidate being sought. It is more likely to be placed in a trade journal or on a specialist website where only the few 'big fish' the employer wants to attract will see it.

REALISTIC VERSUS POSITIVE

Another important decision in designing advertisements concerns how accurate the information contained should be. One option is to use an unashamedly positive approach. The aim is to create an image of the job as an exciting and challenging opportunity for a well-motivated person. Any drawbacks in the contract or less attractive aspects of the job are thus either downplayed or left out of the advertising copy altogether. The alternative is to design a realistic advertisement that mentions all aspects of the job (potentially attractive and unattractive). It might state that the work is complex and technically demanding or that a high degree of job security is unlikely to be given.

As was the case with informal methods, the realistic approach has the advantage of encouraging people to self-select and moves some way towards the 'realistic job preview' that is said to have such a marked effect on reducing staff turnover in the first months of employment (Hom and Griffeth 1995, pp193–203). On the other hand, it can be argued that self-selection is often not in the interests of the employer because too heavy a dose of realism can discourage excellent potential applicants from responding. There is thus a good case for adopting a positive approach at the advertising stage and keeping back some of the potential drawbacks of a job for discussion at the selection interview once the candidates' appetites have been whetted. This is particularly true where the job is genuinely attractive in some respects, but also pretty unattractive in others. An example might be a well-paid and interesting leadership role of temporary duration. Emphasising the positive aspects is necessary to attract applicants who might otherwise be put off by the lack of guaranteed tenure. The more complex business of selling the temporary nature of the position by stressing the opportunities for enhanced long-term employability can be left until a pool of suitable applicants has been attracted.

CORPORATE IMAGE VERSUS EMPHASIS ON THE JOB

Recruitment advertisements also vary greatly in the emphasis they give on the one hand to the organisation as a potential employer and, on the other, to the nature and duties of the job. Some advertisements thus make great play of their well-known brand names, while others put the emphasis on the job. In some cases the name of the employer is omitted altogether, with potential applicants asked to contact an agency.

In part this decision is determined by the extent to which the employer is well known in its target labour markets. People are lured towards 'big names' because they perceive that a spell of employment in such organisations will enhance their future career prospects, self-esteem or social status. However, it also important to be mindful of the potential general publicity a recruitment advertisement incorporating well-known brand names can generate. They can thus have two purposes; to attract applicants and to increase sales of well-known products.

PRECISE VERSUS VAGUE INFORMATION

The research carried out by De Witte (1989) showed above all that job seekers like to have as much basic information as possible in job advertisements and that vague forms of words resulted in considerably lower response rates. He found that advertisements that failed to include clear information about job titles, workplace location and salary levels were significantly less attractive to potential candidates than those that were precise in this regard. Similar conclusions were reached from a huge study of 9,000 job advertisements carried out in 2000 (Focus Central London Training, reported in IRS 2004b). Here also a clear statement of all the skills required by the job-holder was found to have a very positive effect on the number of suitable applications received by recruiters. So what possible justification can there be for the many advertisements that contain only imprecise information? The answer mainly lies in the frequent need to preserve confidentiality.

The absence of precise salary information is relatively common because of potential problems that can arise if other employees see the advertisement and compare their own packages unfavourably with that on offer to job applicants. There may also be a case in some circumstances for making no mention of the employer's name and using an agency to advertise the position. This would be the case if it was thought desirable for existing employees to remain ignorant of the recruitment process. An example might be a situation where an individual's contract is to be terminated with immediate effect and where a replacement is needed to take over very swiftly. In such circumstances there may be insufficient time to advertise the job and fill the vacancy after the previous job-holder has left. In extreme cases it may be deemed desirable further to disguise the organisation's identity by making only very vague references to its markets and location.

However, there is a further possible explanation for the vagueness that is characteristic of many advertisements placed by agencies on behalf of clients – namely, their wish to have on their books as many potential job applicants as possible. The aim of the vague advertisement is thus not primarily to attract candidates seeking the particular job in question, but to generate a large response from people whom the agent may be able to place in other positions at some time in the future.

There is also an argument in favour of vague approaches on the grounds that they contribute towards flexible working. According to this point of view, successful candidates are less likely to come to the job with strong preconceptions about their duties and position in the organisational hierarchy than colleagues recruited via very precise advertisements. In an age when flexible working is becoming increasingly important in many quarters, such arguments can be judged to have some validity. You could certainly use them as part of a case for omitting from advertisements details of hours of work or reporting lines. Moreover, a case can also be made for vaguer approaches on grounds of cost because imprecise wording can often take up less space than detailed information. In recruitment advertising the less wordy the advertisement, the cheaper it is to publish.

PLAIN-SPEAKING VERSUS ELABORATE

There is an ongoing debate among recruitment specialists as to the desirability or utility of incorporating expensive artwork or colour into recruitment advertisements (see IRS 2004b). An interesting selection of views on this topic was featured in *Recruitment Today* in 1996, recruiters putting forward contrasting views. At one extreme is the kind of view identified by John Courtis (1989, p34) that 'too much arty input' can reduce the effectiveness of an advertisement and that the inclusion of straightforward, relevant information is all that is really necessary. The alternative view, expressed by John Ainley, the head of group personnel at W.H. Smith, is that refreshing and distinctive visual approaches are more eye-catching and thus yield more applicants. He also expresses the view that the image of the employer in the labour market is an important consideration, and that stuffy or impersonal approaches are less effective than those that 'read like a conversation' (*Recruitment Today*, February 1996, p7). Much probably depends on the target audience and the approaches adopted by key labour market competitors.

However elaborate in terms of artwork and presentation, it seems clear that certain types of wording are more effective whatever approach is used. Studies by Lunn (1989) and Hill and Maycock (1990), cited by IRS (2001b), suggest that the use of questions in recruitment advertisements helps to generate applications from appropriately qualified people. Instead of simply describing the role, they argue in favour of the approach in which a series of rhetorical questions are asked focusing on the attributes required for the job role (Are you ready for a new challenge? Do others judge you to be a good leader? Do you have an excellent record of achievement at the cutting edge in HRM? If so we want to hear from you' etc.). Hill and Maycock's study found that response rates to advertisements were far more influenced by the presence or absence of questions than they were by the size or presentation style of the advertisement.

REFLECTIVE QUESTION

How elaborate are the advertisements for jobs used by your organisation? Could they be improved by either reducing or increasing their visual distinctiveness?

ANALYSING ADVERTISEMENTS

People management

EXERCISE 9.2

Spend some time looking in detail at the recruitment advertisements published in national newspapers or in trade journals such as *People Management*.

Analyse them in terms of the major categories set out above. See if you can find clear examples of advertisements that fit into each category (eg a wide trawl ad, a wide net ad, a realistic ad, a positive ad).

Then look for examples of poor advertisements that you think are unlikely to attract many applicants. You should

look for advertisements that miss out key pieces of information or those that appear dull or confusing. What is missing? What could be done to improve them?

You may find it useful when carrying out this exercise to read an article by Brian Chandler and Tony Scott, How to write a job ad (*People Management,* 24 November 2005, pp42-43). This can be downloaded from the *People Management* archive on the CIPD's website (www.cipd.co.uk).

KEY ARTICLE 19

Deanne N. Den Hartog, Anne Caley and Philip Dewe, Recruiting leaders: an analysis of leadership advertisements. *Human Resource Management Journal,* Vol. 17, No. 1, pp 58–75

This is a fascinating and very original article looking in detail at the precise wording used in job advertisements for senior management roles published in *The Times* and the *Sunday Times*. The authors analysed 941 separate ads, recording the key words used to describe the kind of leader being sought. They then compared these with the major contemporary theories of effective leadership. Their final conclusions are slightly ambiguous, largely because they found it difficult to interpret exactly what was meant by certain words and phrases, but the article is interesting to read because it includes a good summary of

the literature on effective leadership and discussion about which terms are used most frequently in advertisements for senior managers in the United Kingdom.

Questions

1   How might some of the assumptions behind this research be questioned?

2   Why do so many advertisements fail in practice to articulate the attributes that are being sought in potential job-holders of senior positions?

3   What practical lessons can be learned from this piece of research?

INTERNET RECRUITMENT

The use of the Internet as a recruitment medium has increased substantially in recent years. In the late 1990s, the jobs advertised on the web were mainly in IT or academia, or were specifically for new university graduates. The first years of the twenty-first century have seen an expansion to include vacancies across all areas of work. Over 75 per cent of employers were advertising some jobs on the Internet in 2007 (CIPD, 2007a, p12), while the providers of job-search websites were spending vast amounts of money on television, cinema and radio advertising, sports sponsorship and public relations activities as a means of raising their public profile. To some the rise of web-based recruitment is a revolutionary development, destined fundamentally to change the way the entire recruitment industry operates. In 10 years' time, they argue, most of us will find our jobs via the web, signalling the beginning of the end for more established methods. Others are more sceptical, pointing out the disadvantages of Internet use for recruitment purposes and arguing that it merely represents an important, but in no way revolutionary, addition to the range of methods already in use.

To date the sceptics appear to be winning this argument. Despite the majority of households now having access to the Internet, only 12 per cent of adults first look to the web when seeking a new job, compared with 51 per cent who look first in their local newspaper (Newspaper Society 2005, pp50–51).

EMPLOYER WEBSITES

The most straightforward approach involves maintaining vacancy pages as part of organisations' own websites. Links to these are provided via a home page that people can locate using a search engine, or via other websites such as those operated by recruitment agencies or university careers services. Employer sites are cheap to operate and provide the organisation with plenty of space to sell their jobs to potential applicants in whatever way they wish. According to Frankland (2000), the cost of setting up a fully operational website from scratch is about the same as is required to advertise one job prominently in a national newspaper. It is thus easy to see why web pages carrying job ads have proliferated so quickly: no pain and all gain from the organisation's perspective.

However, the extent of the gain is difficult to evaluate. Because this approach relies on potential employees actively taking the trouble to visit the site, the number of people who will see a particular advertisement at a particular time is relatively limited. According to IRS (2001c), vacancies posted on corporate sites 'are no different in essence to those found on job boards mounted on factory gates, or on notices posted by retailers in their own stores – prospective candidates have to be passing by in order to come across them'. The approach is thus only viable for big-name employers or those with a strong reputation as employers within defined labour markets. Most small and medium-sized employers will not attract sufficient numbers of hits to their websites to be able to rely on this as a means of finding new recruits. Interestingly, it is recruitment websites run by the large public sector organisations (local authorities, the NHS and universities) which attract the most traffic (Newspaper Society 2005, p81).

CYBER AGENCIES

The second form of Internet recruitment involves making use of specialist employment agencies that operate principally on the web, well-known examples being Workthing and Monster.com. These operations are interesting because in many ways they combine the functions traditionally carried out by employment agencies and newspapers. Not only do they advertise the vacancy, but they are also willing to undertake some short-listing on behalf of employers, sending on a selection of the CVs that have been submitted by job-seekers.

Running cyber agencies is a highly competitive business, and it is likely that only a handful of the current plethora will ultimately survive. Schreyer and McCarter (1998, p222) argue that over time a handful of highly sophisticated, international operations will emerge to carry general job vacancies on behalf of the industrialised world. In addition there will be a series of smaller sites with a reputation as the main advertisers of jobs in particular industries or among defined professional groups. Both types of operation will be very profitable and will make use of the most up-to-date software available. They will be interactive, fun to visit and very speedy, offering all manner of services to job-seekers. Achieving this prize of being among the world's favourite job-search websites is an endeavour that justifies the investment of a great deal of money. As a result we can expect to see more and more expensive and sophisticated marketing campaigns as the battle between the big players left in the game evolves. At the time of writing (late 2007) several major cyber agencies have already dropped out of this tournament or been taken over by their rivals, despite having developed an enviable public profile (eg Stepstone Recruitment).

JOBSITES LINKED TO NEWSPAPERS AND JOURNALS

A third category includes all recruitment-based websites that are run in parallel with paper-based operations. Examples include the *Guardian*'s JobsUnlimited site and BigBlueDog operated by the *London Evening Standard*. These sites republish on the Internet advertisements that have also been carried in the job sections of newspapers and journals. It is now usual for employers to pay a fee that leads to the carrying of advertisements in both media. Advantages of the web-based version include the opportunities they give job-seekers to go straight to the employer's own site via a hotlink, to submit a CV instantly by e-mail and to search the job-bank for particular types of vacancy.

JOBSITES OPERATED BY EMPLOYMENT AGENCIES

Just as newspapers operate parallel advertising in paper and Internet forms, established employment agents are also developing a formidable web presence. These allow jobseekers to register with the agency and to browse current vacancies using a search engine. An example is bluearrow.co.uk. In addition, the government's network of job centres now puts details of all its vacancies on the Internet via its Learning and Work Bank. These can be accessed free of charge by anyone with Internet access, and also from jobpoint kiosks in the job centres themselves.

ADVANTAGES AND DISADVANTAGES

There are clear potential advantages associated with Internet recruitment when compared with more traditional approaches. First, as has already been stated, for bigger name employers with the potential to attract 'passing traffic' to a corporate site there are substantial cost savings to be made. These arise in part because there is no longer a need to pay for recruitment advertising in printed media, and partly because these organisations can greatly reduce the number of recruitment brochures they need to print. In addition further savings are achieved by cutting down on the need to use written correspondence or field phone calls. United Biscuits expected to cut their total recruitment costs by half with the establishment of a comprehensive new recruitment site called UBCareers.com, having already saved 85 per cent of their graduate recruitment costs by moving it online from 1999 (Roberts 2001, p7).

As well as reducing costs, web-based recruitment is attractive because it gives the employer access to a potential audience of millions. This will include people who are not actively looking for a new job but who may become interested if they stumble across a particularly original or well-designed advertisement when surfing the Internet. The other great advantage is the speed and ease with which job seekers can respond when they see an opportunity publicised on the web. It can take seconds, and a few clicks of a mouse to send a CV by e-mail to the employer concerned. In tight labour markets, where vacancies can take months to fill, any time saved is valuable to employers. Developments in the fields of online selection and CV-matching software are also significant as they provide a means for shortlisting of candidates to be carried out, in part, electronically.

However, it must also be pointed out that there are considerable disadvantages associated with Internet recruitment, many of which could be said to undermine its effectiveness fundamentally. Some will become less significant over time as technology develops, but there will always be some important drawbacks. Top of the list is the tendency for employers to get bombarded with applications from unsuitable candidates simply because it is so easy to respond speculatively to an advertisement. The result is a need to devote more rather than fewer resources to the shortlisting process. This problem, known as 'spamming', can only be overcome by using some form of electronic online short-listing technology. However, in key respects these are not satisfactory. Most rely on software with the ability to reject CVs that do not include certain key words. This is a very hit and miss kind of approach that inevitably leads to applications from well-qualified candidates being electronically discarded simply because certain words do not appear. Alternative approaches require candidates to complete online application forms that ask more specific questions. Many of these now take the form of psychometric tests. They are much fairer from a candidate's perspective but are expensive to develop properly. They are thus only of great use in fields such as police, army or graduate recruitment where large numbers of people are applying for many vacancies on a year-by-year basis.

Another major drawback for Internet recruitment relates to confidentiality and the fear many people have about allowing their CV to circulate in cyberspace outside their own control. This may be more a problem of perception than reality, but it can act as a barrier to e-recruitment in the same way that a reluctance to submit credit card numbers acts as a barrier to the development of e-commerce more generally. The safeguards with CVs are less satisfactory than is the case with credit cards, meaning that people have good reason to worry about on which screens their personal details will end up. A particular fear is that the

CV will be sent, unsolicited, to one's own boss, who may be wholly unaware that a job search is in progress. Confidentiality issues are a particular problem for senior people who prefer to deal with traditional agencies over which they can exercise more personal control.

Finally there is the whole range of technical problems associated with Internet usage generally. These are summed up by IRS (2001c, p5) as:

> *Bugs in the system, computer crashes and problems caused by recruiters with poor IT skills can lose applications, delay rather than accelerate recruitment, and damage the public image of the organisation. Poorly designed or over-engineered websites represent a further pitfall: slow loading speeds, irritating 'movies' and faulty links are all guaranteed to try the limited patience of online users whose expectations of fast, reliable access are very high.*

It is because of these drawbacks that Internet recruitment has, as yet, failed to impress many employers. While most make use of the Internet, few have a high regard for its effectiveness as a recruitment method. Other more established approaches are ranked much more highly in surveys of employer opinion. The CIPD (2003b, p17) reported that only 7 per cent of its survey respondents ranked the Internet as being the most effective source of new staff. This is far lower than the rankings for satisfaction with newspaper and journal advertisements.

Another way of measuring the effectiveness of the web as a recruitment tool is to establish how many people actually find their jobs via an Internet site. Here too progress to date is limited. A major survey by the Newspaper Society (appropriately published on the web) asked a representative sample of UK Internet users how they had found their current job. Thousands took part in the survey, but only 5 per cent stated that they had been recruited via an Internet site. The volume of vacancies being advertised on the Internet continues to grow and cyber-agencies in particular are gaining greater acceptance by employers, so it is reasonable to conclude that more and more people will find their jobs through e-sources as time goes by.

THE NAKED TRUTH

Internet recruitment is a fast-evolving field. In the early days, employers tended to do no more than put their existing, paper-based recruitment literature online. More recently there has been a growth in the use of interactive features such as questionnaires and games, and much more use of moving pictures and striking graphics. Humour is also being used more, as predictably are features with sexual content.

Asda pioneered these latter approaches with its 'naked truth' campaign aimed at enticing prospective graduate recruits to make

applications. The website featured pictures of recent graduate recruits wearing no clothes, with strategically placed pieces of fruit and cereal packets ensuring that some level of decency was retained. It also included a personality-oriented questionnaire for candidates to complete, to which instant feedback was given. Those who did not give the answers Asda was looking for were then redirected to the site of one of its supermarket rivals. Such approaches are interesting, but must be used with great care. Good candidates are just as likely to be put off as attracted by the use of this kind of imagery.

EXERCISE 9.3

DEBATES ABOUT ONLINE RECRUITMENT

Read the article by Steve Smethurst, The allure of online (*People Management*, 29 July 2004, pp38–40). This can be downloaded from the *People Management* archive on the CIPD's website (www.cipd.co.uk).

This article discusses various viewpoints on the advantages and disadvantages of online recruitment. The major point it makes is that cost savings are by no means the only reason for increased use of the Internet by recruiters. It also provides a more general opportunity to review the effectiveness of recruitment strategies. Critical voices focus on diversity issues and worries that the Internet is not used by many under-represented groups.

Questions

1   Aside from reductions in cost, what other specific advantages associated with e-recruitment are cited by the people interviewed for this article?

2   Which of these points do you find most and least convincing?

3   How far do you agree with the view that Internet recruitment tends to benefit groups who are already well represented in the workforce at the expense of those who are not?

KEY ARTICLE 20

Kristin B. Backhaus, An exploration of corporate recruitment descriptions on monster.com. *Journal of Business Communication*, Vol. 41, No. 2, pp115–136 (2004)

In this article the author, who is US-based, analyses the wording of the recruitment materials posted by corporations on the leading American cyber-agency's website. Her interest is particularly in the words the companies use to describe what they offer as employers and the impression that this gives. In this respect the article is a useful contribution to the literature on employer branding (see Chapter 3), but the article is principally concerned with analysing the different recruitment tactics that are being used by different corporations.

Questions

1   Why do you think corporations put so much more emphasis on describing themselves and their achievements rather than in explaining what they are like to work for as employers?

2   Why do such a small number make reference to pay and benefits?

3   Why is there so little attention given to ethics or diversity?

4   Why is there so little evidence of clear employer branding strategies being in use?

CHAPTER SUMMARY

- While often paired together, recruitment and selection are distinct resourcing activities that involve different kinds of activity.

- Most organisations seek to recruit people internally before looking for external recruits. There are many advantages, but also some disadvantages associated with this practice.

- Recruitment advertising requires resourcing specialists to make choices about the style and forms of words that are most appropriate to attract the number and types of candidates needed.

- The growth of Internet recruitment is the most significant current development in this field. It is used by most employers as a tool for filling some vacancies and is likely to become considerably more widely used in the future. Technical and other difficulties mean that it is less effective at present.

EXPLORE FURTHER

- Three books by John Courtis give an interesting perspective from the point of view of an experienced recruiter. These are *Recruiting for profit* (1989), *Cost effective recruitment* (1985) and *Recruitment advertising: right first time* (1994).

- Various articles in academic textbooks provide an introduction to key debates. Among the most useful are those by Thom Watson (1994), Sue Newell (2005) and Julie Beardwell (2007).

- Books that give an American perspective on recruitment issues include Diane Arthur's *Employee recruitment and retention handbook* (2001), which is full of original and unusual ideas, including a great deal of material on Internet recruitment. US-based academic research on recruitment issues (which is far more extensive than the United Kingdom's) is analysed in *Recruiting employees* by Alison Barber (1998) and by Taylor and Collins (2000) in a chapter that focuses on original approaches being pioneered by IT firms in the United States.

- Marc Orlitzky (2007) provides an up to date summary of US research in the field.

- Internet recruitment has been described, discussed and debated in countless articles published in *People Management* and other journals over recent years. IRS *Employment Review* has given extensive coverage to online recruitment issues in recent editions, while IDS (2000a, 2003b,2006d) has also published major surveys on Internet recruitment together with case studies. Useful books on the subject are *The employer's guide to recruiting on the Internet* by Ray Schreyer and John McCarter (1998) and *E-recruitment: is it delivering?* by Polly Kettley and Maire Kerrin (2003).

CHAPTER 10

Alternative recruitment methods

In this chapter we turn our attention to the methods of recruitment that do not, primarily, involve advertising either in the printed media or online. Informal methods, such as word-of-mouth recruitment or direct applications from job seekers are very common indeed, but have always been controversial because they appear to contravene all the principles of the established 'good practice' approach to recruitment. Nonetheless, they continue because they have much to offer employers. Equally controversial, but for different reasons, is the employment of headhunters to carry out recruitment on behalf of companies. The methods they use frequently irritate employers, but there are significant steps that can be taken to help ensure that the headhunters you work with as a P&D professional operate in such a way as to benefit rather than to harm your organisation's interests. Other types of agency also play a role, notably temping agencies and job centres. But here too there are major drawbacks for employing organisations when considered from an HR perspective. In this chapter we also look at developments in the field of education liaison and at the specialised recruitment methods adopted over the years by graduate recruiters. Finally we focus on discrimination law and the way that it restricts employers' freedom of action in the field of recruitment.

LEARNING OUTCOMES

By the end of this chapter readers should be able to:

- advise about the advantages and disadvantages of informal recruitment methods
- distinguish between different types of agency that play a part in the recruitment process
- deal effectively and professionally with recruitment agents and headhunters
- advise on the approaches to use when recruiting graduates and school leavers
- ensure that recruitment practices comply with all major legal requirements.

In addition, readers should be able to understand and explain:

- the major debates about the merits and legality of informal recruitment
- the framework within which employers interact with the recruitment industry
- major current developments in the field of graduate recruitment
- the legal and ethical framework for recruitment.

INFORMAL APPROACHES

A major government survey carried out in 2002 involved asking over a million people how they had found their current jobs (*Labour Market Trends* 2002). This revealed that informal channels account for a majority of new hires, with word-of-mouth recruitment topping the poll by a considerable margin (see Table 10.1). By contrast the numbers finding their positions through job centres and employment agencies is relatively small. Rather less than a third of all employees are recruited through recruitment advertising, the large majority of whom (75 per cent) read advertisements in local newspapers. The rest of the market is split between trade journals, national newspapers and papers specialising in job advertising (Newspaper Society 2005, p49).

Table 10.1 Recruitment methods in practice

Recruitment method	Men %	Women %
Hearing from someone who worked there	30	25
Reply to an advertisement	25	31
Direct application (eg walk in/on spec)	14	17
Private employment agency	10	10
Job centre	9	8
Other	12	9

Source: Labour Market Trends (2002).

While it is clear that the use of informal methods is very widespread, opinion is divided as to how much they really have to offer employers when compared with formal approaches. Some research findings, such as those of Kirnan *et al* (1989), Blau (1990) and Iles and Robertson (1997), strongly suggest that informal recruitment methods yield a better selection of well-qualified applicants than formal methods. The same studies also found a correlation between informal recruitment, low staff turnover, and high levels of subsequent employee performance (see Barber 1998, pp22–32 for an excellent summary of US research in this area). However, the reasons for these effects are unclear. One possibility is that candidates who are recruited by word of mouth or approach organisations themselves self-select to a greater degree than those finding out about the job from other sources. They come to the job knowing more about the employer and the work duties, and are better placed to decide for themselves whether or not it is suitable for them. The relatively low turnover rates are probably best explained by the likelihood that informal recruits have more realistic perceptions of what the job will be like than those recruited through formal channels.

Aside from the fact that it seems in practice to lead to better performance, other arguments in favour of informal approaches can be made. In terms of cost, they are clearly inexpensive from an organisation's point of view. Some employers offer 'bounty payments' to existing staff who introduce new recruits, but in the main these are relatively modest (see IRS 2001b). Direct approaches from prospective employees cost nothing at all except for some management time. Moreover, it is also possible to argue that informally recruited people are attractive for other reasons:

on several grounds, co-worker referrals can be desirable hires per se. A social tie to an existing employee provides a ready-made avenue of socialization, training, and social support for the new hire. The co-worker responsible for the referral will also have a reputational stake in the success of the person whom he or she referred, providing an additional reason to provide assistance and support to the new hire.

(Baron and Kreps 1999, p342)

Alec Reed (2001, pp23–26) also offers a robust defence of informal recruitment, going as far as to suggest that 'the oft-maligned practice of nepotism' may have a serious role to play in HR strategy. Here too the case is made, in part, with reference to the effect word-of-mouth recruitment has on existing employees. They like it, according to Reed, partly because they enjoy working alongside friends and partly because the practice shows 'the value the company places on them and their opinions … offering implicit praise by displaying a willingness to recruit others of the same ilk'.

Nonetheless, both word-of-mouth and direct approach methods are criticised on the grounds that, by definition, they only reach a very limited target audience. The employer may have a good group of candidates from which to choose but it will not be a very extensive selection – nor is it likely to be representative of the wider community. It could thus be argued that a formal method, such as a recruitment advertisement, might yield an even better pool of candidates if it was designed effectively and printed in an appropriate publication. It may not be the formal methods themselves that are ineffectual, but the manner in which they are deployed. The use of some informal methods, as we shall see later in this chapter, may also cause employers to breach discrimination legislation.

RECRUITMENT IN THE PUBLIC SECTOR

Research shows a substantial difference between preferred methods of recruitment in the public and private sectors. Although both make extensive use of advertising in the local and national press, private sector employers are more likely than their counterparts in the public sector to use other types of approach.

In particular, there is a strong aversion in public sector organisations to recruitment using informal methods (such as word of mouth, formal employee referral schemes or unsolicited applications) and headhunters. In many public sector organisations these methods are not used as a matter of policy, despite their being relatively highly rated by the employers in the private sector who use them routinely.

The main reason is the way that informal methods and headhunting tend to favour groups that are already well-represented in the workforce. While it is considered good practice for all employers to seek to reach out to all groups in the community, it is politically important that public sector organisations do so and are seen to be doing so. This is because it is right for the demographic make-up of public servants to reflect that of the communities they serve, particularly where the individuals concerned exercise some form of statutory authority.

Sources: IRS (1999a), CIPD (2007b).

EXERCISE 10.1

WEB 2.0

Read the following two articles featured in *People Management*. They can be downloaded from the *People Management* archive on the CIPD's website (www.cipd.co.uk).

- Andy Allen, Bravo two zero (*PM Guide to Recruitment Marketing*, June 2007, pp26–28)

- James Brockett, Face to face with social networking (9 August 2007, pp15–17).

While both these articles discuss a broader range of issues, they raise some very interesting questions about the current and future use of social networking sites, blogs, viral campaigns and Second Life as informal recruitment tools. Increasingly employers are making use of these tools, or encouraging employees to

do so, as a means of building up an employer brand or just sourcing potential recruits. They are also sometimes researching candidates' backgrounds using social networking sites such as Facebook and MySpace.

Questions

1   What evidence is presented of employers making use of Web 2.0 applications in a formal sense as a means of recruiting informally?

2   How successful do you think these approaches could be? Why?

3   What are the major drawbacks that are identified?

4   What ethical issues do these kind of practices raise?

KEY ARTICLE 21

Marilyn Carroll, Mick Marchington, Jill Earnshaw and Stephen Taylor, Recruitment in small firms. *Employee Relations*, Vol. 21, No. 3, pp236–250 (1999)

There are few articles reporting academic research about recruitment in the UK HR journals. It is not a subject that has generated a great deal of debate or sparked much interest in the academic community. This article is an exception to the rule. It describes interview-based research focused on small firms in five separate industries. The findings confirm a preference for informal methods of recruitment on the part of small business owners and managers. The reasons for this are discussed.

Questions

1   What are the major strands of the case for the use of formal methods of recruitment on the part of small firms?

2   Why are these not used by small firms in the five sectors studied here?

3   How far do you think that the firms studied here would see their staff turnover rates decline if they were to adopt more formal recruitment methods? Why?

USING AGENTS IN THE RECRUITMENT PROCESS

A variety of different external agencies can be employed to undertake some part of the recruitment process on behalf of employers. In addition to government and voluntary agencies involved in finding jobs for people, there is now a well-established recruitment industry that exists to serve the needs of employers and job seekers in ever more complex and competitive labour markets. It is estimated to employ around 80,000 people and to have an annual turnover in excess of £23 billion (IRS 2004d, p45). From a human resource management perspective this provides interesting opportunities for increasing the effectiveness and efficiency of recruitment activity, but the use of agents also carries risks. In particular, there is a need to establish at the outset exactly what the agent can offer and precisely how much the service is going to cost. The advantages and disadvantages of agents vary considerably with the type of agency service on offer. These can broadly be categorised under four headings, each discussed below.

GOVERNMENT AND VOLUNTARY AGENTS

In addition to the government's employment service and its network of job centres, there are also a number of other state-sponsored organisations that offer employers a free recruitment service. One is the Forces Resettlement Agency, which assists ex-service personnel to find jobs in civilian life. As well as providing its regular job advertising function, the Employment Service also runs a range of training programmes for people who have been out of work for a prolonged period. Their initiatives often involve placing unemployed people in workplaces free of charge in exchange for training. The aim is to improve individuals' skills while giving them an opportunity to gain work experience. From an employer's perspective, as long as there are suitable work and training opportunities, such schemes provide additional employees at low cost. They also allow managers to preview an individual's work before deciding whether or not to offer employment on a longer-term basis.

Some employers are reluctant to advertise posts in job centres despite the fact that they offer free advertising. This is partly because the clientele is mainly comprised of unemployed people, the majority of whom are perceived to be unskilled or low-skilled, and thus inappropriate for many jobs. The other reasons relate to poor past experiences of using job centres. Carroll *et al* (1999) found that many small employers in their qualitative study were both very willing and able to describe difficulties they had had with job centre recruitment, a 'downside' also reported in an IRS survey (2001e). The main difficulties arise from candidates who come to interviews and accept posts because they are pressed into doing so by job centre staff and not because they really want to fill the vacancy. They do this because the job centres are required to ensure that people claiming state benefits are genuinely looking for work. The result is a situation in which managers spend hours interviewing people who have no real interest in the work. Often candidates do not turn up for interview, or if they are successful, subsequently fail to start work.

A number of voluntary bodies also run programmes for unemployed jobseekers either with or without government support. Two examples are Comeback, an agency originally set up by British Rail to find jobs for ex-offenders, and the Shaw Trust, which finds work placements for disabled job seekers.

ADVERTISING AND RECRUITMENT CONSULTANTS

These are private companies that, in return for a fee, will undertake a part of the recruitment process on behalf of employers. They act like any other management consultants, except that they specialise in the recruitment and selection functions. Perhaps the most useful are recruitment advertising agents who assist employers in the drawing up and placing of job advertisements. They are often mistakenly believed only to offer a 'Rolls-Royce service' involving the production of showy artwork for publication in newspapers and careers brochures. While much of their work is at this glossy end of the market, they also have a potentially useful range of services to offer regular job advertisers. This is made possible by the muscle power they have in the recruitment advertising market. Because they represent large numbers of clients and consequently do a great deal of business with newspapers and trade journals, they are able to negotiate substantial bulk discounts, a portion of which can be passed on to employers. The net result is that a large agency is able to give advice on the wording and placing of advertisements while also improving the appearance of the advertising copy and charging a lower fee than would be paid were the employer dealing with the newspaper independently.

Recruitment consultants, by contrast, take over a larger part of the recruitment process. In addition to handling the advertising they will also undertake much of the administration by sifting initial applications and providing employers with a short-list of candidates. Such arrangements are expensive, the client either being charged an hourly fee or an overall sum calculated as 10–20 per cent of the first year's annual base salary for the job in question. Sometimes both approaches are used, a retainer or advance fee being paid, followed by further payments on production of a short-list and the appointment of a candidate. The potential advantage to the employer is access to the agent's expertise and the saving in terms of time associated with outsourcing administrative activity. Such arrangements are particularly appropriate when employers are operating in unfamiliar labour markets (eg overseas) or when a major recruitment drive is being undertaken over a limited period of time. An example might be the launch of a major new tourist attraction by a company with a relatively small P&D function. In such a situation it makes more sense to buy in a one-off recruitment service than to set up a major new in-house facility.

TEMPORARY EMPLOYMENT AGENCIES

As competition has become tougher and more international, the use of temporary staff to cover peaks in business has grown. There are now large numbers of agencies that retain casual employees on their books to serve the needs of employers with short-term vacancies. Traditionally these have operated in the secretarial and clerical field, but there are increasing numbers of agencies specialising in the provision of staff to fill a variety of other functions. Examples are companies that have taken over the running of nurse banks from the hospitals, and the growing number of agencies specialising in the provision of catering and computer staff. It is also possible to find work as a personnel and development specialist on a locum basis through some agencies. In fact over 250,000 agency temps are estimated to be working in the United Kingdom at any one time (National Statistics 2006, p23).

For the employer, temping agencies potentially provide a reliable source of well-qualified staff at very short notice. They will also replace an unsatisfactory temporary worker with someone more suitable if asked. While the primary purpose of such arrangements is to undertake a short-term assignment, caused perhaps by absence or a sudden increase in workload, there are also advantages for employers with longer-term vacancies to fill. First, the agency can provide someone to undertake work during the time that the search is on for a permanent replacement. This can be indispensable if an employee undertaking important work leaves at short notice. Second, these agencies can provide staff on a temporary basis who can later be offered full-time positions. The great advantage of such arrangements from the employer's perspective is the opportunity they give to observe an individual's work prior to making him or her an offer of employment. The employee also gets a realistic job preview and thus accepts a job less blindly than the candidate whose only knowledge of the employer derives from perceptions gained at a selection interview.

The drawback is the cost. Hourly rates for agency workers are invariably double those paid to regular employees. In addition the agencies have traditionally incorporated charges into the contract that place a financial penalty on employers who make permanent offers of employment to their temps. However, this practice is now severely limited thanks to the Conduct of Employment Agencies and Employment Businesses Regulations 2003. The regulations are too complex to describe here in detail, but they do make it possible for an offer of permanent employment to be made to a temporary worker supplied by an agency without a fee being incurred after a short period of time has passed. IRS (2004d) provides a straightforward guide to the regulations.

CABLE & WIRELESS

An interesting innovation introduced by Cable & Wireless plc was the establishment, in 1995, of an in-house employment agency. It has been set up as a subsidiary company with its own managing director, but unlike most agencies it is expected only to break even and not to make a profit. It exists to provide staff for other parts of the Cable & Wireless operation to undertake project work on short-term contracts.

There are two advantages for the company. First, the agency provides specialist support staff, many of whom are ex-employees of the company. Most staff on the agency's books have undertaken a number of different assignments for the company and are thus far more familiar with its business and corporate culture than regular agency employees would be. Perhaps more importantly, the in-house agency is far cheaper. Its requirement only to cover its own costs means that it charges staff out at approximately half the charge-out rates offered by external agencies.

Source: Walker (1996).

HEADHUNTERS AND PERMANENT EMPLOYMENT AGENTS

The fourth group of agencies offering recruitment services to employers has a number of titles. These agencies often call themselves 'recruitment consultants' but are also known by such terms as 'headhunters' and 'executive search consultants'. They differ from the varieties of agent described above in so far as their purpose is the identification of candidates for permanent employment, often in tight labour markets. They operate on a 'no sale, no fee' basis but charge high sums (typically 30 per cent of the first year's salary) when an offer of employment is made. Essentially they act like dating agencies, selling the job to the potential candidate and then trying to sell the candidate to the employer. Their great advantage from an employer's perspective is the opportunity they give to open up confidential channels of communication with high-flying employees working for competitor organisations. As such, they allow recruitment managers to tap into a reservoir of interesting potential applicants who are not actively seeking new jobs.

While it is possible for personnel professionals to build up effective relationships with trusted agents operating in this way, there is a fundamental conflict of interest that has to be managed if any association is to prove fruitful over the long term. The problem arises from the fact that the recruitment industry is highly competitive and makes money only by successfully filling vacancies. There are no prizes for coming second in this cut-throat business, where commission makes up a high proportion of an agent's remuneration. The competitive pressure derives from the low start-up costs or barriers to entry into the business. It is technically very easy to start up an agency – the only requirements are effective selling skills and sufficient contacts in a particular trade or labour market – so there are hundreds of agents competing for relatively scarce rewards. As a result, the agent's overwhelming aim has to be finding candidates for vacancies quickly and at the lowest possible cost. Ideally they want to place individuals already on their books so as to avoid undertaking time-consuming additional research.

By contrast, while employers may want to employ a new person quickly, they have to pay far more attention to the quality of the individual and the likelihood that he or she will perform effectively over a prolonged period. Hence the possibility of a conflict of interest and, on occasions, the presence of hard-selling and sharp practice on the part of the agent. The potential problems are outlined in some detail by Courtis (1989, pp40–49) and by IRS (2004d, pp45–46), whose survey found that 57 per cent of respondents 'had encountered difficulties in their relationship' with agencies. Many of these will be familiar to any HR manager who has experience of recruiting in tight labour markets. A common example is an agent finding a new employee for an organisation, charging a hefty fee, and then returning to poach them 12 months later on behalf of a rival employer. Others include the beefing up of CVs to make candidates appear more experienced than they really are, and agents replying to advertisements placed in professional journals that serious job-seekers would in all likelihood have seen in any event.

In recent years, as labour markets have tightened and commentators have started to coin terms such as 'the war for talent' to describe the process by which employers compete for staff, headhunters have enjoyed several highly profitable years. They thrive in 'war' situations because there is increased opportunity for them to deploy some of their more ruthless practices. Alec Reed (2001, p26) goes as far as to refer to them as 'heat seeking missiles', urging employers to build sophisticated defences in order to match the growing sophistication of the headhunters. He describes the activities of a consultancy that has been set up with the title 'Anti-headhunting UK', which specialises in advising and training employers to improve their security systems and hence to deter headhunters from approaching their staff. These include training reception staff and telephone operators to spot calls from headhunters and to ensure that no useful information is given. It is important, for example, to try to ensure that internal e-mail directories do not get into the hands of headhunters, as e-mail provides the easiest of ways to reach employees who are quite happy in their jobs but who might be interested in moving were a juicy opportunity brought to their attention.

The (then) Institute of Personnel and Development (IPD) recognised the potential conflict of interest between employers and headhunters, and the fact that the recruitment industry had yet to evolve enforced professional standards, with the publication of a special Code of Conduct for Career and Outplacement Consultants. This provides a mechanism whereby employers and candidates can take formal complaints about the conduct of an agency to a disciplinary panel that can give official warnings to, or even expel, individuals from the Institute. It is thus well worth asking agents whether or not they are CIPD members before entering any arrangement with them. (The IPD became the CIPD in July 2000.) Now we have pointed out the potential pitfalls, it is also necessary to stress that it is possible to develop healthy and workable long-term relationships with particular headhunters. Indeed, in some labour markets where headhunters have gained an unassailable position, employers have few practical alternatives if they wish to recruit the best people. But here too conflicts of interest have a tendency to get in the way. This is because it does not generally make good business sense for headhunters to concentrate their time and effort on building up close relationships with one or two clients. This is a risky strategy because too much is lost if the client decides to switch to another firm. It is thus much safer to build up weaker relationships with large numbers of client employers and also necessary in this business to devote a great deal of time to developing new contacts and drumming up new business (Finlay and Coverdill 2002, pp76–82).

The key from the employer's perspective is to agree the ground rules from the start and to make sure that the charging structures are fully explained and understood. Courtis (1989, pp 41–42) and Jenn (2005, pp41–44) make a number of helpful suggestions, including the following:

- Select a headhunter who possesses genuine expertise about your industry and who understands the needs of your organisation.

- Provide the headhunter with as much information as possible about the organisation, the job and the type of person being sought.

- Offer the agency a degree of exclusivity – never use more than one agency for any one assignment.

- Ask for temps who are prepared to become permanent when you and they fit well.

- Pay promptly.

- Explain what selection or rejection criteria you are likely to use.

- Always ask why a particular candidate is being put forward.

Over time such an arrangement should allow the negotiation of better terms than are offered by rival agencies with whom no long-term relationship has been established. The key is to gain an understanding of the labour market and the way headhunters operate. That way it is possible to avoid employing them where to do so is unnecessary, and it is also possible to save on costs.

IRS (2004d) also suggests that employers should be up front with agencies from the start about how they will be assessing performance. The aim is to make it clear to the agency from the start that high standards are expected and that any continuing business relationship is dependent on receipt of a good service.

REFLECTIVE QUESTION

What is your experience of headhunters and recruitment consultants? To what extent have you observed situations in which a conflict of interest is apparent between the needs of employers and the aims of the agent?

DITCHING THE HEADHUNTERS

People management

EXERCISE 10.2

Read the following two articles featured in *People Management*. They can be downloaded from the *People Management* archive on the CIPD's website (www.cipd.co.uk).

- Jenny Hirschkorn, Research and employ (15 January 2004, pp33–35)

- Jane Simms, Zoom at thetop (*PM* guide to recruitment consultancies, April 2006, pp27–28).

The first article explains why larger corporations are increasingly dispensing with the services of headhunters and instead employing their own researchers to carry out the headhunting under their direction. Sometimes these researchers are directly employed by the recruiting companies, sometimes they are hired on a consultancy basis at a fixed fee. The second

article explores sharp practice among headhunters and debates the advantages and disadvantages of their use by employers.

Questions

1   What are the major reasons cited in the first article for the move away from headhunters?

2   Why do you think representatives of companies which employ their own headhunting researchers are so reluctant to talk about it on the record?

3   What examples of poor practice on the part of headhunters are cited in these articles?

4.   What are the major advantages that using headhunters can have for an employer?

ORIGINAL APPROACHES AT CISCO SYSTEMS

The California-based Internet services firm Cisco Systems is widely quoted as being the company that has done most to develop effective new approaches to recruitment practice. Cisco grew very quickly in the late 1990s – a commercial success story that was only possible because of its ability to recruit and subsequently retain highly qualified people in extremely competitive labour markets. Today it employs 30,000 people in 60 countries, having doubled in size each year through the 1990s. Not surprisingly much of its recruitment activity has been carried out online, but other approaches have been used to raise its profile as an employer in order to get people to visit its recruitment websites. Some of Cisco's more interesting activities are the following:

- The company employs a specialised recruitment team which operates separately from the rest of its HR department. In many ways it resembles an in-house headhunting operation.

- The recruitment website includes a fake screen that prospective applicants can access instantly should their boss catch them visiting the Cisco site during working hours.

- Cisco has taken over many rival firms. One of the major motivations has been the opportunity this gives it to employ large numbers of talented new employees. Extra care is taken in the process to ensure that as many technical staff as possible are retained after the takeover.

- Business cards have been distributed at brewery festivals and antique fairs since Cisco discovered that these were leisure interests of many prospective employees.

- Recruitment is considered to be an 'ongoing activity that never stops'. CVs received by jobseekers are not just filed away. Instead the senders are periodically contacted and asked to provide updates.

- Use is made of smart software that informs Cisco's system from where visitors to its website have logged on. If this is a rival firm the system directs it to the recruitment pages.

Source: Taylor and Collins (2000).

KEY ARTICLE 22

Jan Druker and Celia Stanworth, Partnerships and the private recruitment industry. *Human Resource Management Journal*, Vol. 11, No. 2, pp73–89 (2001)

This article is one of very few that examine temporary agency working from the perspective of agencies and employing organisations rather than from the worker point of view. The research described aimed to establish why employers source temporary staff through agencies and to establish whether any fundamental shifts in the nature of agency-employer relationships had occurred at a time of great growth in the number of agency temps in employment.

Questions

1   Why do employers in the UK hire so many more temps than they used to, despite the fact that the wage bill is usually higher as a result?

2   What are the major developments in the recruitment industry outlined in the article?

3   Why do only a minority of organisations appear to have formed close, long-term relationships of a 'preferred-supplier' variety with particular agencies?

EDUCATION LIAISON

Another form of recruitment that is available to employers and is widely used involves recruiting people directly from educational institutions. Most attention is given to graduate recruitment, which has developed its own procedures and professional organisation (the Association of Graduate Recruiters), but equally important at the local level is the recruitment of young people leaving schools and colleges of further education.

Over 400,000 students now graduate from universities in the United Kingdom each year, of whom nearly 300,000 are being awarded their first degree. This figure has doubled since the 1980s and is now planned to increase still further as the government strives for a situation in which half of all school leavers enter higher education. Purely in terms of size, this is thus a very significant labour market in its own right, but it is made more important for employers because among the thousands of new graduates each year are most of the individuals who have the ability to make a real difference to an organisation's future fortunes. According to IDS, employers perceive about one in 60 graduates to be truly of 'high calibre', and view the process of recruiting them as resembling a search for a needle in an ever-growing haystack (IDS 1994c, p13). Attracting these individuals is a competitive business for the larger organisations, and is one in which they are prepared to invest substantial sums of money. This has led not only to the design of more attractive financial and development packages for new graduate recruits, but also to a refinement of the methods used to recruit and select graduates. Year on year demand for graduates continues to grow, but employers also report increasing difficulties in filling their vacancies with suitable candidates. The result is simply greater competition for those who have genuine long-term potential (IRS 2004e).

Part of the problem is that all the graduate recruiters are fishing for the same types of people and are using the same range of recruitment and selection tools to identify them. IRS (2003d) shows that most graduate recruiters seek evidence of the same clusters of generic competencies, irrespective of the graduate's degree subject: communication skills, a results orientation, teamworking skills, analytical skills and business acumen being standard requirements.

The cost of recruiting graduates varies considerably, depending on the size of the campaign launched and the types of methods used. Costs have reduced to an extent recently with the development of net-based graduate recruitment, but it still averages in excess of £5,000 per person recruited. However, this figure disguises huge variations, some organisations spending 15 or 20 times more than others (Jenner and Taylor 2000, p19).

Graduate recruitment is also very time-consuming. Until their recent reorganisation, Courtaulds reported that 37 per cent of its personnel department's time was taken up with this activity (*Personnel Today*, April 1996, p3). Much of the time and money is taken up with sending company representatives to the various universities to talk to groups of students, to staff stands at careers fairs, and to brief careers advisors about the organisation and what it can offer to the right individuals. The more effectively these activities are carried out, the greater the organisation's prospects are of reaching that elusive creature: the well-qualified, well-motivated, intelligent, energetic and mobile graduate with management potential. In addition, there is a need to produce eye-catching literature and websites setting out what is on offer and what kinds of individual the organisation is looking for. The same fundamental decisions have to be taken in designing graduate literature as with the more conventional forms of recruitment advertising discussed above.

The major recruitment methods used are:

- advertising in specialist graduate recruitment directories such as the *Prospects Directories* (published by the Higher Education Careers Services Unit) and *GET* (published by the Hobsons Group)

- attending careers fairs organised by university careers services, student industrial societies and private companies (the daily cost of a basic stand is around £2,500)

- organising employer presentations or events at universities, with 'free' food and drink to generate interest and raise the profile of the organisation

- offering work placement opportunities to students during their vacations

- sponsoring students (usually during their final years) by supplementing their allowances on condition that they subsequently join the sponsoring organisation.

IRS (2004e, p42) shows that sponsorship arrangements are rated as being the most effective graduate recruitment method, along with the provision of work experience placements. Interestingly, national newspaper advertisements were ranked higher in terms of effectiveness than campus-based recruitment activities in this survey. As is the case with the generality of recruitment, Internet sites are ranked relatively poorly in terms of their effectiveness, but are still used by the vast majority of graduate recruiters.

GOLDEN HELLOS

One approach used to recruit people in tight labour markets is to pay them a sum of money in the form of a 'signing on bonus' or 'golden hello'. Such approaches have long been used on an ad hoc basis as a means of attracting senior staff who might otherwise hesitate about leaving their existing employment, or might choose some other employer instead.

In recent years some companies have formalised their procedures and extended them to graduate recruitment. The change has partly come about because of intensified competition for the very best graduate recruits, and partly because graduates are increasingly leaving university with substantial debts (an average of £13–14,000 according to bank surveys). They are therefore considered to be more susceptible to the attractions of golden hellos and more likely to allow the prospect of a windfall payment to influence their decision to join a particular company.

Some public sector organisations have also moved down this road as a means of recruiting people to professions such as teaching and social work where there is a shortage of able graduates.

In 2007/8 leading employers were offering sums of between £2,000 and £6,000 in the form of signing on bonuses or interest-free loans. The Training and Development Agency for Schools was offering £5,000 to trainee teachers in subjects suffering shortages, while one or two financial institutions were offering considerably higher sums (£6–12,000). In more recent years this practice seems to have declined.

It has been argued that the cost of graduate recruitment can be reduced in a number of ways. First, employers can target their recruitment activity on a few specific universities, including those in the localities where they have the greatest presence. They cannot reach such a wide pool of potential recruits this way, but they might be more successful in stimulating interest and thus making themselves attractive to students approaching graduation (IDS 1994, pp13–14). Second, employers can question the need to take on so many graduates by analysing critically their existing training programmes and by considering other sources of graduate-calibre employees. However, while there is always the option of improving career progression and training for employees who have not completed university courses, the costs associated with such strategies may well be high.

Another approach is for graduate recruiters to develop links with universities using the methods long favoured in schools liaison. According to IDS (1998, p1), in addition to providing work experience for students, these have traditionally included providing industry placements for teachers, buying or donating equipment, sponsoring school events, arranging workplace visits for school parties, providing teachers with places on in-house training courses, helping students with project work, running business understanding courses, carrying out mock interviews, mentoring students and encouraging employees to become school governors. All these activities raise the profile of the organisation in the community and, crucially, among school pupils who will be seeking jobs in the near future. It can thus be an important means by which employers improve their position in local labour markets and hope, as a result, to attract a greater number of high-quality applications than their competitors.

Employers have had the opportunity to put such activities on a more formal footing by participating in 'compacts' (IDS 1998). These arrangements are mainly directed at improving the job prospects of school-leavers in areas of high unemployment, and have principally been associated with the inner cities. Essentially a compact is an agreement between an employer and one or more schools to give special consideration to their pupils when recruiting school-leavers into jobs. Participating employers are also expected to provide work placements and are encouraged to take part in school life in the various other ways outlined above. In return, employers get access to so called 'compact graduates' – pupils who have met specific goals. These may include measures of punctuality, attendance, homework completion rates and accreditation in basic English and maths. In theory, therefore, the employer, pupils and school stand to benefit. For organisations based in specific localities with an interest in recruiting school-leavers, such arrangements are worthy of serious consideration. The costs are few and the potential benefits substantial.

School leavers can also be recruited through the network of government-funded careers advisers. Several agencies, including the Learning and Skills Councils, the Training Standards Council, and local and national training providers, collaborate on the development of 'work-based routes' for young people seeking to gain vocational qualifications. Through the use of government grants they encourage employers to recruit young people who are signed up to a structured training programme such as a National Traineeship or a Modern Apprenticeship. From an employer perspective, these schemes provide a source of younger workers who are working towards a specific qualification in a particular field. In addition to the workplace training offered to all employees, these recruits attend further training sessions on a day or half-day release basis at local colleges or the premises of private training providers. The government-funded agents help employers to identify suitable candidates and then monitor their progress in the workplace.

REFLECTIVE QUESTION

How could your organisation's educational liaison activities be improved? What arguments would you employ to persuade managers to pay greater attention to relationships with schools and colleges?

THE END FOR TRADITIONAL GRADUATE RECRUITMENT SCHEMES?

EXERCISE 10.3

Read the following two articles featured in *People Management*. They can be downloaded from the *People Management* archive on the CIPD's website (www.cipd.co.uk).

- Anna Czerny, The fast track broadens (2 September 2004, pp14–15)

- Hashi Syedain, Gown and town (23 March 2006, pp38–39).

The first is a news article reporting the views of delegates attending the Association of Graduate Recruiters' annual conference. It makes it clear that many employers that have recruited large numbers of fresh graduates in the past on to fast-track development schemes are fundamentally reviewing their established practices. Some are even asking whether there remains a business case for

continuing to compete for new graduates at all.

The second article paints a very different picture. It describes the National Graduate Development Programme recently established by local government organisations, its ambitions and successful record to date.

Questions

1   What are the different factors that are combining to make some employers question the value of their graduate recruitment schemes?

2   In what ways are employers altering their approaches in practice?

3   Why is the experience of local government employers apparently so different?

KEY ARTICLE 23

Jeanette Taylor, Recruiting university graduates for the public sector: An Australian case study. *International Journal of Public Sector Management*, Vol. 18, Nos. 6/7, pp514–533 (2005)

In this article Jeanette Taylor sets out the results of a large questionnaire survey undertaken among undergraduate students in Australia aimed at establishing what they are looking for in their first post-graduation jobs and the type of employer they want to work for. She goes on to focus in particular on the implications of the results for public sector employers in Australia. While the findings do not relate to the United Kingdom, the article makes many references to UK literature and explicitly links the experience of the public sector in the United Kingdom to that of Australia. The main conclusion is that although only a minority of students have an interest in public sector work, more effective and well-targeted recruitment campaigns should ensure that a reasonable pool of candidates is available to staff graduate roles in the public services in the future.

Questions

1   In what ways does the article contend that the experiences of public sector workers in the 1980s and 1990s have affected the career intentions of today's new graduates?

2   What evidence is presented to explain why there is a preference for private sector careers among Australian university students?

3   How is it recommended that public sector employers should proceed in order to improve their graduate recruitment records?

4   To what extent does the same message apply in the United Kingdom? Why?

LEGAL AND ETHICAL CONSIDERATIONS

Anti-discrimination law covers the conduct of recruitment activity and must be adhered to if costly legal actions are to be avoided. The relevant legislation is contained in the following Acts of Parliament and subsequent amendments: the Sex Discrimination Act (1975), the Race Relations Act (1976), the Rehabilitation of Offenders Act (1974), the Disability Discrimination Act (1995), the Equality (Sexual Orientation) Regulations (2003), the Employment Equality (Religion and Belief) Regulations (2003) and the Employment Equality (Age) Regulations 2006. Much of this law derives from or is covered by EU directives. As is the case in a number of other areas affecting personnel management, the law in this field is regularly added to, new rulings setting precedents that make clearer requirements in areas which were hitherto ill-defined. Recruiters are therefore advised to keep a close eye on legal developments as well as to develop a thorough grasp of the basic legal principles that have evolved. When in doubt it is best to err on the side of caution so as to deter aggrieved individuals from taking legal action.

In the case of discrimination on grounds of sex, race, disability, sexual orientation, religion or belief, and age, the law operates on the same basic principles. It is, quite simply, unlawful to discriminate unfairly against people on these grounds either directly or indirectly. In the field of recruitment this clearly means that the use of gender-specific terminology in advertisements is unacceptable, as would be any recruitment practice that explicitly discouraged applications from particular racial groups or from disabled persons. For this reason we have increasingly seen new forms of gender-neutral wording developed by job advertisers in recent years. Chambermaids have been replaced with 'room attendants', waiters with 'waiting staff' and firemen with 'fire-fighters'. You also no longer see adverts asking only for manageresses or nursing sisters. Importantly, however, it remains lawful to discriminate on grounds of age if there is objective justification in the form of a strong business case to justify doing so. This means that employers can restrict entry to training schemes as a matter of policy to people who are relatively young (though probably not to people in their 30s and 40s) on the grounds that a reasonable period of employment needs to be possible before retirement following a large investment in an individual's training.

The only defence available to employers in most cases of direct discrimination relates to the presence of a 'genuine occupational qualification', which requires the employer to recruit from a particular group. Examples include the recruitment of models, actors and actresses for theatrical or promotional work, and of people to work in single-sex establishments or situations where decency may be a factor (eg lavatory attendants and prison officers).

Legislation on indirect discrimination is more difficult, but no less important, to grasp. In recruitment this occurs when an advertisement or other recruitment technique favours a significantly greater proportion of one population group covered by the legislation than another. It is unlawful, whether or not there was any intention to discriminate on the part of the employer, and applies to recruitment practices that in themselves do not appear to discriminate unfairly. A classic example would be a height requirement. Were a job to be restricted to people over 6ft tall (as used to be the case with the recruitment of police officers) or under 6ft (as remains the case with the recruitment of cabin crew hired to work on some types of aircraft) it would be indirectly discriminatory because more members of one sex are in a position to comply than the other. In cases such as these a defence of objective justification can be deployed by the employer. The need is to satisfy the tribunal, if called upon to defend itself, that the act of discrimination constitutes 'a proportionate means of achieving a legitimate aim'.

While difficult to prove in practice, organisations can be seen to be inviting claims of unfair discrimination by relying exclusively on internal recruitment or on advertising a post in a newspaper read mainly by members of a specific racial group. In either case it is possible that individuals of one race were disadvantaged when compared with others. The same kind of actions could also be brought against employers where word-of-mouth recruitment significantly disadvantages one racial group.

The law relating to practices that discriminate in favour of disadvantaged groups is less clear. In general terms, the courts have made a distinction between 'positive' or 'reverse' discrimination, which clearly acts to the detriment of a group (in this context usually men), and 'positive action', which assists underrepresented or disadvantaged groups while stopping short of actual discrimination. In practice, however, this distinction is often hard to draw. Human resource professionals are probably best advised to take legal advice from solicitors or from ACAS advisers concerning specific cases. Legal precedents have established that it is unlawful to have quotas for numbers of men and women in particular jobs, but that it is lawful to set targets for increasing the numbers of a particular underrepresented group. Similarly, while it is unlawful to request applications only from women, members of a defined ethnic minority or any other underrepresented group, it is quite lawful to include equal opportunities statements in job advertisements. There is no legal impediment preventing employers from positively discriminating in favour of a disabled person.

ALL-WOMEN SHORTLISTS

The complexities of the law on positive discrimination gained an unusual amount of publicity during the 1990s with the introduction by the Labour Party of 'all-women shortlists' in the selection of prospective parliamentary candidates for some safe seats. The issue here was whether or not such a post came within the legal definition of work. Cases were brought by two men who were deprived of the opportunity to stand for selection. To avoid further actions, and after 35 women had been selected, the party announced that it was to end this policy.

In 2002 the law was changed so that it is now possible for political parties to discriminate positively in this way again.

In serious cases of unlawful discrimination, complaints can also be made to the CIPD on the grounds that a member has breached the Code of Professional Conduct. This goes beyond minimum legal standards to advocate the promotion of equal opportunities for disadvantaged groups other than those currently protected by unfair discrimination laws.

Aside from legal and ethical considerations, there is also a 'business case' that can be advanced in support of rigorous equal opportunities policies and practices, and this is endorsed, in some particulars, by the CIPD. The main thrust of the business case is as follows:

- A commitment to equal opportunities makes the organisation more attractive in the labour market.

- Equal opportunities practices help ensure that the organisation has the widest possible field of candidates from which to choose.

- A commitment to equal opportunities is appreciated by employees, who consequently respond with increased commitment to the organisation.

These arguments are controversial and may not readily be accepted. In particular, there is a fundamental question concerning the costs associated with effective equal opportunities monitoring, and the low priorities such activities inevitably have in very busy workplaces. One can also ask, quite legitimately, why, if the business case is so compelling, there is a need for such a comprehensive body of anti-discrimination law?

REFLECTIVE QUESTION

What are your views on this debate? How convincing a business case could you make in the context of your organisation?

EXERCISE 10.4

THE BUSINESS CASE FOR DIVERSITY

Read the following two articles featured in *People Management*. They can be downloaded from the *People Management* archive on the CIPD's website (www.cipd.co.uk).

- Jenny Hirschkorn, Mirror image (*PM Supplement on Recruitment Consultancies*, April 2004, pp17–20)

- Steve Smethurst, Fair traders (29 November 2007, pp28–31).

The first article puts a strong case for the adoption of policies and practices which encourage the recruitment of a diverse workforce, irrespective of legal requirements. Several examples of good and bad practice are given to illustrate the main argument. The second article focuses on recent efforts made by firms based in the City of London to become more diverse in terms of the people they employ at all levels.

Questions

1   What are the major strands of the case for treating diversity seriously that are presented in these articles?

2   What problems can you see with a policy of recruiting people for their potential rather than their experience?

3   Why might Ford in particular have a strong business case for promoting diversity?

4   Why is this a particularly important issue for City firms in London?

5   What examples of 'positive action' in practice are described in these articles?

- Informal recruitment is frequently criticised as being a means by which inequality in society is perpetuated. However, research shows that it remains both very common and a reasonably effective method of recruiting good staff.

- Employment agents may be government sponsored or private companies. Some specialise in the provision of temporary staff, others in candidates for permanent positions. The activities of headhunters can cause problems for employers as well as providing a useful channel to make confidential approaches to employees working for competitors.

- Graduate recruitment is an expensive and time-consuming activity for organisations. Distinct methods need to be used to reach the brightest new graduates with the best prospects.

- The most able school leavers are best recruited through the development of partnerships with local schools and through the auspices of government sponsored careers agencies.

- Employers must take care in their recruitment activities to avoid breaching anti-discrimination legislation. This protects job applicants from unfair discrimination on grounds of sex, race or disability.

EXPLORE FURTHER

- Every year *People Management* produces a supplement to accompany one of its April issues that focuses on the recruitment industry. These supplements include various articles, many of which focus on developments in recruitment consultancy. They are particularly good sources of information about recruitment advertising agencies.

- Graduate recruitment is examined in depth by Jenner and Taylor in *Recruiting, developing and retaining graduate talent* (2000) and in the annual benchmarking surveys carried out by IRS and published each autumn in *Employment Review*.

- A good source of information on schools-based recruitment is the IDS study, *Business partnerships with schools* (1998).

- There is relatively little material published on headhunters. Two recent books fill the gap somewhat. Although both are written predominantly from the perspective of the headhunters and primarily give advice to them, they are useful sources of knowledge for P&D managers too. These are the books by Finlay and Coverdill (2002) and Jenn (2005).

CHAPTER 11

Selection: the classic trio

The choice of appropriate employee selection techniques is a field in which there is great divergence between the recommendations of academic writers and day-to-day practice in organisations. When applying for a job, most people expect to have to fill in an application form, attend one or more interviews and then receive an offer of employment subject to satisfactory references being provided by the referees they have named. These three methods are labelled 'the classic trio' by Mark Cook (2004). The procedure is expected, because in most cases this is the approach taken by organisations. What is interesting is that this traditional approach continues to dominate in the face of apparently conclusive evidence that other tools of selection have far greater predictive power and are fairer to most candidates. In this and the following chapters we discuss this conundrum in relation to the wide range of different selection methods available to employers. We also assess the advantages and disadvantages of each in different situations, and examine ways in which each might be improved against a range of criteria.

In this chapter we focus on the traditional approaches described above. We concentrate principally on the interview, since this appears to be the one approach to selection that virtually all selectors consider to be indispensable, but also look at the use of application forms and references in the screening process. In the next chapter we consider those selection methods that are less commonly used but that are said to be far more accurate as predictors of job performance.

LEARNING OUTCOMES

By the end of this chapter readers should be able to:

- devise application forms
- draw up a shortlist of candidates
- conduct a selection interview
- make effective use of employment references
- advise on the effectiveness of traditional selection tools.

In addition, readers should be able to understand and explain:

- the theoretical advantages and disadvantages of different selection methods

- employer objectives in the use of interviews, references and application forms.

RESEARCH IN EMPLOYEE SELECTION

There is a long tradition going back to the beginning of the twentieth century of academic research into the relative merits of different selection tools. For the most part, the field has been dominated by occupational psychologists who have worked with a shared set of assumptions concerning personality traits and their relationship to job performance. Foremost among the approaches undertaken have been validity studies, in which a selection process that results in the appointment of several individuals is observed. The scores given to candidates at the selection stage are recorded and compared with their actual performance on the job some months or years later. Different selection methods can then be compared according to how accurately they predict job performance (ie the extent to which candidates who score particularly well at selection achieve higher levels of performance than colleagues who impressed less at the selection stage).

The unit of measurement used in these studies is the correlation coefficient: a measure of how closely scores at the selection stage correlate with those awarded for later performance. Were a selection process to be found to have resulted in a correlation coefficient of 1, it would have predicted the relative performance of employees with perfect accuracy. Conversely, a correlation coefficient score equal to 0 indicates the absence of any predictive accuracy at all – the employer might as well have picked candidates at random. A modest validity study looking at a small group of employees chosen using one selection tool, while interesting, is not especially helpful in allowing generalised judgements to be made about the predictive qualities of any particular selection method. However, over the years many hundreds of such studies have been carried out in many countries that can be combined and assessed together using computer programs. It is the results of such exercises, known as meta-analyses, that have apparently confirmed what many have long believed, namely that traditional methods of selection such as interviews are markedly poorer at accurately predicting job performance than more sophisticated techniques such as personality tests and assessment centres. The results of meta-analyses are illustrated in Figure 11.1. More recent meta-analytic studies have given a rather better press to structured interviews, but provide continuing evidence of the poor predictive powers of the traditional formats that are the more commonly used (see Buckley and Russell 1999, Rynes *et al* 2000, Salgado 2001, Dipboye *et al* 2001, Cooper *et al* 2003, Morgeson *et al* 2007.)

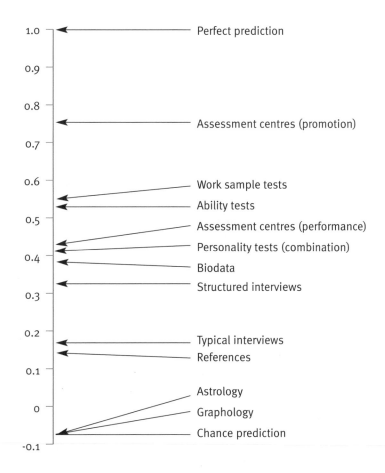

Figure 11.1 Accuracy of some methods of selection

Source: Smith *et al* (1989).

Despite the presence of this research and the accompanying bad publicity for traditional selection methods, there is plenty of evidence to show that they remain very widely used in the appointment of new employees. Successive CIPD surveys looking at recruitment and selection practices show that interviews of one kind or another are almost universally used, that application forms are completed by candidates seeking work in over 80 per cent of organisations, and that references are taken up either before or after interviews by at least three-quarters of employers (see IRS 2002a, CIPD 2007a). The current picture would thus appear to confirm the observation made by Robertson and Makin (1986) that in the United Kingdom 'the frequency of a method's use is inversely related to its known validity'.

However, what is particularly interesting in these surveys is the response of employers when asked to reflect on which selection techniques they found most useful. For all grades of staff, a very clear majority stated that the interview was the most important tool for them in making selection decisions. There is thus clearly a great gulf between the considered views of academics and practitioners about the relative usefulness and value of different selection methods. Possible reasons for this disagreement will be explored in relation to each of the selection methods described in this and the subsequent chapter. It is, however, useful to make one or two general observations at this stage.

First, it should be pointed out that the 'classic trio' are the most straightforward and least expensive of the range of selection methods available to employers. The use of reputable personality and ability tests requires costly training or the employment of trained consultants, to which is added the cost of the tests themselves. The potential expense of an assessment centre is clearly far higher and is not in any case a practical option for small organisations or for the selection of relatively low-skilled personnel. Second, it is important for employers to have an eye on the effect the selection methods they use have on candidates and potential candidates. Such matters have not historically concerned psychologists, who have preferred to concentrate purely on the predictive qualities of each tool.

Furthermore, because application forms, interviews and references are so commonly used, they are expected by job applicants. Too much innovation in the selection procedure might be disorienting, and thus reduce the effectiveness of a candidate's performance. In certain situations the prospect of being judged by the selection methods with the highest validity may actually dissuade good candidates from applying. This is particularly true of assessment centres that require attendance at a two or three-day event and that often include tough assignments.

The reluctance from the candidates' perspective springs from the lack of control they can exercise over the process when the more scientific approaches are adopted. Not only, therefore, are we more comfortable with the classic trio because we expect them and have experienced them before; we also prefer them because we think we understand how they work, and feel that they give us a greater degree of influence over the selection decision.

Mention should also be made of criticisms that have been made of the psychological research itself. Iles and Salaman (1995, pp219–224), Searle (2003) and Iles (2007, pp99-100) argue persuasively that the assumptions on which much validity research is based are open to question. In particular, they take issue with the notion that personality is on the one hand readily measurable, and on the other necessarily stable over time. In other words, they question the very basis on which psychometric studies of selection are based. They also draw attention to the fact that job content varies to a great extent over a period of years, or even months, and that the individual attributes candidates display when selected may be less and less relevant as time passes and the nature of the job develops and changes. It follows from this argument that what is important at selection is finding an individual who generally 'fits in' with the culture and values of the organisation and is sufficiently well qualified to undertake a range of possible tasks. The aim is thus less to 'match' a personality with a job than to screen out people perceived as likely to be dishonest, lazy, difficult to work with or unsatisfactory for a variety of other reasons.

THE USE OF GRAPHOLOGY

An interesting example of the use of selection methods that are neither scientific nor systematic is the use of graphology or hand-writing analysis. Despite firm evidence of its poor predictability (Smith et al 1989, pp86–88; Ben-Shakhar 1989), it appears to be used surprisingly widely. In the United Kingdom it is rare for employers to admit to its use in selection, although some have confirmed that they use it as one of a range of techniques (see North 1994, p3; Cooper *et al* 2003, pp149–152). On the Continent it is much more common, with over three-quarters of smaller French companies believed to use it in employee selection, while a good proportion of employers in Belgium and Germany also apparently believe it has an effective role to play.

A possible reason for the use of graphology is its apparent 'reliability' as a selection tool. People's handwriting tends not to change to any great extent during their adult life, although it can be made neater with effort. It is also a 'reliable' method in so far as different graphologists have been found to reach similar conclusions about a candidate's personality when given the same handwriting sample to analyse – not a situation that typically occurs when several people interview the same candidate at different times.

However, reliability should not be confused with validity. There is also evidence to show that graphology is a poor diviner of important personality traits, and is thus probably a poor predictor of job performance. According to Smith *et al* (1989), when tested, graphologists were unable to distinguish between real and faked suicide notes, and failed to identify which of a range of handwriting samples had been submitted by people diagnosed as neurotic. Further research reported by Watson (1994, p208) and Edenborough (2005, pp 29–30) supports this view, leading them to conclude that, as yet, there is insufficient evidence to support the use of graphology as part of a fair and objective selection procedure.

EXERCISE 11.1

PERFORMANCE-BASED SELECTION

People management

Read the article by Lou Adler, Outside chance (*People Management*, 10 March 2005, pp38–39). This can be downloaded from the *People Management* archive on the CIPD's website (www.cipd.co.uk).

In this opinion piece, Lou Adler draws on many years of recruiting experience to suggest ways in which decision-making about who to hire can be improved in organisations.

Questions

1   What, according to Adler, are the major common errors made by recruiters when selecting staff?

2   To what extent do you agree with Adler's 'five easy-to-learn principles for improving employee selection decisions'?

3   What other action could be taken by organisations seeking to improve their capabilities in this area of practice?

KEY ARTICLE 24

Cliff Lockyer and Dora Scholarios, Selecting hotel staff: why best practice does not always work. *International Journal of Contemporary Hospitality Management,* Vol. 16, No. 2, pp125–135 (2004)

This article persuasively questions the universal utility of the conventional 'best practice' approach to recruitment and selection. It combines a questionnaire survey of practice in 81 Scottish hotels with a case study approach focusing in some detail on the selection practices used in nine hotels. The findings are somewhat contrary to those that are usually reported in the selection and 'best practice' literatures. Hotels that are part of larger chains with centralised P&D functions tend to use the more formal, sophisticated approaches to selection recommended in the best practice literature. Independent hotels, as well as those that are part of chains but that are characterised by very high standards of customer service tend, on the contrary, to recruit and select using informal methods of the kind damned in the literature for lacking predictive validity. Yet staff turnover is lower in the case of

the hotels using informal processes, while they also have far fewer recruitment difficulties. In other words, in this industry it appears that failing to adopt 'best practice' leads to the best staffing outcomes.

Questions

1   Why do independently managed hotels persist with the use of informal recruitment and selection methods?

2   What explanations do Lockyer and Scholarios give for concluding that informal methods can amount to 'best practice' in the hotel industry?

3   How persuasive do you find the conclusion? Why?

4   To what extent might the findings be generalised beyond the Scottish hotel industry and why?

APPLICATION FORMS

In its surveys, the CIPD finds that application forms are used in some shape or form by 80 per cent of respondents (CIPD 2003b). In many larger organisations and in the public sector, they appear to be used for all jobs except those at senior management level, and there are examples of universal usage for all jobs including the most senior. The alternative is to allow or encourage applicants to compose their own curriculum vitae or CV. This practice is widespread in the private sector, but only permitted in 50 per cent of public and voluntary sector organisations. Many employers make use of both approaches, accepting CVs as well as application forms, the CV being the preferred approach in smaller organisations.

From an employer's perspective there are advantages and disadvantages to both application forms and CVs. In principle, the CV is preferable because it gives applicants the freedom to sell themselves in their own way. They are thus able to tailor their applications to their own strengths and are not restricted to fitting relevant information into boxes of predetermined size. Some application forms, because they are so restrictive in their design, may lead to excellent candidates being overlooked. An example might be a form that contains a set of questions and several blank spaces under the heading 'Present employment'. In putting so much emphasis in the form on this aspect, the likelihood is that otherwise good candidates who are not currently in full-time employment will be disadvantaged. A similar problem confronts an applicant who, while in work, is unhappy and is perhaps seeking a new position after just a few weeks or months in this employment. Indeed, a poorly designed application form has been shown to put many applicants off applying in the first place (Jenkins 1983).

However, CVs can be criticised for giving job applicants the opportunity to sell themselves to a potential employer by including material in their applications that is wholly irrelevant to the position being advertised. Similar 'contamination' effects can occur when a CV is particularly attractively presented or structured, leading unwary selectors, perhaps unconsciously, to favour applications from otherwise unimpressive candidates over those of their better-qualified rivals. In extreme cases, candidates engage in sophisticated 'impression management', going to great lengths to dazzle with well-bound, professionally produced CVs with career and other achievements highlighted and a judicious mix of leisure interests. A few, through individual quirkiness or a belief that their career opportunities are enhanced through making themselves memorable, produce CVs that make them unforgettable but also unemployable. It is for this reason that many public sector organisations refuse to accept CVs at all.

Perhaps the best solution is to design separate application forms for each vacancy advertised. This gets round the problem of inappropriate design and allows specific questions to be posed relevant to the job in question. With the development of more sophisticated word-processing and printing equipment, such an approach should be used more frequently, but as yet there is little evidence to suggest that employers have moved away from the standard organisation-wide form that has long been used across the whole range of jobs on offer. Individualisation would also permit the inclusion, where appropriate, of spaces for candidates to write longer descriptive answers to more involved questions.

Whether the application form used is standard or original to the job advertised, it will fulfil a number of distinct functions. According to Smith and Robertson (1993, pp81–82) these are:

- to enable a shortlist of candidates for interview to be drawn up

- to provide information that can be drawn on during the interview

- as a means by which information about good but unsuccessful candidates can be filed away for future reference

- as a means of analysing the effectiveness of the various alternative recruitment media used (see Chapters 9 and 10)

- as a public relations tool enhancing the employer's image as 'an efficient, fair and well-run organisation'.

IRS (1999b, p8) also found evidence of employers using forms 'to capture sensitive information in a non-intimidating way', by which is meant data for equal opportunities monitoring and medical information.

It follows that the best application forms are designed so as to fulfil each of the above functions as effectively as possible. The first three factors require the use of clear, concise language and a layout that allows candidates sufficient space to include all relevant information. The public relations function is best served by good-quality paper and typesetting.

A typical application form includes questions asking for basic biographical information, previous work experience, educational background, vocational training undertaken and future career aspirations. Forms often ask about previous convictions and the applicant's state of health. Asking candidates to include a passport-size photograph is also relatively common, although in practice candidates often fail to do so. Another relatively recent development is the request for information concerning gender and ethnic background to enable organisations to undertake equal opportunities monitoring. More often than not, this is included on a separate form that is detached or removed from the original prior to shortlisting. The question of nationality, by contrast, is usually included in the main body of the form to allow the employer to discuss matters relating to work permits with candidates at their interviews.

THE STANDARD APPLICATION FORM (SAF)

According to Keenan (1995, p397), half of all employers recruiting graduates prefer applicants to complete the standard application form provided by the university careers service. The SAF has been used extensively for many years now, proving to be an effective and fair shortlisting tool. Being designed specifically for new graduates, it is updated each year and is competence-based.

Copies are available at all university careers services establishments and can also be downloaded from the CSU website at www.prospects.ac.uk. The following appears on the current version:

- Personal details (name, contact address/numbers, date of birth, nationality, driving licence, work permit and so on).

- Higher education (dates, courses, expected and achieved results).

- Prior education (A levels, number and dates of GCSE passes at C and above,

grades in English and maths, number of GCSE A grades).

- Work experience (dates, jobs, responsibilities and achievements).

- Geographical location (preferred work locations).

- Personal interests/achievements (spare-time activities, specifically those that included organising and leading or those requiring initiative and creativity).

- Evidence of 'planning, implementation and achieving results' (specific examples required together with an estimation of 'how you measured your success').

- Evidence of 'influencing, communication and team work' (specific examples required with a statement of why the outcomes were satisfactory).

- Evidence of 'analysis, problem solving and creative thinking' (specific example of a problem required, together with a information about alternative

- approaches that could have been used in solving it).
- Additional information (space for candidates to write what they wish plus a question about where they heard about the vacancy).
- Specific skills (languages, IT packages etc).
- Career choice (a requirement for candidates to state their reasons for applying and evidence of their suitability).
- Health declaration.
- Referees (x2).
- Availability for interview.
- Equal opportunities monitoring form.

There are a number of questions commonly included in application forms that are controversial and that are often the subject of heated discussion among recruiters. Examples are those asking applicants to state their age or date of birth, and those asking them to list their hobbies and interests. The latter is a peculiar type of question because it usually has no relevance at all to the ability of candidates to fulfil the requirements of the job. It is also very likely indeed to be answered untruthfully, candidates taking care to include only mainstream or 'politically correct' interests. If candidates' main hobbies are eating fast food, watching 'adult' movies and smoking illegal substances, they are unlikely to include them in the response.

The question of age is more interesting, not least because since 2006 it has become possible to bring an age discrimination claim before an employment tribunal. The new law serves to restrict the extent to which age can be used as a selection criterion, but it does not outlaw such practices altogether. Employers remain free to continue discriminating on grounds of age when they can objectively justify so doing, the test being that the practice in a particular case constitutes 'a proportionate means of achieving a legitimate aim'. Ahead of the passing of the relevant regulations, the government's consultation documents suggested that age discrimination would be lawful on the following grounds:

- for health, safety and welfare reasons
- in order to facilitate employment planning
- to encourage or reward loyalty
- to take account of the need for a reasonable period for employment prior to retirement.

At the time of writing (late 2007) no cases on age discrimination had reached the appeal courts, so it is not yet possible to know exactly how far the courts will ultimately permit continued discrimination on grounds of age, and hence whether or not some long-standing selection practices will have to be abandoned. For example as matters stood it was lawful for age to be taken into account when a vacancy for a position as a supervisor of a group of middle-aged employees was advertised. While the presence of a young supervisor might not necessarily cause problems, many employers might think it very reasonable to include age as one of the criteria used in deciding who to invite for interview. It would then be possible to ensure that there were at least some older people shortlisted. Alternatively to what extent will it be considered lawful for an organisation whose customers are either predominantly from younger or older age groups to reflect these demographic bases when selecting staff for marketing and customer-facing roles?

Perhaps these are further situations in which there is a case for designing different applications for different jobs. The question about age or date of birth would then be included only when judged strictly necessary.

REFLECTIVE QUESTION

Where do you stand in this debate? Can you think of other circumstances in which it might be appropriate to request information about dates of birth?

In the next chapter we examine the use of weighted application forms and biodata. These are methods that enhance the role of application forms in the selection process and that have been found to have relatively high validities when compared with other selection methods.

FRAUDULENT APPLICATIONS

People management

EXERCISE 11.2

Read the article by Steve Smethurst, Faking it (*People Management*, 16 June 2005, pp35–36). This can be downloaded from the *People Management* archive on the CIPD's website (www.cipd.co.uk).

This short article reports the views of various commentators on the subject of untruths being included by job applicants in their CVs and on application forms. It concludes that the problem is widespread, but that employers can take steps to reduce the extent it affects them.

Questions

1   What proportion of CVs are thought to contain inaccurate information which makes candidates appear more impressive than they actually are?

2   Why do you think so few employers carry out checks to ascertain the truth of the information candidates submit to them?

3   What measures does the article suggest could be taken? How far do you think these would reduce the extent of fraud and why?

SHORTLISTING

The next stage in the traditional approach to selection is to boil down the applications received to a shortlist of candidates to invite for interview. Here again, as so often in employee selection, there is a potential tension between the relative merits of methodical and more informal approaches. All descriptions of best practice, including that contained in the (former) IPD's *Guide on recruitment* (1996a, pp5–6), advocate a systematic approach to shortlisting whereby a list of criteria is drawn up from the person specification. Each application form is then judged and scored against these standards. Torrington *et al* (2008) suggest that the drawing-up of criteria is best done by a panel, but that the shortlisting itself should be undertaken on an individual basis, each panel member looking at all application forms separately and drawing up his or her own list. Any candidate chosen by all the screeners is then invited to interview, while any discarded by all is rejected. Panel members then debate the merits of the remaining applicants with regard to the requirements of the person specification until a consensus is reached about who should and who should not be interviewed.

The argument in favour of such an approach is its inherent fairness. It discourages selectors, either consciously or unconsciously, from discriminating unfairly on the basis of factors unrelated to the content of the job. It thus reduces the chances of well-qualified candidates being screened out on account of peculiar handwriting, marital status or place of birth. Research quoted by Cook (2004, p4) found evidence of unfair discrimination on grounds of sex occurring at the shortlisting stage through the stereotyping of men and women as suitable or unsuitable for particular jobs. Other examples of stereotyping that have occurred in the experience of the author include making negative assumptions on the basis of:

- first names that are perceived to be unusual, old-fashioned or associated with low levels of education

- the kind of school (private, grammar or comprehensive) that someone attended

- the fact that a candidate was an ex-army officer.

It goes without saying that it is easier for individual managers who are racially prejudiced to screen out members of ethnic minorities if there is no panel to whom they must justify their actions.

Having put the case for a systematic approach, it is also reasonable to point out the drawbacks. The main problem arises if the criteria drawn up are too exacting, leading to the screening-out of good candidates who fail to respond to questions on the application form with precisely the answers required. An example might be a situation in which the agreed criteria include a requirement for shortlisted candidates to have had some years' experience in a particular role or at a specified level in an organisation. A typical case might be one in which applicants for a personnel management job are required to have worked for a minimum of three years in a senior HR role in manufacturing. While relevant and justifiable, such a parameter might lead to the rejection of the best candidate on the grounds that he or she has only two years' experience as a general manager in a service industry.

There is thus a strong case for allowing a degree of flexibility in the screening of application forms and for avoiding too narrow or bureaucratic an approach. If a candidate looks interesting, for whatever reason, it does no great harm to invite him or her to interview. To reject purely on the basis of an arbitrary set of criteria may be theoretically justifiable, but might well not be in the long-term interests of the organisation.

Wood and Payne (1998, pp77–81) advocate a simple scoring approach which, they argue, allows recruiters to sift hundreds of application forms at a rate of less than two minutes per form, while maintaining a high degree of fairness. Their starting point is the presence of an agreed list of competencies being sought for the job. Each candidate's application form is then rated on a three-point scale (A, B or C) against each competence, an A indicating strong evidence of the competence being sought, B indicating moderate evidence and C indicating little or no evidence. Once two C scores have been awarded the form is rejected. Those with most As are then shortlisted for interview.

? REFLECTIVE QUESTION

How systematic are the approaches to shortlisting used in your experience? What examples of stereotyping have you come across?

SHORTLISTING AT DAEWOO

An example of systematic shortlisting occurred when the Korean industrial corporation Daewoo established a car company in the United Kingdom. The sales arm was set up from scratch in the year following June 1994, requiring the HR department to fill several hundred vacancies in just a few months. The jobs on offer were based at retail stores across the country and at the company's UK headquarters in Hertfordshire. Local newspapers were used for advertising, each leading to the receipt of around 800 completed application forms. The company then had to screen out 90 per cent of these so that the interview stage might become manageable. The aim was to interview four or five applicants for each available position.

This was done in two ways. First, a computer system was used to rank the applicants in each town or city according to the answers given to specific questions on the application form. For the most part, these focused on the amount of work experience applicants had completed in the motor trade or in retailing and finance functions. Other questions asked about length of experience in working with information technology, managing staff, managing budgets and dealing with the public. Experience of unconventional working patterns was also included. The computer screening identified the 'top' 25 per cent of candidates.

The numbers were then further reduced by HR officers examining how applicants had answered other questions relating to experience in previous jobs. Here the focus was on how sales were achieved, what was understood by the term 'customer service', and previous successes applicants could point to in the fields of staff supervision and teamworking.

Source: IDS (1995d, pp10–11).

ONLINE SIFTING

As was explained in Chapter 9, among the disadvantages associated with online recruitment is the sheer number of unsuitable applications that employers can receive when jobs are advertised to a potential audience of several million Internet users. According to IRS (2003e, p38) this is by some margin the most significant problem for employers who use online recruitment; over 75 per cent of respondents had experienced difficulties dealing with large volumes of applications from unsuitable candidates. The problem is particularly acute in areas such as graduate recruitment, where employers actively seek to encourage applications from people who have yet to gain much work experience and thus employ broad criteria (a wide-trawl rather than a wide-net approach). In such circumstances some form of electronic screening technologies needs to be used so that the cost of printing off completed forms and/or CVs, and subsequently reading them, does not become prohibitive. Several approaches can be used, although the evidence suggests that to date they have only been adopted by a minority of organisations (see CIPD 2007a).

ONLINE APPLICATION/BIODATA FORMS

These require job applicants to complete an application form that is questionnaire-based. Its first purpose is to collect straightforward factual information about achievements and personal career history (eg class of degree, years of relevant work experience and current salary). Second, forms usually ask direct questions designed to establish how far the candidate possesses the attributes or competencies the employer wants for the job in question. Once completed, the candidate submits the form and it is scored electronically. Those that do not reach a threshold score are rejected electronically (but hopefully with courtesy), while the others are sent on into the employer's database. IRS (2003e) describes online application procedures that include 'killer questions' designed to sift out unsuitable candidates before they have even completed the form. If one or two of these are answered 'wrongly' the procedure terminates and the candidate is directed to another site.

ONLINE PERSONALITY QUESTIONNAIRES

These are generally established psychometric tests developed by reputable providers that have been adapted for use online from their original paper and pencil formats. Their advantages and disadvantages as tools of selection are debated in Chapter 12; our purpose here is to explain how they can be used as a means of screening out (or screening in) candidates who make applications via a website. As with online application forms, personality questionnaires can be scored electronically, those candidates who do not meet the employer's criteria being sifted out within a few minutes of completing the test.

There are drawbacks to the use of personality tests in this way. First, they are not completed within a set time limit. This allows the candidate greater opportunity to think carefully about what answer is sought and to give that rather than a truthful response. Second, the employer cannot know that it is in fact the candidate who is completing the inventory. Finally, as has been pointed out by McHenry (see Lamb 2000, p12), online testing allows no opportunity to give face-to-face feedback, which has always been considered good practice in the administration of personality tests.

ONLINE ABILITY TESTS

The fact that online tests can be completed by anyone, and not necessarily the candidates themselves, is a particularly acute problem in the case of online ability testing. However, this has not stopped some test providers from developing tools of this kind. As with the other forms of test identified above, these allow poorer candidates to be screened out, meaning that only those achieving the highest scores proceed to the next stage. Two methods seem to be used as a means of reducing the likelihood of 'cheating' (IRS 2001g, p9). First, the tests are designed to be 'game-like in appearance and functionality', so that applicants are not necessarily aware that they are in fact screening tests. Second they are deliberately designed to be enjoyable exercises so that individuals will want to complete them and will be less inclined to get someone else to do so on their behalf.

Whatever drawbacks such tests have at the shortlisting stage, they remain potentially useful later in the selection procedure when candidates can be asked to complete them while sitting in front of a terminal on the employer's own premises.

CV-MATCHING TECHNOLOGIES

The fourth approach differs from the first three in that it makes use of IT to screen out CVs submitted by candidates rather than a form designed by the employer. Here use is made of software that searches for key words in each CV that is submitted (examples are 'teamwork', 'initiative', 'self-confidence' and 'leadership'). Those that mention enough of the key words identified as desirable by the employer are then sent on to the recruiter for further analysis. Those that mention none or insufficient of the key words are rejected electronically with a polite but definitive e-mail.

This whole concept is highly questionable professionally as it introduces a strong element of chance into the shortlisting procedure. Good candidates are rejected simply because they have used one word rather than another, while poor ones slip through the net by chance having chosen a lucky turn of phrase. It is only really justifiable when an employer receives far more CVs electronically than it can begin to cope with. In such circumstances, there is no practicable alternative if applications are to be considered and then answered at all. It is the HR equivalent of a highly popular sporting event for which demand is so great that organisers are forced to allocate tickets via a ballot.

SELF-TEST QUESTIONNAIRES

The final approach differs somewhat from the first four in that the employer does not itself use the results of online testing for shortlisting purposes. Instead a questionnaire is provided that prospective candidates complete, but that is designed to encourage those who score 'poorly' to select themselves out by refraining from making an application. Questionnaires of this kind are 'marked' electronically, allowing e-mail based feedback to be given. Candidates who do not answer the questions in the desired ways are then advised that their applications, if submitted, would be unlikely to succeed.

EXERCISE 11.3

SHORTLISTING GRADUATES ONLINE

People management

Read the article by Victor Dulewicz, Give full details (*People Management,* 26 February 2004, p23). This can be downloaded from the *People Management* archive on the CIPD's website (www.cipd.co.uk).

In this opinion piece, Victor Dulewicz of Henley Management College makes a number of very serious criticisms about some employers' practices when using online shortlisting for candidates applying to join their graduate schemes.

Questions

1   In what ways do the practices described in the article fall short of those you would expect to see

adopted by professional graduate recruiters?

2   Aside from the ethical issues, what business case could be made to persuade these employers to reconsider their approaches?

3   In his penultimate paragraph, Dulewicz bemoans the failure of recruiters to implement a joint approach to graduate recruitment in which candidates would all take the same tests and complete the same application forms. What are the advantages and disadvantages of such a scheme from the perspective of graduate employers?

PROBLEMS WITH INTERVIEWS

As was stated above, there is plenty of apparently authoritative research in support of the claim that traditional selection interviews are poor predictors of future job performance. The term 'traditional' refers to typical, unstructured interviews in which different candidates may be asked quite different questions. The traditional interviewer thus gathers information in a relatively unsystematic manner, and may reach judgements about candidates on a number of different grounds. Anderson and Shackleton (1993), drawing on a wide variety of academic studies from several countries, very effectively summarise the reasons put forward to explain why such interviews have been criticised for their poor predictive validity. The following list is based on their summary:

- The expectancy effect. Undue influence may be given to positive or negative expectations of a candidate formed from his or her CV or application form.

- The self-fulfilling prophecy effect. Interviewers may ask questions designed to confirm initial impressions of candidates gained either before the interview or in its early stages.

- The primacy effect. Interviewers can put too much emphasis on impressions gained and information assimilated early in the interview.

- The stereotyping effect. Interviewers sometimes assume that particular characteristics are typical of members of a particular group. In the case of sex, race, disability, marital status or ex-offenders, decisions made on this basis are often illegal. However, the effect occurs in the case of all kinds of social groups.

- The prototyping effect. Interviewers may look for or favour a particular type of personality regardless of job-related factors.

- The halo and horns effect. Interviewers sometimes rate candidates as 'good' or 'bad' across the board and thus reach very unbalanced decisions.

- The contrast effect. Interviewers can allow the experience of interviewing one candidate to affect the way they interview others who are seen later in the selection process.

- Negative information bias effects. Interviewers can give more weight to perceived negative points about candidates than to those that are more positive.

- The similar-to-me effect. Interviewers sometimes give preference to candidates they perceive as having a similar background, career history, personality or attitudes to themselves.

- The personal liking effect. Interviewers may make decisions on the basis of whether they personally like or dislike the candidate.

- The information overload effect. Interviewers may form judgements based on only a fraction of the data available to them about each individual candidate.

- The fundamental attribution error effect. Interviewers sometimes incorrectly assume that some action on the part of the candidate is or was caused by an aspect of his or her personality rather than by a simple response to events.

- The temporal extension effect. Interviewers may assume that a candidate's behaviour at interview (eg nervousness) is typical of his or her general disposition.

What are we to conclude from this litany of criticisms? The most tempting and apparently rational conclusion would be to consign the traditional interview to the personnel management dustbin on the grounds that selection decisions reached in this manner are inevitably infused with subjectivity, prejudice and displays of cognitive dissonance. However, such action would be hasty. A different view might conclude that the validity of some traditional interviews is probably higher than others. In other words, we might acknowledge that interviews in which the above traps are avoided are likely to have greater predictive power than those in which they feature strongly. It follows that it may not be the interview as a selection tool that is faulty so much as the interviewer. With thought, care, experience and training, it should then be possible consciously to avoid making many of the basic errors that have been described.

REFLECTIVE QUESTION

Where do you stand in this debate? Is it the traditional interview that is faulty or is it the typical interviewer who is responsible for giving the method such a bad press?

THE SURVIVAL OF THE TRADITIONAL INTERVIEW

Another reason for hesitating before abandoning traditional approaches to interviewing is their continued popularity as tools of selection among both managers and candidates. Despite the presence for a number of years of evidence that suggests they are extremely poor predictors of performance, they continue to be the most favoured and frequently used of the available selection techniques. It is wise, therefore, at least to consider whether managers may in fact be right to continue swearing by the interview.

A number of alternative explanations can be put forward to explain the survival of traditional interviewing, some of which have already been touched on. One possibility is that managers have simply remained unaware of the research evidence amassed over the years. Another is that they are aware of the defects of traditional interviews but feel it to be counter-intuitive and therefore discount its relevance. Others accept some of the research evidence but regard themselves as exceptions (ie as good, intuitive interviewers who avoid making the classic errors).

Another explanation is the relatively low cost of carrying out simple one-to-one interviews, and the consequent perception that their efficiency outweighs their ineffectiveness as predictive techniques. In some cases it is also true that unstructured interviews are used as one of a range of selection tools, and that their principal role is to confirm impressions or clear up points left unresolved by the other selection methods. However, the most straightforward and significant explanation is that interviews are not only arranged for the purpose of enabling managers to make predictions about future performance on the job. According to Herriot (1989), there are in fact three key objectives for selection interviews, of which only one is their function as tools of assessment. The others are labelled 'mutual preview' and 'negotiation'.

The mutual preview function refers to the opportunity the interview gives both employer and applicant to meet face to face and exchange information unrelated to the prediction of performance, but nevertheless essential to any recruitment and selection process. In particular, it gives candidates the opportunity to ask questions about the job and the organisation as part of the process whereby they decide whether or not they wish to take the job. Interviewers also have the opportunity to inform candidates about the duties they can expect to undertake and the role they would be expected to fill, were they successful. It must be appreciated that in order to make effective choices about whether or not to accept the position on the terms offered, any candidate needs sufficient information about how the type of work and the organisational environment compare with those of existing or other employers.

The negotiation function is another part of the selection process that can only realistically occur by means of an interview. Here we are concerned with the processes that have to be gone through prior to the issuing and subsequent acceptance of a contract of employment. According to Anderson and Shackleton (1993, p42), matters up for negotiation include start dates, relocation procedures and allowances, training provisions and all other terms and conditions of employment.

A further role played by an interview is that of a labour market public relations exercise. There is every advantage to be gained from sending candidates away (a) believing that they would like the job if subsequently offered it, (b) determined to seek other positions within the organisation if other opportunities present themselves, and (c) willing to speak well of the organisation because of the efficiency, effectiveness, fairness and courtesy displayed towards them. The interview provides the only real opportunity for organisations to carry out this PR function with any degree of success.

Poor selection, on the other hand, leads to damaging, negative PR. If individuals depart perceiving that they have been treated unfairly, incompetently or harshly, they are likely to share their experiences with others. As the word spreads, it almost inevitably becomes embellished and distorted with repetition, which is exactly what we find in the field of consumer affairs. In 1986, the Ford Motor Company discovered that people who are pleased about their cars tell an average of eight others, whereas dissatisfied customers complain about their experiences to at least 22 others (who in turn tell 22 others, and so on). The result is that, in the realm of products and services, organisations lose customers; in the field of selection, organisations lose potential talent. It is not even absurd to believe that individuals treated badly as candidates might withdraw their business from the offending organisation, and that they might encourage others to do so as well. It can thus be contended that giving no interview, as much as giving a bad one, is likely to lead to such occurrences. People expect to be interviewed, and will not feel that they have had a fair hearing or respectful treatment if one is denied.

It can therefore be concluded that the interview has a number of distinct objectives, and that these can be summarised as follows:

- to predict future job performance and behaviour

- to focus on aspects of behaviour and performance that cannot easily be addressed by other methods

- to supply information to the candidate

- to persuade suitable candidates to accept the job offered and join the organisation

- to create goodwill for the organisation.

For these reasons, whatever the potential dangers of relying too heavily on traditional interviews, there is no practical substitute for some form of informal face-to-face meeting between employer and candidate. The interview is the only way in which the range of fragmented information about candidates gathered from the use of other selection techniques can be integrated into a meaningful pattern.

IMPRESSION MANAGEMENT

In 1998 Liz Whalley and Mike Smith published a fascinating book, *Deception in selection*, which examined the different ways in which both employers and potential employees seek to manipulate selection processes and mislead one another. One chapter concerns interviews. Here they set out how candidates for jobs use impression-management techniques to impress interviewers – activities that are far easier to undertake in traditional than in structured types of interview.

One technique involves taking an assertive or proactive approach. Here the candidate confidently exaggerates his or her past achievements or elaborates them somewhat so as to appear more impressive. There is also a tendency for candidates to talk assuredly, but not truthfully, about exciting future plans. When this is done convincingly, interviewers are impressed not only by the achievements themselves, but also by the implication that they provide evidence of attributes such as assertiveness and natural leadership ability. Common examples are a willingness to claim personal credit for some kind of positive outcome or to make out that an outcome was more positive than was the case in truth.

The other major impression-management technique used is defensive or reactive in nature. Here candidates seek to minimise the significance of their perceived weaknesses in a form of 'damage limitation exercises'. In interviews these often focus on reasons for leaving past jobs. Candidates are, for example, frequently reluctant to admit they were fired, or if they admit that, want to make out it was not their fault. They say either that they were made redundant, or that all the fault was on the part of the manager.

Whalley and Smith argue that impression-management of this kind is not necessarily a bad thing. It may reduce the predictive validity of the interview (if interviewers are sufficiently taken in), but it can also provide strong evidence of the ability to create a good impression – a necessary attribute in many management and customer-facing roles.

VARIETIES OF INTERVIEW FORMAT

Interviews and interview questions come in diverse forms. For this reason, when one is about to be interviewed, it is very difficult to predict exactly what will be involved or the general approach to questioning that will be taken. An obvious variable is the number of interviewers: Will the interview be conducted by one person, by two or by a panel?

The one-to-one interview has the advantage of informality and thus helps reduce the artificiality of the process. The intimacy makes it relatively straightforward to gain an interviewee's trust and thus to encourage them to relax. In the view of Munro Fraser (1979, p140), this is the most important objective of any interview:

> *The first requirement of a selection interview is that the interviewee should feel at ease and that he or she should talk freely and frankly. In practically every case, this will depend on the skill of the interviewer. If he behaves in a formal manner,*

asking questions and appearing to evaluate the answers, he will cease to be an interviewer and become an interrogator. There will thus be little chance that the interviewee will behave in his normal manner, and the amount of information he supplies will be minimal.

Against this however are the considerable drawbacks of cosy one-to-one interviews. First, there is the danger alluded to above of information overload. It is very difficult for one interviewer simultaneously to encourage openness by relaxing the candidate while concentrating on what he or she is saying and considering what question is best to ask next. What is gained in informality is lost in effectiveness. Second, having just one interviewer greatly increases the possibility of unfair bias in the final decision. Many of the problems with traditional interviews discussed above – particularly the halo and horns effect, the similar-to-me effect and the personal liking effect – are far less likely to play a part in the evaluation of candidates if multiple interviewers have to justify their thinking to one another.

While drawbacks can be ameliorated to an extent by the presence of two interviewers, it is only in the panel format that information overload and unfair bias are excluded to a satisfactory degree. However, the panel interview (when up to a dozen interviewers are present together) suffers from the very artificiality and formality that are so usefully absent from the one-to-one and two-to-one formats.

Panel interviews are also difficult to arrange, as so many people have to make sure they are available at the same time over a day or two while the candidates are to be seen. According to Anderson and Shackleton (1993, p75), they are also frequently controlled poorly, leading to the presence of unprofessional practices.

Perhaps the best solution of all is the sequential interview, in which the candidate is interviewed by several people over a period of time, but only sees one or two at a time. In principle, such an approach is the best of both worlds. The danger here, however, is that each interviewer or duo simply ask the same questions as each other. The result is a bored candidate and less information on which to make selection decisions. Sequential interviewing thus only lives up to expectations when different interviewers agree in advance which areas of questioning each will cover.

360-DEGREE INTERVIEWING

An intriguing form of interviewing senior managers was instigated in the London Borough of Havering in 1996, when applicants for directorships and the post of chief executive were interviewed by their future subordinates. The thinking behind the innovation was that these people, were they to be successful in their posts, would have to lead and motivate the organisation. How better to test their ability to do so than by getting the staff to interview them? In this case, trade unions were also involved in the process, which lasted three days.

Perhaps more common is the practice whereby members of a team interview future colleagues – a form that could perhaps be labelled 180-degree interviewing. It is most commonly associated with the selection of board directors, but is also used in other situations where effective team membership is crucial to success in a role.

Source: Daly (1996, p1).

VARIETIES OF INTERVIEW QUESTION

Another way that interviews vary is in the type of questions asked. While there are many approaches, three types are given particular attention in the literature: hypothetical, behavioural and stress questions.

HYPOTHETICAL QUESTIONS

Also referred to as problem-solving or situational questioning, this method involves asking candidates how they would react or behave in specific situations. The problems posed will usually be examples of those that might be encountered in the job in question, but there may be situations in which examples from outside work could be used in an attempt to obtain evidence of the candidate's customary reactions to pressured or unusual circumstances. The obvious problem, of course, is the opportunity such questions give the quick-witted candidate to think of the best answer, or the one that is expected. When asked how you would react if a customer complained loudly about sloppy service, it is very easy to say that you would deal with the situation calmly and cool-headedly by taking the complainant to a private area and listening carefully to their points, before judiciously offering discounts or complimentary products. The extent to which people would really manage the situation so professionally and effectively remains open to question: it is far easier said than done.

There is also the problem of asking candidates about situations that they cannot have encountered and would not be expected to deal with anyway without relevant training. In such cases, honest candidates will say, 'I don't really know', or 'I would ask head office what to do' – answers that are likely to do them little credit. Others will make up a plausible response without having any idea about whether they have answered correctly. To that extent, hypothetical questioning can be said to introduce an unsatisfactory element of chance into the interview. Perhaps it is best to use hypothetical questioning only in order to test basic knowledge about the tasks that make up the job in question, and not to ask about social situations or those that are particularly complex.

Examples of hypothetical questions that might be used for an HR post are:

- A customer reports the loss of a wallet or purse. A manager subsequently finds a wallet that matches the description in a locker allocated to a member of staff. What would you do if confronted with this situation?

- Absence rates in Department A are three times higher than in Department B. What steps would you take to analyse the reasons and reduce absence in Department A?

- A female member of staff comes to talk to you confidentially. She claims to have suffered harassment from two work colleagues who have used intimidating language with a sexual content. What do you do?

BEHAVIOURAL QUESTIONS

Less commonly used, but often more effective, are questions that focus on past events in a candidate's life. These are also referred to as 'patterned behaviour description interview' (PBDI) questions, which seek to focus the candidate's attention on critical incidents from his or her past. In so doing, the interviewer hopes to hear of occasions when the interviewee has demonstrated those abilities or behaviours that are most relevant to the job for which he or she is applying. An example might be a job in which decisiveness was seen as a crucial attribute. A behavioural question would then involve asking candidates to describe an occasion when they took a particularly difficult decision or were forced to make an important decision without having as much information as they would have liked.

In putting this question, the interviewer is looking for hard evidence that candidates have acted with sufficient decisiveness in the past. The assumption is then made that, put in a similar situation, they would display the same behaviour in the future.

When asking behavioural questions, it is often necessary to home in on the detail of a critical incident by seeking supplementary information. Once the candidate has given a broad description of a relevant occasion, the interviewer probes more deeply by asking, 'What exactly happened?', 'What was your personal contribution?' or 'Tell me more about how you reacted.' Only when hard evidence of the behaviour in question has been gained can the candidate be deemed acceptable on that count.

It is harder to make up answers to behavioural than hypothetical questions because of the need to give believable answers to the probing supplementaries. They also have the advantage, from the interviewer's point of view, of providing a good basis on which to justify an appointment or promotion. When asked why someone was unsuccessful, it can simply be pointed out that there was no hard evidence given of sensitivity, persuasiveness, creativity or whatever other attributes were deemed important for a job-holder to possess. A very positive review of behavioural interviewing is provided in Jean Barclay's (2001) account of her recent research into the subject.

There are few disadvantages of this approach to interviewing recorded in the research literature although, as was shown in Chapter 8, there are criticisms of the competency frameworks that underpin many of the questions that are asked. However, problems can arise when the behaviours asked about in the interview are not strictly those required to undertake the job effectively. It is actually very difficult to pick three or four key attributes or personality dimensions for any one job and, as a result, different interviewers often end up asking very different questions. There is thus clearly a need to base such questioning on the contents of agreed person specifications, or ideally on discussions with a current holder of the job in question.

REFLECTIVE QUESTION

Would you like to be interviewed using behavioural questions? What are the advantages and disadvantages from the perspective of the candidate?

STRESS QUESTIONS

A third type of question apparently used quite regularly is one that is disparaging or aggressive. These 'stress' questions can also involve deliberately contradicting something the interviewee has said. Sometimes, one suspects, this practice has no real purpose and is carried out only because it is hugely enjoyable for a particular type of sadistic selector. However, some argue that stress interviews are necessary in some circumstances in order to observe, at first hand, reactions to stressful or uncomfortable situations. There is also no clear agreement as to what exactly is encompassed by the term 'stress' in these circumstances. Some people might find being asked to 'sell themselves' highly stressful, while others will not blink an eyelid when given a thorough interrogation.

In general this author would argue that there are precious few circumstances in which there is any case for deliberately putting a candidate under undue stress. Reactions are likely to be as artificial as the behavioural patterns of individuals in any kind of selection interview; moreover, candidates are being asked to produce spontaneous responses in unfamiliar circumstances when, in practice, they would have the opportunity to think about options in advance. There is also a grave danger that the interviewee will react badly, assume that the interviewer has acted unprofessionally, and share their negative experiences with others. In this respect the stress interview can be said to generate bad labour-market PR of the kind described earlier.

Of course, not all interview questions fit neatly into one of these three categories. There is a case for asking easy-going and chatty questions to which there are obvious answers in order to put candidates at their ease and hence glean more meaningful information. Such approaches are particularly useful at the start of interviews when candidates may be less than forthcoming, because they are apprehensive.

However, at all times, there are certain basic rules to follow in posing interview questions. According to Goodworth (1979, pp51–61), these include:

- Ask open-ended questions; that is, those starting with the words 'what', 'when', 'why', 'where', 'which' and 'how'.

- Avoid direct (or 'closed') questions to which the candidate can answer simply 'Yes', 'No', or 'That's right.'

- Avoid asking questions that reveal the answer you want. An example given by Goodworth is, 'We place great faith in our house magazine as a medium of communication. Are you in favour of house journals?'

- Avoid engaging in arguments with interviewees. Restrict yourself to restrained and courteous discussion about issues of importance in the job.

- Ask one question at a time. Avoid the temptation to string one or two together, as this will confuse the candidate.

STRUCTURING INTERVIEWS

The one constructive and consistent message that emerges from the large body of research into selection interviewing is the finding that structured interviews have considerably higher predictive validity than their unstructured equivalents, and recent years seem to have seen a substantial growth in the number of employers taking up this approach (CIPD 2007a, p13). However, academic commentators differ in their interpretations of how substantial an improvement is made by structuring.

Smith *et al* (1989, p9) suggest that structured interviews have validity coefficients of approximately 0.3, although they also refer to studies that have found them to have greater predictive qualities. Anderson and Shackleton (1993, pp49–51), Eder and Harris (1999, pp16–18) and Rynes *et al* (2000), on the other hand, give structured approaches a far better press. They quote meta-analyses that suggest validity coefficients in excess of 0.6 – as effective as any selection technique can ever reasonably be expected to be.

The term 'structured' in the context of selection interviewing has a number of distinguishing features:

- Questions are planned carefully before the interview.

- All candidates are asked the same questions.

- Answers are scored according to agreed rating systems.

- Questions focus on the attributes and behaviours needed to succeed in the job.

While structuring interviews in this way may be a highly effective method of improving their predictive quality, it is not necessarily conducive to the creation of a relaxed atmosphere in which the candidate can easily open up. There is evidence to suggest that unless handled carefully by trained interviewers, structured interviews can be unsatisfactory:

> *The main disadvantage of using a structured interview is that its rigidity can limit the information-gathering process. Instead of exploring an applicant's responses by further questioning during the interview, the process is often rushed in order to get through all the questions on the schedule, and the assessment of the individual can be inaccurate as a result. Also, since the interviewer takes the lead, he or she may dominate the process, denying the applicant sufficient time to provide a considered and accurate response.*
> (Du Plessis 2003, p179)

The artificiality of these approaches may also dissuade candidates from entering into a two-way exchange by asking their own questions. In short, the mutual exchange and negotiation functions are less well served than the assessment function. There are two compromise solutions that help ameliorate these problems: semi-structuring and mixed approaches.

SEMI-STRUCTURING

The interviewer can opt for the approach referred to by Anderson and Shackleton (1993, p72) as 'focused', in which there is a degree of structuring, but also a greater degree of flexibility than a fully structured approach would allow. The interviewer thus plans a series of topics to cover in the interview but follows up what individual interviewees say with supplementary questions. A degree of spontaneity is therefore made possible that permits the candidate some control over the direction of the interview. Meaningful two-way exchange is thus retained.

MIXED APPROACHES

The interviewer can use different questioning techniques at different stages in the interview. Hence, at the start, in order to facilitate mutual exchange and to help the candidate relax, unstructured spontaneous questions are asked. Later, in order to maximise the effectiveness of the assessment function, a greater degree of structuring is introduced, with all candidates asked the same questions. Unstructured approaches are then returned to in the final stages when the negotiation function becomes significant.

KEY ARTICLE 25

Elaine D. Pulakos and Neal Schmitt, Experienced-based and situational interview questions: studies of validity. *Personnel Psychology*, No. 48, pp289–308 (1995).

This American article describes and analyses the findings of a validity study – a common type of approach to research in the field of employee selection. However, this study is unusual in that it focuses on the relative validity of two types of interview strategy rather than focusing on selection interviews in more general terms. It compares the outcomes associated with interviews made up from behavioural questions (referred to here as 'experienced-based questions') and hypothetical questions (referred to here as 'situational questions'). The first step involved obtaining detailed ratings of the performance of over 200 employees in an organisation against specific competences. Each of these people was then invited to a structured interview with a three person-panel, but the strategies adopted were different. Half were asked hypothetical questions designed to predict performance in the key competences, the other half were asked behavioural questions. The extent to which each strategy accurately predicted performance was then established by carrying out a correlation analysis.

The stark conclusion reached for this sample of interviewees was that behavioural interviews were valid predictors of performance and that hypothetical interviews were not. A further study described in the same article finds evidence to suggest that well-designed structured interviews can be better predictors of job performance than cognitive ability tests (see Chapter 12). This finding conflicts with those of most validity studies that have focused on those two selection methods.

Questions

1 What reasons do the authors advance to explain the finding that behavioural interviewing better predicts performance than hypothetical interviewing?

2 What other reasons do you think could
   help explain the finding?

3 To what extent do you think these
   conclusions have a general
   significance for selection policy in
   organisations and why?

PREPARING FOR INTERVIEWS

In this section some of the basic steps that need to be taken in preparing to
interview candidates are outlined. While many of the points may seem
rudimentary, they are frequently handled poorly or forgotten altogether. The key
points are the need to ask questions that are clearly relevant to the job for which
the candidate is applying, and the need, at all times, to be concerned about the
image of the organisation in the potential recruit's mind.

- In writing to invite a candidate for interview, address him or her by name and
  not by a ritualistic mode of address like 'Dear sir or madam'.

- Specify the date, time and place of the interview. Also include a location map
  with details of access for cars and pedestrians, parking and public transport.
  Disabled access arrangements should also be mentioned.

- Indicate in the letter the purpose of the interview by distinguishing between a
  screening interview, speculative discussions and the final decision-making
  event.

- Outline the likely duration of the exercise and the format the interviewee can
  expect (eg panel, one-to one, sequential).

- Include the names and job titles of the interviewers.

- Give details of other aspects of the proceedings so that nothing takes
  candidates by surprise. For instance, if they are expected to undergo a medical
  examination, then they should be advised in advance.

- State what documents applicants need to bring with them (eg proof of
  qualifications, driving licence, indemnity insurance certificate). Specify the
  need to bring originals, not copies.

- Explain how (or whether) expenses will be paid.

- Ask candidates to confirm their intention to attend the interview at the stated
  time and place.

- Close the letter with optimistic or enthusiastic remarks about the forthcoming
  process.

- End by giving a name (not an illegible signature) and methods by which
  candidates can make contact (address, phone number, e-mail etc.).

- Base interview questions on a comprehensive, accurate and up-to-date job
  description.

- Ask questions derived from a meaningful person specification that genuinely discriminates between the 'essential' and the 'desirable' in a fashion that, at least in principle, enables definitive judgements to be made.

- In framing questions for unstructured and semi-structured interviews, refer to the CV or application form so that any inconsistencies or omissions can be followed up.

- Give active consideration to the current environment and to any important business issues of relevance to the vacant job. This background material should be used in question design and can also be imparted to candidates during the interview so that they can answer questions as effectively as possible.

APPLICANT REACTIONS

In recent years, as labour markets have tightened and employers have had to work harder at attracting staff, researchers have focused more extensively on the recruitment aspects of selection interviewing. Several projects have thus been carried out looking at the perceptions of applicants and at which forms and types of interview experience give them the most favourable impression of the organisation.

Among the qualities that applicants rate highly are warmth. They like an interviewer who appears friendly and supportive rather than distant and cold. Second, the research shows that candidates greatly appreciate being interviewed by someone who is informative, who answers their questions frankly and gives them a full picture of the job and the organisation. Candidates are suspicious of interviewers who seem to be overselling the job, because they assume that they are

covering something up. They also tend to be put off by interviews that are very heavily structured and give them little opportunity to put their own case in the way that they want to. Aside from being personable and informative, applicants also want to be assured that their interviewer is competent and is clearly listening to what they are saying.

Body language thus matters a great deal, as does effective preparation on the part of interviewers. These studies provide further evidence of the gains that can be made for organisations that invest time and money in training their interviewers. Perhaps the most dangerous beast of all is the arrogant manager who believes he or she is a 'natural' interviewer whose style cannot be improved with training or thorough preparation

Sources: Whalley and Smith (1998, p96) and Rynes *et al* (2000, pp260–266).

SELECTING PEOPLE TO WORK WITH CHILDREN

EXERCISE 11.4

Read the article by Catherine Waldon of the NSPCC, Questions of trust (*People Management*, 7 March 2002, p27). This can be downloaded from the *People Management* archive on the CIPD's website (www.cipd.co.uk).

This article raises a number of interesting and important issues about the selection of staff to work in schools, children's homes and other children's organisations – situations in which choosing the wrong person can have extremely serious consequences.

Questions

1   Why do some people have concerns about the equal opportunities implications of in-depth preliminary interviewing of the kind advocated in this article?

2   What kind of interview and interview questions do you think would be most appropriate to ask candidates applying to work with children, and why?

3   Aside from interviewing, what other methods of selection should be used when recruiting for these kinds of jobs?

TELEPHONE INTERVIEWING

Telephone interviews are becoming increasingly common, being used mainly by employers as a quick and relatively cheap method of deciding which candidates to invite to a formal face-to-face interview. CIPD (2007a, p13) reports that over 60 per cent of employers now use this approach for some of their jobs, a very substantial growth being recorded in the use of telephone interviewing in recent years.

Aside from cost, the main advantage that supporters of telephone interviewing point to is a supposed reduction in the opportunity for unfair bias on grounds of race, age, disability and other factors that might be unlawful to take into account, or false impressions that lead to good candidates being rejected for insignificant reasons (see IRS 2002b). The extent to which this is true is debatable, and there appears to be little academic research that backs it up. When speaking on the telephone to someone whom we have not met, we have a strong tendency to picture that person in our minds on the basis of the characteristics of his or her voice. These impressions are often wildly inaccurate, as we later find out to our surprise when we meet someone whom we have only got to know on the telephone (the same is true when a radio presenter we are very familiar with appears on television). The suggestion that telephone interviewing reduces the extent to which interviewers leap to conclusions about people must be questionable. In fact they are often more likely to gain an inaccurate impression.

A rather more sound, evidence-based argument is that telephone interviews tend to be more business-like, with interviewers and interviewees focusing on the key questions from the start. There is less general chit-chat and hence a greater focus on the job role itself. It is also argued that the quality of someone's argument comes through more clearly by telephone than it does in a face-to-face interview, because interpersonal factors such as the way people look, dress or carry themselves physically cannot get in the way of judgements about what they are actually saying.

Research carried out by Joanne Silvester (reported in IRS 2002b) found that candidates were consistently rated more poorly in telephone interviews than when interviewed face to face. Interviewers, it would seem, are happier to be critical of someone they have not met personally. This strongly suggests that there is a likelihood of unfair bias occurring where some candidates are interviewed by telephone for a job, while others are seen face to face. The latter invariably achieve greater success rates.

EMPLOYMENT REFERENCES

The reference letter of recommendation or testimonial is the third of the three selection techniques that make up the 'classic trio'. Like interviews and application forms, it is very widely used but has been found to be of limited value by researchers. As a predictor of job performance it has low validity, and has often been found to say more about its author than about its subject.

A number of reasons have been put forward to explain the limitations of references. According to Cooper *et al* (2003, p154), they are 'highly subjective' and 'open to error and abuse' because 'the flow of information is between two people who are unlikely to meet and about an applicant who will never know what is written'. The implication is that employers are generally disinclined to regard the giving of a fair, considered assessment of a former employee as a high priority. The result is carelessness and a reluctance to put a great deal of time or thought into the writing of the reference. Interestingly, only around half of all reference requests sent out by post ever receive a response (IRS 2001h, p11). Furthermore, a number of specific problems have been identified:

- A tendency to give individuals a similar rating when asked about different aspects of their work and personality. If asked to comment separately about someone's social skills, conscientiousness, initiative and attendance records, referees tend to rate candidates as good, moderate or poor on all counts.

- A tendency to give good ratings. It is comparatively rare for employers to receive poor references. While this could be simply because candidates name only people who, they believe, will write a positive assessment, there is also evidence to suggest that employers are generally reluctant to mark someone down in a reference report. A range of average or non-committal ratings or statements thus often indicates a weak performer.

- A tendency, when given a five-point scale, to rank individuals in the centre. Employers seem reluctant to give excellent ratings.

As was the case with interviews, given these damning research findings it is reasonable to ask why references retain their near universal appeal for employers. Here, too, the answer probably lies in the function that references fulfil. According to IRS (2002a, p36), some 70 per cent of references are taken up after the selection decision has been made. The aim is therefore less to assist in the prediction of job performance and more to do with double-checking factual information and seeking confirmation of general impressions gained during the selection process. The reference provides one more piece of information, but is rarely crucial in determining who will get a job.

There are three exceptions to this. The first is the case of internal candidates. In large organisations where people compete for in-house promotions, references are likely to play a more fundamental part in the selection process. In such situations both the selector and the referee will take the process of writing references more seriously. The same kind of influences also come into play in the case of applicants for jobs in professions occupied by relatively few people. Here, although job transfers are occurring between organisations, the chances are that referees know those responsible for the selection of candidates. As a result, references are generally more reliable than they are when the writers and recipients are anonymous to each other. Examples include academic and senior medical appointments. The other exception is the case when a reference reveals that candidates have been less than honest in statements they have made in interviews or on their application forms. Common examples include misleading information about dates of employment, salary, seniority and reasons for leaving previous jobs.

Where references bring dishonesty of this kind to light, they can be crucial in determining that offers of employment are not made. Perhaps the most useful question of all is: 'Would you re-employ this person?' If former employers answer negatively, there is a need to probe further and find out why.

There are three improvements to the process of reference-gathering that researchers have found increase the quality of the information gathered. The first is to contact former employers and named referees by telephone. Doing so is less anonymous and thus increases the chances of a candid and balanced assessment. Provided that the questions asked over the phone are precise and job-related, this approach can work well. It also has the advantage of making it harder for ex-employers to avoid giving references. According to IRS (1999b, p15), 17 per cent of employers take up references by telephone, but this approach is very much used as a fallback and frequently leads to a request for confirmation of key points in writing (IRS 2003e, p37).

The second widely mooted improvement is to design structured assessment forms that relate specifically to the skills and experience necessary to perform well in the job under consideration (Dobson 1989). As with structured interviewing, this requires much more preparation than the placing of a pre-printed form in an envelope. It requires separate forms to be constructed for different jobs, with questions related to the criteria agreed in the job specification. IRS (1999b, p15) reports that as many as 60 per cent of employers use structured forms as a means of gaining references.

The third means by which references can be made more useful is to request more than just one or two. Asking a candidate for permission to approach half-a-dozen referees increases the chances of receiving meaningful information. It also makes it harder for the candidate to name only people who are likely to give unblemished reports. It is for this reason that applicants for positions in the security services are asked to name several referees, including employers whom they left many years previously. Cook (2004, p70–72) gives a positive review to the practice of including peers as well as former supervisors in the list of people to whom references are sent.

Interestingly, the likelihood of eliciting frank and honest references from former employers is perceived to have become harder in recent years, with some interesting legal judgements (IRS 2002a, p34–35) and the presence on the statute books of data protection laws which permit unsuccessful applicants access to references in many circumstances. These have led a number of employers to review policy concerning the giving of references by agreeing to give factual information only or by insisting that references are issued only once they have been approved by P&D managers. In some cases organisations have simply decided that their policy will be to not write references at all. Potentially, referees can be sued by both the ex-employee and their new employer if they knowingly make false statements. According to IDS (1992b, p56):

> An employer who provides a reference owes a duty to the recipient of that reference, usually the new employer. If the recipient of the reference suffers loss as a result of relying on the inaccurate reference, he may be able to claim damages from the writer of the reference. The loss may be the expense of recruiting a replacement employee or, more seriously, the loss consequent upon the incompetence or dishonesty of the employee.

The situation with ex-employees is more complicated because of the range of different grounds on which cases can be brought. These include defamation, injurious falsehood and negligent mis-statement. The law is quite clear that employers owe a duty of care to ex-employees and are thus obliged to take care to write references based on accurate facts. As is the case with most legal issues in personnel management, the law on these matters is complex and subject to adaptation by judges over time.

Perhaps the best approach to the use of references, like so many tools and techniques in human resource management, is not to have too great expectations of them. They are not a panacea; nor are they a substitute for managerial judgement. They have very great limitations, but can nevertheless be useful and informative provided they are treated warily. If they are approached in the full knowledge that they are less than perfect and likely to be overgenerous towards candidates, they have a positive role to play in selection. The danger lies in relying too heavily on them.

EXERCISE 11.5

THE TOMBSTONE

People management

Read the article by Anat Arkin, Burden of proof (*People Management*, 24 February 2005, pp30–32). This can be downloaded from the *People Management* archive on the CIPD's website (www.cipd.co.uk).

In this article contributions made to an online discussion forum set up by CIPD are set out and discussed. Contributors debated the future of the job reference in the context of 'today's litigious society'.

Questions

1   What are 'tombstone references' and why have they become more common in recent years?

2   What, according to the article, are effective ways of eliciting full and accurate information from referees?

3   Why is it argued that we tend to be more cautious about giving full and accurate references than we need be?

KEY ARTICLE 26

Paul J. Taylor, Karl Pajo, Gordon W. Cheung and Paul Stringfield, Dimensionality and validity of a structured telephone reference check procedure. *Personnel Psychology*, No. 57, pp745–772 (2004)

Like Key article 25, this paper from *Personnel Psychology* discusses a validity study. In this case the focus is on the predictive validity of telephone references with applicants' former supervisors. The jobs that the applicants were applying for were all customer-facing roles in a service sector organisation in New Zealand. Importantly, the reference checks carried out here were structured in nature, each referee being asked the same questions about three elements of the applicants' performance: conscientiousness, agreeableness and customer focus. Ratings given by referees were then compared to the ratings achieved by successful candidates following their first and second annual appraisals in their jobs. Regression analysis was then carried out which revealed a moderate correlation between the two sets of scores (0.26). This is described as 'acceptable' by the authors, who point out that the figure is considerably higher than that recorded by validity studies of unstructured reference checks. They thus conclude that since most employers carry out reference checks as a matter of policy, there is much to be gained and little to be lost by developing a structured approach such as the one described here.

Questions

1 What factors might explain why the correlation between the referees' estimates of the applicants' performance and the performance subsequently achieved in the job was so low?

2 On what basis do the authors assert that their reference checking system could be simplified and shortened so that only questions about customer focus are asked?

3 How convincing do you find the conclusion in favour of structured telephone reference checking and why?

CHAPTER SUMMARY

- During the past 20 years, meta-analytic studies have shown that traditional approaches to selection involving interviews, application forms and references comprise a poor method of predicting future job performance. However, they remain the most widely used tools.

- Application forms have a number of distinct functions. They have weaknesses as a shortlisting tool, but usually offer more from an organisation's point of view than CVs.

- Shortlisting procedures are best carried out formally using some form of predetermined criteria. Online shortlisting technologies are developing fast, but as yet are used by a small minority of employers.

- Traditional unstructured interviews are widely considered to have many serious weaknesses. There is thus a good argument for ensuring that interviewers are trained and are able to avoid the pitfalls.

- Interview questions are mainly situational or behavioural. In some circumstances there is also a case for using questions of the 'frank and friendly' or 'stress' variety.

- Academic research strongly suggests that the validity of selection interviews is substantially improved by structuring them. Many employers now use structured or semi-structured interviews. Telephone interviewing is becoming increasingly common.

- References are mostly taken up after the decision to appoint someone has been taken. They are inherently unreliable but can nonetheless play a useful role if handled professionally.

EXPLORE FURTHER

- There is good coverage given to the general topic of research into employee selection in all the current personnel management textbooks. The most accessible books on the topic are *Selection and assessment: a new appraisal* by Mike Smith, Mike Gregg and Dick Andrews (1989), *Recruitment and selection: a framework for success* by Dominic Cooper, Ivan Robertson and Gordon Tinline (2003), *Personnel selection: adding value through people* by Mark Cook (2004) and *Assessment methods in recruitment, selection and performance* by Robert Edenborough (2005).

- There has been a great deal published on the topic of selection interviewing. All the above texts discuss the topic in detail, as do two specialist academic books of edited articles: *Assessment and selection in organisations* edited by Peter Herriot (1989), and *The employment interview handbook* edited by Robert Eder and Michael Harris (1999). More recent research is reviewed by Schmitt and Chan (1998), Rynes *et al* (2000), Salgado (2001) and Cook and Cripps (2005).

- The best general guide to interviewing practice is *Successful selection interviewing* by Neil Anderson and Vivian Shackleton (1993). This is rooted in academic research but is aimed at students and practitioners, and is very accessible.

- A number of other handbooks have been published by experienced selectors that contain helpful advice and are often thought-provoking on the subjects contained in this chapter. These include *Competency-based recruitment and selection* (1998) by Robert Wood and Tim Payne and *Recruitment and selection: a competency approach* (2000) by Gareth Roberts.

- Comparatively little has been written on the subjects of application forms and references. However, Paul Dobson's article on references in the book of articles edited by Herriot (1989) is useful, as are the relevant sections of Mark Cook's general text on selection referred to above. A useful critical perspective on all these approaches is provided by Rosalind Searle (2003).

- The subjects covered in this chapter, particularly selection interviewing, have long been the focus of extensive academic research and debate among occupational psychologists. Online searches of the psychological journals always yield dozens of examples of academic papers on these subjects, including original validity studies.

CHAPTER 12

Advanced methods of employee selection

In recent years, despite the continued prevalence of traditional methods in employee selection, there has been increased interest shown by employers in a range of other techniques. While few have dispensed altogether with interviews, references and application forms, substantial numbers now supplement information gathered from their use with a range of more sophisticated assessment techniques. Such methods cost a great deal more to operate fairly and effectively, but have all performed comparatively well when subjected to analysis by occupational psychologists. As a result, they can probably be said to be the most accurate techniques available in terms of their ability to predict job performance.

In this chapter we complete our discussion of employee selection by examining four specific 'high-validity' selection methods: biodata analysis, ability tests, personality tests and assessment centres. In addition, particular attention is paid to the issue of professionalism and ethicality in the use of selection tests. The chapter concludes with a section outlining the main legal considerations of importance in the management of employee selection.

LEARNING OUTCOMES

By the end of this chapter readers should be able to:

- advise on the sources and standards for biodata, aptitude and personality tests, and assessment centres

- recommend and assist in devising a variety of exercises for use in an assessment centre

- find and evaluate sources of professional advice about psychometric testing and other 'high-validity' selection methods.

In addition readers should be able to understand and explain the:

- benefits and shortcomings of biodata, aptitude and personality tests, and assessment centres

- different situations in which each would or would not be appropriate

- legal and ethical framework for employee selection.

BIODATA

The use of biodata (biographical data) to predict job performance has a long history. According to Furnham (2005, pp196-197), its use can be traced to the early twentieth century, and it has attracted the attention of researchers ever since. However, in the United Kingdom the method has only ever been used by a minority of employers. An IRS survey carried out in 1997 reported its use in 5 per cent of organisations, while a further survey in 1999 found only one employer that used the technique (IRS 1997b, 1999b). More recent CIPD surveys have not registered any use at all, although it is clear that employers are moving in this broad direction through the design of lengthier and more sophisticated application forms, often completed online. The lack of usage is probably because, in spite of its apparent high validity, biodata remains both controversial and costly to develop. In practice it thus tends to be used only in the limited number of situations to which it is most suited.

Selection by means of biodata takes a number of forms, but at base all involve using detailed information concerning an applicant's past to make deductions about his or her likely performance in a future job. Typically, the employer using the approach requires applicants to fill in a detailed questionnaire that contains a large number of items about their work and personal lives. These often take a multiple choice form, allowing for ease of analysis. The questionnaire is usually sent to applicants in the post with a request that it should be returned within a few days. The data collected is then fed into a computer and a score generated. Some companies now take a more direct approach and read out the questions over the telephone, while others use online tests that contain questions of the biodata type. The candidates' answers are then fed directly into the computer for immediate analysis.

The scoring system operates in a similar manner to those operated by insurers and actuaries, the employer screening applicants according to how closely their history or characteristics match those of the better current employees. Just as an insurance company determines its prices and willingness to insure property according to the age of the applicant, location of the house, type of property, type of employment and number of previous claims, the employer using biodata seeks to predict from a range of factual data how effective an employee each applicant is likely to be if appointed. In both cases, experience of the characteristics of previous clients or employees is being used to make predictions about whom to insure or employ in the future.

A biodata questionnaire is effective only if designed separately for each job type. Typically, it involves an employer choosing a sample of existing employees that includes the best and poorest performers. These individuals then complete very extensive questionnaires covering a whole range of issues related to their work history, hobbies and personal circumstances. The results are then analysed and conclusions drawn about which questions most effectively delineate between the good and poor performers. The process can throw up some extraordinary results, as is illustrated by the following quotation:

> Mosel (1952) found the ideal saleswoman was: between 35 and 54 years old, had 13–16 years' formal education, had over five years' selling experience, weighed over

160 pounds, had worked in her next to last job for under 5 years, lived in a boarding house, had worked in her next to last job for over 5 years, had her principal previous experience as a minor executive, was between 4 feet 11 inches and 5 feet 2 inches high, had between 1 and 3 dependants, was widowed and had lost no time from work during the past two years.

(Cook 2004, p75)

Once it is established which attributes are shared by the best current employees, a biodata questionnaire is drawn up containing the questions found to have elicited information about the relevant characteristics. If, for example, it is found that the best employees tend to have achieved GCSE level in Maths and English and that poor employees have not, questions would be included about educational attainment in these subjects. By contrast, if it was found that the age at which employees left school had no statistically significant bearing on whether they were good or poor performers, then no such question would be included.

Opinion among writers is divided over the extent to which biodata questionnaires should include 'hard' and 'soft' questions. Hard questions are those that ask for information of a factual nature that is, at least in theory, objectively verifiable. Examples might be 'How many children do you have?' or 'In which year did you pass your driving test?' By contrast, soft questions are more directly job-related and are closer to items commonly found in psychometric tests. Rather than asking for factual information, their aim is to allow inferences to be made concerning the personality traits shared by better-performing job-holders. The problem here is that they generally do not allow candidates to say that they would react differently according to circumstances. Instead, there is a requirement to opt for one of a number of starker options. An example of a soft question is given by Drakeley (1989, p440):

When people in front of you talked through the beginning of a film at a cinema did you:
i)   ignore them
ii) get up and move
iii) ask them to be quiet
iv) call the manager
v)   none of the above.

Questions such as this have the advantage of directly tapping into personal qualities that are related to the job and are thus readily justifiable. The disadvantage is that, unlike hard questions, they are not easily verified, making it easier for applicants to choose the response they believe is likely to give them the highest score. In the above example, it is not difficult to spot that the employer is looking for evidence of assertiveness. It would thus not be a good idea to answer (i) or (ii), whatever the truth might actually be! Biodata is therefore more commonly associated with the hard variety of questions. Further examples of types of biodata question are provided by Schmitt and Chan (1998, pp163–167) and Furnham (2005, pp196–206).

The use of biodata can be criticised from a number of perspectives. First, it can be perceived as unfair by rejected candidates and may thus have adverse effects on an organisation's image in the labour market. An example known to the author concerns a major UK company that uses biodata to screen out large numbers of applicants for its graduate trainee programme. One of the questions applicants are asked is to identify which university awarded their first degree. The company then rejects all applicants who did not attend one of 10 specific universities. This is very rough on otherwise excellent candidates who may spend a great deal of time completing application forms and researching the company before being rejected on grounds over which they have no control at all. In one case, an applicant who had gained a post-graduate degree at one of the approved institutions was rejected because her first degree had been awarded elsewhere. Another example is quoted by Cooper and Robertson (1995, p124). Here an employer found that there was a significant correlation between people's work performance and their preferred holiday locations. The result was a negative score for future applicants who stated that they enjoyed holidays in Spain.

It is the apparently arbitrary nature of making selection decisions on the basis of such questions that is disturbing, however effective the approach may be at predicting effective job performance. The result can very easily be strong feelings of unfairness and injustice. For these reasons, employers using biodata approaches have to take very great care to avoid using questions that might be construed as unfairly discriminating against one sex, racial group or people with disabilities. Whatever the validity of the method in terms of its ability to predict job performance, it may easily also fall foul of discrimination law.

Biodata has also been criticised on practical grounds. In particular, detractors have pointed to its lack of portability between job types. A questionnaire that is good at predicting the performance of airline stewards will be very different from one that aims to forecast how effective pilots are likely to be. Researchers have also found that biodata questionnaires age fairly rapidly, and thus need to be revised every few years if they are to retain their predictive power. These factors, combined with the need for large numbers of existing employees to take part at the development stage, greatly limit the number of situations in which it is practicable to employ the approach. Smith *et al* (1989, p56) suggest that, in order for a questionnaire to be effective, the sample of existing employees should not generally be less than 300, 'and in any event should be at least four times the number of items in the questionnaire'. It can therefore be concluded that biodata is best used in the following circumstances:

* where large numbers of applications are received for a particular job

* where there are large numbers of existing staff employed in the same position

* where the nature of the work performed is not likely to change to any great degree over time

* where job applications are screened centrally (ie where the process has not been dissolved to separate divisions or business units).

Its use is thus effectively restricted to large organisations aiming to employ the most systematic and valid technique to screen candidates prior to inviting them to an interview or assessment centre.

REFLECTIVE QUESTION

For which particular jobs or professions would you consider biodata to be an effective and efficient selection method?

KEY ARTICLE 27

Elizabeth Gammie, The use of biodata in the pre-selection of fully-accredited graduates for chartered accountancy places in Scotland. *Accounting and Business Research,* Vol. 31, No. 1, pp19–35 (2000)

It is rare to find an article that both discusses in some detail the development of a biodata selection tool and presents evidence as to its validity as a predictor of subsequent performance. This is an example which draws on data from accountancy practices in Scotland. The author argues that her preselection tool based on biodata is a good predictor of which graduates will pass their accountancy exams on the first attempt. She argues that it is a better predictor than the commonly used selection methods (UCAS points achieved prior to university entry, application forms, interviews and references) and, given the large number of applicants for a relatively small number of training places, a great deal more cost-effective.

Questions

1   Why did the author decide to omit questions about personal background and extracurricular activities at school and university?

2   Of the items that were included which might be open to criticism for lacking face validity or being unfair for another reason?

3   If you were responsible for recruiting graduates into accountancy training roles, what practices would you amend having read this article? Why?

ABILITY TESTING

According to the CIPD (2007a), over 70 per cent of larger employers now use some form of ability testing when selecting at least some of their employees. Some use tests of general ability (such as IQ tests), others focus only on literacy or numeracy, while a third group test skills in areas that are more specific to the particular job. This represents a doubling of the number recorded by CIPD in its equivalent survey of 2003 (CIPD 2003b). Usage thus appears to be growing at a substantial rate. However, results from such tests seem most often to be used as a back-up to other selection techniques rather than as the main determinant of hiring decisions. Tests of basic literacy and numeracy tend to be used to weed out the poorest candidates rather than as a means of distinguishing between those considered appointable. It should not be surprising that ability testing is becoming increasingly widely used, as it is the least controversial of the high-validity selection methods, with great potential advantages over other approaches. According to Smith *et al* (1989, p9), Cook (2004, p99) and Furnham (2005, p204), validity coefficients of over 0.5 are achievable using such approaches. Moreover it is a relatively inexpensive technique, making it the selection technique which 'delivers the biggest bang for the buck' in the words of Wood and Payne (1998, p131).

A broad distinction can be made between tests of specific job-related abilities and the more general tests of mental or cognitive ability. The former category includes the use of typing and shorthand tests in the case of applicants for secretarial appointments, tests of hand–eye co-ordination for manual workers and driving tests for potential drivers of heavy goods vehicles. In practice, employers who use such methods are making selection decisions on the basis of a sample of the quality of the work candidates will be able to offer if successful in their applications. In many cases, however, people apply for jobs made up of tasks they have not undertaken previously. In manufacturing this is very common because of the specialised machinery that is often used. In such situations it would clearly be impractical and unfair to expect candidates to be able to demonstrate ability in the principal job duties. One means of getting round this problem is the trainability test, described at length by Downs (1989, pp392–399).

Here the aim is to make deductions about future performance by observing how effectively candidates learn a job-related task when given a standard set of instructions or training from an instructor. It is particularly suited to jobs in which new recruits are required to master new and complex machinery. An example given by Downs (1989, p394) is a test designed by British Airways to assess how quickly aspiring electricians might become sufficiently well-qualified to maintain aircraft engines. Her advice is to develop tests that stretch candidates to the full and, when scoring their performance, to focus on the number and type of errors made.

PRE-EMPLOYMENT TRAINING AT COURTAULDS

An interesting experiment in employee selection was reported in 1997 when Courtaulds set out to select around a hundred new process technicians to work at a new textiles plant in the North-East of England. Prior to opening the plant, the company operated an intensive, 12-week evening training programme for prospective employees. The courses were held in sessions of four hours on two nights a week and took place at a local college. Participants were not paid for attending, but completed a level-3 NVQ qualification, whether or not they were taken on to work in the new plant. The course was run by managers and cost just £1,000 per candidate to provide. The topics covered included process control, safety, basic science, computing and team-building.

Participants were assessed according to their performance in a written examination, but were also scored for teamworking ability and leadership potential. Inferences were also made, from participants' approach to the course, about motivation levels and likely attendance records. The managers responsible were happy with the experiment (though they have stated that in future they will be cutting the length of the programme). Not only did the course successfully identify the most effective employees, it also ensured that a good part of their initial training was already completed when they took up their new posts.

Source: Burke.

A substantial amount of research has been carried out in the field of mental ability testing, with apparently encouraging results. Meta-analyses of many small-scale validity studies carried out in the 1980s seem now to have established, to the satisfaction of most researchers, that tests of intelligence or intellectual ability are among the most effective predictors of job performance available. The main controversy seems to be between those who believe it is possible to devise fairly short pencil-and-paper tests that can deliver meaningful measurements of general intelligence in less than an hour (see Toplis *et al* 2005, pp20–21) and those who argue that a more sophisticated battery of different tests is required to achieve reliable results (Cook 2004, pp117–119).

In theory, tests of mental ability are superior to other selection methods on a variety of counts. The biggest advantage is their transportability: they do not have to be designed afresh for each job, each organisation or even each country. Once a test is accepted as being a valid measurement tool, it can be used across a wide variety of job types in all manner of organisations. There is thus no need for extensive job analysis, as in the case of personality testing, or for development among a specific group of staff, as in the case of biodata. Tests can be bought from a supplier, and training in their use undertaken before they are administered to job applicants at all levels in an organisation.

Test questions come in a variety of forms and are forever being updated and improved by suppliers who operate in a very competitive market. However, most share the same basic format. First, they all contain questions to which there is a right answer – in most cases requiring candidates to pick from a set of multiple choice options. Second, all tests are designed to be taken under examination conditions with a set time limit and standard instructions. Typically, before applicants undertake each type of question, there are practice examples given that can be checked by the instructor to ensure that everyone fully understands what exactly they are expected to do. Another feature shared by all reputable tests is the process by which they are developed. This is a lengthy and costly operation involving hundreds of volunteers to enable the scoring system to reflect the performance of certain 'norm' groups. Norming allows the employer marking the test to know how well a particular candidate has done in comparison with a specified population such as graduates, school-leavers or senior managers.

Some of the most common types of question are illustrated below (Byron and Modha 1991, 1993).

1) *Verbal Reasoning*
    i)   Ocean is to Pond as Deep is to
             a) Shallow b) Well c) Sea d) Lake

    ii) Early is the opposite of
             a) Evening b) Late c) Postpone d) Breakfast

    iii) What means the same as portion?
             a) Whole b) Part c) Chip d) None

    iv) Which would be the third in alphabetical order?
             a) Sevene b) Severn c) Seveen d) Seven

v) Which is the odd one out?
 a) Lock b) Quay c) Bollard d) Anchor

vi) Which is the penultimate letter in the word REST?
 a) R b) E c) S d) T

2) *Numerical Reasoning*

Which number comes next in the following series:

i) 12 10 8 6 4
 a) 3 b) 2 c) 1 d) 0

ii) 1 1 2 3 5
 a) 7 b) 10 c) 8 d) 9

iii) 10 25 12 30 14
 a) 16 b) 50 c) 24 d) 35

iv) 81 27 9 3 1
 a) 0.5 b) 1 c) 0.33 d) 0.166

v) If a set of five screwdrivers costs £4, how much does each one cost?
 a) 50p b) 60p c) 70p d) 80p e) 90p

vi) If a 90–litre tank needs to be filled up using a hose pipe that allows water to flow at 2 litres per second, how many seconds would be needed to fill up the tank?
 a) 180 b) 90 c) 45 d) 22.5 e) 11.25

3) *Analytical Ability*

Janet, Marcus, Eric and Angela sit in this order in a row left to right. Janet changes places with Eric and then Eric changes places with Marcus.
i) Who is at the right end of the row?
ii) Who is to the left of Eric?

James is eight years old and half as old as his brother Humphrey. Jenny is two years younger than James and the same number of years older than Mark.
iii) Who is the oldest?
iv) Who is the youngest?
v) How old is Mark?

Furnham (2005, pp207–208) distinguishes between questions that measure 'cystallised intelligence' and those that measure 'fluid intelligence'. The former consists of specific bits and pieces of knowledge that are picked up over a lifetime. Older people, because they have had more life experience, tend to do well in such tests. Fluid intelligence, on the other hand, is defined as 'the ability to perceive relationships, deal with unfamiliar problems and gain new types of knowledge'. Questions of this type are answered better by younger people, because 'it peaks at the age of twenty'.

Furnham gives examples of the two types of question:

a) Which of these numbers does not belong with the others?
 625 361256 193 144

This requires fluid intelligence to answer and will often be answered more quickly by a schoolchild than a retired person.

   b) Which of the following towns is the odd one out?
      Oslo London New York Cairo Bombay Caracas Madrid

By contrast, this requires crystallised intelligence. You know the answer if you are able to draw on knowledge picked up or learned over time. It is fluid intelligence that seems to be the best predictor of success in a job, particularly among senior managers, and hence contemporary ability tests increasingly feature that type of question. But in practice, the two types of intelligence are correlated. Someone who scores well on one type of test tends also to score well on the other.

Often the questions in tests of mental ability are not in themselves particularly difficult, but become far harder when part of a long questionnaire that has to be completed in a limited period of time. There is also a tendency for the questions to get very much trickier as the test proceeds. This makes it possible for people with a wide range of mental ability to be scored after sitting the same test. A recent innovation in abilities testing is the use of computer software packages. In such situations the candidate answers using a keyboard, and the score is automatically recorded. The great advantage of these packages is the capability they have to tailor the standard of questions to the appropriate level for each individual applicant. If a candidate performs well in the early questions the computer starts generating more difficult problems. As a result, less time is taken to establish the level of mental ability demonstrated in each individual case.

An issue of significance with this kind of test is the extent to which candidates can raise their performance with practice. Opinion is divided on this issue; writers of books aimed at helping candidates to prepare claim that practice improves performance (eg Byron and Modha 1991, p9), while psychologists and test-providers downplay the extent to which this can in fact occur. Toplis *et al* (2005, p73) suggest that retesting candidates with the same test a few days after their first attempt usually leads only to a marginal improvement in performance, a conclusion underlined by research quoted by Wood and Payne (1998, p136) and Whalley and Smith (1998, p120).

In fact, it appears that candidates are quite likely to encounter the same test on a number of occasions, particularly if they are applying for many jobs at the same time. Silvester and Brown (1993) found that 40 per cent of the graduate job-seekers in their sample had completed the same test twice or more for different prospective employers. As a result, the rise of online testing has led, according to Dulewicz (see Allen 2007b, p7), to the existence of a 'Harry Potter' problem. The title derives from the tendency of would-be recruits signing up under the name 'Harry Potter' repeatedly to practice the same test again and again. Clearly the extent to which candidates can prepare will vary from test to test, with some forms of ability test more susceptible than others to this kind of effect. Another variable is the effectiveness of any feedback that a candidate may be given on his or her performance when first attempting a particular type of test.

Whalley and Smith (1998) show that candidates often end up under-performing in ability tests, which is just as problematic for an employer seeking the most able candidate as is over-performance by candidates who are practised test takers. The reasons for poor performance can relate to anxiety or can derive from the adoption of failed 'test-taking strategies' involving 'a trade-off between speed and accuracy'. Here candidates opt to complete the test on time by rushing or even guessing answers rather than risk failing because they have not managed to complete all the questions. Some tests also appear to disfavour members of lower socio-economic groups and some ethnic minorities, while others are biased against people whose first language is not English because of the requirement to complete them speedily (Wood and Payne 1998, p138). That said, research carried out in the United States shows that it is quite possible to design tests that favour members of some ethnic minorities (Cooper *et al* 2003, p128) and that with care and extensive research unbiased tests can be developed.

Kandola *et al* (2000) raise doubts about the way that ability tests are used in practice. Their principal concern relates to the common use of mental ability tests in the selection of senior managers, which they suggest may be inappropriate because factors other than mental ability tend to determine success or failure in such job roles. The studies showing that ability tests have high predictive validity relate to whole populations and not specifically to senior managers, yet employers continue to use them in the selection of their senior people. Their conclusion is that other types of selection method, such as assessment centres, are probably better than ability tests at predicting managerial competence. Others argue that ability tests, and particularly those designed to measure cognitive ability, are unsuitable when all applicants for a particular job are likely to share a similar level of general intelligence (Cooper *et al* 2003, pp127–128).

Ultimately, it is probably wise to accept that no method can be perfect, and that some candidates may perform better than others for a variety of reasons. No predictive selection method is a panacea, and management decisions in this field are bound to contain a measure of error. It can nevertheless be said that, according to current research and against a range of criteria, ability testing is more effective than other methods. Furthermore, it would appear to be a least-worst option across a wide range of selection situations. That said, there are of course plenty of jobs for which too high a level of intelligence would be a drawback. Where duties are purely manual or highly simplistic and repetitive, and where there is no clear upward career path to more interesting work, it can plausibly be argued that they are not best undertaken by people who score highly in tests of mental ability. The result would be boredom, low levels of commitment and high staff turnover. Wood and Payne (1998, pp139–140) thus give good advice when they argue that ability tests are best used conservatively as a means of excluding unsuitable people rather than for identifying top performers.

REFLECTIVE QUESTION

For what jobs in your organisation would mental ability tests be appropriate? For which would they be inappropriate?

EXERCISE 12.1

ONLINE TESTING

Read the article by Vivienne Riddoch, Safety net (*People Management* guide to assessment, October 2007, pp21-24). This can be downloaded from the *People Management* archive on the CIPD's website (www.cipd.co.uk).

This article considers the vigorous debate that exists over the use of online ability tests completed by candidates at home rather than under exam conditions on an employer's premises. Is it possible, the article asks, to devise mechanisms and approaches that either substantially reduce or rule out cheating?

Questions

1   What mechanisms are being developed which seek to prevent cheating from taking place?

2   What other potential problems with online testing are identified?

3   To what extent do you agree with the view that online ability testing has no future and that employers will soon choose to revert back to pencil and paper tests?

PERSONALITY TESTING

The use of tests that purport to measure personality in the selection process is a field of activity that has generated a vast literature and remains highly controversial. It is not within the scope of this book to deal with the very many issues that this long-lasting and wide-ranging debate has encompassed. The aim here is to introduce the topic in general terms and to give an overall assessment of the effectiveness of using personality tests in different situations. While a number of distinct approaches to personality testing have been developed by psychologists, in most selection situations inferences are made about candidates' suitability for a particular position from responses given in answer to personality questionnaires or inventories (mostly pencil-and-paper or on-screen tests produced by commercial organisations). The validity of personality testing ultimately rests on a number of basic assumptions about which psychologists and other researchers have very different ideas, namely that:

- Human personality is measurable or 'mappable'.

- Our underlying personality remains stable over time and across different situations.

- Individual jobs can be usefully analysed in terms of the personality traits that would be most desirable for the job-holder to possess.

- A personality questionnaire, completed in 30 to 60 minutes, provides sufficient information about an individual's personality to make meaningful inferences about his or her suitability for a job.

A large body of research into these questions and the validity of the various psychological instruments developed to map personality has been undertaken.

Nevertheless, opinions among specialists in the field – let alone lay people – differ considerably, making it difficult to come to firm conclusions about the validity of the personality test per se. To a great extent the jury is still out, with test providers and their supporters claiming them to be effective predictors of various aspects of job performance, and others questioning their claims. For reasonably accessible introductions to these debates the following are recommended: Cook and Cripps (2005), Furnham (2005, pp170–196), Cook (2004, pp133–172), Searle (2003, pp191–225), Fletcher (1991, pp38–42), Van der Marsen de Sombrieff and Hofstede (1989, pp353–367) and Kandola *et al* (2000).

For the purposes of this text, and while acknowledging its controversial nature, the broad thrust of the case for personality testing is accepted. When used carefully and professionally, personality tests at least have a potentially useful role to play in the selection procedure. This position appears broadly to be shared by most occupational psychologists working in the field of employee selection. The general consensus is that well-designed tests can, if used properly, predict aspects of job performance reasonably accurately. The problem is the large number of poorly designed tests on the market and misuse by untrained assessors (Smith *et al* 1989, pp77–78; Allen 2007b, p10).

THE BARNUM EFFECT

A classic piece of research carried out in 1958 should act as a warning to those who place great faith in the power of personality testing. In Dr R. Stagner's study – written up under the heading 'The gullibility of personnel managers' – 68 managers completed a personality questionnaire. At the end, each was presented with a written profile summarising the main characteristics of their personalities. They then completed a further questionnaire asking how accurate they believed the profile to be. In all, 50 per cent ranked the profile overall as being 'amazingly accurate' and a further 40 per cent as 'rather good'. However, the researchers had tricked the managers by giving them all the same faked personality profile to assess, instead of genuine summaries of their own personalities.

The experiment shows how very easy it is for the devisers of personality tests to profit from their high face-validity by taking advantage of the fact that the results can appear a great deal more accurate and meaningful than they actually are. Personality tests of this type are said to sell as a result of the 'Barnum effect' – the belief that 'you can fool most of the people most of the time'. Prospective purchasers of tests should, therefore, be highly suspicious of tests that produce profiles similar to those written by astrologers in the tabloid newspapers!

Source: Jackson (1996, pp37–38).

IRS (1997b, p13) reported that the use of personality testing remained stable during the 1990s, with approximately three-fifths of organisations stating that the method forms part of selection procedures for some positions. They were used for all appointments by fewer than 10 per cent of employers. Interestingly, this finding contrasts with the great growth in the use of ability tests over the same period, and may well reflect unease about the accuracy of personality tests in terms of predicting job performance.

CIPD (2007a), drawing on a larger sample of employers, reported that 56 per cent use personality questionnaires for some selection of candidates, the figure being broadly similar for all industrial sectors. The evidence strongly suggests that their use within organisations is mainly restricted to applicants for management and trainee management roles, jobs for which a majority of applicants can now expect to complete personality tests. The one exception appears to be the finance sector where there use is particularly heavy, with over 85 per cent of employers stating that they employ them in the selection of some staff. However, managers appear not to allow the results to have too much influence in actual selection decision-making (IRS 1999b, p12), preferring to use them to back up or inform decisions made primarily through other methods.

All the major personality questionnaires available on the market employ the same basic methodology: the aim being to help assessors in making inferences about an individual's psychological make-up from answers given to a standard set of questions. Underlying this is an acceptance of the idea that people differ one from the other in terms of their personality traits. According to Cooper *et al* (2003, pp22–24) and Furnham (2005, pp180–186), it is now possible to state with some confidence that there are five basic psychological constructs or 'traits' that form the building-blocks of our personalities and explain the differences between us:

- extroversion–introversion (the extent to which we enjoy socialising with others, excitement and change)

- emotional stability (the extent to which we exhibit tension and anxiety)

- agreeableness (the extent to which we avoid conflict and exhibit good nature, warmth and compassion)

- conscientiousness (the extent to which we are well-organised, concerned with meeting deadlines and the making and implementation of plans)

- openness to experience (the extent to which we are imaginative, flexible and view new experiences positively).

Of these emotional stability and conscientiousness appear to be the two that are consistently important determinants of effective performance across the vast majority of job roles. This has led some to argue that the other three are less significant and that personality tests need not be concerned with their measurement. Such views are firmly criticised by Robertson (2001) on the grounds that they are often more important in some jobs than conscientiousness and emotional stability.

Another theory states that the most significant single personality trait as far as predicting effective work performance is concerned is self-esteem (see Furnham 2005, pp211–213) and that a relatively simple test that measures it is thus all that is required. This too is a controversial idea although there is evidence to support it. The problem here is that psychologists have yet to agree among themselves why people with high levels of self-esteem perform better than those with low levels. Is it because they really perform better, or is it because they tend to believe they do and persuade others of this?

Personality questionnaires are designed to assist selectors in finding out where individuals lie on scales like 'the big five'. In so doing, it is claimed, it is possible to predict the manner in which people are predisposed to react in given situations. Using this knowledge, selectors can make inferences about a number of important matters:

- how well the individual's personality matches that believed to be ideal for the job

- how well the individual will fit in with the general organisational culture

- how well an individual's personality or predisposition to behave in a particular way might complement those of existing team members

- whether an individual, otherwise well-qualified, might in fact be unsuitable for a post because he or she scores too high or too low in terms of a particular personality trait.

Even if the results of the personality questionnaire are not themselves crucial determinants of the selection decision, they can flag areas to raise and discuss at the interview stage.

Like mental ability tests, the better personality questionnaires are developed using large numbers of volunteers. Aside from testing the validity of the instrument, this also enables each individual's scores to be compared with those typical of humanity in general or a particular sector of the population. However, personality tests differ in that individuals completing them are not usually given strict time limits. Indeed, it is essential that applicants complete all questions in order to enable a full and well-balanced assessment to be made of their psychological make-up.

Various different forms of question are asked in personality inventories, most of which require applicants to agree or disagree with a statement. In some cases this simply involves choosing one of two options: true or false, yes or no. In others, a three-point scale is used, allowing candidates to state that they are uncertain about the statement or that their answer is 'in between' yes and no. These fictitious examples are from Jackson (1996, p154):

1) I lose my temper over minor incidents.
    a) True b) In between c) False

2) I like giving practical demonstrations in front of others.
    a) True b) Uncertain c) False

3) I double-check for errors when I perform calculations.
    a) True b) Sometimes c) False

A further development of this approach is to give the applicant five options in response to each question. Such questionnaires often make use of a Likert scale, as in the following examples:

1) I like working to strict time deadlines

a) strongly agree
b) agree
c) unsure
d) disagree
e) strongly disagree

2) On TV, drama series are more interesting than factual series
   a) strongly agree
   b) agree
   c) unsure
   d) disagree
   e) strongly disagree

A problem with these approaches is the apparent ease with which candidates can fake their responses in an attempt to make themselves appear more appropriate for the job. If applying for a position as a senior manager, no serious candidate will want to give the impression that they lack decisiveness or assertiveness. On a Likert scale it is not difficult to spot which questions are concerned with these traits and to tailor answers accordingly. In an attempt to reduce faking of this kind, some questionnaires use 'ipsative' or forced-choice questions, in which applicants are required to choose between a number of statements or descriptive words that appear equally desirable or undesirable. The following examples are typical:

1) Would you rather work with people who are:
   a) generous b) hard-working

2) Do you feel that it is best:
   a) to be too assertive b) not to be sufficiently assertive

3) Which word appeals to you most in each of the following pairs?
   a) effective b) pleasant
   a) loyal b) ambitious

4) Rank the following characteristics in order of preference:

Characteristics	Rank Order
Arrogant	_____
Controlling	_____
Irritable	_____
Reticent	_____
Smooth	_____

In tests such as these candidates have to choose one or other option, so they cannot say that they are 'unsure' or that their preference is 'in between'. Another ipsative format asks candidates to choose which of four descriptive words is most, and which is least, appropriate as a description of their personality:

1) a) kind   b) influential   c) respectful d) inventive
2) a) refined   b) adventurous c) tactful   d) content

However, ipsative questions have also been criticised because they set one psychological construct against another. In such a questionnaire, a question does not, for example, simply assess how conscientious someone is: it forces the candidate to choose between a statement concerning conscientiousness and another concerning extroversion. As a result, the fact that someone is both relatively extroverted and relatively conscientious is not recorded. For this reason, the scoring and meaningful interpretation of ipsative tests is particularly difficult to carry out, and raw results can be highly misleading. The extent to which, in practice, they deter faking is also questionable. While it is harder to spot which traits the forced-choice questions are focusing on, it is not impossible to do so for anyone familiar with the way personality questionnaires work.

An alternative approach to the problem of faking personality questionnaires is to include a 'lie-index', also known as a 'social desirability index'. While this does not deter candidates from faking responses, it can help warn the assessor that the truth has been embellished in some way. The approach used is to include in the questionnaire a number of questions to which there is, for the vast majority of individuals, only one honest answer. An example from one of the most widely used tests is a question that invites people to agree or disagree with the following statement:

'I sometimes talk about people behind their backs.'

Anyone claiming to disagree – or even strongly disagree – with this statement is considered by the test devisers to be giving a socially desirable response, as opposed to a true one. If several questions of a similar kind are answered in the same manner, a high social desirability score will show up when the test is analysed. There are two implications for the employer:

- There is an indication that the test in general may not have been completed accurately.

- It may be possible to infer that the candidate is not a particularly honest individual.

Unfortunately for test designers, research has sometimes shown that people who occupy jobs that require very high standards of integrity tend to score badly on lie scales, suggesting that they are not particularly trustworthy. Examples given by Whalley and Smith (1998, p114) include civil servants, bank managers and church ministers. This implies either that these people are major-league liars or that they are genuinely decent characters who really do 'never talk about people behind their backs', who 'never lose their tempers' or who are 'never late for meetings'. If the latter is the case, as it may well be, lie indexes of this kind actually serve to screen out as 'untrustworthy' people who are actually the most conscientious and upright. It is important that test users are aware of this possibility when they come across candidates who have achieved low marks on one of these indices. It is also possible, of course, to make more general inferences about someone's integrity from their answers to other questions in personality tests. Cooper *et al* (2003, pp141–142) describe a study in which a group of ordinary white-collar employees were tested using various methods against a group of convicted white-collar criminals. The criminals were found to score poorly on measures of social conscientiousness, responsibility/ irresponsibility and reliability/unreliability. They also had a disregard for rules and social norms.

A significant and more recent development in personality testing is the use of computers. As in the case of ability testing, software is available that permits candidates to answer questions generated on the screen using the keyboard. The result is far greater speed and accuracy in the scoring of tests. For a number of years, paper-and-pencil tests have made use of technology that allows computer scanners to read score sheets. However, these are often user-unfriendly, leading to confusion on the part of candidates when answering the questions. Perhaps the greatest advance made possible by computer technology is the capacity to generate extensive printouts summarising the main features of the candidate's personality. To some extent this obviates the need for a trained psychologist to be present to interpret the results of the questionnaire. The printout permits individuals with far less extensive training to make meaningful inferences from the results of personality tests. By way of illustration the following extract is taken from a printout generated following the completion of the one such test:

> *Temperamentally, Mr *** has quite a trusting nature and is inclined to believe that people are basically genuine and honest. An easy-going, affable group member, he may occasionally be accused of being overindulgent, and consequently may be taken advantage of. He will generally give people the benefit of the doubt (without being unduly credulous). Social demands do not play a significant part in determining his behaviour. Not being particularly concerned about how others view him, he will prefer to relate casually to others rather than be constantly alert for the need to observe social etiquette. Although his affinity with group activities is above average, he may have difficulty conforming to its rules. He is unlikely to make a popular group member in situations where individualism is strictly discouraged. Somewhat unpretentious, genuine and rather outspoken, when asked for an opinion, Mr *** may on occasions, unintentionally (or otherwise), express himself in a direct and uncalculated manner.*

EXERCISE 12.2

PERSONALITY TESTS IN AN INTERNATIONAL CONTEXT

Read the article by Fons Trompenaars and Peter Woolliams, Model behaviour (*People Management*, 5 December 2002, pp31–35). This can be downloaded from the *People Management* archive on the CIPD's website (www.cipd.co.uk).

In this important article the authors draw on the results of their research to question the value of established approaches to personality testing, particularly with reference to the employment of people to work in overseas countries. In calling for the development of tests that focus on the identification of 'trans-cultural competence', they argue that different types of questions are needed from those that feature on the best established, market-leading personality tests.

Questions

1   What is Trompenaars and Woolliams's major criticism of existing psychometric tests?

> 2   How do they suggest that these can be
>   improved so that they effectively test for
>   'trans cultural competence'?
>
> 3   To what extent do the arguments
>   presented hold true for selection within a
>   UK context?

PROFESSIONAL ISSUES IN THE USE OF SELECTION TESTS

As has been made clear in the above paragraphs, selection by means of either ability or personality tests is a complex field. The theories underpinning their use are sophisticated and subject to disagreement among occupational psychologists. Furthermore, there are a bewildering number of different tests on the market claiming to provide managers with objective methods of predicting job performance. The highly competitive nature of the business and the sizeable costs involved in developing truly robust and valid tests mean that unwary personnel managers can easily find themselves spending too much on buying licences to use questionnaires that are largely ineffective.

In the absence of any detailed statutory regulation, the CIPD has updated its long-standing code of practice on psychological testing with a guide for its members (IPD 1997a). This accepted and made explicit reference to the professional standards drawn up and validated by the specialised professional body for occupational psychologists – the British Psychological Society (BPS). A 'Quick facts' download is also provided at the CIPD website, which includes advice on ethical issues as well as achieving value for money when choosing selection tests. The following six points summarise the most significant points set out in the CIPD guide:

* Selection decisions should not be made through psychological tests alone. If used, they should always form a part of a wider selection process. Inferences made from test results should always be backed up with data from other sources.

* Anyone in the organisation who has responsibility for supervising applicants taking tests, evaluating results or giving feedback should have gained the relevant certificate of competence from the British Psychological Society. In the case of ability tests, these people should be trained and certificated to level A, and in the case of personality tests, to level B.

* Feedback from tests should be given to all candidates – successful as well as unsuccessful – concerning their performance in tests. However, such feedback should be given only by individuals who have been professionally trained in interpreting test results and who are skilled at giving appropriate feedback.

* The only tests that should be used are those 'which have been through a rigorous development process with proper regard to psychological knowledge and processes'. It is also important to ensure that any test used does not discriminate unfairly on grounds of gender, ethnicity or disability.

- Test users should maintain the highest possible standards of confidentiality, with results made available only to those with 'a genuine need to know'.

- Test results should be used to make decisions between candidates only when they are shown to have a clear potential impact on likely performance in the job in question. Test results should not therefore be used as the basis for making decisions based on personal preference for a particular character type.

Perhaps the biggest problem for P&D practitioners is making sure that what they are being sold by the test providers does in fact conform to the above standards. It is very tempting, when being offered an apparently plausible product at a competitive price, to overlook the lack of evidence of BPS approval or a lack of the professional training needed to operate the test. The best advice in such circumstances is to seek professional assistance from a chartered psychologist. The British Psychological Society can recommend appropriate professionals for this purpose. When considering introducing tests or replacing existing products, it is also a good idea to research the issues explored above thoroughly and to familiarise yourself with the alternative products on the market. The bigger and more reputable providers of tests have now formed a professional body (the Business Test Publishers Association) to which the publishers of less sophisticated testing instruments are not admitted. The British Psychological society has also set up an extensive website that provides a good source of information on professional issues in selection testing (www.psychtesting.org.uk). Sources of further reading on this and other relevant topics are given at the end of the chapter.

SIMULATIONS

The most significant contemporary development in the practice areas covered in this chapter is the increasing use of simulation exercises. Sometimes these are used as part of an assessment centre, candidates being asked to react to unexpected occurrences such as might occur if they were to be selected to do the job. More often, however, simulations take the form of sophisticated computer-based exercises which are used to shortlist candidates for interview. Some are bespoke (ie designed for a particular corporation), but it is possible to purchase packages 'off the shelf' which are designed to help weed out the less suitable candidates. In either case the simulation aims to test how far a candidate is comfortable taking decisions and operating in an environment that is similar to the one that they have applied to work in. Producers and users of simulations argue that aside from being useful and effective selection tools, a good simulation also acts as a realistic job preview and thus helps candidates to decide for themselves whether or not they are really suited to a job and if they will enjoy it.

Sources: Smethurst (2006) and Allen (2007c).

KEY ARTICLE 28

Joanna Moutafi, Adrian Furnham and John Crump, Is managerial level related to personality? *British Journal of Management*, Vol. 18, pp272–280 (2007)

This is an interesting recent article describing research into links between personality traits, as measured using two well-known and well-respected psychometric tests, and the level to which managers have been promoted. It is unusual in the size of its sample (900 managers based in UK companies operating in different sectors), which makes the results more robust and generalisable than is the case with smaller studies. Three management levels are defined, the level to which someone has been promoted acting as a proxy measure for job performance. The researchers found positive correlations between management level and conscientiousness, extroversion and intuition. Negative correlations were found between management level and neuroticism, one measure of introversion and sensing. The conclusion is therefore that personality testing is a valid method of predicting managerial performance. The article is also worth reading for its lengthy introduction to some of the psychological theories that underpin the tests that were administered.

Questions

1 Why do you think that the personality trait with the strongest correlation with management level is conscientiousness?

2 Why do you think that the personality trait with the strongest negative correlation with management level is neuroticism?

3 In carrying out their statistical analysis the researchers controlled for age and gender because so many more men were in senior positions than women, and because older people had longer to achieve more promotions. What other factors could usefully have been controlled for and why?

4 How convincing do you find the conclusion that personality tests should be used in the selection of managers?

ASSESSMENT CENTRES

The assessment centre has been referred to as 'the Rolls Royce' of selection methods, and is the approach that has received the best all-round press of any surveyed in this and the previous chapter. Validity studies have consistently found assessment centre techniques to have good predictive ability, and they appear to be liked by candidates too. Perhaps the only drawback, albeit an important one, is the cost associated with their preparation and administration. While the approach can also be used for developmental purposes, the aim here is simply to review its application in the selection field.

Assessment centres involve assembling in one place several candidates who are applying for the same position and putting them through a variety of different tests. Centres can be operated over one day, but usually involve an overnight stay. They will typically include a conventional interview, together with paper-and-pencil tests both of mental ability and personality. In addition, a range of other exercises are included to test a variety of specific competencies. It is the presence of so many different selection tools acting together that is thought to account for the high validity that the approach has been found to possess. This permits assessors to observe candidates' behaviour in a number of distinct situations, removing the need to make inferences based on only one technique (interview, psychometric test, application form and so on).

However, most centres are not exclusively concerned with the identification of underlying personality traits or constructs, as is the case with personality testing. Instead, the aim is to observe actual behaviour in a work-related situation. The concern is not therefore with identifying an underlying predisposition to be assertive, conscientious, sociable or whatever, but to assess each candidate's actual actions and reactions when they are placed in job-related situations. A particular feature of the method is its ability to focus on potential rather than on achievement. Unlike the other commonly used selection methods, assessment centres are not concerned with making inferences about the candidates' likely future performance from evidence of their past activities. Instead, the focus is on anticipating how potential employees are likely to behave, if appointed, from direct observation of their behaviour in circumstances similar to those they are likely to encounter on the job.

A number of researchers have pointed out that, in practice, assessors tend to resist scoring candidates according to specific psychological dimensions, but instead prefer to judge their general performance in each exercise (Woodruffe 1993, pp199–203). In other words, managers who are supposed to be looking out for evidence of specific behaviours when observing an assessment centre activity end up giving high scores to those candidates of whom they have formed a generally good impression, whatever specific behaviours are demonstrated. The result is an apparent preference on the part of managers to see the assessment centre as an extended interview or work sample rather than as a psychometric selection technique. The high validity may thus result as much from the period of time over which candidates are observed as from the combination of selection tools being used together.

According to the CIPD (2007a), assessment centres are used for the selection of some staff by almost half of organisations. However, the extent of their usage increases very steeply with the size of employer (they are used by 75 per cent of organisations employing over 5,000 people, but only by 20 per cent of those employing fewer than 200 staff). There seems to be little variation between industrial sectors, and most larger private and public sector organisations employ the assessment centre approach in the selection of managers, professional grades and new graduates. Furthermore, the use of the method is increasing.

The fact that assessment centres are mainly used by larger organisations is not surprising when the costs associated with the development and running of an effective centre are considered. At the very least, the following activities have to be undertaken and either paid for directly or accounted for in terms of management time:

- analysis of the key competencies required to perform the job in question

- the development of appropriate exercises to measure or permit observation of the competencies

- the purchase of psychometric tests or other proprietary products to use at the assessment centre

- short-listing of applicants to be invited to the centre

- training of assessors and other employees actively involved in conducting the exercises

- food and accommodation at the centre for candidates and assessors

- the presence of senior managers to act as observers and interviewers

- the giving of meaningful feedback to successful and unsuccessful candidates

- evaluation and validation.

When it is considered that, to run an effective assessment centre, it is necessary to have a candidate–assessor ratio of around 2:1, it is easy to see how the costs can mount up – especially when a number of centres are set up for the selection of different staff groups. For this reason, the approach is only really appropriate for the selection of individuals who fall into one or more of the following categories:

- people who will be employed in the most senior positions with large staffs to supervise or sizeable budgets to manage

- people who will be employed to undertake work that is absolutely crucial to the success of the organisation (perhaps jobs in which the making of errors has unusually important consequences)

- people (like graduates) who are expected to remain employed by the organisation for a long period and in whom significant investment will be made.

An advantage of assessment centres is their flexibility. They are not purchased 'off-the-shelf' like psychometric tests, and are not as time-restricted as interviews. There is therefore plenty of scope to introduce exercises that are of specific relevance to the job and the organisation involved. For this reason, each centre is likely to differ from others to a considerable degree. That said, there are a number of exercises and types of exercise that are associated with assessment centres and that are frequently included; these are now discussed.

IN-TRAY EXERCISES

A common exercise used in assessment centres is the in-tray or in-basket test. Here each candidate sits at a desk and is given a pile of documents to read through. The pile consists of a mixture of memos, letters, notes, telephone messages, e-mails and other documents related to the job for which candidates attending the centre are applying. Participants are then given a limited amount of time to read the documents and state what action they would take in each situation. In some tests they are explicitly required to prioritise their actions by listing what they would do, and in what order, on an answer sheet.

The more sophisticated in-tray tests take place over a two or three-hour period and require candidates to digest fairly complex written material before recommending courses of action. It is also possible for assessors to add extra pieces of paper to the in-tray and to take away completed work (the out-tray) at set time-intervals. A further variation involves instructing candidates to demonstrate writing skills by composing a letter or report in reaction to an item in the in-tray. In some centres, candidates are interviewed after completing the test to allow assessors to explore their thinking and the reasons for the decisions they have made.

In-tray exercises have a number of very useful functions. They are relatively straightforward to develop and can be undertaken by all candidates at the same time. However, their greatest advantage is the number of different competencies they require candidates to demonstrate. According to Jansen and de Jongh (1997, p36), these include intelligence, interpersonal sensitivity, planning and organising ability, delegation skills, problem analysis, problem-solving ability and decisiveness. While the test requires candidates to give an indication of their interpersonal style and approach to dealing with colleagues and customers, it clearly does not directly test social skills such as assertiveness or a candidate's ability to negotiate effectively. On the other hand, as Edenborough (2005, p146) points out, there is huge and very valuable scope to tailoring the content quite closely to the organisation's actual day-to-day activities.

GROUP EXERCISES

Interpersonal competence is usually tested by means of a variety of group exercises that a group of four or five candidates carry out together. A common approach is the 'leaderless' project, in which the group is given instructions to carry out a particular task within a time limit, but the members are left to decide for themselves how the project is to be tackled and who is to do what. The aim here is to allow assessors to observe how each candidate behaves in relation to the others. The kind of questions they will be looking for answers to are: Does someone take the lead? Does someone hold back but contribute effectively later? Does someone negotiate between opposing views? Is one candidate more persuasive than the others?

Some assessment centres give groups fairly involved tasks to complete, some of which resemble management games more commonly used for developmental purposes. In some cases the group is presented with a problem to which there is a definite right answer. The assessors then observe which of the candidates played the greatest part in reaching it, and how this was achieved. Other group exercises are open-ended, the instruction being simply to design or build something, to draw up a strategy or action plan, or to agree among themselves a common position on some issue. Often the group is then required to present the solution to the panel of assessors. Such exercises test creativity and the ability to present ideas confidently, as well as a wide range of interpersonal skills. An interesting feature of some group exercises is the use of outdoor environments to allow for greater flexibility in the type of tasks the group is required to undertake.

Other group exercises differ in that candidates are, in turn, assigned leadership roles. The content of the tests is similar but the types of behaviour being observed are different, the emphasis being on how well and by which methods the leader motivates others, exercises effective control or delegates tasks. The difficulty with such approaches arises from the unavoidable presence of competition among candidates who are, after all, applying for the same job. To discourage other group members from undermining the 'leader' it is necessary to point out that other behaviours are also being observed (eg the ability to work as an effective team member).

PRESENTATIONS

Most assessment centres also contain exercises that require candidates to make some kind of presentation or put a case to other participants and assessors. Again, these come in many different forms. At one extreme is the highly unpleasant exercise in which candidates are required to speak off-the-cuff for a few minutes on a subject, without notice. In turn they are simply given a subject and asked to respond immediately. Understandably, many find this very difficult and find themselves either waffling or drying up completely. At the other end of the scale are exercises that test the candidates' ability to make a longer and more considered presentation. Typically this approach involves giving each candidate some information to read – perhaps concerning a specific organisational problem – before explaining that they have a limited period of time to prepare a presentation.

ROLE-PLAYING

A variety of assessment centre exercises employ the services of staff members to play roles of one kind or another. The classic exercise involves observing how a candidate deals with an irate customer, but there is no reason why other job-related scenarios should not be included. Role-playing is a good way of observing how effectively someone deals with subordinates in need of emotional support or effective counselling. It could also be used as a means of scoring candidates in terms of their ability to handle the disciplining of subordinates or negotiations with hard-bargaining suppliers. Another test that makes use of role-playing is the fact-finding exercise, in which candidates are given incomplete written information about an organisational problem. They then each have a limited time to question a role-player with a view to discovering the missing information. In some versions, the person playing the role is under instructions to be evasive or to challenge the line of questioning. According to Jansen and de Jongh (1997, p39), when properly designed, fact-finding exercises allow assessors to evaluate candidates in terms of their intelligence, thoroughness and decisiveness, as well as their interpersonal skills.

Other tests used include exercises requiring candidates to compile an extensive piece of written work in the form of a report, and all manner of problem-solving exercises carried out alone rather than in groups. Organisation-specific exercises include some of the work-sample and trainability selection techniques identified above. Ideally, more than one exercise will be devised to test each of the key behaviours that the assessment centre is concerned with identifying. The aim here is to reduce the extent to which situational factors may obscure a candidate's abilities. It is possible, for example, that one participant might appear to have poor skills of persuasion when observed carrying out a group activity, but will subsequently show considerable persuasive skills in giving a presentation. The more tests that are included to test each key attribute, the more chance there is of seeing the whole picture.

A common method used to demonstrate which exercises are testing which competencies is the assessment centre matrix. An example is shown in Table 12.1.

Table 12.1 Barclays personnel procedures manual: sample assessment centre matrix

Competencies	Exercises					Total	
	GE	IT	PRES	IV	OPQ	WR	
Analysis		X	X			X	3
Business awareness		X		X			2
Competitiveness	X			X	X		3
Decision-making	X	X					2
Drive/enthusiasm			X	X			2
Leadership	X				X		2
Oral communication	X		X				2
Written communication		X				X	2
Planning/organising		X			X		2
Interpersonal sensitivity	X			X	X		3
Achievement/motivation			X		X		2
Total	5	5	4	4	5	2	25

Key
GE = Group Exercise   IV = Interview
IT = In-Tray   OPQ = Occupational Personality Questionnaire
PRES = Presentation   WR = Written Report
Source: IDS (1995b).

Assessment centres throw up particular issues concerning fairness. Aside from the need to ensure that equal opportunities law is complied with and that tests do not unfairly discriminate on grounds of sex, race or disability, there is also a potential problem of unfair bias towards candidates with relevant work experience. A special difficulty arises when internal as well as external candidates are present at the same assessment centre. There are two alternative approaches to coping with this. The first is to take care to design exercises that are job-related but do not give a particular advantage to those with extensive knowledge of the job or the organisation. An alternative is to retain the organisation-specific exercises and then take account of the advantages to internal and experienced candidates at the scoring stage.

THE CIVIL SERVICE SELECTION BOARD

The selection procedures for entry into the UK Civil Service 'fast-stream' are notoriously tough and rigorous. Around 80 per cent of applicants are turned down after the first stage on the basis of biodata analysis and performance in a series of mental ability tests sat at regional testing centres. Those who successfully negotiate these first hurdles are invited to a two-day assessment centre known as the Civil Service Selection Board (CSSB).

Before they arrive at the assessment centre, candidates are informed of the key qualities the service is looking for in new recruits. These include:

- the ability to communicate effectively at all levels

- a strong intellect coupled with common sense

- the ability to think quantitatively

- drive and determination

- readiness to accept responsibility

- awareness of the outside world.

In order to test for these qualities, the CSSB includes two group exercises: an in-tray exercise and a series of written tests that resemble Civil Service work. Candidates are required to assimilate information from several documents, make recommendations, summarise information, draft letters and participate in the running of a committee. At the end, each candidate is given three interviews: two with senior civil servants and one with a psychologist. Eight hundred candidates are invited to CSSBs each year. Of these, 22 per cent go on to the final stage in the selection procedure: a panel interview lasting approximately one hour.

Source: IDS (1995).

EXERCISE 12.3

SELECTING SPIES

Read the article by Charles Woodruffe, *Intelligence test* (*People Management*, 16 May 2002, pp36–37). This can be downloaded from the *People Management* archive on the CIPD's website (www.cipd.co.uk).

This article discusses the recent experiences of MI5 in developing an assessment centre for use in the selection of graduate recruits. The author says very little about what the assessment centre actually contains, but the way it was put together and continues to be managed are explained very effectively.

Questions

1   What aspects of the MI5 assessment centre have led the author to conclude that it is a good example of best practice?

2   How would you define poor practice in the development and management of assessment centres?

3   What characteristics do you think the MI5 centres are designed to identify in applicants? What types of exercise would test for these most effectively?

LEGAL ISSUES IN SELECTION

The principles of current discrimination law were explored in Chapter 10 in the context of recruiting employees. The basic issues – direct, indirect and positive discrimination, genuine occupational qualifications and the role of the statutory commissions – are the same in the field of employee selection. It is thus clearly unlawful to fail to select a well-qualified candidate who has performed well in the selection procedures on the grounds of sex, race, marital status, disability, sexual orientation, age, belief or membership of a trade union.

The most common example of potential indirect discrimination in employee selection is the presence of unintended bias against one gender or racial group in the selection tools used. Great care must thus be taken when undertaking job analysis and formulating person specifications to omit any item that could be construed as favouring one group over another. The same rules apply in the design of application forms, the framing of interview questions and the content of reference request documentation. In these cases, removing items that could be construed as being indirectly discriminatory is a relatively straightforward matter. It is a lot harder to evaluate the 'high-validity' selection methods discussed in this chapter. The extent to which, for example, a question in an aptitude test favours candidates with English as their first language is essentially a matter of opinion rather than a matter of fact. The same is true of biodata criteria, work samples and most assessment centre exercises. It is nevertheless important to give active consideration to these matters so that particular questions or tests can be defended if legal action is taken. If in doubt, it is wise to consult your organisation's solicitors or legal department.

The situation with personality and ability tests bought from suppliers is different, in so far as it is possible to ask, prior to purchase, whether or not the products have been tested among different groups and found to be free of unfair bias against those protected in law. Producers of the well-established tests should also be able to provide evidence that in practice they have been found not to discriminate unfairly. If it is not explicitly stated in the sales literature, it is wise to ask what evidence there is, from the experience of their use in other organisations, that sufficient numbers of women, members of ethnic minorities and disabled applicants are in fact selected. Larger organisations can undertake monitoring of this kind themselves.

Finally it is necessary to make the point that candidates suffering from some forms of disability may have practical difficulties completing tests. Employers need to be aware of this possibility and be prepared to make alternative arrangements. Common examples are visual impairments, dyslexia and injuries that make speedy completion of pencil and paper tests difficult.

KEY ARTICLE 29

Alison Wolf and Andrew Jenkins, Explaining greater test use for selection: the role of HR professionals in a world of expanding regulation. *Human Resource Management Journal*, Vol. 16, No. 2, pp193–213 (2006)

In this article the authors describe their research into the reasons UK employers are using ability and personality tests more frequently than they used to. Drawing on their own case study research and on data from the Workplace Employment Relations Survey, they conclude that contrary to the commonly held view, the reasons have little to do with the increased sophistication and validity of the most widely used proprietary tests, and indeed nothing much to do with their psychometric properties at all.

Questions

1   What three major reasons are identified in this research to explain increased use of psychometric testing in the United Kingdom?

2   What implications do these findings have for the commercial producers of the tests?

CHAPTER SUMMARY

- Biodata is a high validity selection method that is rarely used in practice. It involves selecting people who have similar characteristics and life histories to the more effective existing employees in an organisation.

- Ability testing is a very common and effective selection method, particularly for identifying unsuitable candidates. However, it is far from perfect, tending to favour some groups (such as those who are practised test-takers) and disfavouring others (such as people whose first language is not English).

- Personality testing remains controversial but is widely used in the United Kingdom. Evidence suggests that it is mainly used as a subsidiary selection tool and that recruiters are more influenced by information gained from other sources.

- Psychologists have identified five distinct personality factors that all personality tests seek to measure in some shape or form. A variety of question types are used, individual scores being compared with those of the population as a whole or of specific groups such as graduates or managers.

- Assessment centres are expensive to run but appear to be rated highly by employers and candidates alike. Aside from psychometric tests and interviews, candidates can expect to undertake in-tray exercises, role-plays and group activities, as well as being required to make presentations.

- Care should be taken when using high-validity selection methods to ensure that they operate fairly and are free of bias against any particular group of candidates.

EXPLORE FURTHER

- A number of texts cover all four of the selection methods discussed in this chapter, as well as the legal and ethical issues. The most comprehensive are *Assessment methods in recruitment, selection and performance* by Robert Edenborough (2005), *Personnel selection: adding value through people* by Mark Cook (2004), *Competency-based recruitment and selection* by Robert Wood and Tim Payne (1998) and the book of articles edited by Peter Herriot, *A handbook of assessment in organisations* (1989).

- Aside from coverage in these texts, the application of biodata in selection has received relatively little attention. An exception is two articles in the first issue of *Recruitment and Development Bulletin* (IRS 1990), and the research reported by Neal Schmitt and David Chan in their book on selection (1998). IRS also published a useful article on biodata in 2004 (IRS 2004f). Searle (2003) and Furnham (2005) both include substantial sections on the subject in their books.

- There are numerous specialist texts and a great deal of academic literature covering psychological testing. In addition to coverage in the texts mentioned above, two useful and accessible books are *Psychological testing: a manager's guide* (4th edn) by

Toplis, Dulewicz and Fletcher (2005) and *Understanding psychological testing* by Charles Jackson (1996).

- There are two good books that deal specifically with the subject of assessment centres. These are *Assessment centres: identifying and developing competence* by Charles Woodruffe (1993) and *Assessment centres: a practical handbook* by Paul Jansen and Ferry de Jongh (1997). IDS published a study of assessment centres in 2002 including summaries of the approaches used by a number of companies and public bodies (IDS 2002d).

- Readers seeking information about particular psychological tests are referred to the guides produced by the British Psychological Society and to its website. These are expensive but contain detailed and authoritative reviews of all personality and ability tests recommended by the society. Another useful and unbiased review of the major tests is contained in the article by Richard Bell in *Professional issues in selection and assessment* edited by Mike Smith and Valerie Sutherland (1993).

- Extensive coverage of issues surrounding the use lie-indices is provided in by Whalley and Smith (1998) and Schmitt and Chan (1998).

CHAPTER 13

The new employee

Once a job offer has been made and accepted, a variety of activities are carried out in order to help ensure that the new recruit becomes, as quickly as possible, an effective, confident, engaged and committed member of staff. Many of these are basic administrative tasks such as ensuring that the new starter is placed on the payroll, knows when and where to report on the first day of work, has a desk, telephone and photocopying access or has been issued with the right uniform, equipment, keys or security passes. All these are important activities because they have an impact on first impressions, the appearance of incompetence being a bad message to send out to new employees. However, they are not difficult to achieve and do not raise any significant professional issues. In this chapter we focus on three types of activity that are sometimes complex and that raise important questions. We start by looking at the issuing of contracts of employment, summarising the legal position and setting out the various ways in which terms and conditions can be established and communicated. The question of international diversity in the treatment of contracts of employment is also raised. We move on to look at the establishment of psychological contracts with employees, introducing the major debates in this field and focusing on the importance of establishing mutual expectations at an early stage in the employment relationship. Finally we look at induction processes, stressing their importance and debating why they have a tendency to disappoint in practice.

LEARNING OUTCOMES

By the end of this chapter readers should be able to:

● draw up basic contracts of employment

● write offer letters and written statements of terms and conditions of employment

● advise on legal questions relating to the establishment of employment contracts

● influence the evolution of psychological contracts in their organisations

● give advice about how to convey organisational expectations to new employees most effectively

● design and deliver induction and orientation programmes

● evaluate and review established approaches to induction.

In addition, readers should be able to understand and explain:

● the principles of the law as it relates to contracts of employment and employment status

● international variations in the field of employment contracts

● the concept of the psychological contract and its development over time

● debates about good practice in induction

● the reasons for the continuation of inadequate induction programmes in organisations.

THE BRITISH ANTARCTIC SURVEY

EXERCISE 13.1

Read the article by Becky Allen, *Anoraks welcome* (*People Management*, 13 July 2006, pp8–30). This can be downloaded from the *People Management* archive on the CIPD's website (www.cipd.co.uk).

This article describes the particular problems faced by an organisation based in Cambridge which employs teams of scientists to work in Antarctica. A number of issues relevant to those covered in this chapter are discussed.

Questions

1   What particular issues arise in this organisation in relation to the drawing-up of legal contracts?

2   How would you describe the major features of the psychological contract established with workers employed to staff bases in the Antarctic over the winter period?

3   What are the major aims of the induction programme? What particular problems are can you identify which would make induction processes difficult to handle in this organisation?

Contracts of employment

One of the most common fallacies that people continue to believe is that a contract of employment can exist only as a written document. This leads even those who have worked somewhere for months or years to state quite falsely that they 'do not have a contract', when a contractual relationship was in fact formed on the day they first accepted the offer of employment. For a P&D manager, it is therefore often necessary to remind people continually that the contract of employment is no more or less than an agreement between two parties to create an employment relationship. It can thus quite easily exist only in an oral form or with an offer letter and acceptance forming the only written evidence of its existence.

There are in fact four simple legal tests as to whether or not a contract exists:

- Has an offer of employment been made?

- Has the offer been accepted?

- Does consideration exist (see below)?

- Is there an intention to create legal relations?

The question of consideration relates to the law of England and Wales. In the modern context it means that the employee agrees to perform the job and that the employer agrees to make payments in the form of wages. In other words, the employment relationship can be likened to a bargain in which both parties give something up (time and effort in the case of the employee, and money in the case of the employer). According to Aikin (2001, p10), under Scottish law it is insufficient simply to show that 'consideration' exists. The employment relationship is seen as something more than an economic bargain. Instead, there has to be 'causa', which includes an acceptance of moral obligations on behalf of the two parties.

Legally this is significant, because once a contract of employment exists, both parties owe certain duties to one another that are enforceable at law. These are known as 'implied terms' because they are held by the courts to exist even though neither party has agreed to them in writing. In addition, all employees are entitled to the protection of some statutory employment legislation (laws passed by Parliament). While much dismissal law currently applies only to employees with over a years' continuous service, other legislation applies from day one and is relevant wherever a contract of employment has been agreed. Examples include the right to Statutory Sick Pay, to maternity leave and to a minimum period of notice.

The question of implied terms is more complex because they can vary from situation to situation – for example, where over a period of time employer and employee have both acted as if there was an agreed term or where certain obligations can be said to have emerged through custom and practice. That said, there are common-law implied terms that exist simply because a contract of employment has been agreed. For example, the employer is obliged to pay wages, to treat employees courteously, to provide support to help employees undertake their work, to reimburse expenses incurred in the performance of the job and to provide a safe working environment. In return, employees are expected to be willing to work, to be honest, to co-operate with an employer's reasonable instructions, to be loyal and to take care in performing their duties (ie not to be careless with the employer's property).

While it is important to appreciate that contracts of employment – and therefore duties and obligations – exist whether or not they are agreed in writing, it is far more satisfactory for all parties if there is evidence in writing of both the existence of the contract and its main terms. This will not make the contract any more valid, but will make it far easier to prove if challenged, and puts the relationship on an open, clear footing from the start. There are three types of written document that are most commonly used to provide evidence of the contract and its contents: an offer letter and acceptance, written particulars of the terms and conditions, and other documents expressly incorporated into the contract (eg collective agreements).

OFFER LETTERS

The style and length of offer letters clearly vary greatly from position to position. Where the terms and conditions of employment are standard across the organisation, the offer letter itself can be short and to the point. A copy of the standard terms and conditions can then be enclosed or sent a short time later. Where the contract is unusual or particularly different from the standard, there is a need to write longer and more detailed offer letters. In any case, the following should always be included:

- job title
- start date
- starting salary
- pay date (weekly or monthly)
- hours of work
- any probationary or fixed-term arrangements.

Some employers go further at this stage and make specific mention of bonus schemes, sick pay arrangements, holiday entitlements, pension schemes, periods of notice and other matters. By and large, unless the employee concerned is to be treated differently from others, or unless he or she has specifically asked about these matters at interview, there is no need to include them in the offer letter. What is important is that the letter is dated and that a reply is requested within a certain time. Where this is not done, potential employees are liable to wait several weeks before replying, by which time the job has been offered to another candidate.

WRITTEN PARTICULARS OF EMPLOYMENT

According to the terms of the Employment Rights Act 1996 as amended by the Employment Act 2002, new employees have to be informed in writing of their main terms and conditions within eight weeks of the start of their employment. People whose employment began before 30 November 1993 (when the requirement was first introduced) are also entitled to receive a statement if they request one. The written particulars must cover the following in a single document:

- the names of the employer and employee between whom a contractual relationship has been formed

- the date the employment commenced

- the job title or a brief description of the work concerned

- the amount of pay

- the dates on which pay will be received

- details of bonuses or commission to be paid

- the hours of work

- holiday and holiday pay entitlements

- the place of work.

Where an employee moves to a new job with a new employer but remains in the same parent organisation, continuity of employment is retained. In other words, the employee is not required to work for a further year before being entitled to full employment rights. Where internal moves of this kind have occurred, the written statement is also required to state that such is the case.

Employees also have to be given other documentation, which can be incorporated into the principal statement described above or can be sent separately. These cover:

- sick pay arrangements and other terms and conditions relating to sickness

- notice periods for both employer and employee

- details of any occupational pension arrangements

- the anticipated duration of the contract, if it is temporary

- details of any collective agreements that govern the terms and conditions of employment.

In the case of employees working abroad, there is also a requirement to indicate the duration of the period to be spent overseas and the currency in which payments will be made. Additional allowances and benefits for overseas workers have also to be included.

Finally, the written particulars must include details of relevant disciplinary and grievance arrangements. The full details of procedures do not need to be sent to everyone, but everyone needs to be informed of where they can have access to these documents. As a rule, disciplinary and grievance procedures do not themselves form part of the contract of employment, which is stated clearly in the written particulars. Employees thus have a contractual right to be informed that they exist but cannot use the law either as a means of forcing an employer to apply them or to sue for breach of contract where this has not occurred.

It must again be stressed that the written particulars do not amount to a contract of employment. Even when signed by an employee and returned for filing, they are seen legally only as written evidence of the contract and as such representative only of the employer's view of what the contract itself contains. However, in practice, they are generally accepted by the courts as good evidence of a contract's details, and it is very difficult for employees to suggest otherwise when they have not complained of any inaccuracy previously.

Until 2004 there was little by way of a legal incentive to persuade employers to comply with the requirement to issue written particulars. Where the employer failed to do so, all the employee could do was to ask an Employment Tribunal to require that a statement be issued. This remains the case, but an additional incentive has now been introduced under regulations that form part of the Employment Act 2002. These include a right for Employment Tribunals to award compensation of between two and four weeks' pay to anyone who wins a case of another kind and is found not to have been issued with the written particulars or informed of important changes that mean that any original statement is now out of date. Importantly, however, these regulations also free employers of the obligation to issue a separate statement of terms and conditions when they have already communicated all the relevant information to a new employee in an offer letter or included it in a written contract of employment.

INCORPORATED DOCUMENTS

Notwithstanding the minimum requirements described above, employers often expressly incorporate other documents into contracts of employment. The most common examples are job descriptions, collective agreements and staff handbooks, but there is no reason why other material such as a disciplinary procedure or a set of health and safety rules should not also be incorporated. Whether or not this is done is a matter for the employer, and there are arguments for and against doing so.

Once procedures are incorporated, an employee gains the right to sue the employer if those procedures are not followed. For example, if the staff handbook is incorporated and it states that all employees are entitled to a month's notice, then any employee, even if he or she has not yet completed a month's service, could sue for damages if summarily dismissed. In incorporating these documents, the employer is in effect conveying on employees more generous terms and more extensive rights than they are entitled to at law. The argument against doing so is therefore that this amounts to an unnecessary risk.

However, where an employer wishes to be seen as being fair and applying best practice, there is a good case for incorporating such documents as a means of indicating that all employees will be treated equally well from the start of their employment. Incorporation ensures that this is the case and that exceptions are not made in the case of recent starters. The rationale, as with all commitment to best practice, is that as a result the organisation will be better able to attract, retain and motivate the best available people. Incorporation, if done conspicuously, can make a sizeable contribution to the achievement of this objective.

The second argument in favour of incorporation is the clarity that it can bring to the employment relationship. Provided the documents concerned are written unambiguously, they should act to set out exactly what is expected of each party and thus avoid disputes breaking out about interpretation. For example, where a grievance procedure exists but is not incorporated, and an employee with less than two years' service wishes to complain about his or her manager's actions, there will always be a temptation among some managers either to threaten dismissal if the allegation is not withdrawn, or actually to dismiss the employee. Such action could very easily lead to anger or less co-operation on the part of others, or to calls for collective action. Where the policy is incorporated into contracts of employment, all parties should know where they stand from the start, thus avoiding such situations.

SPECIFIC CONTRACTUAL TERMS

Employers are free in principle to seek to include whatever terms they wish in a contract, and will be able to enforce these at law provided they are not superseded by statutory employment rights. Similarly, in principle, employees are free to accept or reject any offer that is made to them. In practice however, for the vast majority of people contracts take a pretty standard form and it is only in relatively exceptional cases that there is a need to require lengthy notice periods, unusual patterns of hours or peculiar payment arrangements. However, where such is the case, there will be a need to draw up a more substantial, individual written contract rather than relying simply on an offer letter and written particulars.

That said, there are a number of potential express terms that most P&D practitioners are likely to come across at some stage and about which it is wise to have some knowledge. In some cases they can simply be inserted into an offer letter; in others it may be felt more appropriate to include them in a separate written contract. They include the clauses discussed below.

FIXED-TERM CLAUSES

Employing people on a fixed-term basis is common where funding is limited or where the job is clearly of fixed duration. In such cases a termination date clearly needs to be stated in the contract. It is, however, important to remember that the Employment Act 2002 limits the length of time that employers can employ people on a succession of fixed-term contracts to four years unless they can justify their actions.

WAIVER CLAUSES

Where people are employed on a fixed-term basis, they used to be able to be asked to sign a waiver clause, renouncing their right to a redundancy payment on the termination of their employment. This right was abolished by the Employment Act 2002, meaning that any such clause is considered void if issued after 1 October 2002. However, fixed-term contracts entered into before that date will still include valid waiver clauses in many cases.

PROBATIONARY CLAUSES

Many employers initially hire people for a probationary period of six months or a year, at which point their performance is reviewed and a decision taken on whether or not to confirm the appointment. Where this is the case it is important to gain the employee's agreement and to ensure that he or she understands the probationary arrangements together with the consequences of failure.

RESTRAINT OF TRADE CLAUSES

Another common express term that is incorporated into contracts seeks to deter employees from working for rival employers in their spare time or using information gained in their employment to help business competitors (eg by leaking trade secrets).

RESTRICTIVE COVENANTS

These are like restraint of trade clauses, but refer to the period after the employment has ended. They usually seek to prevent employees from taking up employment with competitors for a certain period of time after they leave. They are covered in greater detail in Chapter 17.

CONTRACTS FOR SERVICES

As was seen in Chapter 3, it is increasingly common for people to take on 'atypical' work that does not resemble the traditional 40-hour, Monday–Friday, 9–5.00 form that has dominated for generations.

In these cases it is not always easy to state with certainty that a contract of employment actually exists. It may be that, even though the employees believe themselves to have contracts of employment, albeit on an atypical basis, they are in fact employed as independent contractors through a 'contract for services', which is a very different legal beast. In this case, because the individual concerned is technically self-employed, there are fewer obligations, but far fewer rights too.

In determining whether the relationship is governed by a 'contract of service' (employees) or a 'contract for services' (all workers), employment tribunals are required to look at the facts of each case. It is therefore difficult to identify any overriding general principles that are applied. However, according to Macdonald (1995, p2) the following questions are some of those usually asked when a case falls into the grey area between the two types of status:

*   Is the person in business on his or her own account?

*   Is the work performed an integral part of the company's business?

*   Is the work performed under the direction and control of the company?

- Is the person obliged to do any work given or can he or she choose whether to do so?

- Is the company obliged to give the individual work to do?

- Is the individual required to do the work personally or can he or she see that it is done by someone else?

- To whom do the tools and equipment belong?

- Is a fixed wage or salary paid?

- Is work also taken from other employers?

- Is tax and national insurance deducted by the company?

- Are company benefits such as pensions or holiday pay received?

In recent years the concept of 'mutuality of obligation' has become increasingly significant when the courts are deciding these issues (see O'Kelly and Others v Trusthouse Forte 1983 and Carmichael v National Power 1999). The focus here is on whether or not the employee is able, in practice, to turn down offers of work without ending the employment relationship. Where the answer to this question is 'yes' the likelihood is that a court will judge the applicant to be a 'worker' and not an 'employee'. Some employment rights apply to 'all workers, such as the right not to suffer unfair discrimination, but many others do not. Foremost among these is the right not to be unfairly dismissed, which is a prerogative of employees working under contracts 'of service'.

EXERCISE 13.2

INTERNSHIPS

People management

Read the article by Helen Beckett, All good practice (*People Management,* (9 March 2006, pp38–40). This can be downloaded from the *People Management* archive on the CIPD's website (www.cipd.co.uk).

This article discusses the growing recruitment practice where by large employers take on a number of 'interns' – mainly university students during their summer vacations – to undertake a period of work experience. The practice raises a number of questions about contractual issues.

Questions

1   Why do employers hire interns?

2   What factors would determine the employment status of an intern as far as legal rights are concerned? Why is this a significant issue?

3   What are the major elements you would include if drawing up a contract for an intern? Why?

NATIONAL VARIATIONS

Organisations operating in a number of countries need to comply with local laws concerning the regulation of the employment relationship. While something similar to the contract of employment, as defined in UK law, exists in most countries, there are substantial differences in important areas. First, different countries have different rules concerning who qualifies as an 'employee', different tests being used by the courts to reach decisions. In many countries the key test is the extent to which there is dependency – a less difficult hurdle for workers to clear than the multiple tests used in the UK courts. Second, countries vary to a considerable degree in the extent to which they permit freely agreed contracts to form the basis of an employment relationship. In the United Kingdom, the state has traditionally intervened very little, leaving it up to individual employees and trade unions to negotiate terms and conditions with their employers. Hence, there was until recently no statutory right to paid holiday – or any holiday at all – in the United Kingdom. Now, although various minimum standards must be maintained, there remain few restrictions on what a contract can contain beyond those. Moreover, with the exception of the Health and Safety Executive and Local Authority Health and Safety Officers, the United Kingdom has steered clear of labour inspectorates employed by the government to enforce the minimum standards that are determined by Parliament. It is thus largely left to aggrieved employees or their representatives to bring cases. This is not the case in most EU member states.

It is beyond the scope of this book to go into any great detail about how terms and conditions are determined in other countries. The aim is to flag the fact that substantial differences do exist, especially in the treatment of such special groups as apprentices, seafarers, homeworkers, professional sportsmen/women and agricultural workers. A major area of difference relates to employees of the state, an employment relationship that has not traditionally been governed by freely negotiated contracts in many countries.

Within the European Union there has been a tendency in recent years to harmonise the approaches of the member states, but there are still very considerable differences. Among the most common is the tradition in several European countries for employees to be classed legally either as blue-collar, white-collar, professional or managerial staff, with different contractual standards applying in each case. In others, including the Scandinavian countries, the law explicitly involves trade unions in the determination of all contracts of employment. Other examples are as follows:

- German law prescribes strict conditions under which it is permissible to agree a fixed-term contract.

- In France, at the time of writing (late 2007) most are entitled to a minimum of 30 working days of holiday each year and, in most cases, is limited to a 37-hour working week.

- In Italy the law requires companies to pay their senior managers minimum rates of pay set by union negotiations.

- All Danish contracts of employment must be in writing.

- In Spain employees have a right to take unpaid leave for a period of two to five years once they have been employed in an organisation for at least a year.

REFLECTIVE QUESTION

Which of these approaches would you like to see incorporated into UK law? Which would you argue against?

THE PSYCHOLOGICAL CONTRACT

Formulating and agreeing legally enforceable terms and conditions of employment is not the only form of contract that is established with new employees. Equally important, but rather harder to pin down, are the 'terms' that make up the psychological contract. This concept was first discussed in the 1960s and has since been refined and debated extensively by writers such as Edgar Schein (1980). They see the psychological contract as being concerned with the expectations that employers and employees have of their relationship: what each expects the other to deliver, what each expects to get from the working experience, how each expects to be treated by the other party.

By their nature such expectations are perceived and exist only in people's heads. Unlike contracts of employment, they are unwritten. But this does not mean that the terms of the psychological contract cannot be breached without important consequences. Where employees' expectations are not met, or worse, where changes made by managers mean that long-established expectations are dashed, the result is dissatisfaction, demotivation and higher levels of staff turnover. Loyalty and commitment are lost because employees perceive that their employer has been disloyal in breaching their psychological contract. Rousseau (1995) goes further than Schein and the earlier researchers in stating that the psychological contract contains more than just expectations. She sees it as containing more significant 'promissory and reciprocal obligations', which lead to anger and alienation among employees if breached by the employer.

In recent years there has been a great deal of debate about 'the state of the psychological contract' in the United Kingdom and elsewhere in the world. Many influential voices claim that we are seeing a steady and identifiable shift across industry towards the replacement of an 'old' psychological contract with a 'new' one that is different in important respects. In other words, it is claimed that the expectations and perceived obligations that employees have of and to employers (and vice versa) are changing fundamentally. The old psychological contract is usually characterised as being 'relational' in nature. The expectation is of a long-term relationship on the part of employers and employees, in which job security and career progression are offered by employers in return for loyalty, commitment and discretionary effort on the part of employees. By contrast, the new psychological contract is typically characterised as being 'transactional' in nature. The employer offers employment for a limited period, together with pay and some developmental opportunities, while in return employees undertake a defined set of duties to an agreed standard until such time as their career aspirations are better met by an alternative employer. The relationship is thus less emotional in nature and much more a case of a simple economic exchange.

The shift from old to new is said to be being driven by greater volatility in product markets of the kind discussed in Chapter 2. Because the business environment is becoming increasingly unpredictable and subject to sudden and profound change, this is also reflected in the employment relationship. The result is greater flexibility for employers, but less job security for employees. Commitment is lost in the process, as employees increasingly see their employment as being a short-term opportunity to earn money and develop skills and experience, rather than as the start of a longer-term relationship with their current employer.

The extent to which we are seeing the replacement of relational psychological contracts with those that are transactional is an issue about which researchers are divided. Different studies undertaken in different industries come up with findings that are at variance with one another. Atkinson (2003) shows that most evidence for change comes from smaller-scale studies in which managers, employees and trade union officials are interviewed in depth about their experiences. These tend to produce more evidence of change and of 'breaches' in psychological contracts than the larger-scale questionnaire-based studies such as those conducted by David Guest on behalf of the CIPD. The latter, by contrast have tended to find evidence of the persistence of the 'old' relational contracts as far as most organisations and most jobs are concerned.

REFLECTIVE QUESTION

Think about workplaces in which you have been employed and others with which you are familiar. Can you think of occasions in which someone's psychological contract was breached by their employer? Why did the breach occur? What were the consequences?

Where employers are seeking to change the content (or terms) of psychological contracts, this can in part be achieved by altering the expectations of new employees, as is the case with contracts of employment. The recruitment, selection and induction processes provide an opportunity for the organisation to shape expectations and state what obligations it expects to shoulder in return for the effort, commitment and initiative of employees. It is in the weeks leading up to the start of employment and particularly in the first few weeks of employment that organisations have an opportunity to establish the psychological contract that they would like to see operating, or at least to influence it profoundly. A failure to take this opportunity, as is the case when no written terms and conditions of employment are issued, does not mean that no psychological contract exists. But the expectations will be shaped by fellow employees, past employment experiences and general impressions rather than by managers taking a lead and focusing on the needs of the organisation.

In practical terms, this means it is important to set out clearly and consistently, using a range of communication methods, what are the employer's expectations of the new employee and what he or she can expect to receive in return. This is not something that can be left entirely to line managers, because of the need for consistency. Mixed messages can easily be given out if different people convey different nuances in their communication with employees. It is best if a clear organisation-wide set of expectations is established and communicated effectively to everyone in the same way. Above all this gives managers an opportunity to convey their priorities to new starters, and thus can over time help to deliver cultural change. Examples of the kind of expectations that managers might want to shape on the part of employees could include the following:

- reliability (in terms of lateness and absence)

- honesty and integrity

- professionalism in terms of manners, appearance etc.

- customer focus

- quality of work versus quantity of work

- flexibility

- organisational focus versus departmental focus.

In order to help ensure that the organisational expectations of this kind are met, it is necessary to communicate the other side of the bargain too. Without two sides there is no contract. So it is important to give equal stress to what the organisation offers people who meet its expectations. Examples would be rewards of various kinds, career development opportunities, flexibility in terms of hours, time off and holidays, a decent work–life balance, a pleasant/supportive/exciting/relaxed/dynamic working environment, genuine employee involvement, and a fair-minded, open and straight management style.

EXERCISE 13.3

CAN WE MANAGE PSYCHOLOGICAL CONTRACTS?

Read the article by Rob Briner and Neil Conway, Promises, promises (*People Management*, 25 November 2004, pp42–43). This can be downloaded from the *People Management* archive on the CIPD's website (www.cipd.co.uk).

In this article the authors briefly summarise the history of research into psychological contracts, before questioning the wisdom of organisations trying to manage psychological contracts in their own organisations or to use the concept as a management tool.

Questions

1   Why is it often problematic in practice to set out explicitly what the organisation perceives its own psychological contracts to contain?

2   What are the major features of your psychological contract?

3   To what extent could these be written down and communicated explicitly by your employer? What purpose would it serve?

KEY ARTICLE 30

David Guest and Neil Conway, Communicating the psychological contract: an employer perspective. *Human Resource Management Journal,* Vol. 12, No. 2, pp22–38 (2002)

This article presents the results of a very substantial questionnaire survey of senior CIPD members concerning the management of psychological contracts in their organisations. It is particularly relevant to this chapter because of the inclusion of data and interesting findings on communications with new employees. The article is also interesting in that it is less concerned with an analysis of what the psychological contract contains, and more on ways in which employers use the concept of the psychological contract in their employment relations strategies.

Questions

1   What do the results of the survey tell us about how senior HR people in the UK view the effectiveness of their organisations' communication with new employees?

2   Why do you think only 36 per cent of the respondents said that their organisations make 'deliberate use of the psychological contract as a concept to help them shape their employee relations'?

3   What grounds are there for questioning the validity of this research in terms of how it reflects actual practice in the workplace?

INDUCTION

Once the offer letter has been sent and the basic terms of contract agreed, the final stage in the recruitment and selection process can begin: namely, the induction of new employees. There is some confusion between different writers in the terminology used to describe events and procedures surrounding the arrival of new staff, so it is important to distinguish between different aspects of the subject. For the purposes of this chapter, 'induction' is used as a general term describing the whole process whereby new employees adjust or acclimatise to their jobs and working environments; 'orientation' refers to a specific course or training event that new starters attend; and the term 'socialisation' is used to describe the way in which new employees build up working relationships and find roles for themselves within their new teams.

There is nothing easier than giving new starters a poor induction, simply by neglecting them and failing to consider their basic needs. On the other hand, making it work well is both difficult to achieve consistently and time-consuming. There is also a need to persuade others of the value a well-designed induction has for the organisation. The following quotation puts the nub of the case most effectively:

Few things affect employees more than the way they are first introduced to their job, to their workplace, and to their co-workers. If new employees are treated with indifference, considered a necessary nuisance, left to wait interminably 'till people get around to you', loaded down with incomprehensible policy and procedure manuals, given sketchy introductions to the people and things they encounter, left with their questions unanswered and their curiosity unslaked, they are likely to be far less than fully productive new employees. However, if a new person's and the organisation's human resources department staff carefully plan and implement an effective programme for proper induction and orientation, they are making a wise investment in that person's growth, development and output, and in the organisation's efficiency, productivity and future success.

(Shea 1985, p591)

It is not just a question of creating the conditions for employees to reach their full potential as soon as is possible. Important though that is, there is also a need to minimise the other effects of 'induction crises', such as low morale and resignation. In some industries, as will be seen in Chapter 17, staff turnover is particularly high in the first months of appointment. The result for the organisation is that it suffers avoidable costs, as jobs have to be readvertised and selection procedures used more often than is necessary. Of course, not all early leaving is avoidable, but there is evidence to suggest that effective initial induction has an important contribution to make in encouraging employees to stay who might otherwise have been tempted to leave (see Fowler 1996a, pp1–6).

At base, it is a question of recognising, as Wanous (1992) argues, that starting a new job is a highly stressful experience for the average employee. Adjusting to a new environment, and taking in and committing to memory new procedures and terminology while building up relationships with new colleagues is an onerous, confusing and tiring process. It is made all the more difficult when the employees concerned have moved to new locations or are starting work in an industry with which they are unfamiliar. That said, it is also the case that employees have widely varying requirements when they join a new organisation, and there are thus dangers in making blanket assumptions about what they need to know and how much assistance they will need in adjusting. Putting everyone, regardless of rank or experience, through an extensive, identical, centrally controlled induction programme can well be counterproductive, whatever its intentions, as it will inevitably be inappropriate for some participants.

On the other hand, there are some aspects of induction that, if they are to be managed efficiently, have to be organised on a collective basis and must be provided for all new starters. Examples are fire regulations, security arrangements, canteen facilities, the distribution of organisation handbooks, the setting up of payment arrangements and the completion of forms detailing next of kin in case of emergency. There is thus a good case for running a general induction session covering these matters on a weekly basis and making sure that all new members of staff definitely attend.

In larger organisations, other matters that are traditionally dealt with at orientation sessions held in the first few weeks include a formal welcome from senior management, the setting-up of occupational pension arrangements and general tours of the premises. There is also a need to apprise new employees of current organisation-wide trends and to let them know about centralised administrative arrangements such as expense claims, welfare services and rules covering absence, discipline, holidays and the making of telephone calls. Because these activities do not have to be covered on an employee's first day, and because they are likely to lead to discussion and questioning, they are probably best organised for small groups of new employees to attend some days after their start date. This also allows flexibility in terms of who is invited to each session, so that school-leavers, graduate recruits, senior staff and junior employees are invited to separate sessions. Differentiation of this kind will, of course, not be an option for smaller employers who have relatively few new employees starting each month.

Other matters to be covered during an employee's induction are specific to each department or job. They are therefore the responsibility of line managers to organise. Aside from the basic issues of performance standards, training arrangements and introductions to colleagues, some also argue that there is a need for employers consciously to use the induction period to ensure that the organisation's values and culture are assimilated by the new employee. Achieving this is easier said than done, and there are dangers that too regular a repetition of such points can demotivate employees and actually increase the time it takes them to adjust and reach a good standard of performance.

For organisations seeking, and then trying to hold on to, the Investors in People (IiP) Award, induction is particularly important, as they need to be able to show that there are effective systems in place for introducing new employees to their jobs and organisations. The need to provide evidence inevitably leads P&D managers to develop control systems designed to ensure that the departmental orientation and socialisation processes are carried out to a sufficiently high standard. The most common mechanism for achieving this is a check-list of points that supervisors are required to cover and that new employees tick off or sign when completed. Another means of making sure induction procedures are being followed is for P&D specialists to see new staff formally a month or two after they have started work in order to ascertain how they are getting on and whether or not they have any outstanding questions about what is expected of them.

The other aspect of induction that needs to be worked at is the need for new starters to be made to feel comfortable socially. For strong extroverts this aspect of starting a new job is not a problem: they will relish the opportunity to meet new people and will quickly ensure that they fit in with the prevailing social norms. For others, being new in a department filled with old hands is daunting and can very easily hold back the speed with which they adjust and reach their full potential. More fundamentally, a lack of social ease is likely to discourage new starters from asking questions or being honest about their training needs. Again, there is no great strategy needed to deal with this issue. It is simply a question of reminding people of its existence, asking them to recall how they felt when they started jobs, and suggesting that attention is given to making new starters feel welcome. According to Skeats (1991, p56), an approach that can be successful is the identification of an established staff member to act as mentor or 'buddy' to each new employee. This person should be approximately the same age and have similar status to the new starter, and should have a good working knowledge of the job the newcomer will be doing. The buddy then makes contact before the start date to introduce him or herself and is responsible for showing the newcomer where facilities are located. Ideally they will also take meals together in the first days and discuss some of the prevailing norms and unwritten rules that govern the way the department operates.

IRS (2003d, 2003f) carried out a useful survey looking at current induction arrangements in UK organisations. This involved asking managers what they most liked about their current approaches and what they would like to change given the opportunity. The most striking finding was that only 35 per cent of organisations across the industrial sectors vary the induction they offer depending on the employee. In a good majority of cases, the only induction on offer is one that is standardised across the whole organisation. The minority who vary their processes take one of three alternative approaches:

- offering a core orientation programme supplemented with activities appropriate to the particular role

- customised induction for each specific job

- customising induction for managers and other senior staff.

However, only 30 per cent adopt full customisation (that is just over 10 per cent of all organisations). The study thus concludes that the vast majority of employees put most, if not all, new employees through an induction programme that is to a large degree standardised across their organisations. Moreover, a substantial number of the survey's respondents (two in five) stated that greater standardisation was needed in order to ensure that a consistent message was communicated to all new starters.

Several common problems were identified, chief among them being concern among P&D managers that line managers do not give sufficient attention to induction processes and often fail to carry out the procedure fully or properly. Induction is too often seen as being a personnel affair, with the result that new employees are given little personal attention by their direct supervisors, are given a full workload immediately and are forced to turn to colleagues for assistance. It is also sometimes difficult to persuade line managers of the need to release new starters so that they can attend orientation events such as visits to parts of the organisation that they do not work in. Getting line managers to appreciate the significance of an effective induction and to carry it through with enthusiasm, let alone take responsibility for improving it, appears to be a distant ambition for many working in HR.

This tension between the perspectives of P&D and line managers is interesting to observe and not easy to explain. It may occur because many line managers necessarily have a shorter-term focus than P&D people. Their overwhelming need is to ensure that work gets done now, and they are placed under continual pressure to reduce costs. So releasing valuable new people for orientation training is something they can only do with enthusiasm when they have sufficient other staff to cover the absence. It is thus something of an unaffordable luxury. Another explanation for the lack of enthusiasm on the part of line managers for carrying through induction procedures is that they are often quite tedious, and by their nature need to be repeated regularly. There is thus a tendency to see them as routine aspects of the management role and to delegate them whenever possible.

The same point can be made about the approach taken by many larger corporate HR functions. Running orientation programmes is rarely seen as being glamorous, cutting edge or important work. Instead it is routine, regular and standardised. As a result the task tends to be given to junior training managers, while management attention and resources are focused on other training and development interventions. This is understandable, but does not make good business sense. Few P&D activities are more important than ensuring that new employees receive a timely and effective induction. Failing to provide one is the best way of ensuring that people are ineffective in their roles for longer than they need to be when they first start, unable to maximise their contribution, lacking in confidence when dealing with customers and generally demotivated. Moreover, the likelihood of early leaving is vastly increased by a failure to induct new staff properly.

As far as good practice is concerned, the IRS survey identified a number of features that employers have found serve to improve the experiences of their new starters. These include the following:

- regular updating of induction procedures

- direct consultation with new recruits about how to improve induction

- keeping improvement of induction on the organisational agenda

- making use of several communications methods (eg intranets)

- including job-related training as part of orientation programmes

- producing an accompanying 'welcome' resource pack

- involving senior managers in orientation sessions

- covering informal rules and norms as well as the formal ones.

REFLECTIVE QUESTION

Reflect on the induction you have received when starting new jobs. Which aspects were helpful? How could the process have been improved?

THE TEXAS INSTRUMENTS STUDIES

A classic research exercise designed to investigate the benefits of induction was carried out in the United States in the 1960s by Gomersall and Myers, two occupational psychologists. Working among employees at an electrical assembly plant, they started by ascertaining from existing employees what aspects of the work they had found to be most stressful when they first took up their jobs. Acting on this information, they designed a six-hour orientation programme designed to reduce stress among new starters. The course covered four areas:

- New recruits were assured that failure rates were very low and that the vast majority of starters quickly learned to perform to a satisfactory level.

- They were told to expect some baiting from established employees, but to ignore it because the same treatment tended to be given to all new starters.

- It was suggested that they took the initiative in terms of communication with others, including their new supervisors.

- They were each given some specific

advice about how to build up a good working relationship with their particular supervisors.

A hundred new starters, selected at random, were then put through the new orientation programme, and a further 100 given the standard two-hour course offered by the company. The result was a substantial divergence between the performance of the two groups, with those who had attended the six-hour session achieving higher productivity rates. They also had better attendance records and required less training time than those who had been given the standard two-hour introduction.

Source: Wanous (1992, pp178–179).

EXERCISE 13.4

INDUCTION TIPS

Read the article by Guy Browning, New kid on the block (*People Management*, 15 July 2004, p98). This can be downloaded from the *People Management* archive on the CIPD's website (www.cipd.co.uk).

In this short and amusing article Guy Browning makes a number of serious points about the experience of new employees in an entertaining fashion.

Questions

1 What examples of good and bad practice in handling new employees are described in the article?

2 How many of the poorer types of new employee experience are provided by your organisation?

3 What changes would you recommend were made to your organisation's induction practices? What business case could you advance to justify your recommendations?

KEY ARTICLE 31

Michel Mestre, Alan Stainer and Lorice Stainer, Employee orientation – the Japanese approach. *Employee Relations*, Vol. 19, No. 5, pp443–458 (1997)

Induction, socialisation and orientation of new employees is an under-researched area. This is a rare example of an interesting recent article published in an academic journal on the subject. The writers are based in UK and Canadian universities, but their subject is the approach to the management of new employees that is typically taken in Japanese companies. They contrast these approaches with those that are common in Western organisations and discuss the implications.

Questions

1   Why do you think Japanese approaches to the induction of new employees are so very different from those we tend to use in the United Kingdom?

2   To what extent do you think it is sensible to 'select for attitude and train for skill'? Why?

3   How far in practice would it be possible for a UK firm to adopt the Japanese approach to induction? Why?

CHAPTER SUMMARY

- Contracts of employment exist whether they are in writing or not. Evidence of their content is usually found in offer letters, statements of terms and conditions, and incorporated documents.

- A distinction is made in law between 'employees' working under 'contracts of service' and 'workers' working under contracts for services. Employees enjoy considerably more employment protection rights than workers.

- The psychological contract consists of the expectations and obligations that employees perceive they are owed by their employees and vice versa. The start of employment provides an opportunity for employers to shape the psychological contract to benefit the organisation.

- Timely and effective induction is widely recognised as playing a useful role for employer and employee alike.

EXPLORE FURTHER

- *Contracts* by Olga Aikin (2001) is a good starting-point for further reading on the topic of contracts of employment. Useful information can also be found in most general texts covering employment law. *Hired, fired or sick and tired* by Lynda Macdonald (1995) also provides a readable and easily understood guide to basic contract law as it applies to employment relationships. More detailed guides to legal obligations are found in Duggan (2003) and IDS (2001b).

- International comparisons are less well covered. *Comparative labour law and industrial relations* edited by R. Blanpain (2001) provides a general overview, while *Contracts and terms and conditions of employment*, jointly published by IDS and the IPD (IDS 1995), gives more detail about particular European countries.

- The psychological contract is introduced very effectively in many HR textbooks. Makin *et al* (1996), Sparrow (1998), Pointon and Ryan (2004), Osborn-Jones (2004) and Conway and Bryner (2005) provide helpful guides drawing on the work of the leading researchers.

- Two general management guides to employee induction are Successful induction by Judy Skeats (1991) and Employee induction: a good start by Alan Fowler (1996). Established academic research on the topic is summarised by John Parcher Wanous in Organizational entry (1992). IRS (2003d & f) published two articles which summarise its research into UK induction practices and provide many examples of good and poor practice.

CHAPTER 14

Performance management strategies

Reducing the incidence of poor performance, and improving organisational performance generally, are key priorities for any P&D function. They are complex processes with no easy solutions, which have generated a vast literature exploring all manner of approaches used to enhance both individual and collective performance. This is the first of three chapters exploring aspects of performance management. The aim here is to give an overview of the subject and to put forward a number of distinct approaches that can be used by P&D managers in seeking to improve performance. In Chapter 15 attention turns to performance appraisal systems and in Chapter 16 to the specific issue of absence management. The role of training and development, payment arrangements and employee involvement in enhancing performance levels are recognised, but are covered in less detail than is the case in other books in the series (see Marchington and Wilkinson 2005, Armstrong 2002, Harrison 2005, Gennard and Judge 2005). In this chapter the objective is to address in quite general terms the following question:

What options are open to an organisation seeking to improve the performance of its people?

One answer is to take what Levinson (1973) referred to as an 'asinine' perspective of the employment relationship and to motivate members of staff as one would a donkey, using on the one hand the carrot and on the other the stick: that is to say, a mixture of incentives and disincentives. While both these elements have a part to play, it is important also to recognise that employees are many times more sophisticated than donkeys, and that other strategies are also available for adoption. In particular, it is necessary to give consideration to the underlying causes of limited performance levels and to what might be done to address these. There is also a place for the use of effective negotiation and coaching skills.

LEARNING OUTCOMES

By the end of this chapter readers should be able to:

- evaluate the principal methods for managing performance

- advise on their benefits and shortcomings in particular situations

- set up systems for measuring and obtaining data on performance.

In addition, readers should be able to understand and explain:

- different definitions of the term 'performance management'

- the potential role of job redesign, teamworking, counselling, negotiation, discipline, persuasion and reward in improving performance

- the significance of major contemporary developments in thinking about effective performance management in organisations.

PERSPECTIVES ON PERFORMANCE MANAGEMENT

It is possible to identify two distinct frames of reference for considering the management of performance issues in organisations, and these are associated with different uses of the term 'performance management' (see Table 14.1). The first starts with the idea that it is necessary or desirable for managers to set clearly defined standards with which staff are obliged to comply. These may take the form of sets of rules (eg on lateness, reporting absence, dress-codes), which are formal and usually written down in policy documents. Alternatively, they may be generally accepted but informal types of rules that have become established workplace norms. Examples include expectations about the relationships

Table 14.1 Two perspectives on performance management

Standards-oriented	Excellence-oriented
Focus on remedying poor performance	Focus on enhancing strong performance
Measured at the individual level	Measured at the organisation level
Concern with slippage below defined expectations	Concern with continuous improvement of expectations
Use of disciplinary procedures, incentive-based payments and formal appraisal systems	Use of coaching techniques, improving conditions, enhancing job satisfaction and raising levels of motivation/commitment
Transactional leadership	Transformational leadership

established with customers and senior managers (closeness, informality, formality, type of language used etc) and understandings about who is responsible for dealing with what organisational tasks. In either case, managers establish the standards and performance management focuses on ensuring that staff meet these. The chief concern is thus with poor performance defined as slippage below expected standards.

The alternative perspective sets no defined benchmark, but instead focuses on continual improvement of performance. There is no definition of a satisfactory level of performance. Instead all are expected to strive for improvements all the time, aiming for excellence and the highest possible levels of customer satisfaction. From such a perspective 'performance management' is primarily concerned with maximising levels of commitment, motivation and job satisfaction among staff. In recent years expressions such as 'discretionary effort' and 'discretionary behaviour' have become fashionable. They are used to describe situations in which employees, of their own volition, work beyond their contracts. Superior standards of customer service and organisational performance are the result. It should be a major aim of all managers to create a working environment in which employees want to maximise rather than minimise their individual contribution and that of the teams they work in, and look for opportunities to do so,.

It can be argued that these two perspectives are entirely compatible, if different, and can coexist quite satisfactorily in one workplace. This would be the case where the defined rules and norms that are the focus of the first approach are seen as minimum standards, beyond which the majority of people are expected to aim, and in practice achieve. Compliance with such standards is required, but individual performance is judged using a far broader range of criteria. However, there is a well-rehearsed argument that questions the compatibility of the two perspectives, holding that a rules-based approach by its nature impairs the creation and sustenance of a culture of excellence. Hendry *et al* (2000, p46) make the following observation:

> *The common ground between these two pieces of work lies in the view that measuring people performance is vitiated by the obsession with control and therefore is liable to undermine, rather than contribute to, performance.*

In other words, as soon as management is perceived to be monitoring and evaluating performance according to rules it has imposed, people are deterred from, or less inclined to develop, a high level of organisational commitment.

This is a debate we will return to in Chapter 15 in the context of arguments about the rights and wrongs of formal performance appraisal systems, but the tension runs right through thinking on all the performance management processes we discuss here. The two frames of reference produce different answers to the question posed above about options available to organisations seeking to improve the performance of their people. One answer (associated with the first of our two perspectives) would look to the use of formal performance appraisal systems, to incentive payment systems and to disciplinary procedures. The alternative would start by thinking about workplace conditions, employee satisfaction and effective leadership.

In both cases the aim should always be to link the management of individual performance to the goals of the organisation. The ultimate purpose is the enhancement of organisational performance. This should be reflected in the criteria used to evaluate it and in the methods adopted to improve it. Unfortunately managers often have other criteria in mind, such as the need to impose their personal authority, or enhance their political positions in the organisation or their career prospects. Many performance management initiatives make no contribution whatever to organisation success and should, by rights, be abandoned – but they continue to be pursued for political reasons. It is thus important to bear in mind another key conclusion from the work of Hendry *et al* (2000, p59), namely that 'performance management is about improving performance (this is obvious, but sometimes forgotten).'

EXERCISE 14.1

NETWORK RAIL

People management

Read the article by Rebecca Johnson, Back on track (*People Management*, 1 June 2006, pp24-27). This can be downloaded from the *People Management* archive on the CIPD's website (www.cipd.co.uk).

This is an interesting article which describes changes made at Network Rail since it was taken back into government ownership in 2003. The article very much reflects the view of one manager, and one suspects that others would be less enthusiastic about what has been achieved, but it is a good example of a particular approach being taken to improve performance in a failing organisation.

Questions

1   Which of the two perspectives outlined above dominates thinking among managers at Network Rail?

2   Would it have been possible for the company to have addressed its performance issues using both the above approaches to performance management? Why or why not?

3   How would you advise Network Rail managers to proceed in the future and why?

OBTAINING DATA ABOUT PERFORMANCE

Fundamental to any programme of standards-based performance management is some form of judgement about how an individual employee or team of employees is currently performing. Inevitably this involves devising, however informally, some kind of rating system so that a conclusion can be made as to how far below the expected or optimum standard an individual or team's performance can be judged to be. Measurement then provides the means by which performance improvements are later tracked. It thus forms the cornerstone of any management process aimed at raising standards.

The great problem, of course, arises from the fact that some aspects of performance are more readily measured than others. Moreover, it may be that the most important are those that can be measured only in a subjective way. As a result, there is a danger that judgements about individual or group performance are largely made on the basis of information that is easily quantifiable and that can be collected with a degree of objectivity. Hence, there is a reliance on output measures of one kind or another to judge overall performance, with the result that employees strive to achieve only those quantifiable goals. The results are often damaging, as the following quotation suggests:

> There are countless organisations where the totality of individual performance measures serves to undermine, rather than enhance, corporate performance. We have all seen examples of organisations in which production staff are measured primarily on the basis of output (regardless of quality), sales staff are measured primarily on the basis of orders taken (regardless of whether the order can be met), managers are measured primarily on the basis of reducing costs (regardless of the long-term impact on performance) – and at the end of it all the organisation proclaims itself a 'total quality company'!
>
> (Walters 1995, p18)

The opposite effect can also easily occur, whereby a level of achievement, although deemed poor when measured crudely, was actually a good performance given the environment in which it was achieved. Hence, a director who presides over a year in which corporate profit levels fell may in fact have presided over a good set of figures given the background of a general economic downturn. Similarly, a police force may actually have performed reasonably well despite the fact that crime in its area rose if that rise merely reflected an increase in the number of reported incidents.

It can thus be concluded that too simplistic an approach to the measurement of performance is generally unwise. This is not to say that measures of output or results are irrelevant, but that there is also a need to focus on how they were achieved in order to encourage employees to go about meeting their objectives in a manner that serves the long-term interests of the organisation. A mixture of measures thus needs to be considered when evaluating the level of performance. Some will be output-focused, systematic and quantifiable, while others will be more subjective, focused on processes rather than results and less easily quantified. Output-based measures that are characterised by varying degrees of objectivity, but that can claim to be systematic to some degree include productivity measures, quality measures, and objectives set and met.

PRODUCTIVITY MEASURES

These simply involve assessing an individual's or team's ability to achieve or exceed production targets. In a normal manufacturing operation, it is a question merely of measuring the number of products or parts that individuals produce in a given period of time. Comparisons are then made over time and between different individuals or teams to establish what level of productivity is considered acceptable and hence what level is deemed to be either excellent or poor. Where the quality of products is relatively unimportant, as in the case of products that are very simple and are to be sold cheaply, crude measures of performance such as these may be applicable. In most cases, however, there is also a need to introduce a quality-control element as well so as to ensure that efficiency is not achieved at the expense of poor workmanship and the production of unreliable goods. Hence it is the number of products of acceptable quality that is measured when productivity rates are calculated. Productivity measurement is of course not restricted only to manufacturing operations. The speed with which tasks are completed to required quality standards is a feature of many different kinds of operation – indeed, there is an element of efficiency in most. Examples from the service sector would be the number of customers that a check-out operator deals with in a busy supermarket, the number of trains that arrive at their destination on time and the number of school meals that are cooked and served in a given period of time. In all these cases, as in countless others, measurement is relatively straightforward, with the result that cost comparisons can be made between different units, teams or individuals.

QUALITY MEASURES

While the measurement of quality is often more subjective than is the case with productivity, there are approaches available that increase the level of objectivity. First of all, it is possible to draw up a set of criteria that defines different levels of product quality. Examples of such approaches include the methods used to assess teaching standards in schools and colleges, the star rating for hotels or the standard of service provided in first and standard-class trains and airplanes. An assessor then uses his or her judgement to determine how far the established criteria are being met, and hence the relative level of performance being achieved.

A common approach to performance evaluation where some objective measure of quality is needed involves surveying customer opinion. This can be done by means of a questionnaire sent to a cross section of customers or through the employment of telephone canvassers. Where one individual provides the main contact point between the organisation and its clients, the enquiry can focus on the individual's performance as well as on that of the organisation as a whole. Examples include many sales staff, people employed to maintain and service equipment, and a range of business-service providers. In the case of retail, garage, transport, tourism and catering services, it is common for organisations to undertake spot-checks on individual units by employing assessors to visit premises periodically in the guise of customers. Here too, while there is clearly an element of subjectivity in the judgements reached, standard training and the provision of quality check-lists can both bring some objectivity and permit comparisons to be made between individual units. Internal customers can also be asked to rate the performance of individuals or organisational functions. The P&D function is often most effectively evaluated using such methods, its customers being line managers, senior executives, staff and job applicants.

OBJECTIVES SET AND MET

The third approach to evaluation is that which forms the basis of many performance appraisal systems and is covered in greater detail in Chapter 15.

This involves judging performance according to the extent to which agreed objectives have been met over a set period of time by an individual job-holder, a team of employees or a division of the organisation. There is a strong element of objectivity, because it is usually quite clear whether or not specific objectives have been achieved. However, problems arise where environmental circumstances or the actions of others have had a role in preventing their achievement. In deciding how to rate the performance, it is thus necessary for the assessor to determine how far a failure to meet a specific performance objective was, in fact, avoidable.

The advantage of goal-setting approaches to the measurement of performance over straight productivity and quality assessments is the wide range of jobs that can be encompassed in the system. While many job roles do not specifically have measurable efficiency or quality outcomes, there are few for which some objectives cannot be set and then worked towards over the course of six months or a year.

REFLECTIVE QUESTION

Which of the above approaches to measurement would be suitable as a means of evaluating your performance in your current job? How far would such methods enable a fair performance rating to be determined?

KEY ARTICLE 32

Yuk Lan Wong and Robin Stanley Snell, Employee workplace effectiveness: implications for performance management practices and research. *Journal of General Management*, Vol. 29, No. 2, pp53–69 (2003)

In this most interesting article two academics based in Hong Kong advance a point of view and present a model rather than setting out the results of empirical research. The argument put forward concerns a fundamental question in the field of performance management: what exactly constitutes effective performance on the part of employees? The authors assert that in most organisations far too narrow a view is taken, focusing entirely on the particular tasks that make up the jobs each person is employed to carry out (task performance). In fact, if organisational performance is to be maximised, a far broader view ought to be taken which encompasses three other distinct domains: 'citizenship performance', 'ethical performance' and 'emotional performance'.

Questions

1   How do the authors define the terms 'citizenship performance', 'emotional performance' and 'ethical performance'?

2   How convincing do you find the argument that these are as important features of individual performance as 'task performance' in contributing to organisational success?

3   Why do the authors assert that their theory has greater resonance in the contemporary business environment than was the case in the past?

BEHAVIOUR-ORIENTED APPROACHES

Many commentators and writers have argued that the above approaches, while neatly quantifiable, do not permit a balanced assessment of an individual employee's performance. Instead, they argue that behaviour needs to be assessed as much as outcomes. In other words, it is argued that the processes by which achievements are reached are as important as the achievements themselves. Indeed, some go as far as to argue that the behaviours exhibited by employees should form the whole basis of performance assessments, and that outputs or results should thus be looked at only indirectly (eg Levinson 1976, Murphy and Cleveland 1995). This, it is argued, permits a more just rating of employees and enables more constructive approaches to be devised when considering how performance can be improved. It is fairer, because it focuses on what individuals actually do, thus removing environmental factors and the input of others from the assessment; where only results or objectives achieved are considered, it is not always easy to take account of such distortions. Focusing on employee behaviour and how job tasks are achieved also provides a firmer basis for discussing possible approaches to improving the performance standard.

However, employee behaviour is less readily measured than the criteria used in the results-oriented approaches. As a result, conclusions about performance standards have to be reached without the aid of quantifiable data. Instead, supervisors have to use their own judgement in reaching a balanced verdict. The main methods used are thus direct observation of the employee's performance and the reports of others (peers, subordinates, suppliers, customers etc.) who have observed him or her at work. As with outcome-focused methods, a number of different approaches are used: rating scales, critical incidents and reactive approaches.

RATING SCALES

The most systematic behavioural assessments use rating scales to judge the performance of individual employees over a set period of time. Typically, they will involve Likert scales, with aspects of behaviour that have been agreed to be significant determinants of overall performance scored on a five-point scale. The criteria vary from job to job, but often include scales such as those illustrated in Table 14.2.

Carrell *et al* (1995, pp359–360) argue that, in the case of performance measurement, judgements can be made more valid with the use of non-graphic

Table 14.2 A five-point rating scale

	Excellent	Very good	Good	Average	Poor
Timekeeping					
Appearance					
Communication skills					
Relationship with subordinates					
Relationship with senior staff					
Organisation skills					

rating scales. Here, instead of the supervisors' rating employees as 'excellent', 'good' or 'poor' in respect of an aspect of their behaviour, a series of alternative phrases is provided. The supervisor then chooses the most applicable or appropriate. In the case of personal appearance, this might mean choosing one of the following five options:

- frequently untidy and scruffily dressed

- occasionally untidy and careless about appearance

- generally neatly dressed

- careful about personal appearance

- impeccable appearance and standard of dress.

The advantage of non-graphic scoring is its tendency to reduce the degree to which value judgements are subjective. Although two or more assessors might disagree about what constitutes 'good' appearance, when presented with descriptive phrases such as these they are more likely to agree on how to rate an individual's appearance. This occurs not least because the factors they are expected to consider in reaching a judgement are implied in the phrases themselves.

CRITICAL INCIDENTS

An alternative approach is to focus on actual occurrences to evaluate individual performance. Here, instead of making general judgements about different aspects of an employee's work, attention is focused on incidents that have occurred during the review period that form examples of particularly good or particularly poor performance. It is best if these are recorded at the time, because some that may be significant will inevitably be forgotten or only half-remembered when a formal performance review is held some months after the event. Using this method, the effectiveness of a supervisor's relationships with subordinates, for example, would be judged not in the round or on the basis of a general impression, but with reference to specific episodes that reveal strengths or weaknesses. Occasions when subordinates complained about their supervisor's behaviour, or when someone left citing unfair treatment as a reason, would thus be considered as negative critical incidents. On the other hand, examples of inspired leadership under difficult circumstances, or of occasions when poor working relationships had been improved through the intervention of the supervisor, would be recorded as positive critical incidents.

Although the critical incident approach makes it possible to measure performance quantifiably, its real purpose is to analyse job performance so that measures to improve it can be put in place. It does this by drawing employees' attention to aspects of their performance that are especially effective or that are regarded by the organisation as poor. The employee, with the support of the organisation, can then take steps to increase the number of positive incidents and reduce the number that are recorded as negative.

REACTIVE APPROACHES

While there are advantages in terms of fairness and consistency in using formal and systematic approaches to gathering data about employee performance, in many cases it is necessary to act quickly in response to particular events. Rather than waiting until a formal review to discuss and put right negative critical incidents or other unsatisfactory aspects of job performance, matters have to be dealt with more swiftly. In such cases, the information is gathered and conclusions reached about aspects of performance in a less systematic manner. Often the process starts as a result of an observation made by a supervisor, but an individual may also be investigated following a report from another member of staff, a supplier or a customer. In other cases, evidence of unsatisfactory performance is discovered by chance through overhearing a conversation or stumbling across documents that make it clear that certain performance standards have not been, or are not being, met. The result is a meeting with the person or persons whose actions have resulted in poor performance. Although in some situations this will involve holding a disciplinary hearing, there is in any case a need to check all salient facts before taking any action. Particular care must be taken when information concerning individual poor performance is obtained from fellow employees or some other source that may be questionable (see the boxed text on 'Information gathered through surveillance').

REFLECTIVE QUESTION

Which of the above methods of collecting data about employee performance is used in your organisation? In your experience, what are their advantages and disadvantages?

INFORMATION GATHERED THROUGH SURVEILLANCE

An interesting and potentially disturbing issue that arises from the installation of new technologies in workplaces is their potential use in monitoring employee performance. For some time now, closed-circuit TV cameras have been installed in premises for security purposes. It is not difficult to see how they could also be employed to survey staff at work and then used as a source of evidence against an employee whose performance is alleged to be inadequate. Indeed, it is likely that the installation of security cameras pointed at reception desks or other workplaces will result in slackness or unprofessional conduct being spotted by supervisors. New telecommunications technology also permits employers to eavesdrop on employee telephone calls and e-mails, thus catching employees who are using these systems for private purposes or who are spending too long dealing with routine matters.

It can be argued that such means of gathering information about performance standards amount to an invasion of privacy –

and it is now unlawful when carried out without telling employees that they may be subject to surveillance of this kind. To avoid such accusations there is a need to draw up guidelines or formal policy statements setting out exactly how and when new technologies will be used for performance surveillance purposes. It is also probably unwise to rely solely on data gathered in this way when taking formal action against any employee, even where poor performance is discovered by chance and not as a result of systematic attempts to check on staff in their places of work.

IMPROVING PERFORMANCE THROUGH NEGOTIATION

Having established where and how far performance falls below desirable and achievable levels, the next step is to consider what can be done to raise it. A number of different strategies are available, some of which require greater effort and expense than others. One of the most common in situations where collective employee performance needs to be improved is the negotiation of improvements with workforce representatives. Such approaches are most commonly associated with collective bargaining and trade unions, but are equally applicable wherever the desired performance improvement requires the consent and co-operation of a team of employees. Negotiation is also the approach used where people are employed on a sub-contracted basis.

In a unionised setting, the most common manifestation of negotiation as a means of enhancing performance is productivity bargaining. This occurs when the management side wishes to reorganise working systems or organisational structures in order to facilitate efficiency improvements. In order to achieve this, formal negotiating meetings are then held in order to secure staff-side agreement. Provided negotiations do not break down, the result is a settlement that brings satisfactory benefit to both sides. The union agrees to some or all of the proposed changes in return for concessions in other areas or some form of compensation. A common example would be a negotiation that resulted in base-pay rises in return for greater flexibility in the way that work is organised and carried out. However, increased remuneration is not necessarily an outcome. It is possible that employee representatives will see advantages in the proposals and that they will agree to the changes on the understanding, for example, that additional training is given or that aspects of work organisation or workplace rules of which they disapprove are replaced.

Negotiated solutions can also operate in less formal ways. For example, where a small team of clerical workers is employed to manage a body of work, it is often the case that the most fruitful means of introducing efficiency savings is to negotiate some form of gain-sharing deal. Suggestions as to how work could be organised more productively or the quality of service improved are then brought forward, team members themselves often being the main source of ideas. A new remuneration package is then developed and offered to the team. If it is accepted as a fair deal, the changes are introduced. If it is rejected, managers will consider whether or not to offer an improved package. The same kind of process is equally applicable in the case of individual employees whose performance could be improved were established forms of working to be altered.

Where collective bargaining is not the established mechanism for introducing change into a workplace, negotiated performance improvements are most suited to situations in which there are difficulties in recruiting and retaining good people. Seen purely in cost terms, it will usually be less expensive to impose changes on employees, with management determining any compensation changes unilaterally. Where such approaches are likely to lead to high turnover, and particularly to the resignation of individuals with valuable organisation-specific skills, bargaining in some shape or form is necessary. By giving employees a degree of control over changes in working arrangements and involving them in determining any compensatory settlement, the likelihood of resistance, demotivation and significant resignations is greatly reduced.

IMPROVING PERFORMANCE THROUGH PERSUASION

A very different approach, also relevant in the case both of individuals and groups of employees, involves seeking to persuade or encourage employees to raise performance standards without directly compensating them for their efforts, at least in the short term. The term 'persuasion' in this context is used in an entirely positive way, and is associated with the techniques and skills of effective leadership and coaching. At root, the approach is based on an acceptance of the assumptions concerning human motivation at work described by Douglas Macgregor (1960) as 'Theory Y', whose proponents hold that people are naturally drawn to hard work and responsibility. It thus follows that, if encouraged and given opportunities, people will seek to contribute to the achievement of organisational goals. Macgregor contrasted this with another philosophy of motivation, Theory X, which assumes the average employee to be lazy and liable to avoid work or responsibility. The implication is that staff will not perform to a higher standard without coercion or compensation.

Effective coaching is often explained with reference to the motivation of sportsmen and sportswomen. For many, it is primarily defined as a training and development activity through which skills and knowledge are imparted. However, it can also be seen simply as a form of communication or as a set of diverse activities that all aim to bring out the best in people. According to Kalinauckas and King (1994), the key features of effective coaching include the following:

- active listening

- questioning

- giving praise and recognition

- building rapport

- creating trust

- being non-judgemental

- being candid and challenging

- giving encouragement and support

- focusing on future opportunities.

A good coach thus avoids subjective judgements and criticism. Instead, individual work performance is reviewed constructively and enthusiastically, with a focus on future activities.

Effective leadership often encompasses coaching skills but is generally accepted as having other characteristics too. Writers tend to have different conceptions of what exactly constitutes good leadership, some stressing the significance of qualities acquired and others putting the emphasis on innate personality traits. This debate serves to illustrate that successful leadership can come in a variety of shapes and sizes, and that what may be highly appropriate in one situation may actually be ineffective in another. This is recognised by Bernard Bass (1990), who distinguishes between 'transactional leadership' and 'transformational leadership', and argues that the latter is becoming increasingly relevant in the current business environment. Whereas transactional leaders set objectives and administer a mixture of rewards and penalties to ensure that performance standards are reached, transformational leaders 'broaden and elevate the interests of their employees, generate awareness and acceptance of the purposes and mission of the group and stir their employees to look beyond their own self-interest for the good of the group'. Research carried out by Bass suggests that it is possible to identify four key characteristics shared by transformational leaders:

- charisma (provides vision and a sense of mission, instils pride, gains respect and trust)

- inspiration (communicates high expectations, uses symbols to focus efforts, expresses important purposes in simple ways)

- intellectual stimulation (promotes intelligence, rationality and careful problem-solving)

- individualised consideration (gives personal attention, treats each employee individually, coaches, advises).

As a practical proposition for raising performance standards, the use of persuasive approaches has many attractions. Where carried out effectively, the result is a highly motivated and committed staff capable of sustaining over a prolonged period standards of performance superior to those of competitors. It is thus unsurprising that much recent management literature contains many examples of business success stories brought about through the efforts of charismatic leaders and the development of 'coaching cultures'. However, that does not mean that a strategy of persuasion is universally applicable or that it will always succeed in raising levels of performance. For a start, it is necessary to recognise that truly effective leaders and coaches are a relatively rare breed. Even if it is accepted that theirs are acquirable skills, they are not the kind that can be picked up in a short time or simply by attending training courses. Organisations may thus be unable to adopt persuasive approaches because existing managers and supervisors do not have the ability or the inclination to manage people in that way. Over a period, cultures can be changed and new management techniques introduced, but these inevitably take a good deal of time to bed down and start producing results.

In addition, as Makin *et al* (1996, pp190–191) point out, there are very real difficulties in introducing approaches to management that derive from Macgregor's Theory Y when the assumptions that underlie Theory X have governed management and employee expectations for a long time. In their view, a shift away from a situation in which people expect to be told what to do to one in which they are encouraged to take their own decisions and solve their own problems can easily lead to a 'period of considerable confusion and a resulting drop in levels of performance'. Consequently, the organisation finds itself with no alternative but to re-introduce methods based on the administration of rewards and penalties. It is probably wise to conclude that, as a means of improving standards, persuasion is attractive in principle and in theory, but may not be achievable in practice for many organisations. Where, over a period of time, employees develop the capacity to lead and coach effectively (and to be led and coached), such a strategy can be relied on to drive standards upwards. In other situations there will be a need to adopt other approaches too.

REFLECTIVE QUESTION

What other problems can you think of that might act as barriers to the use of persuasive approaches to performance management? How might they be overcome?

CONSTRUCTIVE USE OF FEEDBACK

Central to the persuasive approach to performance management is the need to develop high levels of trust so that constructive criticism is something that people are prepared both to give and to take. According to Swinburne (2001), most organisations in the United Kingdom are poor in this area. What is needed is the following:

- feedback that is constructive in intent even if it is critical

- a balance of 80 per cent positive feedback to 20 per cent negative

However, the opposite happens in practice. The ratio of positive to negative feedback for most managers is actually 20:80, while for many criticism takes the form of 'a rollicking for doing something wrong' rather than an opportunity to learn from one's mistakes.

Swinburne argues that managers require training in the use of feedback to improve performance so that they are aware of the following 'dos and don'ts':

- DO make comments objective, basing them on actual facts and observations.

- DO focus comments on actions, not people's personalities.

- DO give feedback in a respectful, adult-to-adult manner.

- DO feed back regularly and informally, not only as part of a formal appraisal process.

- DON'T start by setting out solutions: let the individual develop their own.

- DON'T adopt an 'I know best' attitude.

- DON'T focus mainly on the negative aspects of someone's performance.

EXERCISE 14.2

LESSONS FROM SPORTS COACHES

People management

Read the article by Andy Allen, No soft touch (*People Management*, 26 September 2002, pp46–47). This can be downloaded from the *People Management* archive on the CIPD's website (www.cipd.co.uk).

This article reports an interview with Brendan Venter, a highly successful rugby player and coach. Venter's approaches and philosophy are explained as is their source in his professional and rugby playing background.

Questions

1   To what extent do you agree with the view that a fear of failure is the greatest barrier to achievement in a job?

2   In what ways did Brendan Venter's approach to coaching differ from those of traditional sports coaches? How far do you think these accounted for the success of his side?

3   To what extent can useful lessons in effective performance management be learned by managers from sports coaches?

IMPROVING PERFORMANCE THROUGH DISCIPLINE

The use of punitive measures to improve standards of performance is unfashionable at present, and thus tends to be covered in management literature in mainly critical terms. It is seen nowadays as a necessary evil, used where low-trust relationships persist or where other approaches have failed. It is thus portrayed as symbolic of poor or ineffective management. Criticisms go beyond a condemnation of arbitrary punishment or of disciplinary measures applied indiscriminately without proper procedures being followed. It is, for example, pointed out that discipline often has little effect on individual standards of performance, because it fails to address the root causes of the problem. Hence, where the poor performance arises because of a personality clash or problems in the employee's personal life, any number of disciplinary sanctions will not lead to improvements. The other main criticism relates to the demotivating effects of disciplinary action, both on the individual employee who is disciplined and on other employees who may perceive such treatment as iniquitous. While it is agreed that punitive sanctions can effectively deter slackness or carelessness on the part of employees, it is also argued that their overall effect is more damaging in the long term. Applying disciplinary measures, it is said, lowers trust and demotivates employees, leading to less commitment and higher staff turnover.

Although it is correct to argue that a performance management system based entirely on the threat of disciplinary action would be inappropriate for any organisation seeking to succeed in the contemporary business environment, it is also reasonable to assert that discipline still has an important role to play. It is for this reason that an IRS survey carried out in 1995 found that every one of its respondents had a written disciplinary procedure and that, on average, 5 per cent of employees faced some form of disciplinary action each year. A further survey carried out in 2001 found that the most common 'offences' that led to the application of disciplinary sanctions were poor records in absence, performance and timekeeping. In other words, basic performance issues were more frequently dealt with through the use of disciplinary measures than conduct issues such as fighting, alcohol or drug abuse, swearing, theft or infringements of health and safety regulations (IRS 2001i, p7). Moreover the management of discipline was found to remain an area in which HR specialists are heavily involved, taking up between 5 and 20 per cent of HR staff time.

A number of arguments can be advanced in favour of the use of discipline as a remedy for poor performance. The first is very practical and relates to the significance that UK employment tribunals now give to procedural questions when judging cases of unfair dismissal. The requirement that employees who are dismissed on grounds of either ordinary misconduct or poor performance must have received two or three formal warnings before dismissal has created a situation in which employers feel it necessary to discipline any employee who might ultimately be dismissed on account of poor work performance. As a result, the prudent P&D manager who wishes to avoid having to appear before a tribunal and possibly lose a case tends to ensure that disciplinary action is taken whenever a serious individual performance problem materialises. Even when there is no clear expectation of a dismissal and when other approaches are considered more appropriate as potential remedies, formal oral or written warnings are thus issued.

The second argument in favour of disciplinary approaches is based on the notion that the assumptions underlying Macgregor's Theory X have some validity. In other words, it can be argued that some staff in certain organisations and at certain times are essentially uncommitted to their work and liable to minimise the amount of effort they expend in performing it. These employees come to work because they need to and not because they want to. They are thus often unresponsive to positive, coaching-based techniques of performance management and respond only when faced either with the threat of punitive action or some form of pecuniary incentive. Where the latter cannot be afforded, employers are left with no choice but to employ disciplinary approaches.

For the benefits of such approaches to be maximised and the long-term motivational drawbacks minimised, there is a need to ensure that disciplinary measures are applied in a fair and reasonable manner. Arbitrary punishment and perceived unfairness in the way different groups of employees are treated has the effect only of reducing staff morale and hence the general level of commitment. Furthermore, where there is no clear link between poor performance and the taking of specific disciplinary action, any deterrent effect is greatly reduced. It is therefore wise to heed the principles discussed below in managing disciplinary policies and practices.

ESTABLISHED PROCEDURES SHOULD BE FOLLOWED

Procedural issues are covered in greater detail in Chapter 19 in the context of dismissal. It is thus necessary simply to state here that an organisation's disciplinary procedure should always be followed to ensure that all employees are treated consistently. Disciplinary procedures should be explained to new employees and be available in written form for them to see so that no one can claim to be ignorant of their contents at a later stage. Moreover, in the context of performance standards, procedures should always make provision for employees to improve by requiring a number of warning stages before dismissal is considered.

DISCIPLINARY SANCTIONS SHOULD BE APPROPRIATE

In choosing the penalty or punishment to be administered, it is important to ensure that it is neither too harsh nor too lenient. The former risks engendering feelings of injustice or even victimisation, while the latter reduces the power of any subsequent deterrent effect.

It should be remembered that a wide range of possible disciplinary sanctions are available to employers aside from threatening, or carrying out, dismissal. Others include demotion, withholding promotion, changes in responsibilities, the removal of perks or privileges, reductions in bonus or incentive payments and delaying access to training courses. Furthermore, in all cases it is always open to employers either to impose a temporary sanction or simply to warn the employee concerned that a failure to improve standards of performance may lead to taking one or more of the actions mentioned above.

DISCIPLINE SHOULD BE CONSTRUCTIVE IN INTENT

It is important to remember that the purpose of disciplinary action is corrective and not simply punitive. The aim of any formal disciplinary hearing or informal meeting to discuss poor performance should thus not just be to listen to the two sides of an argument before reaching a decision about the sanctions that will be applied. Instead a good deal of attention has to be given to counselling and to agreeing measures designed to ensure that standards improve in the future. It is also important that the whole tone of disciplinary actions is constructive. Carrell *et al* (1995, p704) put the case for positive approaches very succinctly:

> *Positive discipline corrects unsatisfactory employee behaviour through support, respect and people-oriented leadership. The purpose of positive discipline is to help rather than harass the employee. Positive discipline is not an attempt to soft-pedal or sidestep an employee problem. Rather, it is a management philosophy that assumes that improved employee behaviour is most likely to be long lived when discipline is administered without revenge, abuse or vindictiveness.*

For this reason, as Alan Fowler (1996b, p42) points out, it is important for P&D specialists to learn the skills associated with the effective handling of disciplinary matters. In particular, there is a need to develop the ability to control formal disciplinary interviews so as to ensure that they do not simply become occasions for supervisors and subordinates to trade mutual recriminations. Above all, any formal disciplinary hearing must end with an agreed framework for the acceptance by all concerned of future action. It is not only important in itself that disciplinary measures are constructive; it is also important in case the matter ultimately leads to dismissal, because the nature of the discipline sanctioned will be considered by an industrial tribunal in its evaluation of an employer's actions.

REFLECTIVE QUESTION

In your view, for which forms of poor individual performance are disciplinary approaches most suitable? For which are they most poorly suited?

EXERCISE 14.3

SETTING STAFF UP TO FAIL

People management

Read the article by Jean-Francois Manzoni and Jean-Louis Barsoux, Rescue remedy (*People Management*, 14 October 2004, pp6–30). This can be downloaded from the *People Management* archive on the CIPD's website (www.cipd.co.uk).

In this article the authors draw on their own extensive research to argue that most poorly performing employees fail to improve and often perform even more poorly because of the approach towards them that is typically taken by their managers.

Questions

1   What aspects of the way that managers typically tackle poorer performing employees come together to demotivate rather than motivate them?

2   In what ways do employees who feel alienated from their managers harm an organisation?

3   What alternative approaches to the management of poor performers would prevent the 'set-up-to-fail syndrome' from occurring in the first place? What role might the HR function have in helping to encourage these?

IMPROVING PERFORMANCE THROUGH REWARD

The use of financial incentives and bonuses of one sort or another to raise the performance levels of individual employees and teams has a long history. Interest has grown in recent years with the development of profit-related pay schemes and the extension of individual performance-related incentives to a larger number of employees. The use of payment to raise performance standards has already been discussed in the context of negotiated settlements, and the whole issue is covered in far greater detail in other books in this series (see Marchington and Wilkinson 2005, Armstrong 2003). The aim here is therefore to draw readers' attention to the availability of the approach and to the possibility of using non-monetary rewards as part of a strategy to improve performance.

Strategies that make use of reward systems to raise standards of performance are based on the kind of assumptions of human motivation described by Vroom (1964) in his expectancy-valence theory. Quite simply, the theory suggests that people take rational decisions when choosing which course of action they will follow, and that their decision is influenced primarily by their perception of which course will deliver most by way of reward. In the field of performance management, the relevant decisions include the choices of whether to:

- come to work in the morning

- come into work on time

- put in extra effort

- complete work that is dull rather than moving on to more interesting activities

- stay late at work to complete a project

- persevere in building effective working relationships with difficult colleagues.

It follows that employers can influence decisions of this kind by manipulating their remuneration systems. Hence we see examples of all manner of bonus systems that tie salary levels and incentive payments to the achievement of performance outcomes and forms of employee behaviour.

The whole concept of performance-related pay (PRP) has been the subject of criticism over the years. To some, such as Kohn (1993), PRP is always doomed to fail because its capacity to demotivate outweighs its positive motivational effects. This occurs because most people rate their own personal contribution to their organisation more highly than their bosses do. When formally scored to allow remuneration to be distributed, most therefore end up being disappointed. Another criticism derives from the tendency of employees to view PRP as a tool of management control, restricting their own freedom of action and forcing them to carry out their work in the way their managers want them to. Professionally qualified groups are particularly resistant on these grounds. Linked to this is the view that PRP, by its nature, reinforces organisational hierarchies by putting additional power in the hands of supervisors. It is thus the antithesis of decentralised, open management of the type advocated by many management theorists. PRP is also criticised for its tendency to undermine teamworking through its focus on individual rather than collective performance.

PRP can work where the circumstances are suitable (see Gomez Mejia and Balkin 1992, Brown and Armstrong 2000). These include the presence of an individualistic organisational culture and situations in which individual performance can be objectively and meaningfully measured. But it is by no means universally applicable and can very readily disappoint when introduced hastily. It is therefore wise to consider other forms of reward too.

Psychologists traditionally categorise work-based rewards as either 'extrinsic' or 'intrinsic'. Extrinsic rewards are external to the job and tend to be tangible. They therefore include various forms of payment, along with fringe benefits, promotion and the various trappings that tend to accompany advancement up organisational hierarchies (bigger offices and cars, newer computers, larger expense accounts and so on). All of these have a potential role in influencing employees to improve performance levels and to increase the amount of effort they expend at work. Intrinsic rewards, by contrast, are fundamentally inherent to the job and thus tend to be less tangible. Intrinsic motivation is also more difficult to define than extrinsic, with the result that different writers conceive of it in slightly different ways. However, according to Shamir (1991, p152), there are two basic underlying concepts that are generally accepted: first is that intrinsic motivation stems from the expected pleasure of the activity rather than from the results, and second, it is based on self-administered rewards rather than on rewards administered by an external agent.

Shamir goes on to argue that intrinsic rewards are fundamentally concerned with the enhancement of self-esteem and self-worth. They thus involve the development of feelings of influence, purpose, achievement and competence – all of which are brought about through different experiences and behaviours in different people. What leads to increased self-esteem in one person may have little or no effect on another. It follows that managers can do no more than encourage the achievement of intrinsic rewards. By their very nature, they cannot be administered to someone by someone else (as is, by contrast, the case with extrinsic motivation). However, that does not mean that specific actions cannot be taken, because it is possible for employees to be 'rewarded' with opportunities to gain intrinsic rewards. Examples would include giving an employee greater responsibility or a higher level of control over his or her own work. Alternatively, developmental opportunities can be conferred in the form of access to training or through involvement with new projects.

It can also be argued that some forms of extrinsic reward in fact have a positive effect on intrinsic motivation. This is particularly true of praise, which is administered extrinsically but which can have its greatest impact in increasing people's feelings of self-worth. Similar claims can be made on behalf of formal schemes run by employers to recognise exceptional individual performance. In such cases, as with all actions designed to enhance intrinsic motivation, it must be remembered that the nature of the impact varies from individual to individual. It thus follows that managers seeking to improve performance through intrinsic rewards will be successful only if their action is appropriate for the particular employee concerned. Heaping praise on individuals, however genuine the sentiment, will motivate some to strive for even greater improvements in performance, while others may regard it as either patronising or inadequate.

Similarly, some of those chosen as 'employee of the month' and rewarded by having their photograph displayed in a public place will enjoy increased feelings of self-esteem, while others will find the experience embarrassing, patronising and ultimately demotivating. Similar judgements have to be made when deciding how to balance recognition of effective team performance with recognition of specific employees who form part of the team. Some individuals will resent having their own achievements reflected in a team-based reward, while others will prefer that to being singled out for special recognition.

However, there are clear difficulties associated with rewarding different employees in different ways for good performance. These result from the possibility that one individual or group may perceive the action as inequitable and thus demotivating. Hence, formally recognising outstanding performance by one employee – by, for example, mentioning it in a corporate newsletter or team brief – while not giving the same reward to another, equally good, performer may very well lead to feelings of unfairness on this other team member's part. There are thus limits to how far it is possible to reward different personality types in different ways. The sensible approach is to take a very pragmatic, commonsensical line in such situations by making sure that all good performance is recognised, even though in some cases it is done more publicly than in others. Perhaps the best way forward in such situations is simply to ask the employee concerned whether he or she wishes to have outstanding achievements made public or not.

REFLECTIVE QUESTION

In what ways does your organisation formally reward staff who perform exceptionally well? Which of these would you define as extrinsic and which as intrinsic?

KEY ARTICLE 33

Antti Kauhanen and Hannu Piekkola, What makes performance-related pay schemes work? Finnish evidence. *Journal of Management Governance*, No. 10, pp149–177 (2006)

In this extensive article the authors analyse the findings from questionnaires sent to over 19,000 Finnish white collar workers by their unions. The purpose was to ascertain the impact of performance-related pay on individuals and to see whether there was any positive correlation between aspects of scheme design and outcome on motivation levels. Some very clear findings demonstrate that the way a performance-related pay scheme is designed can have a significant impact on its success in practice.

Questions

1 Why are PRP schemes particularly significant from a management point of view in Finland?

2 Why do you think so many employees who claim not to be personally motivated by PRP nonetheless support the use of such schemes?

3 Having read this article, what advice would you give to an organisation that was introducing a new performance-related pay scheme for higher-paid, white collar workers?

4 To what extent do you think the key findings set out in this article would hold true for lower-skilled workers? Why?

IMPROVING PERFORMANCE BY IMPROVING THE WORK ENVIRONMENT

Another approach that draws on notions of intrinsic motivation involves improving performance through the judicious design and redesign of jobs and of the work environment, and by generally seeking to make the experience of work as satisfying as possible. It is based on the idea that employees achieve higher levels of motivation, satisfaction and performance if the jobs they do are made more interesting and challenging. The approach thus goes a great deal further than simply seeking to reward people for performing well: it involves finding ways of adjusting the whole working environment so as to make all jobs in an organisation as intrinsically motivating as possible.

The principles of effective job design were discussed in Chapter 8. Applying these, for example by taking on board the findings of Hackman and Oldham's research (1980), can make a major contribution to maximising the enjoyment and fulfilment that employees get from their work and hence, in turn, increase their contribution and the performance of the organisation. But there are several other significant components that make up the work experience as well.

IMPROVING THE PERFORMANCE OF P&D MANAGERS

In May 1997, *People Management* magazine distributed a questionnaire for readers to fill in and return entitled 'What makes people work harder?' The questions asked readers about their working environment and, more specifically, about the intensity and time commitment required in their jobs. Over 3,000 people responded, and preliminary results were published in July 1997. Among the conclusions reached by the team analysing the responses was that P&D specialists are motivated most when they perceive that their role is meaningful. In this

they differ from other groups who have been studied, notably salespeople, who have been found to have a strong need for 'psychological safety' in the form of support, clarity of objectives and recognition from managers. The survey findings suggest that these features do not have to be created by managers in order to motivate P&D people, because they emerge naturally from the work itself. Clear direction from senior managers, praise and backing for the decisions they take are thus not likely to improve P&D performance to any great extent. Instead the emphasis should be on enhancing the perception that the role is meaningful by ensuring that P&D job-holders feel that they are key members of the organisation and that they are not taken for granted. A perception that the work is demanding also appears to be important in enhancing motivation.

Source: McHenry (1997).

An example is the physical work environment in which people are obliged to work. Where it is perceived as unpleasant, dissatisfaction will set in, leading to low levels of motivation and a higher likelihood of poor work performance. And where conditions are uncomfortable they can make it harder for well-motivated employees to give of their best. Hot, noisy, dark, unattractive or overcrowded workplaces do not just dissatisfy those obliged to work in them, they also reduce energy levels. A working environment that people are keen to leave as soon as they can come the end of their working day is not one in which positive discretionary effort is likely to be found in abundance.

A fascinating area of current research involves investigating which forms of working environment are most productive and which tend to hinder organisational performance. It draws on management and architectural research to recommend ideal forms of office design, temperature level, ventilation, room size, lighting and decoration. A series of articles on these themes was recently published (see Clements-Croome 2000), which suggested that quite substantial improvements could be made to productivity if proper attention was given to the design of appropriate office environments. While one or two specific recommendations are made, such as the suggestion that a building depth of 12 metres is optimal (Leaman and Bordass 2000, p180), the main finding is that people vary in their preferences. Productivity is thus maximised where staff have a high degree of personal control over their own immediate environment. Where this is not possible, it is necessary to survey opinion regularly and to follow up complaints about the environment to compensate for an absence of direct control on the part of individuals. The research also suggests that the maximum number of people who should occupy one office is four or five (Leaman and Bordass 2000, pp184–185). Once the number becomes bigger than this people, perceive a loss of control over their environment and become less productive. This suggests that the tendency to develop large open-plan office arrangements, partly in a bid to raise productivity, may in fact have the opposite effect.

REFLECTIVE QUESTION

Think about different offices in which you have worked. Which gave you most satisfaction and why?

The way that work is organised can also have an important effect on individual performance (see Williams 2002, pp130–137). Those who are obliged to work in highly bureaucratic work environments, for example, find that the requirements on them to meet the demands of 'the system' are demotivating, because these tasks are often tedious and appear unnecessary. In addition, of course, they eat up time and thus in themselves reduce efficiency and effective performance. Such issues have fuelled serious complaints in recent decades from teachers, nurses, doctors and the police, who contend that the increasing bureaucratic demands of their roles reduce rather than enhance the performance of their organisations.

Instability and lack of clarity in terms of organisational structures are further performance-reducing elements of the work context. This is partly because confusion abounds as to who exactly is responsible for what, and partly because a huge amount of time is taken up managing instability and ambiguity. Staff spend their time focusing on, debating and often resisting internal changes rather than serving their customers. Where change is genuinely necessary, effectively justified and supported by employees it can and does enhance performance. But too often the opposite results because change is introduced for the sake of it, or simply so that a senior manager is seen to be 'shaking things up' or 'making a splash' – often moving on to another organisation to make another big splash before the long-term consequences of the first one come home to roost.

Finally, we can point to barriers to effective performance that occur because work systems are poorly designed or break down too often. Often it is a simple question of machinery breaking down and not being repaired quickly enough. In manufacturing plants the result can be very serious indeed if a production line ceases to operate. There is a clear impact on organisational efficiency, but a further longer-term impact on employee satisfaction. Indeed employees may lose out financially in such circumstances because their pay is linked to specific production targets. The same principles, however, apply to almost any workplace, because we all rely increasingly on technically complex tools to carry out the basic tasks of our jobs. Examples are e-mail systems that regularly go offline for hours, photocopiers that are forever breaking down and staying down while a maintenance engineer is called out, lifts that are unreliable, printers that stop printing and any number of software problems caused by viruses and system overloads. The impact on performance is inevitably negative. Not only are we unable to do our jobs to the required standard, but we also become demotivated and cynical about our work, our managers and our organisations.

SMART OFFICES

Read the article by Carol Glover, Room with a view (*People Management,* 8 August 2002, pp24–29). This can be downloaded from the *People Management* archive on the CIPD's website (www.cipd.co.uk).

In this article a number of prize-winning architects and other commentators are interviewed about the thinking behind some modern office building designs. In each case the needs of employees and the organisation's culture are said to drive decision-making, the aim being to maximise organisational performance.

Questions

1   In what ways do traditional office designs reflect an obsession with 'control, status and hierarchy'?

2   How do the approaches to design described in the article serve to reflect moves towards more democratic workplaces?

3   Why are HR objectives so rarely taken seriously when organisations build or rebuild their offices?

IMPROVING PERFORMANCE THROUGH COUNSELLING

Whereas job design and redesign focus on improving aspects of the way work is organised, the use of counselling approaches aims to help employees solve any personal problems, whether related to home or work life, that are affecting motivation and performance on the job. Aside from informal counselling sessions, the two principal, formal vehicles used by employers to address such issues are occupational health services and employee assistance programmes (EAPs). The former are primarily involved in dealing with medical problems and the prevention of illness and injury, but they also often provide counselling services, particularly where employees are suffering as a result of drug addiction, alcoholism or eating disorders. EAPs can also help in these fields, but have a wider remit. EAPs employ trained counsellors as well as people with practical expertise in dealing with issues such as debt, divorce, bereavement, domestic violence and a wide range of legal questions. Counselling can also be the best approach, at least at the start, where performance problems derive from bullying, harassment or workplace stress. (See IDS 2002e for an excellent evaluation of EAPs, and case studies on the role they play in practice.)

The rationale for both these facilities is broadly the same, namely that it is in the employer's interest for employees to be both healthy and content with their lives. It follows that where counselling services are capable of having a positive effect, and where they can be afforded, they are a worthwhile investment as part of a programme to raise standards of performance. That said, even where such services are not provided, it is necessary when faced with a performance problem to ask how far it might be explained by personal difficulties of the sort described above. It is particularly likely in the cases of individuals whose personal level of performance drops after a prolonged period of highly satisfactory working. Where such is believed to be the case, a counselling approach should probably be used in the first instance.

Some organisations take a more proactive approach by trying to identify potential sources of stress before they begin to have a negative impact on work performance. Questionnaire-based tools that are used include the GHQ-12 (General Health Questionnaire) which ascertains how far individual employees are suffering from damaging levels of stress and the OSI (Occupational Stress Indicator), which identifies the sources of the stress. These are reviewed extensively in IRS (2000b and 2000c). They have the advantage of helping to ensure that problems are dealt with before they begin to have a serious effect on individual work performance and become far harder to manage effectively.

CONTEMPORARY THINKING ON PERFORMANCE MANAGEMENT

How to improve and indeed to maximise people's performance at work is one of the most widely researched issues in management. New ideas and perspectives regularly emerge and are debated at length, some going on to influence management philosophies and to inform the development of widely used practical tools and techniques. It is beyond the scope of this chapter for us to look at all emerging perspectives in great detail, but it is helpful briefly to summarise some of those which have attracted most attention in recent years and appear likely to gain greater influence in organisations in the future.

THE PSYCHOLOGICAL CONTRACT

In Chapter 13 we introduced the concept of the psychological contract and explained how it can be a useful way of thinking about and managing employment relationships. Central to much research on psychological contracts has been the idea that negative consequences ensue when managers are perceived as having breached established psychological contracts with employees. Examples of such consequences are increased absence, higher levels of staff turnover and reduced effort. In other words, a failure on the part of managers in an organisation to honour what employees perceive to be the major 'terms' of their psychological contracts is likely to lead to poorer performance on the part of staff.

In some cases a deliberate, conscious decision will be taken to respond to a perceived breach by reducing the amount of effort that employees put in. Minor breaches will lead to a withdrawal of discretionary effort, defined as the willingness of employees to work above and beyond what is strictly required in their legal contracts (see Deery 2005). Major breaches have more serious consequences as employees react by actively seeking to reduce the level of performance, or even to sabotage an organisation's operations in some way (Jermier and Nord 1998). Keeping your word and managing expectations are thus central in the effective management of performance. If promises are made and not kept, performance may fall below the level that it would have been had assurances not been given in the first place. This happens because trust has been broken and an organisation thus moves from being one founded on high trust relationships to one characterised by low trust relationships. Breaches, like wounds, can heal, but it takes a long time and there is always greater vulnerability because the wound never heals completely.

HAPPINESS

Over the past decade there has been considerable development of thinking and research among psychologists in the field of positive psychology. Increasingly, in addition to focusing on mental illness and depression, leading figures have developed thinking about ways of maximising positive emotions and the benefits associated with this. As far as the workplace is concerned the result has been a growing body of evidence that links people's overall emotional state (ie the extent of their happiness) to job satisfaction and hence to superior work performance. In short, the happier people are, the better they tend to perform in their jobs. This is partly because happy people have a more optimistic outlook than unhappy people, and thus tend to be more confident in their work and better able to cope with knocks and set-backs. More generally, however, people who enjoy a positive emotional state have are motivated to come to work, put more effort into their activities and rise more readily to organisational challenges (West 2005; Adams 2007, p180).

Cropanzano and Wright (2001) define 'happy' people as being those who regularly exhibit positive emotions, rarely experience negative emotions and remain in this state over time. In other words, we are thinking here about people whose long-term state of mind is oriented towards positive emotions, not to any kind of transient state of happiness associated with what is currently going on in our lives. Their research demonstrates that such people tend to perform better in their jobs than people who experience more negative emotion more frequently. There is of course a chicken-and-egg argument to be made here. Could it be that success in a job leads to happiness rather than the other way round? This was generally assumed to be the case, but the most recent research tends to suggest that a positive emotional state is something that people bring with them to work from outside and which influences their work more than something which is uniquely generated in the workplace (Marks 2006). However, this does not mean that employment practices cannot influence people's emotional state for the better. West (2005, p39) suggests that the following managerial characteristics can play an important part in fostering 'a culture of positive emotion':

- encouraging good humour
- giving plenty of positive feedback
- exhibiting confidence and enthusiasm
- discouraging aggression between colleagues
- encouraging celebrations of success

Linked to this body of research is another which focuses on the relationship between physical and mental well-being. Increasingly it is being recognised that physical fitness has a major contribution to make to the development and maintenance of positive emotional states (Smethurst 2007b). Encouraging employees to take exercise, for example by providing subsidised gym memberships, and to eat healthily can thus play a role in improving long-term performance, as well as reducing absence. Physical well-being, however, is about much more than fitness. Someone may eat well and have a fit body, but nonetheless be unfit if they are overworking, overstressed and sleeping badly. It is thus helpful to think in terms of a broader category increasingly labelled as 'wellness' and to encourage its development. Employers always have to be careful when trying to extend their influence into people's lives beyond work, because many employees resent such an approach. But there are examples of organisations claiming to have improved performance at work by offering employee assistance programmes, relationship counselling and lifestyle coaching courses, all of which help to foster 'wellness' and hence to increase positive emotion and improve job performance.

KEY ARTICLE 34

Fred Luthans, Positive organisational behavior: developing and managing psychological strengths. *Academy of Management Executive,* Vol. 16, No. 1, pp57–72 (2002)

This article presents an overview and attempts very successfully to synthesise diverse strands of psychological research in the field of 'positive organisational behavior'. It concludes that there are strong grounds for accepting that people who have a positive approach to their lives and their work perform better than those who do not and that there are plenty of actions that organisations can take to enhance positive behaviours on the part of employees.

Questions

1   Why does Luthans argue that self-efficacy is the single most important element in establishing positive organisational behaviours?

2   What, according to Luthans, is the difference between 'self-efficacy' and 'hope'?

3   Why is 'optimism' not always a useful attribute for people to have in the workplace?

4   What initial practical steps would you advise senior managers in your organisation to take if they were interested in developing greater positive organisational behaviour?

STRENGTHS-BASED PERFORMANCE MANAGEMENT

Another interesting approach which is in part also derived from the recent focus on positive psychology is strengths-based management. It is a simple idea, but one that is somewhat counter-intuitive and has, as a result, had less practical influence than the other contemporary ideas discussed above. The approach involves managers focusing on people's strengths rather than on their weaknesses when seeking to improve their performance. This is the opposite of what traditionally happens. Strengths are taken for granted in discussions between managers and staff, the focus of developmental efforts being firmly on identifying weaknesses (nowadays more often described as 'learning opportunities') and putting in place plans of one kind or another to improve performance in those areas. Organisations encourage employees to reflect on their achievements self-critically and to take steps to improve in areas of weakness, for example by taking on roles which broaden their experience (because their work history is too narrowly focused) or working on projects 'outside their comfort-zones'.

In fact, according to extensive research carried out by the Gallup Organisation and popularised by the writer Marcus Buckingham (Buckingham and Clifton, 2001; Buckingham, 2007), a more fruitful approach involves downplaying weaknesses and allowing, and even encouraging, people to focus more on their strengths. According to Buckingham, organisational performance increases when managers match people to tasks at which they excel and allow them to achieve their objectives in ways they find work best for them. According to this philosophy performance management should therefore start by identifying strengths. Managers should find out exactly what their people do excellently, and then give them more of it, reducing the amount of time they spend on activities that play to their weaknesses.

It is a very straightforward way of looking at performance management, but despite millions of copies of Marcus Buckingham's books being sold, the approach only appears to be used by a minority of organisations (Roberts 2006, pp48-49). This is partly thought to be because the idea goes so much against the grain of traditional thinking about performance management, partly because it undermines the central message put forward in influential self-help manuals and employee development seminars (that you can learn to improve in your areas of weakness) and partly because the outcome in practice is an organisation that appears to be managed somewhat chaotically. This last point is very significant, because it relates to the strong preference of managers for standardised practices, conformity to a single organisational approach or culture and bureaucratic systems. These are not sustainable where a pure form of strengths-based performance management is practised because each person is encouraged to meet their objectives in ways which they find most effective. Management itself is much more eclectic in such organisations because management styles vary so much across departments. Marcus Buckingham sums up the consequences as follows:

> *This is about learning week by week which activities bore you, drain you and deplete you, and rewriting your job description under your manager's nose to direct yourself towards the activities you want to do and are good at.*
> (Roberts 2006, p49)

It can thus be argued that strengths-based management is perhaps an example of a good idea in theory, but one that is very hard to adopt efficiently and effectively in practice. It is hard to operationalise because there will always be some activities that all members of a team find boring, draining and self-depleting, but which nonetheless still have to be carried out by someone.

BAE SYSTEMS

Read the article by Tim Smedley, The powers that BAE (*People Management*, 1 November 2007, pp40–43). This can be downloaded from the *People Management* archive on the CIPD's website (www.cipd.co.uk).

This article describes a serious attempt by the UK division of BAE Systems to implement a form of strengths-based performance management for the senior management team. Slightly different approaches were used from the purist ones advocated by Marcus Buckingham.

People management

Questions

1   Why did the company introduce strengths-based management?

2   In what ways did the approach adopted differ from that recommended by Marcus Buckingham?

3   What were the results in practice?

CHAPTER SUMMARY

- It is possible to identify two perspectives on performance management. The first is standards-based and focuses on situations in which performance falls below what a management expects. The second is excellence-focused and aims to find ways of continually improving organisational and individual performance levels.

- Performance can be measured objectively using productivity measures, quality-control measures or evaluations of the extent to which specific objectives have been met. An alternative approach involves focusing on behaviours, or inputs, rather than on outputs.

- In some situations improvements in performance are best achieved through negotiation. This is particularly true of individuals whose skills are in high demand (and who could readily find alternative employment) and of people employed on a subcontracted basis.

- The most difficult but effective means of securing improvements in

performance is persuasion. Central here are the use of active listening, effective coaching, inspirational leadership and constructive feedback.

- The use of formal disciplinary procedures is easy to criticise but they are often necessary in practice. Perceived fairness is essential if demotivating effects are to be minimised, so it is important to follow established procedures, to treat everyone in the same way, and to apply appropriate and constructive sanctions.

- The use of rewards is a long-established means of enhancing employee performance. They can either be extrinsic or intrinsic in nature. The latter involve finding ways of recognising good performance that enhance individual self-esteem and self-worth.

- The design of the work environment can affect performance levels. There is a long tradition of research that has established the features necessary to make a job motivating.

Recently attention has begun to focus on the physical working environment and how this can be designed so as to maximise productivity.

- The final major approach to performance management involves the provision of counselling services. These are most appropriately used where individual performance falls because of personal difficulties faced in or outside the workplace.

- In recent years there has been growing interest in, but limited practical introduction of, emerging ideas about effective performance management. These include the use of a philosophy based on psychological contracts, the adoption of measures to increase personal happiness and strengths-based approaches to performance management.

EXPLORE FURTHER

- A number of books cover several of the topics covered in this chapter. Richard Williams's *Managing employee performance* (2002) provides a good up-to-date summary of academic research in the field, as does *Managing people in organizations* by Jeremy Adams (2007). Two books of articles edited by Richard Steers and his colleagues are also very useful. These are *Motivation and work behavior* (1991/2003) and *Motivation and leadership at work* (1996). A number of *Harvard Business Review* articles gathered together in *Manage people, not personnel* (1990) also cover general issues of performance management.

- The CIPD publishes several books covering the practical aspects of managing performance. Those that specifically cover the subjects included in this chapter are *Coaching* by Paul Kalinauckas and Helen King (1994) (now out of print but available from libraries), *Negotiation: skills and strategies* by Alan Fowler (1996) and *Managing performance* by Michael Armstrong and Angela Baron (2005). The edition of *People Management* dated 11 March 2004 contained several articles focusing

on different aspects of coaching.

- The debate about how best to obtain information on individual performance and how it can be measured is covered comprehensively by Kevin Murphy and Jeanette Cleveland in *Understanding performance appraisal* (1995).

- Derek Torrington has written extensively about disciplinary issues (see Torrington 1998, Torrington *et al* 2008). The use of rewards to improve performance is a major topic area. Good summaries of research in this field can be found in Brown and Armstrong (2000), Thorpe and Homan (2000) and White and Druker (2008).

- *Psychological capital* by Fred Luthans, Carolyn Youssef and Bruce Avolio (2007) is a good introduction to the practical application of positive psychological principles in the workplace. *Understanding psychological contracts at work* by Neil Conway and Rob Briner (2005) provides an excellent introduction to theories about the breach and violation of the psychological contract and their consequences.

CHAPTER 15

Performance appraisal

Performance appraisal can be seen, at least in theory, as a process that brings together all the different approaches to the management of performance identified in Chapter 14 and permits managers to exercise them. It is thus a procedure that can both reward and discipline, a means by which employees can be coached and counselled, and a vehicle through which improvements to performance levels can be negotiated. It also often provides an opportunity for discussion about ways in which the working environment can be improved so as to facilitate better performance on the part of individuals and groups of staff. Moreover, it has the potential to fulfil a range of other organisational objectives in addition to the improvement of performance. It can raise morale, help clarify expectations and duties, improve upward and downward communication, reinforce management control, help validate selection decisions, provide information to support HR planning activities, identify developmental opportunities and improve workforce perception of organisational goals. What is more, it provides information on which to base the selection of individuals for promotion and redundancy, not to mention its potential role as the foundation of incentive reward systems. In theory, it can be portrayed as something of a panacea, so it is no surprise to find that it has generated a vast literature over the years.

Unfortunately, the practice rarely lives up to these high theoretical expectations. Research into the outcomes of performance appraisal systems shows that, far from improving motivation and performance, they can in fact very easily have the opposite effect – particularly when they form the basis for decisions about an individual's remuneration. Indeed, reading the results of some studies, it can easily be concluded that performance appraisal is in practice more of an organisational curse than a panacea. At the very least it can be shown that there is no actual relationship between organisation success (as measured financially) and the presence of performance appraisal (Redman 2001, p62).

Opinion differs about why this is the case, with some writers on the subject questioning the system itself and its underlying philosophy, and others blaming the manner in which it is actually carried out in organisations. Undoubtedly, part of the problem is quite simply that appraising people is fiendishly difficult to do well. Its formality, in so far as it reminds the participants that their working relationships are hierarchical, can serve to set back or even destroy the development of genuine and fruitful relationships between supervisors and subordinates. Furthermore, the frankness and openness that the parties have to show during performance appraisals are a feature of the process with which many are understandably uneasy. Berkley Rice (1985) quotes an acquaintance as saying that appraising a work colleague is 'the equivalent of walking up to a person and saying "Here's what I think of you, baby"' – an uncomfortable activity that most would avoid if they could.

This chapter looks at a number of features of performance appraisal, both in theory and practice. Attention is given to criticisms of the approach and to some of the ethical issues to be considered in introducing and running an appraisal system. We also look at the question of cultural differences, among both occupational groups and people of different nationalities. The relatively new and highly fashionable topic of 360-degree appraisal is considered, before we turn finally to key practical issues for which P&D professionals usually take responsibility.

LEARNING OUTCOMES

By the end of this chapter readers should be able to:

- distinguish between evaluative and developmental aspects of performance appraisal
- make recommendations on the design and installation of appraisal systems appropriate for staff of different cultural backgrounds
- provide advice on the legal and ethical aspects of performance appraisal
- draw up documentation for use in performance appraisals
- arrange appropriate training for appraisers.

In addition, readers should be able to understand and explain the:

- advantages and disadvantages of behavioural and output-based approaches to appraisal
- criticisms made of both the theory and practice of performance appraisal
- principles underpinning effective 360-degree appraisal
- potential implications of the growth in atypical working for performance appraisal.

THE RISE OF PERFORMANCE APPRAISAL

During the 1980s and 1990s performance appraisal became a very widely used management technique. Since then its presence in workplaces has continued to grow, although sometimes different labels are used to describe it. It has a long history, its use having been traced back to the reign of Wei Dynasty in third-century China, but its use in modern times was until recently mainly restricted to managers, army officers and senior civil servants. In western countries it is now very widespread, and it is being increasingly introduced in other regions too. In the UK regular surveys undertaken by IRS and the CIPD show expansion both in the number of organisations using the approach and in the number of employees covered. Adoption of the approach in the public sector has followed practice in the private sector, successive governments advocating its merits and introducing its use in schools, hospitals, universities, and across the civil service. Most local authority employees have also been brought within the remit of schemes during the past ten years. A recent large-scale CIPD survey found that 87 per cent of organisations from across the sectors operated some form of formal appraisal system (Armstrong and Baron 2005, p65).

Many reasons have been suggested for this growth. Some believe it to be linked to the adoption of individualised performance-based pay systems that are filling the gap left by the collapse of industry-level collective bargaining. However, only a minority of schemes (43 per cent according to the 2004 CIPD survey) link appraisal formally to payment. Other factors must also therefore be important. Bach (2005, p297) cites the stimulus given by the requirements of the Investors in People award, and the development of organisation-wide competency frameworks. Other factors that may be significant are the need for organisations to respond to intensified competitive conditions and the need to find ways of managing accelerating change. Theoretically, performance appraisal helps in both scenarios because it encourages employees to focus their attention on management objectives.

Evidence is provided by the trend cited by many authors (Latham and Latham 2000; Iles 2007; Redman 2001; Bach 2005; CIPD 2005, p4; Torrington *et al* 2008) for individual performance appraisal to be linked quite specifically to defined organisational objectives. Such an explicit linkage is a relatively recent phenomenon, even in organisations that have long practised performance appraisal:

> *Historically, this process [appraisal] was often implemented in isolation from other inter-related systems, in particular the organization's strategic plan. Often appraisals were used primarily as an aid to compensation decisions and human resource record keeping. Consequently, the strategic plan document disappeared into employees' bottom desk drawers so that people could continue to pursue 'business as usual'. This occurred because little or no time was spent on considering what employees must do to implement the strategic plan with zeal.*
> (Latham and Latham 2000, pp296–297)

One reason for this, may well be the tendency identified by Bach (2005, pp297–298) for P&D specialists to see performance appraisal as 'an end in itself' rather than a means to an end. This attitude springs from the fact that appraisal produces the data on which to base so many other decisions for which P&D take responsibility, such as employee development, human resource planning and reward management.

Explicit linkage to business goals helps focus employee efforts on organisational priorities, while also ensuring that the performance appraisal process is owned by line managers and not just HR specialists. Commitment to it is higher because it helps add value to the organisation as a whole, rather than simply helping to meet administrative needs.

Along with a change in emphasis has come a development of terminology. The term 'performance appraisal' is still widely used, but other terms now tend increasingly to be used as well. The most common, according to Iles (2007) are those that emphasise the developmental aspects of the appraisal process. Examples are 'personal development review' and 'performance review and development'. According to the CIPD survey, over 70 per cent of employers see their systems as being primarily developmental in character (Armstrong and Baron 2005, p65).

VARIETIES OF PERFORMANCE APPRAISAL

Although performance appraisal comes in a number of shapes and forms, in its most typical incarnation it involves the formal appraisal of an employee's work performance over a set period of time (usually six months or a year) by his or her immediate line manager. In most organisations it has an official character, with some form of report submitted by the line manager that is then placed on the employee's file. As a result, appraisal interviews are acknowledged by all concerned to be significant occasions that require considerable preparation. In many cases, standard forms are provided by P&D departments to help line managers reach judgements about the main aspects of employee performance. The interviews themselves typically last an hour or more to allow proper discussion to take place concerning past performance and the best way to maintain or improve its standard in the future.

In Chapter 14, a divergence of view was identified between those who advocate the measurement of performance on the basis of results or outputs and those who believe it is more effective to focus on behaviours or the way that results are achieved. This dichotomy is also reflected in the literature on performance appraisal, two basic alternative approaches being put forward: behavioural assessments and output-based assessments.

BEHAVIOURAL ASSESSMENTS

Here the supervisor reaches a judgement about overall performance on the basis of his or her evaluation of the employee's general conduct during the assessment period. Although specific outputs may come into the calculation, they are subordinate to a consideration of behaviour, and are used principally to provide evidence of its effective and ineffective aspects. Hence, the appraiser may decide that an appraisee has performed particularly well in the field of customer care, and will justify this judgement with reference to evidence from a number of sources. Some of these will relate to observation of the employee at work, while others will be derived from formal output measures such as the number of customers who stated that they were very satisfied with the service they received from the employee concerned.

The behavioural approach is often associated with a requirement for managers to consider performance against certain criteria already defined and determined elsewhere in the organisation. Typically, this will require a standard form to be completed that obliges the appraiser to score or comment on different aspects of performance. Although the use of such forms can be helpful in guiding managers to those aspects of individual performance that they should consider, they can also be very inflexible, because they do not focus on the specific requirements of individual jobs.

A more sophisticated approach, which is also a good deal more time-consuming, involves using competency frameworks of the kind introduced in Chapter 8. The starting point is the identification of the particular behaviours or competencies are most important for employees in particular jobs or departments to display. In selection processes these frameworks are used as the basis for reaching judgements about likely future performance; by contrast, their use in this context involves assessing past performance. Employees are thus appraised according to how far, in the judgement of their immediate supervisor, they are actually meeting or exceeding the basic requirements of the job in question. Hence, if the competencies identified include conversational French, good interpersonal skills, the ability to work under pressure and an interest in law, then it is against these criteria that the appraisee's actual performance is judged.

OUTPUT-BASED ASSESSMENTS

In the case of some kinds of job it is possible to appraise people on the basis of quantifiable data. The most common examples are those in which employees repeat the same procedure or activity continually, allowing clear measures of their efficiency or effectiveness to be obtained. Such an approach is thus possible in the case of groups such as fruit-pickers, some manufacturing employees, clerical workers who process paperwork, and a wide variety of salespeople. Often such employees will be set some form of target to work towards, against which they are later formally appraised.

The other form of output-based appraisal seeks to apply the target-setting principle to a far wider range of jobs. Under such schemes, specific performance objectives or goals that the employee agrees to complete are set at the start of the appraisal cycle. At the end, the employee's performance is appraised according to how many or how fully these objectives have in fact been achieved. At each annual or six-monthly meeting, the manager reviews past achievements with the employee and then moves on to determine the objectives for the next appraisal period. The level of employee involvement in the determination of objectives varies from organisation to organisation. In some, they are basically set by supervisors, and clearly reflect organisational needs, whereas in others the responsibility is placed on employees to devise their own objectives and to state what action they intend to take to ensure that these are fulfilled. In most cases, a mixture of these two approaches is used, supervisors and subordinates agreeing a set of appraisal objectives that satisfies both the operational needs of the employer and the personal goals of each individual employee concerned. As is shown by the General Electric study described below, employee involvement in the setting of objectives is an important feature of successful output-based appraisal systems.

The debate about which of these two broad approaches is most effective has been a consistent theme of writing about performance appraisal for decades. As long ago as 1957, Douglas Macgregor was questioning the objectivity and motivational qualities of behavioural approaches, and advocating the use of approaches drawing on the 'promising' notion of management by objectives or MbO (Macgregor 1957, p159). Since then, the debate has continued through a period in which goal-setting approaches have become increasingly common.

According to a recent CIPD survey (see Armstrong and Baron 2005, p65), 62 per cent of organisations use objective-setting as the basis of their performance management systems, yet this approach too is often criticised when it is applied to particular job-types. For example, it is often argued that objective-based approaches are unsatisfactory for appraisal of professional staff and many public sector workers (Fletcher 2004, pp127–131). For manual workers in manufacturing industry too, there can be problems as so much hinges on systems working properly and the actions of others. Objective-setting has also come in for a great deal of criticism from writers advocating the use of 'competency frameworks' in performance management. Behavioural approaches are often more appropriate here as means of establishing how far an individual has or has not reached a defined level of 'competency' (see Beer and Ruh 1976, Fletcher 2004).

Vigorous debate over these issues is possible because both the above approaches have distinct advantages and disadvantages. Goal-setting appraisal systems have the virtue of being the more objective of the two, because the overall assessment of performance is based on specific achievements. Behavioural approaches, by contrast, are by their nature far more subjective, however fairly they are actually carried out. It is far easier for supervisors to reflect any like or dislike that they may have for an individual appraisee in a behavioural assessment than in an assessment based on the achievement (or non-achievement) of specific objectives. Such assessments are made all the more unfair because they are not necessarily job-related, but can be heavily influenced by a manager's general view of someone's personality or lifestyle. In addition to objectivity, output-based systems have the advantage of clarity. In other words, they leave each employee in no doubt as to what they need to do over the coming months to secure a favourable appraisal review. Moreover, systems in which individuals are able to participate in the goal-setting process have been found to have significant motivational qualities (Fletcher 2004, p19).

However, there are also drawbacks with results-based approaches that are not present in the behavioural systems. First and foremost, it is often argued that objective-setting is wholly unsuitable for many jobs, because there are so few clear goals to achieve. This is particularly true of those jobs whose the main function is the maintenance of an operation or body of work to a set standard. In such cases there are no specific new objectives to be achieved, let alone goals that are appropriate for individuals to be set. This is true of many unskilled and semi-skilled jobs, but is also the case in a number of professional occupations. Examples include medicine and teaching, where the effectiveness of job-holders' performance is based on the skill with which they carry out day-to-day tasks. Such people's contributions to the achievement of specific initiatives may be important, but none may happen to form an especially significant part of their working lives. It is therefore both unnecessary and unfair, so the argument runs, to judge their performance on the basis of such crude results.

Because they involve judging different employees on the basis of different criteria, goal-setting methods of appraisal also make it very difficult to compare one employee's performance with another's. Although this could be done crudely on the basis of the number of objectives achieved or exceeded, it would be most unfair, given how greatly the nature of objectives varies. Where appraisal results are used to determine promotion, pay and redundancy decisions, it is thus necessary to include behavioural approaches, so as to allow employees to be judged against the same basic criteria.

SMART OBJECTIVES

The acronym SMART is frequently used in the context of performance appraisal to indicate the type of objectives that managers should set. These are as follows:

S – specific

M – measurable

A – achievable

R – realistic

T – timebound

As a general guide this comprises useful advice, helping to create clarity so that all staff know exactly where they stand and what is realistically expected of them.

However, in recent years, as the competitive environment for many organisations has become more turbulent, managers have begun to question whether objective-based appraisal is any longer appropriate. In a fast changing context it is not possible to set objectives for a year – or even six months – ahead that have any kind of utility. Organisational priorities are continually shifting, so what was important a year ago may well now be unimportant. Staff who aim to meet these objectives rather than those reflecting the new realities, are thus as likely to be damaging the organisation's performance as much as helping to maximise it. In such environments, according to Rose (2000), objective-setting is better characterised by an alternative acronym: DUMB:

D – defective

U – unrealistic

M – misdirected

B – bureaucratic

Here, greater flexibility is required and different types of objectives relating to those priorities that do not change, such as the need to provide a good service to customers and the need to innovate.

REFLECTIVE QUESTION

Which jobs in your organisation would be impossible to measure on the basis of objectives met? Would other results-based approaches be more acceptable in these cases?

AIMS OF APPRAISAL

As was indicated in the opening paragraph of this chapter, performance appraisal is potentially useful for managers in many ways. At base, however, there are two fundamental reasons for developing such systems: assessing past and improving future performance. These are also often referred to as the evaluative and developmental objectives of appraisal systems. Although each in itself can be met using either of the basic formats outlined above, research suggests that problems arise from trying to carry out both aims at the same time. In other words, the extent to which it is possible effectively to evaluate and develop an employee by using the same appraisal procedure is questionable.

The incompatibility arises from the different ways in which employees perceive each of these objectives. When the purpose appears to be evaluative, there is naturally a tendency for appraisees to talk up the good aspects of their performance and perhaps to be less forthcoming about the poorer ones. As a result, they tend not to open up about their developmental needs. This is no great problem if the objective of the exercise is indeed evaluative. Managers know that employees are unlikely to tell the whole truth, and can make allowances for this in reaching judgements about each individual's performance. However, it is clearly a problem when there is a wish also to focus on future performance and on any need employees may have for additional training or experience in order to achieve future goals. In order to persuade subordinates to give a wholly frank picture of their own performance, it is necessary not only to stress the developmental aspects of appraisal but also to make quite sure that information gained is not used for evaluative purposes. As soon as employees suspect that their appraisal results are informing decisions about pay, promotion or redundancy the likelihood of an open and honest exchange of information diminishes considerably. For this reason a number of writers have suggested that organisations should make a choice about whether their appraisal system is to be principally used for evaluation or developmental purposes, on the grounds that it is not possible to achieve both effectively (eg Frechette and Wertheim 1985, p225; Anderson 1992, pp188–189; Randell 1994, p237; Murphy and Cleveland 1995, pp107–109).

Others such as Beer and Ruh (1976) have argued that both can indeed be achieved, but that a clear distinction has to be made between the two objectives nonetheless. Their approach involves setting up two wholly distinct organisational procedures with different names, one of which focuses on performance evaluation and the other on development. Meetings associated with the two procedures are then held at different times of the year to reinforce the separation. Fletcher (2004, p28) suggests a different solution involving a single procedure, but one that is both 'results-oriented' and 'competency-based'. Such a system would require supervisors and subordinates to agree objectives at the start of the appraisal cycle, thus permitting performance evaluation to occur at a later date, but would also require the objectives to be developmental in character. So, instead of setting someone performance objectives linked directly to current organisational needs (eg the development of a new appraisal training programme), the goals to be achieved would all relate to the development of an individual's own skills and knowledge (eg the development of competence in the field of employee appraisal).

REFLECTIVE QUESTION

To what extent do you agree with the suggestion that appraisals cannot achieve both developmental and evaluative aims together?

KEY ARTICLE 35

John Milliman, Stephen Nason, Cherrie Zhu and Helen De Cieri, An exploratory assessment of the purposes of performance appraisals in North and Central America and the Pacific rim. *Human Resource Management*, Vol. 41, No. 1 (Spring), pp87–102 (2002)

This article describes a research project that was initially intended to highlight differences between the way that performance appraisals are used, particularly in terms of their aims, in a variety of different countries. However, when designing their questionnaire the authors included items which asked respondents to state for what purposes they thought performance appraisal should be used in addition to stating for what purposes they are currently used in their organisations. The results were very interesting and broadly similar across all the countries. Everywhere it seems, managers are dissatisfied with the extent to which existing systems achieve useful outcomes and would like to see much more use being made of them to achieve a variety of different purposes.

Questions

1 What four possible major purposes for performance appraisal did the authors identify before they designed their research instrument?

2 What were the key differences the survey identified in terms of the way appraisals are used in different countries?

3 Why are managers everywhere apparently so dissatisfied with the extent to which their appraisal systems currently contribute to the achievement of management objectives?

PROBLEMS WITH PERFORMANCE APPRAISAL

Academic research into performance appraisal has rarely focused on its effectiveness in general terms. Instead, the literature consists, on the one hand, of general surveys establishing which approaches are being used and for what purposes, and on the other of case-studies that describe the problems encountered with typical schemes. It is therefore difficult to come to any firm and defensible conclusion about their overall effectiveness in different situations. Instead, it is necessary to focus on potential effectiveness with reference to research that draws attention to faults in the workings of performance appraisal, with a view to suggesting improvements.

Broadly speaking, critiques of performance appraisal come in three distinct forms: criticisms of the way that managers carry them out in practice, criticisms from a practical point of view of the appraisal in general, and theoretical criticisms from those who advocate wholly different approaches to performance management. Each of these is summarised below.

SPECIFIC PRACTICAL PROBLEMS

A number of research studies have drawn attention to the way in which appraisal is carried out in organisations and, in particular, to unfair bias in managerial assessments of performance. Rowe (1986) identified the following problems with rating systems:

- the tendency to give a good overall assessment on the basis that one particular aspect has been accomplished well

- a tendency to avoid giving low ratings, even when deserved, for fear of angering or upsetting a weak performer

- the tendency to give a poor overall assessment on the basis of particularly poor performance in one area

- the tendency to rate employee performance as 'average' or 'good' rather than to use the end-points of rating scales

- the tendency to give particular weight to recent occurrences in reaching judgements about individual performance

- the tendency to give high ratings to people who have performed well historically, whatever their performance over the previous year

- a tendency to refrain, on principle, from giving particularly high ratings

- a tendency to rate subordinates at a lower level than the appraiser achieved when in their position.

Michael Beer (1985) draws attention to problems that can occur in the interview itself. In particular, he criticises the tendency for managers to do all or most of the talking, leaving insufficient opportunity for appraisees to respond or to participate in addressing future objectives. According to Philp (1990), other common problems that can reduce the effectiveness of appraisal interviews result from poor management preparation, leaving insufficient time for a proper discussion to take place, and allowing interruptions to occur during the interview. With flatter hierarchies and fewer managers per subordinate, a more general problem of ignorance can arise. The manager doing the appraisal may simply be insufficiently familiar with what the employee concerned does or how they perform to carry out a reasonable appraisal exercise (Williams 2002, p8).

APPRAISING APPRAISAL AT GENERAL ELECTRIC

A classic research study into the effectiveness of different approaches to performance appraisal was reported in the *Harvard Business Review* in 1965. This was carried out in the General Electric Company in the United States and involved looking in detail at the appraisal experience of 92 male employees. At that time, the company had an established appraisal system in operation that was used to identify developmental opportunities, and also as the basis for setting salary levels.

In order to study employee reactions to different approaches, the managers were divided into two groups. Those in the first group were instructed to use a high-participation approach, whereby appraisees were asked to set their own goals for achieving improved job performance. By contrast, the second group was asked to take a low-participation approach, in which goals were set by the manager and then presented to the employee for comment.

Interviews after the appraisal process, together with an analysis of the number of personal goals achieved, suggested that the high-participation approach was more successful in general terms. It tended to lead to higher levels of motivation and to positive attitudes towards the appraisal system, in addition to the completion of more of the objectives set in the appraisal. However, an interesting finding was that employees who were judged to be performing relatively poorly, and who had thus been criticised in the interviews, appeared to do better under the low-participation regime.

Source: Meyer *et al* (1965).

GENERAL PRACTICAL PROBLEMS

The specific problems described above can in many instances be reduced, or even eliminated, with effective appraisal training and regular evaluation of how appraisal interviewing is working in practice. By contrast, the more general practical problems are rather harder to put right. The first of these was alluded to in the introductory paragraphs: the reluctance of managers to carry out appraisals. A number of reasons have been put forward to explain this phenomenon, ranging from a general dislike of passing judgement on others to an inability to handle the emotional responses that often arise when appraisal ratings are less impressive than employees expected. The appraisal interview, as an activity, does not often fit in well with individual management styles, and this too may explain some managerial reluctance. Where a supervisor has a close and open relationship with his or her subordinates, the formality implicit in appraisal interviewing may well serve to create greater distance between appraiser and appraisee. In such situations, especially ones in which an individual's performance is substandard, supervisors may well feel that a formal appraisal interview is an inappropriate forum in which to discuss performance issues. Instead, subtler approaches are preferred. By contrast, where a supervisor prefers to manage employees from a distance, eschewing close personal contacts, appraisal interviews can reduce distance by providing employees with the opportunity to force a frank and open exchange of views.

Another practical criticism relates to the inevitably political nature of some appraisal decisions. In their research into US executives' perceptions, Longenecker *et al* (1987) found that such political considerations very often led to the 'generation of appraisal ratings that were less than accurate'. What is so interesting about their findings is that this did not arise because of ignorance or carelessness on the part of appraisers, but was carried out quite deliberately after careful consideration. In other words, it appears to be a problem inherent to the appraisal process and thus not easily solved by the provision of better training or standardised paperwork. The general message is neatly summed up by one of the interviewers in their study:

> There is really no getting around the fact that whenever I evaluate one of my people, I stop and think about the impact – the ramifications of my decisions on my relationship with the guy and his future here. I'd be stupid not to. Call it being politically minded, or using managerial discretion, or fine tuning the guy's ratings, but in the end I've got to live with him, and I'm not going to rate a guy without thinking about the fallout. There are a lot of games played in the rating process and whether we admit it or not we are all guilty of playing them at our discretion.

This research brings strongly into question the extent to which appraisal can ever be carried out in anything approaching an objective manner. The implication is that it is therefore bound, as sure as night follows day, to result in a degree of demotivation and dissatisfaction on the part of some employees.

THEORETICAL CRITICISMS

A third critique challenges the assumption that has been accepted so far in this chapter that performance appraisal is great in theory but difficult to carry out well in practice. The view is thus expressed that performance appraisal is wrong in principle and represents an ineffective philosophy of management. The most celebrated critic to put forward this kind of view is W. Edwards Deming, the leading advocate of 'Total Quality Management' (TQM) approaches. His views have been echoed in the work of other gurus too, such as Tom Peters (1989, p495), who described objective-setting approaches to performance appraisal as 'downright dangerous'.

The essence of the case can be summed up in Deming's exhortation to 'replace supervision with leadership'. In short, it is argued that supervision, particularly when it involves the inspection of subordinates' work as a means of achieving quality, is a barrier to the achievement of long-term competitive advantage. Performance appraisal, in reinforcing the significance of the supervisor–

subordinate relationship, is therefore exactly the opposite of what is actually required. According to Deming, it creates fear, encourages the development of adversarial relationships and 'robs' people of their 'right to pride of workmanship'. By its very nature, he argues, appraisal reduces motivation, makes less likely the achievement of genuinely shared objectives throughout the organisation, and so wastes organisational resources.

Other principled criticisms of appraisal are based on the notion that, whereas such approaches to the management of employees were generally appropriate for much of the past 200 years, this is no longer the case. This view is eloquently put forward by Fletcher (2004, pp145–150), who argues that traditional approaches to appraisal are inappropriate for organisations that are knowledge-based, have flatter hierarchies, and need to maximise flexibility in order to compete effectively. Annual performance appraisals, in which the year's achievements are evaluated and new goals set for the coming year, are thus by their nature too inflexible to be useful as tools of performance management. Instead, there is a need to focus wholly on today's business needs, and to recognise that these are likely to change considerably over the course of a year, as will the contribution that individual employees will be expected to make. Moreover, it is argued that because performance appraisal sits uneasily with the ethos that characterises the attitudes of most professional groups, it is an inappropriate approach to take if an organisation wishes to maximise its performance. According to Fletcher (2004, pp129–130), the professional ethos is typified by:

- high levels of autonomy and independence of judgement

- self-discipline and adherence to professional standards

- the possession of specialised knowledge and skills

- power and status based on expertise

- operating, and being guided by, a code of ethics

- being answerable to the governing professional body.

By contrast, the principles of performance appraisal emphasise wholly conflicting characteristics:

- hierarchical authority and direction from superiors

- administrative rules and the following of procedures

- the definition by the organisation of standards and goals

- the demand that primary loyalty be given to the organisation

- the basing of power on one's legitimate organisational position.

It follows that the greater the extent to which professional and 'knowledge' workers are employed, the less appropriate traditional forms of top-down appraisal are for organisations. Similar criticisms have been made about some of the newer public sector schemes, such as those introduced in the NHS and schools. Redman (2001, p73) argues that these 'managerialist interventions' tend to 'undermine the public service values and public accountability of employees'.

REFLECTIVE QUESTION

How far do Fletcher and Redman's views accord with your own experience? Are they he right to suggest that appraisal by supervisors is inappropriate in the case of professionally qualified employees?

KEY ARTICLE 36

David Spicer and Rusli Ahmad, Cognitive processing models in performance appraisal: evidence from the Malaysian education system. *Human Resource Management Journal,* Vol. 16, No. 2, pp214–230 (2006)

This article describes the results of an interview-based research project looking at the decision-making processes employed by those with responsibility for appraising the performance of teachers in state schools in Malaysia. A model of 'cognitive processing' is first introduced and advanced as comprising good practice. Extensive detailed interviews were then carried out to establish how closely and in what ways the appraisers met the requirements of the model when making their decisions. The researchers found considerable variation in the practices employed, particularly finding that the less experienced appraisers did not make as much use of each stage in the model as their more experienced colleagues.

Questions

1   To what extent do you think that the cognitive processing model presented here can reasonably be judged to comprise all elements of a best practice approach?

2   What in particular did more experienced appraisers do that less experienced ones did not?

3   What practical lessons can be learned from this research for organisations seeking to improve the quality of their appraisal processes?

LEGAL AND ETHICAL ISSUES

In practice, the law does not intervene to any great extent in the performance appraisal process itself, but it can nevertheless have an indirect impact in that individual appraisal records inform decisions in the fields of promotion, payment, dismissal, access to benefits and access to training opportunities. There is, to date, a far less extensive body of case law in the United Kingdom dealing with these issues than there is in the United States, where fairness in appraisal systems is now defined quite tightly by the requirements of the law (Carrell *et al* 1995, pp354–355). Nevertheless, the legal principles are clear, and P&D professionals are thus well-advised to bear them in mind when basing important decisions on the results of performance appraisal procedures.

In selecting employees for redundancy, it is quite lawful to use appraisal ratings as one of several selection methods. Indeed, special appraisal exercises can be carried out specifically as part of a redundancy selection programme. Where such an approach is contemplated, there is clearly a need to ensure that the performance criteria used are fair, objective and verifiable by reference to documentary evidence. Performance appraisal ratings and reports can also have a role to play in other forms of dismissal, particularly where employees are dismissed on grounds of poor performance. The appraisals themselves, of course, often form part of the procedure used, whereby employees are formally warned that their performance is unacceptable, given time and assistance to help it to improve, and then dismissed should insufficient improvement have occurred. Employers must always remember in such situations that, were their decision to dismiss to be challenged in court, the fairness and objectivity of formal appraisals would form part of the evidence on which their case would be decided. Paradoxically, performance appraisal results are often produced by dismissed employees as part of their own cases against dismissal. This occurs when supervisors, lacking knowledge of the potential legal consequences, refrain from giving low ratings to their subordinates or choose to give positive performance feedback only. Of course there may be good motivational reasons for taking this approach in the case of poor performers, but it can easily come back to haunt the appraiser if the employee concerned is subsequently dismissed on account of poor performance.

Performance appraisals can also have legal consequences in the fields of discrimination on grounds of sex, race, disability, sexual orientation, religion or belief, and age. This occurs when they are used as the basis of or justification for promoting employees, increasing or decreasing individual pay levels, or selecting employees for new opportunities in the organisation. Here it is necessary to be able to show that the decision was taken objectively and that no unlawful discrimination occurred. Performance ratings that appear to be subjective or arbitrary are therefore unlikely to help in the defence of such cases. Where P&D managers are unhappy about the way that an appraisal has been carried out, or are uncertain whether the criteria used were fair, they are wise to ensure that decisions in these fields are not taken on those grounds alone.

Where appraisal involves explicit scoring of an individual's performance, there is also a need to monitor the results, or at least to keep an eye out for any general biases against particular racial groups and for patterns that show one sex to be achieving higher ratings than the other. Where such biases do appear to be occurring, it is wise to investigate the reasons and to take remedial action through training interventions or by talking to individual managers. If this is not done, the organisation could be open to challenge on the grounds that it is indirectly discriminating against one or other protected group.

Similar considerations apply where pay rates are determined as a result of performance ratings. Here it is equal value law that provides the basis for a legal challenge, for example where an employee believes his or her pay to be unjustifiably lower than that of a comparator of the opposite sex. Where it has been established that the two jobs in question are 'of equal value', it is for the employer to show that any difference in pay is due to 'a genuine material factor, not of sex'. Where the difference arises as a result of disparate appraisal ratings, the employer is likely to lose the case if it cannot satisfy the tribunal that the appraisal procedure operates objectively, that is, without unfair discrimination.

Leaving aside the possibility of legal action, P&D professionals should in any case seek to ensure that principles of natural justice are always applied in the field of performance appraisal to everyone, whatever their sex or race. It is very easy to devise schemes that permit supervisors who are so minded to justify unfair decisions or to use them as a means of advancing the careers of particularly favoured individuals. Apart from being unethical, such activities can have adverse effects for the organisation, in so far as they demotivate employees and contribute towards a poor reputation in key labour markets. Care has to be taken in drawing up policy in this field, in setting up appraisal systems and in training appraisers, in order to minimise the occurrence of such injustices. Where it is suspected that managers are abusing their positions in this regard, there may be a case for disciplinary action; but where that is considered unnecessary, a possible way forward is to ensure that two or more managers rate each employee's performance separately. A further possible solution is to include consideration of the ability to appraise effectively in managers' own performance appraisals.

REFLECTIVE QUESTION

What examples of unethical practice have you observed or suspected are occurring in the field of performance appraisal in your organisation? What would be the most appropriate remedial action to take in such cases?

EXERCISE 15.1

APPRAISAL TECHNOLOGY

People management

Read the article by Roger Trapp, Support system (*People Management*, 12 June 2003, pp40–41). This can be downloaded from the *People Management* archive on the CIPD's website (www.cipd.co.uk).

This article reviews the development of software that aims to make performance appraisal less subjective and inconsistent, while at the same time providing managers with the data they require to appraise people knowledgeably.

Questions

1   What are the major advantages and disadvantages of information systems that track how effectively individual employees are meeting their performance objectives?

2   Which types of jobs and workplaces do you consider are most likely to benefit from the new software and why?

3   Which of the above criticisms of performance appraisal practices could software help to answer? What other problems might be created in the process?

INTERNATIONAL DIFFERENCES

The type of appraisal system described in this chapter is very much the creation of Anglo-Saxon business cultures. In its formality, its requirement for active employee participation and its reliance on frank and open discussion of individual achievement, it fits by and large with the established cultural norms in US and UK organisations. Appraisal systems of this kind are less well established elsewhere, and will not necessarily be processes to which employees with different cultural backgrounds and assumptions will adapt very easily. For this reason, in international organisations it is often difficult and unwise to introduce a single, global approach to employee appraisal. Instead, there is a need to be sensitive to local traditions and to permit managers in each country to operate the performance management systems most appropriate to their populations. The following examples come from diverse sources published over the past few years:

- According to Ling Sing Chee (1994, p154), Singapore Airlines found that they had to adapt their worldwide appraisal system for employees based in Thailand. This arose because it was found that Thais had particular difficulty in highlighting the bad points in an appraisee's performance. The reluctance derives from the Buddhist belief in reincarnation and consequently in the role that 'good and bad deeds' in one's present life plays in determining how one will be reincarnated.

- Fletcher (2004, p143), drawing on the work of Hofstede (see Chapter 2), suggests that many people of Chinese origin are likely to feel uncomfortable when appraised under a system based on Anglo-Saxon assumptions. This is because of their reluctance to assert their own views directly to a superior. As a result, it is argued, appraisers need to be trained to anticipate such a response and to accept that they will have to adapt their appraisal style if they are to achieve a positive outcome.

- Prokopenko (1994, p154) states that in Eastern European countries, although changes are occurring, many of the norms and expectations of the communist era still influence P&D practice. An example of this is the continued diffidence towards performance appraisal that is associated with the bureaucracy characteristic of state-managed organisations before 1990. Because promotion and reward were rarely based on merit or performance, but instead on loyalty and political status, people have been understandably slow to adjust to a situation in which performance appraisal has a constructive role to play in management and motivation.

- Sparrow and Hiltrop (1994, pp558–560) note that performance management operates very differently in France from the way that it does in most UK organisations. Linking this suggestion to Hofstede's (1980) finding that French management culture was characterised by 'high power-distance' and 'high uncertainty-avoidance', they suggest that the Anglo-Saxon model of performance management is ill-suited to French organisations. In particular, the French are uneasy with the notion that subordinates should be involved in objective-setting, being used to more autocratic forms of management and a situation in which decision-making is carried out at the highest levels within organisational hierarchies.

- Laroche and Rutherford (2007, pp188–190) explain that appraisal systems commonly used in Western countries which involve people rating themselves are anathema to people who work in countries such as Russia which have a more hierarchical management culture. Here it is expected that the immediate manager appraises subordinates and Russians have difficulty rating themselves in isolation from their managers' judgement. Similarly the idea that people should be appraised on their ability to meet organisational objectives sits uneasily with a culture in which people focus primarily on pleasing their managers in a more personal sense.

It is thus clear that in this field, as in so many in P&D, it is not possible simply to take a model or approach off the shelf and install it in a subsidiary or branch office anywhere in the world. Care has to be taken, training has to be given and thorough research has to be carried out before it is safe to install such systems or procedures. The more innovative the approach, the more necessary it is to adapt its use in different countries. A good example is 360-degree appraisal of the kind described below. It is hard enough to gain acceptance for its use in countries that Hofstede characterised as having low power-distance work cultures; it would be tougher still in the Latin countries, where high power-distance assumptions prevail.

EXERCISE 15.2

APPRAISAL IN CHINA

People management

Read the article by Pepi Sappal, Cultural evolution (*People Management*, 17 April 2003, pp32–38). This can be downloaded from the *People Management* archive on the CIPD's website (www.cipd.co.uk).

This article discusses the introduction of various aspects of people management to China by western investors and the problems that they often encounter.

Questions

1   What cultural factors described in the article led analysts to warn companies investing in China that performance appraisal 'will never work' there?

2   Why are there grounds for arguing that the Chinese will adopt Western management systems like performance appraisal relatively quickly in the coming years?

APPRAISING A FLEXIBLE WORKFORCE

In their comprehensive review of recent US research into performance appraisal, Murphy and Cleveland (1995) consider possible consequences of increased flexible working practices such as those described in Chapter 2. Although some of their arguments are rather speculative, they make an interesting contribution to wider debates about the most effective approaches to the appraisal of employees. Two conclusions stand out as being particularly interesting.

A PREDICTED INCREASE IN THE USE OF OUTPUT-BASED SYSTEMS

Murphy and Cleveland argue that a number of trends designed to increase operational flexibility are greatly reducing the amount of day-to-day contact between employees and their line managers. This arises from increased homeworking, greater flexibility in terms of precisely when and where individuals work, and a tendency for organisations to develop matrix structures, in which people report to different managers about different areas of their work. In each case, the result is much less opportunity than has traditionally been the case for supervisors to observe their subordinates actually performing their jobs. In such situations it is natural for appraisers to focus more on results in compiling their evaluations than on employee behaviour.

A GENERAL REDUCTION IN THE SIGNIFICANCE OF APPRAISAL AS A MANAGEMENT TOOL

It is also argued that the growth in part-time employment, temporary working and subcontracting will have the effect of downgrading the significance of much traditional appraisal activity. This is because of the lack of internal career progression opportunities for most employees in these peripheral categories. Because two of the main aims of performance appraisal are the identification of candidates for promotion and the determination of long-term individual development needs, it follows that appraisal, as traditionally practised, is less significant in the case of such employees. The result is a need to find other motivational mechanisms and to focus attention on the achievement of short-term performance objectives.

REFLECTIVE QUESTION

How far do you agree with Murphy and Cleveland's conclusions? To what extent do they reflect your experience of managing staff employed on atypical contracts?

CUSTOMER-BASED APPRAISAL

In organisations seeking to develop and maintain the very highest standards of customer service, there has been increased use in recent years of techniques designed to inform managers of the real quality of the customer experience. The importance attached to such evaluations is made clear by their explicit linkage to individual or team-based appraisals. They are particularly useful in appraising managers with responsibility for a defined area of customer service work

(eg a restaurant manager or a manager of local authority services), but in many situations they can and are used to appraise the performance of individual employees.

Redman (2001, pp68–70) identifies three separate approaches:

- the use of customer survey instruments completed at the time that they experience the service or via a future telephone or postal survey

- surveillance by managers of employees at work, the main example being the taping of telephone conversations between staff and customers (used routinely in many call centres)

- 'mystery shopper' approaches, which are in practice used well-beyond the retailing sector and involve the employment of consultants to sample the services offered by the company.

Some have argued that these approaches, because they are often secretive in nature, lack ethicality. Moreover, they imply implicit mistrust of staff on the part of management, which can lead to demotivation. Redman (2001) suggests that the best way to gain acceptance of these approaches is to use them as the basis for rewards but not punitive actions. Good customer-care ratings should be rewarded well; poor ratings seen very much as a developmental opportunity.

A DEFENCE OF PERFORMANCE APPRAISAL

It is clear from reading the literature on performance appraisal that it is far from a perfect management technique. As has been shown, traditional top-down approaches that focus as much on evaluation as development have been widely criticised from a number of angles. Some people find fault in the way that the schemes operate, others dislike the principles on which they are based, while a third group sees them as outdated and inappropriate for today's corporate environment. Although these arguments have some validity, a strong counter-argument can also be put in favour of traditional performance appraisal.

The defence is based on the notion that performance appraisal need not, and indeed should not, be seen as the principal tool for managing performance in organisations. Instead, it should be used in a relatively minor way to achieve only those objectives for which it is best suited. The arguments of its critics all share a common assumption: that performance appraisal should be judged on its ability demonstrably to motivate employees and to enhance their overall performance. This is a tough test to set any single P&D intervention, and performance appraisal is not exceptional in failing to pass. However, that does not mean that it has no role to play at all, or that it cannot be used in tandem with other approaches to performance management.

In the author's view, performance appraisal continues to be used widely not because it has a great contribution to make to enhancing individual motivation at work but because it is an effective tool of management control. At the end of the day, whatever criticisms are made, it retains this key attraction – a feature that becomes more powerful when decisions relating to individual remuneration and promotion are clearly tied to appraisal results. In short, it remains the case that formally setting someone an objective or goal to achieve, and stating that recognition, pay and career opportunities will in part be influenced by that person's ability to achieve it, greatly increases the chances that it will be achieved. The old maxim 'what gets measured gets done' thus applies. In this way, appraisal contributes to organisational performance and the achievement of corporate goals in a steady and unostentatious way. It follows that the main problem with performance appraisal is not its actual effectiveness but the inflated expectations that people have of its ability to achieve far more grandiose organisational outcomes.

The key to using appraisal systems effectively is thus to recognise their limitations. It is true that, for certain groups of employees, it is difficult to formulate clear objectives on which to base performance appraisals, but that does not mean that the approach has no role whatever to play in their management. The problem arises when it is the only tool used to judge their performance. For example, it can be employed usefully and effectively in a relatively modest way as a means of ensuring that medical staff spend sufficient time during the course of a year making a contribution to specific projects, or that technical employees complete important but less interesting tasks that are nevertheless significant for their organisation. In this way it forms a small yet effective part of a wider performance management system. It will demotivate and have damaging consequences only if it is used either ineptly or as the only vehicle by which the organisation communicates its evaluation of an individual's contribution. It can thus be concluded that, with adequate training and experience, performance appraisal remains an important skill for managers to master.

360-DEGREE APPRAISAL

A method of appraising managerial employees that has received a great deal of attention in recent years is 360-degree appraisal (also known as multi-rater feedback), whereby ratings are given not just by the next manager up in the organisational hierarchy, but also by peers and subordinates. Appropriate customer ratings are also included, along with an element of self-appraisal. Once gathered in, the assessments from the various quarters are compared with one another and the results communicated to the manager concerned. The idea itself is nothing new. Management writers, particularly in the United States, have long advocated the use of upward and peer appraisal as a means of evaluating management performance, but such views have taken a good deal of time to become generally acceptable. The past few years have seen the publication of the first major studies of practice in this area, allowing us to reach judgements about the processes involved on the basis of solid evidence. Redman (2001, p65) quotes surveys that show around 40 per cent of major UK companies use it, and 75 per cent of companies in the United States. However, usage in smaller organisations appears to be far less common. The recent CIPD survey into performance management practices found that only 14 per cent of respondents worked in organisations that used 360-degree approaches (Armstrong and Baron 2005, p65).

In theory, 360-degree appraisal is, like many innovations, very attractive. Who better to provide constructive feedback on a manager's performance than his or her own staff? What better source could there be for suggestions about personal developmental needs? What better criteria for promotion to a senior management role than proof of the respect and admiration of peers and subordinates?

In practice it is, of course, far harder to achieve well. First and foremost, there is the problem of objectivity. How is it possible to ensure that peers and subordinates are not rating someone in such a way as to promote their own interests? It would be very tempting to take the opportunity to exercise personal vindictiveness against a manager whom one personally disliked rather than to give a balanced account of that person's work performance. Similarly, where two peers are competing for one promotional opportunity, it is inevitable that they will be tempted into rating each other poorly, however little justification there is for doing so. Second, there is the potential for managerial reprisals against subordinates perceived to have rated them (the managers) poorly and thus set back their careers, or indeed the potential for the reward of subordinates who give 'false' favourable ratings. Third, there is a range of problems that can arise when managers, in a bid to gain high ratings, are tempted to take action that is popular but not necessarily right for the organisation. Finally there are practical problems associated with the delivery of feedback to individuals and the setting-up of formal follow-up meetings to evaluate future progress. The giving of feedback has to be done with a high degree of sensitivity as it is not just one person's view of the individual's performance that is being communicated. Considerable skill is needed to carry out this job and subsequently to use the information as the basis for the development of some form of meaningful personal improvement plan.

It is impossible to remove all these practical problems from the process but, with careful thought and planning, progress can be made. Two conditions in particular stand out as necessary if any such initiative is to be successful:

●   It must be stressed that the appraisal process is to be used solely for developmental purposes. In other words, a situation must be engineered in which no one perceives that promotion or pay are directly linked to the outcome of the process. Although it is true that the result of the developmental process might be better performance, and thus promotion, the link should be no more direct than this.

●   It is necessary to ensure complete confidentiality, so that employees are left in no fear whatsoever that their manager will be able to victimise them on account of the ratings they give or remarks they make. For this reason, the only realistic approach is to produce standard appraisal forms to be used across the whole organisation and returned, once completed, to a central office.

Evidence of participant reactions collected by Mabey (2001) suggests that where safeguards such as these are in place managers being appraised using the 360-degree approach responded favourably and believed the experience to be useful for them and their organisations. It is thus reasonable to conclude that 360-degree appraisal is a technique whose time has come and that it is likely to become seen as standard practice in the near future.

People management

EXERCISE 15.3

EVALUATIVE 360-DEGREE FEEDBACK?

Read the article by Peter Goodge, How to link 360 degree feedback and appraisal (*People Management*, 27 January 2005, pages 46–47). This can be downloaded from the *People Management* archive on the CIPD's website (www.cipd.co.uk).

In this article the author challenges the widely held view that 360-degree appraisal should only have a developmental function. It is both possible and desirable, he argues, to use information garnered from 360-degree feedback exercises to make judgements about a manager's performance.

Questions

1 Why is it important to avoid direct links between pay and the results of 360-degree appraisal?

2 What do you think Peter Goodge means when he refers to 'soft links' between feedback results and manager appraisal?

3 What features of a 360-degree appraisal system does the article cite as comprising good practice?

KEY ARTICLE 37

Ginka Toegel and Jay Conger, 360-degree assessment: time for reinvention. *Academy of Management Learning and Education*, Vol. 2, No. 3, pp297–311 (2003)

At the start of this chapter we identified the problems that arise when there is confusion whether appraisal systems should be used primarily as developmental or as evaluative tools. It was concluded that combining the two was problematic but could be overcome if systems were thoughtfully designed. In this article it is strongly argued that once 360-degree appraisal forms part of the mix, as it increasingly does, the problems associated with systems having a dual purpose (developmental and evaluative) become far greater and are probably insurmountable. They argue that 360-degree assessment is 'something that works beautifully but is now tied to a broken system'. The argument developed here draws on a variety of other research and is itself highly sophisticated. The conclusion is that separate and clearly distinct

systems of 360-degree assessment should be employed in order that both the evaluative and developmental purposes can be met effectively.

Questions

1 Why has 360-degree assessment become so widespread during the past two decades, having hardly been heard of before this?

2 Why are developmental and evaluative objectives particularly difficult to combine in a single system when there is a significant contribution in the form of 360-degree feedback?

3 What proposals do the authors advance for achieving both objectives equally well?

PRACTICAL MATTERS

The day-to-day practice of performance appraisal is not an area of management work that P&D specialists spend a great deal of time undertaking. By its nature, this is primarily a job for line managers and first-line supervisors. With the obvious exception of the appraisal of their own staff, the P&D specialist's role is largely restricted to policy-making and the giving of advice. However, there are two areas in which the P&D function often takes a more hands-on role: in the design of standardised appraisal documentation and in training other managers to carry out effective appraisals. It is to these two areas of activity that we now turn.

DOCUMENTATION

The extent to which there is a need for standard documentation clearly varies, depending on the type of performance appraisal system operated. The more individual the appraisal criteria, the less role there is for any standard form for appraisers to complete. Where appraisal is based on specific objectives or goals set for each employee, the need for documentation is limited to some mechanism whereby managers confirm that they have carried out each appraisal interview. A good deal more is usually required where behavioural approaches are being used, particularly when employees across the organisation are appraised against similar generic criteria.

Those who have sought to identify best practice in the field of appraisal, such as P. B. Beaumont (1993, pp81–82) and Clive Fletcher (2004, pp47–48), argue that a strong element of self-appraisal should be a feature of any well-designed system. Standard documentation has an important role to play here, as it gives employees a clear framework within which to assess their own performance. Typically, the self-appraisal form will be sent to employees at the same time as their supervisors are sent theirs. Both parties then complete these before comparing the content of each other's forms at the appraisal interview itself. Some organisations issue identical forms to appraiser and appraisee, but because the purpose of the self-appraisal is different from that of the employer appraisal, it is probably better if rather different forms are designed. Self-appraisal forms have two main purposes. The first is to provide a means for employees to communicate their own perception of the job and what they believe their strengths and weaknesses to be. The second is to provide an opportunity for them to look forward and state how they would like their career to progress, were they to be given the right training and experience over the coming months. The kind of questions that are included are:

- What parts of your job give you most satisfaction?

- What parts of your job give you least satisfaction?

- How would you assess your technical skills?

- How would you assess your ability to communicate with your colleagues?

- How would you describe your working relationships?

- What do you feel are your main achievements over the past year?

- What did you fail to achieve? Why?

- In what areas do you believe you have the ability to improve?

- What training courses would you like to attend in the coming year?

- What are your career objectives for the coming year?

- What suggestions do you have for ways in which the organisation of work in your department could be improved?

- How might communication in the organisation be improved?

The list is not exhaustive and can clearly be added to and made specifically relevant to particular employee groups, but these questions illustrate the type of approach that is generally taken to self-appraisal forms. The questions are open-ended and thus cannot simply be answered with a simple yes or no. Once completed, therefore, the form provides the basis for constructive discussion in the appraisal interview itself.

Standard forms for appraisers to complete cover similar areas, but also usually include some sections that require formal scoring or rating of performance to be recorded. Hence, while appraisees are asked simply to comment at some length on their communication skills, supervisors will both comment and score them, often using a Likert scale such as those we looked at in the context of employee selection in Chapter 12. Other sections require objectives or targets agreed with the appraisees to be recorded, along with developmental initiatives that are to be taken to assist in their achievement. Typically, appraiser forms also require specific mention to be made of areas that need attention (ie those in which performance is weaker than it should be) and room for the supervisor to write a general summary at the end. The advantage of this last part is the chance it gives to finish on a high note. In other words, where faults or poor performance have been noted early in the form, there is an opportunity for a more general positive statement to be made in order that morale is not too badly damaged.

EXERCISE 15.4

FORCED-RANKING SYSTEMS

Read the following two articles by Anat Arkin published in *People Management* during 2007. They can be downloaded from the *People Management* archive on the CIPD's website (www.cipd.co.uk):

- Force for good, 8 February, pp26–29

- From soft to strong, 6 September, pp30–33

In the first article a method of appraising staff known as 'forced ranking' is discussed in general terms. Essentially it means that managers are required as a matter of policy to rank 20 per cent of their team members as 'good', 70 per cent as 'average' and 10 per cent as 'poor'. In some US companies the bottom 10 per cent are then fired, but the system need not operate in such a brutal fashion. This is demonstrated in the second article which concerns the use of a forced-ranking system in practice at Kimberly-Clark.

Questions

1 Why have so many US companies abandoned forced ranking in recent years?

2   Why is it becoming more common in the United Kingdom?

3   Why do managers at Kimberly-Clark believe that the system has had positive effects for them?

4   What particular problems did they encounter when first introducing their system?

APPRAISER TRAINING

If there is one issue that all writers on appraisal agree about, it is the vital importance of effective training for the people who are going to be carrying out appraisal interviews. The general message is that a badly done appraisal is worse than no appraisal at all in terms of the adverse effect that it has on motivation, job satisfaction, commitment and trust between managers and subordinates. Furthermore, as has been made clear, getting it right is no easy matter. It is not, as some managers like to believe, something that cannot be taught. Just as it is necessary to learn how to interview candidates for new positions effectively, managers also have to learn basic appraisal skills. Aside from the particular features of the scheme in operation, including the use of standard documentation, the following points need to be included in training courses designed to help supervisors develop appraisal interviewing skills:

- the importance of objectivity and consistency

- the need to avoid passing judgement on any aspect of an employee's personality or attitudes that does not relate 100 per cent to his or her performance at work

- the need to prepare thoroughly for all appraisal interviews

- the need to be able to justify with factual evidence any negative comments that are made

- the importance of putting employees at ease and encouraging them to do most of the talking

- the need to stress good aspects of performance as much, or more than, poorer aspects

- the need to take a constructive approach to weaknesses in the employee's performance and to make positive suggestions as to how matters may be improved

- the need to end appraisal interviews on a forward-looking, positive and constructive note.

Appraisal training sessions themselves tend to be highly participatory, exercises of one kind or another, being undertaken as a means of developing the key skills of active listening, the giving of constructive feedback and effective counselling. These take a number of forms. First, there is the kind that involves showing a video to course members in which a particular set of tasks is performed (some well and some badly) by an actor. The group then works out how it would be best to handle an appraisal interview with that individual. Second, there are exercises in which course members or leaders undertake some task in front of the group, such as making a short presentation, and are then formally appraised on their performance. Third, there are role-playing exercises in which course members appraise each other according to the contents of briefs provided by the course leader. In this case, participants can also be asked to give feedback to the appraisers on their performance. In each of these exercises there is scope for introducing unusual or particularly difficult scenarios that appraisers have to tackle. Wherever possible, this should include the appraisal of an employee with a particularly poor performance record, caused in part by emotional or personal difficulties. The importance of developing effective counselling skills is thus emphasised.

Research carried out in the United States suggests that proper training can be highly effective in reducing the extent to which appraisers fall into the most common traps. It also appears to bring substantial improvements to the level of objectivity observed. A review of these studies is provided by Latham and Latham (2000, pp203–204).

APPRAISAL AT JP MORGAN

Latham and Latham (2000) use the example of the bank JP Morgan to illustrate good practice in performance appraisal, but also as an example of a company that has sought to address the concerns about performance appraisal raised in the academic research.

Morgan uses a multi-tier approach so that individual performance is appraised against three distinct sets of criteria:

- core competencies that are relevant to all jobs across the group

- objectives linked to the company's business strategy

- individual performance objectives that are developmental in character.

These objectives are agreed annually by employees and their managers, then formally reviewed after six months to allow for adjustment. There is a strong degree of self-appraisal in the end-of-year evaluation, which operates as part of a 360-degree appraisal system.

Substantial training programmes are used to make appraisers aware of the importance of objectivity and of the dangers associated with the stereotyping and halo and horns effects.

CHAPTER SUMMARY

- The use of performance appraisal has increased substantially in recent years. It is now often linked explicitly to business objectives and to evolving business strategies.

- Appraisals are based either on general behavioural assessments or on the achievement/non-achievement of objectives, or a mixture of these. Another important distinction is between appraisals that are primarily evaluative in their aims and those that are primarily developmental. It is difficult to achieve both these aims in practice using the same system.

- The practice of performance appraisal, particularly when linked to payment, has been the subject of a great deal of criticism. Some argue that the approach is fundamentally flawed, while others have focused on the many practical problems associated with the running of an effective system.

- Numerous legal and ethical issues are associated with performance appraisal. They can be used as the basis of legal claims (and as evidence) in cases brought under sex, race and disability discrimination statutes, equal pay and unfair dismissal. They often play a particularly significant role in redundancy selection policies.

- Many writers have questioned how appropriate performance appraisal as practised in Anglo-Saxon cultural contexts is in other regions. Despite misgivings, there is evidence of the adoption of the approach by multi-national companies in many areas of the globe.

- Recent adaptations of traditional approaches include customer-based appraisal and the very fashionable 360-degree appraisal. The latter appears to be becoming standard practice in many larger organisations and is positively rated by those who participate.

- The HR function does not usually take a direct role in the carrying out of appraisals. It is, however, responsible for the design of systems, for the drawing up of standard documentation and, importantly, for the training of appraisers.

EXPLORE FURTHER

- There is a vast literature covering different aspects of performance appraisal. Two books that cover a great deal of the ground and draw on years of academic research are *Understanding performance appraisal* by Kevin Murphy and Jeanette Cleveland (1995) and *Appraisal and feedback: making performance review work* by Clive Fletcher (2004). Two more recent books which takes particular account of the current trends are *Human performance improvement* by Rothwell *et al* (2007) and *Managing and measuring employee performance* by Elizabeth Houldsworth and Dilum Jirasinghe (2007).

- CIPD and IDS regularly publish the results of case studies and surveys of employer practice in this field. IDS studies include *Performance management* (1992c), *Performance appraisal for manual workers* (1993), *Appraisal systems* (1995a), and two entitled *Performance management* published in 1997 and 2007. The most recent CIPD survey dates from 2005. It can be downloaded free of charge by CIPD members from the institute's website.

Evidence of the way in which debates about performance appraisal have veered this way and that over the years is provided by Gerry Randell (1994) in his contribution to *Personnel management: a comprehensive guide to theory and practice in Britain* edited by Keith Sisson, and in the book of short articles on the subject published by the *Harvard Business Review* in 1990 under the title Manage people, not personnel. Recent research is summarised effectively by Redman (2001), Iles (2007), Bach (2005), Latham and Latham (2000), Williams (2002), Rao (2004) and Latham et al (2007).

- The topic of 360-degree appraisal is covered by Fletcher (2004) and Armstrong and Baron (2005) in the books recommended above, by Peter Ward (1997) in *360-degree feedback*, and by Robert McGarvey and Scott Smith (1993) in their article entitled 'When workers rate the boss', which is included in *Human resources management: perspectives, context, functions and outcomes* edited by Gerald Ferris and Ronald Buckley (1996). Research of interest has been published by Mabey (2001) and Bracken *et al* (2001).

CHAPTER 16

Managing absence

According to recent and extensive employer surveys, the average annual absence rate in the United Kingdom is between 3.3 per cent and 3.7 per cent a year, depending on the criteria used in the study (CBI 2007, CIPD 2007c). This represents seven to nine days per employee, and means that around 200 million working days are being 'lost' annually as a result of absenteeism, a figure that has remained fairly stable for a number of years and puts the United Kingdom towards the bottom of international absence league tables.

The need to reduce absence has risen up the agendas of many P&D managers since April 1994, when the government ceased reimbursing all but the smallest employers for the cost of administering and paying out statutory sick pay (SSP). Henceforward, employers have had to shoulder the bulk of the bill generated as a result of absenteeism in the United Kingdom, estimated by the CBI (2007) to be around £13.4 billion a year. One consequence has been the publication of a great deal more literature about the causes of absenteeism and the various approaches used to reduce the number of days on which employees fail to show up for work. Despite this, absence management remains an area of P&D activity on which commentators and researchers take widely differing positions. It is also a field characterised by the presence of apparently contradictory research evidence.

In this chapter, the management of absence or attendance is viewed as a specialised subfield of performance management. We therefore continue with a number of the themes introduced in Chapters 14 and 15, while also introducing new material that relates specifically to the improvement of absence rates. We first discuss methods used for measuring and costing absence before moving on to focus on its possible causes and the various approaches that have been taken in search of long-lasting remedies. In the main, we are not concerned here with the management of issues arising from chronic illness on the part of employees, which account for around 40 per cent of all absences (CBI 2007). Situations in which people have genuine, long-term illnesses that prevent them from either coming to work or performing effectively when present are distinct P&D activities that are in practice governed by the requirements of the law. These will be dealt with in Chapter 19 in the context of dismissal on grounds of incapability. The focus in this chapter is absence of a different kind: situations in which individuals who could come into work choose not to. This may be on account of a relatively insignificant illness such as a mild headache, stomach upset or cold, or it may be for other reasons.

LEARNING OUTCOMES

By the end of this chapter readers should be able to:

*   set up systems to monitor absence rates

*   estimate the costs of absence and the savings generated by its reduction

*   develop and undertake a programme to reduce absence levels.

In addition, readers should be able to understand and explain the:

*   causes of absenteeism

*   implications of absenteeism for employers and employees

*   potential benefits and shortcomings of alternative approaches to the management of absence.

EXERCISE 16.1

LIVING WITH CANCER

Read the following articles featured in *People Management*. They can be downloaded from the *People Management* archive on the CIPD's website (www.cipd.co.uk):

*   Penny Cottee, Suffering in silence (26 October 2006, pp36–41)

*   Anat Arkin, The C word (24 January 2008, pp28–32).

Both these articles argue that many more workers, one way or another, 'live with cancer' than did previously, as either sufferers or carers, and that employers are generally ill-equipped to deal with their needs effectively. Moreover, their numbers are likely to grow significantly in the future. Ideas are put forward for how the issue can be much better managed.

Questions

1   Why are so many more cancer sufferers working for UK employers than used to be the case?

2   Why is the experience of work so important to cancer sufferers and to their relatives?

3   What approach to the management of this issue could be said to constitute 'best practice' on the part of employers?

MEASURING ABSENCE

Monitoring absence levels is, by all accounts, a prerequisite for the development of policies and practices aimed at their reduction. Without a system for calculating current rates of absence, it is not possible to set targets for its reduction, or even to track the direction of trends across different divisions or among different groups of employees. Measurement must also form the basis of any analysis of the causes of absence, and thus of programmes of remedial action.

The standard and most widely used measure is the crude absence rate expressed as a percentage of 'working days lost'. This is simply calculated by working out the total number of days that employees are contracted to work and dividing it into the number of days on which employees failed to come to work over a given period of time. Multiplying the total by 100 gives the percentage figure. General absence rates of this kind can be calculated for the organisation as a whole, particular departments or staff groupings, or individual employees. Without taking the same approach to measurement and monitoring across the whole organisation, it is impossible to compare department with department. Furthermore, inconsistencies are likely to develop in the approach taken to the management of absence, which can lead to unfairness in the way individual employees are treated.

Absence data can be collected in a variety of ways. Many organisations still rely on time sheets filled in by each line manager and copied weekly or monthly to the payroll department. Others employ systems of self-certification, whereby individuals are required to notify the personnel department of their absence when they return. Larger organisations, and those with integrated computerised personnel systems, will ask line managers to record absences against each employee's record on the database. Reports can then be generated centrally showing how many days have been lost in each department. Perhaps the most technically sophisticated approach is the use of a clock-in/clock-out system, which records hours worked as well as instances of absence. Each of these methods has advantages and disadvantages in particular situations. The clock-in system, for example, is of little use where employees work away from the employer's premises for a substantial proportion of their time. Organisations also frequently experience difficulties in ensuring that line managers do actually record absence on computerised systems.

The measurement process is invariably more complicated than it looks. First, there is a need to establish a clear policy for including the absence of part-time workers, particularly those who have irregular hours of work. Which system should be used to record a part-timer's failure to turn up to work for three hours over a busy lunch-time period? This cannot be recorded as a day lost, so it should be recorded as a portion of a day (eg 37 per cent), as a half day, or as a percentage of that individual's contracted hours in the week in question. Where there are large numbers of part-time employees, organisations can use 'hours lost' rather than 'days lost' as the basic unit of absence for monitoring purposes.

There is also a need to consider what counts as absence and what does not. For example, a decision has to be taken whether holidays or days taken in lieu of overtime payments are included in the calculation. What should be recorded when someone comes into work a few hours late? What about days lost, or partially so, as a result of industrial action or by employees looking for work when under notice of redundancy? What is recorded when someone is absent because he or she has a dental appointment or is required to do jury service? What about maternity leave?

Once decisions have been made on these points, it is possible to calculate a standard absence rate for the organisation, or a part of the organisation, in any given period, and to undertake a meaningful analysis of trends over time. A great advantage of the more sophisticated computerised systems is their capacity for recording and subsequently reporting causes of absence, as well as the ball-park rate. Such systems contain a set of codes or a menu of options listing the whole range of possible reasons for absence that have to be chosen by the person feeding in the statistics. It is then possible to generate overall reports that include or exclude particular causes.

Many have also argued that the crude absence rate expressed as a percentage of time lost is too all-encompassing to be of any great use in analysing absence and planning courses of action aimed at its reduction. In particular, it is said that there is a need to record the number of distinct spells of absence (ie its frequency) as well as the total number of days. This is because one long spell of absence lasting 10 days is considerably less disruptive for the organisation than several short spells that total 10 days. Making such a distinction also allows an employer, in developing strategies to reduce absence, to differentiate between absence that results from a genuine illness and that due to other, less acceptable, causes.

A useful approach is the 'Bradford factor', which was devised by a team of researchers at Bradford University. Here, a points system is used as the unit of analysis, rather than 'days lost'. The formula used to calculate the number of points is $S \times S \times D$, where S is the number of separate spells of absence taken in a year and D is the number of days taken. Hence, someone absent for a total of 10 days in a year taken in a single spell would be recorded as having 10 points ($1 \times 1 \times 10$), whereas someone absent for 10 days in five two-day spells would be given 250 points ($5 \times 5 \times 10$). Such figures are easily calculated by a computerised system and can then be used as a basis for determining at what point individuals are formally interviewed on the subject of their absence record. It also provides a more useful basis for comparing levels across different departments, for setting absence reduction targets, and for tracking progress over time.

It is because of these complexities that benchmarking performance in terms of absence levels against those of competitor organisations becomes an intricate process. Unless everyone applies the same assumptions and rules, meaningful comparisons are difficult. A figure of 1 or 10 per cent means little unless you know what types of absence are included and on what basis the calculation has been made. That is not to say that there is no use at all in comparing figures with those of other employers operating in the same industrial sector, but that great caution should be taken when doing so, and that it should be recognised that figures can be calculated in markedly different ways. In particular, it is important to qualify comparisons made with industry-sector averages or 'norms' published in commercial surveys and in government publications. Indeed, Huczynski and Fitzpatrick (1989, pp158–160) argue that comparing performance against average absence rates for the industry is a fatuous exercise even when it can be done accurately, because the variations within each industry are so great as to make the average figure meaningless. Instead, they suggest that all organisations should set a figure of 3 per cent as their aim, on the grounds that it has been shown to be achievable in all industrial sectors. Taking comfort from the fact that a 5 per cent absence rate is good by industry standards is thus seen as unnecessarily complacent.

REFLECTIVE QUESTION

What is the current absence rate in your organisation? What methods are used to collect the data?

SICKNESS ABSENCE IN BRITAIN 1971–97

A major survey on absence rates among full-time employees in the United Kingdom over several decades was carried out by Tim Barmby and his colleagues, using substantial bodies of data found in the government's *General household and labour force surveys* (Barmby *et al* 1999). Among their findings are the following statistics:

- Absence rates show strong seasonal characteristics, being considerably higher in the winter months than in the summer.

- On average men have lower absence rates than women.

- The lowest average rates are among men under the age of 40 (2 per cent); the male rate then climbs steadily to 7 per cent just before retirement.

- The female rate starts at a similar level to the male rate, but climbs to 4 per cent on

average at age 33; it then begins to climb again in the 50s and 60s to 7 per cent at retirement.

- Employees who continue to work after the retirement age have lower average absence rates than are exhibited by most in the years running up to the retirement age.

- The lowest rates of absence are found in England, with employees in the north having more time off than people in the south. Rates in Wales, Scotland and Northern Ireland are higher than in England, with the highest rates of all being found in the Strathclyde region.

The study makes suggestions as to the reasons for these figures, but reaches no firm conclusions. What do you think might account for the observed patterns ?

COSTING ABSENCE

The process of putting a cost on absence – and thus calculating the value to the organisation of initiatives that help reduce it – is a complex and controversial field. According to an Industrial Society survey (1997b, p11), it is attempted by only 54 per cent of organisations – for the most part, larger employers with the resources to invest in a well-planned costing system. Respondents gave a variety of reasons for not undertaking costing exercises . Some believed the process to be of little value or did not perceive that absence was a priority for them, while others believed such exercises to be too time-consuming. A further group stressed their inability to cost absence accurately because they lacked accurate attendance records or a computerised personnel system.

For those who do attempt to calculate the cost, there is a range of approaches available. The simplest is to calculate it in terms of the earnings paid to absent employees. Where pay is not deducted when people are absent, calculating the overall cost of absence is straightforward. An organisation simply works out the average daily earnings of its employees and multiplies this figure by the number of days on which employees were absent. Figures can also be worked out for subgroups and for particular departments. Hence, if average individual daily earnings in a clerical division employing 20 people are £50 and absence levels average 10 days a year, the total cost would be calculated at £10,000 (20 × 50 × 10). It is this approach that is used by employer organisations and government agencies to estimate the total annual cost of absence in the United Kingdom. The following is an example of such a calculation:

Average daily earnings per employee:	£75
Average number of absences per employee:	7 days
Total number of employees in the United Kingdom:	27 million
Total cost = (£75 × 7) × 27 million =	£14.175 billion

However, such crude figures can act as only rough guides to the actual overall cost. In some ways it overestimates the total cost, because few employers pay their employees full earnings for all the days that they are away. Some pay only the rate of SSP, while others reduce the level during long periods of sickness. In the public sector, it is common for people who are sick for a long period to be put onto half-pay after six months. However, this approach also underestimates costs in a variety of other ways. First, in basing the calculation on average earnings, it fails to take into account employment on-costs such as employers' National Insurance contributions, pension scheme contributions and the cost of any other benefits provided. Second, it does not include other direct and indirect costs incurred by the employer as a result of the absence. These include:

- temporary staff to cover for absent staff

- overtime paid to existing staff who cover

- reduced quality of work or productivity

- disruption to smooth running of systems

- management time spent managing the consequences of individual absences

- low morale or dissatisfaction on the part of colleagues left to cover the work.

Clearly, some of these are indirect and very difficult to quantify in practice; it is nonetheless possible to make estimates and to add these to the direct costs that are straightforward to calculate. A number of approaches used in individual industries to estimate indirect costs is given by Huczynski and Fitzpatrick (1989, pp15–21) and by Bevan and Hayday (2001). Arguably, because greater costs are incurred by frequent short-term absences than by the more manageable long-term variety, these should be reflected in any assumptions used to calculate organisation-wide costs. Perhaps the most substantial costs of all are those associated with a continual need to overstaff the organisation so that absence can be covered. If the absence rate is running at 5 per cent a year, it is necessary to employ 5 per cent more staff than would otherwise be the case in order to allow the organisation to function. In a large organisation employing thousands of people, the total cost is therefore very considerable indeed.

However, it is also important to recognise that a certain amount of absence is unavoidable, because employees inevitably fall ill from time to time. Assumptions of this kind also have to be built in to estimates of the overall costs incurred. Employers can either look at their absence records to work out what proportion of sickness is definitely unavoidable, or make a general assumption about its likely level based on published data. Recent CBI research, for example, states that managers generally agree that around 12 per cent of absence is non-genuine (CBI 2007), suggesting that at least six of the eight days the average employee is absent each year are for genuine ill-health reasons. However, it is reasonable to argue that an absence level of 1.5 per cent, or approximately four days a year per employee, is realistic, since this represents the lowest levels of absence achieved by organisations taking part in the most surveys. Subtracting this figure from the total cost will thus give a more useful estimate of the total avoidable cost.

PRESENTEEISM

The opposite of absenteeism is 'presenteeism', a phenomenon that has received attention in the P&D press recently. The term refers to situations in which employees spend a good deal more time at work than is necessary for them to complete their job tasks. Typically, it involves people arriving very early in the morning and leaving very late at night. They may also come in at the weekend or decline to take their full holiday entitlement. Often it is done in an effort to impress superiors, and can become engrained in the culture of certain work groups. A limited amount of presenteeism is no big problem; indeed, when the workload is high it is useful to have people willing to work extra hours. However, when it is excessive, it can have negative effects. For example, it can make people over-tired and bad-tempered, leading to a deterioration in workplace relationships. People who come in too much also tend to become narrow-minded, as they lack sufficient stimulation from outside the workplace. According to Balcombe (quoted in Industrial Society 1997b), this reduces their capability 'to contribute fresh ideas and different perspectives' or to bring to their work 'a sense of proportion and humour'. Cooper (2001) reports that perceptions of a presentee culture at senior levels in British Telecom resulted in 38 per cent of people stating that they would refuse promotion if it was offered.

Managers should therefore be open to the possibility that individuals or groups of employees are turning into 'presentees', and take steps to discourage such behaviour. This can be done by making clear to them that they are not impressing anyone by their actions and that their careers will not be enhanced as a result. It is also possible for managers actively to set an example by leaving on time themselves.

THE CAUSES OF ABSENCE

It is not easy to identify with confidence what the main reasons for absence are, either in general terms or in particular organisations, because research findings on the issue have tended to differ. Undoubtedly, the uncertainty stems in part from the fact that employees are often unwilling to admit that they have been absent for reasons other than serious illness. However, it is also the case that there are no simple answers to the question, and that a variety of reasons may contribute to an individual employee's being absent from work on a particular day. Moreover, the same reason can often be seen as being more or less justifiable depending on your point of view – a truism neatly summed up by Johns and Nicholson (1982) in their suggested conjugation of the verb 'to be absent':

> I am sometimes prevented from attending work through no fault of my own.
> You lack motivation to attend work regularly.
> They are lazy malingerers, wilfully milking the system.

An Industrial Society survey suggests that managers are often unconvinced by the excuses given by employees to explain their absence. This is illustrated by the differences between what managers believe the major reasons for short-term absence to be and what employees state as their reasons are when completing self-certification forms (see Table 16.1).

Table 16.1 Five main causes of absence

As recorded on certification forms	In managers' opinions
1 Colds and flu	1 Colds and flu
2 Stomach upsets and food poisoning	2 Stress and personal problems
3 Headaches and migraines	3 Sickness of other family member and childcare problems
4 Back problems	4 Low morale/boring job
5 Stress and personal issues	5 Monday morning blues

Source: Industrial Society (1997, p10).

Employers are right to be suspicious of the reasons given by employees when they are absent. A survey of 1,336 employees undertaken by the research company My Voice in 2001, widely reported in the media, found that 56 per cent confessed to taking between one and five 'sickies' in the past year (ie pretending to be ill when actually taking time off for other reasons). As many as 12 per cent said that they had taken more than five days off on the pretence of being ill. When they were asked what the real reasons were, the following topped the poll:

Being tired or hung over:	33 per cent
Stress:	27 per cent
Hating the job:	15 per cent.

Occasionally similar types of admissions are made on a confidential basis to journalists and researchers which give further evidence that the taking of 'sickies' is very widespread. For example it has been reported that one in every three people visiting the Alton Towers theme park on weekdays has taken a day off work to do so 'on a dishonest pretext', only one in 10 apparently feeling any sense of guilt whatsoever (Bolchover 2005, p4).

If this is anywhere near an accurate reflection of the reality, it contains important messages for employers. Not least, it suggests that a great deal could be done to reduce absence levels with some imagination and by resisting counterproductive knee-jerk reactions.

Huczynski and Fitzpatrick (1989) and the Institute of Occupational Health (2003) warn against taking a simplistic view of the reasons for absence, and argue that managers invariably fail in their efforts to improve attendance levels if they take such views. It therefore follows that there is a need to recognise that a variety of different factors may influence absence levels and that, in most cases, this calls for the development of a range of remedial tools.

> *Our argument is that much of what is done by managers to combat absence in their organisations is taken in total ignorance of the causes of absence. Most managers neither understand, nor have investigated the causes of their absence problem. Instead, personal hunches, prejudices and rules of thumb represent the basis on which corrective action is decided. The failure of managers to deal effectively with their absence problem derives, to a large extent, from a lack of proper understanding.*
>
> (Huczynski and Fitzpatrick 1989, p32)

In an influential and often-quoted article published in 1978, Steers and Rhodes developed a process model to illustrate the different influences that determine attendance levels. Their work broke new ground in so far as it recognised first that dissatisfaction with work was not necessarily the most important explanation for absence and, second, that there might be situations in which employees were prevented from attending by 'situational constraints' that included factors other than poor health. They therefore divided the reasons into two broad categories: those concerned with the ability of employees to attend work, and those concerned with their willingness to do so. Their model is useful in that it makes a distinction between first-order or immediate causes of absence and the underlying influences that lead to poor attendance. The model is presented in Figure 16.1.

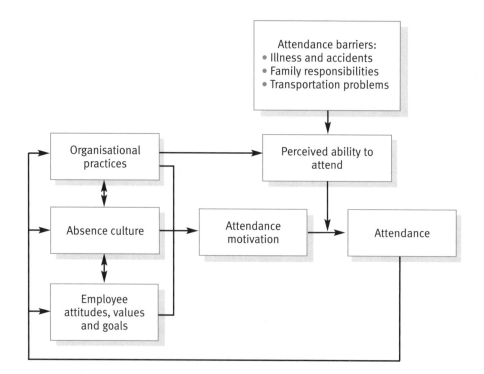

Figure 16.1 Diagnostic model of employee attendance

With reference to the work of Steers and Rhodes, as well as that of other writers who have researched employee attitudes and perceptions, it is possible to divide into five broad categories the various factors, aside from genuine illness, that may explain why one employee opts not to come to work when a colleague employed to do the same job chooses to attend. However, it is important to recognise that these are not distinct categories and that, in many cases, one factor influences another. For example, high absence could be due to boredom at work, which might in turn result from poor supervision and the orientation of the individual's personality. It may also reflect apathy towards life in general, which may in turn be related to home circumstances. Alternatively, the extent to which individuals have a strong social attachment to colleagues may well also derive from a mixture of factors relating to personality, home circumstances and the way the organisation is managed.

EMPLOYEE ATTITUDES

A number of authors have cited research that suggests some people are more prone to absence than others throughout their working lives. The presence of a poor history of attendance was one of the few factors that Keller (1983, p536) found could be used to predict future absence rates with any confidence. Huczynski and Fitzpatrick (1989, p61) go further in suggesting that some 5–10 per cent of individuals in any work group usually account for around 50 per cent of all absence. They go on to point out that studies have consistently shown particular personality types to be more absence-prone than others. It would seem that there is more likelihood that individuals who are tense, anxious and emotionally less stable will be absent more often than colleagues who exhibit traits of introversion and stability. However, research has also suggested that proneness to absence declines as people age. While older workers tend to have longer periods of illness, they tend to take less absence of the short, unauthorised variety than younger employees.

Others have found evidence that attitudes and orientation towards work are correlated with social class and family background. Those who have had instilled in them a strong work ethic tend also to have a pronounced sense of family responsibility and a desire to do their jobs well. Such people tend to have excellent attendance rates and often come into work when, in truth, they are too ill to do so (Steers and Rhodes 1978, p369, Huczynski and Fitzpatrick 1989, p75). Personal attitudes towards work and absence are also shaped by the prevailing values and norms of the work group. Those who have hitherto been absent relatively seldom may become poor attenders if they join a group of employees who share an 'absence culture' (Nicholson and Johns 1985, p378). Conversely, in groups that display a strong work ethic, colleagues are less likely to be absent, for fear of letting down fellow employees or attracting their disapproval (Steers and Rhodes 1978, p368).

HOME CIRCUMSTANCES

A number of authors have argued that family responsibilities are an important 'hidden' cause of absence. According to Sargent (1989, p16), such obligations often produce split loyalties for employees who otherwise exhibit a robust attachment to their jobs or possess a strong work ethic. This is the main reason cited in the literature for the tendency for younger women to have relatively high absence rates, because it is they who are most likely to take time off to care for sick children or elderly relatives. Huczynski and Fitzpatrick (1989, p80) have found from their research that rates of female absenteeism increase as women's families become larger. In the case of women who employ childminders, there may also be an economic incentive to take a day off occasionally, as long as no loss of pay is involved (Harvey and Nicholson 1993, p845).

Transportation difficulties can also affect the propensity to take days off work. The implication is that people who live some distance from their place of work, or have to undertake a difficult journey every morning, are more likely to opt for a day away from work than those whose travel-to-work arrangements are less disagreeable. In such cases it is not dislike of the job that deters people from making the effort to come to work, but the unpleasantness of commuting. Studies have found that it is not just the length of the journey that is off-putting, but that its complexity and cost are also important factors.

In addition, home circumstances may also determine the importance of the economic incentive to come to work. It is often the case that one member of a household earns a great deal more than the others. The second or third income, while useful, is not therefore as essential, and reduces the importance of their work to the members concerned. Because there is less incentive for employees in these categories to earn more, they are less likely to be deterred from being absent by the prospect of losing pay or promotion opportunities. In their research, Huczynski and Fitzpatrick (1989, p53) found instances of employees who wanted part-time work but had to take full-time jobs because that was all that was available; there was thus no incentive or even desire to attend for more than two or three days a week.

THE ECONOMIC CLIMATE

Among the key factors identified in the literature are prevailing economic conditions and, in particular, employees' perceptions of their own job security. Several studies have shown that at times of relatively high unemployment, or when there is fear of an economic downturn, people tend to be more diligent in attending work. It is assumed by Steers and Rhodes (1978, p366) that this occurs because employees fear for their jobs and do not wish to jeopardise their positions at work. Alternatively, as Huczynski and Fitzpatrick (1989, p65) suggest, the correlation could reflect a tendency on the part of managers to clamp down on absence when profit margins are particularly tight. Unsurprisingly, by contrast, absence appears to rise during economic recessions among individuals under formal notice of redundancy.

DISSATISFACTION WITH WORK

The question of a link between job satisfaction and a propensity to be absent is one the most controversial issues in this field. Its importance, when compared to other factors, is downplayed by Nicholson (1976, p734), Steers and Rhodes (1978, p362) and Edwards and Scullion (1984, p566), but is recognised as having potential significance by Huczynski and Fitzpatrick (1989, pp38–40) and Sargent (1989, pp12–13). Steers and Rhodes accept that satisfaction has a part to play, but stress that it is individual expectations and attitudes that determine satisfaction to a great degree.

Despite the conflicting opinions, it is clear from surveys of management perceptions that dissatisfaction with elements of the job and the work environment are believed to have a role to play in explaining absence patterns. In their review of the literature in this field, Huczynski and Fitzpatrick (1989, pp38–51) cite evidence of the significance of the following factors in some cases (the extent to which findings can be generalised remains an open question):

- general boredom with the job

- lack of responsibility and challenge

- forms of work-related stress

- poor working conditions

- work overload

- lack of a defined workplace role

- poor relationships with colleagues

- poor supervision

- frequent internal job moves.

Interestingly, shift-working, although found to increase stress, does not appear to lead to increased absence. On the contrary, research suggests that people working variable shift-patterns have a lower level of absence than those employed on fixed shifts. There is also evidence to suggest that absence decreases as employees become more satisfied with their jobs and, in particular, form strong relationships with colleagues or attachments to a work group or team of which they form a part. This perception is used to explain why absence increases when individuals move from department to department within an organisation, and why attendance tends to deteriorate as an organisation becomes larger (Huczynski and Fitzpatrick 1989, pp46, a 51).

CONTROL SYSTEMS

There is a body of literature that examines absence from work not from the perspective of managers but as a social phenomenon in its own right. Here it is seen less as a managerial problem that can be 'solved' and more as a natural state of affairs arising from the way work is organised in capitalist societies. Nevertheless, there are findings in this literature with important implications for those viewing absence through managerial eyes.

Those writing within sociological frames of reference (notably Paul Edwards and his colleagues) have tended to see absence as a form of unorganised or individual industrial conflict, which they accept as an inherent feature of manager–worker relationships. Seen in this light, absence is not a reaction to dissatisfaction with a particular job at a particular time, but one of a range of means used by employees in resisting management control of the labour process. In discussing their research, Edwards and Scullion (1984, p562) state that 'absenteeism was neither a response by individuals to the physical work environment nor a simple reflection of protest against management control … [but] was the product of the control system'.

Seen in this way, the key variable is the extent and nature of the management control systems in operation. Edwards and Scullion (1984, pp560–564) illustrate this point by contrasting absence rates in two factories. The first, in which there were high rates of absence, was characterised by the presence of intensive control systems and did not allow workers a means of 'challenging' the effort levels and quality standards demanded by managers. The second factory was organised very differently and as a result, in the view of the researchers, had a lower absence level. Here, although the work tasks were unpleasant and mundane, 'workers had sufficiently generous manning levels to enable them to perform their work comfortably, to enjoy a period of leisure at the end of the day and to move around and chat to their mates'. This occurred because of the degree of control that employees exercised over the way they organised their own work. Edwards and Scullion thus concluded that low rates of absence in their case-study companies arose from situations in which managers did not retain 'tight control over the work process', but where an environment had been created 'in which workers accepted managerial requirements as legitimate'.

ABSENCE MANAGEMENT AT TOLLIT & HARVEY

Tollit & Harvey is a long-established small manufacturing company based in Norfolk that produces stationery and office supplies. It employs 170 people, mainly in shop-floor roles. In 1999 its attendance rates were running at 92 per cent, with absences costing the company around £100,000 a year. By 2001 the rate had risen to 99 per cent and absences only cost £15,000 a year.

Managers at the company credit the change to its participation in a project run by an alliance of health authorities and voluntary bodies called Healthy Norfolk 2000. Workers completed questionnaires on a variety of workplace issues that revealed widespread dissatisfaction about their working environment, lack of training opportunities and poor communication. The survey also showed that the more satisfied employees took less time off sick than those who were most dissatisfied.

As a result, a series of measures were taken that combined features of the punitive approach (closer absence monitoring, probationary periods for new employees, return to work interviews), with others designed to improve levels of employee satisfaction. The latter included more multi-skilling and job rotation, greater promotion opportunities, a new air conditioning system, new flooring, better furnished rest areas and more formal communication mechanisms. All these steps were taken in direct response to the survey results.

A second questionnaire survey carried out two years after the first revealed substantially greater levels of staff satisfaction. Productivity generally, as well as levels of absence and lateness have substantially improved.

Source: Arkin (2001a).

REFLECTIVE QUESTION
Think about recent occasions when you have been absent. Which of the above causes played a role in your case?

STRESS AS A CAUSE OF ABSENCE

People management

EXERCISE 16.2

Read the following articles featured in *People Management*. They can be downloaded from the *People Management* archive on the CIPD's website (www.cipd.co.uk).

- Joe Jordan, Strain stoppers (20 November 2003, pp38–40)

- Cary Cooper, Another year down (29 December 2005, pp36–37)

- Emma Clarke, Pressure soars (31 August 2006, pp30–32).

These articles all argue both that the problem of work-induced stress is more common than it used to be and that it is being taken increasingly seriously by employers. The role of the Health and Safety Executive in pressing employers to do more is also highlighted.

Questions

1 Why is 'stress' now such a common cause of absence when it was almost unheard of 20 years ago?

2 What business case could be developed for taking a pro-active approach to the management of stress at work?

3 How do the articles differ in their suggestions as to what employers should do to reduce stress-related absence?

4 Which approach do you think has the best chance of success and why?

KEY ARTICLE 38

Arie Shirom and Zehava Rosenblatt, A panel study of the effects of school positions and promotions on absenteeism in the teaching profession. *Journal of Occupational and Organizational Psychology*, No. 79, pp623–644 (2006)

This article reports the result of a huge quantitative study involving the analysis of attendance records of over 50,000 teachers employed in the Israeli public education sector. The number of days of absence and the number of separate spells of absence were analysed for four separate levels in the school hierarchy. The researchers also looked at the impact of promotion up through this hierarchy on individual absence levels. They concluded that the higher up the hierarchy someone goes, the less absence they tend to take. Another conclusion was that newly promoted teachers take less absence than those who are established in supervisory positions.

Questions

1 Why is absence among teachers more damaging from an organisational point of view than absence among other groups of workers? Why is absence among senior teachers even more damaging?

2 What contribution does this article make to the debate about the major causes of absenteeism?

3 What practical management lessons can be learned from the research described here?

REDUCING ABSENCE LEVELS

A great deal has been written about the methods available to P&D practitioners to help reduce absence levels. However, no consensus has emerged on what might constitute best practice in this field, with the result that this, like the debate about the causes of poor attendance, is a controversial area. Broadly speaking, the different approaches advanced fall into three categories: punitive measures, the use of incentives, and action that addresses the causes of absence with a view to preventing its occurrence. None of these three basic approaches, nor the various techniques they encompass, are mutually exclusive. It is therefore possible to argue that absence can be addressed from a number of different angles at the same time.

PUNITIVE APPROACHES

The most commonly used approach is the use of punitive or disciplinary sanctions, or the threat of so doing. According to the CIPD (2007c), the majority of organisations monitor absence levels centrally, formally interview people about their absence when they return to work, and review absence records when the number of days taken by an individual reaches a predetermined trigger-point. Often these policies are couched in positive terms, the aim in the early stages being to offer help to individuals who may be experiencing some of the problems identified and discussed above in the section on causes of absence. However, they also serve as a means by which employees are informed that their absence has been noted and are warned that, except in cases of serious illness, they are expected to attend. As such, they effectively form the start of a formal disciplinary procedure that will be geared fully into action if the absence becomes persistent.

A variation on this approach is to require all employees returning from a period of absence to complete a sickness form. Such forms usually contain the same kind of questions that would be asked at a return to work interview, but have the appearance of being 'official' and state that they will be kept on an employee's personal file. Again, the aim is to underline the fact that the employer has noticed the absence, and that such conduct will be permitted only in cases of genuine illness. Forms typically ask for quite detailed information, such as that requested below, and require employees to sign a declaration stating that the information given is true:

- On which day did you fall sick?

- When and how did you notify your manager?

- On which day did your sickness end?

- Please specify the symptoms of your sickness.

- Please specify the actions you took to aid your recovery.

The law effectively defines the shape and broad approach that employers take in treating absence as a disciplinary matter. It is quite lawful to dismiss people whose absence records are deemed too high, provided the employer acts reasonably and operates an acceptable procedure. The fact that the sickness is genuine or that medical certificates are presented does not stop an employer from lawfully dismissing someone whose attendance record is persistently poor. This position was confirmed by the judgment of the Court of Appeal in the case of Wilson *v* the Post Office (2000), where an employee was dismissed purely on grounds of poor attendance despite there being no evidence of continuing ill-health. In these cases employees often complain of back pain, minor emotional stress or other conditions that are not, in truth, sufficient to stop them coming to work if they wish to. According to Sargent (1989, pp68–69), these are the important steps to take:

- Investigate the facts to establish how much absence has been taken and whether there are any patterns to suggest that it might not be due to genuine sickness (eg not returning after a holiday, skipping Mondays and Fridays or the day after a staff night out).

- Give employees every opportunity to explain their absence record.

- Give formal written warnings explaining that an improvement is required and that dismissal will result if this does not occur.

Many organisations also, in their formal warnings, set employees specific targets to aim at, so that they know exactly what is expected over a review period. There is no hard-and-fast rule about what the target should be, but a common approach is to use the average rate for the individual's department or work group. A period of six months is considered a reasonable length of time between formal review meetings, although it may be shorter where the record is particularly poor.

In practice, these cases are very much more difficult to deal with than they appear on paper, especially when warnings fail to have the desired effect and dismissal is imminent. Where there is a genuine problem, such as one relating to sickness in a child or parent, handling these matters sensitively but firmly is one of the most unenviable tasks that a P&D manager has to perform. It nevertheless remains important that all cases are handled consistently and in accordance with an agreed procedure or formal absence policy. Otherwise, were a legal case to be brought, the employer would be unable to show that he or she had acted with sufficient reasonableness to satisfy an industrial tribunal.

However, an important caveat concerns situations in which someone has a genuine underlying medical condition that causes regular intermittent absence. In some cases (for example where the problem derives from severe back pain or certain mental conditions), staff may be covered by the Disability Discrimination Act 1995, which protects them from unfair discrimination on grounds of their illness. In such circumstances employers must tread very carefully as dismissal can lead to tribunal cases in which many thousands of pounds may have to be paid by way of compensation. We deal with this issue in greater detail in Chapter 19. Suffice it to say at this stage that employers should treat such cases differently from 'normal' situations in which someone has a poor attendance record. There is a need to consider what steps can be taken to enable the disabled individual to work (ie reasonable adjustments), and it may well be necessary to accept some absence and 'live with it', provided the disruption for the employer is not unreasonable.

Another commonly used application of punitive sanctions involves reducing or docking pay for days or hours not worked. In this field the employer has considerable if limited discretion. At the time of writing (early 2008) organisations are obliged to pay SSP to employees earning over £87.00 a week when they are absent for more than three days. It is only reasonable to refuse this payment where employees fail to notify their employer that they are sick. Self-certification is acceptable to cover the first seven days of absence; thereafter a medical certificate is required if the employer is to continue paying SSP. At present, the weekly rate of SSP set by the government is £72.55.

However, there is a great deal more flexibility for employers seeking to reduce other payments or withdraw payment altogether. Provided employees are made aware of the position through a written statement of terms and conditions of employment, it is permissible for an employer to pay no money at all to employees who are absent, over and above their obligation to pay SSP. A number of employers take this approach in the first weeks of employment if they find that absence rates among new starters are particularly high. Others take a less severe view but nonetheless reduce pay by a proportion for all sickness not covered by a medical certificate. Effectively, such approaches involve fining employees as a deterrent against unauthorised absence.

TIME OFF WORK TO DEAL WITH FAMILY CRISES

Since December 1999 employees have had a new statutory right to take reasonable unpaid leave in order to deal with family emergencies or those involving other people who rely on them for care. The UK legislation specifies the following reasons

- to provide assistance when a dependant falls ill, gives birth or is injured

- to make arrangements for the provision of care for a dependant who is ill or injured

- on the death of a dependant

- due to unexpected disruption or termination of the arrangements for the care of a dependant

- to deal with an incident involving a child during the time when an educational establishment has care of that child.

Importantly, the right is to unpaid time off, employees being required to inform their employers of the intention to take the leave 'as soon as is reasonably practicable'.

Dependants are defined for the purposes of the Act as spouses, children, parents or people 'who live in the same household' as the worker. Tenants, lodgers and employees are specifically excluded. They only become 'dependants' at such time as they rely on the worker for assistance when ill, either directly or through arrangements made with a third party.

The right is enforced through an application to an employment tribunal in one of two ways:

- a claim that an employer has unreasonably refused a request for time off

- a claim that an employer has caused a detriment to be suffered as a result of reasonable time off being taken.

A further set of punitive methods are somewhat longer-term in their effect. These involve taking attendance records into account when making fundamental decisions about individuals' future employment. The most common examples are in:

- selecting candidates for redundancy

- deciding when or whether to promote someone

- determining pay increases or increments

- determining performance-related payments or bonuses

- the allocation of interesting work or new projects.

All or some of these may be a deterrent, provided people know in advance that their absence may count against them in these ways. That said, it is vital that people suffering from serious illness are not included: to do so would be iniquitous and inevitably prompt strong feelings of injustice, low morale and low trust among employees generally. It would also fall foul of the Disability Discrimination Act 1995, as described above and in Chapter 19.

Despite their apparent proliferation, punitive approaches such as these have attracted a great deal of criticism. First, it is argued that they have little effect in reducing absence levels except in the short term (Harvey and Nicholson 1993, p843; Institute of Occupational Health 2003) – a point confirmed in a number of published case-studies. Allen and Torrington (1996, p101), remarking on absence patterns in a case-study company, conclude that it is not the punitive measures themselves that cause a reduction in absence, but the signalling by management that they intend to make absence an issue. The result is a temporary, if substantial, reduction in absence while the 'purge' is on, followed by a return to previous levels – or, in this case, higher levels than before. By contrast, Nicholson (1976) found in a similar study that absence did not decline following a management clampdown, but that employees simply started producing medical notes so as to ensure that their absence was classified as authorised rather than unauthorised.

Others criticise the use of punitive measures in absence control on the grounds that they often operate unfairly. In particular, they make no distinction between absence that, from the perspective of an employee, could be classed as avoidable, and that which is not. Hence, people who take days off to care for a sick relative or because they themselves are genuinely suffering from a minor ailment are treated in the same way as those who simply opt for more leisure time by feigning sickness. True, the effect from the employer's perspective is the same, but if the workforce perceives the approach to be unjust it will lead to other problems such as low morale, higher staff-turnover and reduced work effort (Harvey and Nicholson 1993, p843).

Edwards and Whitston (1993, p31) go further, arguing that the introduction of stricter absence control mechanisms of this kind may actually be counterproductive, because employees resent such initiatives and are inclined to react against them by 'withdrawing the day to day commitment to the enterprise on which [management] had hitherto been able to rely'. In an earlier article, Edwards and Scullion reported an example of such considerations being taken on board by an employer:

> *In one company this was explicitly recognised, with an internal report on absenteeism and its relationship to the company's sick pay scheme arguing that tolerating a certain level of absence could be in the company's interests because other more disruptive expressions of discontent were rendered less likely: absence could be an important safety valve.*
>
> (Edwards and Scullion 1984, p555)

Despite these formidable criticisms, all the survey evidence indicates that most employers continue to operate some punitive techniques, and that they believe them to have a degree of effectiveness (CBI 2007, CIPD 2007c). Furthermore, Harvey and Nicholson's (1993) survey of opinion in the Civil Service strongly suggests that most employees also support the use of penalties to discourage absence, provided they are applied fairly. It would thus appear that many either remain sceptical about the merits of alternative approaches or are unwilling to view unauthorised absence as anything other than a disciplinary matter.

REFLECTIVE QUESTION

How far does your organisation rely on punitive measures to control absence? Have other approaches ever seriously been considered?

ABSENCE IN THE PUBLIC SECTOR

Absence levels in the public sector are considerably higher than they are in the private sector, averaging between 9 and 10 days a year according to the surveys (see CBI 2007, CIPD 2007c). This is double the amount of time typically taken in equivalent private sector roles, and amounts to a substantial cost for the taxpayer. IRS (2004g) reports that nearly half a million days are lost due to absence in the civil service alone, representing a cost to the taxpayer of £370 million. According to the CBI (2007) the overall cost of public sector absence is conservatively estimated at £1.1 billion a year, which it claims 'is enough to build seven new general hospitals'.

Research by Dibben *et al* (2000) (see also James et al 2000) found that absence rates in public sector organisations remain high even where there is in place strong absence management policies of the kind that the government wishes to see operating (eg written policies, occupational health departments, health promotion activities, training for line managers, return to work interviews).

Dibben *et al* conclude that the reasons for persistently high rates of absence in the public sector derive from poor implementation of the 'right' policies. So, for example, although occupational health services are provided, they are frequently under-resourced. Moreover, more generally there are few organisation-level mechanisms in place to ensure that policies are implemented by line managers. This results in poorly co-ordinated systems and substantial uncertainty on the part of managers about how they should manage absence in practice.

However, it is possible to reach a different conclusion from a reading of the evidence put forward by Dibben *et al.* This is based on their finding that the use of punitive approaches was rather less common in the public sector than in the private sector. Private sector employers are substantially

more likely to discipline people with poor attendance records and to use absence records in making redundancy or promotion decisions. Conversely occupational sick pay (ie pay beyond SSP) is more commonly paid in the public sector than in the private sector. While the authors themselves do not reach this conclusion, it is possible to see their research as a ringing endorsement for the effectiveness of punitive approaches to absence management.

EXERCISE 16.3

IS THE SICK-NOTE SYSTEM SICK?

People management

Read the article by Zoe Roberts, Referred pain (*People Management*, 20 May 2004, pp34–36). This can be downloaded from the *People Management* archive on the CIPD's website (www.cipd.co.uk).

This article explains that many GPs dislike being asked to issue sick notes on behalf of their patients and do not take the process seriously. It suggests that larger employers should consider taking the process over themselves through the use of occupational health departments.

Questions

1   Why do you think two-thirds of doctors issue 'sick notes on demand' to their patients?

2   Why might the suggestion that these matters should be dealt with by company doctors and occupational health departments be impractical for most cases of absence?

3   What other possible approaches could usefully be piloted?

ATTENDANCE INCENTIVES

Taking active steps to reward good attendance is a controversial approach to the reduction of absence. Many managers are unwilling to consider such practices because they involve rewarding employees merely for fulfilling a basic term of their contracts. Some argue that this amounts to paying people twice. Others feel that attendance bonuses are unfair because they effectively punish people who, if they are genuinely ill, lose out through no fault of their own. A third set of criticisms relates to the apparent ineffectiveness of incentive approaches when applied in practice.

A number of different methods by which employees can be rewarded for attending every day over a defined period are identified in the literature. Huczynski and Fitzpatrick (1989, p118) provide a long list, which includes the following possibilities:

• **Attendance bonuses.** The payment of additional cash to employees with a perfect or near-perfect attendance record. This can be done on a weekly, monthly, quarterly or annual basis.

- Lotteries. All employees with a perfect attendance record over a week or a month are entered into a prize draw. Winners are then publicly recognised and rewarded with a cash sum or some other prize.

- Adjustments to profit-sharing. Where some form of profit-related pay scheme is in use, the proportion of bonus allotted to individuals is increased if their attendance record is good.

- Well-pay plans. No payments are made over and above SSP for days absent, but extra payments are made for months where attendance is perfect.

- Group-based approaches. Bonuses are paid to every member of a team or department, provided average absence levels reach set targets.

In France some employers have taken to rewarding good attendance with additional holidays, thus replacing unauthorised absence with the authorised variety. Incentive schemes of these kinds appear to be used by a substantial minority of employing organisations. Edwards and Whitston (1989, p10) state that they are operated in around 10 per cent of organisations, while other surveys (Industrial Society 1997b, CIPD 2007c) put the figure somewhat higher. However, according to the Industrial Society, around half of these schemes are non-monetary. That is to say, prizes are offered rather than bonus payments.

ATTENDANCE INCENTIVES AT VICTORIA STATION

At the Victoria Coach Station in London, managers claim to have had considerable success in reducing absence levels by using both attendance bonuses and return-to-work interviews. Between 1987, when the scheme started operating, and 1991, absence levels fell from 16.3 days per year per employee to 9 days.

The incentive scheme was based on a points system calculated using the Bradford Factor described above. It is paid quarterly, but relates to attendance records over the previous 12–month period. Each employee with fewer than 200 points at each review date receives a bonus payment equal to one day's pay. The result is that staff who are off work with genuine illnesses qualify even if they are absent for 200 working days in a single spell. Those who take more than five single days of absence over a year do not qualify, because six spells multiplied by six spells multiplied by six days equals 216 points. After a few years of operation, over three-quarters of the staff were found to be qualifying for the bonus payments.

Source: IDS (1992a, p4).

Opinion is divided over how successful these approaches are in the reduction of absence. Cherrington (1989, p316) found evidence of absence rates declining by 40 per cent in a manufacturing company following the introduction of rewards for good attendance, and others also quote examples of individual schemes that appear to have had a positive effect (Steers and Rhodes 1978, p367). However, by and large the literature comes down against such approaches. Huczynski and

Fitzpatrick (1989, p115) describe a series of studies that suggest either that these approaches are unsuccessful in reducing absence or that, where there is an improvement in attendance, they prove not to be cost effective. The same broad conclusion is reached by the CBI (1997, p17) and the Industrial Society (1997b, p13), who suggest that these are ranked among the least effective approaches by managers, and that they are associated with organisations that have higher than average absence levels.

However, it can be argued that it is unwise to treat all reward plans as being alike, because in reality they differ greatly one from another in terms of their design and value. What is important is to pick out those features of incentive plans that appear to give them the best chance of success. A number of conclusions can be made in this regard. In particular, there is evidence that attendance bonus systems work most effectively when the employees themselves are involved in the design of the scheme (Steers and Rhodes 1978, p367, Huczynski and Fitzpatrick 1989, p121). Another conclusion is that incentive schemes are more appealing to employees who are paid relatively little. Harvey and Nicholson (1993) found that lower-grade civil servants were far more attracted to the prospect than colleagues who earned higher salaries. It can therefore be assumed that such schemes work best where people come to work primarily for money, and are keen to increase their take-home pay in whatever way possible.

The central problem in designing schemes is setting the right level of bonus. On the one hand, the payment or prize must be of sufficient value to act as an incentive, while on the other, if it is too high the scheme will be too costly. A bonus of 10 per cent may be effective as a means of discouraging absence, but it will end up costing the employer a great deal more than was being lost as a result of poor absence levels in the first place. There is also the problem of employees' losing all incentive to attend once they have taken time off in any one review period. In such circumstances, seeing their colleagues collecting the bonus can act only as a disincentive.

An interesting conclusion reached by several authors is that non-monetary or intrinsic rewards are both a relatively effective means of reducing absence and cost very little. Essentially, these involve publicly recognising good attendance. A number of such schemes are described by Huczynski and Fitzpatrick (1989, pp120–121), including one operated at Rank Xerox that involved granting employees who completed a year without any absence a 'perfect attendance award', consisting of a small gift and a certificate. The result was successful, with 31 per cent of the workforce qualifying for the award in 1986. A three-year certificate was then introduced, which 12 per cent of the workforce received. The great potential of such approaches is summed up by Harvey and Nicholson (1993, p854):

> *Many respondents with little or no absence for long periods expressed much pride in the fact, but at the same time many commented on lack of recognition for their attendance. These two responses strongly suggest that reinforcing pride in attendance by explicit recognition of good attendance is likely to be one of the most cost-effective management actions.*

It can thus be concluded, first, that there are great practical problems associated with the introduction and maintenance of monetary-reward systems that pay extra cash to employees who have good attendance records, and, second, that they appear to have only limited success in practice. That said, it is clearly not impossible to make them work well when the circumstances are right and when the main pitfalls associated with their introduction are avoided. On the other hand, there is a strong body of evidence suggesting that non-monetary forms of reward are effective and cost considerably less than the monetary kind. As so often in personnel management, it is important to avoid being swift to criticise and slow to praise – a general rule of particular relevance to absence management.

EXERCISE 16.4

ROYAL MAIL

Read the article by Julie Griffeths, The price is right (*People Management*, 10 November 2005, pp34–35). This can be downloaded from the *People Management* archive on the CIPD's website (www.cipd.co.uk).

This article describes how the Royal Mail managed to reduce absence levels very sharply over a six-month period by rewarding workers with 100 per cent attendance rates with holiday vouchers (worth £150) and entry into a prize draw which awarded 37 cars and 75 sets of holiday vouchers worth £2,000.

Questions

1   How is the Royal Mail able to claim that it saved £80 million as a result of this exercise?

2   What further steps were taken at the same time so that absence rates stayed low following the prize draw exercise?

PREVENTIVE MEASURES

The third set of approaches open to employers wishing to reduce absence levels involves tackling the root causes rather than using penalties and incentives to encourage better attendance. The aim is to assess what factors are motivating employees to stay away from work when they could come in, and to strive to eliminate such factors. It is suggested above that the main causes of absence could broadly be divided into five distinct categories. We now look again at these, reflecting on which preventative measures might have most effect.

The first category of causes was employee attitudes, both those that people bring to their employment and those developed in response to prevailing organisational norms. In the case of the former, little can be done short of seeking to influence people's views through effective leadership. Perhaps the most effective action that employers can take is to give consideration to absence records at the selection stage. References from former employers may have something to offer here, because the information requested is essentially factual and thus does not rely on someone's opinion of an employee. However, great care must be taken in assessing past absence records, for they can be highly misleading. High absence over the previous 12 months might very well have resulted from a one-off illness, and so should not be used as evidence of a general proneness to absence. It is necessary to probe beneath the 'headline figure' by asking the candidate to explain why he or she was absent on so many days. The use of personality questionnaires can also help to screen out people likely to be more prone to absence than others. It is also possible to include some form of attitude survey in selection procedures that could include questions on perceptions of absence from work. The aim here is not simply to weed out those likely to be absent most often, but also to make sure that the right people are appointed to the right jobs, thus reducing the likelihood of absence occurring as a result of dissatisfaction.

Addressing the problems that stem from a prevalent absence culture is a harder task. There are no simple solutions here, but the use of some of the incentive and punitive techniques outlined above, when applied over a sustained period, may have a positive effect. Alternatively, efforts can be made to probe a little more deeply in order to discover the main reasons for the existence of such cultural norms in a particular department. The work of Nicholson and Johns (1985) is useful here, in that it identifies four distinct types of absence culture and suggests different means by which each might be tackled to best effect. For example, they distinguish between situations in which some unauthorised absence is perceived by employees to be an entitlement and those in which employees calculate and then balance the costs and benefits accruing to them when they take a day off. In each case, different managerial actions are needed if employee attitudes are to be changed and the absence culture weakened.

In situations where it is not attitudes that are the problem, but home circumstances, different preventative measures are clearly justified. The aim here should be to give practical help so that employees are able to come to work more easily. It may be possible to allow people to work from home from time to time, or to work more flexible hours so as to allow them to juggle home and work responsibilities more easily. Larger organisations may devise systems whereby people can apply to take unpaid leave in addition to their annual holiday entitlement, or longer career breaks or sabbaticals. It may also be possible to take a more flexible attitude to start and finish times, enabling those with further to travel to cut their journey time by avoiding rush-hour traffic or to use different buses. All these measures cost very little, but may have the effect not only of cutting avoidable absence but also of increasing morale and commitment. Other more costly developments, such as the introduction of childcare facilities, can probably be justified only in terms of other benefits, but are likely to have a positive effect on attendance records.

Other areas of activity that have received a good deal of attention in recent years are occupational health services, counselling sessions and more general forms of employee assistance programmes (EAPs) that aim, amongst other things, to help employees improve their situations both at home and at work. Occupational health services clearly have a direct role to play as far as absence is concerned, because they can help employees to avoid contracting medical complaints. There are also situations in which interventions by an occupational health department can ease the strain of coming to work and thus minimise the occasions on which employees stay at home on account of relatively minor medical conditions. Back pain is one example, as are a whole range of mental and emotional illnesses. EAPs have grown in number in recent years, and cover over 7 per cent of the UK workforce (IRS 2000e). The majority, however, are not provided in house. Most operate off site and are staffed by specialists employed by companies on a consultancy basis. It is through telephone helplines that most employees encounter them, when seeking confidential advice about how to deal with personal matters that relate to either the workplace or non-working life, or both. IRS (2000d) report that take-up rates among employees vary from 3 to 15 per cent of those who are eligible.

In the case of absence rooted in employee dissatisfaction at work or resistance to overbearing control on the part of managers, there is a wide range of preventative actions open to employers. Many are discussed elsewhere in this book – several in the following chapter in the context of staff turnover – so there is no need to cover them in detail here. The following are identified by Huczynski and Fitzpatrick (1989, pp123–127, 144–145) as particularly significant:

- job enrichment
- work rotation
- teamworking
- employee participation
- improving the work environment
- better training in supervision
- improved communication
- improved developmental opportunities.

The benefits of initiatives in these areas are, of course, not restricted to improving attendance. They should also have a general effect on trust, commitment and morale, with positive consequences for staff turnover, employee relations, employee development and, ultimately, competitiveness. However, their effect on absence, in so far as it can be costed, may be used to form part of a business case for their introduction.

Recent research by Cunningham and James (2000) (see also James *et al* 2002) focused on the mechanisms an organisation has in place to help people who have been absent for some time to return to the workplace. They found that there was a correlation between formal processes of this kind and absence rates. In other words, actively managing the return to work experience tends to bring people back earlier and hence reduces overall absence rates. The practices they considered included the extent to which regular contact was maintained with people away on account of long-term sickness, the ability to return on a reduced-hours basis or to lighter work, involvement of occupational health services, counselling provision and modification of job duties to enable a faster return.

ALIEDIM

At the end of their book on absence management, Huczynski and Fitzpatrick (1989) conclude by presenting a 'seven-step approach to absence control' that draws together their main themes. It is given the acronym ALIEDIM, which represents the following steps: Assess, Locate, Identify, Evaluate, Design, Implement and Monitor. They also provide very informative and useful check-lists and activity briefs to assist managers in completing each step, along with a case-study illustrating the model's use in practice.

The first step involves assessing the size of the absence problem and estimating what it is costing the organisation. They suggest that indirect long-term costs be included in the assessment, as well as the obvious and easily quantifiable direct costs. The second step involves locating where in the organisation (ie among which groups of employee) the problem is worst; inevitably, this requires the assembly of comparative statistical data. The third step entails investigating the causes of absence among the groups identified in step 2. Step 4 necessitates evaluating the effectiveness of existing absence-control techniques and deciding how appropriate they are in the light of the investigation undertaken in step 3. That is followed by the design stage (step 5), in which new and more appropriate remedial plans are decided upon, due consideration being given to the range of available options. They are then implemented at step 6. The final stage involves monitoring the results of the initiative against pre-defined criteria.

EVIDENCE-BASED ABSENCE MANAGEMENT

The most recent major contribution to research on absence management in the UK is the extensive study undertaken by Spurgeon *et al* (2007). Here the researchers gained access to a database containing details of every spell of absence over a number of years in 40 separate organisations operating in a variety of industrial sectors, both privately and publicly owned. As a result they were able to analyse over 80,000 absence episodes involving over 30,000 individual employees. The data in their report is very detailed, revealing for example how frequently certain types of absence (stress, back problems, stomach upsets etc) occur among members of different professions, age groups and by gender, as well as how long the spells of absence associated with each of the main causes tend to last.

In terms of practical absence management the key finding was that employers tend to use quite blunt and unsophisticated tools in order to manage absence issues, treating all absences in pretty well the same way. When tried and trusted methods are used (return to work interviews, disciplinary practices, referring people to occupational health departments) they have an impact, but only up to a point. In order to reduce absence levels further, it is argued, employers need to take a far more sophisticated, evidence-based approach which involves treating different types of absence differently.

In particular the authors of the report call for the collection of information which enables managers to understand each individual employee's patterns of absence and then to 'establish reference groups against which individual cases can be managed'. For example, this means treating stress-based absence very differently from absence because of back problems, and both differently again from absence due to cancer. Instead of dealing with all cases through the same policy, a more tailored individual approach is appropriate.

The second major conclusion is that it is possible and makes good business sense for organisations to put in place robust preventative measures. This is described as 'an upsteam strategy to prevent, or at least minimise, bodies falling into the water in the first place by understanding where and why they are falling in' (Spurgeon *et al* 2007, p37). Once it has been established where the highest risks are, managers can go about making improvements to working conditions and to working environment, taking steps to deal with the management styles of individuals or a departmental culture which has the effect of increasing absence. Finally, there is a good case made for promoting healthy living among employee groups whose risk of absence is highest.

EXERCISE 16.5

WELLNESS INITIATIVES

Read the article by Rima Manocha, Well adjusted (*People Management*, 8 April 2004, pp26–30). This can be downloaded from the *People Management* archive on the CIPD's website (www.cipd.co.uk).

This article discusses the apparently novel idea that employers should actively encourage their employees to live more healthy lifestyles. All kinds of benefits can result, including a reduction in absence.

Questions

1   What other factors, aside from fewer incidents of genuine illness, might explain why employee absence reduces following the introduction of a wellness initiative?

2   The article gives a few examples of the types of element that make up wellness programmes. What others might be introduced? Which would be most appropriate for your organisation?

3   What different elements make up the business case for the introduction of wellness initiatives?

Philip James, Ian Cunningham and Pauline Dibben, Absence management and the issues of job retention and return to work. *Human Resource Management Journal*, Vol. 12, No. 2, pp82–94 (2002)

KEY ARTICLE 39

This article reports the results of 30 interviews conducted with HR managers from a variety of UK industrial sectors. The key finding is that most organisations are ill-equipped to deal proactively and effectively with incidences of sick employees returning to work after a period of absence. The authors argue that since most absence in practice results from genuine illness which is not just a few days long in duration, and that since there are major advantages for organisations that are able to help sick employees rehabilitate, the lack of effective management in this area represents a major lost opportunity.

Questions

1   Why are organisations so poor at proactively managing the return to work of sick staff?

2   What is the business case for investing in improving management capabilities in this area?

3   What approaches would you were recommend were adopted by organisations wishing to improve their record of management in this area?

CHAPTER SUMMARY

- Absence rates in the United Kingdom are between 3 and 4 per cent on average. This represents eight or nine days a year and costs organisations around £13 billion.

- Measuring and costing absence enables employers to benchmark their performance, track progress over time and justify investing in policies designed to reduce absence levels.

- Much absence is due to genuine illness, but a great deal more is not. There are, in fact, many different causes of absence including dissatisfaction with work, home circumstances and management control systems. Some people are more prone to take absence than others, so there is a case for using absence records in selection decisions.

- Three basic approaches are used to reduce absence levels: punitive,

reward-based and environmental. The latter involves addressing the root causes of absence, the former two tackle the symptoms.

- Great care must be taken over using punitive approaches because of the requirements of employment law. It is, however, lawful in principal to dismiss someone who is not defined as disabled simply on grounds of poor attendance.

- Attendance incentives are controversial and of questionable utility. However, there is evidence to suggest that non-monetary schemes have a role to play in absence reduction.

- Preventive measures include health promotion campaigns, to provision of occupational health and EAP services and general initiatives designed to improve job satisfaction.

EXPLORE FURTHER

- Good general books on absence written from a management perspective are few and far between. The best is undoubtedly *Managing employee absence for a competitive edge* by Andrzej Huczynski and Michael Fitzpatrick (1989), which, despite being somewhat dated now, provides plenty of ideas together with a summary of research evidence. A shorter book covering practical issues and containing a number of helpful suggestions is *From absence to attendance* by Alistair Evans and Steve Palmer (1997). The research report by Spurgeon *et al* (2007) published by CIPD contains useful background information alongside the detailed results of a fascinating empirical study.

- Publications that review the academic research on absence management (mainly US-based) very effectively, include *Managing employee absenteeism* by Susan Rhodes and Richard Steers, and the chapter by Gary Johns in Robertson and Cooper (2001).

- Measurement and costing issues are effectively explored in two publications from the Institute of Employment Studies (reports 353 and 382) by S. Bevan and S. Hayday.

- Updates on developments in the field of absence management, together with case studies illustrating initiatives undertaken by employers, are covered by IDS which produces a new study of the topic every few years. Case studies also feature alongside statistical tables in the CIPD's annual survey of absence which is available free of charge for members from the institute's website.

- A thought-provoking and critical view of practice in the field of absence management, based on interviews with employees about their perceptions, is *Attending to work: the management of attendance and shopfloor order* by Paul Edwards and Colin Whitston (1993).

- *People Management* regularly features articles on different aspects of absence management. In addition to those cited in the chapter the following are particularly recommended: Beaumont (2005) and Tulip (2006) on the changing nature of occupational health initiatives, Robson (2007) on developing an attendance culture, Simms (2005) on formal absence-reduction initiatives, and the special issue looking at aspects of risk management published on 18 May 2006.

CHAPTER 17

Staff turnover and retention

It is common to hear employers characterise difficulties in staffing their organisations as 'recruitment problems', often summed up in the familiar phrase, 'You just can't get good staff these days'. In fact, many such predicaments are due more to the existence of problems in retaining people. If good staff chose not to resign in the first place there would be no need to wade through such difficulties in recruiting their successors. However, managers are often reluctant to concede this truism, because it may mean implicitly admitting that a frustrating situation is, at least in part, of their own making.

Employees leave organisations for many reasons. While some depart involuntarily as a result of dismissal, redundancy or forced retirement, the vast majority resign of their own volition – some to take up new jobs, others to take a permanent or temporary break from participation in the workforce, some to start new businesses of their own. This chapter focuses on the implications for P&D specialists of voluntary turnover and on its costs for organisations. It starts by looking at recent turnover trends and at the extent to which increases in the number of voluntary resignations can be seen as either positive or negative for employers. The methods used to monitor staff turnover, to calculate its costs and to benchmark results against those of other employers are then examined. This is followed by an analysis of various explanations for voluntary resignations, and consideration of the plans of action that can be adopted to reduce their number. Finally, attention is given to the legal and ethical issues associated with voluntary release.

DEFINING VOLUNTARY RELEASE

Distinguishing between departures from employment initiated by employees and those initiated by the employer is not straightforward. While some cases are clear-cut (eg dismissal for gross misconduct or resignation to take up a job with a competitor), many others result from a mixture of factors. A common example is the resignation of an employee on grounds of serious ill-health, when dismissal would have resulted in any event. Another situation arises with retirement, when it is not always easy to tell how keen individual employees are to quit at a predetermined retirement age. It is also difficult to say with any degree of certainty whether someone 'was pushed' or 'jumped' when he or she resigns when redundancies are threatened.

However, it is important to reach some kind of accepted judgement as to what is defined as voluntary termination if any meaningful comparative analysis is to be undertaken of turnover rates in different departments or among other employers. Perhaps the simplest approach is to use the very broad definition that includes all resignations not formally initiated by the employer. Collecting data of this kind is straightforward and is thus unlikely to take up a great deal of management time. Results can then be adjusted or re-interpreted at the analysis stage to take account of any grey areas such as those identified above.

A further distinction to be made in deciding how to manage turnover levels is that between resignations that might have been avoided and those that would have occurred anyway, irrespective of employer actions. These are often referred to as, respectively, 'controllable' and 'uncontrollable' reasons. The former category includes employees who quit primarily because of dissatisfaction with some aspect of their job or the organisation in comparison with perceived alternative employment opportunities, while the latter encompasses resignations that result from factors such as ill health, the relocation of spouses and other domestic responsibilities. Naturally, it is the controllable resignations that are given most attention when organisations seek to reduce turnover levels. However, there are grey areas here too. Often employers will label a particular resignation as 'unavoidable' when in truth a mixture of avoidable and unavoidable factors caused it to occur. The most common examples involve employees resigning to relocate so as to live with a partner or spouse based elsewhere. On the surface this appears like unavoidable turnover, but couples often weigh up the advantages and disadvantages of either one of them relocating. The one whose interests prevail is usually the one with the best career prospects, highest pay or greatest level of job satisfaction. Good employers lose fewer people for these kinds of 'personal reasons' than poorer ones.

In other ways the distinction between voluntary and involuntary turnover is becoming increasingly significant for organisations with a large number of employees on fixed-term contracts working on specific projects. In organisations where flexible working of this kind has become common, the proportion of resignations categorised as 'involuntary' will also have grown. Whereas previously a situation in which someone left at a time of the organisation's choosing was relatively rare, it is now an accepted part of organisational life. As a result, organisations seeking to monitor voluntary turnover can no longer wholly rely on crude general turnover rates as their main tool of measurement.

REFLECTIVE QUESTION

What factors explained your decision to resign from positions you have held? To what extent are these readily categorised as voluntary/involuntary or controllable/uncontrollable?

TURNOVER TRENDS

A number of surveys are undertaken each year in the United Kingdom to establish overall turnover rates. The largest are those carried out by the CIPD and the CBI, but many others are organised by consultancies and employers' organisations and focus on specific industries. An excellent summary of the data from these and other one-off surveys is published each year in *IRS Employment Review* in January or February.

All the surveys reveal considerable fluctuations in turnover rates over time, in different regions and between different industries. However, the different methodologies and definitions of turnover used mean that the figures can vary quite considerably from survey to survey. Since the late 1990s, the overall national figure reported by the CIPD and CBI surveys has been between 15 and 20 per cent, which is quite high by historical standards, reflecting strong economic conditions and the presence of tight labour markets. The more opportunity people have to move employers, the more likely they are to do so. By contrast, in the early 1990s recessionary conditions led to national turnover rates of only 10 per cent (*Skills needs in Britain*, IFF Research 1993).

Interestingly, in recent years some economists have questioned the causal link between economic conditions and skills shortages (of which high turnover is a symptom). Rather than the former leading to the latter, many believe that in reality the opposite is the case (see Lind Frogner 2002, p23). According to this theory, skills shortages constrain productivity, which leads to lower output and higher unemployment. The ups and downs of the economic cycle are thus created, in part at least, by changes in the labour market. It follows that economic growth is best served by ensuring that there are sufficient numbers of appropriately qualified people available to fill the vacancies that employers create. Substantial investment in training on the part of employers and government may thus be the best way of ensuring that their operations remain competitive over the long term.

Of particular interest to employers seeking to benchmark their turnover rates against appropriate comparators are the figures for turnover in specific industrial sectors, regions and occupational groups. Retention is always hard in the most prosperous areas of the country where unemployment is lowest. The highest turnover levels are invariably found in London, the south east and East Anglia, where rates in excess of 25 per cent were reported in the early 2000s. By contrast, in Northern Ireland, Merseyside and the north east, figures are some 40 per cent lower.

For data on variations between specific industrial sectors it is necessary to rely on smaller-scale surveys, such as that carried out each year by the CIPD. One should not read too much into these results, because of the very small sample sizes used and the inclusion of involuntary as well as voluntary turnover. They do, however, give a general indication of substantial variations between industries, particularly when it is considered that the same industries (call centres, retailing and catering) top the table in most years (see Table 17.1).

Table 17.1 Turnover rates, various industries

Industry	Average turnover 2007 (%)	Industry	Average turnover 2007 (%)
Hotels and catering	32.6	Professional services	20.0
Retail and wholesale	27.5	Health	17.2
Media and publishing	27.1	Community and voluntary	15.2
Construction	27.1	Utilities	15.1
Call centres	24.6	Financial services	14.5
Communications	23.5	Local government	13.7
Manufacturing	20.9	Education	13.1
IT industry	20.8	Central government	6.2
Transport/storage	20.3		

TURNOVER AMONG PERSONNEL SPECIALISTS

According to the Remuneration Economics Surveys, the overall voluntary turnover rate for personnel specialists in the United Kingdom tends to be in the region of 6–7 per cent, pretty low when compared with other occupational groups. The more senior the position, the lower the turnover (in 2000 it was 9.8 per cent among junior personnel specialists but only 4.2 per cent among senior colleagues). As with other occupational groups, there is a marked inclination for older personnel people to remain in their jobs longer than their younger counterparts when given the choice. In 1996, turnover was 8.7 per cent for the under-30s but only 1.7 per cent for over-50s.

Data from these and other surveys suggest that turnover figures also vary quite considerably among people in different occupations. Perhaps unsurprisingly, it appears to be highest among sales staff and those employed to do routine, unskilled work (30–50 per cent), and lowest among management and craft workers (10–20 per cent). In other words, turnover rates are highest among those who possess fewest industry-specific skills. By contrast, there is less movement where individuals are more restricted in their choice of alternative jobs because their skills and experience are less readily transferable. Although they have recently risen (from 9 per cent to 10 per cent in the case of nurses, for example), the lowest turnover levels of all are found in the public sector, despite persistent claims of retention crises resulting from low rates of pay.

EXERCISE 17.1

LABOUR TURNOVER IN LAW FIRMS AND BARRISTERS' CHAMBERS

Read the article by Karen Moloney, Lines of defence (*People Management*, 11 July 2002, pp48–49). This can be downloaded from the *People Management* archive on the CIPD's website (www.cipd.co.uk).

This article reports the views of managers in law firms and barristers' chambers about labour turnover trends and some other associated issues.

Questions

1   Why is labour turnover so much higher among solicitors than it was ten years ago? Why might it be considered more damaging in this industry than in many others?

2   Aside from reducing staff turnover rates, what other advantages accrue to the firms who invest in training and developing their junior staff?

3   Once barristers have secured a place in a chambers, it is rare for them to leave. Turnover rates are very low indeed. Why do you think this is? Can other employers learn anything from the pupilage system operated by barristers' chambers?

DOES TURNOVER MATTER?

There is some debate in the literature about how far employers should be concerned about turnover levels. Some writers have emphasised the potentially positive effects of a continuous transfusion of fresh blood into the organisation. Carrell *et al* (1995, p777) distinguish between 'functional' and 'dysfunctional' turnover, and suggest that the former serves to promote innovative ideas and methods and can thus 'renew a stagnating organisation'. Hom and Griffeth (1995, pp27–30) also draw attention to research that has shown functional turnover to be commoner than the dysfunctional form. The net result is an improvement in productivity as poorer employees quit, leaving a higher proportion of good performers to enhance organisational effectiveness. They also note that high turnover gives employers more opportunity to promote and develop valued staff, and reduces the need to make costly redundancies when there is a downturn in business. More generally, it can be argued that relatively high turnover allows employers to establish greater control over their wage budgets. Where turnover is low and business takes an unanticipated dip, profits fall unless people are laid off. Where turnover is high it is easier to keep wage costs low and profits higher by refraining from recruiting successors to the people who leave.

High turnover is probably least worrying in industries employing people in relatively low-skilled occupations that nevertheless require high levels of customer service (eg fast-food restaurants and telesales operations). According to Kearns (1994, p11), this is because the employer wishes to harness what is, in all likelihood, a short-term burst of enthusiasm on the part of the employee. Such a situation has allowed the various brands of burger restaurant to expand rapidly across the world while coping with annual turnover rates averaging 300 per cent (see Ritzer 1996, p130; Cappelli 2000, p106).

Despite these points, it is safe to conclude that, for most organisations, turnover in excess of 5–10 per cent has more negative than positive consequences. The more valuable the employees in question, the more damaging the resignation, particularly when they move on to work for a competitor. Aside from the costs directly associated with the resignation, there are further good reasons for employers to minimise the numbers of employees leaving. These include productivity losses, impaired quality of service, lost business opportunities, an increased administrative burden and employee demoralisation.

However, it is the direct costs associated with turnover that have received the most attention from writers on this topic, and that provide the meat of the business case for seeking to reduce the frequency of voluntary resignations. The following is a list of potential costs associated with employee attrition, incorporating material from a variety of sources (Fair 1992, IDS 1995e, Cascio 2000, Griffeth and Hom 2001, IRS 2001f). It is clear that some are more readily quantifiable than others:

- direct recruitment costs (advertising, use of agents etc)

- recruitment administration (responding to enquiries and sending out application forms, equal opportunities monitoring)

- selection costs (travelling expenses for candidates, psychometric testing, staff time in interviewing or running assessment centres, checking references)

- development costs (training the new employee using formal and informal development methods, induction training)

- administrative costs associated with resignations (payroll arrangements, calculation of holiday entitlements, pension transfers, conducting exit interviews)

- administrative costs associated with new starters (contract writing, medicals, sending out documentation, issuing uniforms, parking permits, identity badges, company cars etc, relocation expenses for new starter)

- inefficiency in production or service provision (resulting from slackness on the part of the resigner, inexperience of the replacement employee and inefficiencies resulting from a period in which the vacancy is unfilled)

- overtime and costs of hiring temporary workers (during the period between resignation and the hiring of a new member of staff).

Although not all of the above cost implications will apply in any one case of voluntary resignation, several are likely to feature in some way. No one element will in itself necessarily result in a great deal of expenditure, but it is the cumulative effect that gives the business case for attacking turnover its potency.

Estimates of the actual cost of turnover vary considerably, depending on which of the factors listed above are included in the calculation. The level of the final figure also varies with the nature and content of the job under consideration. Ball-park figures are thus of only limited use to P&D specialists seeking to compare the performance of their organisations with others. However, they do give a useful indication of the potential scale of cost implications associated with high turnover.

Fair (1992) suggests that replacement costs equate, on average, to six months' salary of the post in question, rising to two years' salary in the case of very senior posts. J. Douglas Phillips (1990) goes further, suggesting that the total figure averages 1.5 times the annual starting salary. Surveys of employers indicate that, while costs are not generally perceived to be this high, they are nevertheless very significant. Employers participating in the 2007 CIPD survey on labour turnover estimated the average cost of recruitment alone to be £4,333 (see Table 17.2), but here too the figures for senior staff were a good deal higher than for those paid at lower rates.

A simple calculation is all that is required to give an indication of how great the

Table 17.2 Median turnover costs for different occupational groups (2007)

Managers and professionals	£11,000
Technical and administrative	£5,000
Services	£5,000
Manual and craft	£1,174
Average for all employees	£7,750

potential savings can be when staff turnover is reduced, however modestly. For large organisations, particularly those operating in high-attrition sectors such as retailing and catering, the annual 'turnover bill' can easily run into many millions of pounds. Smaller organisations can also soon find that the costs mount up if turnover rates increase too much. Conversely, of course, substantial savings can be made from reducing turnover rates. IDS (2005b) quote the example of a voluntary sector organisation called Positive Steps Oldham which managed to reduce its turnover rates from 38 per cent to 14 per cent over a three-year period. The saving was calculated to be £20,000 per year.

While these figures seem to give incontrovertible justification for attacking turnover and setting out plans for its reduction, it must be remembered that such strategies themselves can cost a great deal of money. There is therefore also a good case for judicious consideration of appropriate courses of action in terms of their likely long-term costs and benefits to the employer.

REFLECTIVE QUESTION

Does your organisation measure its turnover rates? How varied are the figures for different occupational groups?

KEY ARTICLE 40

Steve Hillmer, Barbara Hillmer and Gale McRoberts, The real costs of turnover: lessons from a call center. *Human Resource Planning*, Vol. 27, No. 3, pp34–41 (2004)

There are few articles that examine in detail the costs associated with voluntary staff turnover in particular workplaces. Here the authors have done so, using data they have gathered from a call centre in the United States. They conclude, having made conservative estimates for intangible as well as tangible costs, that the true cost of turnover in this workplace is equivalent to a sum not less than a year's salary.

Questions

1   Why is staff turnover both so high in call centres and so problematic for their managers?

2   To what extent do you think that the researchers have included all the possible sources of cost in their calculations?

3   How far could this methodology be employed in other types of organisational setting?

MEASUREMENT AND BENCHMARKING

Generating meaningful turnover statistics that form a robust basis for the development of remedial plans is a very inexact science. It is easy to misinterpret figures, which can lead to problems in multi-divisional organisations where one unit's turnover rates are compared with others'. A classic example arises from the tendency for turnover to be at its highest in the first months of an individual's employment. For this reason, units that are performing well (and are thus expanding) are very likely to have higher figures than those in relative decline. So great care has to be taken in analysing raw turnover statistics and in using them as a means of formally assessing the performance of particular personnel functions or line managers.

The two most commonly used measures of turnover were discussed in some detail in the context of human resource planning (see Chapter 5). They are the 'wastage index' and the 'stability index'. The former measures crude turnover rates by dividing the number of voluntary resignations over the course of a year by the average number of staff employed in the organisation over the same period. The result is then multiplied by 100 to give a percentage figure. Wastage indices of one form or another are those used by the various government and commercial surveys of turnover described above. By contrast, stability indices effectively discount high turnover in the first months of employment by focusing only on the number of individuals employed for a prolonged period – usually a year – rather than on the number who actually leave. This index is also expressed as a percentage figure, but is calculated by dividing the number of staff with more than one year's service by the total number of employees in post a year ago. Job tenure figures for the UK as a whole are occasionally published by the government using data from the Labour Force Survey. The most recent figures, according to the DTI (2006), are as shown in Table 17.3.

Table 17.3 Job tenure figures for the United Kingdom

Length of service	Percentage of workforce
1 month–2 years:	27
2–5 years:	24
5–8 years:	13
8–12 years:	9
Over 12 years:	24

Interestingly, despite what we read about the 'end of jobs for life' and decreasing employer–employee loyalty, these figures have remained remarkably stable over time. There have been no dramatic reductions in job tenure trends in recent years.

It would be quite possible for an organisation to have a very high wastage rate and, at the same time, a high stability rate – reflecting particularly high turnover in the first year of employment. Alternatively, an employer could have a relatively healthy overall wastage rate but a worryingly low stability rate, reflecting a tendency for individuals to leave once they had completed some years of service. In each case, the most appropriate P&D response as a means of reducing turnover will be rather different. However, the figures themselves are often meaningless until they are put in context by comparing them with those of other departments, divisions and organisations, or with those computed for previous years. As we have seen, substantial turnover levels are part and parcel of life in certain industries at particular times and in particular regions. What is significant, in business terms, is how the results compare with those of key competitors. It is only when figures are benchmarked that they can inform personnel priorities and policies.

Within a single company or conglomerate, in theory, it is relatively straightforward to obtain benchmarking information. An example might be a chain of restaurants or shops, where each unit is very similar to the others. In theory, it would be possible to set up a monitoring system that compared turnover in each unit on the same basis over time, and many such organisations have attempted to do so. However, problems can arise when turnover statistics are used to compare individual managers' performance and not primarily to identify promising methods by which the level of voluntary resignations can be reduced.

Wherever managers feel that they are in any way being judged on the basis of their turnover there will be a strong temptation to 'massage' figures so as to impress their superiors, or at least to avoid their disapproval. This can very easily be done, even where the payroll function is managed centrally, by wrongly recording voluntary resignations that fall into the 'controllable' category as 'involuntary' or 'uncontrollable'. Ways in which such activity can be discouraged include downplaying the extent to which turnover is taken into account in judging management performance, and giving the central personnel function responsibility for undertaking exit interviews and surveys of ex-employees.

Benchmarking against competitors is a less exact activity, but one that can be effectively undertaken by using one of two methods. First, managers can compare their own performance against the figures included in the published government and industry-sponsored surveys of turnover in the United Kingdom. We made reference above to the regular CIPD studies, but there are many others, too by industry federations (such as the Institute of Management, the British Retail Consortium and the Engineering Council) and by commercial research organisations (see IRS 2004h, pp42–48 for details of dozens of published surveys). The alternative approach is to set up or join an informal association of similar employers to enable mutual exchange of information. Such arrangements resemble the long-established 'salary clubs' in their nature and methods.

BP CHEMICALS

Since 1992, BP chemicals division has been benefiting from benchmarking its HR operation against those of similar companies. In the absence of sufficiently detailed published data, managers decided to set up their own benchmarking club. They started by cold-calling their opposite numbers in other large manufacturing firms to enquire whether or not they would be interested in sharing data, but were rejected by many 'for reasons ranging from pressure of work to suspicion of the process and plain secretiveness'.

Eventually they set up arrangements with ten companies, and began exchanging data on a wide variety of HR practices, including voluntary and involuntary turnover. The process then continued with visits to other companies so that judgements could be made about best practice and how policy could be improved in the future. Qualitative research therefore followed on from the initial quantitative benchmarking exercise.

Source: Holt (1994).

REFLECTIVE QUESTION

Does your organisation exchange data of this kind with other employers? What do you think are the main disadvantages of such associations?

EXERCISE 17.2

PRET A MANGER

Read the article by Lucy Carrington, At the cutting edge (*People Management*, 16 May 2002, pp30–31). This can be downloaded from the *People Management* archive on the CIPD's website (www.cipd.co.uk).

This article describes the approach to recruitment that has been adopted by the café chain Pret a Manger. Its thoroughness is highly unusual in the industry, but appears to have resulted in substantially reduced staff turnover: from 130 per cent to 98 per cent.

People management

Questions

1 How can organisations such as Pret a Manger sustain their operations with such high staff turnover rates?

2 Why do you think the recruitment procedure the company has adopted leads to fewer voluntary resignations?

3 What further advantages does the company enjoy as a result of its approach to recruitment?

EXPLAINING TURNOVER

There is a wide variety of possible explanations for voluntary resignations. People become dissatisfied with their jobs for a range of reasons; they may become bored with the content, frustrated by lack of promotion, fed up with their supervisors or irritated by changes in their working environment. In some cases the job may simply fall short of their expectations at the time of appointment. However, such phenomena are only half the story – in most cases, for a resignation to occur, the individual concerned must first perceive that there are better opportunities elsewhere and then secure another position. The complexities of this process were effectively illustrated by William Mobley (1977) in the following 10-stage model of 'the employee turnover decision process':

1. Evaluate existing job.

2. Experience job dissatisfaction.

3. Think of quitting.

4. Evaluate expected utility of search for a new job and the cost of quitting.

5. Decide to search for alternatives.

6. Search for alternatives.

7. Evaluate alternatives.

8. Compare best alternative with present job.

9. Decide whether to stay or quit.

10. Quit.

It is therefore important, when assessing the reasons for turnover and devising remedial plans, to take account not just of employee dissatisfaction, but also of the possible alternatives open to employees, as well as the relative ease with which any such opportunities can be taken up.

Several different methods are available to employers seeking to investigate why employees choose to leave. Here we consider four contrasting approaches: exit interviews, surveys of ex-employees, attitude surveys and quantitative approaches.

EXIT INTERVIEWS

Formal interviews with employees before they leave the organisation are commonly undertaken to develop an understanding of their motivation for resigning. As many as 90 per cent of employers responding to a survey carried out in 2000 claimed to carry them out with at least a sample of their leavers (IRS 2001d). The most straightforward approach is to take the resigner through a questionnaire of direct questions concerning his or her satisfaction with pay, supervisor, development opportunities, relationships with colleagues and job content.

There are, however, a number of problems with such approaches that can serve to reduce their effectiveness. First, there is the tendency for employees to develop a far more optimistic outlook after they have secured a new job and resigned. Their original reasons for seeking alternative employment often get forgotten as they move towards their last day. Such feelings are compounded if counter-offers are made to encourage them to stay, and may disappear completely in the last days as cards are signed, leaving presents bought, affectionate speeches given and farewell parties held. This is often not, therefore, the best time to ask them for an honest and well-balanced assessment of their reasons for quitting.

A further problem arises when supervisors or department heads undertake exit interviews, because leavers will often baulk at implying any criticism of them – particularly if they believe that they will require positive job references in the future. The reason given for leaving may thus conceal the whole truth or may even be entirely false. It is far easier to say that you are leaving because you were offered more money elsewhere or because your spouse is moving, than to state openly that you disapprove of your new manager's style or feel that you have been treated unfairly in some way. According to ACAS (1985, p7), employees often 'simply quote some small incident which proved the last straw' as a means of avoiding the admission of deeper or less tangible factors. Furnham (2001) actually advises leavers to refrain from stating true feelings, especially if they are negative, on the grounds that it is 'unwise to burn your bridges'. Instead he suggests that 'the best piece of advice is two-fold: dissimulate or keep quiet'. Leavers should not say that their work 'was humdrum, stressful or tedious', but that they are moving on to new challenges, upgrading their portfolios or extending their horizons.

It can thus be argued that exit interviews, if used at all, should be undertaken very soon after the resignation has been confirmed, and that they should be carried out by an individual who will not have any role in writing future job references. A personnel officer is very well placed to carry out such work. According to Carrell *et al* (1995, p770), another way of encouraging candour is to explain to the leaver that the aim of the interview is to gather information for improving work conditions. In other words, the individual should be asked directly for his or her opinion on how things can be improved and only indirectly about any personal reasons for resigning. Good general advice about how to conduct a good exit interview, including ways of encouraging honesty, is provided by Macafee (2007).

REFLECTIVE QUESTION

Have you been responsible for conducting exit interviews? If you have, to what extent have you experienced the problems identified above?

A more efficient approach is to use separation questionnaires. These cover the same ground as exit interviews but are completed by the leaver alone and then returned by post. They may be anonymous, but can have advantages over exit interviews when such is not the case. According to IRS (2001d), this is because they 'offer a better opportunity for honesty and frankness'. Moreover, because the questionnaires typically have a multiple-choice answer format, responses are readily recorded in a database. This allows reports to be generated electronically on a regular basis.

THE VALIDITY OF EXIT INTERVIEWS AND QUESTIONNAIRES

Wilkinson (2004) investigated the accuracy of responses given in exit questionnaires by carrying out in-depth telephone interviews with 50 people who had previously been employed as nurses at a large NHS hospital trust, all of whom had resigned voluntarily within the past four years. Questions were put to them about their reasons for leaving in the same order as they appeared on the original leavers' questionnaire and in the same format. This enabled a direct comparison to be made between the responses made by each interviewee to the trust at the time of resignation and those made some months or years later confidentially to an independent researcher.

The results clearly showed substantial differences between the two responses. In fact only 36 per cent of the reasons given for leaving on questionnaires completed at the time of resignation were confirmed in the follow-up interviews. Moreover, of those responses that changed, 88.9 per cent were altered from reasons that could be categorised as 'pull' factors to those that were essentially 'push' factors. By far the most common reason for leaving given in the interviews was dissatisfaction with management, yet this was only stated as being the reason on the questionnaires by a small minority.

This study appears to confirm that departing employees are reluctant to voice the real reasons for their resignations when these are negative. In particular there is a strong reluctance on the part of leavers to make criticisms of their line managers or to complain about matters within the control of line managers. As a result the employer is given a highly misleading impression of why its employees are resigning.

SURVEYS OF EX-EMPLOYEES

A more promising, if less straightforward, approach is to contact former employees some months after they have left in order to ask them for a considered view of their reasons for resigning. While the use of this method is relatively rare, there has been a number of cases covered in the human resource journals that indicate some large organisations are experimenting with it (see IRS 2001d). Candour is further encouraged if the surveys are carried out by independent bodies and are clearly labelled 'private and confidential'.

ATTITUDE SURVEYS

A third approach is to seek the views of employees before they leave and so provide a basis for the development of policies and practices that will deter them from so doing. These too are truly effective only if confidential, so as to maximise the chance of employees' stating honestly how they feel about their jobs, their perceived opportunities, their bosses, colleagues and the organisation as a whole. Questions can also be asked about their current intentions for the future and about their perceptions of alternative career paths open to them. Such approaches enable employers to anticipate in which areas future turnover is most likely to occur, and to gain an insight into the main causes.

QUANTITATIVE APPROACHES

An alternative to the use of surveys is to make use of employee records to compare the data or characteristics of those who leave with those who stay. Although quantitative approaches are unlikely in themselves to give a particularly clear picture of reasons for turnover, they may reveal some interesting general trends, and can usefully supplement information gathered using the three other methods outlined above.

Any number of ratios can be investigated using quantitative analyses. Examples might include comparing leavers with stayers in terms of their age, the distance they travel to work, their shift patterns, pay levels, performance record or length of service. It is also possible to use these techniques to identify the extent to which turnover varies with the type of job undertaken or with the supervision of different managers. As with all quantitative analyses, the data is really useful only when there are large sample sizes available. Such approaches are thus inappropriate for smaller organisations.

KEY ARTICLE 41

Naresh Khatri, Chong Tze Fern and Pawan Budhwar, Explaining employee turnover in an Asian context. *Human Resource Management Journal*, Vol. 11, No. 1, pp54–74 (2001)

This article describes a programme of research aimed at identifying the major antecedents of turnover among employees working in three industries in Singapore. A particularly interesting feature is the finding that the causes of turnover that are believed to have the biggest effect in Western organisations are much less significant in Singapore. The article draws attention to a phenomenon which the authors label 'job-hopping' and which they define as apparently irrational voluntary turnover that is caused by neither dissatisfaction with a job, nor a wish to improve the level of salary. This, it appears, is very common in Singapore.

Questions

1 Why do people job-hop so much in Singapore?

2 What other significant differences do the authors identify between the antecedents of employee turnover in Western countries and those prevailing in Singapore?

3 What advice would you give to an international corporation setting up a subsidiary company in Singapore if it wanted to achieve levels of staff turnover that are well below average?

REDUCING TURNOVER

Once the reasons for resignations have been established and analysed, the next step is to formulate plans to reduce them. Clearly, it is impossible to generalise about the form such plans will take, because they will vary dramatically depending on the causes of turnover in specific organisations. Employers may often find that very different factors explain resignations in each department or business unit. However, there are several possible courses of remedial action that can usefully be considered and that have been shown by researchers to have a positive effect in some circumstances. Two books by Peter Hom and Rodger Griffeth cover this ground particularly well. Hom and Griffeth (1995) is a comprehensive review of recent US research into the management of turnover, while Griffeth and Hom (2001) is a more accessible guide for managers that draws on their earlier research. They describe nine areas for employers to consider. The first six are described as 'robust' methods of controlling turnover, for which there is strong research evidence, and the final three as 'promising' methods:

- realistic job previews
- job enrichment
- workspace characteristics
- induction practices
- leader–member exchange

- employee selection

- reward practices

- demographic diversity

- managing inter-role conflict.

Several of these areas are investigated elsewhere in this book and in others in the series (eg realistic job previews, selection, induction and reward). In the following paragraphs, we therefore focus on the other areas identified by Hom and Griffeth as worthy of consideration.

JOB ENRICHMENT

Psychological research has strongly suggested that employees are far less likely to consider looking for new jobs when they feel fulfilled in their existing roles. According to Hom and Griffeth (1995, p203), the following perceptions of jobs by job-holders are particularly significant:

- There are opportunities for self- and career development.

- The job is meaningful or significant.

- A variety of skills is used.

- There is a high degree of personal responsibility.

- People can work with a degree of autonomy.

- Positive feedback on performance is given.

Increasing the extent to which these features are present in a job leads to its 'enrichment'. There is thus a good case, where retention rates need to be improved, for looking at ways in which job content can be refined in some or all of these directions. In many cases the costs associated with such actions will not be particularly high.

WORKSPACE CHARACTERISTICS

In a series of research papers G. R. Oldham and his colleagues have reported research findings on working environments and their effect on employee satisfaction (see Hom and Griffeth 1995, pp203–205). Their experiments have involved providing similar groups of employees working for the same organisation with radically different office designs, which has led to interesting results. While they have found various factors to be significant, particular attention has been paid to Hom and Griffeth's discovery that large open-plan offices with few dividing walls or partitions tend to reduce employees' feelings of autonomy and significance, and therefore increase dissatisfaction significantly. Overcrowding and darkness make matters worse. It can thus be argued that, except where it clearly matches the established workplace culture, the idea of doing away with partitions to decrease feelings of isolation and to encourage people to identify and socialise with other group members may be mistaken. In

Chapter 9 further research in this area is described in the context of effective performance management.

LEADER–MEMBER EXCHANGE

The suggestion here is that turnover is reduced, particularly in the first months of appointment, if managers have been trained to develop high 'leader–member exchanges' with their subordinates. This term is defined as paying new starters particular attention and actively trying to develop high-trust relationships with them from the start. This involves taking special care to ask employees their opinion about operational matters, giving them influence in decision-making processes and allowing them as much latitude as possible to undertake their job roles in the way they prefer. Essentially it means resisting the display of any feelings of suspicion managers may have, and relying on 'social exchange' rather than 'formal authority' to ensure that work gets done.

Such techniques might be regarded as simply attributes of effective supervisors. The point made by researchers working in the field is that they do not necessarily come naturally to managers and that it is possible to develop appropriate characteristics with formal training.

EXPLORING REASONS FOR TURNOVER AMONG NURSES

In 1996, a large NHS trust hospital in the north of England undertook a detailed investigation of the high turnover rates among junior qualified nurses, which was running at 23 per cent. An independent researcher was brought in to conduct a questionnaire survey of 193 nurses who had left voluntarily over the previous two years, and to undertake interviews with nurse managers about the causes of turnover in their departments. Over 70 per cent of the nurses who had left were still employed in the NHS, and all but 5 per cent had remained in nursing or nursing-related careers.

The questionnaire results showed that 63 per cent had left for reasons that could be categorised as 'controllable'. While a number of reasons for turnover were established, three were particularly significant. These were: a poor working relationship with the supervisor, failure to secure promotion, and general dissatisfaction with aspects of the working environment (including low staffing levels). Of particular interest was the identification of departments in which there was a pattern of poor supervisor–subordinate relationships. It became very clear from the questionnaire that some nurse managers were far more effective motivators than others, and that developing their supervisory skills would lead to improved retention of nurses in their departments.

Source: Burton (1996).

DEMOGRAPHIC DIVERSITY

Research in the United States reported by Hom and Griffeth (1995, pp239–252) has indicated that, on average, women and members of ethnic minorities are more likely than white males to leave jobs voluntarily. Furthermore, studies have shown that this is partly explained by perceptions on the part of these groups that they have been unfairly discriminated against while in their jobs. The point is made that it is irrelevant from a management perspective whether the discrimination is 'imagined' or 'real': it is the perception of inequality that is significant, and that needs to tackled if turnover is to be reduced. The US research found that perceptions of supervisor bias, inequality in pay awards, unsupportive colleagues and blocked careers all contribute towards high turnover among women and ethnic minorities. People also identified extra pressure to perform well and a tendency for the most interesting and highly visible tasks or projects to be given to whites and males as factors in their decision to resign voluntarily.

Such problems are familiar in the United Kingdom but, as yet, little formal research appears to have been undertaken here as regards their specific effect on employee turnover. However, it is reasonable to assume that, at least in some cases, involuntary resignations could be explained by perceptions of unfair discrimination. Clearly the way to tackle this is to introduce and communicate effective equal opportunities policies that managers at all levels are obliged to accept. There is a need not just to monitor the pay and job progression among members of the relevant groups, but also to communicate results and plans of action to employees. Problems with particular supervisors or departments could be effectively identified by means of the survey techniques described above. A good start would be for questions relating to unfair discrimination to be included in exit interview questionnaires.

MANAGING INTER-ROLE CONFLICT

Another reason for turnover identified by Hom and Griffeth (1995, pp252–255) relates to conflicts between the demands of work and family, a problem made worse with recent increases in the number of single-parent families. Research into turnover in the United States suggests that whereas 33 per cent of women cite such conflicts as contributing to their reasons for quitting a job, it was significant for only 1 per cent of men.

Such findings may back a business case for employers to go further than the minimum standard required by the law in the provision of maternity leave (paid or unpaid), career breaks, childcare, day-care for elderly dependants, flexible work schedules and forms of homeworking. Although some of these may be expensive for employers to introduce (particularly in small organisations), they are at least worthy of consideration where the costs do not outweigh those associated with high levels of staff turnover.

In addition to organisation-wide policy initiatives such as those outlined above, employers can also improve staff retention rates simply by giving the issue a far higher profile in the organisation than is often the case. This involves securing senior management commitment by developing a robust business case and then giving responsibility for turnover reduction to individual line managers. It is possible to go as far as to incorporate departmental turnover records into performance appraisal criteria for supervisors, so that career progression or bonus levels are determined in part by success in this area.

Read the article by Jim Dow, Spa attraction (*People Management*, 29 May 2003, pp34–35). This can be downloaded from the *People Management* archive on the CIPD's website (www.cipd.co.uk).

This article describes the experiences of a large, privately owned, country-house hotel in the Scottish borders. It has very low staff turnover in comparison with its competitors, many of its staff having over ten years' service.

Questions

1 Why do you think staff turnover is generally so high in the hotel industry?

2 What factors cited in the article help explain why this particular hotel enjoys low staff turnover? What other factors are likely to have played a part?

3 What problems has the hotel encountered because of its low turnover? What has it done to tackle these?

4 What lessons could be learned from the experience of the Peebles Hydro Hotel by organisations in other industries?

KEY ARTICLE 42

Sarah Robinson, Trevor Murrells and Michael Clifton, Highly qualified and highly ambitious: implications for workforce retention of realising the career expectations of graduate nurses in England. *Human Resource Management Journal*, Vol. 16, No. 3, pp287–312 (2006)

This article reports the results of a very large-scale quantitative research project comparing the plans and relative levels of job satisfaction between two groups of newly recruited NHS nurses: those entering nursing with a degree and those entering with a nursing diploma. The results are relevant to the field of graduate recruitment generally as well as carrying some important messages for NHS managers as the nursing profession moves towards all-graduate entry. The major finding is that future quit-rates are likely to be considerably higher among graduates than non-graduates.

Questions

1 Why do the graduate recruits only start to show serious signs of dissatisfaction and increased intention to leave after a number of years in the nursing profession?

2 Why are the diploma-level entrants less likely than the graduates to express a desire to quit once they are established in the profession?

3 What action would you advise NHS managers to take in the light of the findings of this study?

LEGAL ISSUES

As a general rule, employers do not have the protection of the law in preventing or discouraging employees from leaving their employment, even when they quit in order to join a competitor or set up in a similar business themselves. However, there are two important exceptions that personnel professionals should be aware of so that they can give general advice to line managers in specific cases. These are the implied duty of fidelity in all contracts of employment and specific restraint-of-trade clauses. Another legal issue relevant to voluntary resignations is the right of the employer to be given reasonable notice of the employee's intention to leave.

DUTY OF FIDELITY

All contracts of employment, however informal, are accepted by the courts to contain an implied duty on the part of employees to act in good faith towards their employer. This means that even if no such agreement has been made between the two parties it is nevertheless deemed to exist in law. Rulings in this area are complex and depend very much on the individual circumstances of each case, so personnel specialists are well advised to seek advice from legal experts if at all unsure of their position.

First, if employees are planning to resign in order to set up in direct competition to their employer or to work for a competitor, contract law prevents them from unfairly using their current employer's resources to help them do so. Hence, test cases have found that a milkman about to set up his own delivery business was wrong to have solicited for customers while still employed by a large dairy (Wessex Dairies v Smith 1935), and that employees are liable to pay compensation if they copy lists of customers prior to joining a competitor company (Robb v Green 1895). In both these cases, the individuals were found to have breached their duty of fidelity while employed by their original organisations. However, the courts have made it quite clear that this duty does not prevent ex-employees in the service of a competitor from making use of skills and non-confidential knowledge acquired while working for their previous employer.

In practice, it is sometimes difficult to draw a clear distinction between what is and what is not permitted. The extent of the grey area is illustrated by the example of a driving instructor planning to set up his own business in competition with an existing employer. What is he supposed to say to his existing pupils? Is it a breach of duty to inform them that he is leaving to set up an independent driving school? What if he gives them a business card or home telephone number to enable pupils to make contact with a view to arranging lessons? What if he telephones existing pupils to invite them to continue their instruction with him? At what stage the breach of contract occurs is difficult to state, particularly when pupils have had contact with the individual instructor only and believe it to be in their interests to continue being taught by him.

The duty of fidelity has also been found to extend to the use of 'confidential information' by an ex-employee who has taken up employment with a competitor. Here, too, the case law is far from clear as to what exactly can be defined as being confidential. A recent case, Faccenda Chicken v Fowler 1986, stated clearly that the answer to this question will vary from situation to situation depending on the circumstances. These will include the extent to which a piece of information has been labelled confidential in some way, or the number of individuals in the organisation who have knowledge of it. It is therefore possible to conclude that, except in very clear-cut cases, where an employee has clearly abused his or her position prior to resigning, employers are unlikely to be able to rely on implied contractual terms to stop information, skills or knowledge being used in the service of a competitor.

RESTRICTIVE COVENANTS

Where trade secrets do exist but do not fall within the limited legal definition of the term 'confidential' described above, employers can, and probably should, seek to protect themselves by inserting an express restraint-of-trade clause into contracts of employment. This would clearly be appropriate where an employer wished to keep a particular manufacturing process secret from competitors, or where information about new products being developed or advertising campaigns might be obtained by a rival company via an employee who was in the know. Employees would then have to sign contracts on taking up their employment that clearly stated they were not permitted to work for a direct competitor within a defined period (eg a year) after resigning.

In companies where such circumstances are prevalent, restrictive covenants of this kind can act very effectively to deter employees from resigning voluntarily. Restraining clauses are also common in contracts of employment issued to solicitors, accountants and doctors, where customer connections might permit them to set up in competition in the same area. They are also used by all kinds of other employers whose business might be severely threatened by direct competition from ex-employees.

However, in interpreting restrictive covenants, the courts have tended to uphold the rights of ex-employees to work where and for whom they please, except where the clause is clearly 'in the legitimate interests of the employer' (see IDS 1994b). In other words, if the intention of the clause is simply to restrict the ability of employees to resign, it would be declared to be void by a court. To be enforceable, the restraint-of-trade clause must refer specifically to the passing on of trade secrets or trade connections to another organisation.

A well-known case that illustrates these principles was Greer *v* Sketchley 1979. Here, a senior manager in a dry-cleaning business decided to resign in order to take up employment with a rival company. However, he was constrained from so doing because of a restraint-of-trade clause in his contract of employment that forbade him associating 'with any other person, firm or company' engaged in any similar business in the United Kingdom for a period of 12 months. Believing the clause to be overly restrictive, Mr Greer took his employer to court and succeeded in persuading the court to declare it invalid on the grounds that it was not reasonable to seek to restrict an employee from working anywhere in the country.

According to IDS, in drawing up 'reasonable' restrictive covenants, employers should focus on four areas:

- the nature of the employees' activities (ie restrict ex-employees only in fields directly related to their work, not the business of the organisation as a whole)

- geographical area (ie include in the clause only those geographical areas in which the company has significant business interests)

- duration (ie put only the minimum necessary time-limit on the clause – 12 months is usually sufficient to deter employees from resigning to pass on trade secrets or details of customers)

- employee rank (ie treat senior employees with access to a range of confidential information differently from relatively junior staff with limited knowledge).

There are two broad conclusions that can be made regarding the use of restraint-of-trade covenants. First, it is clearly unreasonable in law to use them as a matter of course in seeking to deter employees from leaving. They have to be specific and restricted to the protection of genuinely confidential information if they are to be upheld by the courts. Second, it is apparent that the more restrictive the clause, the harder it will be to defend in court. Employers are thus wise to restrict the scope of their clauses only to areas in which they clearly have legitimate commercial interests to protect.

NOTICE PERIODS

Employers are strongly advised to include in their contracts of employment specific reference to the amount of notice an employee must give when deciding to leave. Where this is not the case, according to the Employment Rights Act 1996, the employee is entitled to give just one week's notice. Traditionally, most employers have declared the notice period to be the same as the payment period, so that weekly paid staff are required to give a week's notice, whereas their monthly paid colleagues are required to work for a full four or five weeks after handing in their notice. For senior managers it is reasonable to ask for more notice to reflect the need for a more involved procedure in the selection of a replacement. Three months is common for such jobs.

In practice, of course, there is little employers can do to force the employee to work out the full period of notice. Technically they could sue the employee for breach of contract, but the damages that would be awarded would rarely be sufficient to justify the legal expenses incurred. Instead, employers tend to rely on the goodwill of employees and on the fact that they often have an incentive to stay on – if required to do so – to ensure good references in the future. It is also possible for an employer to decline to pay the final pay-packet in circumstances where an employee leaves without giving the notice required in his or her contract.

ETHICAL ISSUES

There are various practices that are, apparently, commonly used by employers when managing voluntary resignations that could be seen as unethical. One, familiar to many employees of smaller businesses, is the use of explicit or implied threats to deter employees from seeking alternative employment. These take the form of the manager's informally disciplining or punishing employees discovered to have applied for new jobs. The punishment can take a number of forms, ranging from verbal castigation and the withdrawal of perks to exclusion from decision-making and the blocking of pay-rises. It is for such reasons that employees often feel that they must keep their job searches secret and conceal from their colleagues the fact that they have visited job centres or attended interviews.

Another heavy-handed practice occurs when resigners are told to leave with immediate effect, and may even be escorted from the premises. Although the practice is most commonly used in cases of dismissal, there have been instances of its use with voluntary releases, when individuals have announced their intention to take up a position with a competitor. The aim is to protect confidential information of the kinds referred to above. However, the extent to which the interests of the employer are really served by immediate departures of this kind is highly questionable. As soon as employees realise that it is likely to occur, they will take steps to prepare for it, including taking home any information they believe will be helpful to them in the future.

It can thus be argued that both of these practices are unprofessional and not conducive to the development of healthy, high-trust relationships with employees. Effectively, they amount to a deliberate attempt to restrict employees from seeking to develop their own careers, and as such are likely to generate dissatisfaction and so encourage more staff to seek alternative employment. In the long term they are liable to increase rather than decrease staff turnover, and to make it harder for employers to recruit and motivate the best people.

REFLECTIVE QUESTION

What other practices that might be described as 'unethical' have you come across in the field of voluntary release? How convincing a business case could you make in arguing for their cessation?

EXERCISE 17.4

CUTTING TURNOVER

Read the following articles featured in *People Management*. They can be downloaded from the *People Management* archive on the CIPD's website (www.cipd.co.uk):

- Steve Smethurst, Batteries recharged (5 May 2005, pp24–27)

- Jane Simms, In their shoes (20 April 2006, pp36–38)

- Emma Clarke, Safety in numbers (11 January 2007, pp44–46).

Each article describes a case study of an organisation which has managed to reduce staff turnover rates. The organisations and the type of staff they employ are diverse

(accountants, managers and retail workers), but in each case carefully though-through management interventions have had a striking impact.

Questions

1 What are the major interventions which are credited with improving staff retention rates in each of these cases?

2 Why were different approaches called for in each of the cases?

3 What general lessons can be learned from the experience of these three organisations?

CHAPTER SUMMARY

- Some staff turnover is unavoidable or involuntary (as in the case of dismissals and retirements), but there is a good case both for monitoring and seeking to minimise that which is avoidable and voluntary.

- Turnover rates are highest when and where the economy is performing well. They reach over 50 per cent in some private sector service industries, falling below 5 per cent among more senior staff in larger corporations and in the public sector.

- Very low turnover, especially at senior levels, can be harmful for organisations. However, in most industries too high a turnover rate is damaging and costly.

- Employers estimate the total costs associated with replacing an average employee to be around £4,000, of which £2,500 is spent recruiting a replacement. It is a good deal higher in the case of management and professional staff.

- The reasons for resignations are many and varied. The major methods used to investigate why people leave are exit interviews, surveys of ex-employees, attitude surveys and quantitative analyses of employee databases.

- Research suggests that several practices are successful at reducing turnover levels. These include enriching jobs, improving the work environment, upgrading the quality of supervision, ensuring that employees perceive they are being treated fairly and developing family-friendly conditions.

- As a rule the law prevents employers from using unreasonable means of trapping employees in one employment. However, in certain circumstances it is permissible to incorporate restrictive covenants in contracts of employment to deter people from resigning to work for direct competitors.

EXPLORE FURTHER

- *Employee turnover* by Peter Hom and Rodger Griffeth (1995) is by far the most comprehensive publication on the topic. All aspects are explored and all established research reviewed. Their more recent book entitled *Retaining valued employees* (2001) is more user-friendly, but also draws on robust academic research.

- *The employee retention handbook* by Stephen Taylor (2002) covers all the topics dealt with in this chapter in greater detail, together with case studies focusing on ways of retaining people in different occupational groups.

- The best source of data on turnover levels in different regions, industries and occupational groups is the online journal *IRS Employment Review*, which regularly

publishes statistics and useful articles on the subject. Their annual benchmarking survey is published early every year. Incomes Data Services has also produced a number of useful publications on the management of turnover.

- Interesting and useful contributions by academic writers researching in this field include articles by Hiltrop (1999), Capelli (2000) and Maertz and Campion (2001).

- Information about initiatives taken by particular employers is often featured in articles published in the CIPD's twice-monthly journal, *People Management*. The CIPD also carries out a large survey each year focusing on employee retention and turnover. This can be downloaded, free of charge if you are a member, from its website.

CHAPTER 18

Redundancy and retirement

After voluntary resignations, the next most common reasons for people leaving employment are retirement and redundancy. In some cases, where the figures add up, people opt to take early retirement or willingly accept an offer of redundancy. In others they are made compulsorily redundant or are forcibly retired by employers once they have reached a certain age. Both events thus occupy something of a grey area between terminations that have an essentially voluntary character and those that are involuntary. Indeed, a voluntary retirement is often a means to avoid making someone compulsorily redundant.

Retirement and redundancy are both covered by an extensive body of law yet, unlike laws on other forms of dismissal, legislation does little more than set a basic minimum standard of employer conduct. Whereas in the case of a termination on account of poor performance, misconduct or ill health, 'best practice' has effectively been determined by Parliament and the courts, in the case of the management of redundancies and retirements many employers prefer to offer far more generous terms than are strictly required by law. This is particularly so in the field of redundancy payments where a clear majority of employers offer severance payments beyond the statutory minimum (IRS 2004i).

In this chapter, a number of aspects of these two specific forms of termination of employment are explored. The main legal requirements in each case are summarised, and some of the approaches that can be used to minimise the distress and disruption associated with involuntary redundancy and forced retirement are assessed. The methods that employers can use to avoid making compulsory redundancies, or at least to reduce their number, are also described.

LEARNING OUTCOMES

By the end of this chapter readers should be able to:

- define the term 'redundancy'

- calculate redundancy payments

- organise job-search and pre-retirement courses

- run or commission the provision of outplacement services

- draw up policies on the management of retirement and redundancy

- determine fair criteria for selecting employees to be made compulsorily redundant.

In addition, readers should be able to understand and explain:

- the main legal issues relating to the management of redundancy and retirement

- best-practice approaches to handling redundancy and retirement over and above what is required by law.

EXERCISE 18.1

THE LEGAL SERVICES COMMISSION

Read the article by Hashi Syedain, A judicious review (*People Management*, 4 October 2007, p37). This can be downloaded from the *People Management* archive on the CIPD's website (www.cipd.co.uk).

This brief article describes how the LSC managed to cut a third of its workforce over five years, while also ensuring that it did not lose its best people.

Questions

1   Why do strong performers tend to leave an organisation voluntarily when future redundancies are rumoured?

2   Why was the approach used by the LSC successful in preventing this from occurring?

3   What other types of initiative might have been used to achieve the same effect or to complement the approach that was taken?

DEFINING REDUNDANCY

In the United Kingdom, the term 'redundancy' is defined by law as a situation in which, for economic reasons, there is no longer a need for the job in question to be carried out in the place where it is currently carried out. Although the selection of employees to be made redundant can take into account their ability to perform the job, individual failings are not the main reason that a job is being lost. The Employment Rights Act (1996) states that redundancy occurs only when a dismissal arises either mainly or wholly for one of the following reasons:

- where the employer has ceased, or intends to cease, carrying on the business in which the employee is or was employed

- where the employer ceases, or intends to cease, carrying out this business at the place where the employee is or was employed

- where the requirements for employees to carry out work of a particular kind have ceased or diminished (or are expected to), and where the employee is employed to carry that work out

- where the requirements to carry out work of a particular kind have ceased or diminished at the place where the employee is employed.

The starting-point is, therefore, a reduction in the need for employees either in general or at a particular location. If such is not the case, whatever the dismissal might be called by those involved, it is not considered a 'redundancy' in legal terms. Although a reduction in the requirement for employees usually results from a reduction in the volume of work, that is not a necessary condition for a legal redundancy to occur. It is quite possible for an expanding business to make redundancies, provided certain types of work are becoming less necessary and the employees concerned are unable to transfer to other jobs. A common example would be a situation in which new technology is introduced to meet increased demand, leading to a requirement for fewer low-skilled employees.

It is important to grasp the legal definition, because it sets out the circumstances in which employees are entitled, as of right, to a redundancy payment. Where the dismissal is mainly for other reasons, such as misconduct or incapability, the employer is not obliged to pay compensation except in cases where individual contracts of employment require it. Redundancies also require a wholly different procedural approach if they are to be judged to have been carried out reasonably by employment tribunals. Moreover, the distinction between true redundancies and other dismissals is also a matter of interest to the Inland Revenue, because redundancy payments below £30,000 are tax free. The practice of making someone redundant and paying a redundancy payment when the above definitions do not in fact apply can thus lead to as much difficulty as situations in which payments are not made to dismissed employees who are truly redundant.

Redundancies fall into the category of 'potentially fair dismissals' as far as employment tribunals are concerned. Like the other kinds of dismissal discussed in the next chapter, employers are therefore legally able to dismiss employees on account of redundancy provided they meet the tribunal's standards of 'reasonableness'. In other words, a redundancy will be judged fair as long as the correct procedures are followed and as long as people are treated equitably. As is the case with all kinds of dismissal, employment tribunals can hear only cases brought by employees with over a years' continuous service after the age of 18.

REDUNDANCY STATISTICS FOR THE UNITED KINGDOM

Given the amount of press coverage in recent years about 'downsizing', 'right-sizing', 'streamlining' and 'rationalising' of workforces, it is remarkable how few people are actually formally made redundant in the United Kingdom each year. The figures vary considerably depending on the economic climate, but never climb beyond a tiny percentage of the total workforce.

The current method of compiling the national figures dates from 1990, when establishments making fewer than ten redundancies at the same time were included. In the years since then the highest number to be made redundant in a single year was 391,000 (in 1991). This means that even at the very peak of the early 1990s recession, fewer than 1.5 per cent of the total UK workforce experienced redundancy. The figure suggests that managements are very successful at finding ways of avoiding compulsory redundancies, such as those described in this chapter.

Aside from calculating the over all figures, the Labour Force Survey also publishes statistics by gender, age, occupational group and industry. The figures show that men are considerably more likely than women to be made redundant, that the highest risk age group is 16–24 (when it is cheapest to let people go), and that workers in manufacturing are the most likely to be made redundant, particularly when they are employed in 'craft and related' occupations.

Sources: IDS (2001c, p3), Redman and Wilkinson (2001, p300) and Heap (2004).

AVOIDING REDUNDANCIES

One of the issues that tribunals look at in judging the reasonableness with which a redundancy programme has been carried out is the extent and nature of the steps taken either to minimise the number of redundancies or to avoid them altogether. A variety of management actions can be taken to avoid making people compulsorily redundant, some of a general nature that help prevent redundancy situations' arising in the first place and others that come into play once it becomes apparent that redundancies are likely or necessary.

LONG-TERM APPROACHES

In publications on redundancy, authors rightly give considerable attention to the approaches that managers can take to prevent, or reduce the likelihood of, redundancies (eg Lewis 1993, Redman and Wilkinson 2006). Each involves planning in order to avoid as far as possible scenarios in which the employer has no alternative but to dismiss employees whose jobs have become redundant. The approaches fall into three broad but distinct categories: effective human resource planning, flexible working practices, and the sponsorship of early retirement incentives.

The arguments for and against human resource planning were explored at length in Chapters 5 and 6 of this book. One strong argument in favour of carrying out formal forecasting of staffing needs is the assistance that the development of human resource plans gives in avoiding redundancy. If one can foresee months or even years ahead a downturn in business levels or a change in business processes likely to reduce an organisation's need to employ people or to undertake work of a particular kind, then one can take steps to reduce the number of compulsory redundancies that will have to be made. For example, an organisation can reduce the number of new employees taken on and focus its attention on retraining and developing existing employees for new roles that they may have to undertake in the future. Such a course of action also permits natural wastage to occur, so that over time the size of the workforce diminishes as people leave voluntarily and are not replaced.

The second long-term activity is the maximisation of flexibility in an organisation, so that where work of a particular kind is expected to grow less, the employees engaged in that work are able to develop new job roles. We explored these issues in Chapter 7. Fowler (1993, pp24–26) usefully distinguishes between 'organisational flexibility', which involves reducing the number of steps in organisational hierarchies and organising employees into multifunctional teams, and 'job flexibility', which requires enlarging and enriching individual jobs so that each employee becomes multi-skilled. Such courses of action make modern organisations more efficient and the employees working within them more adaptable to changing circumstances. Each of these consequences contributes to the avoidance of redundancies.

Other kinds of flexibility with a role to play are the employment of subcontractors to carry out peripheral tasks and the development of flexible contractual terms. Because subcontractors are hired on a temporary or fixed-term basis, it is clearly less expensive to dispense with their services or to renegotiate new terms than is the case with established employees. However, the introduction of such outsourcing may itself reduce job security and increase the likelihood that individual employees will be made redundant. Over time, though, it can be accomplished without harming the prospects of current employees, as long as retraining opportunities are offered to those affected. In smaller, growing organisations such forms of flexibility can be developed as the business expands. Contractual flexibility also contributes by ensuring that an organisation is able to maximise its efficiency through reducing its inherent rigidity. Wherever possible, therefore, staff can be employed on contracts that do not define job content or hours of work too narrowly.

Early retirement is often an attractive way of reducing the extent to which compulsory redundancies are necessary. The Inland Revenue permits organisations to release people after the age of 50 with enhanced pensions, so in most cases such schemes apply only to employees who have reached that age. Many employees find it an attractive option, because it permits them to draw their occupational pensions early (if at a reduced rate) but also permits them to continue working elsewhere on either a full-time or part-time basis. In practice, they are made voluntarily redundant, but are better off financially than they would have been with a straightforward redundancy payment. In most cases the costs are met by using pension fund assets, and so do not have to be drawn from current organisational budgets. In theory, therefore, everyone benefits: the employer loses employees amicably and at low cost, the retiree leaves on acceptable financial terms, and fewer compulsory redundancies are needed from the ranks of other employees. Early retirement is, of course, an option only for organisations with an established occupational pension fund that has successfully attracted members from among its employees. For this reason, it is best categorised as a long-term activity that can help reduce the need to make compulsory redundancies. There is also a significant cost incurred to the pension fund, making it an option that is only realistic for employers whose funds are in surplus.

SHORT-TERM APPROACHES

The above preventative measures will not always have been introduced and will, in any case, often fail to prevent the need for compulsory redundancies. In these circumstances most employers will seek to minimise their number by using a range of other established tools and practices. The most common of these is to ask formally for volunteers, giving long-serving employees in line to receive substantial redundancy payments the opportunity to claim them. However, there are problems. First, this is often more expensive for the employer than when the employees to be made redundant are identified by management. Second, it often allows the most employable and valuable staff to depart, leaving less effective employees in place after the programme of redundancies has been completed.

In practice, the process of seeking volunteers is fraught with difficulty and has to be managed with great care if the many pitfalls are to be avoided. A common problem arises when too many people volunteer for redundancy, leading to a situation in which weaker performers appear to have been rewarded with redundancy while more valued volunteers are left to soldier on until they reach 65 (or whatever the contractual retirement age is). Such situations are common where redundancy terms are excessively enhanced in order to attract a pool of candidates. The result is demotivation among those required to stay on. Another problem relates to people's fear that their careers may suffer or that their relationships with line managers may deteriorate if they are known to have applied unsuccessfully for voluntary redundancy. This may deter people from applying in the first place, but can also lead to further problems of morale if the employee is kept on.

These and other problems can be overcome provided the volunteering process is carefully controlled and planned. The first decision to make involves establishing the coverage of the voluntary scheme. To whom is voluntary redundancy to be offered? Should it be to everyone in the organisation or just to selected grades or departments? Some organisations, particularly those having to effect large numbers of redundancies in a short period of time, will make a blanket offer to all employees, or may exclude only a few groups – such as people in jobs that are to remain and into which others could not be redeployed. Where the redundancies are restricted to limited areas of the organisation, however, it makes sense to target these alone so as to avoid raising expectations among those working in other areas.

It is also possible to target offers on individuals who are performing poorly and who have built up a number of years' service. This can be done by developing a package specifically designed to appeal to them, perhaps including early retirement options. Offers can then be made individually ahead of any general announcement, with a view to developing tailored settlements to suit those whom the organisation most wants to lose. Flexibility over the timing can also be discussed to increase the incentive to volunteer. The other approach is to use the stick as well as the carrot, by indicating that the people concerned are likely to find their jobs disappearing in the post-redundancy structure anyway. As with so much practice in this area employers need to keep half an eye on age discrimination law, but that should not be an insurmountable obstacle provided a clear business case can be advanced to justify a policy.

The next step is to establish the criteria for selecting candidates for redundancy from among those who volunteer. It is important that these are drawn up before the offer is made, in order to avoid raising the hopes of people whom the organisation has no intention of selecting. It can, for example, be made clear that those with good performance and attendance records, long service and valuable skills are unlikely to be selected. A general offer can then be made to all staff within affected departments, which will nevertheless deter from applying those who are still very much wanted.

Other approaches to avoid or minimise redundancies are rather more straightforward. Where there is several months' warning, it is possible to institute a general restriction on all recruitment of new employees. A vacancy in a post that will continue after the redundancy programme has been completed may be advertised internally and filled by someone at risk of redundancy. Another approach is to fill vacancies externally but to do so only on a fixed-term basis. If it is known that redundancies are likely in six months' time, new starters are hired on six-month contracts that can later be extended but that are occupied by people with no expectation of longer-term employment. Where the period is shorter than six months it is better to bring in agency staff or subcontractors.

A recruitment freeze effectively allows the organisation to minimise the number of redundancies it will have to make, as it allows the size of the permanent workforce to diminish by natural wastage. When redundancies are expected, individual employees will often take steps to look for other work in any case, and many will thus resign of their own accord rather than wait to see whether their job will survive the programme of staff reduction. This has cost advantages for employers, in so far as it reduces the number of redundancy payments, but it can be risky if more valuable employees resign, leaving the poorer performers in place.

A further means of reducing redundancies is to cut staff costs in general. The commonest approach is to cut or radically reduce overtime. The result is less pay for employees in return for greater job security. Other approaches include pay freezes and the abandonment of profit-based bonus schemes. Where negotiated with staff representatives, such methods of redundancy avoidance can be the most satisfactory. The reduction of non-pay costs can also be considered: for example, the area of office space can be reduced or less expensive premises rented.

AVOIDING REDUNDANCIES AT VOLKSWAGEN

In 1993, despite a 9 per cent reduction in the size of its workforce, the Volkswagen Group reported a fall in annual sales of over 25 per cent. Relatively inefficient systems of production, combined with high labour costs, had led to a situation in which the company was struggling to compete in international markets. At the start of 1994 it was calculated that, to rectify the situation, DM 2 billion had to be saved from production costs over a two-year period, the equivalent of making 30,000 employees redundant.

In the event, the company managed, by using other approaches, to achieve its cost savings without redundancies. The strategy was to lower production costs for two years while simultaneously introducing innovations in work organisation and production planning. The aim was to have the new production methods in place by the start of 1996, thus improving productivity without needing to make redundancies.

The two-year cost reduction programme had three elements:

- a temporary reduction in the working week to 29 hours, leading to a 10–12 per cent reduction in salaries

- giving younger workers part-time contracts for two years after they had completed their apprenticeships, and offering similar terms to all employees over the age of 55

- offering career breaks to employees to take up places in government-sponsored training establishments.

The trade union agreed to the terms within a month of the publication of the annual results in 1993. The size of the crisis facing the company meant that the workforce accepted the sacrifices as a means of avoiding mass redundancies.

Source: Garnjost and Blettner (1996).

The final approach is redeployment, or finding jobs elsewhere in the organisation for those whose jobs are redundant. This will often mean placing people in posts that are very different from those they currently hold, or relocating them different premises. Where there are flexibility or mobility clauses in the contract of employment, employers are able to redeploy people as they deem appropriate. If individuals refuse a reasonable offer of alternative employment in such circumstances, there is no obligation on the employer to pay a redundancy payment.

Where there is uncertainty about the suitability of a post, in law employees have the right to a four-week trial period before deciding whether or not to accept. A different situation arises where jobs are available elsewhere in the organisation but are thought unsuitable to offer to redundant workers because they are lower paid, of lower status or located hundreds of miles away. Employers should not make any assumptions about people's interest in or willingness to take up such jobs. All possibilities need to be explored before redundancies take effect.

KEY ARTICLE 43

Lea Waters, Experiential differences between voluntary and involuntary job redundancy on depression, job-search activity, affective employee outcomes and re-employment quality. *Journal of Occupational and Organizational Psychology*, No. 80, pp279–299 (2007)

This article, describing research into the impact of redundancy on the people who are made redundant, serves as a reminder as to just how major a negative effect it can have on people's lives. It also demonstrates that the impact of voluntary redundancy is a great deal less negative in practice than is the case with compulsory redundancy.

The research involved following a substantial group of Australian workers through redundancy, job search and into their next jobs. Various questionnaire-based tools were used to assess their perceptions of future opportunities, job security, retrospective job satisfaction and levels of depression.

Questions

1   How is the concept of the psychological contract useful in making a distinction between the perceptions of people made redundant voluntarily and compulsorily?

2   Why do people made redundant involuntarily continue to experience high levels of depression even after they have secured and started new jobs?

3   Why do they demonstrate less commitment towards their new employers than those who took voluntary redundancy?

4   What practical lessons can be learned from this research about making people redundant and hiring people who were formally redundant?

SELECTING PEOPLE FOR REDUNDANCY

The now-substantial body of case law on the selection of employees for redundancy is based on straightforward principles: that the employer, in choosing which staff to make redundant, must use criteria that are fair and objective. If this is judged not to be the case, the test of 'reasonableness' will have been failed and the dismissals will be declared unfair by an employment tribunal. Some selection criteria fall into the 'automatically unfair category'. If these are found to have been used, the tribunal will not even get as far as debating the issue of reasonableness. Automatically unfair criteria, as in all cases of unfair dismissal, include the following:

- a trade union reason (ie selection because an employee either is or is not a member of a trade union, or took part in trade-union activities or refused to take part)

- pregnancy

- sex, marital status, race, disability, sexual orientation or religion/belief

- as a means of victimising an employee who has asserted legitimate statutory rights.

Aside from these automatically unfair selection methods, many others are acceptable provided they are fair and objective. While 'last in first out' (LIFO) has traditionally been the most common approach, and is accepted as fair by tribunals, in recent years it has been used less frequently (only five employers taking part in an IRS survey continued exclusively to use LIFO – see IRS 2004i, p13). This is because managers have sought to use criteria that better distinguish staff with ability and potential. There is also a question mark over the lawfulness of LIFO systems as a result of the introduction of age discrimination law. Other commonly used methods include the following:

- skill or competence

- performance records

- attendance records

- record of conduct

- health

- qualifications

- age

- attitude.

While some of the above, such as attendance, are easy to verify objectively, others are not. How, for example, is it possible to judge an employee's attitude or commitment in an objective fashion? The answer, according to Fowler (1993, p108), is to ensure that there is evidence to back the decision and that the latter is not based on a subjective judgement and does not arise from a personality clash. He suggests that where a choice has to be made between two employees, and only one has volunteered for unpleasant tasks in the past or taken the initiative in a specific case, it will be reasonable to take that into account when deciding which person is to be made redundant. What is important is the presence of some kind of evidence (letters, reports, mentions in performance appraisal records etc) that could be used to show a tribunal that the selection was based on objective criteria.

The same care must be taken when using other methods. Attendance, for example, is a potentially fair criterion. Where there are grounds for believing that an employee's state of health is likely to lead to poor attendance in the future, it is reasonable to take that into account. What is important is that the judgement is made on objective grounds and can be justified if necessary at a tribunal. What is not acceptable is to single out one employee for redundancy on health grounds while failing to apply the same criteria to others. Moreover, it would be unfair to base a redundancy on a poor health record in past years where there was evidence that a full recovery had been made. Where the employee concerned falls under the definition of 'disabled' in the Disability Discrimination Act 1995, very great care must be taken in using attendance or estimations of future health as criteria. We will return to this topic at length in Chapter 19. Suffice it to say at this stage that it is unlawful to select a disabled person for redundancy for a reason connected to the disability.

According to the CIPD's *Guide on redundancy* (IPD 1996b), tribunals are increasingly looking with favour on points systems as a means of selection when redundancies are made. Such an approach involves taking into account a number of criteria from among those listed above and weighting them according to the perceived future needs of the organisation. Each employee within the group to be considered for redundancy is then scored against the others, and the employees with the lowest tallies are then selected. According to IRS (2004i, p14), the following criteria are commonly used:

- length of service

- qualifications/relevant experience

- disciplinary record

- attendance

- adaptability/flexibility.

Where such systems are used it is important, wherever possible, to avoid any perception of subjectivity. It must thus be decided at the beginning what points are to be awarded for what factors. So defined numbers of points must be awarded (or deducted from a base starting point) for each day of absence in a particular period, for numbers of GCSEs, for written warnings, for performance appraisal scores and so on. It is essential that everyone in the selection pool is treated the same way by being scored fairly against identical criteria.

A wholly different approach to the selection of staff for redundancy is to start by developing a new organisational structure, identifying which jobs will be present in the organisation after the redundancy programme has been completed, and which roles or duties those jobs will entail. This is the kind of approach used by organisations undergoing a planned downsizing operation, and has been used extensively in public sector organisations, as well as those that have been privatised. In such situations, the new structure is agreed and job descriptions and person specifications, or competency frameworks, drawn up for the jobs that remain. Where a job remains essentially unchanged and is currently undertaken by a single person, that person is then 'slotted in' and told that he or she will not be made redundant. Others then apply for the jobs in the new structure and, if necessary, undergo a competitive selection process. Where two or three jobs of a particular type are disappearing, to be replaced by a single job, the application procedure is 'ring-fenced' so that only those currently employed to undertake the roles in question compete for the new position. Those that are unsuccessful are then selected for redundancy. The advantage of this arrangement is the control that it gives managers over the selection process. Its great disadvantage is its effect on morale and teamworking, as employees compete with one another for positions in their own organisations. Of course, it remains the case that the selection criteria have to be both fair and objective, and capable of being justified in court if necessary.

REFLECTIVE QUESTION

Which of these approaches to the management of redundancy have you experienced or observed? In your view, which is least distressing for the individuals involved, and why?

BREAKING THE NEWS

Telling people that they are at risk of redundancy and then subsequently that they have been selected is a very difficult task. Except where very large redundancy payments are on offer, it is probably impossible to carry out this task without causing substantial disquiet. However, the stress suffered can be reduced with careful planning and by following a few sound rules. Rothwell (2000) suggests the following:

- make the process as transparent as possible

- keep people informed throughout periods of uncertainty

- plan any meetings with great care, anticipating questions and ensuring that you are fully aware of how selection criteria are to be applied

- hold one-to-one meetings as well as larger collective sessions

- choose a suitable time so that individuals are not faced with major responsibilities immediately after hearing the bad news

- arrange a follow-up meeting to discuss detailed matters a day or two after the meeting at which the news is broken.

KEY ARTICLE 44

Adrian Furnham and K. V. Petrides, Deciding on promotions and redundancies. *Journal of Managerial Psychology*, Vol. 21, No. 1, pp6–18 (2006)

This is a fascinating article. Its findings are not at all unexpected, but research questions are important ones that have rarely been asked, and the methodology used is unusual. The researchers put together 16 separate 'vignettes' of information about fictional employees which made reference to their intelligence, length of experience and motivation. Their gender was apparent from their names and their age indicated by their length of experience. 183 volunteer managers were asked to imagine that they were running their own company and employed the people described in the vignettes. They were then asked to rate them each according to a seven-point rating scale in terms of their suitability for promotion and the likelihood that they would be made redundant should such a situation arise.

Questions

1 Why do you think the managers might have rated experienced men more highly than experienced women, but unintelligent men more poorly than unintelligent women?

2 Why do people rate motivation more highly than intelligence or experience when thinking about who should be selected for redundancy?

3 What are the major strengths and weaknesses of the methodology adopted by these researchers?

PROVIDING HELP FOR REDUNDANT EMPLOYEES

One area of redundancy management in which the law does not intervene to any great extent is the provision of counselling and assistance to employees who are under notice of redundancy. All that the law requires is that such employees should be given reasonable time off work to look for a new position or to undergo job-search training once they have received notice of redundancy. However, because few cases have been brought, it remains unclear what exactly 'reasonable time off' means. At present, it depends on the facts in particular cases (eg the nature of the job, the extent of expected difficulties in finding comparable work and the need for retraining). That said, the survey evidence suggests that most large employers offer further practical assistance to employees who are going to be dismissed on account of redundancy, and many also provide counselling where necessary (see IDS 2001c, IRS 2004i).

According to Fowler (1993, pp181–184), there are two broad stages in counselling redundant employees. The first is helping them to come to terms with their fate and to understand the reasons. The second is future oriented, and involves helping them to see the future as an opportunity to make new plans for their careers. Although in practice both issues are dealt with together, the first is a prerequisite for the second. It is only when people have successfully 'put initial feelings of resentment, anger and fear behind them' that they are psychologically able to face the future constructively. For this reason, Fowler argues strongly that professional, trained counsellors should be employed to carry out this work. Where well-meaning but untrained people attempt to carry out counselling, the result is often counterproductive. If there are no trained in-house counsellors there is, therefore, a good case for hiring external specialists. The other great advantage of bringing in outsiders is the experience they have of dealing specifically with redundancy situations. Moreover, employees are more likely to open up and talk freely to outsiders than they are to colleagues who will be remaining with the organisation. Established employee assistance programmes (EAPs), should an organisation have them in operation, can obviously be used as providers of counselling services.

A number of employers also offer to provide services of a more practical kind for employees under notice of redundancy. These are usually known as outplacement or career consultants and specialise, on the one hand, in the provision of advice to individuals and, on the other, in running job-search courses or workshops for groups of employees. In both cases, the content of outplacement programmes covers similar grounds. The following is a typical list:

- sources of further employment
- options for part-time and self-employed work
- analysis of skills
- application forms or CV preparation
- interviewee skills
- advice about retraining
- salary negotiation.

Some outplacement consultants also operate as headhunters and are thus in a position to give more assistance than simply advice. This raises a potential conflict of interest, which may mean that the advice given is not sufficiently unbiased. The CIPD Code of Conduct for Career and Outplacement Consultants deals with this issue, along with others concerning the appropriate system of payment and the question of proper qualifications. Managers considering employing consultants should thus take note of the Code and make sure that potential providers adhere to its contents and are CIPD members.

Aside from formal outplacement and counselling, there are many other ways in which employers can give helpful and practical assistance to employees seeking new positions. First and foremost, they can offer more than just time off to look for a job by permitting the use of company facilities as well. Secretarial assistance can be given in the preparation of CVs and in other aspects of the job-search process; company cars can be used; and employers can waive any routine restraint-of-trade clauses that might otherwise prevent employees from working for competitors. Larger companies can offer retraining courses or pay for redundant employees to attend training events elsewhere. Managers can also get in touch with professional contacts and other employers in the area to see whether opportunities exist for those whose jobs are going.

Another option, as mentioned above, is redeployment to another location within the same organisation, if necessary with further training provided. Employees are more likely to show interest in such opportunities if allowances are paid to assist with removal expenses and if the career prospects are perceived as good. Employers also sometimes negotiate re-hire agreements, whereby ex-employees are employed as subcontractors or consultants after they have been made redundant. Again, such arrangements are unlikely to be attractive or feasible for most, but may prove satisfactory for some redundant employees. Another approach is the establishment of a recall arrangement, whereby employees are given advance notice of any jobs advertised at their old place of work following their redundancy.

The final area of support that employers often choose to give reflects the possibility that ex-employees will spend a period without work following their redundancies. For some, this will mean applying for state benefits and surviving with a greatly reduced standard of living. For others, such as those leaving with substantial redundancy payments, a period out of the workforce may be more welcome. In either situation, there is a need for psychological preparation and sound financial advice. Some organisations make funds available to employees to organise their own counselling or training in these areas. They might, for example, add a sum of a few hundred pounds to the final redundancy payment to fund individual financial advice. Others take a more proactive role, laying on courses covering benefit entitlements and investment for employees who are leaving without a job to go to.

REFLECTIVE QUESTION

If you were to be made redundant, what other forms of help and support would you like to have? Which of those described here would be of most use to you?

EXERCISE 18.2

GOOD AND BAD PRACTICE IN REDUNDANCY MANAGEMENT

People management

Read the article by Jane Pickard, When push comes to shove (*People Management*, 22 November 2001, pp30–35). This can be downloaded from the *People Management* archive on the CIPD's website (www.cipd.co.uk).

This article debates what exactly is good practice and bad practice in the handling of redundancies. It questions some of the commonly held views about good practice and reflects on the advantages that can be gained from taking extra care over how redundancies are planned and executed.

Questions

1   On what grounds does the article question the use of performance measures as the basis for selecting people for redundancy?

2   Is there a better alternative? If so what is it?

3   What different strands could make up a business case in favour of treating people as well as possible during a redundancy exercise?

REDUNDANCY PAYMENTS

Since 1965, the law has set out minimum levels of compensation to which redundant employees are entitled. In most cases, the rules are straightforward and have remained unchanged for 30 years. The main features as of 2008 are as follows:

- The amount due to redundant employees depends on their length of service with the employer.

- The calculation is based on the number of continuous years' service and the employee's weekly salary at the time the notice period expires.

- If the weekly salary varies, the average figure for the 12 weeks preceding termination is taken into account.

- Only completed years count.

- The maximum weekly salary that can be used as the basis for the calculation is determined by the government. At the time of writing (2008) it is £330.

- The maximum number of years' service that can be used as the basis of the calculation is 20.

- Only employees with more than two years' continuous service are entitled to redundancy payments.

- The formula for the calculation is as follows:

    - For every completed year between the ages of 41 and 65: 1.5 weeks' pay.

    - For every completed year between the ages of 22 and 41: 1 week's pay.

    - For every completed year between the ages of 18 and 22: 0.5 week's pay.

However, the statutory scheme is widely recognised as very much a minimum standard. The CIPD's guide on redundancy recommends that higher redundancy payments are made 'if at all possible, as the statutory sums are often too small to adequately compensate for the loss of a job'. The 20–year rule, combined with the £330 earnings limit, mean that the largest payment that employers are currently obliged to make is £9,900 – not a great deal for someone in his or her 60s with over 20 years' service. As a result, many have introduced more generous arrangements to ensure that those leaving are treated fairly. According to IRS (2004i, pp15–17), the ways in which improvements to the statutory package are made vary from organisation to organisation. Examples from their survey include the following:

- doubling the statutory minimum

- increasing the number of weeks' pay used in the calculation (often to one month per year of service)

- making additional ex gratia payments for each completed year of service (eg 5 per cent of salary per year)

- disregarding the statutory earnings limit.

There are rarely any problems in calculating and communicating the entitlements due to full-time employees with unbroken periods of service. However, difficulties often arise where work patterns take a less standard form and where periods of employment have been temporarily broken. Cases have also been brought over the question of what figure represents a week's pay. Is it just base pay, or are overtime payments and bonuses to be considered too? The law states that all contractual payments should be included but is silent on the question of what figure should be used as the basis of calculations where weekly earnings fluctuate from one month to the next. In such cases, tribunals are forced to look at the facts in each individual case with a view to establishing what is 'reasonable'. Another common problem occurs in the case of employees who have completed a number of years' service as full-timers but have then opted for part-time work. Unjust though it may be, at present employers are permitted to calculate redundancy compensation on the basis of the current part-time salary, thus disregarding however many years have been completed as a full-time employee. In all such cases it must be stressed that employers have the discretion to award more generous terms, and they often choose to do so as a means of avoiding additional unpleasantness and bad feeling.

The continued presence of age-based criteria in the calculation of redundancy payments is surprising given the introduction of age discrimination law in 2006. The opportunity was not taken at this time to amend the statutory minimum redundancy payments scheme simply because the EU directive covering age discrimination did not require this. Interestingly, however, the government specifically included in the age discrimination regulations the right for employers to retain schemes which are more generous than the state scheme and which mirror its key features.

REFLECTIVE QUESTION

What level of redundancy payments does your organisation pay? What are the reasons for calculating them in the way that it does?

MANAGING THE SURVIVORS

An important feature of the successful management of a redundancy programme is the attention given to those who remain employed in the organisation after the dismissals have taken place. Ultimately, the long-term success or failure of the redundancy programme depends on these people's ability to come to terms with new structures and working practices. In practice, as anyone who has experienced such a situation can verify, it is not always easy to bring about a soft landing. Like soldiers who have survived a bloody battle, employees left to run organisations in the absence of colleagues can suffer from strong feelings of guilt and shell shock. Added to this, it is likely that there will be some who would have preferred to take voluntary redundancy had they been given the chance, and who experience demotivation as a result.

The CIPD *Guide on redundancy* provides sound advice on approaches to managing these issues and reducing the likelihood that survivors will lack 'commitment, enthusiasm and initiative'. First and foremost, the guide stresses the need to manage the redundancy process in a fair and open way. Survivors are more likely to recover and look forward if they are satisfied that the dismissal of colleagues was truly unavoidable in the circumstances and was handled professionally. There is thus a need not only to select redundant employees fairly, to provide fair levels of compensation and to offer practical assistance, but also to make sure that these matters are communicated effectively to all employees, whether or not they are individually affected by the redundancy programme. Second, it is important that communication with staff is two-way and that managers respond to suggestions and criticisms from employees at different stages throughout the process.

The other emotion that survivors often display is fear, arising from concern that further redundancies will follow and that they may be next in line. If this is not dealt with, organisations will find that they have difficulty retaining the very individuals they most need to ensure future prosperity. Extra attention has to be given to reassuring employees of their value and continued employment prospects. The CIPD guide suggests that this is best achieved by line managers' putting time aside to meet employees individually both to reassure and to listen. Once more, two-way communication is vital to success.

THE MAZE PRISON REDUNDANCY PROGRAMME

Between 1998 and 2000, the prison service in Northern Ireland faced a very difficult P&D situation. As the 'peace process' proceeded, nearly all prisoners who were members of paramilitary groups were released, stage by stage, from the top-security Maze Prison. This meant the disappearance of 1,300 jobs out of a total workforce of 3,271 (a 40 per cent reduction). However the redundancy process was complicated by the fact that it could have been stopped and thrown into reverse at any stage should paramilitary ceasefires come to an end. Managers had to be prepared for this eventuality, but also needed to be mindful of their responsibility to run an effective prison service for the province over the long term.

In the event, mainly due to very generous redundancy packages provided by the government, around 200 more people volunteered for redundancy than was necessary. Unfortunately these tended to be the more senior and experienced officers, leaving the Service with a dilemma. Should it refuse some of the requests for voluntary redundancy (from senior people) while making compulsory redundancies among more junior staff? Or should it allow all those who volunteered to take redundancy and promote people into their roles? In the event the latter route was chosen, leading to a situation after 2000 in which many senior officers are newly promoted.

The opportunity was taken to restructure the organisation and to improve its record on managing diversity. A big investment in training was made and fresh blood brought in at all levels.

A substantial outplacement programme was used in the early stages of the process, involving families of staff as well as the officers themselves. Consultants provided this service over a two-year period, giving advice in workshops to 900 employees. The total cost of the redundancy programme, including payments, was £147 million – considerably over £100,000 per redundant employee. At that price, it could be argued, it is just as well that the programme has been judged a success.

Source: Johnson (2001b).

OTHER LEGAL ISSUES

As in many areas of resourcing practice, in the field of redundancy there is a great deal of relevant employment law that it is beyond the scope of this book to explore in detail. Readers are thus recommended to turn to specialised texts, such as those identified at the end of this chapter, for more detail on these topics. Here, therefore, we simply give a short description of a number of significant legal issues that P&D managers should be aware of when approaching the management of a redundancy programme.

COLLECTIVE CONSULTATION

The law requires employers to undertake meaningful consultation exercises with trade unions in situations where they are recognised and where members are under threat of redundancy. To that end employers have to disclose in writing to relevant trade union representatives the number of employees likely to be dismissed and details of the groups of employees at risk. Moreover, the proposed selection criteria must be outlined, together with the method that will be used in selection and the proposed redundancy payments. Where trade unions are not recognised employers are obliged to arrange for the election of workforce representatives to carry out the same function. Sufficient numbers must be elected to allow representation of all key groups who are to be affected.

The timescale for consultation is a minimum of 30 days where between 20 and 99 employees are to be made redundant, and 90 days if more than 100 are affected. Where fewer than 20 redundancies are proposed, there is still a requirement to consult, but not to any predetermined timescale and not on a collective basis. The consultation process has to be more than a formality. In other words, employers are required to seek agreement with trade union representatives on such issues as ways of minimising numbers and of mitigating the consequences.

INDIVIDUAL CONSULTATION

Irrespective of whether or not collective consultation is being undertaken, and additional to it, is the requirement on employers to undertake reasonable consultation with individual employees who are at risk of redundancy. Each should be seen formally, at regular intervals, during the weeks or months leading up to the redundancies. The purpose is to explore possibilities for redeployment, to allow the employees to comment on selection criteria or scoring processes, and to discuss ways of ameliorating the effects of the redundancies. Where proper consultation of this kind does not occur, it is possible for employers to lose subsequent unfair dismissal claims on the grounds that they have not met all the procedural requirements expected by the law.

NOTIFICATION

Whether or not a trade union is recognised, employers proposing to make 20 or more employees redundant are obliged to notify the Department of Trade and Industry (DTI) in writing. Standard forms are produced for this purpose and the timescales are the same as those for trade union consultation. The DTI also has to be informed which trade unions, if any, are involved.

THE NEED TO DISMISS

An important legal technicality is the requirement that employees have to be formally dismissed in order to qualify for the receipt of a tax-free redundancy payment. Employees who volunteer for redundancy must, therefore, not resign. Instead they have to express an interest in being made redundant and then must wait to be dismissed by the employer.

'BUMPING'

'Bumped' or transferred redundancies occur when an employee whose job is to be made redundant is given a position elsewhere in the organisation, leading to the dismissal of someone else. In other words, an occupant of a position whose own job is not being made redundant is dismissed in order to retain the services of an employee whose job is being removed.

The courts have ruled that such manoeuvres are potentially 'reasonable' where it can be shown that the business clearly benefits as a result. It is thus unacceptable to bump simply in order to find a job for a particularly liked person who would otherwise be redundant; it has to be shown that there are sound operational reasons to justify the action. Where that is the case, it is acceptable to pay a redundancy payment to the bumped individual, despite the fact that his or her job is not itself affected.

> ## MURRAY *ET AL V* FOYLE MEATS (1999)
>
> The question of whether or not bumping was a lawful practice has been the subject of much debate in legal circles, some cases suggesting that it was acceptable and others that it was not. In 1999 the House of Lords reached a judgment in a case called Murray *et al v* Foyle Meats, which appears to have settled both this and a range of other thorny legal issues.
>
> The Law Lords ruled that when faced with a situation in which it was not clear whether a dismissal was or was not for legitimate reasons of redundancy, tribunals should ask three straightforward questions:
>
> • Has the employee been dismissed?
>
> • Has there been an actual or prospective cessation or diminution in the need for employees to carry out work of a particular kind?
>
> • Is the dismissal wholly or mainly attributable to this state of affairs?
>
> If the answer to all three questions is 'yes', then it is a redundancy and the tribunal can proceed to consider the question of reasonableness (ie the manner of the dismissal, fairness of selection, procedure used and so on).
>
> This ruling suggests that bumped redundancies are acceptable in principle (ie are potentially fair reasons for dismissal). However, the procedures used and selection methods adopted must operate fairly in practice.

OFFERS OF ALTERNATIVE WORK

Where employees under threat of redundancy are offered suitable alternative work by their employer before they are dismissed and refuse to take the offer up, the employer is under no obligation to pay them a redundancy payment. Where redundancy payments are substantial, the suitability of the new job offer is often a contentious issue. Tribunals have tended to avoid applying general principles in cases of this kind, preferring to look at the facts and take into consideration the employee's reasons for rejecting the offer. Where the job is in the same location, pays the same salary, is of a similar status and is within the capability of the employee concerned, it is likely that a refusal to accept would be found unreasonable by a tribunal.

The law also provides for four-week trial periods to be offered to employees where new jobs are offered on terms different from those on which the previous contract was based. At the end the employee has to decide whether or not the work is suitable. Again, where an employee who has been given every assistance to settle into the new position resigns for trivial reasons, the employer is entitled to refuse the redundancy payment. Here, too, tribunals judge reasonableness by looking at the particular facts in each case rather than setting down hard-and-fast principles.

WAIVER CLAUSES

Until October 2002, staff employed on a fixed-term basis for one year or more could be required as a condition of their employment to sign contracts containing redundancy 'waiver clauses'. These then formed the basis of an agreement between employer and employee that there would be no liability for redundancy payments on the expiry of the contract. It was a standard and straightforward matter in most cases, but could become complicated when individuals were employed over a period of time on a succession of separate fixed-term contracts. In such cases each new contract had to be treated separately, a new waiver clause being signed at the time of each renewal. The right of employers to benefit from waiver clauses of this kind was abolished from 1 October 2002, but the old law still applies where fixed-term contracts were entered into before that date.

INDIVIDUAL CASES

So far in this chapter the topic of redundancy has been examined from a collective perspective. It has therefore been seen from the perspective of managers faced with decisions involving groups of employees. However, there are also occasions when individuals are dismissed for reasons of redundancy – situations that tend to be handled rather differently. Although the basic legal principles remain the same, there is no requirement to inform the Secretary of State, and the process may be managed in a less formal and standardised fashion.

This kind of situation arises when, for example, one member of a team has to be dismissed. Examples might be losing one teacher from a school when the number of pupils declines, or needing to dismiss one of a pool of clerical workers following the introduction of new technology. In such circumstances, the use of impersonal approaches, such as putting people under formal notice that they are at risk of redundancy and making them undergo highly formalised selection procedures, is too brutal. What is needed is a great deal more sensitivity and confidentiality.

First, where they are not already laid down in a redundancy policy, it is necessary to agree the selection criteria that will be used in choosing the individual to be dismissed. Instead of asking generally for volunteers, the next step involves privately approaching individuals who might be interested in taking voluntary redundancy and establishing whether or not this is the case. If no one expresses an interest in leaving, the individual to be compulsorily dismissed should then be informed and discussions carried out with him or her personally to explore alternative opportunities and the extent to which practical assistance can be given to help him or her find a new position. The principles of reasonableness are thus adhered to, just as in the case of collective redundancies, but the manner in which the process is managed is made more appropriate to the case of the individual concerned.

THE LAW ON RETIREMENT

Age discrimination law was introduced in the United Kingdom from October 2006. It included a great deal of quite controversial new law on the management of mandatory retirements. Within a few weeks the government's approach was challenged in the courts by a charity which campaigns for older people's rights called Heyday. At the time of writing (early 2008) their case challenging the legality of continued mandatory retirement under the terms of the relevant European directive is awaiting a decision from the European Court of Justice. This is expected in 2009 and until then the tribunal service has stayed all cases that have been lodged in the United Kingdom. Matters are thus unclear, and it is possible that the situation will change quite profoundly if the government loses the Heyday case. If that does not happen the following will continue to be the key legal requirements:

- It is lawful to dismiss at a set retirement age of 65 or higher, provided a statutory procedure is followed.

- Mandatory retirement ages between 60 and 65 can continue, but only if the employer can objectively justify them.

- There is a duty on employers to write to employees between six months and a year before they reach the retirement age informing them that they will be retired unless they exercise their right to request to continue working.

- If the employee replies requesting to work beyond the set date, the employer must give the request serious consideration, hold a meeting to discuss the matter with the employee if the request is not granted, give a final decision in writing within 14 days and allow an appeal.

- There is no list of reasons given in the regulations for legitimately turning down requests, so in theory an employer could simply make it its policy to mandatorily retire everyone at a set age.

- When a request is accepted it is possible for the employer to set a new retirement date and to go through the procedure again six months before the employee reaches that age.

The main reason that this is so controversial and unsatisfactory arises from the fact that at the same time that the new procedure was introduced, thanks to age discrimination law, the exemption that previously prevented people who were over 65 (or the normal age for retirement in an organisation if lower than 65) from bringing cases of unfair dismissal was abolished. Previously employers were encouraged to keep people on past 65 because it was so easy to dismiss them lawfully if, perhaps as a result of age, their performance or absence became problematic. Now that unfair dismissal law applies to all of whatever age, employers face the need to take people through lengthy capability procedures and to give warnings before they can lawfully dismiss someone who is over 65 and whose performance has begun to decline. However, at the same time a procedure which permits mandatory retirement at 65 with no good reason has also been introduced. Surely, the critics quite reasonably argue, the effect in practice is to encourage employers to dismiss at 65 when previously before the advent of age discrimination law they would have kept people on. In other words, the practical result of age discrimination law is to make it more rather than less likely that employers will mandatorily retire people.

EARLY RETIREMENT

Many larger employers offer employees the opportunity, if they so wish, to retire early. A survey undertaken by the CIPD (2003c) indicates that a clear majority welcomes the opportunity to take early retirement, and that very few choose to carry on working having made the decision to retire. Although people with private savings or personal pensions that have performed particularly well may be able to retire before their contractual dates, the term 'early retirement' is more commonly associated with membership of the employer's occupational pension scheme. Precise terms and methods of calculation vary from organisation to organisation, but most employers will in some circumstances pay a reduced pension to retirees who leave before the contractual retirement age. Where employees have accrued sufficient pension rights to provide a satisfactory income, such offers are very tempting – especially if there is a possibility of continuing to work on a part-time or consultancy basis.

However, in order to prevent a general exodus of highly valued employees, most employers also reserve the right to refuse requests for early retirement. Where the financial liability of the pension fund is increased by such arrangements, scheme trustees also have a right of veto. Where redundancies are in the offing, managers often improve the early retirement provisions somewhat in order to provide an incentive for older employees to take up the opportunity. In so doing, they reduce the number of compulsory redundancies, while much of the cost is shouldered by pension scheme funds.

XR ASSOCIATES

In 1991, in order to sweeten the incentive to take early retirement at a time when large numbers of redundancies were being made, Ford UK set up a consultancy company called XR Associates. It was unusual in that it was staffed entirely by ex-Ford employees over the age of 50 who had accepted offers of early retirement. In return, they were guaranteed 90 days' work a year on a consultancy basis with either Ford or one of its suppliers. After two years of operation, it was reported that XR employed 400 people, including a third of the managers who had left Ford in that period. By 1996 there were 600 consultants.

XR people work on one-off projects on behalf of the company, rather than simply working in their pre-retirement roles. They are paid daily rates at a level commensurate with the type of work undertaken. They can take as much or as little work as they please, some opting to work three or four days a week and others reducing their commitment to one day. The advantage for the company is the ability that it gives to call on experienced people with a knowledge of the business to undertake project work. This leaves full-time managers free to carry out day-to-day duties.

Source: IDS (1996, p17).

PREPARING EMPLOYEES FOR RETIREMENT

In her book on retirement, Phil Long (1981, pp38–50) puts a very good case for the provision by employers of effective pre-retirement training. Without it, she claims, employees often experience shock and prolonged depression when they suddenly find that they no longer have jobs to go to. The sense of loss and lack of purpose in life leads many to deteriorate mentally and physically:

> *The emergence from the world of work is as much a culture shock as the entry, yet in neither situation is there much preparation. The young school leaver, entering his or her first job, usually finds a supportive environment, however informal this might be. By contrast, the newly retired have to adjust to an equally novel situation unaided and for many the transition can be a difficult one. ... Three score years of being indoctrinated in the Protestant work ethic, which stresses the virtues and values of work, is no preparation for what should be a period in which to do one's own thing. Unfortunately few have been educated to use their leisure in a creative way.*

In France and in the Scandinavian countries, governments are actively involved either in providing or promoting pre-retirement training courses. In the United Kingdom, although some local authorities operate events of this kind, it is mainly up to employers to do so.

The contents of pre-retirement training courses appear to be fairly standard. In practice, there is usually a need to blend group-based training with individual counselling and advisory sessions. Wherever possible, spouses should be invited to attend along with the prospective retirees. According to Long (1981, p49), the following are typical issues to be covered:

* understanding pension provision

* taxation of savings

* investment of lump sums and annuities

* social security entitlements

* health and nutrition

* safety in the home

* developing leisure activities

* re-employment and part-time working

* moving house

* drawing up wills.

In addition, courses include sessions designed to help people to adjust psychologically to the idea of retiring. These involve explaining what difficulties might be encountered and suggesting approaches to managing the transition. Reynolds and Bailey (1993), in their book on pre-retirement training, give a good deal of attention to this topic and offer helpful advice for those delivering training of this kind. Drawing on their experience, they provide a depressing description of the emotional problems that people suffer when they are required to retire. However, they also show how it is possible to work through the initial feelings of shock, denial and depression in order to adjust and accept retirement as the new, normal state of affairs. Unsurprisingly, a major part of this process is the development of new interests and the revival of those left dormant during busy working lives. The taking-up of voluntary work or part-time paid work is also a possibility. By all accounts, one method of avoiding the psychological problems associated with retirement is to find ways of phasing it in over a period of a year or two. A number of larger organisations have well-established schemes of this kind that permit employees gradually to reduce their working hours as they approach the date of retirement. Ideally, in order to attract employees, such schemes should not involve too great a loss in income.

The importance of pre-retirement preparation is also stressed by Vickerstaff *et al* (2004), but their research among older people from three large organisations found that it tends to be offered rather too late to be of maximum value. They also found much support for the idea of 'downshifting' in the years immediately prior to retirement, but established that many employers and employees think that it is not a serious option due to its impact on subsequent pension entitlements.

POST-RETIREMENT CONTACT

The final area of activity that contributes to the smooth transition into retirement is the maintenance of formal contacts with the organisation. These can take a wide variety of forms. At one extreme, there is the continuation of an economic relationship, whereby the retiree is hired again, but on a casual or part-time basis, and thus continues to come in to work from time to time. For professional and managerial staff, an option is to work on a consultancy basis. In such cases the employee is freed from having to come into work at set times, but is still required to provide advice or to undertake specific projects.

At the other end of the scale is the organisation of social events. Where organisations operate social clubs or provide weekend trips, Christmas parties and evening functions for staff, it is possible to invite retired employees too. The larger, more paternalistic organisations go further, setting up benevolent funds for retirees in order to provide, or assist in the provision of, private health care, sheltered housing and holidays.

REFLECTIVE QUESTION

What formal contact does your organisation maintain with retirees? To what extent could greater use be made of retirees' skills and expertise?

People
management

EXERCISE 18.3

POSTPONING RETIREMENT

Read the following two articles featured in *People Management*. They can be downloaded from the *People Management* archive on the CIPD's website (www.cipd.co.uk).

- Roger Trapp, A life's work (6 May 2004, pp8–39)

- Rebecca Johnson, An idea past its sell-by date? (1 November 2007, pp26–39).

These articles cite several reasons for expecting many more older people to remain in the workforce in the future than has traditionally been the case. Examples are given of organisations that have offered flexible retirement options, or even abandoned fixed retirement altogether, and of the consequences.

Questions

1   What are the main factors that are making people more willing and able to work beyond the 'normal' retirement age for their occupation?

2   Why have some employers been reluctant to accede to requests from individuals to work beyond their normal retirement date while others have actively encouraged later retirement?

3   Why are employers still so reluctant to appoint new staff over the age of 50?

4   Think about an individual you know who was forced to retire at a certain age. What would have been the advantages and disadvantages from the employer's point of view of continuing to employ that person for some years?

KEY ARTICLE 45

Marjorie Armstrong-Strassen, Organisational practices and the post-retirement employment experience of older workers. *Human Resource Management Journal*, Vol. 18, No. 1, pp36–53 (2008).

This article starts with the premise that as the population in many countries ages significantly over the coming decades and labour markets tighten, organisations will need to attract older people into jobs (including those who are past normal retirement ages) and will also be keen to retain existing employees in employment until and beyond such ages. Using a large sample of older Canadian workers, the research described sought to establish how big an impact HR practices that are tailored to meet the needs of older people can have on decisions by people in these age groups to continue working or to return to work after retiring. The significance of other factors was also tested such as 'perceived fair treatment by the organisation' and 'perceived respect from one's work group'. The main finding was that HR practices are very important indeed as factors which influence people's decision about whether to retire and whether to return to work after having retired. Moreover, and significantly, it was not just HR practices in the fields of flexible working and reward that were significant. The whole range of 'good practice' approaches have just as big an impact in practice, including access to training and development opportunities.

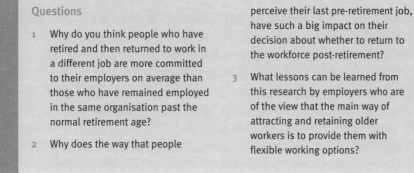

Questions

1   Why do you think people who have retired and then returned to work in a different job are more committed to their employers on average than those who have remained employed in the same organisation past the normal retirement age?

2   Why does the way that people perceive their last pre-retirement job, have such a big impact on their decision about whether to return to the workforce post-retirement?

3   What lessons can be learned from this research by employers who are of the view that the main way of attracting and retaining older workers is to provide them with flexible working options?

CHAPTER SUMMARY

- The introduction of age discrimination law in the United Kingdom in 2006 has had a substantial impact on the law and practice of managing redundancy and retirement.

- The term 'redundancy' is narrowly defined in UK law, limiting the number of situations in which people can claim a redundancy payment as of right. To qualify, a dismissal must derive directly from a reduction in the need for workers to carry out particular kinds of work.

- There are numerous ways that employers can seek to avoid making compulsory redundancies. These include recruitment freezes, asking for volunteers, offering early retirement and redeploying staff to new duties.

- In law, employers have wide scope to choose their own redundancy selection criteria. Provided the system is fair and objective, both in principle and operation, it will be acceptable to an employment tribunal.

- There is a statutory minimum redundancy payment calculated according to length of service and age. In practice the majority of employers offer terms that are substantially more generous. This leads to situations in which people are keen to be made redundant.

- Care must be taken when managing a redundancy programme to consider the future needs of survivors as well as those who will be leaving.

- Consultation on both an individual and collective basis is an expectation of the law on redundancy. A failure to consult meaningfully or to allow sufficient time for meaningful consultation will lead tribunals to declare the dismissals unfair.

- Under age discrimination law it is lawful to retire people mandatorily at the age of 65 or at some other later date provided a statutory procedure is followed.

- It is good practice and makes sound business sense for employers to take some care in preparing employees for retirement. Maintaining post-retirement contact, particularly in the case of long serving staff, is also recommended.

EXPLORE FURTHER

- Two excellent general texts covering all aspects of redundancy management are *Redundancy* by Alan Fowler (1999b) and *The successful management of redundancy* by Paul Lewis (1999). A good introduction to the issues, together with some critical analysis, is provided by Redman and Wilkinson (2006).

- Legal aspects are well covered in employment law handbooks and textbooks. The most up-to-date case law is described in the various loose-leaf subscription services covering legal issues. Incomes Data Services and Industrial Relations also regularly publish articles on redundancy law. A broad summary is provided by the CIPD's guide to redundancy handling written by lawyers from Hammond Suddards Edge (2003).

- Surveys and case studies looking at redundancy and retirement practices are published from time to time by IRS in *Employment Review* and by IDS studies. An excellent and quite extensive general survey of practice in the United Kingdom focusing on the legal aspects, but covering others too, by Simon Deakin and Frank Wilkinson was published in the journal *Labour* in 1999. Similar surveys covering practice in other major EU countries appeared in the same edition.

- Two publications on the preparation of employees for retirement are *How to design and deliver retirement training* by Peter Reynolds and Marcella Bailey (1993) and *Retirement: planned liberation?* by Phil Long (1981). The CIPD's 2003 survey of attitudes to ageing, pensions and retirement is a good guide to the perceptions and preferences of the working population (CIPD 2003c). Vickerstaff *et al* (2004) contains extensive analysis of qualitative data looking at the same issues.

- The impact of age discrimination law on retirement is covered effectively in the CIPD's *Managing age: a guide to good practice* (2007d) and by the IDS *Employment Law Supplement on Age Discrimination* (2006).

CHAPTER 19

Dismissals

Dismissing individual employees, however strong the justification, is undoubtedly the most difficult task that P&D practitioners are required to undertake. Since 1971, as the law of unfair dismissal has developed, it has become a task that can very easily lead to costly and time-consuming legal actions when carried out poorly. For both these reasons it tends to be an area of work that other managers have little inclination to take over. When carried out effectively, it enhances the reputation and authority of P&D practitioners in the organisation, raising their profile and giving them greater influence. By contrast, when carried out sloppily, the result is tribunal actions, bad publicity, ill feeling and even industrial action. It is thus a key skill for any aspiring P&D specialist to learn.

The unpleasantness of dismissal and the risks associated with carrying it out poorly mean that there is always a temptation to put it off or avoid taking action wherever possible. Yet this can often lead to greater problems at a later date. It is thus an area of P&D work requiring the exercise of considerable skill and judgement, as well as being a significant means by which P&D practitioners justify their role. Furthermore, dismissal and the disciplinary procedures associated with its management typically consume a great deal of time.

Inevitably, given its centrality to the topic, the law occupies much of this chapter – in particular, its requirements as to the handling of dismissals. In this field, recourse to legal action is very common indeed. Between 1 million and 2 million people are technically dismissed from their jobs in the United Kingdom every year (many through compulsory retirements), of whom around 10 per cent subsequently bring employment tribunal claims (Knight and Latreille 2000, National Statistics 2006, p11). This means that a majority of UK employers face unfair dismissal claims in any one five-year period, while a quarter find themselves on the losing side (IDS 1995a, p5).

LEARNING OUTCOMES

By the end of this chapter readers should be able to:

- manage the process for dismissing employees on grounds of ill-health or misconduct

- compile the documentation required in the dismissal process

- advise line managers and other colleagues about the major requirements of the law as it relates to dismissal

- distinguish between gross and 'ordinary' misconduct

- distinguish between unfair and wrongful dismissal.

In addition, readers should be able to understand and explain:

- the legal concept of 'reasonableness'

- automatically fair, automatically unfair and potentially fair reasons for dismissal

- the importance of following correct procedures when dismissing employees

- the role of the ACAS code of practice and the role that can be played by ACAS itself.

INTRODUCTION TO THE LAW OF UNFAIR DISMISSAL

The law of unfair dismissal in the United Kingdom dates from 1971, when it was included among a host of other measures in the Industrial Relations Act of that year. Although much of this legislation was later repealed, the measures relating to dismissal and the employment tribunal system have remained on the statute book and have developed over time as new regulations have been introduced and legal precedents set. For some time, the basic principles have been well established, and now form the basis of the manner in which dismissals are carried out by most employers. To an extent, therefore, it is possible to argue that best practice in this field is synonymous with the principles of the law. The only substantial way in which best practice and legislation part company arises from current regulations that exclude certain groups of employees from protection. By far the largest of these comprises employees who have completed less than a years' continuous service, but many casual workers, subcontractors and office holders are also excluded.

For these reasons, it is essential for anybody with responsibility for the dismissal process to gain a sound basic knowledge of unfair dismissal law. The best way of avoiding the time, expense and inconvenience of appearing in court to justify one's action in dismissing someone is to anticipate the consequences of that action and to make sure that there is no case to answer. This is why even though only a minority of P&D managers are ever called to give evidence to a tribunal, they should all be familiar with the relevant law and legal processes, and allow this knowledge to guide their actions.

When an employment tribunal is faced with a claim of unfair dismissal, and when it is satisfied that a dismissal has actually taken place, it is required to ask two questions:

- Is the reason for the dismissal one of the potentially fair reasons identified in law?

- Did the employer act reasonably in treating the reason as sufficient to justify the dismissal?

Only if the answer to the first question is 'yes' will the second even be considered. In other words, if it cannot be established at the outset that the dismissal has actually occurred for a bona fide reason, the employer's case will fail, and the tribunal will not get round to considering the issue of the employer's 'reasonableness'.

When reaching a judgment about the first question, the burden of proof is on the employer. The tribunal thus expects the employer's representatives to show that they dismissed the individual for one of the reasons laid down as fair or potentially fair in the relevant statutes. For the second question, the burden of proof shifts and becomes neutral, so that the tribunal considers the facts and makes its decision without requiring either side to prove its case. In employment tribunals, as in all civil courts, the standard of proof is 'on the balance of probabilities' and not, as in criminal courts, 'beyond reasonable doubt'.

FAIR AND UNFAIR REASONS

In considering the reason for dismissal, the tribunal has to decide into which of three categories a particular case can be classified. These are: automatically unfair, automatically fair and potentially fair. Only if it decides that the reason is 'potentially fair' will the second question (ie reasonableness) be considered. If it finds the reason to be either automatically fair or unfair it will reach an immediate judgment.

The list of automatically unfair reasons has grown over the years. At the time of writing (2008), it comprises the following:

- Dismissal for a reason relating to pregnancy or maternity.

- Dismissal for a health and safety reason (eg refusing to work in unsafe conditions).

- Dismissal because of a spent conviction.

- Dismissal for refusing to work on a Sunday (retail and betting workers only).

- Dismissal for a trade union reason.

- Dismissal for taking official industrial action (during the first 12 weeks of the action).

- Dismissal in contravention of the part-time workers or fixed-term employees' regulations.

- Dismissal for undertaking duties as an occupational pension fund trustee, employee representative, member of a European Works Council or in connection with jury service.

- Dismissal for asserting a statutory right (including rights exercised under the Employment Rights Act, as well as those connected with the Working Time Regulations, the National Minimum Wage Regulations, the Public Interest Disclosure Act and the Information and Consultation of Employees Regulations; the right to request flexible working, the right to time off for dependants, the right to adoptive, parental or paternity leave, the right to be accompanied at disciplinary and grievance hearings and the claiming of working tax credits).

- Dismissals that take place before the completion of the disciplinary and dismissal procedures (DDPs) required by the Statutory Disputes Resolutions Regulations (2004).

These last requires further explanation. The 2004 Dispute Resolution Regulations require employers to dismiss using a basic procedure. In most cases this will have three necessary steps:

Step 1:   The employer sends the employee a letter setting out the nature of the circumstances that may lead to the employee's dismissal.

Step 2:   The employer invites the employee to discuss the issue at a meeting at which both parties put their views across. After the meeting the employer informs the employee about the outcome. If it is a dismissal, then the right of appeal is confirmed.

Step 3:   The employee exercises his or her right to appeal and a further meeting is conveyed for this purpose.

In cases of automatically unfair dismissal, with the exception of these DDPs,, there is no one-year qualifying period, so the right not to be unfairly dismissed applies to all who work under contracts of employment from their first day of work. At the time of writing it is anticipated that the 2004 Statutory Disputes Resolution Regulations will be repealed in their entirety, probably from April 2009. So after that date we will return to a situation where by all dismissals for automatically unfair reasons apply from the first day of employment and thus do not take effect only once a year's continuous service has been completed.

There are now only two automatically fair reasons for dismissing employees. The first concerns situations in which employees take unofficial industrial action, by which is meant action that has not been sanctioned by a union executive. Effectively, employers have immunity from liability where a dismissal occurs directly as a result of unofficial industrial action. The other category of dismissals in which employers can dismiss automatically without breaching unfair dismissal law are those that relate to safeguarding national security. In most cases, this will apply only to certain government employees working in the intelligence services or armed forces, but may also conceivably be relevant to some private sector employers, such as those engaged in weapons production.

The vast majority of cases fall into the third category of potentially fair dismissals, and it is in these that the issue of the employer's reasonableness and the circumstances of individual cases become relevant issues. The law states that there are five potentially fair reasons: capability, conduct, redundancy, statutory restrictions and 'some other substantial reason'. A new category comprising dismissals taking place after eight weeks of official industrial action was effectively created in 1999, the period being increased to 12 weeks in 2004, and a further one comprising dismissals that take place for a reason relating to the transfer of an undertaking where an economic technical or organisational reason applies in 2006. The original five potentially fair reasons are defined below.

Capability

This term is defined broadly as encompassing skill, aptitude, health or 'any other mental or physical quality'. In other words, it is potentially fair to dismiss employees who, in the judgement of the employer, are incapable of carrying out their work because they are ill-qualified, incompetent or too sick to do so.

Conduct

Poor conduct or misconduct on the part of an employee is also deemed to be a potentially fair reason for dismissal. The most common instances involve absenteeism, lateness, disloyalty, refusal to carry out reasonable instructions, dishonesty, fighting, harassment, drunkenness and swearing.

Redundancy

This term relates to economic dismissals that meet the definitions laid down. They are discussed at length in Chapter 18.

Statutory restrictions

This category is intended to cover situations in which employers cannot continue to employ particular individuals in a job because they are legally barred from doing so. The two examples most frequently given relate to foreign nationals who do not have work permits (or whose permits have run out) and drivers who lose their licences.

'Some other substantial reason'

The final category has attracted criticism in so far as it is seen as being something of a 'catch-all', permitting employers to dismiss on a variety of grounds not covered by the other fair or potentially fair reasons. The question of how substantial the reason is in practice is a matter for the courts. Over the years the following reasons for dismissal have been included:

- business reorganisations that do not result in redundancies
- pressure from customers

- termination of temporary contracts

- staff mutinies

- misrepresentation of qualifications at interview.

REFLECTIVE QUESTION

What other cases have you come across that could be classed as 'some other substantial reason'?

REASONABLENESS

Having established that the reason for the dismissal is indeed one of the above 'potentially fair' ones, employment tribunals next go on to judge how reasonable the employer has been, given the circumstances of the case, in deciding to dismiss the employee concerned. It is thus on the issue of 'reasonableness' that most unfair dismissal cases hang. The following quotation from the Employment Rights Act 1996 sets out the approach that is taken:

> *The determination of the question of whether a dismissal was fair or unfair, having regard to the reasons shown by the employer, shall depend on whether in the circumstances (including the size and administrative resources of the employer's undertaking) the employer acted reasonably or unreasonably in treating it as a sufficient reason for dismissing the employee; and that question shall be determined in accordance with equity and the substantial merits of the case.*

For a number of years tribunals interpreted these words in different ways, but since the judgment in the case of Iceland Foods *v* Jones [1983] an accepted standard test has operated. Since that time, members of tribunals have not simply asked whether, in their view, the course of action taken by the employer was what they themselves would have done in the circumstances, but whether or not it fell within a band of reasonable responses. It is thus quite possible that a decision to dismiss might not be what the members of the tribunal believe should have occurred, given the facts of the case, but will nevertheless be found fair because the employer's action was one that fell within a range of approaches that could be considered reasonable.

In judging reasonableness, tribunals look at a number of factors relating to the individual and the organisation concerned. They will, for example, wish to satisfy themselves that the employer treats all staff alike in deciding to dismiss. Where it is shown that, in similar circumstances, an employer has acted inconsistently in dismissing one employee while retaining the services of another, it is likely that the dismissal will not be found to have been 'reasonable'. However, tribunals also like to see account taken of an employee's past record, especially in questions of conduct. This means that staff who have been employed for a good number of years and have impeccable disciplinary records are expected to be treated rather more leniently than colleagues with less service and records of poor conduct. Where relevant, tribunals will also investigate how far employers have sought to avoid the dismissal. Such matters are particularly associated with dismissals due to ill health, where there may be alternative jobs or duties that employees can carry out, even though they are no longer fit to undertake their existing job.

The size and relative resources of the employer concerned are also issues considered when judging 'reasonableness'. A large organisation employing hundreds of people will thus be judged against different standards from those expected of a small business employing half a dozen. In the former case, it would probably be unreasonable to dismiss someone who was sick but expected to return to work in five or six months' time. For a small business, by contrast, such an action might be necessary to permit it to continue in operation. Similarly, a large employer will have more opportunities than a small counterpart to find alternative work for an employee struck down with a serious illness such as multiple sclerosis or a severe neck injury.

The other major issue that tribunals are currently required to look at in judging 'reasonableness' is the procedure used. Since the landmark case of Polkey *v* Deyton Services Ltd [1987], the question of the procedure used to carry out the dismissal has become central to tribunal decision-making. Prior to that date, there were cases of tribunals' disregarding procedural deficiencies on the grounds that it made no difference to the final outcome – namely the decision to dismiss. At the time of writing (2008) thanks to the Dispute Resolution Regulations (2004) the position in respect of procedure is complex and not entirely clear. However, as of April 2009 when they are due to be repealed, we will return to the situation as set out in the Polkey judgement. In practice, this means that, in dealing with employees in matters of ill health, misconduct or poor performance, as well as redundancy and the other potentially fair reasons, employers are obliged to adopt the procedures recommended by ACAS in its advisory handbooks. Although these are not prescribed by law, they are still the yardstick by which tribunals now judge reasonableness, and so have formed the approach used by most employers. Moreover, employers will be found to have dismissed unfairly if they do not follow their own prescribed procedures in all significant respects.

The most widely used ACAS code is that concerned with discipline. The current version dates from 2001 and forms the model that employers are expected to follow when dealing with poor conduct, work performance and poor attendance. Based on the principles of natural justice, it includes the following basic features, the last of which is now a statutory requirement:

- Organisations should have written disciplinary procedures, and not handle cases on an ad hoc basis.

- There is a need to state who has the authority to take what action at each stage of the procedure.

- The procedure should clearly specify what employee action or lack of action will be treated as sufficiently serious for formal procedures to be invoked.

- Provision must be made for employees to be informed of the complaint against them and to have every opportunity to state their case.

- In the case of poor performance a fair-warnings system must be in place to ensure that employees are given at least one warning and thus the opportunity to improve before being dismissed.

- Provision should be made for a right to appeal, and an individual or committee should be specified to whom appeal may be made.

- Employees should have the opportunity to be accompanied at any serious formal hearing by a trade union representative or work colleague of their choice.

THE DISCIPLINARY CONUNDRUM

A problem for P&D practitioners managing disciplinary issues is how to resolve the tensions inherent in procedures such as those recommended by ACAS, tensions that pull in two very different directions. The problem arises from a situation in which the procedure is at once supposed to be both corrective in intent and also the mechanism by which lawful dismissals take place. Often the two aims conflict.

The problem is best illustrated with an example. A common situation is that of an employee who has become seriously demotivated (for whatever reason) and whose standard of performance drops. He or she starts arriving late, phones in sick on Mondays, ceases to complete work tasks on time and becomes a disruptive influence on other members of the department. In theory, such a situation needs action to be taken that addresses the employee's lack of motivation and seeks to provide new challenges and incentives. Giving a formal oral warning and setting attendance and performance targets is thus an inappropriate course of action, because it is likely to demotivate further. It may also lead to a breakdown in trust between the employee concerned and his or her line manager.

Yet any P&D manager who has seen many such situations in the past knows that, in all likelihood, there is no practical means by which the employee's level of motivation can be lifted. He or she is unsuitable for

promotion, has already alienated work colleagues and has formed an apathetic attitude towards training and development opportunities. There is thus a strong probability that this situation will lead to dismissal if the employee concerned does not voluntarily resign first. In order for the dismissal to be fair, and to protect the organisation from possible legal challenge, the P&D response is to start the disciplinary procedure.

Therein lies the problem. There are two conflicting requirements. First there is a need to meet with the employee formally, to inform him or her that he or she can be represented or accompanied by a colleague or union official, to warn that his or her performance is unsatisfactory, to give an opportunity to state his or her own case, and then to send a letter that confirms the outcome and informs the employee of the right to appeal.

Second, there is a need to find ways of looking forward positively, of offering opportunities, and of seeking to remotivate the employee concerned. In practice, this is fiendishly hard to achieve. The very act of setting up a formal hearing, particularly in the case of relatively senior staff, signals a breakdown in trust. However positive and helpful the managers present at the hearing try to be, invariably the fact that the procedure has started at all will have the opposite effect.

MISCONDUCT AND POOR PERFORMANCE

A common misconception is that an employer must always start disciplinary proceedings at the start of the ACAS-recommended procedure with an oral warning. In most cases, such as those involving poor attendance, persistent lateness, minor mistakes or instances of negligence, or failure to carry out legitimate instructions, this is indeed the appropriate approach to take. However, where more serious instances of poor performance or breaches of discipline occur, it is well within the definition of 'reasonableness' to start the procedure with a written warning, final written warning or even summary dismissal (ie dismissal without notice), when the circumstances are apt. This latter case occurs where the breach of discipline comes within the definition of 'gross misconduct'. There is no clear statutory definition of this term, and employers are within their rights to decide for themselves what is to be treated as gross misconduct in their own workplaces. Provided their list is broadly reasonable and provided people know that breaches may lead to summary dismissal, it is acceptable in principle to dismiss without notice on these grounds – provided, of course, that all employees are treated alike. These offences typically include the following:

- theft, fraud or deliberate falsification of records

- fighting or assault on another person

- deliberate damage to company property

- serious incapability through alcohol or drug use

- serious negligence causing unacceptable loss, damage or injury

- serious acts of insubordination.

This list is meant to provide examples, and is therefore not definitive or exhaustive. It does, however, indicate the degree of seriousness that an incident must reach if it is to justify summary dismissal. Whether or not misconduct is to be construed as 'gross' inevitably depends on particular circumstances. Drinking three pints of beer at lunchtime may not even qualify as any kind of misconduct in many jobs, but where someone works as a driver, dispensing chemist, or operator of dangerous machinery, it would in all likelihood justify summary dismissal. Similarly, depending on the job and organisation, careless breaches of confidentiality can either be irrelevant or highly damaging.

In practice, managers do not often find themselves debating whether or not an act of gross misconduct has occurred. That much is usually pretty clear. The problem is deciding whether the organisation's response should be to dismiss the individual or individuals concerned (which it would be within its rights to do) or to give written warning. Factors to take into account include whether it is a first breach of discipline, the nature of any mitigating circumstances, the extent to which the employee shows remorse, and their persuasiveness in stating that the offence will not be committed again. It is inevitable that subjective judgements come into play here, with employees who have potential, who are hard to replace or whose work is generally valued, treated more leniently than less-favoured colleagues. Provided there are genuine, defensible reasons for this, some inconsistency will be justifiable should the matter be raised in a tribunal. What is important is that these judgements be not clouded by personal likes and dislikes or grudges.

Procedure also plays a significant role in tribunal decisions concerning the reasonableness of dismissals for gross misconduct. It is not acceptable to fire someone in a fit of temper on the spot (however tempting that course of action can be on occasions). If the dismissal is to meet the legal definition of 'fairness', the following eight steps need to be taken:

1 Inform the employee or employees concerned that they are under suspicion of committing an act of gross misconduct.

2 State that a full and fair investigation will now take place to establish exactly what has occurred.

3 State that the individual(s) will be suspended on full pay while the investigation proceeds.

4 Inform them that a formal hearing will be held when the investigation has been completed, at which they have the right to be represented and will have every opportunity to state their case.

5 Formally investigate the issue, taking formal statements from any witnesses and keeping a written record of all relevant evidence.

6 Hold a hearing within five working days.

7 Put the case to the employee or employees and allow them to respond.

8 Make a decision either to dismiss or to take other action short of dismissal.

In addition to the above, organisations are expected to make provision for dismissed employees to appeal to a more senior manager, and to inform them of this right at the time of their dismissal.

Dismissals on grounds of poor performance are classed as being for a reason of incapability, but in practice they are dealt with in a very similar way to acts of ordinary misconduct (ie those that do not give rise to summary dismissal). In both case employers are required to give at least one warning prior to dismissal, and to allow the employees concerned sufficient time to show that their conduct or capability has improved. In cases of poor performance employers are expected to provide constructive assistance to employees in the form of training or additional support where to so would be reasonable. Only after these efforts have been made, and two or more warnings given is it safe to dismiss. Here, as with cases of gross misconduct it is necessary to hold proper hearings at which representatives can be present, and to allow some form of formal appeal.

WHITBREAD PLC *V* HALL

The significance of procedure in determining the outcome of unfair dismissal cases was firmly reiterated in the case of Whitbread *v* Hall (2001). This concerned the dismissal on grounds of gross misconduct of an employee who admitted falsifying stock control records. The reason was found to be one that was potentially fair, but the manner of the dismissal was unreasonable because there were deficiencies in the procedure adopted. The main problem here was the fact that the

same area manager both investigated the issue and subsequently conducted the disciplinary hearing herself. Moreover, proper consideration was not given to all the facts of the case. So the employer was found to have dismissed the employee unfairly even though he had openly admitted carrying out the offence. The employer appealed to the Employment Appeals Tribunal and then to the Court of Appeal. At all stages the applicant won his case.

KEY ARTICLE 46

Jill Earnshaw, Lorrie Marchington, Eve Ritchie and Derek Torrington, Neither fish nor fowl? An assessment of teacher capability procedures. *Industrial Relations Journal*, Vol. 35, No. 2, pp139–152 (2004)

This article reports the results of an extensive government-funded research project into the effectiveness of capability procedures established to improve the quality of teaching in English schools. The procedures follow ACAS guidelines, requiring head teachers to manage poor performance through a system of formal warnings combined with constructive assistance. For this project the researchers carried out over 500 semi-structured telephone interviews with head teachers and union officials from 13 different local education authorities. They found that the procedures rarely had the effect of improving performance, that they led to many teachers taking stress-related absence and that many, in practice, resigned.

Questions

1   What were the major reasons for teachers' performance being labelled 'unsatisfactory?

2   Why are formal capability procedures only used by head teachers as 'a last resort'?

3   In what different ways were capability procedures found to be unsatisfactory?

4   What suggestions are made for an improved approach to the management of poor performance on the part of teachers?

ILL-HEALTH DISMISSALS

Of all the tasks that P&D professionals have to undertake, by far the most unpleasant is to dismiss employees because they are no longer fit to work. It is particularly hard when the individuals involved are supporting other family members and when there is no possibility of providing financial assistance through a pension or other insurance scheme. Where it is believed that the illness is terminal, the process becomes even more difficult. However, that said, it remains a task that has to be carried out from time to time, and one that has to be done lawfully as well as sensitively.

It is very difficult to give any kind of general definition of 'reasonableness' in such cases, because the law requires above all that each individual case is treated on its own merits. However, the basic considerations are the following:

- Long-term illness is a potentially fair reason for dismissal.

- The decision to dismiss need not be taken on medical grounds alone. It is at root a management issue, which has to be determined against the background of the available medical evidence.

- Jobs should be kept open for sick individuals for as long as is practically possible wherever there is a reasonable expectation that they will be able to return to work in the foreseeable future.

- Sick-pay arrangements are wholly irrelevant. There is no right for an employee to have his or her job held open until sick pay ends, nor are employers permitted to dismiss at this point for no other reason than that no further payments are being made.

The decision to dismiss has thus to be taken in the light of individual circumstances and so cannot be determined by written policy. Where the employee's duties cannot practicably be covered by others, the employer will be justified in dismissing the sick employee in order to hire a replacement after a relatively short period of time. By contrast, where covering through the use of temporary employees, overtime or departmental reorganisation is possible, and where the employee's illness is believed to be long-term and yet temporary, the 'reasonable' employer is expected to keep the job open, and not to dismiss.

Such judgements are impossible without medical evidence, so tribunals expect employers to take all possible steps to obtain it. In most cases this is no problem, because employees have no objection to a letter of enquiry being sent to their GP or specialist. Indeed, they themselves will often provide copies of medical reports to their employers. However, employees are not obliged to do so, and are legally entitled to refuse their employer access to a report once it has been written. There are also situations in which doctors refuse to send reports to employers because they believe that to do so would be potentially damaging to the employee's health or chances of speedy recovery. Often these concerns arise when doctors do not wish their patients to see the full content of such reports. Employees who are sick can also be invited to see a company doctor or medical practitioner employed by an employer's occupational health service. Here too, though, they are under no obligation to attend.

From the P&D manager's perspective, the more information that is provided the better, but the tribunals only require that efforts be made to obtain that evidence. Often this will include formally warning employees concerned that their job is at risk if they do not co-operate. Where no medical evidence is forthcoming despite all reasonable steps being taken to obtain it, and the employer has good reason to believe the illness to be sufficiently serious to justify dismissal, the decision to dismiss will generally be held to be fair by a tribunal. Where it is written into contracts of employment that employees are obliged to submit to a medical examination when they are sick for a prolonged period, the issuing of formal warnings is more easily accomplished.

As in other cases of unfair dismissal, tribunals also pay attention to the procedural arrangements when judging the employer's reasonableness. In ill-health cases, they will look at how far the employer has kept in touch with employees during their illness, how far they have been consulted and informed about the possible consequences of their continued ill health, and whether or not colleagues or trade union representatives have been present at meetings. Here too there is a need, wherever possible, to give formal consideration to taking action short of dismissal. Among the questions that ACAS suggests should be asked are these:

- Could the employee return to work if some assistance were provided?

- Could some reorganisation or redesign of the job speed up a return to work?

- Is alternative, lighter or less stressful work available, with retraining if necessary?

- Could reorganisation of the work group produce a more suitable job?

- Could early retirement be considered, perhaps with an enhanced pension or an ex gratia payment?

- Have all possibilities been discussed with the employee and his or her representative?

To these could be added the possibility that a temporary replacement could be appointed on a fixed-term basis, or the suggestion that the employee works part-time or from home during convalescence. It may also be possible to offer help in bringing the employee in to work and taking him or her back home at the end of the day.

All the above are the kind of questions a tribunal will ask when judging reasonableness in a case of dismissal on grounds of ill health. These issues become a great deal more important where the dismissed employee is able to bring a claim under the Disability Discrimination Act 1995 (DDA). Compensation levels are often considerably higher in these cases, particularly where the individual concerned is unlikely to find new employment for some time. In these cases employers will be found to have discriminated unlawfully if they do not make 'reasonable adjustments' to working practices or the physical working environment to accommodate the needs of a disabled employee. The burden of proof in these matters is on the employer, although its size and resources are taken into account in judging reasonableness. For larger employers there is thus an expectation that wheelchair ramps and disabled toilets will be installed, that duties will be reorganised to allow a disabled person to occupy a post, that the employee concerned will be allowed to take more absence (eg to attend medical appointments) and in some circumstances will be allowed to work from home. In other words the law expects that employers will not prevent a disabled person from continuing to work unless it would be unreasonable to expect the required adjustments to be made.

The Disability Discrimination Act only applies where the worker concerned is judged to be disabled under the following rather complex definition:

> *has a physical or mental impairment which has a substantial and long-term adverse effect on their ability to carry out normal day-to-day activities.*

While certain medical conditions are excluded (such as hay fever, illnesses deriving from body piercing, and one or two socially undesirable mental conditions), almost any other impairment is included provided it leads to the loss of a key bodily function and prevents the sufferer from carrying out 'normal day-to-day activities'. This last requirement means that some people who consider themselves disabled do not qualify because their illnesses only prevent them from carrying out unusual activities. Under this legislation you are not disabled because you cannot play football, or ride a mountain bike, or lift very heavy weights, it must be standard daily tasks that cannot be performed. Importantly the expression 'long term' is taken to mean a condition that has lasted, or might reasonably be expected to last, for 12 months or longer. So it covers most serious illnesses, including conditions that return having lasted more than 12 months at some stage in the past.

Where someone is believed to fall into the category of 'disabled' under the terms of this Act, it is essential that great care is taken in managing their case. They should certainly not be dismissed without first consulting with them about possible adjustments that could be made to enable them to continue working in some capacity. No assumptions should be made about their willingness to work and serious consideration must be given to requests for reasonable adjustments to be made. Only once these possibilities have been discarded as clearly unreasonable is it safe to dismiss. Failure to do so is likely to lead to legal action that is a good deal more costly than typical unfair dismissal cases. DDA claims also succeed much more often in practice. In addition there are risks of attracting adverse publicity in the local press.

BRITISH SUGAR V KIRKER

The potential size of awards that can be made under the Disability Discrimination Act (1995) was illustrated in this case dating from 1998. Mr Kirker was selected for redundancy on grounds of poor performance and an assessment of his future potential performance. He argued successfully that these decisions were heavily influenced, in practice, by the employer's perception of his disability (he was visually impaired).

The tribunal agreed that there were good grounds to infer unfair discrimination on grounds of disability. He was awarded £103,146 (well beyond what can be awarded in unfair dismissal cases), partly to take account of the anticipated problems he would have finding new employment.

In some respects, greater difficulties are caused in situations where employees who are sick continue to come into work despite the fact that they are incapable of adequately performing their jobs. The problem is made worse when such staff have to take time off to undergo medical examinations or to be treated in hospital. In the case of a long-term sickness that results in poor performance and intermittent periods of absence, it is not always easy to judge under which procedure (misconduct, performance or ill-health) it should be managed. This is made all the harder when employees are unwilling to admit that they are seriously ill, for fear of losing their jobs. In such situations, the principles set out above are the same. There is a need to reassure the employees concerned and to deal with the situation as sensitively as possible but ultimately, if no recovery materialises, there is a need to take all reasonable steps to obtain medical evidence and to consider dismissing on grounds of ill-health. Again, provided the above procedural steps have been followed, the dismissal would be defensible at a tribunal, and a legal challenge would therefore be unlikely.

REFLECTIVE QUESTION

How far does your organisation follow the above principles in handling ill-health dismissals? In what ways could your procedures be improved?

OFFENCES COMMITTED OUTSIDE WORK

An interesting area of employment law concerns the response that employers should make when employees commit criminal offences that have no direct bearing on their work. As a general rule, the courts take the view that convictions of this kind should have no lasting effect on the individual's employment, and it is unfair to dismiss someone on those grounds alone.

However, exceptions have been made where courts have judged that the offence effectively breaches an employer's trust, or where potential harm might be done to the business if the employment was to continue. Examples have included acts of dishonesty, indecency and violence committed outside working hours and away from the premises. Dismissal may also be fair, provided no industrial action is threatened, where other employees find the individual's continued employment to be unacceptable.

Nor should imprisonment necessarily lead to dismissal, although in many cases it would amount to a breach of trust and confidence.

Where terms of imprisonment are short (eg for non-payment of a fine), where the disciplinary record of the individual concerned has been good and where the business can function without appointing a permanent replacement, there is a case for arguing that summary dismissal is unfair, both legally and ethically. In such cases, because the employee is known to be returning to work in a few weeks' time, the case should be treated as would an absence due to ill-health.

Longer terms of imprisonment are different. In most instances, even where there is no clear loss of trust and confidence, the contract of employment can be judged to have been frustrated by the inability of the employee to attend. Such is the case automatically after a six-month period. Dismissal is an option in such circumstances but unnecessary, as frustration of a contract renders the formal act of dismissal unnecessary. The law of unfair dismissal will thus not apply and the only legal challenge possible would be in the civil courts on the rather spurious basis that the contract had not in fact been frustrated.

DOCUMENTATION

As has already been made clear, it is necessary, in managing and carrying out individual dismissals, to bear in mind the possibility that a tribunal case might be brought. It is therefore important that affairs are dealt with in such a way as to ensure that, if the dismissed employee decides to launch a legal action, the organisation is well placed to defend it. In any event, where the dismissal has been carried out lawfully and the procedure used has been fair, the aggrieved employee will be less likely to take the organisation to tribunal. Making sure that the documentation associated with the dismissal is in order has a significant role to play in the deterrence process, because documentary evidence is crucial for a tribunal seeking to judge how reasonable the procedural aspects of the dismissal were. There is no point in undertaking all the necessary procedural steps if, at the end of the day, it cannot be shown that this actually occurred. Documentary evidence and the accounts of witnesses are the only means open to a tribunal to make such judgments, and documents tend to be rather more reliable.

Perhaps the most important document of all is the organisation's disciplinary procedure. Since 1993 all employers with more than 20 staff have been obliged to have a written disciplinary procedure, and to make it available to staff through incorporation in an employee handbook or inclusion among the various pieces of information that now have to be given to all new starters within two months of the beginning of their employment (see Chapter 13). If no such document exists, or if a dismissal has been carried out without adopting these procedures, the organisation will lose credibility in the eyes of a tribunal, and may not be seen to have acted 'reasonably'. Ex-employees could also quite honestly claim that they did not know what the procedure was and were put at a disadvantage as a result.

In practice, most organisations base their written procedures on that outlined in the ACAS advisory handbook entitled *Discipline at work*, although they may adapt it to meet local needs. In particular, the list of offences considered to be acts of 'gross misconduct' may be extended to cover the particular circumstances of the organisation concerned.

Other documents that it is important to draw up correctly are any letters sent to the employee prior to his or her dismissal. Here again there is a need to be able to demonstrate that the employee was made fully aware of his or her rights and of the consequences of future actions, and had been issued with clear warnings. The same is true in cases of ill health and in many of the occurrences that fall under the heading 'some other substantial reason'. It is necessary not only to keep employees informed of their rights and obligations, but to be able to prove that this occurred and thus that any dismissal was carried out with procedural fairness. To that end, employers are well advised to write to employees after any meeting or formal hearing, stating the outcome and the reasons for any decisions taken. Above all, there is a need for clarity so that there is no room for debate later about what was said. If the warning is final, it is vital that the letter confirming the outcome of the hearing states that such is the case.

In the ACAS handbook covering discipline there is an appendix that contains a number of example letters on which it is suggested employers base correspondence with employees who either are under threat of dismissal or have been dismissed. In each case the right to appeal is stressed and explained, as is the right to representation at any formal hearing. A suggested letter to be sent to doctors is also included for adaptation in cases of ill health. In the case of formal letters to employees, it is good practice to send two copies and to ask the member of staff concerned to sign one, stating that they have received it and understood its contents, before returning it. There is then no possibility of an employee's claiming later that no correspondence was received.

A further consideration to bear in mind is the right of tribunal applicants to 'discovery and inspection' of documentary evidence. This means that, in preparing their case, they have a right not only to ask only what documents exist but also to see any that are relevant, and to take copies. Where confidential matters are included, the tribunal chairman is given the disputed papers and makes a judgment as to whether or not they should be made available to the applicant. For this reason, care must be taken in compiling minutes of any meetings or hearings that took place, to ensure that their content is clear and not readily misinterpreted.

EXERCISE 19.1

AVOIDING UNFAIR DISMISSAL CLAIMS

People management

Read the article by Emma Grace, How to ... avoid unfair dismissal claims (*People Management*, 7 February 2002, pp48–49). This can be downloaded from the *People Management* archive on the CIPD's website (www.cipd.co.uk).

This article gives employers a simple checklist of actions to take and pitfalls to avoid when handling disciplinary cases. It stresses the importance of procedures and of being seen to have acted in a procedurally correct manner.

Questions

1   Why are employers who follow all the steps set out in this article less likely to face tribunal claims than those who do not?

2   In your view, should employers be able to defend themselves in situations when they have not followed the full procedure on the grounds that it would have made no difference to the final outcome?

3   Why has the organisation of the appeal stage become a more significant issue for employers than was the case until recently?

NOTICE PERIODS

One of the classes of information that has to be provided for all employees within two months of their start-date is the period of notice that they have to give their employer when they resign and that they can expect to receive if dismissed. This is not simply a matter for the contract of employment, because there are also minimum notice periods required by statute (Employment Rights Act 1996) linked to an employee's length of service:

- Continuous service of between four weeks and two years entitles the employee to a minimum of one week's notice.

- Continuous service of between two and 12 years entitles the employee to one week's notice for each completed year.

- After 12 years' continuous service the minimum notice period remains 12 weeks.

These limits apply wherever no specific mention of notice periods is made in contracts of employment. However, if the contract specifies longer (eg 12 weeks for everyone), then that overrides the statutory minimum and must be given, whatever the circumstances of the case. It is interesting to note that employees who resign voluntarily are required to give only a week's notice where no separate contractual agreement has been made.

There are two situations in which an employer can summarily dismiss an employee without notice. The first is where the dismissal results from gross misconduct of the kind discussed above. The second is where the employee has acted in such a way as to have effectively 'repudiated' the contract of employment. In most cases, these two categories overlap, but there are situations in which courts have found repudiation to have occurred even though it could not be said that the employee concerned had committed an act of gross misconduct. Examples include a sportswriter who publicly criticised his employers at a press conference, and a shop steward who made unauthorised use of a password to enter a colleague's computer.

In practice of course, with the exception of redundancies, most dismissals are intended to take immediate effect. Employees are thus not required to work the notice to which they are entitled. What usually happens is that employees are offered 'pay in lieu of notice', a lump sum covering the number of weeks to which they are entitled. The law accepts such payments as marking the end of the contractual employment relationship, and judges their receipt by employees as marking the effective date of termination.

In the case of more senior jobs, perhaps where the individuals employed have access to sensitive or confidential commercial information, it is not in the employer's interest to dismiss with pay in lieu of notice. To do so would immediately free the individual concerned of all contractual obligation and permit him or her to take up a post with a competitor within a few days or weeks of the dismissal. For jobs where this situation could arise, employers insert into the original contract of employment a clause that gives them the option of requiring the dismissed employee to take 'garden leave'. In practice this means that the employee, once dismissed, remains on the payroll during the period of notice but is not required to undertake any work. Instead he or she is expected to stay at home (gardening or undertaking some other pastime – hence the above expression) until the period of notice has been completed. Often this occurs where the employees concerned have held very senior positions and have been entitled to six or 12 months' notice.

UNFAIR DISMISSAL CLAIMS

As was mentioned in the introduction to this chapter, it is not at all unusual for organisations to have unfair dismissal cases launched against them by aggrieved ex-employees. The cost to the individuals concerned is very low, so they may feel that they have nothing to lose and everything to gain by bringing an action. At the very least, many hope to receive something by way of an out-of-court settlement, even where their case is comparatively weak.

Dismissed employees are required to make a claim in writing to the secretary of tribunals via their regional tribunal office. In cases of alleged unfair dismissal, the application must be received by the office within three months of the effective date of termination. A standard ET1 form must now be used to launch a claim. The tribunal officer then sends a copy of this form to the employer, who is required to issue a 'notice of appearance' within 14 days using the ET3 form. A notice of appearance states whether the claim is to be contested, and, if so, on what grounds. At this stage, all that is required is a brief statement of which statutory provisions form the basis of the defence, and not a detailed statement describing events surrounding the dismissal. That said, the notice of response is significant because, once completed, the grounds of any defence cannot easily be changed. Employers who later embellish their 'stories' to present at tribunal will invariably be asked why they did not make reference to new salient points at the time that they completed their ET3. Failure to provide a good explanation suggests unreliability and will not impress the tribunal.

The next stage involves the setting of a date for the hearing and the preparation of cases. In many circumstances this will be preceded a case management discussion with an employment judge (formerly tribunal chairman) at which arrangements for the exchange documents, schedule of loss and witness statements are determined. The purpose is to clarify beforehand the issues about which there is a dispute, so as to reduce the length of time the hearing actually takes. Where the crux of the matter is clear and the issues in dispute straightforward, tribunals will proceed to a hearing without the need for lengthy 'pleadings' of this kind.

In practice, most cases brought never get so far as a hearing, either because they are withdrawn or because they are settled out of court beforehand. Intervention from officers employed by ACAS facilitates most withdrawals and settlements, making their role crucial to the way the system operates. The conciliation arm of ACAS becomes involved as a result of its statutory duty to seek settlements between parties before cases are formally presented before a tribunal. All ET1 applications and notices of response are copied to ACAS, together with other relevant documents, to allow officers to judge the prospects of reaching such a settlement. Where they decide to proceed, they contact the parties, review the strength of the respective cases, and then either advise one party to withdraw or seek to negotiate a financial settlement. Of the cases received by ACAS for conciliation, fewer than a third actually go on to a full tribunal hearing. Where agreement between the parties is reached in this way, it is deemed binding in law only where it has been confirmed in writing. ACAS provide a COT3 form for this purpose.

QUALIFICATIONS AND REMEDIES

All those who have been employed for a period of a year or more by the organisation from which they are dismissed have the right not to be unfairly dismissed, and are therefore able to bring a tribunal case against their former employers. There are a few exceptions (eg, crown employees, police officers, and some domestic servants) but, in most cases, provided the individual is an employee and not a self-employed contractor, the same statutory rights apply. There is also a need to have been employed continuously for a year without contractual breaks. Only when the reason for dismissal is one of those classed as 'automatically unfair' is there no one-year qualifying period.

In cases of unfair dismissal, where a tribunal finds in favour of an employee, a number of options is open to it by way of remedy. First, it can require that the applicant is re-employed either in the same position (re-instatement) or in a comparable one (re-engagement). However, in practice, this occurs in only a handful of cases, because the vast majority seek compensation. In determining the sum the applicant is to receive, tribunals make two distinct calculations: the basic award and the compensatory award. The first is calculated in the same way as a statutory redundancy payment (see Chapter 18), taking into account the salary level and the length of service of the individual concerned. To this is added the compensatory award, which seeks to take account of losses sustained by the employee as a result of the dismissal. At present (2008) there is a ceiling of £9,900 on basic awards and £63,000 on compensatory awards, but in practice average awards in cases of unfair dismissal fall well below these maximum figures. In 2006/07 the median figure was only £3,800, in part reflecting the way that tribunals reduce the value of compensation to reflect any contributory fault on the part of the applicant. The cost to the employer thus derives less from the award itself, and more from legal costs and management time expended in the preparation of a case.

The one-year qualifying period, together with the statutory maximum payments and the restricted way that compensation is calculated, has been criticised on the grounds that it tips the balance of justice heavily in favour of the employer. Prior to 1999 a two-year qualifying period was required, but back in 1970s it was only six months. The reasons for the continued requirement to have completed a full year's service remain controversial. The major reasons given are, first, the belief that less than a year is too short a period of time for employers to determine whether they wished to employ someone over the long term, and second, the belief that employment protection legislation increases unemployment by acting as a deterrent to employers' considering the employment of new staff. In both cases, it was concern for the needs of small and growing businesses that most appears to have influenced government thinking over the years (see Davies and Freedland 1993, p561). Despite these arguments, many disagree with the qualifying period and maximum penalties. It can thus be expected that campaigns to change the law in these areas will continue.

REFLECTIVE QUESTION

What is your view about these issues? What effect would a return to the pre-1980 regulations have for your organisation?

THE ACT OF DISMISSAL

There is no definite right or wrong way to inform people that they are being dismissed, because the circumstances of each case are very different. In cases of gross misconduct, the news may well come as a shock to some employees, while in other cases, where a lengthy procedure has been followed, the response is more likely to be anguish. Employees may become abusive, but such cases are relatively rare.

Whatever the circumstances, this is a difficult and cheerless task. Some of the general rules to follow are these:

- Prepare for the meeting at which the dismissal is to take place very thoroughly.

- Be certain of the facts of the case and the precise reasons the decision to dismiss has been arrived at.

- Organise practical matters such as pay in lieu of notice before the meeting takes place.

- Consider in advance the likely reaction of the individual and prepare an appropriate response.

- Talk to employees concerned firmly but sympathetically. It is important that they understand that the decision is final, but they should be given as much practical assistance in planning for their future as is possible. Where the services of outplacement specialists would be helpful, consider offering these.

- Wherever possible, avoid the need for employees to leave immediately. There is nothing more humiliating and liable to cause ill-feeling than being frog-marched off the premises like a criminal when there is no intention on the employee's part of causing damage or removing company property.

EXERCISE 19.2

LIFTING THE CAP

Read the news article by Zoe Roberts, Lords call for unfair dismissal review (*People Management*, 29 July 2004, p8). This can be downloaded from the *People Management* archive on the CIPD's website (www.cipd.co.uk).

In this article is explained that the Law Lords expressed concern about the cap of £55,000 on compensatory awards that then applied in cases of unfair dismissal. The cap (£63,000 in 2008) means that some victorious claimants who have lost out financially by much higher sums can not be recompensed. To gain more by way of an award they are required to take a separate claim to the county court or High Court alleging breach of the implied term of contract known as 'trust and confidence' (see Chapter 13).

Questions

1   Do you think that employees who are dismissed unjustly should have the right to claim for injury to feelings, as is the case in discrimination cases?

2   What arguments could be advanced for leaving the cap on compensatory awards at £63,000?

3   Why is the cap on unfair dismissal awards described in the article as being 'a political hot potato'?

KEY ARTICLE 47

Sue Corby, Unfair dismissal disputes: a comparative study of Great Britain and New Zealand. *Human Resource Management Journal*, Vol. 10, No. 1, pp79–92 (2000)

In this interesting article the author describes her in-depth comparative study of the different aspects of unfair dismissal law in the United Kingdom and in New Zealand, where it is known as 'unjustified dismissal'. She shows how the two systems are similar, while pointing out the main differences and their practical impact. The article concludes with a discussion about how the UK system might be improved were some aspects of the New Zealand approach to be adopted.

Questions

1   How do the UK and New Zealand systems compare in terms of:

- accessibility?
- speed?
- informality?
- potential cost to the claimant?
- likely outcome?

2   To what extent do you agree with Sue Corby's recommendations as to how the UK system might be improved by taking on some features of the New Zealand system? Why?

WRONGFUL DISMISSAL

In some situations, employees who do not qualify for unfair dismissal rights or who believe they should receive more by way of compensation than is permitted under unfair dismissal law can choose instead to sue their ex-employers for damages under the law of wrongful dismissal. Until 1994 such cases could be heard in the civil courts only, requiring considerable expenditure on the part of the applicant. However, since then jurisdiction over claims worth up to £25,000 has passed to employment tribunals, making the wrongful dismissal route more attractive.

Cases of wrongful dismissal differ from those of unfair dismissal in that they do not rely on statute. The question of how reasonably an employer has acted is thus not at issue. What matters is whether or not the dismissal contravened the terms of the employee's contract of employment. The court is thus asked to rule whether the employer was entitled to dismiss the employee for a particular reason in the way that occurred, given the nature of the particular contractual terms agreed.

There are two situations in which someone who has been dismissed might choose to sue for wrongful rather than unfair dismissal. The first is where the employee, for whatever reason, does not have the protection of unfair dismissal law. This might apply to people with less than a year's service, people whose continuity of employment has been temporarily broken and people over the age of 65. Second, it might apply in cases where the damages that could be gained might reasonably be expected to exceed those likely to be offered as an unfair dismissal award. An example would be a highly paid person who was summarily dismissed and whose contract entitles him or her to three months' notice.

However, no claim of wrongful dismissal can be successful unless the terms of the contract of employment have been breached by the employer. In practice, this can happen very easily, because many employers explicitly incorporate disciplinary procedures into all contracts. In some cases, it is the contents of an employee rulebook or staff handbook that are incorporated; in others it is the terms of collective agreements with trade unions. Often these documents include lists of offences that may be considered to constitute gross misconduct, rules for selecting people for redundancy and details of ACAS-type disciplinary procedures. Where that is the case, any employee of whatever age, whether or not he or she has a years' continuous service, can expect the terms of the contract to be honoured. If he or she is then dismissed in contravention of those terms, there is a possibility that there will be a sound case under wrongful dismissal law.

BEST PRACTICE

As has been shown, in most situations best practice in the field of dismissal is effectively defined by law. It is thus only at the margins that employers seeking to implement 'best practice' approaches across all fields of employee resourcing activity can improve on the legal requirements as far as procedure is concerned. Perhaps the only major area where improvement can be made is in applying the same principles to all employees regardless of length of service or age. In making it clear that everyone will be treated according to the ACAS code from the very start of their employment, an employer extends the principles of natural justice to all, and could claim to be going as far as it is possible to go in treating employees fairly when conduct or capability are in need of improvement.

That said, best practice in dismissal should not be concerned just with procedural matters; the manner in which the procedures are operated is also important. Employers could therefore look at improving the training of managers in these fields, at the clarity of documentation and at ways of improving the investigation stage of any enquiry.

Moreover, in the field of dismissals on account of ill health there are a number of improvements that can be made on the statutory requirements. Here it is a question of handling matters sensitively and seeking to give as much practical and financial assistance as is possible. No employer who terminates contracts in these circumstances without making appropriate and adequate provision for a sick employee's future, either through a pension scheme or other funds, can reasonably claim to be operating 'best practice'.

CHAPTER SUMMARY

- The law of unfair dismissal is firmly established and effectively sets the standards to which organisations must adhere when dismissing employees. Legal action in this field is easy and inexpensive to take. It is therefore very common and is something that most employers are used to dealing with.

- Unfair dismissal law defines certain reasons for dismissal as being 'automatically unfair'. Where one of these is found to be the principle reason for a dismissal, the applicant wins the case irrespective of the circumstances. Employers effectively have no defence to deploy. The reverse is true of automatically fair dismissals.

- Potentially fair reasons for dismissal comprise the most common reasons that people are in fact dismissed. They include misconduct, incapability and redundancy. In these cases the employer wins the case if it can satisfy the tribunal that it acted reasonably in the manner in which it carried out the dismissal. Consistency of treatment as between different employees and the procedure used are important factors taken into account by tribunals.

- Acts of gross misconduct can lawfully lead to summary dismissal. Of particular importance here is whether or not the individual concerned knew that his or her actions might lead to dismissal on grounds of gross misconduct. Ordinary misconduct comprises offences such as lateness, rudeness or a minor breach of an employer's rules. In such circumstances summary dismissal is unreasonable. Warnings must be given before dismissals take place.

- Capability dismissals that relate to poor performance also require warnings to be given. Those that concern ill health are more complex requiring judgments to be made about the likelihood of a recovery. Particular care must be taken where the individual concerned falls within the purview of the Disability Discrimination Act.

- Tribunal awards in cases of unfair dismissal are typically quite modest. But a great deal of management time may be expended in defending a claim, and there are legal costs to pay where professional advice is taken. Poor publicity can also result.

EXPLORE FURTHER

- There are many books on the market that offer a straightforward guide to unfair dismissal law. Good starting points are *Employment law* by Deborah Lockton (2006), *Employment law in context* by Brian Willey (2003), *Employment law: an introduction* by Stephen Taylor and Astra Emir (2006) and *Essentials of employment law* by David Lewis and Malcolm Sargeant (2007).

- More detailed treatments by specialist lawyers and academics are found in *Labour law* by Simon Deakin and Gillian Morris (2005), *Unfair dismissal: law* *practice & guidance* by Michael Duggan (1999) and *Labour law* by Stephen Anderman (2000).

- The law in this field develops at a fair pace, often rendering books more than year or two old out of date. Readers are therefore advised to turn also to journals for details of new legislation and case law. *People Management*, *IDS Brief* and IRS *Industrial Relations Law Bulletin* regularly include guidance notes focusing on key legal issues geared for practitioners rather than lawyers.

CHAPTER 20

Demonstrating added value

In Chapter 1 it was argued that P&D professionals add value for their organisations in two distinct ways:

- by carrying out an important and necessary set of organisational tasks to a higher standard and/or at lower cost than can be achieved by competitors

- by contributing directly to the achievement of specific organisational goals.

The first involves striving to achieve excellence in the management of ongoing core P&D activities; the second involves participating directly in the formation and realisation of organisational strategy. Both are equally important if the P&D function is to be respected, valued and influential within an organisation. Inability to add value in either of these ways means that the P&D function is failing in its chief purposes. The consequences are a lack of credibility and respect from other managers, difficulty in securing resources for programmes, and a questionable future existence.

Much of this book has focused on the tools, techniques and ideas that are available on the resourcing front to enable P&D professionals to add value in one of these ways through the attraction and retention of good people, the maximisation of their performance, the facilitation of change and proficient administration. Increasingly, however, commentators rightly argue that merely achieving added value is not enough. In order to gain and retain organisational influence, P&D people need to be able to demonstrate the significance of their contribution. It is therefore necessary to evaluate what is achieved in terms of 'added value' in hard, credible terms that are readily understood and accepted by managers, shareholders and influential observers such as financial analysts and other opinion formers. The best performers in the field of employee resourcing not only make a valuable contribution to their organisation's success, but can also show that they do so. Robust evaluation also provides a basis for future performance improvement, by providing the means for us to track the outcomes of our activity over time. It is with these issues that this chapter is concerned.

LEARNING OUTCOMES

By the end of this chapter readers should be able to:

- collect and manipulate resourcing data for the purposes of demonstrating added value

- assess the scope, costs and benefits of resourcing programmes

- measure the effectiveness of resourcing activities in the fields of recruitment, selection, performance management, absence and turnover reduction

- monitor the outcomes of resourcing activities to ensure continued business relevance

- distinguish between different types of evaluation criteria

- explain the role played by the major methods of evaluation used in the resourcing field.

In addition, readers should be able to understand and explain:

- the importance evaluating resourcing interventions effectively

- debates about human capital measurement and reporting

- the role played by evaluations of effectiveness, efficiency and fairness

- evolving practices in the evaluation of P&D interventions.

THE CASE FOR FORMAL EVALUATION

Accurate evaluation of the P&D contribution to organisational performance has always been a problematic notion. This is because so many of the outcomes are intangible and not readily measured. They are also complex and difficult to isolate from other initiatives in terms of their impact. How, for example, is it possible to measure meaningfully the value gained by an organisation through sponsoring an aspiring P&D professional through a CIPD course? The cost in terms of fees, materials and time off for study runs to several thousand pounds, but what is the payback for the organisation and over what timescale is the investment recouped? The truth is that it is impossible to calculate in monetary terms with any degree of accuracy. The answer in any case will vary from individual to individual and organisation to organisation, and will depend on the type of circumstances that arise. The problem is illustrated when we try to list some of the likely outcomes that should derive as a result of completing a course in people resourcing:

- costly tribunal cases avoided

- improved selection decisions

- better-targeted recruitment campaigns

- reduced absence levels

- improved work performance

- fewer early leavers

- more effective redundancy management.

Some of these (such as staff turnover and absence) are readily measured and expressed in cost terms, but others result from a range of activities being carried out in the organisation by many people. It is very difficult to isolate the impact of the CIPD course and calculate its value with any degree of accuracy.

However, the fact that evaluation cannot be perfect should not stop us from formally reviewing our activities in terms of their contribution, from tracking progress over time, comparing performance with other organisations and from seeking wherever possible to quantify the value that is added. Maximising the credibility of the P&D function is one outcome, but there are also more direct advantages that can accrue for the organisation as a whole, particularly in industries that are knowledge-intensive and rely very heavily on effective employee performance to achieve competitive advantage. In such industries, according to Becker *et al* (2001, pp8–9), investment decisions, and hence the value of the company's shares, are increasingly made on the basis of non-financial information. Analysts who advise investors are interested in the relative ability of organisations to attract and retain talented individuals, to manage change well, to develop professional management systems and to innovate effectively. There is thus a good case for formally evaluating organisational performance against such indicators, for expressing the results in a readily understood manner and for disseminating them widely.

Non-financial indicators of organisation performance can play a direct role in public sector organisations too, especially where they are competing for contracts with private sector counterparts. Local authorities and government departments, for example, will look at an organisation's P&D policies and practices when deciding to which organisations (private or public) they are going to award contracts. Ministers and local politicians do not want to be found to have paid large sums of public money to organisations that turn out to be providing low-cost services on the back of unprofessional people management practices. They are thus interested in recruitment and selection policy, will look for evidence of effective human resource planning, and have a preference for organisations that maintain accurate personnel records. They also want to be assured that their suppliers are acting lawfully, so human resource expertise is also in itself a substantial asset for organisations operating in these areas of activity.

REFLECTIVE QUESTION

To what extent does your organisation formally evaluate the impact of its P&D activities? What about the core people resourcing activities? How far does any information gathered inform future policy developments?

HUMAN CAPITAL REPORTING

In recent years a great deal of interest has been developing in the idea that public companies should be required by law to report annually on their human capital as well as giving the detailed financial information that is currently included in their annual reports. In other words, in addition to reporting publicly each year on the value of physical assets and their profit and loss for the financial year, specific types of information about their people should also be included so as to allow shareholders and potential investors to make judgements about how effectively the organisation is managed. The case was summed up by the CIPD's former director general, Geoff Armstrong (2003), as follows:

> We have seen huge corporate failures where rigorously measured, audited and apparently conscientiously managed firms have gone bust because they have focused too narrowly on their drivers of value. Although it is well known that by far the highest proportion of stock market capitalisation is in intangible assets – mainly people and brands – companies have sleepwalked to disaster by using only traditional accounting measures. The impact that human capital can have on markets is huge. In advanced economies the only distinctive asset that cannot be imitated easily is the skills, talent and know-how of people. Now is the time to move beyond the rhetoric of 'people are our most important asset' and start developing processes that effectively measure and report on the contribution of that asset.

While this idea is easily expressed and the arguments for its adoption compelling, there remain problems with putting it into practice. How exactly can 'human capital' be accurately measured and reported on in any kind of standard format to permit inter-company comparisons?

Answers to this question have been provided by two important recent reports. The first, published in 2003, was that of the Accounting For People Taskforce chaired by Denise Kingsmill. You can download this free of charge from the website (www.accountingforpeople.gov.uk). Here it was argued that it was impractical to require organisations to publish the same types of 'indicators or metrics' about their human capital, but that a measure of consistency could nonetheless be achieved if directors were required to set out in annual reports details of their approach to human capital measurement and their understanding of links between this and their businesses' performance. The second report put flesh on these bones. This was published by the CIPD's own human capital taskforce in 2003, and included within it a 'Human Capital External Reporting Framework'. While accepting the need to avoid rigid requirements about what data to disclose, the taskforce suggests four headings under which relevant information should be provided:

* acquisition and retention of people

* learning and development

* human capital management (refers principally to general HR policies and strategies)

* performance.

In each case, it is argued, directors should give a narrative statement explaining how the company approaches these areas of activity, and the report suggests several statistical indicators that could be used to back up the points made in these statements. The framework can be downloaded free of charge from the CIPD's website (www.cipd.co.uk/changeagendas) and was published in *People Management* (26 June 2003, pp44–45). An example that has great relevance to people resourcing activities is as follows:

Acquisition and retention

Narrative:	How the firm sources its supply of human capital: composition of the workforce in terms of diversity and employment relationships (full-time, temporary and so on). Policies for the retention of key skills.
Primary indicators:	Average number of vacancies as a percentage of total workforce per month/year. Ratio of internal to external recruitment for job vacancies. Salaries and benefits costs – breakdown by full-time and temporary worker costs. Average length of time taken to fill vacancies. Staff turnover – averages for different levels of management and employees.
Secondary indicators:	Composition of workforce in terms of age, sex or race. Costs of recruitment. Length of service distribution (eg percentage less than two, ten and twenty years). Return on human capital (profits/payroll and training costs). Evidence of skills shortage or shortfall of skill between what is required and that possessed by job applicants.

For some time it looked as if the government would be legislating to require disclosure of human capital measurements of this kind, at least for the larger companies listed on the London Stock Exchange. The Kingsmill Taskforce report was welcomed by the secretary of state for Trade and Industry, and many commentators assumed that in a few years time human capital reporting would become standard practice. However at the time of writing (2008) it appears that the hopes of the proponents of forced disclosure have been dashed.

Company annual reports published since January 2006 have had to contain a mandatory operating financial review (OFR) which is intended to give an overview of the company's position, including information about its objectives, its strategy, its past performance and its future prospects, including information on brands, research and development activity, market position and relationships with stakeholders such as customers, suppliers and employees'. However, OFRs fall well short of requiring any detailed disclosure of human capital measurements as were recommended by the Accounting for People Taskforce. In order to comply in practice, companies are able to make quite bland statements about people being important to them and setting out their total headcount. The government says that it intends to review how effectively the OFR system is working – including human capital management reporting – in 2010, after the new system has bedded down (DTI 2004), so the debate about compulsory disclosure continues for now. Of course this means that individual organisations, whether they are publicly listed companies or not, can still opt to measure their human capital systematically and indeed benefit from disclosing the information to potential investors. Several, including Unilever, the Royal Bank of Scotland and the RAC have already taken this decision (Brown 2004, p38).

REFLECTIVE QUESTION

The government appears to have been effectively lobbied by corporations that were concerned about the consequences of mandatory reporting requirements in the human capital field. What arguments do you think would have been advanced by opponents of human capital reporting? Why do you think they were successful in persuading the government to water down its original proposals?

LESSONS FROM *JAMIE'S KITCHEN*

EXERCISE 20.1

Read the article by Harry Scarbrough, Recipe for success (*People Management*, 23 January 2003, pp32–35). This can be downloaded from the *People Management* archive on the CIPD's website (www.cipd.co.uk).

This article uses the example of the television programme *Jamie's Kitchen* to illustrate the way that human capital is developed. It goes on to report on research that suggests human capital measurement is more significant to some organisations than others and takes very different forms in different industries.

Questions

1   Why has the idea of human capital taken so long to become established? Why is it still resisted or disregarded by so many managers?

2   Why do some firms focus their human capital measurement processes on all employees, while others focus on specific groups such as managers or people of unusually high talent?

3   To what extent do you agree with Harry Scarbrough's conclusion that elaborate measurement systems are 'of little use' to organisations that rely very heavily on individual skills and to those whose competitive advantage derives principally from their tangible assets?

KEY ARTICLE 48

Juanita Elias and Harry Scarbrough, Evaluating human capital: an exploratory study of management practice. *Human Resource Management Journal*, Vol. 14, No. 4, pp21–40 (2004)

This article draws on interviews carried out in 11 case study companies, all UK-based, aimed at establishing what approaches to human capital reporting are used in practice. In the absence of any legal requirement to publish the outcomes of evaluation exercises, organisations were found to have designed there own systems intended purely for internal use. As a result a substantial variety was found in the type of approaches used and their underlying purpose.

Questions

1   Why is accurate human capital evaluation so difficult to achieve in practice?

2   Explain the difference between approaches to human capital reporting which have a 'talent focus' and those which have a 'customer focus'.

3   What is the practical impact of human capital measurement and reporting on the HR function in organisations?

EVALUATION CRITERIA

The first step in setting up formal systems of evaluation is to determine exactly what criteria we are going to use to evaluate the performance of resourcing activities. Several different approaches are available, none of which are mutually exclusive. No one approach is better than the others and there is thus a good case for undertaking evaluating activity using a variety of different criteria.

EFFECTIVENESS, EFFICIENCY AND FAIRNESS

At root, the evaluation of most core resourcing activities involves answering three basic questions:

- Are we doing what we are doing as effectively as possible?

- Are we doing it as efficiently as possible?

- Are we doing it as fairly as possible?

The first question concerns the fulfilment of organisational objectives in the resourcing field. It involves asking how far in practice an intervention, activity, policy or practice achieves what it sets out to achieve. It also leads to consideration of possible alternative methods that might achieve the same set of objectives more effectively. In Chapter 14 we set out the various approaches that are available when faced with a case of poor performance. None is more effective than the others in general terms, but there are circumstances in which a particular approach could be expected to yield more effective results. For example, an organisation that tends to take a disciplinary route may well find that it achieves better and faster outcomes using counselling or coaching techniques where the source of a performance problem lies outside the workplace.

The second question recognises that effectiveness cannot be the only measure used to evaluate HR activity and that value-for-money considerations also need to be taken into account. It is often the case that the most effective approach is a great deal more expensive than viable alternatives. A Rolls Royce may be a very reliable, comfortable and attractive car, but there are far more economic means of getting from one place to another without losing too much by way of effectiveness. The same is true of resourcing practice. In Chapter 12, for example, we described the assessment centre as the Rolls-Royce of selection methods, a claim backed up by research findings over many decades. However, it is also the most expensive. Widespread use of assessment centres in an organisation may well lead to the selection of a highly effective workforce, but the costs involved are so great (both directly and in terms of management time) to make the method unfeasible for use in the selection of most staff.

In most areas of organisational activity, effectiveness–efficiency trade offs are all that managers have to consider when carrying out formal evaluations. However, in the P&D field a third criteria – fairness – is of equal importance. This is because effectiveness and efficiency can readily be undermined where people perceive a practice to operate unfairly. An example can be found in Chapter 18, where we discussed alternative methods of selection for redundancy. Using the 'last in first out' method may be effective, in that it reduces the workforce by the required number swiftly and consistently, retaining the services of the most experienced people. It is also the most efficient method, being straightforward, easily administered and resulting in the lowest level of redundancy payments. Nevertheless, it may also be perceived by the workforce as being thoroughly unfair, leading to hard working younger people losing their jobs, while others who would happily take voluntary redundancy remain employed.

Fairness needs to be considered as an evaluation criterion for two good business reasons, irrespective of its role in an ethical approach to the management of people. First, it clearly plays an important role in meeting legal obligations. Discrimination law is evidently based on the concept that all should be treated equally irrespective of personal characteristics that have no necessary effect on work performance (such as sex, race, disability or trade union membership). The concept of fairness is also central to unfair dismissal law with its expectation that employers will operate fair procedures when disciplining employees, and will adhere to the principle of consistency when dealing with different individual cases. Employers who do not act fairly are thus very much more likely to lose employment tribunal cases than those who do. More importantly, they are also much more likely to find themselves faced with the need to appear in front of a tribunal in the first place.

The second reason for evaluating activities in terms of their fairness concerns the effect that unfairness has on employee motivation and commitment. The surest way to raise staff turnover, reduce job satisfaction, increase absence, lower productivity and engender low trust relationships at work is to pursue policies that are inequitable. Management perspectives on the relative fairness or unfairness of a practice are unimportant here. All that matter are employee perceptions. There is thus a need for practices not just to be fair in their operation, but also to be seen to be fair.

UNINTENDED CONSEQUENCES

When undertaking formal evaluations it is also useful to consider a fourth issue, although it will apply rather less often than effectiveness, efficiency and fairness. This involves asking whether or not there are any unintended consequences of a P&D intervention that serve to undermine its effectiveness, efficiency or fairness. It is possible that a particular programme or policy achieves effectiveness, efficiency and fairness when judged purely on its own terms, but has some form of knock-on effect that requires attention.

The most common examples are programmes that work well in the short term, but have unintended longer-term consequences that cancel out the initial benefits. An example given by Becker et al (2001, p47) concerned a bank where a decision was taken to shift gradually from full-time to part-time working for basic customer service roles. Not only was this cheaper in terms of the overall budget, but it afforded greater flexibility and allowed the bank to tap into a growing supply of women seeking part-time work. However, while cost savings and performance improvements were achieved initially, over the longer term the policy was judged to have been damaging. This was because the part-time workers appointed were not on the whole interested in moving up into full-time supervisory roles. Moreover, in moving to part-time working the bank had run down many of 'the training and development opportunities that had historically prepared tellers for promotion'. The result was considerable difficulty over time in finding people who were both able and willing to take on more senior roles. The bank had to recruit from outside for the first time, paying higher salaries to attract people and spending a great deal more on their training and development. The long-term result was increased payroll costs.

FORWARD AND BACKWARD-LOOKING CRITERIA

A criticism that is often made of traditional financial measures of organisational activity, such as annual reports to shareholders and sets of accounts, is that they reflect past performance rather than future potential. It is possible to use reports of past performance to make assumptions about the future, but more information is needed in addition for any kind of realistic assessment to be made. Becker *et al* (2001) use the terms 'lagging' and 'leading' indicators to describe the distinction between two approaches to evaluation of organisational performance, arguing that many P&D measures are effective 'leading indicators' that provide information about likely future performance.

In practice, proper evaluation of an organisation's P&D performance makes use of both forward and backward-looking criteria. Data on past performance needs to be collected and reported regularly, allowing progress to be tracked, problem areas identified and action plans formulated. In this way past evaluation data becomes the platform for improved future performance. An example would be the collection of information on voluntary staff turnover levels in different departments or business units, as shown in Table 20.1. This shows us that retention rates are improving over all, but that the pattern varies in different parts of the organisation. The data also suggests that dramatic improvements have been made in one department (D), while another (E) has seen its situation worsen. The reasons for these trends can be investigated and any lessons learned applied more generally.

Table 20.1 Voluntary staff turnover rates by department (annual %)

Dept	2003	2004	2005	2006	2007	2008
A	15	12	19	16	15	15
B	25	23	20	21	17	16
C	11	10	9	11	12	10
D	23	26	25	10	9	9
E	17	17	15	18	20	20

Future-oriented evaluation usually takes the form of a cost–benefit analysis. Past data, together with management judgement, is used to establish the likely outcomes of particular interventions such as a new supervisors' training course, the introduction of psychometric tests or an attendance incentive scheme. Wherever possible these outcomes are then expressed in financial terms and the total compared with the costs of carrying them out. Methods of costing staff turnover were described in Chapter 17, while other matters such as recruitment and selection costs are readily calculated. Using this kind of data it then becomes possible to make the following kind of analysis. This is a simple example of a new two-day work experience programme for 100 school leavers being proposed by a large department store. The students will attend in small groups over a three-week period. It is anticipated that ten students will be recruited into permanent jobs (half the number of vacancies currently available) as a result of the programme and that turnover in the first year among this group will be half that of colleagues recruited through newspaper advertisements (20 per cent as opposed to 40 per cent).

Costs

Management time (3 hours per student @ £14.50 per hour):	£4,350
Staff time (5 hours per student @ £6.00 per hour):	£3,000
Administration/set-up costs:	£700
Food and drink (2 days @ 3.75 per student per day):	£750
Clothing/laundry costs @ £2.50 per student:	£250
TOTAL COST:	£9,050

Benefits

Reduction in recruitment cost (estimated at £14,000) by 50%:	£7,000
Reduction in turnover costs (estimated at £2,500 per leaver):	£5,000
Total benefit:	£12,000
Balance = £12,000 – £9050 =	£2,950

To that figure could be added additional sales resulting from positive publicity and benefits gained from the presence of effective performers in the workplace in future years. Figures for these benefits are not readily calculated, but it is possible to argue intuitively that they would accrue. The future-oriented evaluation can thus be confirmed as positive, making a decision to go ahead with the programme readily justified. It will pay for itself (and more) over the course of a year.

QUANTITATIVE EVALUATION CRITERIA

As a means of demonstrating added value and progress over time, and of making comparisons with other organisations, the favoured approach is the use of quantitative criteria. These are readily understood, clear and unambiguous measures of performance on a range of P&D indicators. Some are also readily and meaningfully expressed in financial terms as in the previous example. Between them, the major books written about evaluating HR interventions list hundreds of examples (see Holbeche, 1999, pp64–65; Becker *et al* 2001, pp62–75; Cascio *et al* 2008). Some types of quantitative information are easily collected and calculated using a straightforward personnel information system. The following examples relate specifically to the employee resourcing issues covered in this book:

- voluntary staff turnover rates
- absence rates
- accident rates
- average speed with which vacancies are filled
- candidate acceptance rate
- proportion of recruits from ethnic minorities
- proportion of staff who have been formally appraised in the past 12 months
- number of tribunal cases fought
- overtime worked in the past year
- number of formal grievance/disciplinary hearings.

A second category comprises measures that use this and other classes of data to create ratios of the kind used by accountants to evaluate financial performance. Examples such as the following can be expressed in terms of cost. The standard approach is to use a measure of 'full-time equivalents' rather than the crude number of employees working under part-time and full-time contracts.

- profit generated per employee in the past year
- sales per employee in the past year
- recruitment cost per new recruit
- labour costs as a proportion of total costs
- absence costs as a proportion of staff costs
- voluntary turnover costs as a proportion of staff costs
- HR department costs as a proportion of total costs.

A third category comprises quantitative data that is not usually collected as a matter of course in organisations, so it requires the development of evaluative tools such as questionnaires. These can either ask for opinions or test knowledge. Examples are as follows:

- proportion of employees who are satisfied with their work

- proportion of employees who are satisfied with their supervision/management

- proportion of employees who consider the employer to act ethically/equitably

- proportion of employees who are clear about organisational goals/objectives

- proportion of employees who are clear about their own objectives/goals.

The final category of measures relates to the HR function itself and how effectively it is rated by users in the organisation. Examples are as follows:

- proportion of employees who are aware of the content of HR policies on recruitment, diversity, absence and the like

- satisfaction rates among managers with the services and advice provided by the HR function

- knowledge among managers of key HR policies and objectives.

REFLECTIVE QUESTION

Can you think of any other quantitative evaluation indicators that would be useful to set as key criteria in your organisation? Which would you estimate were the most important in terms of their contribution to organisational performance?

QUALITATIVE EVALUATION CRITERIA

Qualitative evaluation is less helpful than the quantitative variety when it comes to demonstrating in a very clear, crisp way that objectives are being met and value being added.

It is nevertheless useful to carry out for a number of reasons. Its major advantage is that it helps to provide explanations of why objectives are not being fully met and thus can form the basis of future improvements. Quantitative evaluation might, for example, show that 75 per cent of employees are uncertain of their personal objectives for the current year. Such a statistic would be a matter of concern for P&D specialists in an organisation that practised objective-based performance appraisal, but as a raw figure it can do no more than cause concern. It is only through qualitative evaluation, undertaken through questionnaires or focus groups, that a clear and objective view can be formed about why the appraisal system is working poorly and about what could be done to improve it in the future. Second, qualitative evaluation provides more detail and so helps an organisation to gain a far richer understanding of processes and perceptions than is possible using basic quantitative measures. It is only through the use of qualitative approaches that the real reasons for high or low employee absence rates in different departments can be understood. The reasons may be complex, hard to articulate, mixed together or changing over time. Quantitative evaluation rarely provides information about these factors, so it needs to be backed up with qualitative approaches.

Third, it is possible to argue that the results of qualitative evaluation can themselves be used effectively as part of the process by which the performance of the P&D function is formally reported. Qualitative evaluation may not allow ready comparison of different units within an organisation, or with external competitors (as is the case with quantitative data), but it is nonetheless a useful tool that serves to back up key messages and to add background colour to the numbers-based data. An example might be the formal evaluation of a new 360-degree appraisal system of the type described in Chapter 15. A questionnaire can be sent out to managers and employees asking them to rate the scheme according to their own experience in quantitative terms. The result would be interesting and useful data on the extent to which the exercise had in fact been carried out, its usefulness as perceived by appraisers and appraisees, and how far specific objectives set for it had in fact been met. All this would be expressed in terms of proportions of employees and managers agreeing with certain statements or ranking elements of the system on five-point scales. The following year a similar exercise could be carried out and the scores compared in some kind of formal report. However, the inclusion of additional qualitative information gathered from the questionnaire would help to give meaning to the quantitative data. Particularly well-articulated responses could be used to sum up the views of a large group of respondents, adding to the credibility and effectiveness of the evaluation exercise. Hence feedback such as the following might be included in the evaluation report:

I found the experience of being appraised using the 360-degree system unsettling but useful. It drew my attention to certain weaknesses of which I had not been aware and which I am now addressing.

In our department the 360-degree exercise was carried out too quickly. Forms were handed out and collected again after an hour. This did not give sufficient time for proper reflection.

It was good to have the opportunity to appraise my manager, but I would have liked more questions on the form to have focused on strengths and fewer on weaknesses.

EVALUATING RECRUITMENT PROCESSES

Using the criteria set out above, the following example describes how an organisation might go about formally evaluating its recruitment processes. We start with three evaluation questions:

1   Do our recruitment practices yield enough suitable candidates to enable us to select sufficient numbers of high-calibre employees?

2   Could a sufficient pool of suitable candidates be attracted using less expensive methods?

3   Are the recruitment methods used fulfilling the organisation's equal opportunities responsibilities?

The first question focuses on the effectiveness of recruitment practices. Asking it will lead to consideration of whether too few sufficiently qualified candidates are applying for jobs. It may be the case that those of the very highest calibre are not being caught in the recruiters' net. The second question focuses on efficiency. It leads to consideration of the relative merits of different recruitment methods in terms of their cost. It is also possible that too many applications are being received, leading to unnecessary expenditure in terms of the time spent on administration. The third question considers the fairness of recruitment processes. Subsequent questions might focus on the extent to which applicant pools are, or are not, representative of all sections of the community.

Answering these questions is a good deal harder than asking them. However, it is possible to move some way to finding answers by using quantitative and qualitative approaches.

Quantitative approaches involve comparing various recruitment methods with each other in terms of their results. We might, for example, choose to compare the effectiveness of using a recruitment advertisement designed by an advertising agency with a similar but less elaborate version set by a newspaper. Which one brought in the greater number of applications? Which one yielded the highest-quality applications? Is there a difference between them in terms of the subsequent performance or turnover rates among selected employees? The same kind of analysis can be undertaken to compare the results of national newspaper advertising with local newspapers, or simply comparing formal with informal recruitment methods. The larger the organisation, the more meaningful the analysis will be. However, it is important to be careful not to read too much into a relatively small sample of cases; plenty of other factors aside from the recruitment method might explain any differences discovered.

Quantitative evaluations of recruitment methods are routinely carried out by many large employing organisations. The main vehicle used is the job reference number, which employees are asked to quote when they respond to advertisements in newspapers, job centres, careers centres and other venues. Employers wishing to compare the different methods include a different reference number in each advertisement and then undertake quantitative comparisons like those described above.

By contrast, qualitative evaluation methods try to locate potential problems with recruitment practices in terms of the three criteria identified above, and consider possible missed opportunities. The aim is to think constructively about ways in which improvements can be made. While a number of approaches are possible, the most common involve asking both successful and unsuccessful candidates to evaluate their experiences during the recruitment process and to compare them with those they have encountered in the past. Reaching successful candidates is straightforward; it is less easy to gather meaningful information from those who have not been offered jobs. One way of doing so is to offer all candidates feedback on their performance at the selection stage.

Such activity is often seen as being solely for the benefit of candidates, but this is not the case: it also provides a good opportunity for employers to gain constructive qualitative feedback on their own recruitment processes from the candidates' perspective.

Other forms of qualitative evaluation might involve investigating the length of time the organisation took to respond to enquiries and formal applications, or evaluating how effectively telephonists and receptionists respond to enquiries about actual or possible vacancies. It may be that good candidates are put off applying because of a lack of courtesy on the part of the employer. Another common form of qualitative evaluation focuses on investigating ways of reducing the number of words in an advertisement without diminishing its effectiveness.

EVALUATION METHODS

Having described the different criteria that can be used in carrying out formal evaluations of resourcing activities, we now need to turn in more detail to the evaluation processes themselves. We start with those that are straightforward and can be employed without the assistance of consultants or expert knowledge. There are a number of alternatives here, some of which were mentioned above by way of illustration. These are not mutually exclusive and can be used in combination with one another. However, some are more useful than others at evaluating performance against different types of criteria.

BENCHMARKING

Bramham (1997, p1) defines benchmarking very succinctly:

Benchmarking is simply the systematic process of comparing your business with others, or parts of your own with one another, to test how you stand and to see whether change is needed. Usually you will identify examples of superior performance, and when you do you should set out to emulate and even better them.

Internal benchmarking is the most common form of this, and the easiest to set up and run. It occurs in larger organisations where several units or departments carry out similar types of activity and operate in the same kinds of labour market. The major examples are 'chain operations' such as supermarkets, hotels or hospitals where a single organisation owns and operates several workplaces in different locations. It is just as feasible, however, to carry out internal benchmarking between different departments within the same workplace, or in organisations that simply wish to compare the relative importance of two business units. All that is required is the collection of data such as that identified above on the same basis across the organisation. Comparisons can then be made and there can be an attempt made to establish the reasons for differential performance. Ideally, over time, the performance of the whole organisation improves.

External benchmarking is less common and more problematic. First, of course, there is likely to be a reluctance on the part of organisations that either compete or believe that they will compete in the future to share information with one another. Even where they do so, it will not be in the interests of the better performing organisations to assist the poorer performers by sharing more than raw benchmarking data. Where this kind of constructive outcome is sought, it is necessary to find partners who run similar operations but do not compete directly. The best examples are service organisations that operate in entirely different geographical areas (eg a bus company in Edinburgh and one in Southampton). Sharing quite detailed information is useful to both parties in these kinds of relationship.

Alternative approaches are less satisfactory, but are nonetheless often worth pursuing. Examples are:

- Simply sharing raw data and no more. This enables organisations to know where they stand in terms of key indicators such as employee turnover, absence, sales per employee, cost per recruit, size of HR department and so on, but does not allow them further information to establish why they stand where they do. An employer that finds itself doing relatively well in such exercises or sees an improvement over time can use this information as an effective means of demonstrating added value.

- Informal benchmarking. This involves steering clear of systematic, formal schemes, but nonetheless using information that comes your way to establish how you are performing on key indices vis-à-vis competitors. The main sources of information are stories in newspapers and trade journals, and knowledge that is brought with them by new staff who have been hired from a competitor.

- Using published data. Quite a lot of resourcing-related benchmarking data is published and freely available in libraries. Some is even included in books such as this. It is possible to use this in order to compare your own organisation's performance with that of others. The surveys included regularly in publications such as *IDS Study* and *IRS Employment Review* are excellent sources of such information.

A number of consultants specialise in setting up and running detailed benchmarking exercises, while similar activities also form a part of what employers' associations have to offer their members. Aside from membership fees, there is usually an additional charge to pay to gain access to the full data, but the result is information that is robust because all participating organisations have completed the same questionnaires with the same sets of explanatory notes.

REFLECTIVE QUESTION

Which other organisations would it be most useful for yours to benchmark against? To what extent would it be either possible or desirable to exchange information with these organisations?

TESCO

People management

Read the article by John Purcell, Nick Kinnie and Sue Hutchinson, The multipack scan (*People Management*, 15 May 2003, pp36–37). This can be downloaded from the *People Management* archive on the CIPD's website (www.cipd.co.uk).

This article describes a programme of research that involved surveying links between employee satisfaction, operational efficiency and financial performance in four Tesco supermarkets. The store that scored worst on measures of staff satisfaction also performed poorly in terms of financial results.

Questions

1   Why do you think that dissatisfaction on the part of staff with HR policies, line management, job influence and low levels of staff commitment should be associated with relatively high levels of inefficiency and wastage?

2   What other possible explanations can you think of that might explain these apparent correlations?

3   How would Tesco be able to benefit from having commissioned this benchmarking study?

HUMAN RESOURCE AUDITING

The audit approach, like benchmarking, involves an organisation comparing its own performance against that of others, but here the comparison is made with standards which are generally acknowledged to constitute 'good practice' or the best attainable results. The approach is thus, by its nature, most appropriate for organisations that are seeking as a matter of policy to be 'employers of choice' or leaders in their field.

The starting point is the results of large-scale research exercises which link certain P&D practices to positive business outcomes across a range of different industries. The best known such studies have been carried out by Mark Huselid and his colleagues (see Huselid *et al* 1997, Becker *et al* 2001, Marchington and Wilkinson 2008), but a wide range of others, including a number carried out in the United Kingdom are reviewed by Boselie *et al* (2005). These kind of studies, as well as those which focus on the approach to HRM adopted in the fastest growing organisations, consistently find a correlation between the presence of particular practices and superior business performance. These tend to be the more sophisticated and costly approaches to the management of people, so they are not going to be an option in organisations that are heavily constrained by cost. However, where it is practicable to employ them, and where an organisation actively seeks to be recognised as an excellent employer, it follows that these are the standards to which it should aspire. The major examples from the resourcing field are:

- recruitment practices that maximise the pool of qualified candidates (ie substantial investment in recruitment)

- the use of sophisticated selection methods (such as those assessed in Chapter 8)

- a high percentage of jobs filled through internal promotion
- formal HR planning systems
- extensive induction/early training programmes
- regular performance appraisals for all staff
- a high degree of self-management/teamworking
- a high proportion of staff in HR roles
- outsourcing of routine HR functions (like recruitment and pay roll)
- well-communicated strategic goals
- participative decision-making
- a commitment to job security wherever possible
- a high profile for diversity management.

The aim is then to audit the firm's own performance against that of 'good practice' as defined by these research findings. The method used is to develop an audit tool (or detailed questionnaire) that mirrors the questions asked by the researchers responsible for these studies. Examples of the kind of questions that could be included are:

i) What proportion of new employees in the past year were selected using psychometric tests?
    a)   100%
    b)   75%–100%
    c)   50%–75%
    d)   25%–50%
    e)   Less than 25%

ii) To what extent is the following statement a true reflection of practice in the organisation?

> 'Employees are actively encouraged to participate in decision-making at the operational level'

    a)   Always true
    b)   Sometimes true
    c)   Occasionally true
    d)   Usually untrue
    e)   Always untrue

iii) How many people are employed in the organisation for each HR specialist?
    a)   Fewer than 150
    b)   150–200
    c)   200–250
    d)   250–300
    e)   More than 300

In the case of each question in the audit tool, a score can be given (eg a=40, b=20, c=10, d=5, e=0) and a total figure calculated. This will show how the organisation compares with the 'best practice employers', but it also allows comparisons to be made between different units and improvements to be tracked over time. HR auditing tools also provide a means by which the areas that need most attention can be readily identified.

EQUALITY AUDITING

Dr Carol Woodhams of Plymouth University recently led a team that created a computer-based audit tool aimed at helping managers of small and medium-sized businesses to avoid sex discrimination claims in the Employment Tribunal. 'Breakthrough' consists of hundreds of specific questions that managers are asked to answer, covering the whole range of P&D policies and practices that do (or more often do not) operate in their organisations. Once the multiple choice answers are fed into the programme, a report is produced electronically, setting out in summary in what ways the organisation is pursuing good practices and in what ways it is leaving itself open either to a moderate or a high risk of litigation. To date hundreds of small firms have undergone an audit and received advice about how to improve their practices as a result.

SURVEY-BASED EVALUATION

A third way of evaluating the contribution made by the P&D function involves surveying opinion within the organisation – best seen as taking the form of a customer-satisfaction survey. Ideally such surveys should be carried out annually, using the same sets of questions so that progress can be tracked over time. Surveys can be divided into two main types, those that focus on management opinion of the HR function and those that gather information about employee attitudes and knowledge.

Management surveys are straightforward to compile in a questionnaire format, and can often be distributed and returned electronically. Typically they consist of multi-choice questions with five possible answers (eg very satisfied, satisfied, neither satisfied nor dissatisfied, dissatisfied, very dissatisfied) about each of the key services offered by the HR function or each of its major objectives. Most management surveys will also include space for extensive qualitative feedback to be given. The difficulty with straightforward 'satisfied/dissatisfied' questionnaire surveys of this kind, according to Cathy Cooper's article about Fidelity International (2001, p42), is that managers simply use them as 'an opportunity to have a go at HR'. The way to avoid this occurring, and to ensure that attention is focused on outcomes rather than on whose responsibility they are, is to phrase questions carefully. At Fidelity they changed the emphasis of questions from 'How good or bad is HR at doing this or that?' to 'As a management population, of which HR is a part, how well do we do these things?'

Surveys of employees are rather different, but equally useful as part of a wider evaluation exercise. The most common approaches involve surveys of employee attitudes and of employee knowledge. The latter is principally of relevance to employee development processes. The former is concerned with discovering how people feel about their work, how far they are satisfied in their jobs, how fairly they perceive that they are treated and how committed they believe themselves to be. Buckingham and Coffman (1999, p28) used focus group research to come up with 12 questions that they subsequently asked thousands of employees in different organisations. These are well-formulated, specific questions that focus on possible sources of dissatisfaction rather than simply asking employees whether or not they are happy at work:

- Do I know what is expected of me at work?

- Do I have the materials and equipment I need to do my work right?

- At work, do I have the opportunity to do what I do best every day?

- In the last seven days have I received recognition or praise for good work?

- Does my supervisor, or someone at work, seem to care about me as a person?

- Is there someone at work who encourages my development?

- At work, do my opinions count?

- Does the mission/purpose of my company make me feel that my work is important?

- Are my co-workers committed to doing quality work?

- Do I have a best friend at work?

- In the last six months have I talked to someone about my progress?

- At work, have I had opportunities to learn and grow?

These questions were found to link directly to at least one of four business outcomes: productivity, profitability, staff retention and customer satisfaction. They can thus be judged to operate as a pretty effective yardstick by which the quality of an organisation's people management practices can be judged.

REFLECTIVE QUESTION

What other questions would you like to see added to this list if you were to undertake a similar exercise in your organisation? Which would you remove from the list and why?

GOAL-BASED EVALUATION

The fourth commonly used evaluation method is in many ways the most straightforward, being the P&D function's equivalent of an individual performance appraisal exercise. It also the method that is best used for determining how effectively specific strategic objectives are being met. At base, the approach simply involves a P&D function setting itself objectives for the months ahead, ideally choosing goals that fit the requirements of the 'SMART' acronym described in Chapter 15 (specific, measurable, achievable, realistic and time-bound). The more directly related these objectives are to organisational strategic objectives, the more appropriate they are to set. Evaluation can subsequently be made on the basis of how far in practice objectives have been met for a particular yearly, half-yearly or quarterly period. Examples from the resourcing field might be as follows:

- to solicit 250 applications from computer science graduates by February

- to redesign and launch a new company induction programme by April

- to train all managers appointed during the past two years in new assessment-centre scoring methodology by June

- to complete consultation on the introduction of 360-degree appraisal by August.

A danger with goal-based evaluation systems, as with individual performance appraisals run along similar principles, is that the context can easily change, leaving you chasing targets that are no longer priorities for the organisation. Objectives must thus be flexible and able to be reviewed, removed or added to at any time. It is also important not to set too many separate objectives for any one time period. What matters is to fully achieve those that are really essential and genuinely contribute to organisation performance. These are what Ulrich (see Becker *et al* 2001, p80) has referred to as the 'doables' and 'deliverables' that 'really make a difference'. Where there is a written organisational strategy with clear operational goals, the priorities for the P&D function should derive directly from these documents.

Becker *et al* (2001, p33) give a good example of ways in which P&D objectives can be tied directly to organisational objectives and need to change when the organisational strategy changes. They cite the example of a large US retail banking operation that decided to shift from a service-oriented strategy to one based on sales. Prior to the change, the P&D programmes were all related to improving the quality of customer service. This was the focus of induction and other training programmes; it provided the basis of the performance appraisal system and also the competency framework on which selection decisions were made. Little attention was given to the building of relationships between individual bank tellers and customers. Instead tellers were considered to be 'overheads' rather than a 'source of revenue growth', and hence dispensable. No great efforts were made to retain them, and their pay was kept relatively low. Once the shift to a sales-oriented strategy was contemplated, the need was for people, skills and knowledge that would allow increased cross-selling of products to existing customers. New values thus had to be stressed in the induction programmes, a new competency framework developed on which to base recruitment of sales-oriented people, and a performance appraisal system developed that rewarded different behaviours. Importantly policies had to be introduced to discourage turnover among tellers so as to allow the building of longer-term individual relationships with customers.

THE ROLE OF CONSULTANTS IN DEMONSTRATING ADDED VALUE

For many organisations, a good starting point when looking to start systematic evaluation of P&D activities is to sign up with a firm of consultants who specialise in this area. The most useful are those that are well established and can provide robust, detailed benchmarking information. An example is the Saratoga Europe group, who run a well-regarded scheme. Organisations pay an annual fee and then provide the consultant with detailed information on their performance against 12 human resource management indicators. The data has to be submitted in a standard format so that the consultant is certain that all participating employers are including and excluding the same types of figures. So, for example, there is a standard definition of voluntary staff turnover to ensure that participants are only measuring the same types of resignation. Each year, detailed confidential reports are produced giving average and median figures for each indicator. It is thus possible for participants to see exactly how they compare with other employers.

The next stage involves setting targets for improved performance against the indicators and putting in place policy initiatives aimed at ensuring that these objectives are met. The initial benchmarking exercise also helps identify the areas that require most improvement. This information can then form the basis of internal surveys to establish exactly why performance is particularly poor against that particular indicator.

Source: Littlefield and Merrick (2000, pp32–34).

CUTTING-EDGE APPROACHES TO EVALUATION

In recent years, larger corporations and specialist consultants have begun to develop approaches to the evaluation of P&D programmes that are a great deal more sophisticated and complex than those described so far in this chapter. Many features of the newer approaches are problematic and it will take some years before they become widely accepted. It is beyond the scope of this book to describe these approaches in great detail, but it is useful to know about their development and to consider how far they may become standard in years to come. A good introduction to some of the approaches, with exercises to complete, is provided by Cascio (2000).

Different terms are used to describe the cutting-edge approaches. Some use the term 'balanced scorecard' and have developed this attractive idea, while others use the language of accounting specialists by thinking in terms of 'return on investment' or 'human asset accounting'. Whatever terminology is used, the core principles are the same. The evolving methods all involve measuring the impact of P&D activities on organisation performance in financial terms. Because this is not easily done, it is necessary to make various assumptions about cause and effect and to employ techniques that are akin to standard accounting conventions. In the financial world, however, there are generally accepted accounting practices (GAAPs) that everyone understands and accepts. It will take some time for such standardisation to occur in the P&D field, if it ever does, so for the time being there are on offer several different systems, mainly developed by different firms of consultants. Many of the approaches described above are used in combination in these kind of exercises.

An often-quoted example is the exercise carried out by the Sears Group in the United States (see Rucci *et al* 1998, Holbeche 1999, pp68–71, Becker *et al* 2001, p28). It serves to illustrate very well what results these activities are intended to bring. At Sears over a period of some years, a great deal of data was collected by task forces about employee development and teamworking, and customer needs and satisfaction, and about revenue growth, sales per square foot and other financial measures. Central to the exercise was the way that the company sought to capture 'soft issues' such as staff satisfaction by using hard measurements. This was done through the use of questionnaire surveys. Correlations were then made between changes in the P&D indicators and improvements in the financial performance of different business units (ie benchmarking). The analysis allowed the company to make the following statement:

> *A 5 point improvement in employee attitudes will drive a 1.3 point improvement in customer satisfaction which in turn will lead to a 0.5 per cent improvement in revenue growth.*

The key process that makes this kind of analysis possible is the isolation of the effects of a particular P&D intervention. Among the 'ten strategies' for achieving this aim, Phillips *et al* (2001) suggest the following (the other seven being variations on these three):

- The use of control groups. Here a workforce is divided into two groups as if taking part in a scientific experiment. In practice two separate business units would be used. One is subjected to the new P&D intervention (new selection method, new performance management system, a turnover or absence reduction programme etc) while practices for the other group remain unchanged. Differences are then measured over time.

- The use of trend line analyses. Here performance (eg sales levels, production costs, customer satisfaction ratings) is tracked before and after the implementation of a P&D intervention, and the extent to which improvements occur in excess of expected projections is measured.

- Participant estimates. Employees and managers are asked to give a reasoned estimate of the extent to which any performance improvements derive directly from an HR intervention. Standard questionnaires are used to enable ready collation of the data.

The next stage involves calculating an estimate of the value added in monetary terms. In the case of sales or output increases this is straightforward, but calculating the monetary value of improved customer satisfaction, reduced employee turnover or improved product quality is a good deal harder. However, many organisations have developed methods that enable them to do so. Most involve tapping into the expertise of experienced staff. For example, a sales manager with long experience will be able to estimate how great a difference in terms of repeat sales is typical as between a satisfied and a dissatisfied customer. Similarly a head receptionist will be able to work out how great a cost is sustained in terms of management and staff time as a direct result of a new, inexperienced employee replacing an established receptionist on his or her team. Product quality can be measured in terms of customer satisfaction, but also using defect rates, the cost of replacing faulty products, or waste generated because of mistakes, all of which are readily expressed in financial terms. Which method is used will depend on the specific activities of the organisation concerned.

Once the impact of P&D activities has been measured in financial terms, it becomes possible to calculate a figure for 'return on investment'. This is simply done by working out the cost of the P&D intervention in terms of staff time, consultants' fees, equipment and overheads. The following formula is then applied:

return on investment = (benefits less cost/cost) × 100

A simple example might be the introduction of assessment centres as a method of selecting sales staff in a computer company. Such an intervention is reasonably straightforward to cost. The results could be expected to include:

- improved levels of new business (eg £400,000 of new business per year generated per year, as opposed to £300,000 before the introduction of assessment centres)

- improved repeat sales levels

- enhanced customer satisfaction ratings

- lower turnover among new graduates (eg down from 50 per cent over two years to 25 per cent)

- higher levels of employee satisfaction.

Using the methods outlined above these benefits are converted into monetary values. Finally a calculation is made of return on investment, possibly:

Total programme costs: £ 250,000

Estimated total benefits: £750,000

$$\frac{(750,000 - 250,000)}{(250,000)} = 2$$

$2 \times 100 = 200$

ROI = 200%

In their book, Phillips *et al* (2001) describe several real life applications of these techniques. Examples include the calculations of return on investment after the implementation of the following types of P&D interventions:

- a programme to reduce incidences of sexual harassment

- a competency-based pay scheme

- an absence reduction programme

- a stress management programme

- a safety awareness programme

- two examples of training and development initiatives.

The results were by no means perfect in any of these cases, but a very real attempt was made to evaluate common forms of P&D intervention in the same terms as are used to estimate the outcomes of forms of capital investment. There can be no question that added value was clearly demonstrated as a consequence.

REFLECTIVE QUESTION

What is your opinion of evolving practice in the field of P&D evaluation? To what extent do you agree with the view that this kind of activity will become standard P&D practice in large corporations over the next 10 years?

EXERCISE 20.3

HUMAN ASSET WORTH

Read the article by Andrew Mayo, A thorough evaluation (*People Management*, 4 April 2002, pp36–39). This can be downloaded from the *People Management* archive on the CIPD's website (www.cipd.co.uk).

This article starts by setting out some of the problems associated with some of the most commonly used approaches to human asset accounting such as the balanced scorecard. It goes on to argue that organisations stand to gain a great deal if they try to measure the 'total asset worth' of individual employees, focusing on the measurement both of financial and non-financial 'value added'. A method of achieving this is briefly described.

Questions

1 What is Mayo referring to when he writes about the 'non-financial added value' created by individual staff?

2 For what practical purposes could managers use data collected about each employee's 'human asset worth'?

3 What problems can you identify with the approach to evaluating employee contribution outlined by Andrew Mayo?

KEY ARTICLE 49

Wesley Hagood and Lee Friedman, Using the balanced scorecard to measure the performance of your HR information system. *Public Personnel Management*, Vol. 31, No. 4, pp543–556 (2002)

This article is a rare example of a published case study which sets out in some detail how an organisation has developed measures for evaluating the effectiveness of an HR intervention and uses it in practice. This article focuses on the effectiveness of the HR information system used by the CIA in Washington DC.

Questions

1 In what way did the adoption of a methodology based on the balanced scorecard enhance the effectiveness of measures that had been used to evaluate the performance of the HRIS beforehand?

2   What are the advantages and disadvantages associated with the calculation of a single score of effectiveness derived from several other very different types of measures?

3   How could the methodology used in this case study be adapted in order to measure the effectiveness of an organisation's selection procedures or its absence management practices?

CHAPTER SUMMARY

- Formal evaluation of resourcing programmes enhances the credibility of the function within organisations and provides a basis for successful bids for future investment. HR-oriented outcomes are also increasingly taken into account by investment analysts.

- In the future, it is possible that companies will be required to disclose detailed information relating to their human capital in their annual reports. At present only quite broad statements are required.

- Core resourcing activities are best evaluated in terms of their effectiveness, efficiency and fairness. Evaluation can be forward-looking, backward-looking or a combination of both.

- Evaluation can be either quantitative or qualitative in nature. Which approach is used depends on the type of evaluation exercise and the way that results are going to be reported.

- The major methods of evaluation used are benchmarking, audit-based, survey-based and goal-based. Each has a role to play and all can be used in combination.

- In recent years, cutting-edge approaches to evaluation have been developed. These involve expressing the impact of P&D interventions in monetary terms.

EXPLORE FURTHER

- Evaluation issues such as those described in this chapter are rarely covered in texts on resourcing topics, with the exception of those concerned with employee selection. The best introductions are books that look at the evaluation of human resource management programmes in general terms. Good recent examples are *The HR scorecard: linking people, strategy and performance* by Brian Becker, Mark Huselid and Dave Ulrich (2001), *The human value of the enterprise* by Andrew Mayo (2001), *The human resources scorecard: measuring the return on investment* by Jack Phillips, Ron Stone and Patricia Pulliam Phillips (2001) and

Investing in people: financial impact of human resource initiatives by Wayne Cascio, John Boudreau and Patrick Ramstad (2008).

- John Bramham (1997) writes principally about benchmarking, but also introduces other forms of evaluation and assesses the importance of the issue in general terms.

- The debate about mandatory human capital reporting is been covered extensively in the HR press in recent years. Good summaries of the idea and its implications are provided by Brown (2004), IRS (2003c) and IRS (2004c).

CHAPTER 21

People resourcing strategy

Ever since 'human resource management' started to supersede 'personnel administration' in the 1980s and 1990s it has become generally accepted that organisations that wish to maximise their competitive advantage need to take a strategic approach to the management of their people. This means pursuing policies that are both coherent in terms of their impact and designed to help the organisation achieve its broad strategic aims. It also means thinking about the practice of managing people strategically, focusing on the achievement of clearly defined, long-term HR objectives. While it is common to read about reward strategies and employment relations strategies alongside general HR strategies, relatively little has been written about the development of strategy in the resourcing field. The term 'people resourcing strategy' is not widely used, and has never been fully defined in the literature. This chapter makes an attempt to do this. It sets out examples of ways in which organisations do and don't take a strategic approach to the major activities discussed in this book, then discusses the lessons to be learned from some of the most influential theories of strategic HRM. Finally it addresses the specific issue of labour market competition, and strategies organisations can develop to help ensure they are better placed than their competitors to recruit and retain the best available people.

LEARNING OUTCOMES

By the end of this chapter readers should be able to:

- identify the different ways in which organisations can take a strategic approach to the management activities discussed in this book

- state how organisations can take steps to align their people resourcing activities with the business strategies being pursued by their organisations

- develop a strategy for effectively competing in the labour market.

In addition, readers should be able to understand and explain:

- the major theories concerning linkages between business strategy and HR strategy

- critiques of approaches to HR strategy making which focus on altering HR practice so as to match strategic organisational objectives

- the determinants of effective labour market competition.

TAKING A STRATEGIC APPROACH

On one level it is possible to describe an organisation's people resourcing activities as having a strategic character simply because of the manner in which they are carried out by management. The term 'strategy' in this context means taking a planned, well-thought-out, evidence-based approach to the various different P&D activities explored in this book. Instead of activities being carried out in a reactive, ad hoc or ill-considered manner, there is a clearly defined coherence and purpose. Hence an organisation might have develop and put into practice an absence management strategy, an employee retention strategy or a talent management strategy. In each case a long-term objective or set of objectives needs to be set, and decisions made about how those objectives are going to be met in practice. These will be influenced by the context of the organisation and by the expectations of staff, managers, shareholders and customers.

Strategic thinking and practice in the people resourcing area is most commonly evident when organisations embark on discrete episodes or projects such as expansions, retractions, reorganisations and structural change management exercises. Here it is usual for a project management team to be assembled and a well-thought-through, if adaptable, plan drawn up which is then followed.

Hence when large retailers open new stores they are more likely to act strategically than they are to act in an ad hoc manner in the way that they go about the staffing process. Human resource planning exercises are undertaken to establish how many people will be required, with what level of skills and experience. Care is then taken to ensure that these people are recruited at the right time so that a new team can be selected, inducted and trained in time for the date the new store or branch opens. Similar care tends to be taken when organisations are required to downsize. Layoffs are planned at some length, consultation taking place as required by law, and the most appropriate method chosen for the selection of staff to be made redundant. It is usual for a recruitment freeze to be introduced, for a redeployment register to be established and not at all uncommon for outplacement training to be provided too. Cascio (2002) provides several examples of strategic downsizing in practice, going on to set out some rules to follow and mistakes to avoid.

Cultural change is harder to bring about and to plan strategically in any kind of systematic way. But here too there is evidence that many organisations at least attempt to take a strategic approach. Campaigns of activity are planned by teams of managers which involve communicating messages to staff and consulting with them. Reward mechanisms are established to encourage new ways of thinking and these are included explicitly as individual objectives in performance appraisal exercises. Several examples of successful programmes of this kind are provided by Millmore *et al* (2007, pp225–232), drawing on a range of published case studies. They argue that in many instances the most effective approaches are 'bottom up' in nature rather than 'top down'. By this they mean that initiatives are taken in parts of the organisation rather than being very publicly co-ordinated centrally. Initiatives are taken by line managers, involving their staff and resulting in the establishment of a shared vision of some kind. The HR function then becomes involved by developing interventions, policies and practices which support this, for example by providing appropriate training and development opportunities.

EXERCISE 21.1

MIDLAND HEART

People management

Read the article by Penny Cottee, Change of heart (*People Management*, 10 August 2006, pp42–44). This can be downloaded from the *People Management* archive on the CIPD's website (www.cipd.co.uk).

The article describes a carefully planned change-management project that met with an apparent high level of success at a large city-based housing association. It involved the merger of four regional offices, the introduction of new technology, further cost-saving measures and major changes to established procedures.

Questions

1   What were the strategic objectives identified by managers at the start of the process described in the article?

2   What evidence is provided of a 'strategic approach' being taken to the management of the project?

3   What do you think might have happened if a more 'ad hoc' approach had been taken?

Such evidence as there is therefore suggests that when people resourcing activities are carried out as part of a distinct project, an approach that can be labelled 'strategic' is typically taken. However, this is not the case when it comes to the way that organisations manage the same resourcing activities over the long term on a day-to-day basis. Here, it would seem, most organisations take an approach to core resourcing activities that is closer to the 'ad hoc' than to the 'strategic' end of the scale. We saw in Chapter 6, for example, how much less prevalent the practice of formal human resource planning is nowadays when compared with the position two or three decades ago, in Chapter 18 how rarely organisations plan the retirement of staff in a considered manner (despite the known advantages of doing so) and in Chapter 16 how most organisations tend to use rather 'blunt tools' when tackling absence rather than more sophisticated, targeted approaches that are more likely to bring about sustained reductions in the amount of time off that employees take. Millmore (2003) reached the same conclusion in his study investigating the extent to which UK organisations take a strategic approach to recruitment and selection. His work is particularly useful because of the way he has developed tests of 'strategicness' against which to judge organisational practice. The criteria he suggests should be used as a means of judging whether organisations are or are not 'strategic' in the way they handle the recruitment and selection of staff are:

- Recruitment and selection practices should reflect the organisation's strategic plans. In other words, the job descriptions and person specifications used should clearly link to current and future organisational priorities. Hence, if the adoption of new technologies is a key component of organisational strategy, a need for people with the competence and experience to work with them, or at least to learn to work with them should be central to recruitment practices and selection decisions.

- A long-term focus should be apparent. The organisation is not simply seeking to fill its need for staff quickly with like-for-like replacements 'with the emphasis on meeting the immediate needs of a vacancy at a highly localised level', but is thinking longer-term about recruiting people with the attributes that will be required increasingly in the future.

- A 'bridging mechanism' for translating long-term plans and organisational priorities into practical recruitment and selection policies and practices. In most cases this will take the form of some kind of formal human resource planning activity, the organisation being in a position to forecast its likely future demand for and supply (internal and external) of labour with reasonable accuracy.

Millmore terms these criteria 'three interdependent primary features', necessary minimum attributes of an approach to recruitment and selection that can be labelled 'strategic'. However, he goes on to suggest further secondary criteria which emerge from the adoption of the first three. In other words he argues that where an organisation operates practices that have the three primary features, it is very likely that two further features of the recruitment and selection policies will follow, will hence be apparent and can therefore form further criteria against which the extent to which the approach being used can be judged as having a 'strategic character'.

- A sophisticated and complex approach to recruitment and selection, a reasonably wide array of methods being used as appropriate and a relatively 'diverse and exacting' set of person specifications being in use when recruiting for different categories of job.

- Recruitment and selection processes which are accorded high status as activities within the organisation. Evidence for this can be found in the relative level of expenditure on recruitment and selection activities and the involvement of many stakeholders (not just the immediate supervisor assisted by an HR officer).

- The use of approaches that are clearly sensitive to the impact on candidates and which, in particular, facilitate 'informed self-selection decisions'.

Millmore's research found precious little evidence of any 'strategic' recruitment and selection being a carried out in the organisations he surveyed when judged against these simple criteria. Indeed he found no examples whatever of any recruitment exercises meeting all his criteria at the same time. As far as the primary criteria were concerned 'taken together it could be argued, perhaps very generously, that 8 per cent of recruitment and selection exercises are being strategically driven' (Millmore 2003, p101).

KEY ARTICLE 50

Dail Fields, Andrew Chan, Syed Akhtar and Terry Blum, Human resource management strategies under uncertainty: how do US and Hong Kong Chinese companies differ? *Cross Cultural Management,* Vol. 13, No. 2, pp171–186 (2006)

The research discussed in this article involved sending the same questionnaire to managers in the US state of Georgia and Hong Kong with a view to establishing how their HR strategies vary in the face of tightening labour market conditions. They found very considerable differences. The Hong Kong companies tended to increase their investment in training and to make more explicit the links between reward and performance. The reverse was the case in the United States.

Questions

1   What principal explanation do the authors give for their findings?

2   To what extent do you find these convincing and why?

3   What major strategic responses, in people resourcing terms, would you expect would be adopted by UK firms facing similar circumstances, and why?

ALIGNING HR PRACTICES WITH BUSINESS STRATEGY

A prominent theme in the academic literature on HRM strategy has long been the idea that organisations should explicitly align their HR activities with their long-term strategic objectives. Indeed, for many writers and consultants this has become the major test used to establish the extent to which an organisation's HR function is or is not acting 'strategically'. The clearer the alignment between HR activity and organisational strategic objectives, the clearer it is that a coherent HR strategy is being pursued (see Boxall and Purcell 2008, p56). The idea of strategic alignment is closely associated with contingency or 'best fit' approaches to HRM, in which HR practices and approaches are quite deliberately selected from a range of alternative possibilities so as to ensure that they 'fit' most comfortably with the organisation's strategic objectives. When fully achieved, it can be shown that the organisations that have the 'best fit' as far as their HR practices are concerned also prosper financially and stand a better chance of gaining competitive advantage. This happens because the HR practices in use are most appropriate as a means of supporting the achievement of the organisation's competitive strategy.

Hence, where an organisation's business strategy is focused on achieving, steady, continuous, long-term organic growth (ie: growth from within rather than by acquiring other firms), the appropriate HR strategy involves prioritising the development of people through effective career management activities. The aim is to select people with potential, to provide them with attractive internal career progression opportunities, to invest in their development and to find ways of tying them into the business for the long term through the use of share options and other longer-term profit-related rewards. On the employee relations side partnership approaches designed to engender high-trust relationships and a shared long-term interest between employer and employee are most appropriate. Achieving fit of this kind will enhance business performance compared with competitors whose HR practices fit less well with the organisation's strategy.

Over recent years a number of academics and consultants have published contingency models which set out, albeit often in a somewhat simplistic manner, the major different types of business strategy and the most appropriate packages of HR practices which align most closely with them. Some of these models have become highly influential and have spawned a considerable literature comprising research studies that aim to evaluate their utility in practice (Marchington and Wilkinson 2008, and Boxall and Purcell 2008, both provide an extensive survey of this body of literature). The models range across the whole HR field, including many areas of practice which are beyond the scope of this book. But resourcing activities often play a central role, and it is thus appropriate that a chapter on 'people resourcing strategy' should focus in some detail on the content of the major models.

MILES AND SNOW

The model advocated by Miles and Snow (1978) has been influential in the business strategy literature and has had a particularly significant impact on thinking about HR strategy over the past few decades. This is due in large part to an often-cited study by Doty et al (1993) which provided good evidence that organisations whose HR practices were aligned appropriately to the contingencies in the Miles and Snow model outperformed competitors whose practices were less well aligned.

Miles and Snow identify three major types of business strategy: the defender strategy, the prospector strategy and the analyser strategy. Organisations that do not pursue one of these are labelled 'reactors'. This fourth group consists of organisations that do not have a clearly identifiable organisational strategy. The assertion is that they tend to perform badly in competitive environments and so their approach is not presented alongside the other three as an 'ideal' type.

The defender strategy involves the organisation protecting its existing market share and growing slowly, steadily and incrementally. Surplus profits are reinvested in the organisation to build up its strength over would-be competitors, the major purpose being to maintain competitive advantage. A suitable military metaphor is a medieval castle with thick walls and full of soldiers able to withstand attack from any who dare to try to seize ground that is already held. Examples of defender organisations are the large clearing banks, the major retail organisations and international organisations that are the established market leaders in their fields. The McDonald's restaurant chain is a good example. They are leading players in their industries, established, strong and capable of withstanding competitive charges from smaller rivals. The Pearl Group is a major financial services provider that meets the definition of a defender. One of its major office buildings located near to Peterborough is built like a modern-day castle, with a drawbridge, turrets and a courtyard – a very visual statement of the organisation's long-established strategy.

By contrast prospectors are highly opportunistic and flexible. Innovation and the search for new market opportunities are the chief features. They have an entrepreneurial approach, take risks and have a tendency to move in and out of industries. Manufacturing organisations frequently take this approach, particularly those operating in high-tech environments where continual innovation is essential to survival. The appropriate military metaphor here is the armoured tank. These organisations move across battlefields, taking ground for short periods of time before moving on in search of new conquests. Smaller start-up organisations have no choice but to take this approach, as do larger organisations whose competitive environments are unpredictable and volatile. Drugs companies, electronics manufacturers, private-sector media organisations are all examples.

The third strategic approach categorised by Miles and Snow is the 'analyser'. These organisations combine features of the other two types. On the one hand they tend to be a sizeable, established presence in an industry, but they also diversify into new markets and indeed new industries when opportunities present themselves. They are like castles from which tanks occasionally emerge to seek new ground to conquer. Analysers are often known for being 'second-to-market', which means that they wait and watch the prospectors carve out new markets (and make all the mistakes) before coming in themselves a few years later to compete with them, making full use of their well-known brand names and financial largesse. The Virgin Group is often cited as a classic example of a company that follows this strategy. The result is that it has a presence in many industries, some for the long term, others for relatively short periods.

In the case of each of these three strategies different kinds of people resourcing strategy are appropriate. In order to maximise their success they need to adopt approaches that are aligned with their business strategies. In the case of the defender, the need is for a stable organisational structure in which jobs are well defined and quite specialised. Their market power enables them to exercise a degree of control over their business environments, so flexibility is not as important as it is in smaller organisations. Instead there is a need to maximise efficiency, so the structures are designed to achieve this. It is in organisations of this kind that traditional approaches to human resource planning and succession planning remain in use. There are well-developed internal labour markets, people often being appointed into junior positions early in their careers and then promoted up the career ladder internally over time. Graduate recruitment is thus highly significant and will have a great deal of resources allocated to it. Selection methods tend to be sophisticated, enough time being taken to ensure that the right people are offered jobs. Subsequent investment in training and development is also extensive, the psychological contract being rooted in the notion of long-term commitment on both sides. Jobs are designed quite narrowly so as to maximise the machine-like efficiency which defender organisations require. Performance appraisal systems will be standardised and linked directly to organisational objectives, while HR bureaucratic policies and a central HR function tend to play a leading role.

The opposite approach is necessarily taken by prospectors. Here flexibility is key, so contracts of both the legal and psychological variety tend to be short term. Multi-skilling is the norm, job descriptions (if they exist) being broad and subject to regular change. People are recruited as and when particular expertise or experience is required, opportunistic and informal recruitment and selection being used much of the time. Costs are kept to a minimum, so bureaucratic approaches to HRM do not make sense. Formal HR planning is unlikely to occur, as are substantial annual recruitment programmes aimed at graduates or school leaver. Instead a variety of recruitment methods are used to bring people in at different levels. Use is made of recruitment agents, different types of advertising and informal approaches. Decision-making in the people resourcing field is delegated to line managers wherever possible, as is responsibility for performance management. HR managers see their role as to provide advice and support rather than to determine how managers carry out their jobs. Prospectors regularly work in networks of other organisations, collaborating on projects and forming alliances. Outsourcing of activities is common, as is the use of subcontractors and agency staff.

In the case of analysers a mixture of the two extreme approaches outlined above is appropriate. The model of the 'flexible firm' we looked at in Chapter 7 is appropriate for them because of its clear core–periphery distinction. In analyser companies there will always be a need for a core of long-term employees to manage the organisation's more stable, core businesses and to staff its corporate HQ. But beyond that, opportunism and flexibility are needed to maximise the ability to compete in new markets when opportunities are identified. Analysers are thus divisional in terms of their structure, and while they often have a well-defined corporate image and a pronounced set of corporate values, each part will necessarily pursue rather different HR policies and practices within that broad framework.

PORTER

Michael Porter's (1985) model of generic business strategies has been as influential as Miles and Snow's, and like theirs has been taken up by researchers specialising in HRM to test the idea that organisations enjoy greater success when their P&D practices are closely aligned with their overall business strategies. In the case of Porter's model, studies of the HR implications are particularly associated with Schuler and Jackson (1987), but many others have carried out research using the same premises.

Porter identifies two major types of business strategy which he suggests that organisations must choose from. The first is a strategy based on 'cost leadership' which means that the key source of competitive advantage lies in providing goods or services at a highly competitive price. Consumers are attracted to the organisation because it can provide them with what they are looking for more cheaply than competitors can. Low-cost retailers such as Kwik Save, Aldi and those that sell everything at discount rates are examples of organisations that compete in this way. The major alternative is a strategy based on 'differentiation'. This involves charging higher prices for goods and services that are either of higher quality than those provided by competitors or more innovative in some way. In the retail world a high-quality department store and a supermarket like Waitrose or Marks & Spencer are examples of differentiators.

Porter goes on to argue that each of the two strategies can be applied to a broad market (eg national or international) or to a niche or narrowly focused market, for example one which is very localised or specialised in terms of its tastes. These ideas are not controversial. What has attracted criticism is the further claim that companies will do less well financially if they fall in between the two stools, for example by seeking to compete on price and quality at the same time. A mixed strategy, according to Porter, invariably leads to poorer financial performance than one that is clearly either cost-based or involves clear differentiation. The extent to which this holds true is questionable in the UK retailing market, where the market is now dominated by chains which specifically appeal because they stick a range of products that are both cheap and of high quality, alongside those that are either cheap or of high quality.

Despite the criticisms, the Porter/Schuler and Jackson models are important and influential as far as the determination of HR strategy is concerned. Where an organisation is clearly intent on pursuing a cost-leadership strategy it makes sense for its P&D policies and practices to be low-cost too. Otherwise it will find it hard to make sufficient profit to thrive. This does not necessarily mean that wage levels need to be low because it is possible to employ fewer people more efficiently and to gain a cost advantage that way. It does, however, tend to require people resourcing systems that are less comfortable from an employee's perspective, and which are often associated with higher levels of turnover as a result. In order to maximise efficiency, jobs tend to me quite specific and narrowly defined. This keeps training costs to a minimum and makes it possible to operate a standardised, routine approach to recruitment, selection and induction.

Organisational rhetoric in such organisations can often be enlightened, forward-looking and employee-friendly, but the reality tends to be different simply because at the local level managers are given strict budget targets to meet which have very little slack. So efforts are continually focused on keeping staffing costs down. There is, as a result, a reluctance to give people overtime and a continual intensification of work so that each employee expends greater effort and is increasingly productive. Cost leaders are typically intolerant of absence, taking a firm disciplinary line, have no interest in sophisticated approaches to selection or performance management, and will be happy to risk dismissing employees in an unlawful way on the grounds that few cases actually go to tribunal and it is possible to settle most ahead of any hearing. It is hard to maintain a high standard of ethics in the way that people are managed, while also pursuing a competitive strategy that requires continual pressure to reduce costs.

By contrast where a strategy of differentiation is pursued, cost control is a less all-embracing feature of organisational life. More important is the effective recruitment, retention and motivation of the best people. Without them, the strategy can not work. Hence budgets are made available for sophisticated recruitment campaigns, lengthy selection processes and five-star, gold-plated induction experiences. Where innovation is central, a great deal of time, attention and money is given to appropriate training and development activities, while performance management practices are tailored to meet the needs of the key groups. The last thing an organisation pursuing a strategy of this type needs is the development of low-trust relationships between staff and management. There is a need to encourage the sharing of knowledge, so reward and recognition of individual contribution is needed. People need to feel valued, so they are managed as individuals rather than as one of a group of staff.

EXERCISE 21.2

ITV

People management

Read the article by Rima Evans, Telly vision (*People Management*, 22 March 2007, pp24–29). This can be downloaded from the *People Management* archive on the CIPD's website (www.cipd.co.uk).

This article focuses on a major new HR initiative called 'Imagine' that has been introduced by HR managers at the broadcaster ITV. The objectives and origins of the initiative are explored in some detail.

Questions

1   How would you characterise ITV's current business strategy using the Porter and Miles and Snow models?

2   To what extent do you think the 'Imagine' project can be seen as being well aligned to the organisation's business strategy?

3   To what extent can the 'Imagine' project be seen as a strategic intervention designed to bring about cultural change in the organisation?

OTHER MODELS

Several other academics and consultants have published other models over the years, all of which in rather different ways link HR policy and practice to organisations' strategic objectives or to their position in competitive product markets. Some have achieved greater influence than others, but none have generated as much interest as the two outlined above in terms of attempts being made to test their validity with reference to financial outcomes. It is beyond the scope of this chapter to look in detail at each of these models, but it is worth mentioning some of them and how they differ from those derived from the Porter and Miles and Snow models.

One approach that has attracted the interest of several commentators is to focus on the stages in the life-cycle of a typical firm (see Sisson and Storey 2000). Here it is very plausibly argued that organisations that are small and growing require rather different HR practices from those that are large, successful and in their maturity, and those which are in decline. Affordability plays a role here because firms that are struggling to survive in their present form, as well as small start-up organisations, will inevitably have fewer resources to devote to HR activities than those that are successful, sizeable and resource-rich. Hence we find many more examples of sophisticated approaches to the major people resourcing functions

(HRP, recruitment, selection, induction, performance management, absence management retirement etc) being used in large corporations than we do in smaller organisations and those that are declining in terms of their market share. The same broad principles are reflected in the Boston Consulting Group model (see Purcell 1989) and in the Lengnick-Hall model (Lengnick-Hall and Lengnick-Hall 1988), both of which focus in large part on the extent to which an organisation is expanding and expects to expand further in the future. They go on to argue that the focus of HR policy ought to be different in each case in order to achieve strategic alignment.

A rather different set of assumptions underpins James Walker's contingency model (Walker 1992). Here the focus is on the rate of environmental change to which an organisation is subject, and the extent of its complexity. This has the advantage over the other modes of incorporating of public sector organisations and others that are non-commercial in nature. In terms of people resourcing practices the big difference between organisations operating in fast-changing, volatile environments and those whose environments are reasonably stable and predictable is the extent to which flexibility is central. Where the environment is stable a long-term approach can be taken to resourcing the organisation. Reasonably sophisticated policies can be established and bureaucratic systems set up to administer HR matters. Change occurs in defined, manageable episodes, and it is feasible to structure organisations in an efficient (if inflexible) hierarchical manner. The less stable the environment, the greater the need for a capacity for flexibility.

ALTERNATIVE VIEWS OF THE HR–BUSINESS STRATEGY LINK

In terms of academic fashion the thinking that lies behind the models described above had its heyday in the 1980s and 1990s. That does not mean to say that they have no relevance today – that is far from the case – but it is true to say that the assumptions that underlie the models are no longer universally accepted as being the best way for the P&D function in organisations to contribute to the achievement of competitive advantage. Two major alternative schools of thought about the link between HR policy and practice and organisational strategy have developed, both of which have proved highly influential. These can be termed the 'best practice school' and the 'resource-based view school'. In both cases there are particular implications for the development of practice in the area of people resourcing.

BEST PRACTICE APPROACHES

Over the past 10 to 15 years a group of researchers have challenged the basic idea that organisations maximise their financial success by adopting approaches in the HR field which are explicitly 'aligned' to their business strategies. One of the leading figures in the development of 'best practice thinking' is Jeffery Pfeffer:

> *Contrary to some academic writing and to popular belief, there is little evidence that effective management practices are 1) particularly faddish (although their implementation may well be), 2) difficult to understand or to comprehend why they work, or 3) necessarily contingent on an organisation's particular competitive strategy.*
>
> (Pfeffer 1994, pp27)

Pfeffer's research in this area has involved identifying the most successful organisations in terms of growth and profitability, and then seeking to establish through interviews with managers and staff in what ways their HR activities contribute to that success. In other words he has sought to discover what it is HR-wise that the most successful organisations do and that less successful organisations do not. In carrying out his research he looked at organisations that were of very different sizes and were pursuing varied business strategies. His major finding was that these contextual factors had much less relevance than is often thought. In practice the most successful organisations all pursued a similar broad approach to HRM, which in his view was a major determinant of their success.

Similar conclusions were reached by Mark Huselid (1995) using a different methodology. His studies have involved large-scale distribution of questionnaires across most major industries in the United States, which ask managers in some detail about their HRM practices. He has then taken this data and analysed it with reference to indicators of the organisations' business performance. Here too a clear link has been established between superior financial performance and particular approaches to HRM. Similar approaches have been used by UK-based researchers (see Wood and Albanese 1995, Fernie and Metcalf 1996, Guest and Conway 2000). The upshot is a situation in which there is now a considerable body of evidence which backs up the idea that there is a definable approach to HRM that can be termed 'best practice' and which appears to help all organisations, whatever their business strategy or market position, to maximise their financial performance over the long term. Guest (2000) sums the case up:

> *Human resource practices exercise their positive impact by (i) ensuring and enhancing the competence of employees, (ii) by tapping their motivation and commitment, and (iii) by designing work to encourage the fullest contribution from employees. Borrowing from elements of expectancy theory (Vroom 1964, Lawler 1971), the model implies that all three elements should be present to ensure the best outcome. Positive employee behaviour should in turn impact upon establishment level outcomes such as low absence, quit rates and wastage, as well as high quality and productivity.*
>
> (Guest 2000, p2)

Important elements of the 'bundle' of best practice approaches that these researchers have identified relate to people resourcing activities. First, in order to maximise motivation and commitment it is important that employees perceive themselves to be in secure jobs. Clearly it is never possible to guarantee people full security, and it is becoming steadily harder and harder to do so as the product markets that organisations operate in become increasingly global, competitive and volatile. However, this body of research clearly indicates that a response which involves ditching job security and replacing it with a highly flexible approach to staffing is likely to hinder the achievement of a strong financial performance. In other words, organisations that wish to thrive need to find ways of becoming more flexible, while also retaining high levels of commitment on the part of their staff – people for whom job security is important.

It is a difficult balance to achieve, but it is by no means impossible. To start with some of the ideas put forward by Peter Reilly (2002) under the heading 'mutual flexibility' can be adopted (see Chapter 7). The focus here is on the adoption of flexible working practices that benefit both employers and employees, and the avoidance of those that are unattractive to employees. Second, it is possible to commit to internal recruitment policies so that people whose jobs are no longer viable can be redeployed into new jobs and be given new opportunities within the same organisation. Third, it is possible to carry out human resource planning exercises so that the extent of redundancies or job losses caused through reorganisation are planned for well ahead of time, remedial action being taken to reduce wherever possible the extent of compulsory redundancies.

A second commonly cited element in the 'best practice bundle' is a sophisticated approach to recruitment and selection when external candidates are being sought. The approaches that should be used are those that are known to maximise the chances of the best performers being selected. Inevitably this means that recruitment and selection need to be carried out with care, and that sufficient time needs to be taken in order to get the decision right. As far as recruitment is concerned, 'best practice' requires that applications are solicited from a reasonably wide field of appointable people. This is achieved partly through the use of carefully planned and well-targeted advertising campaigns, and partly by taking steps more generally to maintain a good reputation in core labour markets. At the selection stage the techniques that are known to have the highest predictive validity should be used to support in-depth, structured interviews. Ideally this will include psychometric testing and, if affordable, some form of assessment centre or work-sample exercises. Key is the involvement of a variety of people, and decision-making based primarily on the experience and attributes required to do the job, rather than on any personal 'gut feelings' or subjective criteria.

Performance management also needs to be relatively sophisticated if it is to meet best practice standards. Autocratic management styles, in particular, need to be avoided. This is because they tend to demotivate in themselves and frequently trigger the resignation of good performers, but also because they discourage people from putting forward ideas about how processes can be improved or questioning their managers' thinking. As far as possible the presence of status differences should be minimised and a culture of openness encouraged. The use of 360-degree appraisal sends a strong signal that this is a the organisation's intended approach. People should be encouraged to contribute to decision-making so that they feel genuinely valued. Appraisals should have a developmental focus wherever possible and, where performance-related pay is used, great care must be taken to ensure that the way the system operates does not have the effect of demotivating people who rank their own performance rather more highly than their managers do. At all times performance management systems need both to operate fairly and be seen to do so.

RESOURCE-BASED VIEWS

The resource-based view of the firm (often abbreviated to RBV) has its origins in the 1950s and has always had considerable influence in thinking about business strategy. However, it is only over the last 15 years or so that its application to HRM has become prominent (Allen and Wright 2008). This is largely because it provides an alternative perspective on the link between HRM and business strategy than those advanced either by proponents of strategic alignment or by those who favour best practice thinking. Key is the notion articulated very effectively by Cappelli and Singh (2002) that organisations are often better off developing business strategies which reflect their existing human resource base than they are seeking continually to realign their HR practices and workforce so that they 'match' the business strategy.

So what we have here is a way of thinking about business strategy, HRM strategy and the link between them that is fundamentally different from those more traditional approaches outlined above. The starting point is not the external environment, but the existing internal resources or assets that the organisation has, including in large part its people. First and foremost RBV involves identifying what attributes the organisation's existing resources have which make them distinctly beneficial when compared to those of competitors. Barney (1991) suggested that the focus should be on understanding which resources are:

- valuable
- rare
- inimitable (ie: hard for competitors to replicate)
- non-substitutable.

These provide the basis of existing competitive advantage and can be improved further so as to sustain and strengthen that competitive advantage.

A good number of the assets that give organisations a degree of competitive advantage are resources of a nun-human kind, like location of activities or buildings, brand reputations and financial solvency. But increasingly it is accepted that the key differentiators are human in nature, particularly knowledge of one kind or another, experience and specialised skills. Increasingly the term 'human capital' is used to describe these attributes, the implication being that long-term competitive advantage is best attained and sustained by those organisations that are able to find ways of developing and growing their stock of human capital. Under RBV thinking, business strategies emerge, often quite opportunistically, as a result of competitive processes. The organisations that are best placed to provide a service or manufacture a product get the business, and their capacity to do so depends on their internal resources.

What contribution can people resourcing activities make? The answer inevitably will vary from organisation to organisation depending on its current situation. The aim will always be to reinforce and further develop the human assets that the organisation has at its disposal which give it its competitive advantage. Hence, where a particular knowledge base is identified as providing a key source of advantage in the market, the people resourcing contribution will involve taking steps that foster it and help in its further development. There is thus a role for quite sophisticated human resource planning, and in particular for the planning of individual developmental activities, the aim always being to ensure that the key areas of knowledge are not lost, but are enhanced. Recruitment and selection is also key, the aim being to replenish the organisation with people who are both willing and able to absorb and assimilate the knowledge needed to maintain the organisation's position when existing staff resign or retire. Effective employee retention is crucial to resource-based approaches to strategy-making because a failure to keep key human assets, and particularly their loss to competitors, can profoundly weaken the resource base which creates competitive advantage.

Beyond the knowledge base, another key attribute of organisations that often gives them competitive advantage is their unique culture. Knowledge can be readily replicated by a competitor, but cultures are far harder to create. It is not in the gift of managers to do so: the best they can aim for is influence over the development of an organisational culture. So, if an organisation is lucky enough to have a culture which contribute towards its competitive edge, there is under RBV thinking a good case for identifying this, treasuring it and fostering it. For example, an organisation may have developed a culture that is characterised by a 'can do' attitude on the part of people, where discretionary effort is regularly deployed, where people co-operate and collaborate willingly, where there are high-trust, open relationships between staff and managers and where people interact creatively. Such a culture is an enormous asset. It is difficult for a competitor that is less fortunate to create, so the need is to find ways of fostering it, encouraging its further development and celebrating it. Key here is a need for managers to consider very carefully how structural or policy changes they may be planning might disturb the culture or weaken it in such a way that it is diminished. It is also important not to bring forward interventions that have the effect of triggering voluntary resignations among people who are immersed in the positive culture and help to foster its further development.

COMPETING IN THE LABOUR MARKET

So far in this chapter the idea of 'people resourcing strategy' has been seen as either deriving from or contributing to the wider HR and business strategy of an organisation. In other words we have defined 'strategicness' in the people resourcing context in terms of the extent to which people resourcing activities in some way link with an organisation's wider business strategy – either deriving from a defined business strategy, or supporting an emerging business strategy. These are the assumptions that underlie most recent research on HR strategy, and which are reflected in the examples of practical applications which are published in professional journals and publicised at conferences attended by HR managers. There is, however, a completely different perspective that can be taken. This involves defining people resourcing strategy less in terms of its relationship with business strategy, and more in terms of an organisation's strategy towards its labour markets.

When labour market conditions are tight, unemployment low and skilled, experienced recruits relatively hard to find, the freedom of manouevre for organisations as far as recruiting and retaining people becomes severely constrained. Such conditions have prevailed in the United Kingdom for several years now, and are likely to continue to do so for the foreseeable future (Leitch 2006). In such circumstances resourcing activities inevitably become more important, consuming more expenditure and rising up the HR agenda ahead of other priorities. The tighter an organisation's labour markets, the more significant it becomes to recruit and then to retain more effective and committed performers than its competitors are able to. The term 'a war for talent' is often used in this context (eg Cappelli 2000, Larkan 2007), and as is the case when taking an army into battle, the chances of succeeding are greatly enhanced if a appropriate strategy is formulated and put into action.

Higgs (2004) suggests that employers have much to gain from 'segmenting' their employment markets and positioning themselves strategically in accordance with such an analysis. He presents a model which suggests four potential basic strategic choices (see Figure 21.1). There are two variables. One is the amount of money the employer is willing or able to pay. The other is not fully explained, but is labelled 'culture', and appears to refer to the extent to which employees are treated in a professional or ethical manner. One strategic choice is therefore to be 'an employer of cash' whereby employees are treated quite harshly, perhaps autocratically or by being expected to work excessive hours, but are nonetheless rewarded well. Such a strategy involves attracting good recruits with large pay packets and then retaining them by ensuring that they will have to take a pay cut if they opt to work elsewhere.

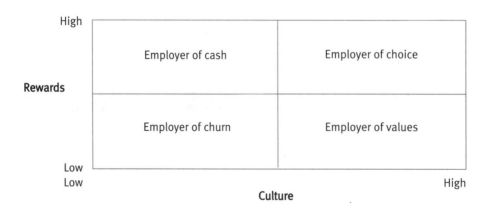

Figure 21.1 Four strategic approaches to the labour market

According to Neil (1996, pp184, 192), such an approach is used at the News International publishing group, allowing the company to buy acceptance from its employees of a range of 'low-commitment/high-control' HR practices. The opposite strategy involves paying poorly, perhaps rather less than the going market rate, but compensating by treating staff conspicuously better than would-be competitors do. Higgs labels this the 'employer of values' strategy. Such approaches have traditionally been associated with work in the public services, where pay has tended to be relatively low, but the work remains attractive because it is perceived as meaningful and rewarding by employees who also enjoy a superior level of job security.

The top right quartile in Figure 21.1 is labelled 'employer of choice', a term that is increasingly commonly used to describe an organisation which sets out to achieve an excellent labour market reputation by both paying well and treating people well. Examples of such organisations, many of which operate in the professional and financial services sectors, are found in the annual *Sunday Times* survey of the best 100 companies to work for in the UK (see www.timesonline.co.uk/tol/life_and_style/career_and_jobs/best_100_companies).

Finally, in the bottom left-hand corner is the box labelled 'employer of churn'. In such organisations pay is lousy, as is the way that employees are treated. The result is high staff turnover. In a tight labour market, where people have choice about where they work, such organisations find it hard to recruit and keep good staff. In recent years they have tended to rely on workers recruited overseas as well as on people who have very low skills and are thus incapable of finding alternative jobs. As a result, a number of companies that have traditionally been 'employers of churn' have taken the decision to reposition themselves. A good example is McDonald's, which had been forced to witness the ignominy of having the term 'McJob' included in the *Oxford English Dictionary* and defined as meaning a poorly paid job without prospects. In recent years the company has actively sought to improve its labour market image, aiming to become an employer of choice (Overell 2006).

Within the 'employer of choice' category, it is possible to identify further divisions, the idea here being that there are distinctly different ways of achieving 'employer of choice status'. Which a particular organisation chooses will in large part be determined on the type of labour market conditions it faces. A potentially useful approach involves simply classifying organisations according to the relative strengths of their internal and external labour markets, the rationale being that different approaches to HR in general, and people resourcing activities in particular, are appropriate in each case. Figure 21.2 represents a simple two-axis, four-way illustration. The top left quadrant represents employers whose external labour markets are tight and who thus struggle to recruit people, but who are in a position to offer long-term career development opportunities because their internal labour markets function effectively. They are labelled 'developers' because the best option available to them is to sell themselves to potential recruits as employers who will help people develop themselves and their careers. By contrast, moving to the top-right quadrant we have employers whose external labour markets are tight, but

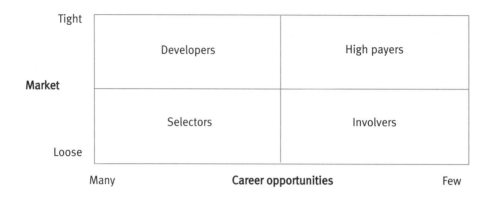

**Figure 21.2 Classifying organisations according to the strengths of their internal
and external labour markets**

who cannot for one reason or another provide many attractive career
development opportunities. Such organisations often tend to be small and
specialised. The only option open to them if they want to recruit and retain
the best people is thus to pay above the market rate, hence the label 'high
payers'.

In the lower half of Figure 21.2 we can place organisations that have relatively
little difficulty recruiting and retaining. On the right-hand side are larger
organisations, with plenty of career paths available to people. In a loose labour
market such organisations are highly attractive to job-seekers, the consequence
being that they receive large numbers of applications whenever they advertise
jobs and plenty of unsolicited applications when they don't. They therefore
have the luxury of being able to pick carefully who they wish to employ. As a
result, employee selection is the focus of their resourcing activities, plenty of
money being spent on graduate recruitment exercises and on sophisticated
selection techniques, so that they can maintain their position as an employer
of choice.

Finally on the bottom right are 'involvers'. These are employers who are able to
offer most employees few development opportunities but who also, often
because they are one of relatively few employers of particular types of staff in a
region, find that they have relatively few problems recruiting new people. The
main problem they face is thus the presence of dissatisfied staff who are
trapped in their jobs, unable to move up the career ladder internally, but who
also have few alternative job opportunities open to them. The danger in such
circumstances is that low levels of trust will develop between staff and
management, leading in some cases to the establishment of an adversarial
industrial relations climate. The priority therefore, for an aspiring employer of
choice, is to involve staff in decision-making, to ensure that jobs are well
designed and to try as hard as possible to maintain good levels of job
satisfaction.

ONLINE GAMING

Read the article by Catherine Edwards, Raised stakes (*People Management,* 9 March 2006, pp25–27). This can be downloaded from the *People Management* archive on the CIPD's website (www.cipd.co.uk).

This article concerns the HR practices being developed in two organisations operating in the international online gaming industry. The industry is growing very rapidly, as are the organisations that operate the best-used websites. However, they are also characterised by an unusual extent of uncertainty about their future.

Questions

1   What different factors make the future uncertain for online gambling companies?

2   Using the models described in this chapter, how would you characterise their business and employment market strategies?

3   To what extent are the resourcing policies and practices being developed appropriate to these strategies?

QUEEN BEE RESOURCING STRATEGIES

Finally in this chapter it is necessary to assess an approach to people resourcing strategy that is controversial, but also apparently increasingly common. This involves organisations focusing their efforts in terms of labour market competition not on the generality of employees but very much on the few who are identified as being highly talented. Such approaches are advocated to different degrees by Hiltrop (1999), Woodruffe (1999), Williams (2000), Cappelli (2000) and Larkan (2007).

The case for a 'queen bee' approach rests on the assumption that there are in all areas of work individuals who have particularly rare and sought-after skills which give them the capacity to 'make a real difference' to an organisation's performance. Their individual contribution is often rated by managers as being five or 10 times more useful to them and their organisations than the average performer. Not only are they exceptional performers in their current roles, but they also have considerable potential for further development in the future. Queen bees typically have a reputation that spreads well beyond the organisations they work for, making them desirable 'catches' as far as headhunters are concerned and the targets of poaching raids by rival employers. Recruiting and retaining such people clearly gives an organisation a competitive advantage in its industry, but to do so particular efforts have to be made. A queen-bee resourcing strategy thus involves lavishing particular attention, opportunities, perks and often money on these relatively few, highly talented individuals. The strategy is judged to be successful when the queen bees are retained for substantial periods and the organisation is successful in attracting the services of further queen bees.

The problem with this approach is its capacity for demotivating average performers who may well be less enamoured of the talents of their queen bee colleagues and hence resent the 'special treatment' that they enjoy. The danger arises because there are many more average performers than there are queen bees and thus considerable potential damage can be done if they become demotivated and dissatisfied. An organisation can thus readily end up retaining its outstanding performers, but losing many more of the kind who are solid, reliable and effective, and on whom the organisation relies over time to deliver a good level of service to its customers. The problem is compounded by the way that queen bees understandably tend to have a keen sense of their own worth and thus display little natural loyalty to any one organisation. Keeping them thus tends to be expensive and time-consuming.

KEY ARTICLE 51

Steven Poelmans, Nuria Chinchilla and Pablo Cardona, The adoption of family-friendly HRM policies: competing for scarce resources in the labour market. *International Journal of Manpower,* Vol. 24, No. 2, pp128–147 (2003)

This article reports the results of a questionnaire survey undertaken in Spain which aims to establish what factors lead organisations to commit to family-friendly employment practices. Various hypotheses are tested, several of which surprisingly are found not to be proven. The key finding is that the tightness of the labour market is a major determinant of whether or not organisations adopt family-friendly policies.

Questions

1   Why do the authors argue that Spanish employers face rather different issues when it comes to adopting family-friendly employment practices than is the case in other countries?

2   Why do you think that this study found so little support for the proposition that organisations adopt family-friendly policies in order to improve performance and reduce absenteeism?

3   What are the major weaknesses you can identify with this study? To what extent do these undermine the validity of its conclusions?

4   Using the models presented above, explain in what circumstances the adoption of conspicuously generous family-friendly practices might contribute most to a people resourcing strategy.

CHAPTER SUMMARY

- Organisations vary in the extent to which they take a strategic approach to their people resourcing activities. They most commonly employ strategic thinking when managing specific projects.

- Much research on HR strategy, including people resourcing strategy, is concerned with identifying ways of effectively aligning HR practices with the organisation's strategic objectives.

- More recently alternative approaches have achieved great influence. These include best practice thinking and the resource-based view of the firm.

- A different way of conceptualising people resourcing strategy is to think about it in terms of competing in the labour market in a strategic fashion.

- Many organisations now set themselves the aim of becoming 'employers of choice'. Such a status can be achieved in a number of ways. Which is most appropriate in which conditions is in large part determined by labour market conditions.

- A queen-bee strategy involves focusing management efforts on the recruitment and retention of outstanding performers. A danger with such an approach is the risk that average performers will be demotivated in response.

EXPLORE FURTHER

- To the author's knowledge there are no books, book chapters or journal articles that focus on the idea of 'people resourcing strategy' in general terms. There are, however, many excellent books that provide comprehensive introductions to the idea of strategic HRM more generally. Schuler and Jackson (2007), Millmore *et al* (2007) and Boxall and Purcell (2008) are all recent and recommended.

- Marchington and Wilkinson (2008) contains good, accessible chapters covering best-fit models, best practice thinking and the resource-based view of the firm. The resource-based view is covered succinctly by Allen and Wright (2007).

CHAPTER 22

Debates about the future of work

The writer Mark Twain famously observed that 'prediction is difficult, especially when the predictions relate to the future', but this has never stopped people trying to predict how the world will develop by thinking through the consequences of a continuation of current trends. A great deal of future-gazing has always gone on in the fields of management and business, because so much rides on the ability to anticipate coming trends so as to enable an organisation to cash in more quickly and effectively than its competitors. The history of modern industry is littered with examples of once great business empires that are now no more simply because they did not adapt their operations quickly enough in response to evolving customer preferences, new technologies or government thinking. Fortunes can thus be made or lost, depending on the accuracy or inaccuracy of predictions. As a result managers are always keen to read and to hear the views of those who claim to be able to see the future, can set out what it is going to mean for organisations and can justify their views with a plausible case. Individuals who can articulate these kinds of messages effectively can themselves become rich through book sales, conference speeches and media appearances. It is not surprising, therefore, that vigorous and very interesting debates about future management practices continually evolve and thrive.

In recent years the attention of the futurologists has increasingly turned to people management issues and to many of the areas of employment practice covered in this book. This principally stems from a belief that the contribution made by individuals – indeed by an organisation's human resources in general – is becoming increasingly central to the achievement of competitive advantage. As was explained in Chapter 20, for a large proportion of organisations, human capital is now the key determinant of long-term business success, outweighing or at least equalling in significance other forms of capital (land, buildings, equipment, finance and so on). The way people are managed is thus accepted as being a central determinant of business success. Moreover, governments have become increasingly interested as they seek to bolster their nations' fortunes in a global economy. Government ministers are as keen as managers of organisations to grasp the significance of current and future trends, so that they can regulate and develop interventions that help to create and sustain international competitive advantage. As a result a great deal of government research funding is now being channelled into projects that contribute to our understanding of the future of work.

In this final chapter we explore the major debates that are developing about the future of work and raise questions about the accuracy of some of the more prominent recent predictions. The case is put for and against the likelihood that we are about to witness very radical change. We then go on to look at two topic areas of general significance to people resourcing activities that are likely to become more important in the future: the concept of emotional intelligence and the management of knowledge.

LEARNING OUTCOMES

By the end of this chapter readers should be able to:

- evaluate the cases for and against a radically different 'future of work'

- advise on the use of 'emotional intelligence' competencies in employee selection and performance management

- evaluate the implications of the development of 'knowledge work' from a management perspective.

In addition, readers should be able to understand and explain:

- the major contours of debates about 'the future of work' and their implications for organisations.

- the concepts of emotional intelligence and knowledge management.

DEBATES ABOUT THE FUTURE OF WORK

Debates about the future of work and how the P&D function will look as the twenty-first century unfolds are necessarily different from the others that have been explored in this book. Self-evidently this is because arguments cannot be based on hard evidence and must be speculative in nature. We can extrapolate current trends forward and we can also place bets on likely future technological advances, but we cannot know with any certainty whether our predictions will in fact be realised. As was shown in Chapter 6, discontinuities have a habit of occurring and surprising even the most well-informed authorities, rendering formerly confident forecasts obsolete. There are also of course very different views about what should happen in the future, and it is not at all clear which of today's competing visions about paths to take, if any, will ultimately win the day.

However, a lack of hard evidence about the future has not stopped many writers from developing quite sophisticated theses about what we can expect over the coming decades. Indeed, helping managers to understand and come to terms with the evolving business environment has developed into a highly profitable industry. Thousands of books are published each year aiming to assist managers in this task, with top authors becoming multi-millionaires in the process (see Collins 2000, p19; Arkin 2001b). Hundreds of thousands of managers contribute towards further fat cheques for so-called 'management gurus' to hear them speak on the international conference circuit, while millions of pounds more are spent each year on consultants' fees with the same aim in mind. Much of what these people have to say is useful and interesting, but it is important to remember that they are not impartial observers. They have a vested interest in persuading us that the world is changing rapidly and that if we do not radically alter what we are doing we, and our organisations, have a bleak future to look forward to. The more successful they are at persuading us of the 'ever accelerating pace of change', the more opportunities there are for new editions of books, the emergence of new buzzwords and the further development of the gurus' own industry. This would not matter too much were the message to fall on thoughtful and sceptical ears. Unfortunately the rhetoric is deployed with such evangelical fervour and is repeated so frequently through different forms of media that managers tend to accept it as received wisdom in quite an unquestioning way. This means that faulty assumptions sometimes cloud decision-making and that the gurus' messages can become self-fulfilling prophecies.

In the last few years these messages have been authoritatively challenged in some of the publications that have been written by participants in the ESRC's (Economic and Social Research Council) future of work programme. Led by Peter Nolan of Leeds University, this is a large-scale government-funded research programme that has involved some 30 teams of researchers in many UK universities. Their findings have, on the whole, been a great deal more cautious than the views of the management gurus, suggesting a future for working life that is not so different from the one we currently experience. Evolution rather than revolution is their message. As yet, however, despite the appearance of hundreds of publications deriving from ESRC future of work projects, their message continues to be somewhat muffled out by sexier, but less well-founded, predictions of radical change just around the corner.

Although we have called for a dose of hard-headed scepticism about claims made for the future, it is important not to ignore everything that is being said by professional futurologists. P&D professionals need to have a view about the way their work may evolve during their careers and can only gain in credibility by developing robust views about the debates that rage in this field. It is difficult to sum these up in a few hundred words, without oversimplifying the arguments. A whole book is really necessary to do proper justice to the various claims that are made about the future, so recommendations for further reading are given at the end of the chapter. However, it is possible to summarise some of the key strands in the arguments that are put forward, many of which build on ideas explored earlier in the book about internationalisation, technological change and flexibility.

Central to the future of work debate is the notion of 'a new economy' that is said to be in the process of replacing 'the old economy' in Western, industrialised countries. The new economy is sometimes conceived as being service-based (ie principally consisting of non-manufacturing activities), but more often nowadays as being 'knowledge-based'. This means that organisations exist for the purpose of making and distributing knowledge (information or intellectual services). The main thrust of the predictions is that most people will, in the future, be engaged in different types of work than has historically been the case. The claim is based on the idea that most manufacturing jobs, along with more routine administrative work will no longer exist in the countries such as the United Kingdom. Labour-saving new technology will account for some of these jobs, while millions of others will effectively be 'exported' to developing countries. The work that we will carry out instead will be of two basic types:

- knowledge-work (developing new technologies, creating new knowledge, R&D etc)

- people-based service provision of the kind that machines cannot carry out (care-work, work that leads and inspires others, creative work).

There is nothing especially controversial about these claims, although it is wise to be cautious about the extent and speed with which their proponents say that developments will take place. What is more questionable is the further claim that the way work will be organised in 'the new economy' will be fundamentally different from the way we currently do things in 'the old economy'. While different commentators, use different terms to describe what they think will happen, several of the most influential (eg Charles Handy, Jeremy Rifkin, William Bridges) argue that the concept of 'the job' as we have come to know it is on the way out. In its place will come a variety of other arrangements that have more in common with forms of self-employment. Instead of perceiving ourselves as belonging to an organisation, we will have 'portfolio careers', undertaking different assignments on a temporary basis for many different organisations.

Handy likens this future state of affairs to the life of an actor playing different types of roles for a limited period of time for different sorts of organisation (television, film, advertising, theatre and so on). Flexible working through agency work, temporary contracts and self-employment will thus become the norm. This will happen, it is claimed, primarily because of the increasing volatility of the business environment (see Chapter 2). The less organisations are able to forecast their own futures with any degree of certainty, the less able they will be to make any kind of long-term commitment to employees. Moreover, technological developments and the rise of knowledge-work will mean that the work we do is increasingly suited to a jobless economy. Much of the work will be able to be carried out at home on a teleworking basis and will be project-based. Knowledge workers with expertise will thus be required to sell their services to organisations as and when they can, and will not be able to anticipate a lengthy employment relationship. Linked to these predictions is a further one that has been downplayed recently, but that was confidently asserted ten years ago. This is the belief that we will all have a great deal more leisure time in the new economy than we have been accustomed to enjoying in the old one. More holidays, more time out in further education, earlier retirement and shorter hours have all been forecast by one or more authors in this context.

If these analyses are right, there are clearly major implications for P&D

specialists. The way we attract people, select them, seek to retain them, motivate them, develop them and reward them will in the future be utterly different from the way things are today. The most significant consequence will be a change in the basic power relationship between employers and employees. With a host of potential employers to work for, the possibility of working largely from home and sought-after expert knowledge in their heads, people will be able to choose who they work for and under what types of terms and conditions. They may choose to enter into a long-term relationship with one organisation, but it will not necessarily be exclusive and could be terminated very easily at any time. Administrative requirements will be wholly different in such a world too. There would be no more standard contracts of employment or organisation-wide HR policies to implement. Payment would be individualised to a far greater degree than at present, while the concept of determining and recording holiday entitlements would seem very old-fashioned indeed.

It is interesting to speculate on the shape of a typical P&D function in such a world. It is likely that most of the activities would themselves be outsourced and that all efforts would be focused on developing a strong corporate reputation for providing interesting and challenging work. But is this really going to happen? Are we really heading fast towards a world in which people no longer have or desire 'jobs' and in which staff choose their employers rather than the other way round? How accurate are the predictions that are being made about the 'new economy'? As was stated above, it is impossible to say with a strong degree of confidence. Some of these predictions are based on a very logical analysis of what can be expected to occur as new technologies and the process of globalisation develop further. However, there are grounds for doubting some of the wilder claims, or at least for concluding that their significance for the workforce as a whole is severely exaggerated.

An important source of evidence is the trend towards atypical working examined in Chapter 7, a phenomenon that is often used by proponents of paradigm shifts in workplace relations themselves to justify earlier predictions. The following quotation from Charles Handy's most recent book is typical:

> It had been foolhardy then, at the start of the Thatcher years in Britain [1981], to prophesy that by the year 2000 less than half of the working population would be in conventional full-time jobs on what are called 'indefinite period contracts'. The rest of us would either be self-employed, or part-timers, perhaps temps of one sort or another, or out of paid work altogether. We would need, I said, a portfolio of different bits and pieces of paid work, or a collection of clients and customers, if we wanted to earn a living. ... As it turned out, by the year 2000 the British labour force on those indefinite period contracts in full-time employment had fallen to 40 per cent and the BBC World Service was running programmes on the theme 'What Future for Men?'.
>
> (Handy 2001, pp3–5)

Unfortunately, such claims are highly misleading. It is true that if you add together part-time workers, temporary workers, self-employed people, people in full-time education, unemployed people and those who have taken early retirement, you have a sum that is higher than the number employed on a full-time permanent basis. But the situation was not actually that different in 1981 when Handy made his 'foolhardy' forecast. There have been modest increases in atypical forms of working since then, mainly in part-time contracts, but these were largely continuations of existing trends. To use this as the basis for a claim that we are now largely a workforce made up of portfolio workers as defined in the quotation is simply untrue. We would have to have witnessed a vastly greater increase in temporary working and self-employment for this prediction to have been substantiated. In fact, the 1990s saw a modest decline in self-employment, while the period since 1997 has seen a sharp decline in temporary employment as a proportion of total employment (McOrmond 2004, p30; National Statistics 2006, pp24–25), remaining a great deal lower than in most other industrialised economies.

The number of self-employed people has begun to increase again, but the rate of increase is gradual and is largely accounted for by the banking and finance sectors, where jobs have been shed leading people to set up their own businesses, and in the building and construction industries, which are booming and provide excellent opportunities for self-employed people ((Lindsay and McCaulay 2004; National Statistics 2006, p23). There is no evidence whatever of major underlying shifts away from permanent employment towards short-term contracts and self-employment.

A second source of information on current trends that can furnish evidence for the future of work debate is the figures on job tenure. If it were true that we are heading towards a world of temporary assignments instead of permanent full-time jobs, we would expect to see a substantial decline occurring over recent years in the length of time we spend in each of our jobs. However, as was explained in Chapter 17, this is not at all evident from the government's statistics. Average job tenure has fluctuated up and down with economic conditions over the years, but has remained within the same broad bands throughout the past 30 years. It was four years and nine months in 1975, and four years and ten months a quarter of a century later (Gregg and Wadsworth 1999, p115). Clearly, there is no evidence of any dramatic shift here.

Moreover, a quarter of the UK workforce has already been employed in the same place for over 12 years. It is true that average male job tenure has fallen somewhat and that the biggest increases have been in the figures for women with children, but we would have had to see substantially greater changes to judge the 'new economy' thesis to be proven. In short, while some sectors have seen a shift towards shorter periods of employment, the overall picture for the labour force is not greatly different. We can thus conclude that as yet, despite the claims of some gurus, there is little evidence of any kind of fundamental shift in working relationships along the lines of their forecasts.

A third type of evidence concerns the nature of the work that we are performing. If the prophets of a 'knowledge-based' economy are correct in their claims, we would expect to see a strong trend towards knowledge-based employment. Here too the evidence is patchy. Research undertaken by Peter Nolan and his colleagues at Leeds University shows that the fastest growing occupational groups in the United Kingdom are a mixture of knowledge-based and non-knowledge-based (Nolan 2001, p31). The top 10 list includes software engineers, technicians and consultants (all types of knowledge-worker) but these are outweighed by growth in relatively low-paid service sector jobs such as shelf-fillers, nursery nurses, domestic staff, educational assistants and welfare workers. The group that saw by far the biggest growth of all during the 1990s was hairdressers (a 302 per cent increase). Again we seem to be seeing a continuation of long-term trends away from manufacturing towards services of different kinds, but no paradigm shift solely towards knowledge work.

Another objection to some of the 'future of work' predictions is their apparent determinism. Proponents argue that the changes they anticipate are going to be technologically driven and that they are therefore in some way inevitable. The fact that people themselves may object and seek to stop the developments happening (or limit their effects) does not seem to be considered. Linked to this is an assumption that people will soon learn to be comfortable with portfolio working, or may even welcome it. No consideration seems to be given to the inherent insecurity of these types of employment and the probability that people will act in such a way as to gain greater security. It may well turn out to be the case that the majority of people will opt for employment rather than the promise of 'employability' wherever they can. It follows that workers with considerable market power derived from their specialist knowledge will be actively seek a traditional 'job' where it is on offer and will tend to steer clear of employers offering only temporary assignments. The result will be an incentive for employers to offer contracts of the full-time, open-ended variety that are supposedly on the way out. It will take a significant shift in established attitudes towards work for people readily to accept life as a portfolio worker. It is true that there is some evidence of a more flexible mindset on the part of the 'Generation Y' people in their early 20s (Pollock and Cooper 2000, Woodruffe 2000), but only time will tell whether their avowed comfort with insecurity will remain when they begin to shoulder domestic responsibilities. All the current evidence suggests that people seek security and prefer to develop their careers with their existing employers. Moreover, employers continue in the large majority of cases to meet their expectations in these respects (see White *et al* 2004, Emmott 2004).

In addition there is the question of regulation – another factor that is largely ignored in the visions of the futurologists. It is quite possible to envisage a situation in which work insecurity becomes a major political issue and politicians will be required to respond with legislation to deter employers from moving towards atypical contractual arrangements. At the European level such debates are already well rehearsed. A great deal of work has already been carried out both in Brussels and through other EU governments to examine ways of bringing greater regulation to the labour market using regulatory mechanisms. The following quotation from a European Commission publication on *The future of work* illustrates the kind of thinking that is developing:

> *The question is whether Europe, after the establishment of economic and monetary union, will have the resources – and whether it wishes to use them as*

part of its social policy – to put a halt to this creeping job insecurity which flies in the face of its values of solidarity (including solidarity between men and women). What balance should it strike between much-needed adaptation of its labour force to international competition and the social cohesion it sees as vital?

(European Commission 2000, p33)

It is thus reasonable to conclude that P&D specialists should be cautious in responding to the cries of 'change now or die' emanating from conference platforms and management books with dramatic titles. They may be right in their messages about the future, but there is little evidence to date of any kind of fundamental changes occurring, and there are reasons to doubt that the 'new world of work' will ever materialise in the way its advocates suggest. A 'new economy' is emerging but it seems clear, at least for the foreseeable future, that will co-exist alongside the 'old economy' rather than replacing it. It might be a good thing for the UK economy if the transformation occurred more rapidly, particularly in respect of skills acquisition (see Taylor 2004), but it is the slowness of change that tends to concern contemporary commentators and not its rapidity.

In fact, a compelling case can be made in favour of the view that the UK employment scene has already gone through its major transformation and that the period ahead will be characterised by relative stability in comparison with the past two decades. We may actually see a deceleration rather than an acceleration of the pace of change. It is easy when looking to the future to forget just how major the changes that have occurred since the 1970s have been. These have included a substantial fall in manufacturing employment and the rise of the service sector, large-scale privatisation of state-owned enterprises, the demolition of the established system of national-level collective bargaining as a means of determining terms and conditions, increases in immigration from overseas, huge falls in trade union membership, the establishment and growth of the Internet, huge increases in regulation, the feminisation of many workplaces, globalisation of many industries and a tightening of labour markets due to lower birthrates. The practices that managers have had to develop in response to these and other trends have been a major focus of this book. Could it be that the future of work 'has already happened' to a great extent and that consolidation rather than further change is the likely dominant theme for the next 20 years?

Above it was argued that there is little disagreement between commentators about one prediction. That is that the industries that will dominate economies such as the United Kingdom's over the coming decades will be of two major types; personal care and knowledge-based. There will be less unskilled work, while some existing skills will become less desirable from an employer's perspective. The effective management of people employed to work in the personal care and knowledge-based industries is thus likely to move up the P&D agenda, and indeed already is doing so in many organisations. Below, two topic areas of relevance to these trends are introduced; emotional intelligence and knowledge management.

SUSAN GREENFIELD'S PREDICTIONS

EXERCISE 22.1

Read the article by Susan Greenfield, Flexible futures (*People Management*, 23 October 2003, pp52–53). This can be downloaded from the *People Management* archive on the CIPD's website (www.cipd.co.uk).

In this short article Baroness Greenfield of Oxford University sets out some of her thoughts about the future of work. Some of her views are similar to those of Charles Handy and others who believe in a radically different future working environment. In other respects her predictions differ somewhat.

Questions

1   What different factors does Greenfield identify that will bring about the changes she envisages?

2   What major weaknesses can you identify in her arguments?

3   What do you think would be the major implications for you as an HR professional if her predictions of 'imminent change' were to prove accurate?

KEY ARTICLE 52

Peter Nolan, Shaping the future: the political economy of work and employment. *Industrial Relations Journal*, Vol. 35, No. 5, pp378–387 (2004)

This article is the editorial which opened a special edition of the *Industrial Relations Journal* on different aspects of the 'future of work debate'. In it, as well as introducing some of the key points from the articles which followed, Peter Nolan takes the opportunity to introduce the ESRC's Future of Work research programme and to tackle head on some of the myths perpetuated by people he describes as 'well-paid visionaries' about contemporary labour market trends. In particular he takes aim at those who argue that a move away from employment (the death of the job) is at all imminent.

Questions

1   Why, according to Nolan, is it plain wrong to argue that new technologies will replace people, leaving a world in which there are too few jobs to occupy for the population of Western industrialised countries such as the United Kingdom?

2   Why is it wrong to assert that self-employment and temporary work will increasingly replace traditional employment in the future?

3   On what basis does Nolan argue that the research commissioned by the Future of Work programme 'reveals good and bad news for paid and unpaid work in the UK'?

EMOTIONAL INTELLIGENCE

The concept of emotional intelligence came to prominence in the 1980s and 1990s through the work of American psychologists such as Howard Gardner, Peter Salovey and John Mayer. However, credit for bringing the term to a wider audience must be given to Daniel Goleman, who wrote several very accessible books and articles on the subject in the late 1990s and continues to preach his message. Goleman has also carried out his own research, which suggests that emotional intelligence is a particularly significant ingredient in effective leadership and is not something that is necessarily associated with intelligence as conventionally conceived (see Goleman 1998; Cook and Cripps 2005, p51). There is even now a UK-based journal specifically dedicated to emotional intelligence and related topics (see IRS 2000f, p6). Often abbreviated to Ei or EQ, 'emotional intelligence' is best understood as a defined group of personality traits or competencies that some people exhibit to a greater degree than others, but that can be developed over time. Salovey and Mayer (1989) describe four distinct elements:

- the ability to perceive how oneself and other people are feeling

- the ability to access or generate emotions in oneself as means of assisting thought

- the ability to understand emotions and emotional reactions to events

- the ability to manage or regulate emotions in oneself and others.

Goleman (1998) defines EQ slightly differently with reference to five separate components:

- self-awareness (of motivations, strengths and weaknesses)

- self-regulation (controlling emotions and channelling them constructively)

- motivation (being internally driven to achieve goals)

- empathy (understanding emotional reactions in others)

- social skill (eg working well with others, building rapport).

Emotional intelligence differs from IQ in that it takes account of irrational as well as rational reactions to different types of situation. But it is also about making intelligent use of one's own emotions and responding effectively to emotional responses in others.

The claim that emotional intelligence (or something very similar) exists and is significant is not new or revolutionary, being rooted in centuries of psychological research and practice (Woodruffe 2001, pp27–28). What is new is the extent to which proponents of the theory now believe EQ to contribute to effective performance in the workplace. Goleman, in his research on effective leaders, goes as far as to claim that up to 85 per cent of success in the contemporary business world can be accounted for by emotional intelligence and only 15 per cent by cognitive ability (IQ). It follows that organisations should ascribe greater prominence than they have done historically to this group of competencies when recruiting, selecting, managing and developing their staff.

While many more cautious analysts have questioned the magnitude of Goleman's claims and believe him to be exaggerating their importance, few dispute the basic idea that the intelligent use of emotions is an attribute that helps raise standards of performance in a number of roles – namely those that hinge to a good degree on the effectiveness of dealings with other people. EQ is not especially useful for people whose main interaction at work is with machines, land or animals. Technical competencies are clearly more important for them. However, for those whose jobs involve managing or serving others in more than a routine manner, a compelling case in favour of the significance of emotional intelligence can be made. The increase we continue to see in the number and prominence of people-oriented jobs thus also accounts for the growth in interest in the EQ concept.

While most of the writing on emotional intelligence has focused on its part in effective leadership, it is clear that the same broad principles apply to many service sector jobs involving direct and prolonged contact with customers. It therefore stands to reason that these types of competencies should be influential factors in recruitment and development practices for such roles. The use of emotional competencies in employee selection is controversial and is apparently opposed by Goleman himself (IRS 2000f, p8). However, case study evidence suggests that it is being increasingly used and that positive results can be identified:

- In the 1990s L'Oreal, a cosmetics company, tried selecting some of their sales agents on the basis of their emotional intelligence, while retaining existing selection practices for others. It subsequently found that the first group outsold the second to the tune of $90,000 per year. Staff turnover rates were also 63 per cent lower in the first group than in the second (IRS 2000f).

- In 2002 it was reported that British Telecom was boasting of a 36 per cent rise in its customer satisfaction rates. Apparently this occurred after a reorganisation of their service management centres using assessments of emotional intelligence to select staff for different roles. Structured interviews and a competency-based questionnaire were used to identify which staff were best suited to roles that involved customer contact, and which were best allocated to administrative jobs. BT concluded that 80 per cent of its employees' success in serving customers derived from emotional intelligence, and 20 per cent from technical competencies.

The major providers of personality tests are now developing instruments that specifically seek to measure emotional intelligence, and a number are already on the market. Those developed by reputable companies using proper validation mechanisms are likely to be used with increasing success in the selection of people for customer-oriented roles.

More generally, EQ would seem to comprise a set of competencies that P&D specialists themselves should seek to develop. This is particularly true for those whose jobs involve frequent interaction with staff in circumstances that precipitate emotional responses. Those with responsibility for hands-on handling of disciplinary issues, cases of poor performance, dismissals and absence particularly stand to benefit. Development programmes that focus on the effective handling of emotion (in oneself and others) are thus worthy of serious consideration. It is true that these competencies can be learned with experience and proper training, raising the effectiveness of the P&D function and the respect in which it is held. The following quotation illustrates the type of understanding that can be usefully developed and applied in more tense encounters:

> There are only two ways to deal with emotion. If you have aroused the emotion because of something you did which you now accept is wrong, then an early apology will defuse the situation. On many occasions, however, this may not be appropriate. In these circumstances the only solution is to let the emotion run its course. This can be encouraged in two ways. Attentive, but silent listening, and the occasional use of reflective questions. Silence can be difficult to maintain as there is a strong temptation to jump in and correct inaccuracies. Reflective questions do what their name suggests; they use a summary of what the person has just said and reflect it back, without evaluation. For example, 'You feel you've been undervalued by the firm – is that it?' The effect is to allow the emotion to run its course. High levels of emotion are difficult to maintain without support from others, either in the form of agreement or argument. With no evaluation, the emotional level tends to steadily decrease.
>
> (Makin *et al* 1996, p202)

In some books on emotional intelligence, writers have begun to go on to explore the notion of the 'emotionally intelligent organisation' (see Goleman 1998, Weisinger 1998), although it is always stated that it will take some years for research on this topic to take place. The idea, though, is attractive in principle and could assist in the achievement of competitive advantage. On one level an emotionally intelligent organisation can simply be characterised as one that is made up of emotionally intelligent people, but it also goes a great deal further. Such organisations, because of the orientation of their people, are said to have developed strong values that combine to make them more effective and understanding workplaces. These include the following:

- a commitment to work–life balance
- openness and high-trust working relationships
- creativity and innovation formed through collaborative working
- a willingness to share ideas and resources
- a supportive as opposed to a competitive climate.

REFLECTIVE QUESTION

To what extent would you characterise your organisation (or parts of it) as 'emotionally intelligent'? What steps would need to be taken in order to encourage the development of such characteristics?

EXERCISE 22.2

EQ IN CALL CENTRES

People management

Read the article by Malcolm Higgs, Good call (*People Management*, 23 January 2003, pp48–49). This can be downloaded from the *People Management* archive on the CIPD's website (www.cipd.co.uk).

In this article Malcolm Higgs describes a programme of research in which he and his colleagues sought to establish a link between emotional intelligence and effective performance on the part of call centre workers. Their results suggest that call centre managers should alter their traditional approaches to recruitment.

Questions

1   In what ways are the personality traits shared by effective call centre workers any different from those you would expect to find shared by most good employees working in customer service roles?

2   To what extent do you agree with the argument that call centres should avoid recruiting intuitive people and why?

3   Why do you think older women make the best call centre workers?

KEY ARTICLE 53

Laura Thi Lam and Susan L. Kirby, Is emotional intelligence an advantage? An exploration of the impact of emotional and general intelligence on individual performance. *Journal of Social Psychology*, Vol. 142, No. 1, pp133–143 (2002)

These researchers set out to establish how far in practice, if at all, people with relatively high levels of emotional intelligence are able to perform more effectively than co-workers who are equally intelligent as measured conventionally, but lack emotional intelligence. This is an example of a kind of laboratory-based methodology that is common in psychology, but which can lack face-validity for many management researchers because the studies are not carried out in a workplace setting. Here the subjects were all undergraduate students, while the method used comprised questionnaire-based tests measuring IQ, EQ/EI and cognitive performance. The conclusions are based on a quantitative analysis of the results.

Questions

1.   Why do you think the researchers found that the capacity to 'understand emotions' had no apparent impact on the capacity to perform the task, whereas there was an effect in relation to 'perceiving emotions' and 'regulating emotions'?

2.   What explanation is given for why people with high levels of emotional intelligence do not in practice find that their own emotions interfere with their ability to complete tasks satisfactorily?

3.   What criticisms can be made of the methodology used in this study? To what extent do these make you question the validity and generalisability of the conclusions the authors reach?

KNOWLEDGE MANAGEMENT

Knowledge management is another notion of general relevance to the material included in this book, and this chapter in particular, which has attracted a great deal of interest in recent years. Originating in the 1980s, the term is linked to a range of other fashionable buzzwords such as 'intellectual capital' and 'the learning organisation'. Like other recent additions to the vocabulary of management thinkers, knowledge management and the ideas that flow from an understanding of its aims are compelling in theory. However, as is the often the case, there is a tendency to exaggerate both the extent to which the idea is new and its significance for managers operating in the real (as opposed to the theoretical) world.

At base we are concerned here with the consequences of the view that our business environment is changing fundamentally from being essentially 'industrial' in nature to 'post-industrial'. The new world differs from the old one in several respects, but central is its knowledge-based nature. Wealth is now principally generated, so it is argued, through the creation and application of knowledge:

> *In these environments, wealth creation is less dependent on the control of resources and more dependent on the exercise of specialist knowledge, or the management of organizational competences. We can no longer blame the mismanagement of tangible resources for failures in a knowledge-based society. We now need to turn our attention to the management of the intangible. Managerial systems remain important, but it is the management of intangible assets that is now argued to be at the heart of the managerial process.*
>
> (Swart 2007, pp450–451)

The trend is most clearly apparent in the nature of the work that we are now required to perform. Historically, the majority of the working population were not obliged to use their minds to any great extent in the workplace. Most people went to work and performed a range of routine tasks that were prescribed for them by managers. They were not required or even invited to be creative, or to innovate, or to make use of their knowledge in any other way. It is argued that the position today is wholly different. Most of us can now be categorised, in some shape or form, as 'knowledge workers', fitting in somewhere to the following four-way classification provided by Laudon and Starbuck (1997, p299):

- people who process or preserve data
- people who interpret information and act upon it
- people who generate new information
- people who apply accumulated knowledge.

We are hired less for what we can offer in physical terms and more because of what we know and our ability to apply that knowledge. Brinkley and Lee

(2006) estimate that 48 per cent of the UK workforce is now employed in knowledge-based industries, the number having grown significantly over the past decade, and up from only 17 per cent at the start of the twentieth century (see Storey and Quintas 2001, p346). It follows that organisations depend to an increasing extent on the knowledge that is held in the heads of their employees in order to develop and retain competitive advantage. 'Intellectual capital', by which is meant the relevant content of human brains, is thus a more significant determinant of commercial success than the ownership of land, tools and machines.

What does all this mean for human resource management? An answer is provided in the following two quotations from Holbeche (1999, p424) and Micklethwait and Wooldridge (1996, p147) respectively:

> The challenge of managing intellectual capital is ensuring that it does not walk out of the door.

> The secret of managing knowledge workers, like the secret of making a martini, lies in the mixing.

One result is some shifting in the traditional power relationship between employers and employees. Micklethwait and Wooldridge (1996, p136) rightly state that:

> the modern masters of the universe are the gilded few who have had the good fortune to be born bright – lawyers, scientists, stockbrokers, skilled mechanics, indeed everyone who can make connections and generate ideas more rapidly and imaginatively than his peers.

The more useful your knowledge, and the rarer your capacity to apply it, the more desirable you are from an employer's point of view. In a knowledge economy, employees are less readily dispensable than they once were. Losing an employee involves losing some portion of the organisation's intellectual capital. There are clear implications for P&D professionals in general, and resourcing specialists in particular:

- The retention of knowledge workers becomes a central organisational objective. It follows that they must be managed effectively and that substantial effort needs to be put into motivating them and enhancing their job satisfaction. A degree of turnover, however, is needed in order to bring new knowledge into the organisation from outside.

- A sophisticated approach must be taken to performance management. Knowledge workers do not have to submit to clumsy, bullying or incompetent treatment. If they do not like the way they are being managed, they can go and work elsewhere.

- Recruitment and selection are crucial processes. It is essential that organisations engaged in knowledge work attract the best possible pool of candidates and devise methods of selecting new employees that are able correctly to identify those with appropriate knowledge or the ability to develop it.

- Redundancy management processes need to focus on the need to retain significant or valuable knowledge at the disposal of the organisation.

Aside from the effective management of knowledge workers, organisations also need to ensure that they are managed in such a way as to foster the sharing of existing knowledge and the creation of new knowledge. This is important first because it is through sharing knowledge among groups of people that new knowledge is created. Innovation and creative thinking, both central capacities for organisations competing in a knowledge economy, are a great deal more likely to occur when people spark ideas off one another, argue out their differences and put their expertise at the disposal of one another. The result is a situation in which human capital is converted into intellectual capital (Swart 2007, p453). Second, sharing knowledge is important because it helps to increase the stock of knowledge available to the organisation. It means that the organisation as a whole is better qualified to address problems, develop future strategies and prosper in an increasingly volatile environment. In short, the more staff know about more things, the more effective they are at performing their knowledge-based roles.

It is useful here to introduce the distinction between explicit and tacit forms of knowledge. Explicit forms of knowledge are those that can be readily identified. The material contained in this book is one example, as is any set of ideas or information that can be readily communicated through books, briefing documents, articles, television programmes, lectures, training events or computer programmes. Explicit knowledge is relatively easily grasped and transferred from one person to another. It can also be measured to an extent (ie organisations can maintain databases on who has completed certain training courses, who has particular qualifications and so on). Tacit knowledge, by contrast is much harder to get a handle on, but is thought by many to be equally important to organisations. Nonaka and Takeuchi (1995) say that it includes 'subjective insights, intuitions and hunches', while Holbeche (1999) sees it as consisting of 'intangibles such as know-how, information on stakeholder relationships, experiences and ideas'. Micklethwait and Wooldridge (1996, p143) prefer the following starker definition:

> *The informal, occupational lore generated by workers grappling with everyday problems and passed on in cafeterias, not the official rules written down in company manuals and transmitted in compulsory training sessions.*

This kind of informal knowledge is seen by many analysts to be equally or even more important than explicit knowledge in cultivating organisational learning. Tacit knowledge is also often the ultimate source of new knowledge. A business idea starts as a hunch, is shared informally with colleagues who assess its possibilities and bring their experience to bear on it. It is then raised more formally and discussed at formal meetings before being developed further. At some stage in the process it becomes explicit knowledge, but it did not start out that way.

Encouraging people to have ideas and to share them is thus an important role for P&D professionals in knowledge-based organisations. This can be done in a number of different ways. First, opportunities need to be provided for people to gain a range of experiences. In so doing their minds are stimulated, new ways of approaching familiar issues are observed and more knowledge created. Job rotation schemes achieve these aims, but are not always practical or desirable. Secondments to other parts of the organisation (if possible internationally) are a good way of developing knowledge, but much can also be achieved through inter-disciplinary teamworking, mentoring and attendance at training events that include participants from different branches of the business. Attendance at conferences and external training events also achieves the same outcomes. When it comes to tacit knowledge, all that can be done to facilitate its transfer around the organisation is to provide sufficient opportunity. Social events are important here, as are recreational activities. We are just as likely to learn useful things from someone visiting from overseas at the dinner table as we are from formal meetings with them.

There also needs to be active encouragement for people to share knowledge, and this should be reflected in reward and recognition systems. It is not easy to achieve because knowledge is so difficult to measure and pin down. However, it is not impossible to include an estimate of knowledge sharing prominently in employees' performance objectives (either formally or informally) and subsequently to allow assessments to influence decisions about pay or promotion. Scarbrough *et al* (1999, pp39–40) draw attention to less tangible forms of reward such as 'status, reputation and recognition which can be conferred on knowledge-leaders in a particular field'.

However, formal systems are often not necessary. What is needed is the creation of a culture in which sharing is encouraged. Praise and genuine gratitude from managers and colleagues are sometimes all that is necessary by way of reward.

A third way that P&D people can encourage sharing of knowledge is by helping to promote a high-trust/high-security culture. Where levels of trust are low and where people fear unnecessarily for their future job security they are much more likely to hoard knowledge. This is because doing so enhances their status and makes them more indispensable as individuals. Why help to develop other people by sharing knowledge if this increases the likelihood that you (rather than others) will lose your job or lose some element of your role that you value? In a volatile business environment there will always be an element of job insecurity, but a great deal can be done to minimise the extent to which it becomes a factor in determining the actions of employees. Where knowledge workers are concerned, for example, it does not make sense to employ people on fixed-term contracts or to withhold information about future human resource plans. Perceptions of insecurity are also minimised through the genuine promotion of employee involvement, and generally through the use of an open style of management.

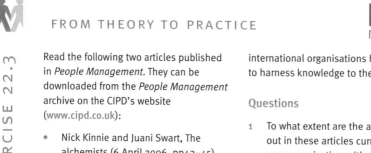

People management

FROM THEORY TO PRACTICE

EXERCISE 22.3

Read the following two articles published in *People Management*. They can be downloaded from the *People Management* archive on the CIPD's website (www.cipd.co.uk):

- Nick Kinnie and Juani Swart, The alchemists (6 April 2006, pp42–45)

- Peter Williamson, Sphere of influence (12 October 2006, pp32–34).

Both these articles describe simple tools which can be used by P&D managers to think about what they can do practically to make knowledge management more effective in their organisations. In addition, the article by Peter Williamson contains several examples of how international organisations have been able to harness knowledge to their advantage.

Questions

1   To what extent are the approaches set out in these articles currently used in your organisation, either formally or informally?

2   In what ways could more formal use be made of them in practice?

3   What business case could you put forward for the adoption of more formal knowledge management activities in your organisation?

A CRITIQUE OF KNOWLEDGE MANAGEMENT

It is difficult to take issue with the central ideas put forward by the proponents of knowledge management. They are right to remind us that knowledge (explicit and tacit) is the source of much competitive advantage and that this should be recognised in our approach to the management of organisations. They are also correct in identifying a breed of 'knowledge workers' who require different types of supervision or leadership from traditional approaches if their talents are to be fully harnessed. However, it is also the case that the ideas are too frequently dressed up in evangelical rhetoric that only serves to dazzle audiences and to exaggerate the significance of what is being said.

In truth, while many of us can now be loosely defined as 'knowledge workers', we are not for the most part individually indispensable to our employers. Nor, alas, are most of us members of headhunted classes who are actively sought by competing employers because of our exceptional knowledge. Talk of fundamental shifts in the power balance between employers and employees is thus untrue in most organisations. Some sectors that have these characteristics have grown in recent years, mainly those in the professional services sector (advertising, public relations, consultancy, IT, law and the like). For these the knowledge management literature has a great deal to offer. The same is true of departments (such as R&D or engineering) in larger organisations operating in other sectors. However, for most employees in most organisations this is not the case. Their knowledge is not as invaluable to their organisations as is suggested in the literature.

Most of the recent growth in employment has been in the provision of other types of services. While expertise and qualifications are required to undertake these jobs, it is not true to say that the capacity to innovate or leverage knowledge is any kind of prerequisite for success. Such organisations will benefit from shared ideas and new thinking on ways of attracting business or organising things more efficiently, but the capacity to harness the knowledge of employees is less of a priority than getting on with the job of serving their customers.

We can thus conclude by saying that knowledge management theory provides the basis of a useful contribution to P&D practice. It is not, however as universal in its application as many commentators lead us to believe. There is a 'knowledge economy' and there are 'knowledge workers' who require careful management, but as yet these represent a relatively small section of the total economy. There is nothing to be gained, and may be some danger, in applying knowledge management principles in situations where they are not appropriate

---

EXERCISE 22.4

SHELL

Read the article by Lucie Carrington, Oiling the wheels (*People Management*, 27 June 2002, pp31–34). This can be downloaded from the *People Management* archive on the CIPD's website (www.cipd.co.uk).

This article provides an excellent case study of a knowledge management project that has developed over time and yielded major benefits. It also explores some of the problems encountered and explains how these were managed.

Questions

1   Why is the approach described in the article particularly appropriate for large, international organisations?

2   Aside from the savings that have been made as result of the knowledge-sharing networks, what other business benefits have accrued because of Shell's use of a web-based approach to knowledge management?

3   How has the problem of 'knowledge hoarding' been overcome?

KEY ARTICLE 54

S. J. van Zolingen, J. N. Stremer and M. Stooker, **Problems in knowledge management: a case study of a knowledge-intensive company.** *International Journal of Training and Development*, Vol. 5, No. 3, pp168–183 (2001)

In this article the authors start with a lengthy literature review focusing on the major stages in a knowledge management process and some of the key problems that previous researchers have drawn attention to when theory is put into practice in this area. The second half of the article comprises a

very useful case study focusing in detail on practical knowledge management in a large Dutch professional services company. Some major issues are debated in the process.

Questions

1   What does this article tell us about the

significance of tacit knowledge and the methods used to 'manage' it?

2   What are the best organisational structures and cultures for the maximisation of effective knowledge management?

3   What were the major problems encountered by the case study organisation (ICT Ltd) in effectively managing knowledge?

SCENARIO PLANNING

It is impossible to predict something as complex as 'the world of work' with any serious degree of confidence in one's accuracy. Yet it is as important as ever, because the pace of change in our business environment is increasing so much that organisations must think seriously about the future and plan so that when the future becomes the present they are in a position to maximise the opportunities and meet the threats more effectively than their competitors. This is as important for managers of people as it is for those whose primary concerns lie in other fields of management practice.

The most effective approach is to think in terms of 'multiple futures' rather than just a single future. This enables organisations to plan for a range of possible future scenarios rather than putting all eggs in the one basket and betting on one particular scenario being fulfilled. HR consultants at PriceWaterhouseCoopers recently worked with academics at Oxford University to develop scenario thinking about how the world of work may develop between now and 2020 (PWC 2007). They surveyed 3,000 recent graduates before eventually coming up with three distinct bundles of ideas. These were each labelled with colours:

- An orange world of work in which the dominant trend is the growth of small, specialised organisations working in a networked fashion. In this scenario larger organisations, particularly multinationals, have less power and significance in the world economy than they do at present.

- A green world of work in which the large corporations grow in influence, but are increasingly regulated and restricted by an expectation on the part of customers that they will act in a socially responsible manner. The need to tackle climate change and ensure environmental sustainability dominate the corporate HR agenda.

- A blue world of work in which huge global corporations dominate markets and have greater power than many states. Skills shortages mean that the packages and careers provided for those who work for these corporations are very generous, but technology also permits closer supervision of them.

In practice, of course, no one such scenario may turn out to dominate in quite the way this body of work implies. Elements of each coloured scenario may well turn out to progress in tandem with others from a different colour to forge a more complex and varied future. Alternatively, of course, other unforeseen developments may come to dominate. However, the process of engaging in this kind of thinking and the collection of evidence to back up the ideas remains useful and interesting. Not only is it useful to think about and prepare for different possible futures on behalf of your organisation and the areas of P&D practice you are responsible for, it is also very helpful when planning your own career and in determining what choices you are going to make now in order to make sure that you are best placed to take up future opportunities when they arise.

CHAPTER SUMMARY

- In recent years, several influential writers have forecast substantial changes to the nature of the work we do and the way employment is organised. While many of their views are logical and interesting, there is as yet little hard evidence to support the main thrust of their arguments.

- The term 'emotional intelligence' describes a group of human attributes that are said to be increasingly significant in management and service sector work. They concern the ability to manage one's own emotions and those of others. Writers agree that emotional intelligence can be learned with experience and appropriate training.

- 'Knowledge management' comp a set of practices that are appropriate to organisations operating in the 'knowledge economy'. From a P&D perspective they include the effective management of knowledge workers and the development of structures and cultures that foster the sharing of knowledge. Despite the rhetoric that surrounds these ideas, they are not universally applicable.

- The most fruitful and interesting approach to preparing for an unpredictable future involves thinking in terms of a range of possible scenarios and planning to meet each, rather than to focus plans on one single future vision.

EXPLORE FURTHER

- There are numerous books and articles in print that deal with aspects of the 'future of work' debate. A good starting point is the work of *Economist* journalists John Micklethwait and Adrian Wooldridge. Their two books published in 1996 and 2000 introduce the debates and discuss them. *People Management* published a special edition on the future of work containing several articles in December 2001. Other recommended texts are those by Scase (2000) and Williams (2007), particularly Chapter 11. Storey

(2001) also provides an excellent summary of the debate.

- Karoly and Panis (2004) provide a very lucid and thoughtful analysis of the future of work debate from a US perspective, their principal messages having strong relevance for the United Kingdom too. Taylor (2002 and 2004) draws effectively on the research emanating from the ESRC future of work project to summarise current trends. His papers can be downloaded, free of charge, from the website (www.leeds.ac.uk/esrcfutureofwork). The case against revolutionary change is best put by Nolan (2004).

- The best introduction to emotional intelligence is found in the books and articles of Daniel Goleman. His original book was published in 1996 under the title *Emotional intelligence: why it can matter more than IQ*. This was followed by *Working with emotional intelligence* in 1998. Both books sold millions of copies. An excellent summary of research in the field and its implications for P&D managers is provided by IRS (2000f). More critical perspectives are developed by Davie *et al* (1998) and Woodruffe (2001).

- Knowledge management is the subject of hundreds of texts published in recent years. Among the most useful from a P&D perspective are the books by Stewart (1997), Boisot (1998) and Horibe (1999). Armstrong (2001) includes a helpful introductory chapter, a more comprehensive treatment being provided by Storey and Quintas (2001). Collins (2000) provides an interesting critical perspective. Two CIPD publications of interest are those by Scarbrough *et al* (1999) and Beaumont (2001). Summaries of more recent research and the interesting points about the HR implications are provided by Swart (2007) and Salaman (2007).

Bibliography

ACAS. (1985) *Labour turnover.* London: ACAS.

ACAS. (1988) *Absence.* London: ACAS.

ACAS. (2001) *Discipline at work: the ACAS advisory handbook.* London: ACAS.

ACKERS, P. (2005) Employment ethics, in T. Redman and A. Wilkinson (eds), *Contemporary human resource management*, 2nd edn. Harlow: FT/Prentice Hall.

ADAMS, J. (2007) *Managing people in organizations: contemporary theory and practice.* Basingstoke: Palgrave Macmillan.

ADLER, L. (2005) Outside chance. *People Management*, 10 March. 38–39.

AIKIN, O. (2001) *Contracts*, 2nd edn. London: Institute of Personnel Development (IPD).

AINSPALL, N. and DELL, D. (2001) *Engaging employees through your brand.* Conference Board report no. R-1288-01-RR. London: Conference Board. Online version available at: www.conferenceboard.org [accessed 11 April 2008].

ALIMO-METCALFE, B. and ALBAN-METCALFE, J. (2003) Under the influence. *People Management*, 6 March. 32–35.

ALLEN, A. (2002) No soft touch. *People Management*, 26 September.

ALLEN, A. (2007a) Bravo two zero. *People Management Guide to Recruitment Marketing,* June. 26–28.

ALLEN, A. (2007b) Niche work if you can get it. *People Management Guide to Assessment*, October. 4–11.

ALLEN, A. (2007c) Even better than the real thing. *People Management Guide to Assessment*, October. 17–19.

ALLEN, B. (2006) Anoraks welcome. *People Management*, 13 July. 28–30.

ALLEN, C. (2000) The hidden organisational costs of using non-standard employment. *Personnel Review*, Vol. 29, No. 2.

ALLEN, C. and TORRINGTON, D. (1996) It all depends on your frame of reference: a study of absence, in A. McGoldrick (ed), *Cases in human resource management.* London: Pitman.

ALLEN, M. and WRIGHT, P. (2008) Strategic management and HRM, in P. Boxall, J. Purcell and P. Wright (eds), *The Oxford handbook of human resource management.* Oxford: Oxford University Press.

AMOORE, L. (2004) Risk, reward and discipline at work. *Economy and Society*, Vol. 33, No. 2. 174–196.

ANDERMAN, S. (2000) *Labour law: management decisions and workers rights*, 4th edn. London: Butterworth.

ANDERSON, G. (1992) Performance appraisal, in B Towers (ed), *The handbook of human resource management.* Oxford: Blackwell.

ANDERSON, N. and SHACKLETON, V. (1993) *Successful selection interviewing.* Oxford: Blackwell.

ANDERSON, N. and SHACKLETON, V. (1994) Informed choices. *Personnel Today*, 8 November.

ARKIN, A. (1999) First class stamp. *People Management annual review of the recruitment advertising industry 1999*, supplement to *People Management*, 15 July.

ARKIN, A. (2001a) A Norfolk broadside. *People Management*, 19 April.

ARKIN, A. (2001b) Flea enterprise. *People Management*, 13 September.

ARKIN, A. (2003) Perfect fit. *People Management*, 25 September.

ARKIN, A. (2005a) Social smokers *People Management*, 1 September. 28–30.

ARKIN, A. (2005b) Burden of proof. *People Management*, 24 February. 30–32.

ARKIN, A. (2007a) The generation game. *People Management*, 29 November. 24–27.

ARKIN, A. (2007b) Force for good? *People Management*, 8 February. 26–29.

ARKIN, A. (2007c) From soft to strong. *People Management*, 6 September. 30–33.

ARKIN, A. (2008) The C word. *People Management*, 24 January. 28–32.

ARMISTEAD, C., BEAMISH, N. and KIELY, J. (2001) *Emerging skills in a changing economy: evolution of the customer service professional.* Colchester: Institute of Customer Service.

ARMSTRONG, G. (2003) Just how intangible is this asset? *People Management*, 12 June. 23.

ARMSTRONG, M. (2001)*Human resource management practice*, 8th edn. London: Kogan Page.

ARMSTRONG, M. (2003) *A handbook of human resource management practice*, 9th edn. London: Kogan Page.

ARMSTRONG, M. and BARON, A. (2005) *Performance management: the new realities*, 2nd edn. London: IPD.

ARMSTRONG-STRASSEN, M. (2008) Organisational practices and the post-retirement employment experience of older workers. *Human Resource Management Journal*, Vol. 18, No. 1. 36–53.

ARTHUR, D. (2001) *The employee recruitment and retention handbook,* New York: Amacom.

ATKINSON, C. (2003) Exploring the state of the psychological contract: the impact of research strategies on outcomes. Paper presented to the CIPD Professional Standards Conference, Keele University, 2003.

ATKINSON, J. (1984) Manpower strategies for the flexible organisation. *Personnel Management*, August.

ATWATER, L., PENN, R. and RUCKER, L. (1991) Personal qualities of charismatic leaders. *Leadership and Organisation Development Journal*, 12 December.

BACH, S. (2000) From performance appraisal to performance management, in S. Bach and K. Sisson (eds), *Personnel management: a comprehensive guide to theory and practice*. Oxford: Blackwell.

BACH, S. (2005) New directions in performance management, in S. Bach (ed), *Managing human resources: personnel management in transition*, 4th edn. Oxford: Blackwell.

BACKHAUS, K. (2004) An exploration of corporate recruitment descriptions on monster.com. *Journal of Business Communication*, Vol. 41, No. 2. 115–136.

BACKHAUS, K. and TIKOO, S. (2004) Conceptualizing and researching employer branding. *Career Development International*, Vol. 9, No. 4/5. 501–516.

BADARACCO, J. and WEBB, A. (1995) Business ethics: a view from the trenches. *California Management Review*, Winter.

BALCOMBE, J. (1997) Quoted in *Industrial Society*.

BARBER, A. (1998) *Recruiting employees*. Thousand Oaks, Calif.: Sage.

BARCLAY, J. (2001) Improving selection interviews with structure: organisations' use of behavioural interviews. *Personnel Review*, Vol. 30, No. 1.

BARMBY, T., ERCOLANI, M. and TREBLE, J. (1999) Sickness absence in Great Britain: new quarterly and annual series from the GHS and LFS, 1971–1997. *Labour Market Trends*, August.

BARNEY, J. (1991) Firm resources and sustained competitive advantage. *Journal of Management*, Vol. 17, No. 1. 99–120.

BARON, J. and KREPS, D. (1999) *Strategic human resources: frameworks for general managers*. New York: Wiley.

BARTHOLOMEW, D. J. (ed) (1971) *Manpower planning: Selected readings*. London: Penguin.

BASS, B. M. (1990) From transactional to transformational leadership: learning to share the vision.

Organizational Dynamics, Winter. Reprinted in R. M. Steers, L. W. Porter and G. A. Bigley (eds) (1996), *Motivation and leadership at work*, 6th edn. Singapore: McGraw-Hill.

BAXTER, L. and MACLEOD, A. (2007) Unhappy endings. *People Management*, 5 April. 38–40.

BEARDWELL, J. (2007) Recruitment and selection, in J. Beardwell and T. Claydon (eds), *Human resource management: a contemporary approach*, 5th edn. London: FT/Pitman.

BEARDWELL, J. and CLAYDON, T. (2007): *Human resource management: a contemporary approach*, 5th edn. London: FT/Pitman.

BEARDWELL, I., HOLDEN, L. and CLAYDON, T. (eds). (2004) *Human resource management: a contemporary perspective*, 4th edn. London: FT/Pitman.

BEAUCHAMP, T. and BOWIE, N. (1997) *Ethical theory and business*, 5th edn. Upper Saddle River, N.J.: Simon & Schuster.

BEAUMONT, D. (2005) Absence minded. *People Management*, 14 July. 36–38.

BEAUMONT, P. B. (1993) *Human resource management: key concepts and skills*. London: Sage.

BEAVAN, R., BOSWORTH, D., LEWNEY, R. and WILSON, R. (2005) *Alternative skills scenarios to 2020 for the UK economy*. Cambridge: Cambridge Econometrics.

BECKER, B. E., HUSELID, M. A. and ULRICH, D. (2001): *The HR scorecard: linking people, strategy and performance*. Cambridge, Mass.: Harvard Business School Press.

BECKETT, H. (2006) All good practice. *People Management*, 9 March. 38–40.

BEER, M. (1985) Note on performance appraisal, in M. Beer and B. Spector (eds), *Readings in human resource management*. New York: Free Press.

BEER, M. and RUH, R. (1976) Employee growth through performance management. *Harvard Business Review*, July/August.

BELL, D. and HART, R. (2003) Annualised hours contracts: the way forward in labour market flexibility. *National Institute Economic Review*, Vol. 185, No. 1. 64–77.

BEN-SHAKHAR, G. (1989) Non-conventional methods in personnel selection, in P. Herriot (ed), *Assessment and selection in organisations*. Chichester: Wiley.

BERGER, L. A. and BERGER, D. R. (eds). (2004) *The talent management handbook: creating organizational excellence by identifying, developing and promoting your best people*. New York, McGraw Hill.

BEVAN, D. (2007) Ethics and HRM, in J. Storey (ed), *Human resource management: a critical text*. London: Thomson.

BEVAN, S. and HAYDAY, S. (2001) *Costing sickness absence in the UK*. IES Report 382. Brighton: Institute of Employment Studies.

BHATTACARYYA, D. K. (2002) *Human resource planning*. New Delhi: Excel.

BIBBY, A. (2002) Home start. *People Management*, 10 January. 36–37.

BLACK, B. (1999) National culture and labour market flexibility. *International Journal of Human Resource Management*, Vol. 10, No. 4. 592–605.

BLANCHFLOWER, D. G., SALEHEEN, J. and SHADFORTH, C. (2007) *The impact of recent migration from Eastern Europe on the UK economy*. London: Bank of England.

BLANPAIN, R. (ed) (2001) *Comparative labour law and industrial relations*. London: Kluwer.

BLAU, G. (1990) An empirical analysis of employed and unemployed job search behavior. *Industrial and Labor Relations Review*, No. 45.

BLAU, R. (2002) Creative fusion. *People Management*, 18 April.

BLYTON, P. (1998) Flexibility, in M. Poole and M. Warner (eds), *The handbook of human resource management*. London: Thomson Business Press.

BOISOT, M. (1998) *Knowledge assets: securing competitive advantage in the information economy.* Oxford: Oxford University Press.

BOLCHOVER, D. (2005) *The living dead: switched off, zoned out.* Chichester: Capstone.

BOSELIE, P., DIETZ, G. and BOON, C. (2005) Commonalities and contradictions in research on human resource management and performance. *Human Resource Management Journal*, Vol. 15, No. 3. 67–94.

BOXALL, P. and PURCELL, J. (2008) *Strategy and human resource management*, 2nd edn. Basingstoke: Palgrave Macmillan.

BOYZATIS, R. E. (1982) *The competent manager.* New York: Wiley.

BRACKEN, D. W., TIMMRECK, C. W., FLEENOR, J. W. and SUMMERS, L. (2001) 360 feedback from another angle. *Human Resource Management*, Vol. 40, No. 1, Spring.

BRAMHAM, J. (1987) Manpower planning, in S. Harper (ed), *Personnel management handbook.* London: Gower.

BRAMHAM, J. (1988) *Practical manpower planning*, 4th edn. London, Institute of Personnel Management (IPM).

BRAMHAM, J. (1994) *Human resource planning,* 2nd edn. London: IPD.

BRAMHAM, J. (1997) *Benchmarking for people managers: a competency approach.* London: Chartered Institute of Personnel and Development (CIPD).

BREWSTER, C., HEGEWISCH, A., LOCKHART, T. and MAYNE, L. (1993) *Flexible working patterns in Europe.* London: IPM.

BRIDGES, W. (1995) *Jobshift: how to prosper in a workplace without jobs.* London: Nicholas Brealey.

BRINER, R. and CONWAY, N. (2004) Promises, promises. *People Management*, 25 November.

BRINKLEY, I. and LEE, N. (2006) *The knowledge economy in Europe.* London: Work Foundation.

BROCKETT, J. (2007a) Flexicurity knocks. *People Management*, 19 April. 16–17.

BROCKETT, J. (2007b) Face to face with social networking. *People Management,* 9 August. 15–17.

BROOKS, I. and WEATHERSTON, J. (2004) *The international business environment: challenges and changes*, 3rd edn. London: FT/Prentice Hall.

BROWN, A, RODDAN, M., JORDAN, S. and NILSSON, L. (2007) The time of your life. *People Management*, 26 July. 40–43.

BROWN, D. (2002) Success in all shapes and sizes. *People Management*, 24 October. 25.

BROWN, D. (2004) Capital vetters. *People Management*, 30 September. 38–41.

BROWN, D. and ARMSTRONG, M. (2000) *Paying for contribution.* London: Kogan Page.

BROWN, G. (1993) Finding new employees for high reliability operations, in D. Gowler, K. Legge and C. Clegg (eds), *Case studies in organisational behaviour and human resource management.* London: Paul Chapman.

BROWNING, G. (2004) New kid on the block. *People Management*, 15 July.

BRYSON, C. (1999) Managing uncertainty or managing uncertainly? in J. Leopold, L. Harris and T. Watson (eds), *Strategic human resourcing.* London: FT/Pitman.

BUCHANAN, D. (1982) High performance: new boundaries of acceptability in worker control, in J. Hurrell and C. Cooper (eds), *Job control and worker health.* Chichester: Wiley.

BUCKINGHAM, M. and COFFMAN, C. (1999) *First break all the rules: what the world's greatest managers do differently.* London: Simon & Schuster.

BUCKINGHAM, M. (2007) *Go put your strengths to work.* New York: Simon & Schuster.

BUCKINGHAM, M. and CLIFTON, D. (2001) *Now, discover your strengths.* London: Gallup Organisation.

BUCKLEY, M. R. and RUSSELL, C. J. (1999) Validity evidence, in R. W. Eder and M. M. Harris (eds), *The employment interview handbook*. Thousand Oaks, Calif.: Sage.

BURACK, E. and MATHYS, N. (1996): *Human resource planning: a pragmatic approach to manpower staffing and development*, 3rd edn. Northbrook, Ill.: Brace-Park Press.

BURCHELL B., LADIPO, D. and WILKINSON, F. (eds) (2002) *Job insecurity and work intensification*. London: Routledge.

BURKE, R. J. (2002) Organizational transitions, in C. Cooper and R. Burke (eds), *The new world of work: challenges and opportunities*. Oxford: Blackwell.

BURTON, N. (1996) The retention and turnover of D-grade nurses. Unpublished MSc dissertation, UMIST, Manchester.

BUTCHER, S. (2005) Recovery plan. *People Management*, 28 July. 34–36.

BUTLER T. and WALDROOP J. (1999) Job sculpting: the art of retaining your best people. *Harvard Business Review*, September–October.

BYRON, M. and MODHA, S. (1991) *How to pass selection tests*. London: Kogan Page.

BYRON, M. and MODHA, S. (1993) *Technical selection tests and how to pass them*. London: Kogan Page.

CALDWELL, C. (2007) No easy answers on immigration. *Financial Times*, 19 October.

CAMPOS E CHUNA, R. (2002) Privatization and outsourcing, in C. Cooper and R. Burke (eds), *The new world of work: challenges and opportunities*. Oxford: Blackwell.

CAPELLI, P. (1999) Rethinking employment, in R. Schuler and S. Jackson (eds), *Strategic human resource management*. Oxford: Blackwell.

CAPELLI, P. (2000) A market-driven approach to retaining talent. *Harvard Business Review*, January–February.

CAPELLI, P. and SINGH, H. (2002) Integrating strategic human resources and strategic management. In D. Lewin, O. Mitchell and P. Sherer (eds), *Research frontiers in industrial relations and human resources*. Madison, Wisc.: Industrial Relations Research Association (IRRA).

CARRELL, M. R., ELBERT, N. F. and HATFIELD, R. D. (1995) *Human resource management: global strategies for managing a diverse workforce*, 5th edn. New Jersey: Prentice Hall.

CARRINGTON, L. (2002a) At the cutting edge. *People Management*, 16 May.

CARRINGTON, L. (2002b) Oiling the wheels. *People Management*, 27 June.

CARRINGTON, L. (2005) A bridge too far? *People Management*, 11 August. 24–28.

CARRINGTON, L. (2007) The skills equation. *People Management*, 23 August. 24–28.

CARROLL, M., MARCHINGTON, M., EARNSHAW, J. and TAYLOR, S. (1999) Recruitment in small firms: processes, methods and problems. *Employee Relations*, Vol. 21, No. 3.

CARTWRIGHT, S. and COOPER, C. (2000) *HR know-how in mergers and acquisitions*. London: CIPD.

CARTWRIGHT, S. and SCHOENBERG, R. (2006) Thirty years of mergers and acquisitions research: recent advances and future opportunities. *British Journal of Management*, Vol. 17 (special edition). S1–S5.

CASCIO, W. F. (2000) *Costing human resources: the financial impact of behavior in organizations*, 4th edn. Cincinnati, Oh.: South Western.

CASCIO, W. F. (2002) Strategies for responsible downsizing. *Academy of Management Executive*, Vol. 16, No. 3. 80–91.

CASCIO, W. F., BOUDREAU, J. W. and RAMSTAD, P. (2008) *Investing in people: financial impact of human resource initiatives*. New York: Prentice Hall/Financial Times.

CERIELLO, V. with FREEMAN, C. (1991) *Human resource management systems: strategies, tactics and techniques*. New York: Lexington.

CHANDLER, B. and SCOTT, T. (2005) How to write a job ad. *People Management*, 24 November. 42–43.

CHARTERED INSTITUTE OF PERSONNEL AND DEVELOPMENT (CIPD) (2002a) *Work, parenting and careers: survey report*. London: CIPD.

CIPD (2002b) *The guide to work life balance*. London: CIPD.

CIPD (2002c) *Employment law: survey report*. London: CIPD.

CIPD (2003a) *HR's contribution to international mergers and acquisitions*. London: CIPD.

CIPD (2003b) *Labour turnover: survey report*. London: CIPD.

CIPD (2003c) *Age pensions and retirement: attitudes and expectations, survey report*. London: CIPD.

CIPD (2004) *Employee absence 2004: a survey of management policy and practice*. London: CIPD.

CIPD (2005) *Flexible working: impact and implementation, an employer survey*. London: CIPD.

CIPD (2007a) *Recruitment, retention and turnover*. London: CIPD.

CIPD (2007b) *Employer branding: the latest fad or the future of HR?* London: CIPD.

CIPD (2007c) *Absence management, annual survey report*. London: CIPD.

CIPD (2007d) *Managing age: a guide to good employment practice*. London: CIPD.

CIPD (2007e) *The changing HR function; transforming HR?* London: CIPD.

CHERRINGTON, D. J. (1989) *Organisational behaviour: the management of individual and organisational performance*. Boston and London: Allyn & Bacon.

CLAKE, R. (2007) How to make flexible working work. *People Management*, 11 January. 48–49.

CLARKE, E. (2006) Pressure soars. *People Management*, 31 August.30–32.

CLARKE, E .(2007) Safety in numbers. *People Management*, 11 January. 44–46.

CLAUS, L. (2007) Get a virtual grip. *People Management*, 23 August. 38–39.

CLEMENTS-CROOME, D. (ed). (2000) *Creating the productive workplace*. London: E & FN Spon.

COLLING, T. (2000) Personnel management in the extended organisation, in S. Bach and K. Sisson (eds), *Personnel management: a comprehensive guide to theory and practice*, 3rd edn. Oxford: Blackwell.

COLLING, T. (2005) Managing human resources in the networked organisation, in S. Bach (ed), *Managing human resources: personnel management in transition*, 4th edn. Oxford: Blackwell.

COLLINS, D. (2000) *Management fads and buzzwords: critical-practical perspectives*. London: Routledge.

CONFEDERATION OF BRITISH INDUSTRY (CBI). (1997) *Managing absence in sickness and in health*. London: CBI.

CBI. (2000) *Cutting through red tape: the impact of employment legislation*. London: CBI.

CBI. (2007) *The CBI /AXA absence and labour turnover survey*. London: CBI.

CONFERENCE BOARD. (2001) *Engaging employees through your brand*. www.Conferenceboard.org.

CONTACTBABEL. (2007) *UK Contact centres in 2007 – the state of the industry*. London: Contactbabel.

CONWAY, N. and BRINER, R. (2005) *Understanding psychological contracts at work*. Oxford: Oxford University Press.

COOK, M. (2004) *Personnel selection: adding value through people*, 4th edn. Chichester: Wiley.

COOK, M. and CRIPPS, B. (2005) *Psychological assessment in the workplace: a manager's guide*. Chichester: Wiley.

COOPER, C. (2000) BT announces clampdown on damaging long hours culture. *People Management*, 27 April.

COOPER, C. (2001) Win by a canvas. *People Management*, 25 January.

COOPER, C. (2005) Another year down. *People Management*, 29 December. 36–37.

COOPER D., ROBERTSON I. and TINLINE, G. (2003) *Recruitment and selection: a framework for success*. London: Thomson.

CORBY, S. (2000) Unfair dismissal disputes: a comparative study of Great Britain and New Zealand. *Human Resource Management Journal*, Vol. 10, No. 1. 79–92.

CORDERY, J. and PARKER, S. K. (2007): Work organisation, in P. Boxall, J. Purcell and P. Wright (eds), *The Oxford handbook of human resource management*. Oxford: Oxford University Press.

COTTEE, P. (2006a) Suffering in silence? *People Management*, 26 October. 36–41.

COTTEE, P. (2006b) Change of heart. *People Management*, 10 August. 42–44.

COURTIS, J. (1985) *The IPM guide to cost-effective recruiting*. London: IPM.

COURTIS, J. (1989) *Recruiting for profit*. London: IPM.

COURTIS, J. (1994) *Recruitment advertising: right first time*. London: IPD.

COWLING, A. and WALTERS, M. (1990) Manpower planning: where are we today? *Personnel Review*, 19 March.

CROPANZANO, R. and WRIGHT, T. A. (2001) When a happy worker is really a productive worker: a review and further refinement of the happy productive worker thesis. *Consulting Psychology Journal: Practice and Research*, Vol. 53, No. 3. 182–199.

CUNNINGHAM, I. and JAMES. P. (2000) Absence and return to work: towards a research agenda. *Personnel Review*, Vol. 29, No. 1.

CZERNY, A. (2004) The fast track broadens. *People Management*, 2 September.

CZERNY, A. (2005) Double trouble. *People Management*, 2 February. 14–15.

DALY, N. (1996) Staff sit in on top job interviews. *Personnel Today,* 16 July.

DALZIEL, M. M. (2004): Competencies: the first building block of talent management, in L. Berger and D. Berger (eds), *The talent management handbook: creating organizational excellence by identifying, developing and promoting your best people*. New York: McGraw-Hill.

DANIELS, K. (2004) *Employment law for HR and business students*. London: CIPD.

DAVIDSON, E. (2003) A break with tradition. *People Management*, 10 July.

DAVIE M., STANKOV, L. and ROBERTS, R. (1998) Emotional intelligence: in search of an elusive construct. *Journal of Personality and Social Psychology*, Vol. 75, No. 4.

DAVIES, A.C.L. (2004) *Perspectives on labour law*. Cambridge: Cambridge University Press.

DAVIES, P. and FREEDLAND, M. (1993) *Labour legislation and public policy*. Oxford: Clarendon Press.

DAVISON, J. and REES MOGG, W. (1997) *The sovereign individual: the coming revolution, how to survive and prosper in it*. London: Macmillan.

DE WITTE, K. (1989) Recruiting and advertising, in P. Herriot (ed.), *Assessment and selection in organisations*. Chichester: Wiley.

DEAKIN, S. and MORRIS, G. (2005) *Labour law*, 4th edn. Oxford: Hart.

DEAKIN, S. and WILKINSON, F. (1996) *Labour standards – essential to economic and social progress*. London: Institute of Employment Rights.

DEAKIN, S. and WILKINSON, F. (1999) The management of redundancies in Europe: the case of Great Britain. *Labour*, Vol. 13, No. 1. 41–89.

DEERY, S. (2005) Love me or lose me. *People Management*, 24 November. 36–37.

DEMPSEY, M. and MCKEVITT, D. (2001) Unison and the people side of mergers. *Human Resource Management Journal*, Vol. 11, No. 2.

DEN HARTOG, D., CALEY, A. and DEWE, P. (2007) Recruiting leaders: an analysis of leadership advertisements. *Human Resource Management Journal*, Vol. 17, No. 1. 58–75.

DEPARTMENT FOR EDUCATION AND EMPLOYMENT. (2000) *Labour market and skill trends*. London: DfEE.

DEPARTMENT OF EMPLOYMENT (DoE). (1971) *Company manpower planning*. London: HMSO.

DoE. (1987) *Employers' labour use survey*. London: HMSO.

DEPARTMENT OF TRADE AND INDUSTRY (DTI). (1999) *The Unfair Dismissal and Statement of Reasons for Dismissal (varying of qualifying period) Order 1999 – regulatory impact assessment*. London: DTI.

DTI. (2004) Hewitt announces plans to strengthen corporate Britain. News release, 5 May.

DTI. (2006) *Collective redundancies – employers' duty to notify the secretary of state. Full regulatory impact assessment*. London: DTI.

DEVARO, J., LI, R. and BROOKSHIRE, D. (2007) Analysing the job characteristics model: new support from a cross-section of establishments. *International Journal of Human Resource Management*, Vol. 18, No. 6. 986–1003.

DEVINE, M. and LAMMIMAN, J. (2000) Original synergy. *People Management*, 13 April.

DIBBEN, P., JAMES, P. and CUNNIGHAM, I. (2000) Absence management in the public sector: crossing the boundaries towards and ideal model. Paper presented at the British Academy of Management Annual Conference, Edinburgh.

DICKEN, P. (2007) *Global shift: mapping the changing contours of the world economy*, 5th edn. London: Sage.

DIPBOYE, R. L., GAUGLER, B. B., HAYES, T. L. and PARKER, D. (2001) The validity of unstructured panel interviews: more than meets the eye. *Journal of Business and Psychology*, Vol. 16, No. 1. 35–49.

DOBSON, P. (1989) Reference reports, in P. Herriot (ed), *Handbook of assessment in organisations*. Chichester: Wiley.

DONKIN, R. (1997) Self employment: predictions of the portfolio career are wide of the mark. *Financial Times*, 8 October.

DOTY, D. H., GLICK, W. H. and HUBER, G. P. (1993) Fit, equifinality and organizational effectiveness: a test of two configurational theories. *Academy of Management Journal*, Vol. 36. 1196–1250.

DOUGLAS PHILLIPS, J. (1990) The price-tag on turnover. *Personnel Journal*, December.

DOW, J. (2003) Spa attraction. *People Management*, 29 May.

DOWNS, S. (1989) Job sample and trainability tests, in P Herriot (ed), *Handbook of assessment in organisations*. Chichester: Wiley.

DRAKELEY, R. (1989) Biographical data, in P Herriot (ed), *Handbook of assessment in organisations*. Chichester: Wiley.

DRUKER, J. and STANWORTH, C. (2001) Partnerships and the private recruitment industry. *Human Resource Management Journal*, Vol. 11, No. 2. 73–89.

DRUMMOND, J. (2004) A matter of principle. *People Management*, 17 June. 42.

DU PLESSIS, D. (2003) Contemporary issues in recruitment and selection, in R. Weisner and B. Millett (eds), *Human resource management: challenges and future directions*. Sydney: Wiley.

DUGGAN, M. (1999) *Unfair dismissal: law, practice and guidance*. Welwyn Garden City: CLT Professional.

DUGGAN, M. (2003) Wrongful dismissal and breach of contract Welwyn Garden City, Emis.

DULEWICZ, V. (2004) Give full details. *People Management*, 26 February.

DYER, L. and ERICKSEN, J. (2007) Dynamic organizations: achieving marketplace agility through workforce scalability, in J. Storey (ed), *Human resource management: a critical text,* 3rd edn. London: Thomson.

EARNSHAW, J., MARCHINGTON, L., RITCHIE, E. and TORRINGTON, D. (2004) Neither fish nor fowl? An assessment of teacher capability procedures. *Industrial Relations Journal*, Vol. 35, No. 2. 139–152.

ECONOMIST. (1997) *The world in 1998*. London: Economist Publications.

ECONOMIST. (1998) *The world in 1999*. London: Economist Publications.

ECONOMIST. (1999) *The world in 2000*. London: Economist Publications.

ECONOMIST. (2000) *The world in 2001*. London: Economist Publications.

EDENBOROUGH, R. (2005) *Assessment methods in recruitment, selection and performance*. London: Kogan Page.

EDER, R. and FERRIS, G. (eds). (1989) *The employment interview: theory, research and practice*. Newbury Park, Calif.: Sage.

EDER, R. and HARRIS, M. M. (1999) *The employment interview handbook*. Thousand Oaks, Calif.: Sage.

EDWARDS, C. (2005) Remote control. *People Management*, 16 June. 30–32.

EDWARDS, C. (2006) Raised stakes. *People Management,* 9 March. 24–27.

EDWARDS, C. Y. and ROBINSON, O. (2001): Better part-time jobs? A study of part-time working in nursing and the police. *Employee Relations*, Vol. 23, No. 5.

EDWARDS, J. (1983) Models of manpower stocks and flows, in J. Edwards *et al* (eds), *Manpower planning: strategy and techniques in an organisational context*. Chichester: Wiley.

EDWARDS, M. (2005) Employer and employee branding, in S. Bach (ed), *Managing human resources*, 4th edn. Oxford: Blackwell.

EDWARDS, P. and SCULLION, H. (1984) Absenteeism and the control of work. *Sociological Review,* 31 March.

EDWARDS, P. and WHITSTON, C. (1989) *The control of absenteeism: an interim report.* Warwick Papers in Industrial Relations, no. 23.

EDWARDS, P. and WHITSTON, C. (1993) *Attending to work: the management of attendance and shopfloor order*. Oxford: Blackwell.

EIKHOF, D. R., WARHURST, C. and HAUNSCHILD, A. (2007) What work? What life? What balance? Critical reflections on the work–life balance debate. *Employee Relations,* Vol. 29, No. 4. 325–333.

ELIAS, J. and SCARBROUGH, H. (2004) Evaluating human capital: an exploratory study of management practice. *Human Resource Management Journal*, Vol. 14, No. 4. 21–40.

ELLIOTT, R. and MURLIS, H. (1996) The state of the art in the public sector, in H. Murlis (ed), *Pay at the crossroads*. London: IPD.

EMMOTT, M. (2004) Britain's real working lives. *People Management*, 30 June. 14–15.

EMPLOYMENT TRIBUNAL SERVICE (2007) *Annual report and accounts*. London: HMSO.

EQUAL OPPORTUNITIES COMMISSION (EOC). (1986) *Fair and efficient: guidance on equal opportunities policies in recruitment and selection procedures*. Manchester: EOC.

EUROPEAN COMMISSION. (2000) *The future of work*. London: Kogan Page.

EVANS, A. and PALMER, S. (1997) *From absence to attendance*. London: CIPD.

EVANS, R. (2006) Variety performance. *People Management*, 23 November. 26–31.

EVANS, R. (2007) Telly vision. *People Management,* 22 March. 24–29.

FAIR, H. (1992) *Personnel and profit: the pay-off from people*. London: IPM.

FARNHAM, D. (1995) *The corporate environment*, 2nd edn. London: IPD.

FARNHAM, D. (2005) *Managing in a strategic business context*. London: CIPD.

FERNIE, S. and METCALF, D. (1996) *Participation, contingent pay, representation and workplace performance: evidence from Great Britain.* Discussion Paper 232, Centre for Economic Performance, London School of Economics.

FERRIS, G. R. and BUCKLEY, M. R. (1996) *Human resource management: perspectives, context, functions and outcomes.* Englewood Cliffs, N.J.: Prentice Hall.

FIELDS, D., CHAN, A., AKHTAR, S. and BLUM, T. (2006) Human resource management strategies under uncertainty: how do US and Hong Kong Chinese companies differ? *Cross Cultural Management*, Vol. 13, No. 2. 171–186.

FIELDS, M. (2001) *Indispensable employees.* Franklin Lakes, N.J.: Career Press.

FINE, S. and GETKATE, M. (1995) *Benchmark tasks for job analysis.* N.J.: Lawrence Erlbaum.

FINLAY, W. and COVERDILL, J. E. (2002) *Headhunters: matchmaking in the labor market.* Ithaca, N.Y.: Cornell University Press.

FINN, W. (2000) Screen test. *People Management*, 22 June.

FISHER, C. and RICE, C. (1999) Managing messy moral matters: ethics and HRM, in J. Leopold, L. Harris and T. Watson (eds), *Strategic human resourcing: principles, perspectives and practices.* London: FT/Pitman.

FLEETWOOD, S. (2007) Why work–life balance now? *International Journal of Human Resource Management*, Vol. 18, No. 3. 387–400.

FLETCHER, C. (1991) Personality tests: the great debate. *Personnel Management*, September.

FLETCHER, C. (2004) *Appraisal and feedback: making performance review work*, 3rd edn. London: CIPD.

FLOOD, P., GANNON, M. and PAAUWE, J. (1996) *Managing without traditional methods: international innovations in human resource management.* Wokingham: Addison Wesley.

FLORKOWSKI, G. (1998) Human resource flows, in M. Poole and M Warner (eds), *The handbook of human resource management.* London: Thomson Business Press.

FOMBRUN, C. (1996) *Reputation: realizing value from the corporate image.* Boston, Mass.: Harvard Business School Press.

FORDE, C. and SLATER, C. (2005) Agency working in Britain causes, character and consequences. *British Journal of Industrial Relations*, Vol. 43, No. 2. 249–271.

FOWLER, A. (1993) *Redundancy.* London: IPM.

FOWLER, A. (1996a) *Employee induction: a good start*, 3rd edn. London: IPD.

FOWLER, A. (1996b) How to conduct disciplinary interviews. *People Management*, November.

FOWLER, A. (1996c) *Negotiation: skills and strategies*, 2nd edn. London: IPD.

FOWLER, A. (1998) *The disciplinary interview.* London: IPD.

FOWLER, A. (1999) *Managing redundancy.* London: IPD.

FRANCIS, H. and KEEGAN, A. (2006) The changing face of HRM: in search of balance. *Human Resource Management Journal*, Vol. 16, No. 3. 231–249.

FRANKLAND, G. (2000) If you build it, they will come. *People Management*, 16 March.

FRECHETTE, H. and WERTHEIM, E. G. (1985) Performance appraisal, in W. R. Tracey (ed), *Human resources management and development handbook.* New York: Amacom.

FRIED, Y., CUMMINGS, A. and OLDHAM, G. R. (1998) Job design, in M. Poole and M. Warner (eds), *The handbook of human resource management.* London: Thomson Business Press.

FRIEDMAN, M. (1963) *Capitalism and freedom.* Chicago: University of Chicago Press.

FULLER, S. R. and HUBER, V. (1998) Recruitment and selection, in M. Poole and M. Warner (eds), *The handbook of human resource management.* London: Thomson Business Press.

FURNHAM, A. (2001) Catharsis with your cards: exit interviews with departing employees help companies to learn about themselves. *Financial Times*, 28 August.

FURNHAM, A. (2005) *The psychology of behaviour at work*, 2nd edn. Hove: Psychology Press.

FURNHAM, A. and PETRIDES, K. V. (2006) Deciding on promotions and redundancies. *Journal of Managerial Psychology*, Vol. 21, No. 1. 6–18.

GAMBLES, R., LEWIS, S. and RAPOPORT, R. (2006) *The myth of the work–life balance: the challenge of our time for men, women and societies*. Chichester: Wiley.

GAMMIE, E. (2000) The use of biodata in the pre-selection of fully-accredited graduates for chartered accountancy places in Scotland. *Accounting and Business Research*, Vol. 31, No. 1. 19–35.

GAN, M. and KLEINER, B. H. (2005) How to write job descriptions effectively. *Management Research News*, Vol. 28, No. 8. 48–54.

GARNJOST, P. and BLETTNER, K. (1996) Cutting labour costs without redundancies, in J. Storey (ed), *Blackwell cases in human resource and change management*. Oxford: Blackwell.

GARSTEN, C. and WULFF, H. (2004) *New technologies at work*. Oxford: Berg.

GENNARD, J. and JUDGE, G. (2005) *Employee relations*, 4th edn. London: CIPD.

GILLEN, T. (1995) *Positive influencing skills*. London: IPD.

GLOVER, C. (2002) Room with a view. *People Management*, 8 August.

GOLEMAN, D. (1996) *Emotional intelligence: why it can matter more than IQ*. London: Bloomsbury.

GOLEMAN, D. (1998) *Working with emotional intelligence*. London: Bloomsbury.

GOMEZ MEJIA, L. and BALKIN, D. (1992) *Compensation, organizational strategy and firm performance*. Cincinnati, Oh.: South Western.

GOODWORTH, C. (1979) *Effective interviewing for employment selection*. London: Hutchinson.

GRACE, E. (2002) How to avoid unfair dismissal claims. *People Management*, 7 February.

GRATTON, L. (2004) Feel the burnout. *People Management*, 15 July.

GRAYSON, D. and HODGES, A. (2001) *Everybody's business: managing risks and opportunities in today's global society*. London: Dorling Kindersley.

GREENFIELD, S. (2003) Flexible futures. *People Management*, 23 October.

GREENFIELD, S. (2006) When the chip comes in. *People Management*, 12 October. 42–43.

GREENHALGH, R. (1995) *Industrial tribunals*, 2nd edn. London: IPD.

GREENWOOD, M. R. (2002) Ethics and HRM: a review and conceptual analysis. *Journal of Business Ethics*, Vol. 36, No. 3. 261–279.

GREGG, P. and WADSWORTH, J. (1999) *Job tenure 1975–98*, in P. Gregg and J. Wadsworth (eds), *The state of working Britain*. Manchester: Manchester University Press.

GRIFFETH, R. W. and HOM, P. W. (2001): *Retaining valued employees*. Thousand Oaks, Calif.: Sage.

GRIFFETHS, J. (2004) Council taps new talent pools to ease shortages. *People Management*, 16 September.

GRIFFETHS, J. (2005) The price is right. *People Management*, 10 November. 34–35.

GRIFFETHS, J. (2006) Masculine wiles. *People Management*, 27 October. 20–21.

GUEST, D. (2000) Human resource management, employee well-being and organisational performance, Paper given at the CIPD Professional Standards Conference, University of Warwick.

GUEST, D. and CONWAY, N. (2000) *The psychological contract in the public sector*. London: CIPD.

GUEST, D. and CONWAY, N. (2002) Communicating the psychological contract: an employer perspective. *Human Resource Management Journal*, Vol. 12, No. 2. 22–38.

HACKETT, P. (1995) *The selection interview*. London: IPD.

HACKMAN, J. R. and OLDHAM, G. R. (1980) *Work redesign*. Reading, Mass.: Addison-Wesley.

HADDOCK, C. and SOUTH, B. (1994) How Shell's organisation and HR practices help it be both global and local, in D Torrington (ed), *International human resource management: think globally, act locally*. London: Prentice Hall.

HAGOOD, W. and FRIEDMAN, L. (2002) Using the balanced scorecard to measure the performance of your HR information system. *Public Personnel Management*, Vol. 31, No. 4. 543–556.

HAKIM, C. (1990) Core and periphery in employers' workforce strategies: evidence from the 1987 E.L.U.S. survey. *Work, Employment and Society*, 4 February.

HALL, K. (2005) Global division. *People Management*, 24 March. 44–45.

HALL, L. and ATKINSON, C. (2006) Improving working lives: flexible working and the role of employee control. *Employee Relations*, Vol. 28, No. 4. 374–386.

HAMMOND SUDDARDS EDGE. (1999) *Dismissal*. London: IPD.

HAMMOND SUDDARDS EDGE. (2003) *Redundancy handling*. London: CIPD.

HANDY, C. (1989) *The age of unreason*. London: Business Books.

HANDY, C. (1994) *The empty raincoat: making sense of the future*. London: Hutchinson.

HANDY, C. (2001) *The elephant and the flea: looking backwards to the future*. London: Hutchinson.

HARRISON, R. (2005) *Learning and development*. London: CIPD.

HARRISON, R., NEWHOLME, T. and SHAW, D. (2005) *The ethical consumer*. London: Sage.

HARRY, W. (2007) East is east. *People Management*, 29 November. 36–38.

HARTER, J., SCHMIDT, F. L. and HAYES, T. L. (2002) Business-unit-level relationship between employee satisfaction, employee engagement and business outcomes: a meta-analysis. *Journal of Applied Psychology*, Vol. 87, No. 2. 268–279.

HARTER, J., SCHMIDT, F. L. and HAYES, T. L. (2003) *Wellbeing in the workplace and its relationship to business outcomes: a review of the Gallup studies*. Washington, DC: American Psychological Association/Gallup. Available online at: http://media.gallup.com/DOCUMENTS/whitePaper—Well-BeingInTheWorkplace.pdf [accessed 11 April 2008].

HARVARD BUSINESS REVIEW. (1990) *Manage people, not personnel*. Boston, Mass.: Harvard Business School.

HARVEY, J. and NICHOLSON, N. (1993) Incentives and penalties as a means of influencing attendance: a study in the UK public sector. *International Journal of Human Resource Management*, 4 April.

HAYWARD, N. and DOUGLAS, H. (2004) Survival strategy. *People Management*, 28 October. 46–47.

HEAP, D. (2004) Redundancies in the UK. *Labour Market Trends*, May. 195–201.

HEERY, E. and SALMON, J. (eds). (2000) *The insecure workforce*. London: Routledge.

HENDERSON, D. (2001) *Misguided virtue: false notions of corporate social responsibility*. London: Institute of Economic Affairs.

HENDRY, C., WOODWARD, S., BRADLEY, P. and PERKINS, S. (2000) Performance and rewards: cleaning out the stables. *Human Resource Management Journal*, Vol. 10, No. 3.

HENEMAN, H., JUDGE, T. and HENEMAN, R. (2000) *Staffing organizations*. Boston, Mass.: Irwin McGraw-Hill.

HERCUS, T. (1992) Human resource planning in eight British organisations: a Canadian perspective, in B Towers (ed), *The handbook of human resource management*. Oxford: Blackwell.

HERRIOT, P. (ed) (1989) *A handbook of assessment in organisations*. Chichester: Wiley.

HERZBERG, F. (1966) *Work and the nature of man*. Cleveland: World Publishing.

HERZBERG, F. (1968) One more time: how do you motivate employees? *Harvard Business Review*, January–February.

HIGGINBOTTOM, K. (2003) Image conscious. *People Management*, 6 February.

HIGGS, M. (2003) Good call. *People Management,* 23 January.

HIGGS, M. (2004) Future trends in HRM, in D. Rees and R. McBain (eds), *People management: challenges and opportunities.* Basingstoke: Palgrave Macmillan.

HILL, J. and MAYCOCK, A. (1990) The design of recruitment advertising featuring questions which have a thematic content. Paper presented to the British Psychological Society Conference.

HILLMER, S., HILLMER, B. and MCROBERTS, G. (2004) The real costs of turnover: Lessons from a call center. *Human Resource Planning*, Vol. 27, No. 3. 34–41.

HILTROP, J.-M. (1999) The quest for the best: human resource practices to attract and retain. *European Management Journal*, Vol. 17, No. 4.

HIRSCH, M. S. and GLANZ, E. (2006) Tomorrow's world of recruitment. *People Management*, 18 May. 48.

HIRSCHKORN, J. (2004) Research and employ. *People Management*, 15 January.

HIRSCHKORN, J. (2004) Mirror image. *People Management supplement: guide to recruitment consultancies*, April. 17–20.

HIRSH, W., POLLARD, E. and TAMKIN, P. (2000) *Free fair and efficient? Open internal job advertising.* Brighton, Institute of Employment Studies.

HOBBY, J. (1995) Farewell notes. *Personnel Today*, July.

HOFSTEDE, G. (1980) *Culture's consequences: international differences in work-related values.* Beverley Hills, Calif.: Sage.

HOFSTEDE, G. and HOFSTEDE, G. F. (2005) *Culture and organisations: software for the mind,* 2nd edn. London: McGraw-Hill.

HOLBECHE, L. (1999) *Aligning human resources and business strategy.* London: Butterworth Heinemann.

HOLMAN, D., WALL, T., CLEGG, C., SPARROW, P. and HOWARD, A. (eds). (2002) *The new workplace: a guide to the human impact of modern working practices.* Chichester: Wiley.

HOLMAN, D., WALL, T., CLEGG, C., SPARROW, P. and HOWARD, A. (eds). (2005) *The essentials of the new workplace: a guide to the human impact of modern working practices.* Chichester: Wiley.

HOLT, B. (1994) Benchmarking comes to HR. *Personnel Management*, June.

HOM, P. and GRIFFETH, R. (1995) *Employee turnover.* Cincinnati, Oh.: South Western.

HOPE, K. (2005) Scots missed. *People Management*, 13 October. 16–17.

HORIBE, F. (1999) *Managing knowledge workers.* Toronto. Wiley.

HOULDSWORTH, E. and JIRASINGHE, D. (2007) *Managing and measuring employee performance.* London: Kogan Page.

HOWARD, S. (2000) Pressing ahead. *People Management annual review of the recruitment advertising industry 2000.*

HOWARD, S. (2001) Cooling-off period. *People Management annual review of the recruitment advertising industry 2001.*

HUBBARD, N. and PURCELL, J. (2001) Managing employee expectations during acquisitions. *Human Resource Management Journal*, Vol. 11, No. 2.

HUCZYNSKI, A. and FITZPATRICK, M. (1989) *Managing employee absence for a competitive edge.* London: Pitman.

HUDDART, G. (1995) A whole new ball game. *Personnel Today*, January.

HUSELID, M. (1995) The impact of human resource practices on turnover, productivity and corporate financial performance. *Academy of Management Journal*, Vol. 38, No. 3. 635–672.

IFF RESEARCH. (1993) *Skill needs in Britain*. London: HMSO.

ILES, P. (2007) Employee resourcing and talent management, in J. Storey (ed), *Human resource management: a critical text,* 3rd edn. London, Thomson.

ILES, P. and ROBERTSON, I. (1997) The impact of selection procedures on candidates, in P. Herriot (ed), *Assessment and selection in organisations*. Chichester: Wiley.

ILES, P. and SALAMAN, G. (1995) Recruitment, selection and assessment, in J. Storey (ed), *Human resource management: a critical text*. London: Routledge.

INCOMES DATA SERVICES (IDS). (1992a) *Controlling absence*. IDS Study 498 (January). London: IDS.

IDS. (1992b) Recruitment: *Employment Law* supplement 64. London: IDS.

IDS. (1992c) *Performance management*. IDS Study 518 (November). London: IDS.

IDS. (1993) *Performance appraisal for manual workers*. IDS Study 543 (December). London: IDS.

IDS. (1994a) Graduates. *IDS Focus* No. 71, August.

IDS. (1994b) *Staff turnover*. IDS Report 661 (March). London: IDS.

IDS. (1995a) *Appraisal systems*. IDS Study 576 (April). London: IDS.

IDS. (1995b) *Assessment centres*. IDS Study 569 (January). London: IDS.

IDS. (1995c) The jobs mythology. *IDS Focus* No. 74, March.

IDS. (1995d) *Large scale recruitment*. IDS Study 581 (July). London: IDS.

IDS. (1995e) *Managing labour turnover*. IDS Study 577 (May). London: IDS.

IDS. (1996) *Older workers*. IDS Study 595 (February). London: IDS.

IDS. (1997) *Performance management*. IDS Study 626 (May). London: IDS.

IDS. (1998) *Business partnerships with schools*. IDS Study 658 (November). London: IDS.

IDS. (1999) The changing shape of personnel management. *IDS Focus* No. 90, Summer.

IDS. (2000a) *On-line recruitment*. IDS Study Plus (Winter). London: IDS.

IDS. (2000b) *Outsourcing HR administration*. IDS Study 700 (December). London: IDS.

IDS. (2000c) Going global. *IDS Focus* No. 95, Summer.

IDS. (2000d) *Work–life balance*. IDS Study 698 (November). London: IDS.

IDS. (2001a) The way we work now. *IDS Focus* No. 100, Winter.

IDS. (2001b) *Contracts of employment*. London: IDS.

IDS. (2001c) *Managing redundancy*. IDS Study Plus (Autumn). London: IDS.

IDS. (2002a) *Teleworking*. IDS Study 729 (May). London: IDS.

IDS. (2002b) *Annual hours*. IDS Study 721 (January). London: IDS.

IDS. (2002c) *Flexitime schemes*. IDS Study 725 (March). London: IDS.

IDS. (2002d) *Assessment centres*. IDS Study 735 (September). London: IDS.

IDS. (2002e) *Employee assistance programmes*. IDS Study Plus (Winter). London: IDS.

IDS. (2003a) *Outsourcing HR administration*. IDS Study 746 (Spring). London: IDS.

IDS. (2003b) *Recruitment practices*. IDS Study 751 (June). London: IDS.

IDS. (2005a) *Homeworking*. IDS Study 793 (March). London: IDS.

IDS. (2005b) *Employee retention*. IDS Study 807 (October). London: IDS.

IDS. (2006a) *Flexible working*. IDS Study 834 (November). London: IDS.

IDS. (2006b) *Annual hours*. IDS Study 815 (February). London: IDS.

IDS. (2006c) *Flexitime schemes*. IDS Study 822 (May). London: IDS.

IDS. (2006d) *Online recruitment*. IDS Study 819 (April). London: IDS.

IDS. (2006e) Age discrimination. *Employment Law* supplement, August.

IDS. (2007) *Performance management*. IDS Study 839 (February). London: IDS.

INDUSTRIAL RELATIONS SERVICES (IRS). (1990) Succession planning. *Recruitment and Development Report*, No. 2 (February).

IRS. (1995) Discipline at work – the practice. *Employment Trends*, No. 591, September.

IRS. (1997a) The changing nature of the employment contract. *Employment Trends*, No. 635, July.

IRS. (1997b) The state of selection: an IRS survey. E*mployee Development Bulletin*, No. 85, January.

IRS. (1999a) Cost effective recruitment: an IRS survey of employers' experience. *Employee Development Bulletin*, No. 115, June.

IRS. (1999b) The business of selection: an IRS survey. *Employee Development Bulletin*, No. 117, November.

IRS. (2000a) Making a success of succession. E*mployee Development Bulletin*, No. 132, December.

IRS. (2000b) Measuring workplace stress: the GHQ-12. *Employee Health Bulletin*, No. 14, April.

IRS. (2000c) Stress auditing – the OSI. *Employee Health Bulletin*, No. 16, August.

IRS. (2000d) Life after merger: managing change at Lloyds TSB. *Employment Trends*, No. 709, August.

IRS. (2000e) Phone a friend. *Employee Health Bulletin*, No. 13, February.

IRS. (2000f) Emotional intelligence – mind games for the future of work. *Employee Development Bulletin*, No. 122, January.

IRS. (2000g) Merger ahead? Make sure HR is part of the deal. *Employment Trends*, No. 706, June.

IRS. (2001a) Managing flexible workers. *Employment Trends*, No. 723, March.

IRS. (2001b) Putting on a brave face. *Employment Review*, No. 738, October.

IRS. (2001c) All aboard the online express. *Employee Development Bulletin*, No. 134, February.

IRS. (2001d) A final word before you go.... *Employee Development Bulletin*, No. 134, February.

IRS. (2001e) Think local: using job centres for recruitment. *Employee Development Bulletin*, No. 139, July.

IRS. (2001f) Benchmarking labour turnover 2001/2002, part 1. *Employment Review*, No. 741, December.

IRS. (2001g) Screen test. *Employee Development Bulletin*, No. 140, August.

IRS. (2001h) Checking out new recruits. *Employee Development Bulletin*, No. 135, March.

IRS. (2001i) Managing discipline at work. *Employment Trends*, No. 727, May.

IRS. (2002a) The check's in the post. *Employment Review*, No. 752 (34–42)

IRS. (2002b) I've got your number: telephone interviewing. *Employment Review*, No. 756 (34–36).

IRS. (2002c) Internal applicants – handle with care. *Employment Review*, No. 748 (p35–38)

IRS. (2003a) Fail to plan, plan to fail . *Employment Review*, No. 790 (p 42–48)

IRS. (2003b) Setting the tone: job descriptions and person specifications. *Employment Review*, No. 776. 42–48.

IRS. (2003c) Human capital – not just another term for HR? *Employment Review*, No. 768. 14–16.

IRS. (2003d) Competencies in graduate recruitment and selection. *Employment Review*, No. 783. 44–48.

IRS. (2003d) Induction to perfection: the start of a beautiful friendship. *Employment Review*, No. 772. 34–40.

IRS. (2003e) Spinning the recruitment web. *Employment Review*, No. 767. 34–40.

IRS. (2003f) The best conditions for the start of a beautiful friendship. *Employment Review*, No. 771. 34–40.

IRS. (2004a) Systems error? How HR chooses and uses information systems. *Employment Review*, No. 812. 9–16.

IRS. (2004b) A graphic illustration: getting the best from recruitment ads. *Employment Review*, No. 805. 42–48.

IRS. (2004c) Human capital reporting: proving the value of people. *Employment Review*, No. 802. 9–15.

IRS. (2004d) Agencies, employers and the new regulations. *Employment Review*, No. 795. 45–48.

IRS. (2004e) Graduate recruitment 2004/5: upturn and optimism. *Employment Review*, No. 811. 40–48.

IRS. (2004f) Biodata: this is your life. *Employment Review*, No. 795. 42–44.

IRS. (2004g) Civil service absence cost £370 million in 2002. *Employment Review*, No. 792. 20–21.

IRS. (2004h) Research – measuring and managing labour turnover: part two. *Employment Review*, No. 794. 42–48.

IRS. (2004i) Communicating bad news: managing redundancy. *Employment Review*, No. 803. 11–17.

INDUSTRIAL SOCIETY. (1997a) *Appraisal.* London: Industrial Society.

INDUSTRIAL SOCIETY. (1997b) *Managing best practice: maximising attendance.* London: Industrial Society.

INDUSTRIAL SOCIETY. (2000) *Maximising attendance: managing best practice.* London: Industrial Society.

INSTITUTE OF ECONOMIC AFFAIRS. (2001) Regulation and the small firm. *Economic Affairs*, Vol. 21, No. 2.

INSTITUTE OF EMPLOYMENT RIGHTS (IER). (2000) *Social justice and economic efficiency.* London: IER.

INSTITUTE OF OCCUPATIONAL HEALTH (IOH). (2003) *Managing attendance at work: an evidence-based review.* Birmingham: IOH.

INSTITUTE OF PERSONNEL AND DEVELOPMENT (IPD). (1992) *Performance management in the UK: an analysis of the issues.* London: IPD.

IPD. (1996a) *Guide on recruitment.* London: IPD.

IPD. (1996b) *Guide on redundancy.* London: IPD.

IPD. (1997a) *Guide on psychological testing.* London: IPD.

IPD. (1997b) Key facts: redundancy. *People Management*, February.

INSTITUTE OF PERSONNEL MANAGEMENT (IPM). (1992) Statement on human resource planning. London: IPM.

IPM. (1993) *Flexible working patterns in Europe.* London: IPM.

JACKSON, C. (1996) *Understanding psychological testing.* Leicester: British Psychological Society.

JACKSON, S. E. and SCHULER, R. S. (1990) Human resource planning: challenges for industrial/organisational psychologists. *American Psychologist,* Vol. 45. Reprinted in G. R. Ferris and M. R. Buckley (eds) (1996), *Human resources management: perspectives, context, functions and outcomes*, 3ird edn. Englewood Cliffs, N.J.: Prentice Hall.

JACKSON, T. (2002) *International HRM: a cross-cultural approach.* London: Sage.

JAMES, H. (2001) *The end of globalization: lessons from the Great Depression*. Cambridge, Mass.: Harvard University Press.

JAMES, P., CUNNINGHAM, I. and DIBBEN, P. (2002) Absence management and the issues of job retention and return to work. *Human Resource Management Journal*, Vol. 12, No. 2. 82–94.

JAMES, P., DIBBEN, P. and CUNNINGHAM, I. (2000) Missing persons. *People Management*, 23 November.

JAMES, P. and LEWIS, D. (1992) *Discipline*. London: IPM.

JANSEN, P. and DE JONGH, F. (1997) *Assessment centres: a practical handbook*. Chichester: Wiley.

JEFFERSON, M. (1997) *Principles of employment law*, 3rd edn. London: Cavendish.

JENKINS, J. (1983) Management trainees in retailing, in B. Ungerson (ed), *Recruitment handbook*. Aldershot: Gower.

JENN, N. G. (2005) *Headhunters and how to use them*. London: Economist/Profile Books.

JENNER, S. and TAYLOR, S. (2000) *Recruiting, developing and retaining graduate talent*. London: FT/Prentice Hall.

JERMIER, J. M. and NORD, W. (1998) Industrial sabotage, in M. Poole and M. Warner (eds), *The handbook of human resource management*. London: Thomson Business Press.

JOHNS, G. (2001) Contemporary research on absence from work: correlates, causes and consequences, in I. Robertson and C. Cooper (eds), *Personnel psychology and HRM*. Chichester: Wiley.

JOHNS, G. and NICHOLSON, N. (1982) The meaning of absence: new strategies for theory and research, in B. Straw and L. Cummings (eds), *Research in organisational behaviour*. London: JAI Press.

JOHNSON, G. and BROWN, J. (2004) Workforce planning not a common practice, IPMA–HR study finds. *Public Personnel Management*, Vol. 33, No. 4. 379–388.

JOHNSON, R. (2001a) Doubled entente. *People Management*, 3 May.

JOHNSON, R. (2001b) Escape from the past. *People Management*, 11 January

JOHNSON, R. (2001c) *Service excellence = reputation = profit*. Colchester: Institute of Customer Service.

JOHNSON, R. (2006) Back on track. *People Management*, 1 June. 24–27.

JOHNSON, R. (2007a) The nicer splice. *People Management*, 22 February. 37–38.

JOHNSON, R. (2007b) Sharing the load. *People Management*, 9 August. 40–42.

JOHNSON, R. (2007c) An idea past its sell-by date? *People Management*, 1 November. 36–39.

JORDAN, J. (2003) Strain stoppers. *People Management*, 20 November.

JOYNT, P. and MORTON, B. (eds) (1999) *The global HR manager*. London Colchester: IPD.

KAKABADSE, A. and KAKADBADSE, N. (2002) *Smart sourcing: international best practice*. Basingstoke: Palgrave.

KALINAUCKAS, P. and KING, H. (1994) *Coaching: realising the potential*. London: IPD.

KANDOLA, B., STAIRS, M. and SANDFORD-SMITH, R. (2000) Slim picking. *People Management*, 28 December.

KAROLY, L. A. and PANIS, C. W. A. (2004) *The 21st century at work: forces shaping the future workforce and workplace in the United States*. Santa Monica, Calif.: RAND Corporation.

KAUHANEN, A. and PIEKKOLA, H. (2006) What makes performance-related pay schemes work? Finnish evidence. *Journal of Management Governance*, No. 10. 149–177.

KEARNS, P. (1994) Measuring the effectiveness of the personnel function. *IRS Employment Trends*, No. 564.

KEENAN, T. (1995) Graduate recruitment in Britain: a survey of selection methods used by organizations *Journal of Organizational Behavior*, Vol. 16.

KELLER, K. (2000) Building and managing corporate brand identity, in M. Scultz *et al* (eds), *The expressive organisation: linking identity, reputation and the corporate brand*. Oxford: Oxford University Press.

KELLER, R. T. (1983) Predicting absenteeism from prior absenteeism: attitudinal factors and non-attitudinal factors. *Journal of Applied Psychology*, Vol. 68, No. 3.

KERSLEY, B., ALPIN, C., FORTH, J., BRYSON, A., BEWLEY, H., DIX, G. and OXENBRIDGE, S. (2006) *Inside the workplace: findings from the 2004 Workplace Employment Relations Survey*. Abingdon: Routledge.

KETTLEY, P. and KERRIN, M. (2003) *E-recruitment: is it delivering?* Brighton: Institute of Employment Studies.

KHATRI, N., FERN, C. T. and BUDHWAR, P. (2001) Explaining employee turnover in an Asian context. *Human Resource Management Journal*, Vol. 11, No. 1. 54–74.

KINNIE, N. and ARTHURS, A. (1993) Will personnel people ever learn to love the computer? *Personnel Management*, June.

KINNIE, N. and SWART, J. (2006) The alchemists. *People Management*, 6 April. 42–45.

KIRNAN, J., FARLEY, J. and GEISINGER, K. (1989) The relationship between recruiting source, applicant quality and hire performance: an analysis by sex, ethnicity and age. *Personnel Psychology*, Vol.. 42.

KNIGHT, K. G. and LATRIELLE, P. L. (2000) Discipline, dismissals and complaints to industrial tribunals. *British Journal of Industrial Relations*, Vol. 38, No. 4. 533.

KODZ J., HARPER, H. and DENCH, S. (2002) *Work–life balance: beyond the rhetoric*. Institute for Employment Studies Report No. 384. Brighton: IES.

KOHN, A. (1993) Why incentive plans cannot work. *Harvard Business Review*, September/October.

KRAUT, A. I. and SAARI, L. M. (1999) Organization surveys: coming of age for a new era, in A. Kraut and A. Korman (eds), *Evolving practices in human resource management*. San Francisco, Calif.: Jossey Bass.

LABOUR MARKET TRENDS. (2002) Labour market spotlight. *Labour Market Trends*, August.

LAMB, J. (2000) Move to online tests threatens quality of recruitment process. *People Management*, 20 July.

LARKAN, K. (2007) *The talent war: how to find and retain the best people for your company*. London: The Times.

LAROCHE, L. and RUTHERFORD, D. (2007) *Recruiting, retaining and promoting culturally different employees*. New York: Butterworth Heinemann.

LATHAM, G. and LATHAM, S. (2000) Overlooking theory and research in performance appraisal at one's peril: much done, more to do. In C. Cooper and E. Locke (eds), *Industrial and organizational psychology: linking theory with practice*. Oxford: Blackwell.

LATHAM, G., SULSKY, L. M. and MACDONALD, H. (2007) Performance management, in P. Boxall, J. Purcell and P. Wright (eds), *The Oxford handbook of human resource management*. Oxford: Oxford University Press.

LAUDON, K. and STARBUCK, W. (1997) Organizational information and knowledge, in A. Sorge and M. Warner (eds), *The IEBM handbook of organizational behaviour*. London: Thomson Learning.

LEA, R. (2001) *The work–life balance and all that: the re-regulation of the labour market*. London: Institute of Directors.

LEAMAN, A. and BORDASS, B. (2000) Productivity in buildings: the killer variables, in D. Clements-Croome (ed), *Creating the productive workplace*. London: E & FN Spon.

LEAP, T. and CRINO, M. (1993) *Personnel/human resource management*, 2nd edn. New York: Macmillan.

LEGERE, C. L. J. (1985) Occupational analysis, in W. R. Tracey (ed), *Human resources management and development handbook*. New York: AMACOM.

LEGGE, K. (1997) The morality of HRM, in C. Mabey (ed), *Experiencing human resource management*. London: Sage.

LEITCH, S. (2006) *Prosperity for all in the global economy – world class skills: final report*. London: HM Treasury.

LENGNICK-HALL, C. and LENGNICK-HALL, M. (1988) Strategic human resource management: a review of the literature and a proposed typology. *Academy of Management Review*, Vol. 13, No. 3. 454–470.

LEVINSON, H. (1973) Asinine attitudes toward motivation. *Harvard Business Review*, January–February.

LEVINSON, H. (1976) Appraisal of what performance? *Harvard Business Review*, July–August.

LEWIS, D. and SARGEANT, M. (2007) *Essentials of employment law*, 9th edn. London: CIPD.

LEWIS, P. (1993) *The successful management of redundancy*. Oxford: Blackwell.

LEWIS, R. D. (1996) *When cultures collide: managing successfully across cultures*. London: Nicholas Brealey.

LIFF, S. (2000) Manpower or human resource planning – what's in a name? in S. Bach and K Sisson (eds), *Personnel management; a comprehensive guide to theory and practice*, 3rd edn. Oxford: Blackwell.

LIND FROGNER, M. (2002) Skills shortages. *Labour Market Trends*, January.

LINDSAY, C. and McCAULAY, C. (2004) Growth in self-employment in the UK. *Labour Market Trends*, October. 399–404.

LING SING CHEE (1994) Singapore Airlines: strategic human resource initiatives, in D Torrington (ed), *International human resource management: think globally, act locally*. London: Prentice Hall.

LITTLEFIELD, D. and MERRICK, N. (2000) Realm of peers. *People Management*, 7 December.

LIVY, B. (1988) Personnel recruitment and selection methods, in B. Livy (ed), *Corporate personnel management*. London: Pitman.

LOCKTON, D. (2006) *Employment law*, 5th edn. London: Macmillan.

LOCKYER, C. and SCHOLARIOS, D. (2004) Selecting hotel staff: why best practice does not always work. *International Journal of Contemporary Hospitality Management*, Vol. 16, No. 2. 125–135.

LONG, P. (1981) *Retirement: planned liberation?* London: IPM.

LONGENECKER, C. O., SIMS, H. P. and GIOIA, D. A. (1987) Behind the mask: the politics of employee appraisal. *American Academy of Management Executive*. Reprinted in G. R. Ferris and M. R. Buckley (eds) (1996) *Human resources management: perspectives, context, functions and outcomes*, 3rd edn. Englewood Cliffs. N.J.: Prentice Hall.

LOVERIDGE, R. and MOK, A. (1979) *Theories of labour market segmentation: a critique*. The Hague: Martinus Nijhoff.

LUNN, T. (1989) In pursuit of talent. *International Journal of Hospitality Management*. 89–96.

LUTHANS, F. (2002) Positive organisational behavior: developing and managing psychological strengths. *Academy of Management Executive*, Vol. 16, No. 1. 57–72.

LUTHANS, F., YOUSSEF, C. M. and AVOLIO, B. J. (2007) *Psychological capital*. Oxford: Oxford University Press.

MABEY, C. (2001) Closing the circle: participant views of a 360 degree feedback programme. *Human Resource Management Journal*, Vol. 11, No. 1.

MACAFEE, M. (2007) How to conduct exit interviews. *People Management*, 12 July. 42–43.

MACDONALD, I. (1995) *Hired fired or sick and tired*. London: Nicholas Brealey.

MACGREGOR, D. (1957) An uneasy look at performance appraisal. *Harvard Business Review*, May–June.

MACGREGOR, D. (1960) *The human side of enterprise.* New York: McGraw-Hill.

MAERTZ, C. P. and CAMPION, M. A. (2001) 25 years of voluntary turnover research: a review and critique, in I. Robertson and C. Cooper (eds), *Personnel psychology and HRM.* Chichester: Wiley.

MAKIN, P., COOPER, C. and COX, C. (1989) *Managing people at work.* Leicester: British Psychological Society/Routledge.

MAKIN, P., COOPER, C. and COX, C. (1996) *Organizations and the psychological contract.* Leicester: British Psychological Society.

MANOCHA, R. (2002) Cut out for the role. *People Management*, 2 May.

MANOCHA, R. (2003) Game plan. *People Management*, 6 November.

MANOCHA, R. (2004) Bonding agents. *People Management*, 11 November.

MANOCHA, R. (2004) Well adjusted. *People Management*, 8 April.

MANZONI, J.-F. and BARSOUX, J.-L. (2004) Rescue remedy. *People Management,* 14 October.

MARCHINGTON, M. and WILKINSON, A. (2002) *People management and development: human resource management at work*, 2nd edn. London: CIPD.

MARCHINGTON, M. and WILKINSON, A. (2005) *Human resource management at work*, 3rd edn. London: CIPD.

MARCHINGTON, M. and WILKINSON, A. (2008) *Human resource management at work*, 4th edn. London: CIPD.

MARKS, N. (2006) Merrily on high. *People Management*, 28 December. 30–31.

MARLOW, S. (2002) Regulating labour management in small firms. *Human Resource Management Journal*, Vol. 12, No. 3. 25–44.

MARSH, C. (1991) *Hours of work of women and men in Britain.* Manchester: Equal Opportunities Commission.

MAYO, A. (2001) *The human value of the enterprise: valuing people as assets – monitoring, measuring, managing.* London: Nicholas Brealey.

MAYO, A. (2002) A thorough evaluation. *People Management*, 4 April.

McBEATH, G. (1992) *The handbook of human resource planning: practical manpower analysis techniques for HR professionals.* Oxford: Blackwell.

McGARVEY, R. and SMITH, S. (1993) When workers rate the boss. *Training Magazine*, March. Reprinted in G. R. Ferris and M. R. Buckley (eds) (1996), *Human resources management: perspectives, context, functions and outcomes*, 3rd edn. Englewood Cliffs, N.J.: Prentice Hall.

McGREGOR, A. and SPROULL, A. (1992) Employers and the flexible workforce. *Employment Gazette*, May.

McHENRY, R. (1997) The secrets of making staff work harder. *Personnel Management*, July.

McORMOND, T. (2004) Changes in working trends over the past decade. *Labour Market Trends*, January. 25–35.

MESTRE M., STAINER A. and STAINER L. (1997) Employee orientation – the Japanese approach. *Employee Relations*, Vol. 19, No. 5. 443–458.

MEYER, H. H., KAY, E. and FRENCH J. R. P. (1965) Split roles in performance appraisal. *Harvard Business Review*, January–February.

MICHAELS, E., HANDFIELD-JONES, H. and AXELROD, B. (2001) *The war for talent.* Boston, Mass.: Harvard Business School Press.

MICKLETHWAIT, J. and WOOLDRIDGE, A. (1996) *The witch doctors*. London: Heinemann.

MICKLETHWAIT, J. and WOOLDRIDGE, A. (2000) *A future perfect: the challenge and hidden promise of globalisation*. London: Heinemann.

MILES, R. E. and SNOW, C. C. (1978) *Organization strategy, structure and process*. New York: McGraw-Hill.

MILLMAN, J., NASON S., ZHU, C. and DE CIERI, H. (2002) An exploratory assessment of the purposes of performance appraisals in North and Central America and the Pacific rim. *Human Resource Management*, Vol. 41, No. 1 (Spring). 87–102.

MILLMORE, M. (2003) Just how extensive is the practice of strategic recruitment and selection? *Irish Journal of Management*, Vol. 24, No. 1. 87–108.

MILLMORE, M., LEWIS, P., SAUNDERS, M., THORNHILL, A. and MORROW, T. (2007) *Strategic human resource management: contemporary issues*. Harlow: FT/Prentice Hall.

MILWARD, N., BRYSON, A. and FORTH, J. (2000) *All change at work? British employment relations 1980–1998, as portrayed by the Workplace Industrial Relations Survey series*. London: Routledge.

MINTZBERG, H. (1976) Planning on the left-side and managing on the right. *Harvard Business Review*, July–August.

MINTZBERG, H. (1994) *The rise and fall of strategic planning*. New York: Prentice Hall.

MOBLEY, W. (1977) Intermediate linkages in the relationship between job satisfaction and employee turnover. *Journal of Applied Psychology*, No. 62. 237-240. Reprinted in R. Steers and L. Porter (eds) (1987), *Motivation and work behaviour*. New York: McGraw-Hill.

MOLONEY, K. (2000) History repeating. *People Management*, 6 July.

MOLONEY, K. (2002) Lines of defence. *People Management*, 11 July.

MORAN, M. (2003) *The British regulatory state*. Oxford: Oxford University Press.

MORGESON, F. P., CAMPION, M. A., DIPBOYE, R. L. and HOLLENBECK, J. R. (2007) Reconsidering the use of personality tests in personnel selection contexts. *Personnel Psychology*, Vol. 60, No. 3. 683–730.

MORRIS, D. (2001) The employment law implications of charity mergers. *Employee Relations*, Vol. 23, No. 3.

MORRIS, H., WILLEY, B. and SACHDEV, S. (2002) *The corporate environment: a guide for human resource managers*, 2nd edn. London: FT/Pitman.

MOUTAFI, J., FURNHAM, A. and CRUMP, J. (2007) Is managerial level related to personality? *British Journal of Management*, Vol. 18. 272–280.

MUNRO FRASER, J. (1979) *Employment interviewing*. Plymouth: Macdonald and Evans.

MURPHY, K. R. and CLEVELAND, J. N. (1995) *Understanding performance appraisal: social, organisational and goal-based perspectives*. Thousand Oaks, Calif.: Sage.

NATIONAL RESEARCH COUNCIL. (1999) *The changing nature of work: implications for occupational analysis*. Washington DC: National Academy Press.

NATIONAL STATISTICS. (2006) *Labour market review*. Basingstoke: Palgrave Macmillan.

NEIL, A. (1996). *Full disclosure*. Basingstoke: Macmillan.

NEWELL, S. (2005) Recruitment and selection, in S. Bach (ed), *Managing human resources: personnel management in transition*, 4th edn. Oxford: Blackwell.

NEWSPAPER SOCIETY. (2005) *Recruitment choice: a practical guide to the recruitment advertising market*. London: Newspaper Society.

NICHOLSON, N. (1976) Management sanctions and absence control. *Human Relations*, 29 February.

NICHOLSON, N. and JOHNS, G. (1985) The absence culture and the psychological contract – who's in control of absence? *Academy of Management Review*, Vol. 10. 397, 407. Reprinted in R. Steers and L. Porter (eds) (1987), *Motivation and work behavior*. New York: McGraw-Hill.

NIKANDROU, I., PAPALEXANDRIS, N. and BOURANTAS, D. (2000) Gaining employee trust after acquisition: implications for managerial action. *Employee Relations*, Vol. 22, No. 4.

NKOMO, S. M. (1987) Human resource planning and organization performance: an exploratory analysis. *Strategic Management Journal*, No. 8. 387–392.

NOLAN, P. (2001) Shaping things to come. *People Management*, 27 December.

NOLAN, P. (2004) Back to the future of work. Available online at: www.leeds.ac.uk/esrcfutureofwork/downloads/events/colloquium_2004/nolan_paper_0904.pdf [accessed 11 April 2008].

NOLAN, P. (2004) Shaping the future: the political economy of work and employment. *Industrial Relations Journal*, Vol. 35, No. 5. 378–387.

NONAKA, I. and TAKEUCHI, H. (1995) *The knowledge creating company*. New York: Oxford University Press.

NORTH, S. J. (1994) Employers turn to handwriting tests. *Personnel Today*, December.

O'DOHERTY, D. (2000) Towards human resource planning? in I. Beardwell and L. Holden (eds), *Human resource management: a contemporary perspective*, 3rd edn. London: Pitman.

O'REILLY, N. (1997) Promotion system too complex. *Personnel Today*, March.

ORLITZKY, M. (2007) Recruitment strategy, in P. Boxall, J. Purcell and P. Wright (eds), *The Oxford handbook of human resource management*. Oxford: Oxford University Press.

OSBORN-JONES, T. (2004) Managing human talent, in D. Rees and R. McBain (eds), *People management: challenge and opportunities*. Basingstoke: Palgrave.

OVERELL, S. (2006) Fast forward. *People Management*, 9 February. 26–31.

PARKER, S. and WALL, T. (1998) *Job and work design*. London, Sage.

PARRY, E. and TYSON, S. (2007) Technology in HRM: the means to become a strategic business partner, in J. Storey (ed), *Human resource management: a critical text*, 3rd edn. London: Thomson.

PEARN, M. and KANDOLA, R. (1993) *Job analysis: a manager's guide*, 2nd edn. London: IPM.

PEOPLE MANAGEMENT. (2004) BA chaos blamed on lack of staff. *People Management*, 2 September.

PERKINS, S. J. (1997) *Globalization: the people dimension*. London: Kogan Page.

PERSONNEL TODAY. (1995) Data projection. *Personnel Today*, September.

PETERS, T. (1989) *Thriving on chaos*. London: Pan.

PETTMAN, B. (1975) *Labour turnover and retention*. Epping: Gower.

PFEFFER, J. (1994) *Competitive advantage through people*. Boston, Mass.: Harvard University Press.

PFEFFER, J. and SUTTON, R. (2006) The real brain teaser. *People Management*, 20 April. 28–30.

PHILLIPS, J., STONE, R. and PULLIAM PHILLIPS, P. (2001) *The human resources scorecard: measuring the return on investment*. London/Boston, Mass.: Butterworth Heinemann.

PHILLIPS, L. (2007) Games of skill. *People Management*, 31 May. 24–29.

PHILP, T. (1990) *Appraising performance for results*, 2nd edn. London: McGraw-Hill.

PHILPOTT, J. (2007) Something wikid this way comes. *People Management*, 13 December. 28–31.

PHILPOTT, J. and DAVIES, G. (2006) No turning back? *People Management*, 14 September. 26–30.

PICKARD, J. (2000) The truth is out there. *People Management*, 3 February.

PICKARD, J. (2001) When push comes to shove. *People Management*, 22 November.

PICKARD, J. (2004) Should I stay or should I go? *People Management*, 25 March.

PICKARD, J. (2007) Spring in its step. *People Management guide to HR outsourcing*, February.

PINNINGTON, A., MACKLIN, R. and CAMPBELL, T. (eds) (2007) *Human resource management: ethics and employment*. Oxford: Oxford University Press.

PITT, G. (2007) *Employment law*, 6th edn. London: Sweet and Maxwell.

POELMANS, S., CHINCHILLA, N. and CARDONA, P. (2003) The adoption of family-friendly HRM policies: competing for scarce resources in the labour market. *International Journal of Manpower*, Vol. 24, No. 2. 128–147.

POINTON, J. and RYAN A. J. (2004) Reward and performance management, in I. Beardwell, L. Holden and T. Claydon (eds), *Human resource management: a contemporary approach*. London: FT/Prentice Hall.

POLLOCK, L. and COOPER, C. (2000) Teenage picks. *People Management*, 24 August.

POLLERT, A. (1987) *The flexible firm: a model in search of a reality (or a policy in search of a practice?)*. Warwick Papers in Industrial Relations, No. 19. University of Warwick.

POLLERT, A. (1988) The flexible firm: fixation or fact? *Work, Employment and Society*, 2 March.

PORTER, M. (1985) *Competitive advantage: creating and sustaining superior performance*. New York: Free Press.

PROKOPENKO, J. (1994) The transition to a market economy and its implications for HRM in Eastern Europe, in P Kirkbride (ed), *Human resource management in Europe: perspectives for the 1990s*. London: Routledge.

PULAKOS, E. D. and SCHMITT, N. (1995) Experience-based and situational interview questions: studies of validity. *Personnel Psychology*, No. 48. 289–308.

PURCELL, J. (1989) The impact of corporate strategy on human resource management, in J Storey (ed), *New perspectives on human resource management*. London: Routledge.

PURCELL, J. and HUTCHINSON, S. (2007) Front-line managers as agents in the HRM–performance causal chain: theory, analysis and evidence. *Human Resource Management Journal*, Vol. 17, No. 1. 3–20.

PURCELL, J. and KINNIE, N. (2007) HRM and business performance, in P. Boxall, J. Purcell and P. Wright (eds), *The Oxford handbook of human resource management*. Oxford: Oxford University Press.

PURCELL, J., KINNIE, N. and HUTCHINSON, S. (2003b) The multipack scan. *People Management*, 15 May.

PURCELL, J., KINNIE, N., HUTCHINSON, S., RAYTON, B. and SWART, J. (2003a) *Understanding the people and performance link: unlocking the black box*. London: CIPD.

PWC (2007) *Managing tomorrow's people: the future of work to 2020*. London, Price Waterhouse Coopers. Available online at www.peoplemanagement.co.uk/pwc/tomorrowspeople [accessed January 2008].

RANDELL, G. (1994) Employee appraisal, in K Sisson (ed), *Personnel management: a comprehensive guide to theory and practice in Britain*, 2nd edn. Oxford: Blackwell.

REDMAN, T. (2001) Performance appraisal, in T. Redman and A. Wilkinson (eds), *Contemporary human resource management: text and cases*. London: FT/Prentice Hall.

REDMAN, T. and WILKINSON, A. (2006) Downsizing, in T. Redman and A. Wilkinson (eds), *Contemporary human resource management: text and cases*. London: FT/Prentice Hall.

REED, A. (2001) *Innovation in human resource management: tooling up for the talent wars*. London: CIPD.

REILLY, P. (1996) *Human resource planning: an introduction*. Brighton: Institute for Employment Studies.

REILLY, P. (2001) *Flexibility at work*. Aldershot: Gower.

REILLY, P. (2002) Labour market stalls. *People Management*, 16 May.

REYNOLDS, P. and BAILEY, M. (1993) *How to design and deliver retirement training*. London: Kogan Page.

RHODES, S. R. and STEERS, R. M. (1990) *Managing employee absenteeism*. Reading, Mass.: Addison Wesley.

Ri5 (2007) Fast forward. *People Management guide to recruitment marketing*, June. 8–12.

RICE, B. (1985) Performance review: the job nobody likes. *Psychology Today*. Reprinted in G. R. Ferris and M. R. Buckley (eds) (1996), *Human resources management: perspectives, context, functions and outcomes*, 3rd edn. Englewood Cliffs, N.J.: Prentice Hall.

RIDDELL, P. (2001) Premier league. *People Management*, 31 May. 37–38.

RIDDOCH, V. (2007) Safety net. *People Management guide to assessment*, October. 21–24.

RIFKIN, J. (1995) *The end of work: the decline of the global labour force and the dawn of the post-market era.* New York: Puttnam.

RITZER, G. (1996) *The McDonaldization of society: an investigation into the changing character of contemporary social life*, rev. edn. Thousand Oaks, Calif.: Pine Forge.

RAO, T. V. (2004) *Performance management and appraisal systems.* Thousand Oaks, Calif.: Sage.

ROBINSON, S., MURRELLS, T. and CLIFTON, M. (2006) Highly qualified and highly ambitious: implications for workforce retention of realising the career expectations of graduate nurses in England. *Human Resource Management Journal*, Vol. 16, No. 3. 287–312.

ROBERTS, G. (2000) *Recruitment and selection: a competency approach*, 2nd edn. London: CIPD.

ROBERTS, Z. (2001) United Biscuits to halve costs by recruiting online. *People Management*, 30 August.

ROBERTS, Z. (2004) Referred pain. *People Management,* 20 May.

ROBERTS, Z. (2004) Lords call for unfair dismissal review. *People Management*, 29 July.

ROBERTS, Z. (2006) Lay down the flaw. *People Management*, 26 October. 48–49.

ROBERTSON, I. (2001) Undue diligence. *People Management,* 22 November.

ROBERTSON, I. and MAKIN, P. (1986) Management selection in Britain: a survey and critique. *Journal of Occupational Psychology*, Vol. 61.

ROBINSON, P. (2000) Insecurity and the flexible workforce: measuring the ill-defined, in E. Heery and J. Salmon (eds), *The insecure workforce.* London: Routledge.

ROBSON, F. (2007) How to develop an attendance culture. *People Management*, 31 May. 42–43.

RODGER, A. (1952) *The seven point plan.* London: National Institute for Industrial Psychology.

ROSE, M. (2000) Target practice. *People Management*, 23 November.

ROTHWELL, J. (2000) How to break the news of redundancies. *People Management*, 23 November.

ROTHWELL, S. (1995) Human resource planning, in J. Storey (ed), *Human resource management: a critical text.* London: Routledge.

ROTHWELL, W. J., HOHNE, C. K. and KING, S. B. (2007) *Human performance improvement: building practitioner performance.* Oxford: Elsevier.

ROUSSEAU, D. (1995) *Psychological contracts in organizations.* Thousand Oaks, Calif.: Sage.

ROWE, T. (1986) Eight ways to ruin a performance review. *Personnel Journal*, January.

RUCCI, A. J., KIRN, S. P. and QUINN, R. T. (1998) The employee–customer–profit chain at Sears. *Harvard Business Review*, January/February.

RUGMAN, A. (2000) *The end of globalization.* London: Random House.

RYNES, S., BRETZ, R. and GERHART, B. (1991) The importance of recruitment in job choice: a different way of looking. *Personnel Psychology*, No. 44.

RYNES, S., BARBER, A. and VARMA, G. (2000) Research on the employment interview: usefulness for practice and recommendations for future research, in C. Cooper and E. Locke (eds), *Industrial and organizational psychology.* Oxford: Blackwell.

SAKO, M. (2006) Outsourcing and offshoring: implications for productivity of business services *Oxford Review of Economic Policy*, Vol. 22, No. 4. 499–512.

SALAMAN, G. (2007) Managers' knowledge and the management of change, in J. Storey (ed), *Human resource management: a critical text,* 3rd edn. London: Thomson.

SALGADO, J. F. (2001) Personnel selection methods, in I. Robertson and C. Cooper (eds), *Personnel psychology and HRM.* Chichester: Wiley.

SALOVEY, P. and MAYER, J. (1989) Emotional intelligence. *Imagination, Cognition and Personality*, Vol. 9, No. 3.

SAMBROOK, S. (2005) Exploring succession planning in small, growing firms. *Journal of Small Business and Enterprise Development,* Vol. 12, No. 4. 579–594.

SAMUEL, P. J. (1969) *Labour turnover: towards a solution.* London: IPM.

SAPPAL, P. (2003) Cultural evolution. *People Management*, 17 April.

SARGENT, A. (1989) *The missing workforce: managing absenteeism.* London: IPM.

SCARBROUGH, H. (2003) Recipe for success. *People Management*, 23 January.

SCARBROUGH, H., SWAN, J. and PRESTON, J. (1999) *Knowledge management: a literature review.* London: IPD.

SCASE, R. (2000) *Britain in 2010: the new business landscape.* Oxford: Capstone.

SCHEIN, E. (1980) *Organizational psychology.* Englewood Cliffs, N.J.: Prentice Hall.

SCHMITT, N. and CHAN, D. (1998) *Personnel selection: a theoretical approach.* Thousand Oaks, Calif.: Sage.

SCHREYER, R. and MCCARTER, J. (1998) *The employers' guide to recruiting on the Internet.* Manassas Park, Va.: Impact.

SCHULER, R. and JACKSON, S. (1987) Linking competitive strategies with human resource management. *Academy of Management Executive*, Vol. 1, No. 3. 207–219.

SCHULER, R. S. and JACKSON, S. E. (2007) *Strategic human resource management*, 2nd edn. Oxford: Blackwell.

SCHULTZ, M., HATCH, M. J. and LARSEN, M. H. (2000) *The expressive organisations.* Oxford: Oxford University Press.

SCHUYLER, M. (2006) Using workforce analytics to make strategic talent decisions, in R. P. Gandossy, E. Tucker and N. Verma (eds), *Workforce wake-up call.* Hoboken, N.J.: Wiley.

SEARLE, R. H. (2003) *Selection and recruitment: a critical text.* Milton Keynes: Open University/Palgrave.

SENEVIRATNA, C. (2001) Dependants' day. *People Management,* 6 December. 38–40.

SHACKLETON, J. R. (2005) Regulating the labour market, pp128–143 in P. Booth (ed), *Towards a liberal utopia?* London: Institute of Economic Affairs.

SHACKLETON, V. and NEWELL, S. (1989) Selection procedures in practice, in P Herriot (ed), *Handbook of assessment in organisations.* Chichester: Wiley.

SHAMIR, B. (1991) Meaning, self and motivation in organisations. *Organisation Studies*, 12 March.

SHEA, G. F. (1985) Induction and orientation, in W. R. Tracey (ed), *Human resources management and development handbook.* New York: AMACOM.

SHIROM, A. and ROSENBLATT, Z. (2006) A panel study of the effects of school positions and promotions on absenteeism in the teaching profession. *Journal of Occupational and Organizational Psychology*, No. 79. 623–644.

SIDDIQUE, C. M. (2004) Job analysis: a strategic human resource management practice. *International Journal of Human Resource Management*, Vol. 15, No. 1. 219–244.

SILVER, M. (1983) Forecasting demand for labour using labour productivity trends, in J. Edwards *et al* (eds), *Manpower planning: strategy and techniques in an organisational context.* Chichester: Wiley.

SILVESTER, J. and BROWN, A. (1993) Graduate recruitment: testing the impact. *Selection and Development Review*, Vol. 9, No. 1.

SIMMS, J. (2003) The generation game. *People Management*, 6 February.

SIMMS, J. (2005) Better by design. *People Management*, 29 September. 24–29.

SIMMS, J. (2006a) Zoom at the top. *People Management guide to recruitment consultancies*, April. 27–28.

SIMMS, J. (2006b) In their shoes. *People Management*, 20 April. 36–38.

SISSON, K. and STOREY, J. (2000) *The realities of human resource management: managing the employment relationship*. Buckingham: Open University Press.

SISSON, K. and TIMPERLEY, S. (1994) From manpower planning to strategic human resource management? in K. Sisson (ed), *Personnel management: a comprehensive guide to theory and practice in Britain*, 2nd edn. Oxford: Blackwell.

SKEATS, J. (1991) *Successful induction: how to get the most from your new employees*. London: Kogan Page.

SMEDLEY, T. (2007a) Underneath the arches. *People Management*, 26 July. 28–31.

SMEDLEY, T. (2007b) The powers that BAE. *People Management*, 11 November. 40–43.

SMETHURST, S. (2004) Onto a winner. *People Management*, 29 January.

SMETHURST, S. (2004) The allure of online. *People Management*, 29 July.

SMETHURST, S. (2005a) Chicken coup. *People Management*, 13 January.

SMETHURST, S. (2005b) Faking it. *People Management*, 16 June. 35–36

SMETHURST, S. (2005c) Batteries recharged. *People Management*, 5 May. 24–27.

SMETHURST, S. (2006) The window test. *People Management*, 26 January. 28–30

SMETHURST, S. (2007a) Fair traders. *People Management*, 29 November. 28–31.

SMETHURST, S. (2007b) Core values. *People Management*, 25 January. 24–25.

SMITH, A. R. (1976) The philosophy of manpower planning, in D. J. Bartholomew (ed), *Manpower planning*. London: Penguin.

SMITH, A. R. (ed) (1980) *Corporate manpower planning*. London: Gower.

SMITH, K. (1996) Managing without traditional strategic planning: the evolving role of top management teams, in P. Flood *et al* (eds), *Managing without traditional methods: international innovations in human resource management*. Wokingham: Addison Wesley.

SMITH, M. and ROBERTSON, I. (1993) *The theory and practice of systematic personnel selection*. London: Macmillan.

SMITH M., GREGG, M. and ANDREWS, D. (1989) *Selection and assessment: a new appraisal*. London: Pitman.

SMITH, M. and SUTHERLAND, V. (1993) *Professional issues in selection and assessment*, Vol. 1. Chichester: Wiley.

SORELL, T. and HENDRY, J. (1994) *Business ethics*. Oxford: Butterworth-Heinemann.

SPARROW, P. (1998) New organisational forms, processes, jobs and psychological contracts: resolving the HRM issues, in P. Sparrow and M. Marchington (eds), *Human resource management: the new agenda*. London: FT/Pitman.

SPARROW, P. (2002) The Future of work, in D. Holman, T. Wall, C. Clegg, P. Sparrow and A. Howard (eds), *The new workplace: a guide to the human impact of modern working practices*. Chichester: Wiley.

SPARROW, P., BREWSTER, C. and HARRIS, H. (2004) *Globalizing human resource management*. London: Routledge.

SPARROW, P. and COOPER, C. (2003) *The employment relationship: key challenges for HR*. London: Butterworth-Heinemann.

SPARROW, P. and HILTROP, J. M. (1994) *European human resource management in transition*. London: Prentice Hall.

SPEECHLY, N. (1994) Uncertainty principles. *Personnel Today*, May.

SPICER, D. and AHMAD, R. (2006) Cognitive processing models in performance appraisal: evidence from the Malaysian education system. *Human Resource Management Journal*, Vol.16, No. 2. 214–230.

SPURGEON P., MAZELAN P., BARWELL F. and FLANAGAN H. (2007) *New directions in managing employee absence: an evidence-based approach*. London: CIPD/Active Health Partners.

STAINER, G. (1971) *Manpower planning*. London: Heinemann.

STALK G., EVANS P. and SHULMAN L. E. (1992) Competing on capabilities: the new rules of corporate strategy. *Harvard Business Review*, March–April.

STEERS, R. M., PORTER, L. W. and BIGLEY, G. M. (1996) *Motivation and leadership at work*, 6th edn. Singapore: McGraw-Hill.

STEERS, R. M. and RHODES, S. (1978) Major influences on employee attendance: a process model. *Journal of Applied Psychology*, Vol. 63. 391–407. Reprinted in R. Steers and L. Porter (eds) (1987), *Motivation and work behavior*, 4th edn. New York: McGraw-Hill.

STEVENS, J. (2005) *Managing risk: the human resources contribution*. London, LexisNexis Butterworths.

STEWART, T. (1997) *Intellectual capital: the new wealth of organizations*. London: Nicholas Brealey.

STILES, P. (2007) A world of difference. *People Management*, 15 November. 36–40.

STOREY, J. (2001) Looking to the future, in J. Storey (ed), *Human resource management: a critical text*, 2nd edn. London: Thomson Learning.

STOREY, J. and QUINTAS, P. (2001) Knowledge management and HRM, in J. Storey (ed), *Human resource management: a critical text*, 2nd edn. London: Thomson Learning.

STRACHAN, A. (2004) Lights, camera, interaction. *People Management,* 16 September. 44–46.

STREDWICK, J. and ELLIS, S. (2005) *Flexible working*. London: CIPD.

STREDWICK, J. and KEW, J. (2005) *Business environment: managing in a strategic context*. London, CIPD.

SWART, J. (2007) HRM and knowledge workers, in P. Boxall, J. Purcell and P. Wright (eds), *The Oxford handbook of human resource management*. Oxford: Oxford University Press.

SWINBURNE, P. (2001) How to use feedback to improve performance. *People Management,* 31 May.

SYEDAIN, H. (2006) Gown and town. *People Management*, 23 March. 38–39.

SYEDAIN, H. (2007) A judicious review. *People Management*, 4 October. 37.

TAYLOR, A. (2007) UK immigration may be close to peak. *Financial Times*, 24 July.

TAYLOR, J. (2005) Recruiting university graduates for the public sector: an Australian case study *International Journal of Public Sector Management,* Vol. 18, No. 6/7. 514–533.

TAYLOR, M. S. and COLLINS C. J. (2000) Organizational recruitment: enhancing the intersection of research and practice, in C. Cooper and E. Locke (eds), *Industrial and organizational psychology*. Oxford: Blackwell.

TAYLOR, P. J., PAJO, K., CHEUNG, G. W. and STRINGFIELD, P. (2004) Dimensionality and validity of a structured telephone reference check procedure. *Personnel Psychology*, No. 57. 745–772.

TAYLOR, R. (2002) *Britain's world at work – myths and realities*. ESRC Future of Work Programme Seminar Series. Leeds University.

TAYLOR, R. (2004) *Skills and innovation in modern workplaces.* ESRC Future of Work Programme Seminar Series. Leeds University.

TAYLOR, S. (2002) *The employee retention handbook.* London: CIPD.

TAYLOR, S. and EMIR, A. (2006) *Employment law: an introduction.* Oxford: Oxford University Press.

THI LAM, L. and KIRBY, S. L. (2002) Is emotional intelligence an advantage? An exploration of the impact of emotional and general intelligence on individual performance. *Journal of Social Psychology*, Vol. 142, No. 1. 133–143.

THORPE, R. and HOMAN, G. (eds) (2000) *Strategic reward systems.* London: FT/Prentice Hall.

TOEGEL, G. and CONGER, J. (2003) 360-degree assessment: time for reinvention. *Academy of Management Learning and Education*, Vol. 2, No. 3. 297–311.

TOKAREK, M. (2006) How to manage intercultural communication. *People Management*, 26 October. 66–67.

TOPLIS, J., DULEWICZ, V. and FLETCHER, C. (2005) *Psychological testing: a manager's guide*, 4th edn. London: CIPD.

TORRINGTON, D. (1994) *International human resource management: think globally, act locally.* London: Prentice Hall.

TORRINGTON, D. (1998) Discipline and dismissals, in M. Poole and M. Warner (eds), *The handbook of human resource management.* London: International Thomson Business Press.

TORRINGTON, D., HALL, L. and TAYLOR, S. (2008) *Human resource management,* 7th edn. London: FT/Prentice Hall.

TRAPP, R. (2003) Support system. *People Management,* 12 June.

TRAPP, R. (2004) A life's work. *People Management*, 6 May.

TRAPP, R. (2004) Older and wiser. *People Management,* 23 December.

TREFRY, M. (2006) A double-edged sword: organizational culture in multicultural organizations. *International Journal of Management*, Vol. 23, No. 3. 563–576.

TRIST, E. L., HIGGIN, G. W., MURRAY, H. and POLLOCK, A. B. (1963) *Organisational choice: capabilities of groups at the coal face under changing technologies.* London: Tavistock.

TROMPENAARS, F. and WOOLIAMS, P. (2002) Model behaviour. *People Management*, 5 December.

TULGAN, B. (2007) Drill inspection. *People Management*, 22 February. 44–45.

TULIP, S. (2006) Better buys. *People Management,* 20 April. 40–41.

ULRICH, D., LOSEY, M. and LAKE, G. (eds) (1997) *Tomorrow's HR management.* New York: Wiley.

VAN DER MARSEN, D. E., SOMBRIEFF, P. and HOFSTEDE, W. (1989) Personality questionnaires and inventories, in P Herriot (ed), *A handbook of assessment in organisations.* Chichester: Wiley.

VAN ZOLINGEN, S. J., STREMER, J. N. and STOOKER, M. (2001) Problems in knowledge management: a case study of a knowledge-intensive company. *International Journal of Training and Development*, Vol. 5, No. 3. 168–183.

VICKERSTAFF, S., BALDOCK, J., COX, J. and KEEN, L. (2004) *Happy retirement? The impact of employers' policies and practices on the process of retirement.* Bristol: Joseph Rowntree Foundation/Policy Press.

VROOM, V. (1964) *Work and motivation.* New York: Wiley.

WALDON, C. (2002) Questions of trust. *People Management,* 7 March.

WALKER, J. (1992) *Human resource strategy.* McGraw-Hill, New York.

WALKER, L. (1996) Instant staff for a temporary future. *People Management*, January.

WALTERS, M. (ed.) (1995) *The performance management handbook.* London: IPD›

WANOUS, J. P. (1992) *Organizational entry.* Reading, Mass.: Addison Wesley.

WARD K., GRIMSHAW, D., RUBERY, J. and BENYON, H. (2001): Dilemmas in the management of temporary work agency staff. *Human Resource Management Journal*, Vol. 11, No. 4. 3–21.

WARD, P. (1997) *360-degree feedback*. London: IPD.

WARREN, C. (2006) Cell block HR. *People Management*, 12 October. 26–31.

WATERS, L. (2007) Experiential differences between voluntary and involuntary job redundancy on depression, job-search activity, affective employee outcomes and re-employment quality. *Journal of Occupational and Organizational Psychology*, Vol. 80. 279–299.

WATKINS, J. (2003) Direct line. *People Management*, 15 May. 42–43.

WATKINS, J. (2003) A mini adventure. *People Management*, 6 November.

WATSON, T. (1994) Recruitment and selection, in K Sisson (ed), *Personnel management: a comprehensive guide to theory and practice in Britain*, 2nd edn. Oxford: Blackwell.

WEISINGER, H. (1998) *Emotional intelligence at work*. San Francisco, Calif.: Jossey-Bass.

WES, M. (1996) *Globalisation: winners and losers*. London: Institute for Public Policy Research.

WEST, M. (2005) Hope springs. *People Management*, 13 October. 38–39.

WETHERLY, P. and OTTER, D. (eds) (2008) *The business environment: themes and issues*. Oxford: Oxford University Press.

WHALLEY, L. and SMITH, M. (1998) *Deception in selection*. Chichester: Wiley.

WHIDDETT, S. and KANDOLA, B. (2000) Fit for the job? *People Management*, 25 May.

WHITE, G. and DRUKER J. (2008) *Reward management: a critical text*, 2nd edn. London: Routledge.

WHITE, K. (2004) Year we go, year we go. *People Management*, 17 June.

WHITE, M., HILL, S., MILL, C. and SMEATON, D. (2004) *Managing to change? British workplaces and the future of work*. Basingstoke: Palgrave Macmillan.

WHITENACK, A. (2001) *Brand marketing basics*. Available online at www.experience.com [accessed 2001].

WILKINSON, K. (2004) An investigation into nurse turnover and the validity of the exit interview questionnaire. Unpublished MA dissertation, Manchester Metropolitan University.

WILLIAMS, C. (2007) *Rethinking the future of work*. Basingstoke: Palgrave Macmillan.

WILLIAMS, H. (2002) Strategic planning for human resources, in J Leopold (ed), *Human resources in organisations*. London: FT/Prentice Hall.

WILLIAMS, M. (2000) *The war for talent*. London: CIPD.

WILLIAMSON, P. (2006) Sphere of influence. *People Management*, 12 October. 32–34.

WILLEY, B. (2003) *Employment law in context*, 2nd edn. London: FT/Prentice Hall.

WILLOCK, R. (2005) Employer branding is key in fight for talent. *Personnel Today*, 17 May. 4.

WILLS, J. (1997) Can do better. *Personnel Today*, June.

WOLF, A. and JENKINS, A. (2006) Explaining greater test use for selection: the role of HR professionals in a world of expanding regulation. *Human Resource Management Journal*, Vol. 16, No. 2. 193–213.

WONG, Y. L. and SNELL, R. S. (2003) Employee workplace effectiveness: implications for performance management practices and research. *Journal of General Management*, Vol. 29, No. 2. 53–69.

WOOD, R. and PAYNE, T. (1998) *Competency based recruitment and selection*. Chichester: Wiley.

WOOD, S. and ALBANESE, M. (1995) Can we speak of high commitment management on the shop floor? *Journal of Management Studies*, Vol. 32, No. 2. 1–33.

WOODHALL, J. and WINSTANLEY, D. (2001) The place of ethics in HRM, in J. Storey (ed), *Human resource management: a critical text*, 2nd edn. London: Thomson Learning.

WOODRUFFE, C. (1993) *Assessment centres: identifying and developing competence*, 2nd edn. London: IPD.

WOODRUFFE, C. (1999) *Winning the talent war.* Chichester: Wiley.

WOODRUFFE, C. (2000) Keep X on the files. *People Management,* 20 July.

WOODRUFFE, C. (2001) Promotional intelligence. *People Management*, 11 January.

WOODRUFFE, C. (2002) Intelligence test. *People Management*, 16 May.

WRIGHT, M. and STOREY J. (1994) Recruitment, in I. Beardwell and L. Holden (eds), *Human resource management: a contemporary perspective.* London: Pitman.

ZEMKE, R., RAINES, C. and FILIPCZAK, B. (2000) *Generations at work.* New York: Amacom.

CASES

British Sugar *v* Kirker (1998) IRLR 624

Carmichael *v* National Power (1999) ICR 1226

Durant *v* FSA (2003) EWCA Civ 1746

Faccenda Chicken *v* Fowler (1986) Court of Appeal

Greer *v* Sketchley (1979) IPLR 445

Haddon *v* Van den Bergh Foods (1999) IRLR 672

Hussein *v* Saints Complete House Furnishers (1979) IRLR 337

Iceland Foods *v* Jones (1983) ICR 17

Murray *et al v* Foyle Meats (1999) House of Lords

Northern Joint Police Board *v* Power (1997) IRLR 610

O'Kelly and others *v* Trusthouse Forte (1983) ICR 728

Polkey *v* Deyton Services (1987) IPLR 134

Robb *v* Green (1895) Court of Appeal

Wessex Dairies *v* Smith (1935) Court of Appeal

Whitbread PLC *v* Hall (2001) IRLR 275

Wilson *v* Post Office (2000) IRLR 834

Name index

Note: this index lists individuals quoted or mentioned in the text, either as HR authors or in other contexts, and organisations mentioned as employers and in similar contexts. It does not include authors given purely as reference sources, either within the text or in the 'explore further' sections, or the names of co-authors not given in the text. Names of countries are included in the subject index.

Subject index

A sommelier pours wine into a "Beaujolais Nouveau bath" at a Tokyo resort.
Source: Photo by Shizuo Kambayash/Courtesy of AP Wide World Photos.

an essay): "My new page turning obsession did not go down too well with my new life partner. When on our first night in the Maldives and expecting some form of conjugal rites [she found] herself in second place to a fictional 11-year-old trainee wizard and something called the Sorting Hat."[102]

The *streaking* fad hit college campuses in the mid-1970s. This term described students who ran nude through classrooms, cafeterias, dorms, and sports venues. Although the practice quickly spread across many campuses, it was primarily restricted to college settings. Streaking highlights several of a fad's "naked truths:"[103]

● The fad is nonutilitarian—it does not perform any meaningful function.
● The fad often spreads impulsively—people do not undergo stages of rational decision making before they join in.
● The fad diffuses rapidly, gains quick acceptance, and dies.

Fad or Trend?

Chrysler's PT Cruiser was the talk of the town when it came out in 2000. With its 1930s-gangster getaway-car looks, cutely compact size, and innovative features—such as a panel in the back that you can use as a picnic table—the PT was hot. Chrysler sold 145,000 of them in 2001. By 2003, PT Cruiser sales slumped to 107,759 cars, and Chrysler offered discounts to keep the miniwagon moving. In fall 2005, Chrysler launched a revamped version—the grille and front end looked more like other new Chrysler models, and it upgraded the interior. The PT Cruiser's sales curve—a 25 percent fall from peak to trough—suggests the market for funky, retro three-quarter-sized wagons generated a lot of excitement at the beginning. But instead of being a hot new model for young trendsetters, the car appealed to graying baby boomers—the median age of owners is 50 years old. Are retro cars a fad or a trend? The jury is still out—especially because General Motors also launched its Chevy HHR—a retro car that according to GM executives was inspired by a 1949 Chevrolet Suburban, *not* the PT Cruiser.[104]

The first company to identify a trend and act on it has an advantage, whether the firm is Starbucks (gourmet coffee), Nabisco (Snackwells low-fat cookies and crackers), Taco Bell (value pricing), or Chrysler (retro cars). Nothing is certain, but

Johnny Earle turned his nickname—
"Cupcake"—into a booming business. His
T-shirts featured cupcakes in unlikely places
(for example, one with a cupcake and
crossbones) and became a popular fad.
Source: Courtesy of JohnnyCupcakes.com.

some guidelines help to predict whether the innovation will endure as a long-term trend or if it's just a fad destined to go the way of hula hoops, pet rocks, and little rubber spiders called Wally Wallwalkers that slowly crawled down walls.[105]

● Does it fit with basic lifestyle changes? If a new hairstyle is hard to care for, this innovation isn't consistent with women's increasing time demands. However, the movement to shorter-term vacations is more likely to last because this innovation makes trip planning easier for harried (and broke) consumers who want to get away for a few days at a time.
● What are the benefits? The switch to poultry and fish from beef came about because these meats are healthier.
● Can we personalize it? Enduring trends tend to accommodate a desire for individuality, whereas styles such as Mohawk haircuts or the grunge look are inflexible and don't allow people to express themselves.
● Is it a trend or a side effect? An increased interest in exercise is part of a basic trend toward health consciousness, although the specific form of exercise that is "in" at any given time will vary (e.g., low-impact aerobics versus Pilates).
● What other changes occurred in the market? Sometimes *carryover effects* influence the popularity of related products. The miniskirt fad in the 1960s boosted hosiery purchases substantially. Now, sales of these items are in decline because of today's more casual styles.
● Who adopted the change? If working mothers, baby boomers, or some other important market segment don't adopt the innovation, it is not likely to become a longer-term trend.

Global Diffusion

OBJECTIVE

Why is that products succeed in one culture may fail in another if marketers fail to understand the differences among consumers in each place?

Innovations know no geographic boundaries; in modern times they travel across oceans and deserts with blinding speed. Just as Marco Polo brought noodles from China and colonial settlers introduced Europeans to the "joys" of tobacco, today multinational firms conquer new markets when they convince legions of foreign consumers to desire what they make.

As if understanding the dynamics of one's culture weren't hard enough, these issues get even more complicated when we consider what drives consumers in other cultures. The consequences of ignoring cultural sensitivities can be costly. Think about problems a prominent multinational company such as McDonald's encounters as it expands globally:

- During the 1994 soccer World Cup, the fast-food giant reprinted the Saudi Arabian flag, which includes sacred words from the Koran, on disposable packaging it used in promotions. Muslims around the world protested this borrowing of sacred imagery, and the company had to scramble to correct its mistake.
- In 2002, McDonald's agreed to donate $10 million to Hindu and other groups as partial settlement of litigation involving its mislabeling of French fries and hash browns as vegetarian (it cooked them in oil tainted with meat residue).
- Also in 2002, the company abruptly cancelled its plans to introduce its new McAfrika sandwich in its Norwegian restaurants. The CEO of McDonald's in Norway acknowledged on national television that introducing this menu item at a time of growing famine in Africa was "coincidental and unfortunate."
- In India, the company doesn't sell any of its famous beef hamburgers. Instead, it offers customized entrees such as a Pizza McPuff, McAloo Tikki (a spiced-potato burger), Paneer Salsa McWrap, and even a Crispy Chinese burger, to capitalize on the great popularity of Chinese food in India. It makes its mayonnaise without eggs, and all stores maintain separate kitchen sections for vegetarian and non-vegetarian dishes. Workers from the nonvegetarian section must shower before they cross over to the other area.
- In 2005, McDonald's introduced the spicy Prosperity Burger in nine countries from South Korea to Indonesia in recognition of the Lunar New Year.
- The chain's Big Tasty burger is an 840 calorie behemoth that consists of a 5.5 ounce beef patty slathered in smoky barbecue sauce and topped with three slices of cheese. The menu entrée was first introduced in Sweden, and it's now available in other parts of Europe as well as in Latin America and Australia. McDonald's worldwide operations are now far bigger than its U.S. domestic business, and it's no longer the case that menu innovations originate here—regional operations are just as likely to create their own offerings.[106]

In this section, we'll consider some of the issues that confront marketers who want to understand the cultural dynamics of other countries. We'll also consider the consequences of the "Americanization" of global culture. As U.S. (and to some extent, Western European) marketers continue to export Western popular culture to a globe full of increasingly affluent consumers, many customers eagerly replace their traditional products with the likes of McDonald's, Levi's, and MTV. But, as we'll also see, there are plenty of obstacles to success for multinational firms—especially Yankee ones.

Rather than ignore the global characteristics of their brands, firms have to manage them strategically. That's critical because future growth for most companies will come from foreign markets. In 2002, developed countries in North America, Europe, and East Asia accounted for 15 percent of the world's population of 6.3 billion. By 2030, according to the World Bank, the planet's population will rise to 9 billion—and

90 percent of these people will live in developing countries. And, the Web no longer concentrates in the West: According to Jupiter Research, by 2012 there will be 292 million Chinese Internet users compared to 241 million in the United States.

Think Globally, Act Locally

As corporations compete in many markets around the world, the debate intensifies: Should an organization develop separate marketing plans for each culture, or should it craft a single plan to implement everywhere? Let's briefly consider each viewpoint.

Adopt a Standardized Strategy

As Procter & Gamble strategizes about the best way to speak to consumers around the world, the company finds large segments in many countries who share the same outlooks, style preferences, and aspirations. These include teenagers, working women who try to juggle careers and families, and baby boomers. As the head of P&G's Global Health and Feminine Care division explains, "We're seeing global tribes forming around the world that are more and more interconnected through technology. If you focus on the similarities instead of the differences [in these tribes], key business opportunities emerge." Brand managers for example find that teenage girls everywhere have the same concerns and questions about puberty so the company can speak to them on its beinggirl.com Web site and make the same content available in 40 countries.[107]

Proponents of a standardized marketing strategy argue that many cultures, especially those of industrialized countries, are now so homogenized that the same approach will work throughout the world. If it develops one approach for multiple markets, a company can benefit from economies of scale because it does not have to incur the substantial time and expense to develop a separate strategy for each culture.[108] This viewpoint represents an **etic perspective**, which focuses on commonalities across cultures. An etic approach to a culture is objective and analytical—it reflects impressions of a culture as outsiders view it.

Adopt a Localized Strategy

Unlike Disney World in Orlando, visitors to the Walt Disney Studios theme park at Disneyland Paris don't hear the voices of American movie stars narrating their guided tours. Instead, European actors such as Jeremy Irons, Isabella Rossellini, and Nastassja Kinski provide commentary in their native tongues.

Disney learned the hard way about the importance of being sensitive to local cultures after it opened its Euro Disney Park in 1992. The company got slammed because its new location didn't cater to local customs (such as serving wine with meals). Visitors to Euro Disney from many countries took offense, even at what seem to be small slights. For example, initially the park only sold a French sausage, which drew complaints from Germans, Italians, and others who believed their own local version to be superior. Euro Disney's CEO explains, "When we first launched there was the belief that it was enough to be Disney. Now we realize that our guests need to be welcomed on the basis of their own culture and travel habits."[109]

Disney applies the lessons it learned in cultural sensitivity to its newer Hong Kong Disneyland. Executives shifted the angle of the front gate by 12 degrees after they consulted a *feng shui* specialist, who said the change would ensure prosperity for the park (see Chapter 13). Disney also put a bend in the walkway from the train station to the gate to make sure the flow of positive energy, or *chi*, did not slip past the entrance and out to the China Sea. Cash registers are close to corners or along walls to increase prosperity. The company burned incense as it finished each building, and it picked a lucky day (September 12) for the opening. One of the park's main ballrooms measures 888 square meters because eight is a lucky number in Chinese culture.

And because the Chinese consider the number four bad luck, you won't find any fourth-floor buttons in hotel elevators. Disney also recognizes that Chinese family dynamics are different so it revamped its advertising: Print ads showed a grandmother, mother, and daughter who wear tiaras at the park. In China, bonding between parents and children is difficult because of the culture's hierarchical nature so an executive explains, "We want to say it's OK to let your hair down." Camping out with stopwatches, the company's designers discovered that Chinese people take an average of 10 minutes longer to eat than Americans. So they added 700 extra seats to dining areas.

Ironically, some locals feel Disney tries *too* hard to cater to local customs—activists raised a ruckus when the company announced it would serve the traditional Chinese dish of shark's fin soup at wedding banquets held in the park. The species is endangered, and one group distributed T-shirts that depicted Mickey Mouse and Donald Duck holding knives and leering over three bleeding sharks. Nonetheless, Disney forges ahead with localized products. One of its latest ventures is in India, where it's making animated films with the voices of Bollywood stars. It's also making a Hindi version of its TV hit *High School Musical*—set against a backdrop of cricket instead of basketball.

Disney's experience supports the view of marketers who endorse an **emic perspective**, which stresses variations across cultures. They feel that each culture is unique, with its own value system, conventions, and regulations. This perspective argues that each country has a *national character*, a distinctive set of behavior and personality characteristics.[110] A marketer must therefore tailor its strategy to the sensibilities of each specific culture. An emic approach to a culture is subjective and experiential—it attempts to explain a culture as insiders experience it.

Sometimes this strategy means a manufacturer has to modify what it makes or a retailer has to change the way it displays the product so that it's acceptable to local tastes. When Wal-Mart started to open stores abroad in the early 1990s, it offered a little piece of America to foreign consumers—and that was the problem. It promoted golf clubs in soccer-mad Brazil and pushed ice skates in Mexico. It trained its German clerks to smile at customers—who thought they were flirting. Now Wal-Mart tries to adapt to local preferences. Its Chinese stores sell live turtles and snakes and lure shoppers who come on foot or bicycle with free shuttle buses and home delivery for refrigerators and other large items.[111]

In some cases, consumers in one place simply do not like some products that are popular elsewhere, or their different lifestyles require companies to rethink their designs. IKEA finally realized that Americans use a lot of ice in their drinks and so they didn't buy the smaller European glasses the stores stocked. The Swedish furniture chain also figured out that compared to Europeans, Americans sleep in bigger beds, need bigger bookshelves, and like to curl up on sofas rather than sit on them.[112] Snapple failed in Japan because the drink's cloudy appearance and the floating pulp in the bottles were a turnoff. Similarly, Frito-Lay stopped selling Ruffles potato chips (too salty) and Cheetos (the Japanese didn't appreciate orange fingers after they ate a handful).[113] The company still makes Cheetos in China, but the local version doesn't contain any cheese, which is not a staple of the Chinese diet. Instead, local flavors come in varieties such as Savory American Cream and Japanese Steak.[114]

Cultural Differences Relevant to Marketers

So, which perspective is correct—the emic or the etic? As you might guess, the best bet probably is a combination of both. Some researchers argue that the relevant dimension to consider is **consumer style**—a pattern of behaviors, attitudes, and opinions that influences all of a person's consumption activities—including attitudes toward advertising, preferred channels of information and purchase, brand loyalty, and price consciousness. These researchers identified four major clusters of consumer styles when they looked at data from the United States, the United Kingdom, France, and Germany:[116]

1 Price-sensitive consumers
2 Variety seekers
3 Brand-loyal consumers
4 Information seekers

Given the sizable variations in tastes within the United States alone, it is hardly surprising that people around the world develop their own unique preferences. Panasonic touted the fact that its rice cooker kept the food from getting too crisp—until the company learned that consumers in the Middle East like to eat their rice this way. Unlike Americans, Europeans favor dark chocolate over milk chocolate, which they think of as a children's food. Sara Lee sells its pound cake with chocolate chips in the United States, raisins in Australia, and coconuts in Hong Kong. Crocodile handbags are popular in Asia and Europe but not in the United States.[117]

The language barrier is one obvious problem that marketers who wish to break into foreign markets must navigate. Travelers abroad commonly encounter signs in tortured English such as a note to guests at a Tokyo hotel that proclaims, "You are invited to take advantage of the chambermaid," a notice at a hotel in Acapulco that reassures people that "The manager has personally passed all the water served here," or a dry cleaner in Majorca who urges passing customers to "drop your pants here for best results." And local product names often raise eyebrows to visiting Americans who might stumble on a Japanese coffee creamer called Creap, a Mexican bread named Bimbo, or even a Scandinavian product to unfreeze car locks named Super Piss.

Chapter 13 noted some gaffes U.S. marketers made when they advertised to ethnic groups in their own country. Imagine how these mistakes multiply outside the United States! One technique marketers use to avoid this problem is *back-translation*, where a different interpreter retranslates a translated ad back into its original language to catch errors. Here are some errors that could have used a bit of back-translation:[118]

● The Scandinavian company that makes Electrolux vacuum cleaners sold them in the United States with this slogan: "Nothing sucks like an Electrolux."
● Colgate introduced Cue toothpaste in France—this also happens to be the name of a well-known porn magazine.
● When Parker marketed a ballpoint pen in Mexico, its ads were supposed to say, "It won't leak in your pocket and embarrass you." The translation actually said "It won't leak in your pocket and make you pregnant."
● Fresca (a soft drink) is Mexican slang for lesbian.
● Ford had several problems in Spanish markets. The company discovered that a truck model it called Fiera means "ugly old woman" in Spanish. Its Caliente model is slang for a streetwalker. In Brazil, Pinto is a slang term for "small male appendage."
● When Rolls-Royce introduced its Silver Mist model in Germany, it found that the word *mist* translates as excrement. Similarly, Sunbeam's hair-curling iron, called the Mist-Stick, translates as manure wand. To add insult to injury, Vicks is German slang for sexual intercourse, so the company had to change its name to Wicks in that country.
● Toyota encountered a similar problem in France, where its MR2 roadster sounds like "M-R-deux," which sounds a lot like *merde*—crap.
● Recently, Buick had to scramble to rename its new LaCrosse sedan the Allure in Canada after discovering that the name comes awfully close to a Québécois word for masturbation.
● IKEA had to explain that the Gutvik children's bunk bed is named "for a tiny town in Sweden" after German shoppers noted that the name sounded a lot like a

phrase that means "good f***." IKEA has yet to issue an explanation for its Fartfull workbench or its Jerker computer table.[119]

Does Global Marketing Work?

So, what's the verdict? Does global marketing work or not? Perhaps the more appropriate question is, "*When* does it work?" Although the argument for a homogenous world culture is appealing in principle, in practice it hasn't worked out too well. One reason is that consumers in different countries have varying conventions and customs, so they simply do not use products the same way. Kellogg, for example, discovered that in Brazil people don't typically eat a big breakfast—they're more likely to eat cereal as a dry snack.

In fact, significant cultural differences even show up within the same country— we certainly feel that we've traveled to a different place as we move around the United States. Advertisers in Canada know that when they target consumers in French-speaking Quebec their messages must be much different from those they address to those in English-speaking regions. Ads in Montreal tend to be a lot racier than those in Toronto, reflecting differences in attitudes toward sexuality between consumers with French versus British roots.[120]

Some large corporations such as Coca-Cola have successfully crafted a single, international image. Still, even the soft drink giant must make minor modifications to the way it presents itself in each culture. Although Coke commercials are largely standardized, the company permits local agencies to edit them so they highlight close-ups of local faces.[121] To maximize the chances of success for these multicultural efforts, marketers must locate consumers in different countries who nonetheless share a common *worldview* (see Chapter 11). This is more likely to be the case among people whose frame of reference is relatively more international or cosmopolitan, or who receive much of their information about the world from sources that incorporate a worldwide perspective.

Who is likely to fall into this category? Two consumer segments are particularly good candidates: (1) affluent people who are "global citizens" and who come into contact with ideas from around the world through their travels, business contacts, and media experiences; and (2) young people whose tastes in music and fashion are strongly influenced by MTV and other media that broadcast many of the same images to multiple countries. For example, viewers of MTV Europe in Rome or Zurich can check out the same "buzz clips" as their counterparts in London or Luxembourg.[122]

A large-scale study with consumers in 41 countries identified the characteristics people associate with global brands, and it also measured the relative importance of those dimensions when consumers buy products.[123] The researchers grouped consumers who evaluate global brands in the same way. They identified four major segments:

1 **Global citizens**—The largest segment (55 percent of consumers) uses the global success of a company as a signal of quality and innovation. At the same time, they are concerned whether companies behave responsibly on issues such as consumer health, the environment, and worker rights.

2 **Global dreamers**—The second-largest segment, at 23 percent, consists of consumers who see global brands as quality products and readily buy into the myths they author. They aren't nearly as concerned with social responsibility as are the global citizens.

3 **Antiglobals**—Thirteen percent of consumers are skeptical that transnational companies deliver higher-quality goods. They dislike brands that preach American values, and they don't trust global companies to behave responsibly. They try to avoid doing business with transnational firms.

4 **Global agnostics**—The remaining 9 percent of consumers don't base purchase decisions on a brand's global attributes. Instead, they evaluate a global product by the same criteria they use to judge local brands and don't regard its global nature as meriting special consideration.

Marketing Opportunity

The huge popularity of a humble local product that Brazilian peasants traditionally wear—*Havaianas*, or flip-flops—illustrates the diffusion of global consumer culture as consumers hunger for fresh ideas and styles from around the globe. Brazilians associate the lowly shoes, which sell for $2 a pair, so strongly with poor people that the expression *pe de chinelo*, or "slipper foot," is a popular slang term for the downtrodden. The main buyers in Brazil continue to be blue-collar workers, but now fashionable men and women in cities from Paris to Sydney wear the peasant shoes to trendy clubs and in some cases even to work.

How did these flip-flops make the leap to fashion statement? In an attempt to boost profit margins, a company named Alpargatas introduced new models in colors such as lime green and fuchsia that cost twice as much as the original black- or blue-strapped sandal with a cream-colored sole. Then, it launched newer styles, including a masculine surf model. Middle-class Brazilians started to adopt the shoes and even the country's president wore them in public. The fashion spread as a few celebrities, including supermodels Naomi Campbell, Kate Moss, and Brazil's own Gisele Bündchen, discovered the flip-flops. Company representatives helped fuel the fire as they gave out free sandals to stars at the Cannes Film Festival. The result: Alpargatas's international sales zoomed from virtually zero to more than 5 million sandals sold around the world.[127]

Marketing Pitfall

Critics in other countries deplore the creeping Americanization of their cultures because of what they view as excessive materialism. City officials in Oaxaca, Mexico, successfully fought to bar McDonald's from installing its arches in the town's central plaza.[132] One French critic summarized this resistance to the diffusion of American culture; he described the Euro Disney theme park as "a horror made of cardboard, plastic, and appalling colors—a construction of hardened chewing gum and idiotic folklore taken straight out of a comic book written for obese Americans."[133] A lot of the criticism focuses on the unhealthy American diet—and its appeal to others.

In the United States, two-thirds of adults and almost one-third of children are overweight. In other countries with traditionally healthy diets, the invasion of fast food and candy has taken its toll. In Greece, considered the birthplace of the Mediterranean diet that emphasizes olive oil, fresh produce, and fish, authorities struggle with an epidemic of obesity (three-quarters of the adult population is overweight or obese) and obesity rates for children skyrocket. Today even small towns overflow with pizza and fast-food outlets. Italy and Spain are not far behind, with more than 50 percent of adults overweight.[134]

The Diffusion of Consumer Culture

Coca-Cola is the drink of choice among young people in Asian countries, and McDonald's is their favorite restaurant.[124] The National Basketball Association sells $500 million of licensed merchandise every year *outside* of the United States.[125] Walk the streets of Lisbon or Buenos Aires, and the sight of Nike hats, Gap T-shirts, and Levi's jeans will accost you at every turn. The allure of American consumer culture spreads throughout the world.

However, it's not simply about exporting American culture. In a global society, people are quick to borrow from *any* culture they admire. For example, the cultural scene in Japan influences many Koreans because they believe the Japanese are sophisticated consumers. Japanese rock bands are more popular in Korea than Korean bands, and shoppers eagerly snap up other exports such as comic books, fashion magazines, and game shows. A Korean researcher explains, "Culture is like water. It flows from stronger nations to weaker ones. People tend to idolize countries that are wealthier, freer, and more advanced, and in Asia that country is Japan."[126]

A survey in Beijing found that nearly half of all children under 12 think McDonald's is a domestic Chinese brand![128] The West (and especially the United States) is a net exporter of popular culture. Many consumers equate Western lifestyles in general and the English language in particular with modernization and sophistication, and numerous American brands slowly but surely insinuate themselves into local cultures. Indeed, some global brands are so widespread that many are only vaguely aware of their countries of origin. In surveys, consumers routinely guess that Heineken is German (it's really Dutch) and that Nokia is Japanese (it's Finnish).[129]

American television inspires knockoffs around the world. But to be fair, many U.S. viewers don't realize that American reality show hits such as *Big Brother* and *American Idol* started out as European concepts that U.S. producers imported. In fact the U.K. version of *Big Brother* briefly went off the air after a fight broke out and housemates threatened to kill each other. The German version attracted accusations of "shameless voyeurism" after a female contestant had her nipple pierced on live TV—without anesthetic.[130]

Still, American TV formats attract many imitators. Some local shows "borrow" from American programs; the German hit *Das Traumschiff* (the "Dream Ship") is a remake of the old American hit *Love Boat*. Versions of *The Apprentice* appear all over the globe—though elsewhere Donald Trump is replaced by local figures such as a German soccer-team manager, a billionaire Arab entrepreneur, and a Brazilian ad agency CEO. Each local version reflects the country's culture—contestants sell flowers in London, hot dogs in Frankfurt, and rolled fish in Finland.[131] Not everyone is treated quite as harshly as the American losers either—in Finland contestants are gently told, "You're free to leave."

OBJECTIVE 8

How does Western (and particularly American) culture have a huge impact around the world, though people in other countries don't necessarily ascribe the same meanings to products as we do?

Emerging Consumer Cultures in Transitional Economies

In the early 1980s the Romanian Communist government broadcast the American TV show *Dallas* to point out the decadence of Western capitalism. This strategy backfired: The devious (but rich!) J. R. Ewing became a revered icon in parts of Eastern Europe and the Middle East. A popular tourist attraction outside of Bucharest includes a big white log gate that announces (in English) the name, "South Fork Ranch."[135] Western "decadence" appears to be infectious.[136]

More than 60 countries have a gross national product of less than $10 billion, and there are at least 135 transnational companies with revenues greater than that. The dominance of these marketing powerhouses creates a **globalized consumption ethic**. Tempting images of luxury cars, glam rock stars on MTV, and modern appliances that make life easier surround us wherever we turn. People the world over begin to share the ideal of a material lifestyle and value well-known brands that symbolize prosperity. Shopping evolves from a wearying, task-oriented struggle to locate even basic necessities to a leisure activity. Possessing these coveted items becomes a mechanism to display one's status (see Chapter 12)—often at great personal sacrifice.

After the downfall of communism, Eastern Europeans emerged from a long winter of deprivation into a springtime of abundance. The picture is not all rosy, however. It's not easy for many people who live in **transitional economies** to attain consumer goods. This term describes countries such as China, Portugal, and Romania that struggle as they adapt from a controlled, centralized economy to a free-market system. In these situations rapid changes occur on social, political, and economic dimensions as the populace suddenly is exposed to global communications and external market pressures.[137]

Some of the consequences of the transition to capitalism include a loss of confidence and pride in the local culture, as well as alienation, frustration, and increased stress as citizens sacrifice their leisure time to work ever harder to buy consumer goods. The yearning for the trappings of Western material culture is perhaps most evident in parts of Eastern Europe, where citizens who threw off the shackles of communism now have direct access to coveted consumer goods from the United States and Western Europe—if they can afford them. One analyst observed, "As former subjects of the Soviet empire dream it, the American dream has very little to do with liberty and justice for all and a great deal to do with soap operas and the Sears Catalogue."[138] A study that looked at how Chinese consumers think about Western brands showed that their interpretations depended on how they think about the

As this Brazilian ad reminds us, globalization is an integral part of the marketing strategy of most major corporations.
Source: Courtesy of Electrolux.

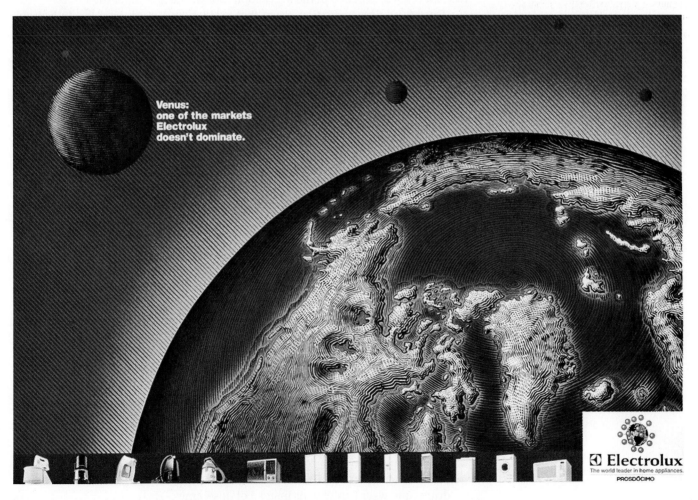

Venus:
one of the markets
Electrolux
doesn't dominate.

Electrolux
The world leader in home appliances.
PROSDÓCIMO

history of relations between China and the West. The researchers in fact identified four different narratives in their sample: West as liberator, as oppressor, as subjugated, and as partner. Depending on the narraitve they endorse, people view Western brands as instruments of democratization, domination, a way to erase past Chinese humiliations, or as instruments of economic progress.[139] A somewhat similar approach identifies various ways that people regard technology in their lives:[140]

- *The Techtopian* sees technology as social progress.
- *The Work Machine* regards it as an economic engine to drive growth and development.
- *The Green Luddite*, blames technology for the destruction of craftsmanship and traditional ways of life.
- *The Techpresssive* regards technology as a way to attain pleasure.

As the global consumption ethic spreads, rituals and product preferences in different cultures become homogenized. For example, some urbanites in Muslim Turkey now celebrate Christmas though gift-giving is not customary in many parts of the country—even on birthdays. In China, Christmas fever grips China's newly rising urban middle class as an excuse to shop, eat, and party. People there snap up Christmas trees, ornaments, and Christian religious objects (even though the street vendors who peddle photos of Jesus and Mary can't always identify who they are). Chinese consumers embrace Christmas because to them the holiday is international and modern, not because it's a traditional Christian celebration. The government encourages this practice because it stimulates consumer spending. To make the holiday even merrier, China exports about $1 billion worth of Christmas products every year, and its factories churn out $7.5 billion of the toys people worldwide put under their trees.[141]

Does this homogenization mean that in time consumers who live in Nairobi, New Guinea, or the Netherlands will all be indistinguishable from those in New York or Nashville? Probably not, because the meanings of consumer goods mutate to blend with local customs and values. For example, in Turkey some urban women use their ovens to dry clothes and their dishwashers to wash muddy spinach. Or a person in Papua New Guinea may combine a traditional clothing style such as a *bilum* with Western items such as Mickey Mouse shirts or baseball caps.[142] These processes make it unlikely that global homogenization will overwhelm local cultures, but it is likely that there will be multiple consumer cultures, each of which blends global icons such as Nike's pervasive "swoosh" with indigenous products and meanings. In Vietnam for example local fast-food chains dominate the market as they duplicate a McDonald's approach—but add a local flavor. The country's hugely successful Kinh Do red and yellow outlets sell specialties like dried squid buns. In the Philippines, the Jollibee Foods Corp. burger chain also copies the McDonald's look—and it outsells McDonald's there.[143]

Creolization occurs when foreign influences integrate with local meanings. Chapter 15 pointed out that modern Christianity adapted the pagan Christmas tree into its own rituals. In India handicapped beggars sell bottles of Coke from tricycles, and Indipop, a popular music hybrid, mixes traditional styles with rock, rap, and reggae.[144] As we saw in Chapter 13, young Hispanic Americans bounce between hip-hop and *Rock en Español*, blend Mexican rice with spaghetti sauce, and spread peanut butter and jelly on tortillas.[145] In Argentina, Coca-Cola launched Nativa, a soft drink flavored with the country's traditional *yerba mate* herbal tea, as part of a strategy to broaden its portfolio with products it makes from indigenous ingredients.[146]

The creolization process sometimes results in bizarre permutations of products and services when locals modify them to be compatible with their customs. Consider these creolized adaptations, for example:[147]

- In Peru, Indian boys carry rocks they paint to look like transistor radios.
- In highland Papua New Guinea, tribespeople put Chivas Regal wrappers on their drums and wear Pentel pens instead of nosebones.

- Bana tribespeople in the remote highlands of Kako, Ethiopia, pay to watch *Pluto the Circus Dog* on a View-Master.
- When an African Swazi princess marries a Zulu king, she wears a traditional costume of red touraco wing feathers around her forehead and a cape of window-bird feathers and oxtails. But guests record the ceremony on a Kodak movie camera while the band plays "The Sound of Music."
- The Japanese use Western words as a shorthand for anything new and exciting, even if they do not understand what they mean. They give cars names such as Fairlady, Gloria, and Bongo Wagon. Consumers buy *deodoranto* (deodorant) and *appuru pai* (apple pie). Ads urge shoppers to *stoppu rukku* (stop and look), and products claim to be *yuniku* (unique).[148] Coca-Cola cans say, "I feel Coke & sound special," and a company called Cream Soda sells products with the slogan, "Too old to die, too young to happy."[149] Other Japanese products with English names include Mouth Pet (breath freshener), Pocari Sweat ("refreshment water"), Armpit (electric razor), Brown Gross Foam (hair-coloring mousse), Virgin Pink Special (skin cream), Cow Brand (beauty soap), and Mymorning Water (canned water).[150]

CHAPTER SUMMARY

Now that you have finished reading this chapter you should understand why:

 1 Styles are like mirrors that reflect underlying cultural conditions.

The styles prevalent in a culture at any point in time reflect underlying political and social conditions. We term the set of agents responsible for creating stylistic alternatives a culture production system (CPS). Factors such as the types of people involved in this system and the amount of competition by alternative product forms influence the choices that eventually make their way to the marketplace for consideration by end consumers.

 2 We distinguish between high and low culture.

Social scientists distinguish between high (or elite) forms and low (or popular) forms of culture. Products of popular culture tend to follow a cultural formula and contain predictable components. However, these distinctions blur in modern society as marketers increasingly incorporate imagery from "high art" to sell everyday products.

 3 Many modern marketers are reality engineers.

Reality engineering occurs when marketers appropriate elements of popular culture to use in their promotional strategies. These elements include sensory and spatial aspects of everyday existence, whether in the form of products that appear in movies, scents pumped into offices and stores, billboards, theme parks, or video monitors they attach to shopping carts.

 4 New products, services, and ideas spread through a population. Different types of people are more or less likely to adopt them.

Diffusion of innovations refers to the process whereby a new product, service, or idea spreads through a population. Innovators and early adopters are quick to adopt new products, and laggards are very slow. A consumer's decision to adopt a new product depends on his or her personal characteristics as well as on characteristics of the innovation itself. We are more likely to adopt a new product if it demands relatively little behavioral change, is easy to understand, and provides a relative advantage compared to existing products.

 5 Many people and organizations play a role in the fashion system that creates and communicates symbolic meanings to consumers.

The fashion system includes everyone involved in creating and transferring symbolic meanings. Many different products express common cultural categories (e.g., gender distinctions). Many people tend to adopt a new style simultaneously in a process of collective selection. According to meme theory, ideas spread through a population in a geometric progression much as a virus infects many people until it reaches epidemic proportions. Other perspectives on motivations for adopting new styles include psychological, economic, and sociological models of fashion.

6   **Fashions follow cycles.**

Fashions follow cycles that resemble the product life cycle. We distinguish the two extremes of fashion adoption, classics and fads, in terms of the length of this cycle.

7   **Products that succeed in one culture may fail in another if marketers fail to understand the differences among consumers in each place.**

Because a consumer's culture exerts such a big influence on his or her lifestyle choices, marketers must learn as much as possible about differences in cultural norms and preferences when they do business in more than one country. One important issue is the extent to which we need to tailor our marketing strategies to each culture. Followers of an etic perspective believe people in many cultures appreciate the same universal messages. Believers in an emic perspective argue that individual cultures are too unique to permit such standardization; marketers must instead adapt their approaches to local values and practices. Attempts at global marketing have met with mixed success; in many cases this approach is more likely to work if the messages appeal to basic values or if the target markets consist of consumers who are internationally rather than locally oriented.

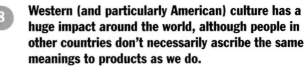 **8**   **Western (and particularly American) culture has a huge impact around the world, although people in other countries don't necessarily ascribe the same meanings to products as we do.**

The United States is a net exporter of popular culture. Consumers around the world eagerly adopt American products, especially entertainment vehicles and items they link to an American lifestyle (e.g., Marlboro cigarettes, Levi's jeans). Despite the continuing "Americanization" of world culture, some people resist globalization because they fear it will dilute their own local cultures. In other cases, they practice creolization as they integrate these products with existing cultural practices.

KEY TERMS

Acceptance cycles, 622
Advergaming, 612
Art product, 606
Branded entertainment, 610
Classic, 622
Collective selection, 618
Consumer style, 629
Continuous innovation, 615
Cooptation, 602
Craft product, 606
Creolization, 634
Cultural categories, 617
Cultural formula, 608
Cultural gatekeepers, 604

Cultural selection, 603
Culture production system (CPS), 604
Diffusion of innovations, 616
Discontinuous innovation, 616
Dynamically continuous innovation, 616
Early adopters, 614
Emic perspective, 629
Etic perspective, 628
Fad, 623
Fashion, 617
Fashion acceptance cycle, 622
Fashion system, 617
Gadget lovers, 615

Globalized consumption ethic, 632
Innovation, 616
Innovators, 614
Laggards, 614
Late adopters, 614
Lead users, 605
Meme theory, 621
Plinking™, 612
Product placement, 610
Reality engineering, 608
Tipping point, 621
Transitional economies, 633
Trickle-down theory, 619
Voice of the consumer, 605

REVIEW

1 What is collective selection? Give an example.
2 Describe a culture production system (CPS) and list its three components. What is an example of a CPS with these three components?
3 Define a cultural gatekeeper, and give three examples.
4 Describe the difference between arts and crafts.
5 What is a cultural formula? Give an example.
6 What is "new vintage?" How is this an example of reality engineering?

7 Define product placement and list three examples of it. How is this practice the same or different from branded entertainment?
8 What is advergaming? Give an example.
9 What is the diffusion of innovations?
10 Who are innovators? Early adopters? Laggards?
11 Describe the differences among continuous innovations, dynamically continuous innovations, and discontinuous

innovations, and provide an example of each. Which type are consumers least likely to adopt as an innovation?

12 What are the differences among *fashion, a fashion*, and *in fashion*?

13 What are cultural categories and how do they influence product designs?

14 Summarize some of the major approaches we can use to understand fashion from the perspectives of psychologists, economists, and sociologists.

15 What is an example of a meme?

16 What is the trickle-down effect? List some reasons why it is no longer as valid as it used to be.

17 What is the difference between a fad, a fashion, and a classic fashion life cycle?

18 What is the difference between an emic and an etic perspective on globalization?

19 Why is the United States a net exporter of popular culture?

20 What country provides an example of a transitional economy?

21 Define creolization and provide an example.

CONSUMER BEHAVIOR CHALLENGE

■ DISCUSS

1 Watchdog groups have long decried product placements because they blur the line between content and advertising without adequately informing viewers. And the networks themselves appear to be divided on how far they want to open the gate. According to one study, the effectiveness of product placements varies by product category and type of placement. Consumers indicate product placements have the most influence on their grocery, electronics, and apparel purchases. The most common platform for a placement is to get a brand shown on a T-shirt or other piece of an actor's wardrobe.[151] What do you think about this practice—under what conditions is product placement likely to influence you and your friends? When (if ever) is it counterproductive?

2 The chapter described a few instances where consumers sold their kids' "naming rights" to corporations—mostly for charitable purposes. Would you do this—why or why not?

3 Is advertising an art or a craft? Which should it be?

4 Movie companies often conduct market research when they produce big-budget films. If necessary they will reshoot part of a movie when viewers say they don't like it. Some people oppose this practice—they claim that movies, or books, songs, plays, or other artistic endeavors should not conform to what the market wants, lest they sacrifice their integrity. What do you think?

5 The chapter describes the traditional acceptance cycle for hit songs. How has the availability of music online altered this cycle? What are the ramifications of these changes for the music acceptance cycle?

6 Because of higher competition and market saturation, marketers in industrialized countries try to develop Third World markets. Asian consumers alone spend $90 billion a year on cigarettes, and U.S. tobacco manufacturers push relentlessly into these markets. We find cigarette advertising, that often depicts glamorous Western models and settings, just about everywhere— on billboards, buses, storefronts, and clothing—and tobacco companies sponsor many major sports and cultural events. Some companies even hand out cigarettes and gifts in amusement areas, often to preteens. Should governments allow these practices, even if the products may be harmful to their citizens or divert money poor people should spend on essentials? If you were a trade or health official in a Third World country, what guidelines, if any, might you suggest to regulate the import of luxury goods from advanced economies?

7 Comment on the growing practice of reality engineering. Do marketers "own" our culture? Should they?

8 Critics of the cultural consequences of standardization often point to Starbucks as an example of a company that succeeds because it obliterates local customs and drives small competitors out of business.[152] Where do you stand on patronizing mom-and-pop stores versus national chains?

9 If you worked in marketing research for a cosmetics firm, how might you apply the lead user concept to help you identify new product opportunities?

10 Boots with 6-inch heels were a fashion rage among young Japanese women a few years ago. Several teens died after they tripped over their shoes and fractured their skulls. However, followers of the style claim they are willing to risk twisted ankles, broken bones, bruised faces, and other dangers the platform shoes cause. One teenager said, "I've fallen and twisted my ankle many times, but they are so cute that I won't give them up until they go out of fashion."[153] Many consumers around the world seem willing to suffer for the sake of fashion. Others argue that we are merely pawns in the hands of designers, who conspire to force unwieldy fashions down our throats. What do you think? What is and what should be the role of fashion in our society? How important is it for people to be in style? What are the pros and cons of keeping up with the latest fashions? Do you believe that we are at the mercy of designers?

■ APPLY

1 The chapter mentions the Hush Puppy shoe fad. Clearly, it's a matter of time before consumers tire of these shoes and move on. What can the company do to prolong the life of this brand?

2 If you were a consultant to a toy company, what would you forecast as the next big trend in this market? Survey toy stores and watch what kids play with to help you with your prediction.

3 How might the rise of peer-to-peer music sharing influence the structure of the music CPS? One guess is that this method erodes the dominance of the big labels because listeners are more likely to access music from lesser-known groups. Survey your friends to determine whether this in fact is happening—do they listen to a wider variety of artists or simply download more from the big-time groups?

4 Read several romance or action novels to see if you can identify a cultural formula at work. Do you see parallels among the roles different characters play (e.g., the hero, the evildoer, the temptress, etc.)?

5 Watch 12 hours of TV and keep a log of all product placements you see. What are the dominant products shows insert?

Case Study

SLUMDOG: FAD OR FASHION?

"And the Oscar goes to . . . *Slumdog Millionaire.*" This line was delivered eight times in Hollywood at the 81st Annual Academy Awards. Not bad for a film produced on a mere shoestring by Hollywood standards (budget of $15 million). It is the story of a young man from the slums of Mumbai who overcomes all odds to beat a television quiz show—the Indian equivalent of the show *Who Wants to Be a Millionaire?* and wins an award of 20,000,000 rupees.

The movie was a hit with worldwide critics, but the audience reaction in India was mixed. Many Indians claim that this movie cannot be considered a credit to India because its director is British, and the lead actor, Dev Patel is also from England. However, Indians are proud of A. R. Rahman, a well-known Indian musician, for his Oscar-winning film score.

It's hard to deny that the film turned the world's attention to India. Some were excited by the global interest, but others were not pleased. They felt that the film did not depict the "real" India. Many from Dharavi, the Mumbai slum featured in the film, protested that the name "Slumdog" was derogatory. In an interview, director Danny Boyle responded, ". . . basically it's a hybrid of the word 'underdog'—and everything that means in terms of rooting for the underdog and validating his triumph—and the fact that he obviously comes from the slums."

Whatever one's attitudes toward the filmmakers' rights to portray poverty and injustice in India, it's clear that the film increased awareness of what UNICEF estimates as 11 million children who currently live on the streets of India. *Slumdog* has, in fact, been credited with inspiring a boost in donations to organizations that fight homelessness in India including Railway Children, SOS, Children's Villages of India, and Save the Children. Railway Children reports Web site visits at 10 times what they were before the film, and many groups report an increase in donations.

DISCUSSION QUESTIONS

1 Can you give specific examples of how *Slumdog Millionaire* is part of the culture production system? Specifically, what are the three major subsystems, and who are the cultural gatekeepers in this context?

2 What does it mean that critics of the film are concerned about India's underlying "cultural category"?

3 How do you predict the film's success will influence the popularity of Bollywood productions—will it spark a fad or a fashion?

Sources: Nithin Belle, "New-Found Celebrity Status of the Three Slumdog Children May Get Upset," *McClatchy-Tribune Business News* (February 24, 2009); Gigil Varghese, "Better Times Await Child Stars," *McClatchy-Tribune Business News* (March 3, 2009); Fareed Zakaria, "A Slumdog in Heat," *Newsweek* (February 9, 2009); Niraj Sheth and Eric Bellman, "Slumdog Success Gets Mixed Reviews in India," *Wall Street Journal* (February 24, 2009); "Success of Slumdog Millionaire Is Aiding Charities," *PR Newswire* (March 3, 2009).

NOTES

1. www.abcnews.go.com/GMA/AmericanFamily/Story?id=3397793&page=2, accessed August 15, 2007.
2. www.allhiphop.com, accessed June 25, 2009; www.undergroundhiphop.com, accessed June 25, 2009.
3. www.hiphopcapital.com, accessed June 25, 2009.
4. Marc Spiegler, "Marketing Street Culture: Bringing Hip-Hop Style to the Mainstream," *American Demographics* (November 1996): 29–34.
5. Nina Darnton, "Where the Homegirls Are," *Newsweek* (June 17, 1991): 60; "The Idea Chain," *Newsweek* (October 5, 1992): 32.
6. Cyndee Miller, "X Marks the Lucrative Spot, but Some Advertisers Can't Hit Target," *Marketing News* (August 2, 1993): 1.
7. Ad appeared in *Elle* (September 1994).
8. Spiegler, "Marketing Street Culture: Bringing Hip-Hop Style to the Mainstream"; Joshua Levine, "Badass Sells," *Forbes* (April 21, 1997): 142.

9. Jeff Jensen, "Hip, Wholesome Image Makes a Marketing Star of Rap's LL Cool J," *Advertising Age* (August 25, 1997): 1.

10. Alice Z. Cuneo, "GAP's 1st Global Ads Confront Dockers on a Khaki Battlefield," *Advertising Age* (April 20, 1998): 3–5.

11. Jancee Dunn, "How Hip-Hop Style Bum-Rushed the Mall," *Rolling Stone* (March 18, 1999): 54–59.

12. Teri Agins, "The Rare Art of 'Gilt by Association': How Armani Got Stars to Be Billboards," *Wall Street Journal* (September 14, 1999), www.wsj.com, accessed September 14, 1999.

13. Eryn Brown, "From Rap to Retail: Wiring the Hip-Hop Nation," *Fortune* (April 17, 2000): 530

14. Martin Fackler, "Hip Hop Invading China," *Birmingham News* (February 15, 2002): D1.

15. Maureen Tkacik, "'Z' Zips into the Zeitgeist, Subbing for 'S' in Hot Slang," *Wall Street Journal* (January 4, 2003); Maureen Tkacik, "Slang from the 'Hood Now Sells Toyz in Target," *Wall Street Journal* (December 30, 2002), www.wsj.com, accessed December 30, 2002.

16. www.hiphop-elements.com/article/read/4/6319/1, accessed July 9, 2005; www.bevnet.com/reviews/pimpjuice, accessed July 9, 2005; www.sohh.com/thewire/read.php?contentID=6893, accessed July 9, 2005; www.undercover.com.au/news/2005/mar05/20050324_usher.html, accessed July 9, 2005.

17. Arthur, Damien, "Authenticity and Consumption in the Australian Hip Hop Culture," *Qualitative Market Research* 9 no. 2 (2005): 140.

18. "European Hip Hop," *Wikipedia*, http://en.wikipedia.org/wiki/European_hip_hop, accessed July 30, 2007.

19. David Carr, "Vibe Magazine, Showcase for Hip-Hop and R&B, Dies at 16," *New York Times* (July 2, 2009), www.nytimes.com/2009/07/02/arts/music/02vibe.html?_r=1, accessed July 2, 2009.

20. Elizabeth M. Blair, "Commercialization of the Rap Music Youth Subculture," *Journal of Popular Culture* 27 (Winter 1993): 21–34; Basil G. Englis, Michael R. Solomon, and Anna Olofsson, "Consumption Imagery in Music Television: A Bi-Cultural Perspective," *Journal of Advertising* 22 (December 1993): 21–34.

21. Spiegler, "Marketing Street Culture: Bringing Hip-Hop Style to the Mainstream."

22. Craig Thompson and Gokcen Coskuner-Balli, "Countervailing Market Responses to Corporate Co-optation and the Ideological Recruitment of Consumption Communities," *Journal of Consumer Research*, 34 (August 2007): 135–52.

23. Grant McCracken, "Culture and Consumption: A Theoretical Account of the Structure and Movement of the Cultural Meaning of Consumer Goods," *Journal of Consumer Research* 13 (June 1986): 71–84.

24. Richard A. Peterson, "The Production of Culture: A Prolegomenon," in Richard A. Peterson, ed., *The Production of Culture, Sage Contemporary Social Science Issues* 33 (Beverly Hills, CA: Sage, 1976); Elizabeth C. Hirschman, "Resource Exchange in the Production and Distribution of a Motion Picture," *Empirical Studies of the Arts* 8, no. 1 (1990): 31–51; Michael R. Solomon, "Building Up and Breaking Down: The Impact of Cultural Sorting on Symbolic Consumption," in J. Sheth and E. C. Hirschman, eds., *Research in Consumer Behavior* (Greenwich, CT: JAI Press, 1988), 325–51. For a study that looked at ways consumers interact with marketers to create cultural meanings, cf. Lisa Peñaloza, "Consuming the American West: Animating Cultural Meaning and Memory at a Stock Show and Rodeo," *Journal of Consumer Research* 28 (December 2001): 369–98. Cf. also Markus Giesler, "Conflict and Compromise: Drama in Marketplace Evolution," *Journal of Consumer Research* 34 (April 2007): 739–53. For a study that looked at ways consumers interact with marketers to create cultural meanings, cf. Peñaloza, "Consuming the American West: Animating Cultural Meaning and Memory at a Stock Show and Rodeo."

25. Richard A. Peterson and D. G. Berger, "Entrepreneurship in Organizations: Evidence from the Popular Music Industry," *Administrative Science Quarterly* 16 (1971): 97–107.

26. Paul M. Hirsch, "Processing Fads and Fashions: An Organizational Set Analysis of Cultural Industry Systems," *American Journal of Sociology* 77, no. 4 (1972): 639–59; Russell Lynes, *The Tastemakers* (New York: Harper and Brothers, 1954); Michael R. Solomon, "The Missing Link: Surrogate Consumers in the Marketing Chain," *Journal of Marketing* 50 (October 1986): 208–19.

27. Michael R. Solomon, *Conquering Consumerspace: Marketing Strategies for a Branded World*, (New York: AMACOM, 2003).

28. C. K. Prahalad and Venkatram Ramaswamy, "Co-Opting Customer Competence," *Harvard Business Review* (January–February 2000): 79–87; Eric von Hipple, "Users as Innovators," *Technology Review* 80 (January 1978): 3–11; Jakki Mohr, *Marketing of High-Technology Products and Services* (Upper Saddle River, NJ: Prentice Hall, 2001).

29. Byrnes, Nanette, "Xerox's New Design Team: Customers," *BusinessWeek* (May 7, 2007): 72.

30. Howard S. Becker, "Arts and Crafts," *American Journal of Sociology* 83 (January 1987): 862–89.

31. Herbert J. Gans, "Popular Culture in America: Social Problem in a Mass Society or Social Asset in a Pluralist Society?" in Howard S. Becker, ed., *Social Problems: A Modern Approach* (New York: Wiley, 1966).

32. www.thomaskinkade.com/magi/servlet/com.asucon.ebiz.home.web.tk.HomeServlet, accessed June 25, 2009; Karen Breslau, "Paint by Numbers," *Newsweek* (May 13, 2002): 48.

33. Martin Forstenzer, "In Search of Fine Art Amid the Paper Towels," *New York Times on the Web* (February 22, 2004).

34. Annetta Miller, "Shopping Bags Imitate Art: Seen the Sacks? Now Visit the Museum Exhibit," *Newsweek* (January 23, 1989): 44.

35. Kim Foltz, "New Species for Study: Consumers in Action," *New York Times* (December 18, 1989): A1.

36. Arthur A. Berger, *Signs in Contemporary Culture: An Introduction to Semiotics* (New York: Longman, 1984).

37. Michiko Kakutani, "Art Is Easier the 2d Time Around," *New York Times* (October 30, 1994): E4.

38. www.geico.com/about/commercials/music/cavemen, accessed June 25, 2009.

39. Brooks Barnes and Suzanne Vranica, "Why Advertising's Cavemen Are Going Totally Hollyrock," *Wall Street Journal* (March 5, 2007): B1; Nina M. Lentini, "Doh! Looks Like 7-Eleven Stores May Get Homered," *Marketing Daily* (March 30, 2007), www.mediapost.com, accessed March 30, 2007.

40. Michael R. Solomon and Basil G. Englis, "Reality Engineering: Blurring the Boundaries Between Marketing and Popular Culture," *Journal of Current Issues and Research in Advertising* 16, no. 2 (Fall 1994): 1–17.

41. Austin Bunn, "Not Fade Away," *New York Times* (December 2, 2002), www.nytimes.com, accessed December 2, 2002.

42. Tim Arango and Brian Stelter, "Messages with a Mission, Embedded in TV Shows," *New York Times* (April 1, 2009), www.nytimes.com/2009/04/02/arts/television/02gates.html, accessed April 1, 2009.

43. Marc Santora, "Circle the Block, Cabby, My Show's On," *New York Times* (January 16, 2003), www.nytimes.com, accessed January 16, 2003; Wayne Parry, "Police May Sell Ad Space," *Montgomery Advertiser* (November 20, 2002): A4.

44. This process is described more fully in Michael R. Solomon, *Conquering Consumerspace: Marketing Strategies for a Branded World* (New York: AMACOM, 2003); cf. also T. Bettina Cornwell and Bruce Keillor, "Contemporary Literature and the Embedded Consumer Culture: The Case of Updike's Rabbit," in Roger J. Kruez and Mary Sue MacNealy, eds., *Empirical Approaches to Literature and Aesthetics: Advances in Discourse Processes* 52 (Norwood, NJ: Ablex, 1996), 559–72; Monroe Friedman, "The Changing Language of a Consumer Society: Brand Name Usage in Popular American Novels in the Postwar Era," *Journal of Consumer Research* 11 (March 1985): 927–37; Monroe Friedman, "Commercial Influences in the Lyrics of Popular American Music of the Postwar Era," *Journal of Consumer Affairs* 20 (Winter 1986): 193.

45. Stephanie Clifford, "Bravo Shows Move Further into Licensing Products," *New York Times* (April 12, 2009), www.nytimes.com/2009/04/13/business/media/13bravo.html?scp=1&sq=Stephanie%20Clifford,%20%93Bravo%20Shows%20Move%20Further%20into%20Licensing%20Products&st=cse, accessed April 13, 2009.

46. www.alibinetwork.com/index.jsp, accessed June 25, 2009; www.reputationdefender.com, accessed June 25, 2009.

47. James Bandler, "Only in the *Star!* Demi Moore's Brown Dress Turns White!" *Wall Street Journal* (April 14, 2004): B1.

48. Jeff Zaslow, "Meet John 'Your Ad Here' Smith," *Wall Street Journal* (March 16, 2006): D3.

49. Stuart Elliott, "In 'Trust Me,' a Fake Agency Really Promotes," *New York Times* (January 21, 2009), www.nytimes.com, accessed January 21, 2009.

50. Fara Warner, "Why It's Getting Harder to Tell the Shows from the Ads," *Wall Street Journal* (June 15, 1995): B1.

51. Quoted in Simona Covel, "Bag Borrow or Steal Lands the Role of a Lifetime, Online Retailer Hopes to Profit from Mention in 'Sex and the City,'" *Wall Street Journal* (May 28, 2008), http://online.wsj.com/article/SB121184149016921095.html?mod=rss_media_and_marketing, accessed May 28, 2008; www.bagborroworsteal.com, accessed June 25, 2009.

52. "Top 10 Product Placements in First Half of '07," *Marketing Daily* (September 26, 2007), www.mediapost.com, accessed September 26, 2007.

53. Nat Ives, "'Advertainment' Gains Momentum," *New York Times* (April 21, 2004), www.nytimes.com, accessed April 21, 2004.

54. Brian Steinberg, "Getting Izze to Izzie on 'Grey's Anatomy': How PepsiCo Placed Beverage Brand in ABC Show Without Paying a Thing," *Advertising Age* (April 1, 2009), www.adage.com, accessed April 1, 2009.

55. Claire Atkinson, "Ad Intrusion Up, Say Consumers," *Advertising Age* (January 6, 2003): 1.

56. Motoko Rich, "Product Placement Deals Make Leap from Film to Books," *New York Times* (June 12, 2006), www.nytimes.com, accessed June 12, 2006.

57. Quoted in Amy Schatz And Suzanne Vranica, "Product Placements Get FCC Scrutiny, Concern Focuses on Rise in Use by Advertisers, Disclosure to Viewers," *Wall Street Journal* (June 23, 2008): B3.

58. Stuart Elliott, "Greatest Hits of Product Placement," *New York Times* (February 28, 2005), www.nytimes.com, accessed February 28, 2005.

59. Benjamin M. Cole, "Products That Want to Be in Pictures," *Los Angeles Herald Examiner* (March 5, 1985): 36; see also Stacy M. Vollmers and Richard W. Mizerski, "A Review and Investigation into the Effectiveness of Product Placements in Films," in Karen Whitehill King, ed., *Proceedings of the 1994 Conference of the American Academy of Advertising*, 97–102; Solomon and Englis, "Reality Engineering: Blurring the Boundaries Between Marketing and Popular Culture."

60. Cristel Antonia Russell, "Investigating the Effectiveness of Product Placements in Television Shows: The Role of Modality and Plot Connection Congruence on Brand Memory and Attitude," *Journal of Consumer Research* 29 (December 2002): 306–18; Denise E. DeLorme and Leonard N. Reid, "Moviegoers' Experiences and Interpretations of Brands in Films Revisited," *Journal of Advertising* 28, no. 2 (1999): 71–90; Barbara B. Stern, and Cristel A. Russell "Consumer Responses to Product Placement in Television Sitcoms: Genre, Sex and Consumption," *Consumption, Markets and Culture* 7 (December 2004): 371–94.

61. Jack Neff, "Clearasil Marches into Middle-School Classes, *Advertising Age* (November 2006): 8; Bill Pennington, "Reading, Writing and Corporate Sponsorships," *New York Times on the Web* (October 18, 2004); Caroline E. Mayer, "Nurturing Brand Loyalty: With Preschool Supplies, Firms Woo Future Customers and Current Parents," *Washington Post* (October 12, 2003): F1.

62. Louise Story, "More Marketers Are Grabbing the Attention of Players During Online Games," *New York Times* (January 24, 2007), www.nytimes.com, accessed January 24, 2007; Shankar Gupta, "King of the Advergames," www.mediapost.com, accessed December 22, 2006; "Plinking," *Fast Company* (April 2007): 31; Sarah Sennott, "Gaming the Ad," *Newsweek* (January 31, 2005): E2; "Advertisements Insinuated into Video Games," *New York Times* (October 18, 2004), www.nytimes.com, accessed October 18, 2004; "Advergaming" Center for Media Research (October 24, 2007), www.research@mediapost.com, accessed October 24, 2007; Tim Zuckert, "Become One with the Game, Games Offer Brands a Unique Way to Be the Entertainment—Not Just Sponsor It," *Advertising Age* (June 16, 2008), www.adage.com, accessed June 16, 2008.

63. Stephanie Clifford, "Advertising Dairy Queen, the Video Game," *New York Times* (December 23, 2008), www.nytimes.com, accessed December 23, 2008.

64. Nick Wingfield, "Sony's PS3 to Get In-Game Ads," *Wall Street Journal* (June 4, 2008): B7; Jeffrey Bardzell, Shaowen Bardzell, and Tyler Pace, *Player Engagement and In-Game Advertising*, (November 23, 2008), www.onetooneinteractive.com/otoinsights/research-studies/player-engagement-and-in-game-advertising, accessed June 4, 2008.

65. Damien Cave, "Dogtown, U.S.A.," *New York Times* (June 12, 2005), www.nytimes.com, accessed June 12, 2005.

66. Emily Nelson, "Moistened Toilet Paper Wipes Out After Launch for Kimberly-Clark," *Wall Street Journal* (April 15, 2002), www.wsj.com, accessed April 15, 2002.

67. Robert Hof, "The Click Here Economy," *BusinessWeek* (June 22, 1998): 122–28.

68. Eric J. Arnould, "Toward a Broadened Theory of Preference Formation and the Diffusion of Innovations: Cases from Zinder Province, Niger Republic," *Journal of Consumer Research* 16 (September 1989): 239–67; Susan B. Kaiser, *The Social Psychology of Clothing* (New York: Macmillan, 1985); Thomas S. Robertson, *Innovative Behavior and Communication* (New York: Holt, Rinehart and Winston, 1971).

69. Jan-Benedict E. M. Steenkamp, Frenkel ter Hofstede, and Michel Wedel, "A Cross-National Investigation into the Individual and National Cultural Antecedents of Consumer Innovativeness," *Journal of Marketing* 63, no. 7 (1999): 55–69.

70. Susan L. Holak, Donald R. Lehmann, and Fareena Sultan, "The Role of Expectations in the Adoption of Innovative Consumer Durables: Some Preliminary Evidence," *Journal of Retailing* 63 (Fall 1987): 243–59.

71. Hubert Gatignon and Thomas S. Robertson, "A Propositional Inventory for New Diffusion Research," *Journal of Consumer Research* 11 (March 1985): 849–67.

72. Eric Pfanner, "Agencies Look Beyond Focus Groups to Spot Trends," *New York Times* (January 2, 2006), www.nytimes.com, accessed January 2, 2006.

73. For more details see Gordon C. Bruner II and Anand Kumar, "Gadget Lovers," *Journal of the Academy of Marketing Science* 35, no. 3 (2007): 329–39.

74. Normandy Madden, "Japan's Latest Fads—Marketable in U.S.? While Some Ideas Seem Pretty Out There, Many Are Moving to Mass Market. Here's What to Watch," *Advertising Age* (June 16, 2008), www.adage.com/results?start=20&endeca=1&...&N54294965798&Ns=P_Ranking|1, accessed June 16, 2008.

75. www.xbitlabs.com/news/multimedia/display/20090601150239_Microsoft_Unveils_Motion_Sensing_Game_Controller_for_Xbox_360.html, accessed June 25, 2009.

76. Everett M. Rogers, *Diffusion of Innovations*, 3rd ed. (New York: The Free Press, 1983).

77. Umberto Eco, *A Theory of Semiotics* (Bloomington: Indiana University Press, 1979).

78. Fred Davis, "Clothing and Fashion as Communication," in Michael R. Solomon, ed., *The Psychology of Fashion* (Lexington, MA: Lexington Books, 1985): 15–28.

79. Melanie Wallendorf, "The Formation of Aesthetic Criteria Through Social Structures and Social Institutions," in Jerry C. Olson, ed., *Advances in Consumer Research* 7 (Ann Arbor, MI: Association for Consumer Research, 1980): 3–6.

80. Grant McCracken, "Culture and Consumption: A Theoretical Account of the Structure and Movement of the Cultural Meaning of Consumer Goods," *Journal of Consumer Research* 13 (June 1986): 71–84.

81. Kimberly Castro, "Michelle Obama Boosts J. Crew," *U.S. News & World Report* (April 3, 2009), www.usnews.com/blogs/luxe-life/2009/04/03/michelle-obama-boosts-j-crew.html, accessed June 25, 2009.

82. "The Eternal Triangle," *Art in America* (February 1989): 23.

83. Elva Ramirez, "How Clothes Make the Car, Fashion Gives Autos Cues on Hues," *Wall Street Journal* (January 11, 2008): B1; Sally Beatty, "Fashion's 'It' Colors: How Runway Dresses, Cars—Even Washer-Dryers—Turned Shades of Blue, Brown," *Wall Street Journal* (February 4, 2005), www.wsj.com, accessed February 4, 2005.

84. Herbert Blumer, *Symbolic Interactionism: Perspective and Method* (Upper Saddle River, NJ: Prentice Hall, 1969); Howard S. Becker, "Art as Collective Action," *American Sociological Review* 39 (December 1974): 767–76; Richard A. Peterson, "Revitalizing the Culture Concept," *Annual Review of Sociology* 5 (1979): 137–66.

85. For more details, see Kaiser, *The Social Psychology of Clothing*; George B. Sproles, "Behavioral Science Theories of Fashion," in Michael R. Solomon, ed., *The Psychology of Fashion* (Lexington, MA: Lexington Books, 1985): 55–70.

86. C. R. Snyder and Howard L. Fromkin, *Uniqueness: The Human Pursuit of Difference* (New York: Plenum Press, 1980).

87. Linda Dyett, "Desperately Seeking Skin," *Psychology Today* (May–June 1996): 14; Alison Lurie, *The Language of Clothes* (New York: Random House, 1981). Note: Until very recently the study of fashion focused almost exclusively on women. Some researchers today also probe the meanings of the fashion system for men, but not nearly to the same extent. Cf. for example Susan Kaiser, Michael Solomon, Janet Hethorn, Basil Englis, Van Dyk Lewis, and Wi-Suk Kwon, "Menswear, Fashion, and Subjectivity," paper presented in Special Session: Susan Kaiser, Michael Solomon, Janet Hethorn, and Basil Englis (Chairs), "What Do Men Want? Media Representations, Subjectivity, and Consumption," at the ACR Gender Conference, Edinburgh, Scotland, June 2006.

88. Harvey Leibenstein, *Beyond Economic Man: A New Foundation for Microeconomics* (Cambridge, MA: Harvard University Press, 1976).

89. Nara Schoenberg, "Goth Culture Moves into Mainstream," *Montgomery Advertiser* (January 19, 2003): 1G.

90. Georg Simmel, "Fashion," *International Quarterly* 10 (1904): 130–55.

91. Maureen Tkacik, "'Z' Zips into the Zeitgeist, Subbing for 'S' in Hot Slang," *Wall Street Journal* (January 4, 2003), www.wsj.com, accessed January 4, 2003; Tkacik, "Slang from the 'Hood Now Sells Toyz in Target."

92. Grant D. McCracken, "The Trickle-Down Theory Rehabilitated," in Michael R. Solomon, ed., *The Psychology of Fashion* (Lexington, MA: Lexington Books, 1985): 39–54.

93. Charles W. King, "Fashion Adoption: A Rebuttal to the 'Trickle-Down' Theory," in Stephen A. Greyser, ed., *Toward Scientific Marketing* (Chicago: American Marketing Association, 1963): 108–25.

94. Alf H. Walle, "Grassroots Innovation," *Marketing Insights* (Summer 1990): 44–51.

95. Robert V. Kozinets, "Fandoms' Menace/Pop Flows: Exploring the Metaphor of Entertainment as Recombinant/Memetic Engineering," *Association for Consumer Research* (October 1999). The new science

of memetics, which tries to explain how beliefs gain acceptance and predict their progress, was spurred by Richard Dawkins who in the 1970s proposed culture as a Darwinian struggle among "memes" or mind viruses. See Geoffrey Cowley, "Viruses of the Mind: How Odd Ideas Survive," *Newsweek* (April 14, 1997): 14.

96. Malcolm Gladwell, *The Tipping Point* (New York: Little, Brown and Co., 2000).

97. "Cabbage-Hatched Plot Sucks in 24 Doll Fans," *New York Daily News* (December 1, 1983).

98. http://hub.guitarhero.com/index_us.html, accessed June 25, 2009; John Lippman, "Creating the Craze for Pokémon: Licensing Agent Bet on U.S. Kids," *Wall Street Journal* (August 16, 1999), www.wsj.com, accessed August 16, 1999; "Turtlemania," *The Economist* (April 21, 1990): 32.

99. Anthony Ramirez, "The Pedestrian Sneaker Makes a Comeback," *New York Times* (October 14, 1990): F17.

100. Madden, "Japan's Latest Fads—Marketable In U.S.?"

101. www.badfads.com, accessed June 25, 2009.

102. Quoted in Stephen Brown and Anthony Patterson, "You're a Wizard, Harry!" Consumer Responses to the Harry Potter Phenomenon," *Advances in Consumer Research* 33, no. 1 (2006): 155–160

103. B. E. Aguirre, E. L. Quarantelli, and Jorge L. Mendoza, "The Collective Behavior of Fads: The Characteristics, Effects, and Career of Streaking," *American Sociological Review* (August 1989): 569.

104. Joseph B. White, "From Fad to Trend," *Wall Street Journal* (June 21, 2005), www.wsj.com, accessed June 21, 2005.

105. Martin G. Letscher, "How to Tell Fads from Trends," *American Demographics* (December 1994): 38–45.

106. Peter Gumbel, "Big Mac's Local Flavor," *CNNmoney.com* (May 2, 2008), http://money.cnn.com/2008/04/29/news/companies/big_macs_lo-cal.fortune/index.htm, accessed May 2, 2008; Geoffrey A. Fowler, "For Prosperity Burger, McDonald's Tailors Ads to Asian Tastes," *Wall Street Journal* (January 24, 2005), www.wsj.com, accessed January 24, 2005; Saritha Rai, "Tastes of India in U.S. Wrappers," *New York Times* (April 29, 2003), www.nytimes.com, accessed April 29, 2003; Gerard O'Dwyer, "McD's Cancels McAfrika Rollout," *Advertising Age* (September 9, 2002): 14; McDonald's to Give $10 Million to Settle Vegetarian Lawsuit," *Wall Street Journal* (June 4, 2002), www.wsj.com, accessed June 4, 2002; "Packaging Draws Protest," *Marketing News* (July 4, 1994): 1.

107. www.beinggirl.com/en_US/home.jsp, accessed June 25, 2009; Carol Hymowitz, "Marketers Focus More on Global 'Tribes' Than on Nationalities," *Wall Street Journal* (December 10, 2007): B1.

108. Theodore Levitt, *The Marketing Imagination* (New York: The Free Press, 1983).

109. Geoffrey A. Fowler, "Main Street, H.K.: Disney Localizes Mickey to Boost Its Hong Kong Theme Park," *Wall Street Journal* (January 23, 2008): B1; Merissa Marr, "Small World: Disney Rewrites Script to Win Fans in India; China, Latin America Are also in Turnaround," *Wall Street Journal* (June 11, 2007): A1; Laura M. Holson, "The Feng Shui Kingdom," *New York Times* (April 25, 2005), www.nytimes.com, accessed April 25, 2005; Keith Bradsher, "Disneyland for Chinese Offers a Soup and Lands in a Stew," *New York Times* (June 17, 2005): A1; Paulo Prada and Bruce Orwall, "Disney's New French Theme Park Serves Wine—and Better Sausage," *Wall Street Journal* (March 12, 2002), www.wsj.com, accessed March 12, 2002.

110. Terry Clark, "International Marketing and National Character: A Review and Proposal for an Integrative Theory," *Journal of Marketing* 54 (October 1990): 66–79.

111. Geraldo Samor, Cecilie Rohwedder, and Ann Zimmerman, "Innocents Abroad? Wal-Mart's Global Sales Rise as It Learns from Mistakes; No More Ice Skates in Mexico," *Wall Street Journal* (May 16, 2006): B1.

112. Marc Gobé, *Emotional Branding: The New Paradigm for Connecting Brands to People* (New York: Allworth Press, 2001).

113. Norihiko Shirouzu, "Snapple in Japan: How a Splash Dried Up," *Wall Street Journal* (April 15, 1996): B1.

114. Glenn Collins, "Chinese to Get a Taste of Cheese-Less Cheetos," *New York Times* (September 2, 1994): D4.

115. Laurel Wentz, "Americans Cry 'Racism' over Absolut Poster," *Advertising Age* (April 14, 2008): 6 (2).

116. Martin McCarty, Martin I. Horn, Mary Kate Szenasy, and Jocelyn Feintuch, "An Exploratory Study of Consumer Style: Country Differences and International Segments," *Journal of Consumer Behaviour* 6, no. 1 (2007): 48.

117. Julie Skur Hill and Joseph M. Winski, "Goodbye Global Ads: Global Village Is Fantasy Land for Marketers," *Advertising Age* (November 16, 1987): 22.

118. Shelly Reese, "Culture Shock," *Marketing Tools* (May 1998): 44–49; Steve Rivkin, "The Name Game Heats Up," *Marketing News* (April 22,

1996): 8; David A. Ricks, "Products That Crashed into the Language Barrier," *Business and Society Review* (Spring 1983): 46–50.

119. Mark Lasswell, "Lost in Translation," *Business* (August 2004): 68–70.

120. Clyde H. Farnsworth, "Yoked in Twin Solitudes: Canada's Two Cultures," *New York Times* (September 18, 1994): E4.

121. Hill and Winski, "Goodbye Global Ads."

122. MTV Europe, personal communication, 1994; see also Teresa J. Domzal and Jerome B. Kernan, "Mirror, Mirror: Some Postmodern Reflections on Global Advertising," *Journal of Advertising* 22 (December 1993): 1–20; Douglas P. Holt, "Consumers' Cultural Differences as Local Systems of Tastes: A Critique of the Personality-Values Approach and an Alternative Framework," *Asia Pacific Advances in Consumer Research* 1 (1994): 1–7.

123. Douglas B. Holt, John A. Quelch, and Earl L. Taylor, "How Global Brands Compete," *Harvard Business Review* (September 2004): 68–75.

124. Normandy Madden, "New GenerAsians Survey Gets Personal with Asia-Pacific Kids," *Advertising Age International* (July 13, 1998): 2.

125. Adam Thompson and Shai Oster, "NBA in China Gets Milk to Sell Hoops," *Wall Street Journal* (January 22, 2007): B1; "They All Want to Be Like Mike," *Fortune* (July 21, 1997): 51–53.

126. Calvin Sims, "Japan Beckons, and East Asia's Youth Fall in Love," *New York Times* (December 5, 1999): 3.

127. Miriam Jordan and Teri Agins, "Fashion Flip-Flop: Sandal Leaves the Shower Behind," *Wall Street Journal* (August 8, 2002), www.wsj.com, accessed August 8, 2002.

128. Elisabeth Rosenthal, "Buicks, Starbucks and Fried Chicken, Still China?" *New York Times* (February 25, 2002), www.nytimes.com, accessed February 25, 2002.

129. Special Report, "Brands in an Age of Anti-Americanism," *Business-Week* (August 4, 2003): 69–76.

130. Suzanne Kapner, "U.S. TV Shows Losing Potency Around World," *New York Times* (January 2, 2003), www.nytimes.com, accessed January 2, 2003; "Big Brother Nipple Sparks Outrage," *BBCNews* (September 10, 2004), www.bbcnews.com, accessed September 10, 2004.

131. Laurel Wentz and Claire Atkinson, "Apprentice Translators Hope for Hits All over Globe," *Advertising Age* (February 14, 2005): 3(2).

132. Julie Watson, "City Keeps McDonald's from Opening in Plaza," *Montgomery Advertiser* (December 15, 2002): 5AA.

133. Alan Riding, "Only the French Elite Scorn Mickey's Debut," *New York Times* (1992): A1.

134. Elisabeth Rosenthal, "Fast Food Hits Mediterranean; A Diet Succumbs," *New York Times* (September 23, 2008), www.nytimes.com, accessed September 23, 2008.

135. Professor Russell Belk, University of Utah, personal communication, July 25, 1997.

136. Material in this section adapted from Güliz Ger and Russell W. Belk, "I'd Like to Buy the World a Coke: Consumptionscapes of the 'Less Affluent World,'" *Journal of Consumer Policy* 19, no. 3 (1996): 271–304; Russell W. Belk, "Romanian Consumer Desires and Feelings of Deservingness," in Lavinia Stan, ed., *Romania in Transition* (Hanover, NH: Dartmouth Press, 1997): 191–208; see also Güliz Ger, "Human Development and Humane Consumption: Well Being Beyond the Good Life," *Journal of Public Policy and Marketing* 16 (1997): 110–25.

137. Professor Güliz Ger, Bilkent University, Turkey, personal communication, July 25, 1997.

138. Erazim Kohák, "Ashes, Ashes . . . Central Europe After Forty Years," *Daedalus* 121 (Spring 1992): 197–215; Belk, "Romanian Consumer Desires and Feelings of Deservingness."

139. Lily Dong and Kelly Tian. "The Use of Western Brands in Asserting Chinese National Identity," *Journal of Consumer Research* 36 (October 2009).

140. Robert V. Kozinets. "Technology/Ideology: How Ideological Fields Influence Consumers' Technology Narratives," *Journal of Consumer Research* 34 (April 2008): 865–81.

141. David Murphy, "Christmas's Commercial Side Makes Yuletide a Hit in China," *Wall Street Journal* (December 24, 2002), www.wsj.com, accessed December 24, 2002.

142. This example courtesy of Professor Russell Belk, University of Utah, personal communication, July 25, 1997.

143. James Hookway, "In Vietnam, Fast Food Acts Global, Tastes Local," *Wall Street Journal* (March 12, 2008), http://online.wsj.com/article/Sb120528509133029135.html?mod=mm_hs_marketing_strat, accessed March 12, 2008.

144. Miriam Jordan, "India Decides to Put Its Own Spin on Popular Rock, Rap and Reggae," *Wall Street Journal* (January 5, 2000), www.wsj.com, accessed January 5, 2000; Rasul Bailay, "Coca-Cola Recruits Paraplegics for 'Cola War' in India," *Wall Street Journal* (June 10, 1997).

145. Rick Wartzman, "When You Translate 'Got Milk' for Latinos, What Do You Get?" *Wall Street Journal* (June 3, 1999).

146. Charles Newbery, "Coke Goes Native with New Soft Drink," *Advertising Age* (December 1, 2003): 34

147. Eric J. Arnould and Richard R. Wilk, "Why Do the Natives Wear Adidas: Anthropological Approaches to Consumer Research," *Advances in Consumer Research* 12 (Provo, UT: Association for Consumer Research, 1985): 748–52.

148. John F. Sherry, Jr. and Eduardo G. Camargo, "May Your Life Be Marvelous: English Language Labelling and the Semiotics of Japanese Promotion," *Journal of Consumer Research* 14 (1987): 174–188.

149. Bill Bryson, "A Taste for Scrambled English," *New York Times* (July 22, 1990): 10; Rose A. Horowitz, "California Beach Culture Rides Wave of Popularity in Japan," *Journal of Commerce* (August 3, 1989): 17; Elaine Lafferty, "American Casual Seizes Japan: Teen-agers Go for N.F.L. Hats, Batman and the California Look," *Time* (November 13, 1989): 106.

150. Lucy Howard and Gregory Cerio, "Goofy Goods," *Newsweek* (August 15, 1994): 8.

151. "Product Placement, Sampling, and Word-of-Mouth Collectively Influence Consumer Purchases," Center for Media Research (October 22, 2008), www.mediapost.com, accessed October 22, 2008; Brian Steinberg and Suzanne Vranica, "Prime-Time TV's New Guest Stars: Products," *Wall Street Journal* (January 12, 2004), www.wsj.com, accessed January 12, 2004; Karlene Lukovitz, "'Storyline' Product Placements Gaining on Cable," *Marketing Daily* (October 5, 2007), www.mediapost.com, accessed October 5, 2007.

152. Craig J. Thompson and Zeynep Arsel, "The Starbucks Brandscape and Consumers' (Anticorporate) Experiences of Glocalization," *Journal of Consumer Research* 31 (December 2004): 631–42.

153. Calvin Sims, "For Chic's Sake, Japanese Women Parade to the Orthopedist," *New York Times* (November 26, 1999), www.nytimes.com, accessed November 26, 1999.

MINTEL

SECTION 5 MINTEL MEMO AND DATASET EXERCISE

Mintel Memo

TO: Consumer Research Dept.
FROM: The Big Boss
RE: Sacred food segmentation and positioning

We need to try to expand our presence in the kosher food market. Are we positioning ourselves in this category as effectively as we could? Are we aiming for the right target segments?

Please provide us with actionable recommendations for segmentation and positioning strategies based on this information. As you analyze the data in the tables provided, remember to focus on general trends with an eye on specific subgroups (e.g., age, household income, education, etc.) that show a statistically significant difference in their responses—especially when there is some reason based on what you have learned in this section about consumer behavior to believe that this difference is important.

When you write your memo, please try to incorporate relevant concepts and information you learned when you read the designated chapters!

What can we learn from the following data to help our company position itself in the kosher food market?

Number of Respondents		1,538	441	240	341	335
Respondent Categories			Household Income		Education	
Respondent Sub-categories		Total	$25,000–$49,999	$100,000+	High School or Less	College Graduate
			(A)	(B)	(A)	(B)
Question	Answers	%	%	%	%	%
How much do you know about kosher food?	Know a lot	13	11	18	9	14
(Comparison of Column Proportions)				A		A
	Know some	58	52	65	50	61
				A		A
	Know nothing	30	37	17	40	24
			B		B	

Comparison of Column Proportions results are based on two-sided tests with significance level p < 0.05. Letters appearing in the column category denote a significant difference between the number immediately above the letter and the category associated with that particular letter. For example, the "B" in the High School or Less category above denotes a significant difference between the percentage of participants with an educational level of high school or less who specify knowing nothing about kosher (40%) and the percentage of participants who had graduated from college (24%).

To access the complete Mintel questionnaires and datasets, go to MyMarketingLab at www.pearsonglobaleditions.com/mymarketinglab. If you are not using MyMarketingLab, visit this book's Companion Website at www.pearsonglobaleditions.com/solomon.

ABC model of attitudes a multidimensional perspective stating that attitudes are jointly defined by affect, behavior, and cognition

Absolute threshold the minimum amount of stimulation that can be detected on a given sensory channel

Acceptance cycles a way to differentiate among fashions in terms of their longevity

Accommodative purchase decision the process of using bargaining, coercion, compromise, and the wielding of power to achieve agreement among group members who have different preferences or priorities

Acculturation the process of learning the beliefs and behaviors endorsed by another culture

Acculturation agents friends, family, local businesses, and other reference groups that facilitate the learning of cultural norms

Activation models of memory approaches to memory stressing different levels of processing that occur and activate some aspects of memory rather than others, depending on the nature of the processing task

Activity stores a retailing concept that lets consumers participate in the production of the products or services being sold in the store

Actual self a person's realistic appraisal of his or her qualities

Adaptation the process that occurs when a sensation becomes so familiar that it no longer commands attention

Advergaming online games merged with interactive advertisements that let companies target specific types of consumers

Advertising wear-out the condition that occurs when consumers become so used to hearing or seeing a marketing stimulus that they no longer pay attention to it

Affect the way a consumer feels about an attitude object

Affluenza well-off consumers who are stressed or unhappy despite of or even because of their wealth

Age cohort a group of consumers of approximately the same age who have undergone similar experiences

Agentic goals an emphasis on self-assertion and mastery, often associated with traditional male gender roles

AIOs (activities, interests, and opinions) the psychographic variables researchers use to group consumers

Allegory a story told about an abstract trait or concept that has been personified as a person, animal, or vegetable

Allocentric person who has a group orientation

Alternate-reality game an application that blends online and off-line clues and encourages players to collaborate to solve a puzzle

Androgyny the possession of both masculine and feminine traits

Animism cultural practices whereby inanimate objects are given qualities that make them somehow alive

Antibrand communities groups of consumers who share a common disdain for a celebrity, store, or brand

Anticonsumption the actions taken by consumers involving the deliberate defacement or mutilation of products

Antifestival an event that distorts the symbols associated with other holidays

Approach–approach conflict a person must choose between two desirable alternatives

Approach–avoidance conflict a person desires a goal but wishes to avoid it at the same time

Archetypes a universally shared idea or behavior pattern, central to Carl Jung's conception of personality; archetypes involve themes—such as birth, death, or the devil—that appear frequently in myths, stories, and dreams

Art product a creation viewed primarily as an object of aesthetic contemplation without any functional value

Aspirational reference group high-profile athletes and celebrities used in marketing efforts to promote a product

Associative network a memory system that organizes individual units of information according to some set of relationships; may include such concepts as brands, manufacturers, and stores

Atmospherics the use of space and physical features in store design to evoke certain effects in buyers

Attention the assignment of processing activity to selected stimuli

Attentional gate a process whereby information retained for further processing is transferred from sensory memory to short-term memory

Attitude a lasting, general evaluation of people (including oneself), objects, or issues

Attitude object (Ao) anything toward which one has an attitude

Attitude toward the act of buying (A_{act}) the perceived consequences of a purchase

Autonomic decision when one family member chooses a product for the whole family

Autotellics individuals who enjoy touching products to experience them

Avatar manifestation of a Hindu deity in superhuman or animal form. In the computing world it has come to mean a cyberspace presence represented by a character that you can move around inside a visual, graphical world

B2C e-commerce businesses selling to consumers through electronic marketing

Baby boomer a large cohort of people born between the years of 1946 and 1964 who are the source of many important cultural and economic changes

Balance theory a theory that considers relations among elements a person might perceive as belonging together, and people's tendency to change relations among elements in order to make them consistent or "balanced"

Basking in reflected glory the practice of publicizing connections with successful people or organizations to enhance one's own standing

Behavior a consumer's actions with regard to an attitude object

Behavioral economics the study of the behavioral determinants of economic decisions

Behavioral influence perspective the view that consumer decisions are learned responses to environmental cues

Behavioral learning theories the perspectives on learning that assume that learning takes place as the result of responses to external events

Behavioral targeting e-commerce marketers serve up customized ads on Web sites or cable TV stations based on a customer's prior activity

Being space a retail environment that resembles a residential living room where customers are encouraged to congregate

Binary opposition a defining structural characteristic of many myths in which two opposing ends of some dimension are represented (e.g., good versus evil, nature versus technology)

Bioterrorism a strategy to disrupt the nation's food supply with the aim of creating economic havoc

Blissful ignorance effect states that people who have details about a product before they buy it do not expect to be as happy with it as do those who got only ambiguous information

Blogs messages posted online in diary form

Body cathexis a person's feelings about aspects of his or her body

Body image a consumer's subjective evaluation of his or her physical self

Boomerang kids grown children who return to their parents' home to live

Brand advocates consumers who supply product reviews online

Brand community a set of consumers who share a set of social relationships based on usage or interest in a product

Brand equity a brand that has strong positive associations in a consumer's memory and commands a lot of loyalty as a result

Brand loyalty repeat purchasing behavior that reflects a conscious decision to continue buying the same brand

Brand personality a set of traits people attribute to a product as if it were a person

Branded entertainment a format where advertisers showcase their products in longer-form narrative films instead of commercials

Brandfests a corporate-sponsored event intended to promote strong brand loyalty among customers

BRIC the bloc of nations with very rapid economic development: Brazil, Russia, India, and China

Bromance a relationship characterized by strong affection between two straight males

Business ethics rules of conduct that guide actions in the marketplace

Business-to-business (B2B) e-commerce internet interactions between two or more businesses or organizations

Business-to-business (B2B) marketers specialists in meeting the needs of organizations such as corporations, government agencies, hospitals, and retailers

Buyclass theory of purchasing a framework that characterizes organizational buying decisions in terms of how much cognitive effort is involved in making a decision

Buyer the person who actually makes the purchase

Buying center the part of an organization charged with making purchasing decisions

C2C e-commerce consumer-to-consumer activity through the Internet

Carbon footprint the impact human activities have on the environment in terms of the amount of greenhouse gases they produce; measured in units of carbon dioxide

Cascades a piece of information shared in a social network triggers a sequence of interactions (much like an avalanche)

Category exemplars brands that are particularly relevant examples of a broader classification

Chavs British term that refers to young, lower-class men and women who mix flashy brands and accessories from big names such as Burberry with track suits

Chunking a process in which information is stored by combining small pieces of information into larger ones

Classic a fashion with an extremely long acceptance cycle

Classical conditioning the learning that occurs when a stimulus eliciting a response is paired with another stimulus that initially does not elicit a response on its own but will cause a similar response over time because of its association with the first stimulus

Closure principle the *Gestalt* principle that describes a person's tendency to supply missing information in order to perceive a holistic image

Co-branding strategies linking products together to create a more desirable connotation in consumer minds

Co-consumers other patrons in a consumer setting

Cognition the beliefs a consumer has about an attitude object

Cognitive learning theory approaches that stress the importance of internal mental processes. This perspective views people as problem solvers who actively use information from the world around them to master their environment

Cognitive processing style a predisposition to process information. Some of us tend to have a *rational system of cognition* that processes information analytically and sequentially using roles of logic, while others rely on an *experiential system of cognition* that processes information more holistically and in parallel

Cohesiveness the degree to which members of a group are attracted to each other and how much each values their membership in this group

Collecting the systematic acquisition of a particular object or set of objects

Collective selection the process by which certain symbolic alternatives tend to be jointly chosen over others by members of a society

Collectivist culture cultural orientation that encourages people to subordinate their personal goals to those of a stable in-group; values such as self-discipline and group accomplishment are stressed

Communal goals an emphasis on affiliation and the fostering of harmonious relations, often associated with traditional female gender roles

Communications model a framework specifying that a number of elements are necessary for communication to be achieved, including a source, message, medium, receivers, and feedback

Comparative advertising a strategy in which a message compares two or more specifically named or recognizably presented brands and makes a comparison of them in terms of one or more specific attributes

Comparative influence the process whereby a reference group influences decisions about specific brands or activities

Compensatory decision rules a set of rules that allows information about attributes of competing products to be averaged in some way; poor standing on one attribute can potentially be offset by good standing on another

Compliance we form an attitude because it helps us to gain rewards or avoid punishment

Compulsive consumption the process of repetitive, often excessive, shopping used to relieve tension, anxiety, depression, or boredom

Computer-mediated environment immersive virtual worlds

Conditioned response (CR) a response to a conditioned stimulus caused by the learning of an association between a conditioned stimulus (CS) and an unconditioned stimulus (UCS)

Conditioned stimulus (CS) a stimulus that produces a learned reaction through association over time

Conformity a change in beliefs or actions as a reaction to real or imagined group pressure

Connexity a lifestyle term coined by the advertising agency Saatchi & Saatchi to describe young consumers who place high value on being both foot-loose and connected

Conscientious consumerism a new value that combines a focus on personal health with a concern for global health

Consensual purchase decision a decision in which the group agrees on the desired purchase and differs only in terms of how it will be achieved

Consideration set the products a consumer actually deliberates about choosing

Conspicuous consumption the purchase and prominent display of luxury goods to provide evidence of a consumer's ability to afford them

Consumed consumers those people who are used or exploited, whether willingly or not, for commercial gain in the marketplace

Consumer a person who identifies a need or desire, makes a purchase, and/or disposes of the product

Consumer addiction a physiological and/or psychological dependency on products or services

Consumer behavior the processes involved when individuals or groups select, purchase, use, or dispose of products, services, ideas, or experiences to satisfy needs and desires

Consumer confidence the state of mind of consumers relative to their optimism or pessimism about economic conditions; people tend to make more discretionary purchases when their confidence in the economy is high

Consumer-generated content a hallmark of Web 2.0; everyday people voice their opinions about products, brands, and companies on blogs, podcasts, and social networking sites and film their own commercials they post on Web sites

Consumer hyperchoice a condition where the large number of available options forces us to make repeated choices that drain psychological energy and diminish our ability to make smart decisions

Consumer identity renaissance the redefinition process people undergo when they retire

Consumer satisfaction/dissatisfaction (CS/D) the overall attitude a person has about a product after it has been purchased

Consumer socialization the process by which people acquire skills that enable them to function in the marketplace

Consumerspace marketing environment where customers act as partners with companies to decide what the marketplace will offer

Consumer style a pattern of behaviors, attitudes, and opinions that influences all of a person's consumption activities—including attitudes toward advertising, preferred channels of information and purchase, brand loyalty, and price consciousness

Consumer tribe group of people who share a lifestyle and who can identify with each other because of a shared allegiance to an activity or a product

Consumption communities Web groups where members share views and product recommendations online

Consumption constellation a set of products and activities used by consumers to define, communicate, and perform social roles

Contamination when a place or object takes on sacred qualities because of its association with another sacred person or event

Contemporary Young Mainstream Female Achievers (CYMFA) modern women who assume multiple roles

Continuous innovation a modification of an existing product

Contrast stimuli that differ from others around them

Conventions norms that regulate how we conduct our everyday lives

Co-optation a cultural process by which the original meanings of a product or other symbol associated with a subculture are modified by members of mainstream culture

Core values common general values held by a culture

Cosmopolitanism a cultural value that emphasizes being open to the world and striving for diverse experiences

Cosplay a form of performance art in which participants wear elaborate costumes that represent a virtual world avatar or other fictional character

Cougars older women who date younger men

Country of origin original country from which a product is produced. Can be an important piece of information in the decision-making process

Craft product a creation valued because of the beauty with which it performs some function; this type of product tends to follow a formula that permits rapid production, and it is easier to understand than an art product

Creolization foreign influences are absorbed and integrated with local meanings

Crescive norms unspoken rules that govern social behavior

Crowdsourcing similar to a firm that outsources production to a subcontractor; companies call upon outsiders from around the world to solve problems their own scientists can't handle

Cult products items that command fierce consumer loyalty and devotion

Cultural capital a set of distinctive and socially rare tastes and practices that admits a person into the realm of the upper class

Cultural categories the grouping of ideas and values that reflect the basic ways members of a society characterize the world

Cultural formula a sequence of media events in which certain roles and props tend to occur consistently

Cultural gatekeepers individuals who are responsible for determining the types of messages and symbolism to which members of mass culture are exposed

Cultural selection the process by which some alternatives are selected over others by cultural gatekeepers

Culture the values, ethics, rituals, traditions, material objects, and services produced or valued by the members of a society

Culture jamming the defacement or alteration of advertising materials as a form of political expression

Culture production system (CPS) the set of individuals and organizations responsible for creating and marketing a cultural product

Custom a norm that controls basic behaviors, such as division of labor in a household

Cybermediary intermediary that helps to filter and organize online market information so that consumers can identify and evaluate alternatives more efficiently

Database marketing tracking consumers' buying habits very closely, and then crafting products and messages tailored precisely to people's wants and needs based on this information

Decay structural changes in the brain produced by learning decrease over time

Decision polarization the process whereby individuals' choices tend to become more extreme (polarized), in either a conservative or risky direction, following group discussion of alternatives

Deethnicization process whereby a product formerly associated with a specific ethnic group is detached from its roots and marketed to other subcultures

Deindividuation the process whereby individual identities get submerged within a group, reducing inhibitions against socially inappropriate behavior

Demographics the observable measurements of a population's characteristics, such as birthrate, age distribution, and income

Desacralization the process that occurs when a sacred item or symbol is removed from its special place, or is duplicated in mass quantities, and becomes profane as a result

Determinant attributes the attributes actually used to differentiate among choices

Differential threshold the ability of a sensory system to detect changes or differences among stimuli

Diffusion of innovations the process whereby a new product, service, or idea spreads through a population

Digital native young people who have grown up with computers and mobile technology; multitaskers with cell phones, music downloads, and instant messaging on the Internet. Who are comfortable communicating online and by text and IM rather than by voice

DINKS acronym for Double Income, No Kids; a consumer segment with a lot of disposable income

Discontinuous innovation a new product or service that radically changes the way we live

Discretionary income the money available to a household over and above that required for necessities

Divestment rituals the steps people take to gradually distance themselves from things they treasure so that they can sell them or give them away

Doppelgänger brand image a parody of a brand posted on a Web site that looks like the original but is in fact a critique of it

Drive the desire to satisfy a biological need in order to reduce physiological arousal

Drive theory concept that focuses on biological needs that produce unpleasant states of arousal

Dynamically continuous innovation a significant change to an existing product

Early adopters people who are receptive to new products and adopt them relatively soon, though they are motivated more by social acceptance and being in style than by the desire to try risky new things

Echo Boomers people born between 1986–2002, also known as Gen Y and Millennials

Economics of information perspective in which advertising is an important source of consumer information emphasizing the economic cost of the time spent searching for products

Ego the system that mediates between the id and the superego

Ego-defensive function attitudes we form to protect ourselves either from external threats or internal feelings

80/20 rule a rule-of-thumb in volume segmentation, which says that about 20 percent of consumers in a product category (the heavy users) account for about 80 percent of sales

Elaborated codes the ways of expressing and interpreting meanings that are more complex and depend on a more sophisticated worldview, which tend to be used by the middle and upper classes

Elaboration likelihood model (ELM) the approach that one of two routes to persuasion (central versus peripheral) will be followed, depending on the personal relevance of a message; the route taken determines the relative importance of the message contents versus other characteristics, such as source attractiveness

Elaborative rehearsal a cognitive process that allows information to move from short-term memory into long-term memory by thinking about the meaning of a stimulus and relating it to other information already in memory

Electronic recommendation agent a software tool that tries to understand a human decision maker's multiattribute preferences for a product category by asking the user to communicate his or her preferences. Based on that data, the software then recommends a list of alternatives

sorted by the degree that they fit with the person's preferences

Embeds tiny figures inserted into magazine advertising by using high-speed photography or airbrushing. These hidden figures, usually of a sexual nature, supposedly exert strong but unconscious influences on innocent readers

Emic perspective an approach to studying for (or marketing to) cultures that stresses the unique aspects of each culture

Encoding the process in which information from short-term memory enters into long-term memory in a recognizable form

Enculturation the process of learning the beliefs and behaviors endorsed by one's own culture

Episodic memories memories that relate to personally relevant events; this tends to increase a person's motivation to retain these memories

Esteem need prioritizing the needs of the individual above those of the group

Ethnic subculture a self-perpetuating group of consumers held together by common cultural ties

Ethnocentrism the belief in the superiority of one's own country's practices and products

Etic perspective an approach to studying (or marketing to) cultures that stresses commonalities across cultures

Evaluative criteria the dimensions used by consumers to compare competing product alternatives

Evoked set those products already in memory plus those prominent in the retail environment that are actively considered during a consumer's choice process

Exchange a transaction in which two or more organizations or people give and receive something of value

Expectancy disconfirmation model states that we form beliefs about product performance based on prior experience with the product and/or communications about the product that imply a certain level of quality; when something performs the way we thought it would, we may not think much about it. If it fails to live up to expectations, this may create negative feelings. On the other hand, we are satisfied if performance exceeds our initial expectations

Expectancy theory the perspective that behavior is largely "pulled" by expectations of achieving desirable outcomes, or positive incentives, rather than "pushed" from within

Experience the result of acquiring and processing stimulation over time

Experiential hierarchy of effects an attitude is initially formed on the basis of a raw emotional reaction

Experiential perspective an approach stressing the *Gestalt* or totality of the product or service experience, focusing on consumers' affective responses in the marketplace

Exposure an initial stage of perception during which some sensations come within range of consumers' sensory receptors

Extended family traditional family structure in which several generations live together

Extended problem solving an elaborate decision-making process, often initiated by a motive that is fairly central to the self-concept and accompanied by perceived risk; the consumer tries to collect as much information as possible, and carefully weighs product alternatives

Extended self the external objects we consider a part of our self-identity

Extinction the process whereby a learned connection between a stimulus and response is eroded so that the response is no longer reinforced

Fad a very short-lived fashion

Family branding an application of stimulus generalization when a product capitalizes on the reputation of its manufacturer's name

Family financial officer (FFO) the individual in the family who is in charge of making financial decisions

Family identity the definition of a household by family members that it presents to members and to those outside the family unit

Family life cycle (FLC) a classification scheme that segments consumers in terms of changes in income and family composition and the changes in demands placed on this income

Fantasy a self-induced shift in consciousness, often focusing on some unattainable or improbable goal; sometimes fantasy is a way of compensating for a lack of external stimulation or for dissatisfaction with the actual self

Fashion the process of social diffusion by which a new style is adopted by some group(s) of consumers

Fashion acceptance cycle the diffusion process of a style through three stages: introduction, acceptance, and regression

Fashion system those people and organizations involved in creating symbolic meanings and transferring these meanings to cultural goods

Fear appeals an attempt to change attitudes or behavior through the use of threats or by highlighting negative consequences of noncompliance with the request

Feature creep the tendency of manufacturers to add layers of complexity to products that make them harder to understand and use

Fertility rate a rate determined by the number of births per year per 1,000 women of childbearing age

Figure-ground principle the *Gestalt* principle whereby one part of a stimulus configuration dominates a situation whereas other aspects recede into the background

Fixed-interval reinforcement after a specified time period has passed, the first response an orgamism makes elicits a reward

Fixed-ratio reinforcement reinforcement occurs only after a fixed number of responses

Flow state situation in which consumers are truly involved with a product, an ad, or a Web site

Food culture pattern of food and beverage consumption that reflects the values of a social group

Food poverty the inability of consumers to obtain healthy and affordable food due to limited accessibility to stores, the availability of healthy choices, the affordability of healthy options, and general nutritional awareness

Foot-in-the-door technique based on the observation that a consumer is more likely to comply with a request if he or she has first agreed to comply with a smaller request

Fortress brands brands that consumers closely link to rituals; this makes it unlikely they will be replaced

Freegans a takeoff on *vegans*, who shun all animal products; anticonsumerists who live off discards as a political statement against corporations and materialism

Freemium a free version of a product that's supported by a paid premium version. The idea is to encourage the maximum number of people to use the product and eventually convert a small fraction of them to paying customers

Frequency marketing a marketing technique that reinforces regular purchasers by giving them prizes with values that increase along with the amount purchased

Frugalistas fashion-conscious consumers who pride themselves on achieving style on a limited budget

Functional theory of attitudes states that attitudes exist *because* they serve some function for the person. Consumers who expect that they will need to deal with similar situations at a future time will be more likely to start to form an attitude in anticipation

Gadget lovers enthusiastic early adopters of high-tech products

Gatekeeper the person who conducts the information search and controls the flow of information available to the group

Gemba Japanese term for the one true source of information

Gen X people born between 1965–1985

Gen Y people born between 1986–2002; also known as Echo Boomers and Millennials

Gender convergence blurring of sex roles in modern society; men and women increasingly express similar attitudes about balancing home life and work

Gender-bending products a traditionally sex-typed product adapted to appeal to the opposite gender

Geodemography techniques that combine consumer demographic information with geographic consumption patterns to permit precise targeting of consumers with specific characteristics

Gestalt meaning derived from the totality of a set of stimuli, rather than from any individual stimulus

Gift-giving ritual the events involved in the selection, presentation, acceptance, and interpretation of a gift

Global consumer culture a culture in which people around the world are united through their common devotion to brand name consumer goods, movie stars, celebrities, and leisure activities

Globalized consumption ethic the global sharing of a material lifestyle including the valuing of well-known multinational brands that symbolize prosperity

Goal a consumer's desired end state

Gray market the economic potential created by the increasing numbers of affluent elderly consumers

Green marketing a marketing strategy involving an emphasis on protecting the natural environment

Greenwashing inflated claims about a product's environmental benefits

Gripe sites web sites consumers create specifically to log complaints about a company

Grooming rituals sequences of behaviors that aid in the transition from the private self to the public self or back again

Group dieting online communities devoted to excessive weight loss

Guerrilla marketing promotional strategies that use unconventional locations and intensive word-of-mouth campaigns

Habitual decision making choices made with little or no conscious effort

Habitus ways in which we classify experiences as a result of our socialization processes

Halo effect a phenomenon that occurs when people react to other, similar stimuli in much the same way they responded to the original stimulus

Heavy users a name companies use to identify their customers who consume their products in large volumes

Hedonic consumption the multisensory, fantasy, and emotional aspects of consumers' interactions with products

Helicopter moms overprotective mothers who "hover" around their kids and insert themselves into virtually all aspects of their lives

Heuristics the mental rules of thumb that lead to a speedy decision

Hierarchy of effects a fixed sequence of steps that occurs during attitude formation; this sequence varies depending on such factors as the consumer's level of involvement with the attitude object

High-context culture group members tend to be close-knit and are likely to infer meanings that go beyond the spoken word

Hoarding unsystematic acquisition of objects (in contrast to collecting)

Homeostasis the state of being in which the body is in physiological balance; goal-oriented behavior attempts to reduce or eliminate an unpleasant motivational state and return to a balanced one

Homogamy the tendency for individuals to marry others similar to themselves

Home shopping parties a gathering where a company representative makes a sales presentation to a group of people who have gathered in the home of a friend or acquaintance

Homophily the degree to which a pair of individuals is similar in terms of education, social status, and beliefs

Host culture a new culture to which a person must acculturate

Household according to the U.S. Census Bureau, an occupied housing unit

Hybrid ad a marketing communication that explicitly references the context (e.g., TV show) in which it appears

Hyperopia the medical term for people who have farsighted vision; describes people who are so obsessed with preparing for the future that they can't enjoy the present

Hyperreality the becoming real of what is initially simulation or "hype"

Icon a sign that resembles the product in some way

Id the system oriented toward immediate gratification

Ideal of beauty a model, or exemplar, of appearance valued by a culture

Ideal self a person's conception of how he or she would like to be

Identification the process of forming an attitude to conform to another person's or group's expectations

Identity marketing a practice whereby consumers are paid to alter some aspects of their selves to advertise for a branded product

Idiocentric a person who has an individualist orientation

Illusion of truth effect telling people that a consumer claim is false can make them misremember it as true

Impression management our efforts to "manage" what others think of us by strategically choosing clothing and other cues that will put us in a good light

Impulse buying a process that occurs when the consumer experiences a sudden urge to purchase an item that he or she cannot resist

Incidental brand exposure an experimental technique that involves showing product logos to respondents without their conscious awareness

Incidental learning unintentional acquisition of knowledge

Index a sign that is connected to a product because they share some property

Individualism one of Hofstede's cultural dimensions: The extent to which the culture values the welfare of the individual versus that of the group

Individualist culture cultural orientation that encourages people to attach more importance to personal goals than to group goals; values such as personal enjoyment and freedom are stressed

Inertia the process whereby purchase decisions are made out of habit because the consumer lacks the motivation to consider alternatives

Influence network a two-way dialogue between participants in a social network and opinion leaders

Influencer the person who tries to sway the outcome of the decision

Influencer programs a strategy to start online conversations about brands by encouraging (and perhaps compensating) bloggers to write about them

Information search the process by which the consumer surveys his or her environment for appropriate data to make a reasonable decision

Initiator the person who brings up the idea or identifies a need

Innovation a product or style that is perceived as new by consumers

Innovators people who are always on the lookout for novel developments and will be the first to try a new offering

Insourcing making things yourself that you used to buy from others

Instrumental conditioning also known as operant conditioning, occurs as the individual learns to perform behaviors that produce positive outcomes and to avoid those that yield negative outcomes

Instrumental values goals endorsed because they are needed to achieve desired end states, or terminal values

Intelligent agents software programs that learn from past user behavior in order to recommend new purchases

Interactive mobile marketing real-time promotional campaigns targeted to consumers' cell phones

Interference one way that forgetting occurs; as additional information is learned, it displaces the earlier information

Internalization deep-seated attitudes become part of our value system

Interpretant the meaning derived from a sign or symbol

Interpretation the process whereby meanings are assigned to stimuli

Interpretivism as opposed to the dominant positivist perspective on consumer behavior, instead stresses the importance of symbolic, subjective experience and the idea that meaning is in the mind of the person rather than existing "out there" in the objective world

Invidious distinction the use of status symbols to inspire envy in others through display of wealth or power

Involvement the motivation to process product-related information

j.n.d. (just noticeable difference) the minimum difference between two stimuli that can be detected by a perceiver

Juggling lifestyle working mothers' attempts to compromise between conflicting cultural ideals of motherhood and professionalism

***Kansei* engineering** a Japanese philosophy that translates customers' feelings into design elements

Kin-network system the rituals intended to maintain ties among family members, both immediate and extended

Knowledge function the process of forming an attitude to provide order, structure, or meaning

Knowledge structure organized system of concepts relating to brands, stores, and other concepts

Laddering a technique to uncover consumers' associations between specific attributes and general values

Laggards consumers who are exceptionally slow to adopt innovations

Late adopters the majority of consumers who are moderately receptive to adopting innovations

Lateral cycling a process in which already-purchased objects are sold to others or exchanged for other items

Latitudes of acceptance and rejection in the social judgment theory of attitudes, the notion that people differ in terms of the information they will find acceptable or unacceptable. They form latitudes of acceptance and rejection around an attitude standard. Ideas that fall within a latitude will be favorably received, but those falling outside of this zone will not

Lead users involved, experienced customers (usually corporate customers) who are very knowledgeable about the field

Learning a relatively permanent change in a behavior caused by experience

Licensing popular marketing strategy that pays for the right to link a product or service to the name of a well-known brand or designer

Life course paradigm this perspective views behavior at any stage in life or given point in time as the product of one's actions or responses to earlier life conditions and the way the individual has adapted to social and environmental circumstances

Limited problem solving a problem-solving process in which consumers are not motivated to search for information or to rigorously evaluate each alternative; instead they use simple decision rules to arrive at a purchase decision

List of Values (LOV) scale identifies consumer segments based on the values members endorse and relates each value to differences in consumption behaviors

LOHAS an acronym for "lifestyles of health and sustainability"; a consumer segment that worries about the environment, wants products to be produced in a sustainable way, and who spend money to advance what they see as their personal development and potential

Long tail states that we need no longer rely solely on big hits (such as blockbuster movies or best-selling books) to find profits. Companies can also make money if they sell small amounts of items that only a few people want—if they sell enough different items

Long-term memory (LTM) the system that allows us to retain information for a long period of time

Look-alike packaging putting a generic or private label product in a package that resembles a popular brand to associate the brand with the popular one

Looking-glass self the process of imagining the reaction of others toward oneself

Low-context culture in contrast to high-context cultures that have strong oral traditions and that are more sensitive to nuance, low-context cultures are more literal

Low-involvement hierarchy of effects the process of attitude formation for products or services that carry little risk or self-identity

Low-literate consumer people who read at a very low level; tend to avoid situations where they will have to reveal their inability to master basic consumption decisions such as ordering from a menu

M-commerce the practice of promoting and selling goods and services via wireless devices including cell phones, PDAs, and iPods

Market beliefs a consumer's specific beliefs or decision rules pertaining to marketplace phenomena

Market maven a person who often serves as a source of information about marketplace activities

Market segmentation strategies targeting a brand only to specific groups of consumers who share well-defined and relevant characteristics

Masculinism study devoted to the male image and the cultural meanings of masculinity

Masculinity/femininity one of Hofstede's cultural dimensions: The degree to which a culture clearly defines sex roles

Masked branding strategy that deliberately hides a product's origin

Mass class a term analysts use to describe the millions of global consumers who now enjoy a level of purchasing power that's sufficient to let them afford many high-quality products

Mass customization the personalization of products and services for individual customers at a mass-production price

Materialism the importance consumers attach to worldly possessions

Megachurches very large churches that serve between 2,000 and 20,000 congregants

Membership reference group ordinary people whose consumption activities provide informational social influence

Meme theory a perspective that uses a medical metaphor to explain how an idea or product enters the consciousness of people over time, much like a virus

Memory a process of acquiring information and storing it over time so that it will be available when needed

Mental accounting principle that states that decisions are influenced by the way a problem is posed

Mere exposure phenomenon the tendency to like persons or things if we see them more often

Metaphor the use of an explicit comparison ("A" is "B") between a product and some other person, place, or thing

Metaverse the network of virtual worlds where people interact in 3-D immersive digital environments

Metrosexual a straight, urban male who exhibits strong interests and knowledge regarding product categories such as fashion, home design, gourmet cooking, and personal care that run counter to the traditional male sex role

Microcultures groups that form around a strong shared identification with an activity or art form

Microloans Small sums—typically less than $100—banks lend to entrepreneurs in developing countries

Millennials people born between 1986–2002; also known as Echo Boomers and Gen Y

Minipreneurs one-person businesses

Modeling imitating the behavior of others

Modified rebuy in the context of the buy-class framework, a task that requires a modest amount of information search and evaluation, often focused on identifying the appropriate vendor

Monomyth a myth with basic characteristics that are found in many cultures

More a custom with a strong moral overtone

Motivation an internal state that activates goal-oriented behavior

Motivational research a qualitative research approach, based on psychoanalytic (Freudian) interpretations, with a heavy emphasis on unconscious motives for consumption

Multiattribute attitude models those models that assume that a consumer's attitude (evaluation) of an attitude object depends on the beliefs he or she has about several or many attributes of the object; the use of a multi-attribute model implies that an attitude toward a product or brand can be predicted by identifying these specific beliefs and combining them to derive a measure of the consumer's overall attitude

Multigenerational marketing strategy an appeal to people of different ages with imagery from an older generation that also turns on younger consumers

Multiple pathway anchoring and adjustment (MPAA) model a model that emphasizes multiple pathways to attitude formation

Multiple-intelligence theory a perspective that argues for other types of intelligence, such as athletic prowess or musical ability, beyond the traditional math and verbal skills psychologists use to measure IQ

Multitasking processing information from more than one medium at a time

Myth a story containing symbolic elements that expresses the shared emotions and ideals of a culture

Name-letter effect all things equal we like others who share our names or even initials better than those who don't

Narrative product information in the form of a story

Need a basic biological motive

Need for affiliation the need to be in the company of others

Need for power the need to control one's environment

Need for uniqueness the need to assert one's individual identity

Negative reinforcement the process whereby the environment weakens responses to stimuli so that inappropriate behavior is avoided

Negative word of mouth the passing on of negative experiences involved with products or services by consumers to other potential customers to influence others' choices

Network effect each person who uses a product or service benefits as more people participate

Neuromarketing a new technique that uses a brain scanning device called functional magnetic resonance imaging (fMRI), that tracks blood flow as people perform mental tasks. Scientists know that specific regions of the brain light up in these scans to show increased blood flow when a person recognizes a face, hears a song, makes a decision, senses deception, and so on. Now they are trying to harness this technology to measure consumers' reactions to movie trailers, choices about automobiles, the appeal of a pretty face, and loyalty to specific brands

New info shopper consumers who almost automatically search for information online before they buy

New task in the context of the buyclass framework, a task that requires a great degree of effort and information search

Noncompensatory decision rules decision shortcuts a consumer makes when a product with a low standing on one attribute cannot make up for this position by being better on another attribute

Normative influence the process in which a reference group helps to set and enforce fundamental standards of conduct

Norms the informal rules that govern what is right or wrong

Nostalgia a bittersweet emotion; the past is viewed with sadness and longing; many "classic" products appeal to consumers' memories of their younger days

Nuclear family a contemporary living arrangement composed of a married couple and their children

Object in semiotic terms, the product that is the focus of a message

Objectification when we attribute sacred qualities to mundane items

Observational learning the process in which people learn by watching the actions of others and noting the reinforcements they receive for their behaviors

Opinion leader person who is knowledgeable about products and who frequently is able to influence others' attitudes or behaviors with regard to a product category

Organizational buyers people who purchase goods and services on behalf of companies for use in the process of manufacturing, distribution, or resale

Paradigm a widely accepted view or model of phenomena being studied; the perspective that regards people as rational information processors is currently the dominant paradigm, although this approach is now being challenged by a new wave of research that emphasizes the frequently subjective nature of consumer decision making

Parental yielding the process that occurs when a parental decision maker is influenced by a child's product request

Parody display deliberately avoiding status symbols; to seek status by mocking it

Part-list cueing effect a strategy to utilize the interference process in memory; when a marketer presents only a portion of the items in a category to consumers, they don't recall the omitted items as easily

Pastiche mixture of images

Perceived age how old a person feels as compared to his or her true chronological age

Perceived risk belief that a product has potentially negative consequences

Perception the process by which stimuli are selected, organized, and interpreted

Perceptual defense the tendency for consumers to avoid processing stimuli that are threatening to them

Perceptual filters past experiences that influence what stimuli we decide to process

Perceptual map a research tool used to understand how a brand is positioned in consumers' minds relative to competitors

Perceptual selection process by which people attend to only a small portion of the stimuli to which they are exposed

Perceptual vigilance the tendency for consumers to be more aware of stimuli that relate to their current needs

Permission marketing popular strategy based on the idea that a marketer will be much more successful in persuading consumers who have agreed to let them try

Personality a person's unique psychological makeup, which consistently influences the way the person responds to his or her environment

Personality traits identifiable characteristics that define a person

Persuasion an active attempt to change attitudes

Physiological need a basic need required to maintain survival of the organism

Pleasure principle the belief that behavior is guided by the desire to maximize pleasure and avoid pain

Plinking™ act of embedding a product or service link in a video

Plutonomy an economy that a small number of rich people control

Podcasting an audio broadcast that people listen to on portable MP3 players or laptops

Point-of-purchase (POP) stimuli the promotional materials that are deployed in stores or other outlets to influence consumers' decisions at the time products are purchased

Popular culture the music, movies, sports, books, celebrities, and other forms of entertainment consumed by the mass market

Pop-up stores temporary locations that allow a company to test new brands without a huge financial commitment

Positioning strategy an organization's use of elements in the marketing mix to influence the consumer's interpretation of a product's meaning vis-à-vis competitors

Positive reinforcement the process whereby rewards provided by the environment strengthen responses to stimuli and appropriate behavior is learned

Positivism a research perspective that relies on principles of the "scientific method" and assumes that a single reality exists; events in the world can be objectively measured; and the causes of behavior can be identified, manipulated, and predicted

POSSLQ (Persons of Opposite Sex Sharing Living Quarters) U.S. Census designation for unmarried couples who cohabitate

Power distance one of Hofstede's cultural dimensions: The way members perceive differences in power when they form interpersonal relationships

Prediction market an approach based on the idea that groups of people with knowledge about an industry are jointly better predictors of the future than are any individuals

Priming properties of a stimulus that evoke a schema that leads us to compare the stimulus to other similar ones we encountered in the past

Principle of cognitive consistency the belief that consumers value harmony among their thoughts, feelings, and behaviors and that they are motivated to maintain uniformity among these elements

Principle of least interest the person who is least committed to staying in a relationship has the most power

Principle of similarity the *Gestalt* principle that describes how consumers tend to group objects that share similar physical characteristics

PRIZM (Potential Rating Index by Zip Market) clustering technique that classifies every zip code in the United States into one of 66 categories, ranging from the most affluent "Blue-Blood Estates" to the least well off "Public Assistance," developed by Claritas, Inc.

Problem recognition the process that occurs whenever the consumer sees a significant difference between his or her current state of affairs and some desired or ideal state; this recognition initiates the decision-making process

Product complementarity the view that products in different functional categories have symbolic meanings that are related to one another

Product line extension related products to an established brand

Product placement the process of obtaining exposure for a product by arranging for it to be inserted into a movie, television show, or some other medium

Product signal communicates an underlying quality of a product through the use of aspects that are only visible in the ad

Profane consumption the process of consuming objects and events that are ordinary or of the everyday world

Progressive learning model the perspective that people gradually learn a new culture as they increasingly come in contact with it; consumers assimilate into a new culture, mixing practices from their old and new environments to create a hybrid culture

Propinquity as physical distance between people decreases and opportunities for interaction increase, they are more likely to form relationships

Prospect theory a descriptive model of how people make choices

Psychographics the use of psychological, sociological, and anthropological factors to construct market segments

Psychophysics the science that focuses on how the physical environment is integrated into the consumer's subjective experience

Punishment the learning that occurs when a response is followed by unpleasant events

Purchase momentum initial impulses to buy in order to satisfy our needs increase the likelihood that we will buy even more

QR code the next generation of barcodes that activate a browser on a smartphone when photographed

Queuing theory the mathematical study of waiting lines

Rational perspective a view of the consumer as a careful, analytical decision maker who tries to maximize utility in purchase decisions

Reality engineering the process whereby elements of popular culture are appropriated by marketers and become integrated into marketing strategies

Reality principle principle that the ego seeks ways that will be acceptable to society to gratify the id

Recall the process of retrieving information from memory; in advertising research the extent to which consumers can remember a marketing message without being exposed to it during the study

Reciprocity norm a culturally learned obligation to return the gesture of a gift with one of equal value

Recognition in advertising research the extent to which consumers say they are familiar with an ad the researcher shows them

Reference group an actual or imaginary individual or group that has a significant effect on an individual's evaluations, aspirations, or behavior

Refutational arguments calling attention to a product's negative attributes as a persuasive strategy where a negative issue is raised and then dismissed; this approach can increase source credibility

Relationship marketing the strategic perspective that stresses the long-term, human side of buyer-seller interactions

Resonance a literary device, frequently used in advertising that uses a play on words (a double meaning) to communicate a product benefit

Reputation economy a reward system based on recognition of one's expertise by others who read online product reviews

Response bias a form of contamination in survey research in which some factor, such as the desire to make a good impression on the experimenter, leads respondents to modify their true answers

Restricted codes the ways of expressing and interpreting meanings that focus on the content of objects, which tend to be used by the working class

Retail theming strategy where stores create imaginative environments that transport shoppers to fantasy worlds or provide other kinds of stimulation

Retrieval the process whereby desired information is recovered from long-term memory

Retro brand an updated version of a brand from a prior historical period

Reverse product placement fictional products that appear in TV shows or movies become popular in the real world

Reward power a person or group with the means to provide positive reinforcement

RFID (response frequency identification device) a small plastic tag that holds a computer chip capable of storing a small amount of information, along with an antenna that lets the device communicate with a computer network. These devices are being implanted in a wide range of products to enable marketers to track inventory more efficiently

Rich media elements of an online ad that employ movement to gain attention

Risky shift the tendency for individuals to consider riskier alternatives after conferring with a group than if members made their own decisions with no discussion

Rites of passage sacred times marked by a change in social status

Ritual a set of multiple, symbolic behaviors that occur in a fixed sequence and that tend to be repeated periodically

Ritual artifacts items (consumer goods) used in the performance of rituals

Role theory the perspective that much of consumer behavior resembles actions in a play

Sacralization a process that occurs when ordinary objects, events, or people take on sacred meaning to a culture or to specific groups within a culture

Sacred consumption the process of consuming objects and events that are set apart from normal life and treated with some degree of respect or awe

Safety need the need to maintain a secure environment

Salience the prominence of a brand in memory

Sandwich Generation a description of middle-aged people who must care for both children and parents simultaneously

Schema an organized collection of beliefs and feelings represented in a cognitive category

Script a learned schema containing a sequence of events an individual expects to occur

Search engine optimization the process of devising online entries to maximize the likelihood they will appear when consumers search for a term online

Search engines software (such as Google) that helps consumers access information based upon their specific requests

Self-actualization a higher-order need for self-fulfillment and harmony

Self-concept the beliefs a person holds about his or her own attributes and how he or she evaluates these qualities

Self-perception theory an alternative (to cognitive dissonance) explanation of dissonance effects; it assumes that people use observations of their own behavior to infer their attitudes toward some object

Semiotics a field of study that examines the correspondence between signs and symbols and the meaning or meanings they convey

Sensation the immediate response of sensory receptors (eyes, ears, nose, mouth, fingers) to such basic stimuli as light, color, sound, odors, and textures

Sensory marketing marketing strategies that focus on the impact of sensations on our product experiences

Sensory memory the temporary storage of information received from the senses

Sensory overload a condition where consumers are exposed to far more information than they can process

Sensory signature A unique characteristic of a brand conveyed on a perceptual channel (e.g., fragrance)

Sexting the growing trend of young people posting sexually suggestive photos of themselves online

Sex-typed traits characteristics that are stereotypically associated with one gender or the other

Shaping the learning of a desired behavior over time by rewarding intermediate actions until the final result is obtained

Shopmobbing strangers organize online around a specific product or service and arrange to meet at a certain date and time in a real-world store to negotiate a group discount

Shopping orientation a consumer's general attitudes and motivations regarding the act of shopping

Short-term memory (STM) the mental system that allows us to retain information for a short period of time

Shrinkage the loss of money or inventory from shoplifting and/or employee theft

Sign the sensory imagery that represents the intended meanings of the object

Simile comparing two objects that share a similar property

Sleeper effect the process whereby differences in attitude change between positive and negative sources seem to diminish over time

Social aging theories a perspective to understand how society assigns people to different roles across the life span

Social class the overall rank of people in a society; people who are grouped within the same social class are approximately equal in terms of their income, occupations, and lifestyles

Social judgment theory the perspective that people assimilate new information about attitude objects in light of what they already know or feel; the initial attitude acts as a frame of reference, and new information is categorized in terms of this standard

Social loafing the tendency for people not to devote as much to a task when their contribution is part of a larger group effort

Social marketing the promotion of causes and ideas (social products), such as energy conservation, charities, and population control

Social media the set of technologies that enable users to create content and share it with a large number of others

Social mobility the movement of individuals from one social class to another

Social need a need to be accepted by others

Social networking a growing practice whereby Web sites let members post information about themselves and make contact with others who share similar interests and opinions or who want to make business contacts

Social power the capacity of one person to alter the actions or outcome of another

Social pressure the power of others to influence what we do regardless of our internal beliefs

Social stratification the process in a social system by which scarce and valuable resources are distributed unequally to status positions that become more or less permanently ranked in terms of the share of valuable resources each receives

Sociometric methods the techniques for measuring group dynamics that involve tracing communication patterns in and among groups

Sociometry techniques allow researchers to systematically map out communication patterns among group members

Sock puppeting a company executive or other biased source poses as someone else to tout his organization in social media

Source attractiveness the dimensions of a communicator that increase his or her persuasiveness; these include expertise and attractiveness

Source credibility a communications source's perceived expertise, objectivity, or trustworthiness

Spacing effect the tendency to recall printed material to a greater extent when the advertiser repeats the target item periodically rather than presenting it over and over at the same time

Spectacles a marketing message that takes the form of a public performance

Spendthrifts consumers who derive pleasure from large-scale purchasing

Spokescharacters the use of animated characters or fictional mascots as product representatives

Spontaneous recovery ability of a stimulus to evoke a weakened response even years after the person initially perceived it

Spreading activation meanings in memory are activated indirectly; as a node is activated, other nodes linked to it are also activated so that meanings spread across the network

Stage of cognitive development the ability to comprehend concepts of increasing complexity as a person matures

Standard learning hierarchy the traditional process of attitude formation that starts with the formation of beliefs about an attitude object

State-dependent retrieval people are better able to access information if their internal state is the same at the time of recall as when they learned the information

Status crystallization the extent to which different indicators of a person's status (income, ethnicity, occupation) are consistent with one another

Status hierarchy a ranking of social desirability in terms of consumers' access to resources such as money, education, and luxury goods

Stimulus discrimination the process that occurs when behaviors caused by two stimuli are different, as when consumers learn to differentiate a brand from its competitors

Stimulus generalization the process that occurs when the behavior caused by a reaction to one stimulus occurs in the presence of other, similar stimuli

Storage the process that occurs when knowledge in long-term memory is integrated with what is already in memory and "warehoused" until needed

Store image a store's "personality," composed of such attributes as location, merchandise suitability, and the knowledge and congeniality of the sales staff

Straight rebuy in the context of the buy-class framework, the type of buying decision that is virtually automatic and requires little deliberation

Subculture a group whose members share beliefs and common experiences that set them apart from other members of a culture

Subjective norm an additional component to the multiattribute attitude model that accounts for the effects of what we believe other people think we should do

Subliminal perception the processing of stimuli presented below the level of the consumer's awareness

Superego the system that internalizes society's rules and that works to prevent the id from seeking selfish gratification

Superstitions beliefs that run counter to rational thought or are inconsistent with known laws of nature

Surrogate consumer a professional who is retained to evaluate and/or make purchases on behalf of a consumer

Susceptibility to interpersonal influence the extent to which an individual needs to have others think highly of him or her

Symbol a sign that is related to a product through either conventional or agreed-on associations

Symbolic interactionism a sociological approach stressing that relationships with other people play a large part in forming the self; people live in a symbolic environment, and the meaning attached to any situation or object is determined by a person's interpretation of these symbols

Symbolic self-completion theory the perspective that people who have an incomplete self-definition in some context will compensate by acquiring symbols associated with a desired social identity

Syncretic decision purchase decision that is made jointly by both spouses

Synoptic ideal a model of spousal decision making in which the husband and wife take a common view and act as joint decision makers, assigning each other well-defined roles and making mutually beneficial decisions to maximize the couple's joint utility

Taste culture a group of consumers who share aesthetic and intellectual preferences

Terminal values end states desired by members of a culture

Theory of cognitive dissonance theory based on the premise that a state of tension is created when beliefs or behaviors conflict with one another; people are motivated to reduce this inconsistency (or dissonance) and thus eliminate unpleasant tension

Theory of reasoned action an updated version of the Fishbein multiattribute attitude theory that considers factors such as social pressure and A_{act} (the attitude toward the act of buying a product), rather than simply attitudes toward the product itself

Theory of trying states that the criterion of behavior in the reasoned action model of attitude measurement should be replaced with *trying* to reach a goal

Tie strength the nature and potency of the bond between members of a social network

Tightwads consumers who experience emotional pain when they make purchases

Time poverty a feeling of having less time available than is required to meet the demands of everyday living

Tipping point moment of critical mass

Total quality management (TQM) management and engineering procedures aimed at reducing errors and increasing quality; based on Japanese practices

Trade dress color combinations that become strongly associated with a corporation

Transformative Consumer Research (TCR) promotes research projects that include the goal of helping people or bringing about social change

Transitional economies a country that is adapting from a controlled, centralized economy to a free-market system

Tribal marketing strategy linking a product's identity to an activity-based "tribe" such as basketball players

Trickle-down theory the perspective that fashions spread as the result of status symbols associated with the upper classes "trickling down" to other social classes as these consumers try to emulate those with greater status

Tweens a marketing term used to describe children aged 8 to 14

Twitter a popular social media platform that restricts the poster to a 140 word entry

Two-factor theory the perspective that two separate psychological processes are operating when a person is repeatedly exposed to an ad: repetition increases familiarity and thus reduces uncertainty about the product but over time boredom increases with each exposure, and at some point the amount of boredom incurred begins to exceed the amount of uncertainty reduced, resulting in wear-out

Two step flow model of influence proposes that a small group of *influencers* disseminate information since they can modify the opinions of a large number of other people

Übersexual male who is similar to a metrosexual but who also has traditional masculine qualities

U-commerce the use of ubiquitous networks that will slowly but surely become a part of us, such as wearable computers or customized advertisements beamed to us on our cell phones

Uncertainty avoidance one of Hofstede's cultural dimensions: The degree to which people feel threatened by ambiguous situations and have beliefs and institutions that help them to avoid this uncertainty

Unconditioned stimulus (UCS) a stimulus that is naturally capable of causing a response

Underground economy secondary markets (such as flea markets) where transactions are not officially recorded

Unipolar emotions emotional reactions that are either wholly positive or wholly negative

Unplanned buying when a shopper buys merchandise she did not intend to purchase, often because she recognizes a new need while in the store

Urban myth an unsubstantiated "fact" that many people accept as true

User the person who actually consumes a product or service

Utilitarian function states that we develop some attitudes toward products simply because they provide pleasure or pain

VALS2™ the Values and Lifestyles segmentation system developed by SBI International

Value a belief that some condition is preferable to its opposite

Value system a culture's ranking of the relative importance of values

Value-expressive function states we develop attitudes toward products because of what they say about him or her as a person

Variable-interval reinforcement the time that must pass before an organism's response is reinforced varies based on some average

Variable-ratio reinforcement you get reinforced after a certain number of responses, but you don't know how many responses are required

Variety seeking the desire to choose new alternatives over more familiar ones

Video blogging (vlogging) posting video diaries on sites such as YouTube or photos on Flickr

Viral marketing the strategy of getting customers to sell a product on behalf of the company that creates it

Virtual community of consumption a collection of people whose online interactions are based on shared enthusiasm for and knowledge of a specific consumption activity

Virtual goods digital items that people buy and sell online

Virtual identity the appearance and personality a person takes on as an avatar in a computer-mediated environment like Second Life

Virtual worlds immersive 3D virtual environments such as Second Life

Voice of the consumer an approach to new product development that solicits feedback from end customers well before the company puts a new product on the market

Voluntary simplifiers people who believe that once basic material needs are satisfied, additional income does not lead to happiness

Von Restorff effect techniques like distinctive packaging that increase the novelty of a stimulus also improve recall

Want the particular form of consumption chosen to satisfy a need

Warming process of transforming new objects and places into those that feel cozy, hospitable, and authentic

Web 2.0 rebirth of the Internet as a social, interactive medium from its original roots as a form of one-way transmission from producers to consumers

Web bullying one or more people post malicious comments about someone online in a coordinated effort to harass them

Weber's Law the principle that the stronger the initial stimulus, the greater its change must be for it to be noticed

Widgets small programs that users can download onto their desktops, or embed in their blogs or profile pages, that import some form of live content

Wiki online program that lets several people change a document on a Web page and then track those changes

Wisdom of crowds a perspective that argues under the right circumstances, groups are smarter than the smartest people in them; implies that large numbers of consumers can predict successful products

Word of mouth (WOM) product information transmitted by individual consumers on an informal basis

Zipf's Law pattern that describes the tendency for the most robust effect to be far more powerful than others in its class; applies to consumer behavior in terms of buyers' overwhelming preferences for the market leader in a product category

Name

Page numbers with "n" refer to end note number.

Aaker, David A., 393n
Aaker, Jennifer L., 44n, 139n, 140, 176n, 201n, 249n, 301n, 519n
Abelson, R. P., 293n
Abolt, Andreas, 352n
Abouzahr, Mahmoud, 439–440
Abraham, Chris, 311n
Achenreiner, Gwen Bachmann, 469n
Adamy, Janet, 271n
Adaval, Rashmi, 132n
Adkins, Natalie Ross, 337n
Adler, Alfred, 244
Adler, Jerry, 227n
Adler, Rick, 556n
Adler, Robbie I., 229n
Affias, Rochelle, 270
Afrika Bambaataa, 433
Aggarwal, Pankaj, 106n
Agins, Teri, 601n, 631n
Agrawal, Jagdish, 303n
Aguirre, B. E., 625n
Ahlering, R. F., 414n
Ahrensa, Anthony H., 222n
Ahuvia, Aaron, 192n
Aikman, Troy, 587
Ajzen, Icek, 293n
Akon, 604
Aksoy, Lerzan, 393n
Alba, Joseph W., 125n, 138n, 139n, 336n, 345n, 349n, 362n
Albanese, Paul J., 224n
Alden, Dana L., 583n
Allen, Chris T., 123n, 129n
Allen, Douglas E., 334n
Allen, Michael W., 93n
Allen, Woody, 69
Allsopp, J. F., 247n
Allyson, June, 556
Alm, Richard, 490–491n
Al Maktoum, Rashid bin Saeed, 510–511
Al Nahyan, Zayed Bin Sultan, 497, 510–511
Alpert, Frank, 88n, 356n
Alpert, Judy I., 388n
Alpert, Lewis, 261n
Alpert, Mark I., 308n, 309n, 388n
Al Sayer, Naser Mohammed, 439
Alsop, Ronald, 45n, 143n, 351n, 359n
Alt, Matt, 209n
Altman, Irwin, 200n
Alwitt, Linda F., 293n, 504n
Ames, B. Charles, 448n
Amjad, Steven, 398n
Anand, Punam, 285n, 585n
Anderson, Chris, 354n, 451n
Anderson, Erin, 449n
Anderson, Hans Christian, 203
Anderson, Helen H., 309n
Anderson, Laurel, 545n
Anderson, Ronald D., 64n
Andre 3000, 601

Andreasen, Alan R., 58n, 396n
Andrews, Edmund L., 462n, 508n
Andrews, I. R., 416n
Andrews, J. Craig, 303n, 416n
Andruss, Paula Lyon, 469n
Angier, Natalie, 503n
Anglin, Linda K., 380n
Aniston, Jennifer, 304
Antonidies, Trinske, 548n
Arango, Tim, 608n
Areni, Charles S., 388n
Armani, Emporio, 601
Armstrong, Gary, 470n
Armstrong, Katrina, 256n
Armstrong, Lance, 410, 503
Arndorfer, James B., 125n
Arndt, Johan, 424n, 425n
Arnold, Mark J., 171n
Arnold, Stephen J., 207n
Arnould, Eric J., 68n, 182n, 412n, 451n, 522n, 583n, 613n, 634n
Aronoff, J., 240n
Aronson, Eliot, 304n
Arora, Neeraj, 167n
Arsel, Zeynep, 248n, 637n
Asai, Masaaki, 570n
Ashford, Susan J., 198n
Ashmore, Richard D., 220n
Askegaard, Søren, 178n, 268n, 271n, 522n, 544n
Aspan, Maria, 90n, 548n
Assael, Henry, 259n
Assmus, Gert, 298n
Atkinson, Claire, 611n, 632n
Atkinson, R. C., 131n
Aylesworth, Andrew B., 100n, 285n
Azhari, A. C., 304n

Baar, Aaron, 137n, 213n, 283n, 435n, 529n, 540n
Babin, Barry J., 381n, 392n
Back, K., 414n
Bagozzi, Richard P., 143n, 293n, 296n, 392n, 398n
Bahr, Howard M., 584n
Baig, Edward C., 167n
Bailay, Rasul, 634n
Bailenson, Jeremy N., 193n
Bakalar, Nicholas, 105n
Baker, Julie, 378n
Baker, Michael J., 304n
Baker, Stacy Menzel, 142n, 182n, 540n
Baker, Stephen, 300n, 412n
Baladi, Joseph, 289
Balakrishnan, Melodena Stephens, 204
Ball, A. Dwayne, 200n
Ball, Deborah, 174n, 226n, 271n, 577n
Ball, Jeffrey, 51n
Bamossy, Gary J., 178n, 268n, 517n, 548n
Bandler, James, 610n
Bandura, Albert, 130n
Banner, Lois W., 222n
Bannon, Lisa, 207n, 222n, 468n
Barak, Benny, 554–555n
Baranauckas, Carla, 454n
Barbaro, Michael, 125n, 485n
Barbosa, David, 44n

Bardzell, Jeffrey, 612n
Bardzell, Shaowen, 612n
Barnes, Brooks, 96n, 300n, 470n, 494n, 525n, 608n
Baron, Alma S., 461n
Baron, Robert A., 120n, 156n, 282n, 355n
Barone, Michael J., 285n
Barth, E., 508n
Barth, Frederik, 517n
Barthel, Diane, 580n
Bartlett, Frederic, 426–427
Barton, Roger, 103n
Basu, Kunal, 349n, 380n
Batra, Rajeev, 168–169n, 381n
Baumeister, Roy F., 193n, 485n
Baumgardner, Michael H., 138n
Baumgarten, Steven A., 419n
Baumgartner, Hans, 293n
Baumgartner, Michael H., 303n
Baumrucker, Craig, 82n
Beaglehole, Ernest, 203n
Beales et al, 356n
Bearden, William O., 95n, 246n, 293n, 394n, 409n, 417n
Beatty, Sally, 618n
Beatty, Sharon E., 178n, 285n, 339n, 459n
Beck, Ernest, 389n
Beck, Glenn, 57
Beck, Melinda, 556–557n
Becker, B. W., 177n
Becker, Howard S., 606n, 618n
Beckham, David, 213, 493, 568
Beckham, Victoria, 213, 493, 568
Beckmann, Suzanne C., 271n
Beeghley, Leonard, 490n, 505n
Begley, Sharon, 132n
Bekin, Caroline, 180n
Belch, George E., 304n, 307n, 309n, 311n
Belch, Michael A., 304n, 309n, 311n
Belk, Russell W., 44–45n, 141n, 142n, 158n, 162n, 182n, 203n, 204n, 246n, 259n, 357n, 397n, 399n, 420n, 454n, 516n, 576n, 581n, 582n, 583n, 587n, 588n, 591n, 632n, 634n
Bell, Stephen, 199n
Belle, Nithin, 638
Bellenger, Danny N., 201n
Bellizzi, Joseph A., 85n, 207n, 387n
Bellman, Eric, 210n, 493n, 638
Belluck, Pam, 72n, 86n
Belsky, Gary, 342n
Bem, Daryl J., 288n
Bem, Sandra L., 208n
Benet-Martinez, Veronica, 176n
Bengtsson, Anders, 228n
Bennett, Jessica, 468n
Bensinger, Ken, 588n
Berenson, Alex, 473n
Berger, Arthur A., 110n, 608, 608n
Berger, D. G., 604n
Berger, Ida E., 293n
Berger, Kenneth J., 356n
Berger, Paul D., 209n
Bergiel, J. Blaise, 127n
Bergstein, Brian, 303n
Berning, Carol K., 397–398n
Berthon, Pierre, 45n

Company

Subject